Cultural Encounters

Cultural Encounters: China, Japan, and the West

Essays Commemorating 25 Years
of East Asian Studies
at the University of Aarhus

*Edited by Søren Clausen, Roy Starrs,
and Anne Wedell-Wedellsborg*

AARHUS UNIVERSITY PRESS

AARHUS UNIVERSITY PRESS
Building 170
Aarhus University
DK-8000 Aarhus C, Denmark

Cover illustration:
Sadahide (1807-73), *Englishman, trading in Yokohama.*
The Japan Ukiyoe Museum.

Contents

Social Encounters

Political Encounters

CONTENTS

Introduction

The Department of East Asian Studies at the University of Aarhus can be traced back to a modest beginning in the late 1960s when a position in Sinology was established as part of the Department of Linguistics. Against a backdrop of political upheaval in China — the Cultural Revolution — and student movements in the West, the newly established Chinese section soon took off in a direction quite incompatible with the linguistic parent Department. When the Chinese section was finally set up as an independent Department in 1973, it already had a well-established profile as a unit dedicated to modern and contemporary East Asia research, based on the idea of inter-disciplinary integration, i.e. the combination of classical orientalist training in language and history with the social scientific and cultural approaches of a whole range of other fields of study. The metamorphosis of East Asian studies at the University of Aarhus that took place in the late 1960s and early 1970s is embodied in the person of Else Glahn, the 'founding mother' and first teacher of the Chinese section, who brought with her a solid classical sinological training (she was a student of the late Swedish master sinologist Bernhard Karlgren) as well as a vivid interest in contemporary East Asia. Her wide range of knowledge as well as her personal qualities constitute the first and fundamental condition for the successful establishment of the Department, and it is only natural that this volume, celebrating the first 25 years of East Asian Studies in Aarhus, is dedicated to her. When Else Glahn retired in 1986 she left behind her an Department with a solid foundation in China and Japan studies and a comparatively young staff covering East Asian languages, culture, history, politics and society.

Knud Lundbæk, now Professor emeritus of medicine and a lifelong con amore sinologist, has also contributed to the bridging of classical sinology with contemporary East Asia studies at the Department. In 1970 he presented the Department with a valuable collection of old books reflecting the genesis and maturation of European sinology, and this 'Lundbæk collection' has been continuously expanding ever since. It is therefore quite appropriate that Knud Lundbæk, who has authored several learned works on the history of sinology, should be placed first in this volume with his essay on the establishment of European sinology.

The Department of East Asian Studies produced a number of spinoffs during the 1980s, prime among which are the China Information Office and the East Asia Area Studies Program. The China Information Office was started as a cooperative enterprise by a number of young graduates associated with the Department in 1981. During the first few years the office had a full-time staff of three, but eventually it settled down to a structure consisting of one full-time and several part-time positions. The office publishes a newsletter which furnishes up-to-date information and analysis concerning economic and political development in China and East Asia generally. It also provides translation and consultancy services to Danish businesses and government institutions.

The East Asia Area Studies Program was launched in 1984 as a joint effort by the Department of East Asian Studies and the Department of Political Science. It is a two year full-time study program designed for senior students and young graduates majoring in economics, law, sociology, journalism, etc., allowing the students to combine their field of study with an extensive and intensive area knowledge, which also includes either basic Chinese or basic Japanese language. The program teaches subjects in the fields of East Asian society and culture, economics and politics, etc., and it also involves intensive language courses, study trips to East Asia and a wide range of guest lectures. The East Asia Area Studies Program is a very popular and successful study program which admits 20 students every second year and is now running its sixth class (the 1994-96 class).

After its first quarter century of existence, the Department of East Asian Studies now stands as the main center for non-Western studies at the University of Aarhus. Although still mainly focusing on modern Asian society and culture, the Department today participates in the full range of Asian studies including linguistics and premodern history, as the selection of essays in this volume makes apparent. The Department has a full-time staff of seven teachers (four in Chinese, three in Japanese), not including staff members at the China Information Office and those from the Department of Political Science involved with the East Asian Area Studies Program. In a wider sense, thus, the permanent number of East Asian Area specialists associated with the Department is around ten, most of whom have contributed to this volume (essays by Bjarke Frellesvig, Roy Starrs, Du Wenwei, Anne Wedell-Wedellsborg, Stig Thøgersen, Søren Clausen and Clemens Stubbe Østergaard). We are

also grateful to three former colleagues for their contributions: Vibeke Børdahl, Kirsten Refsing and Flemming Christiansen.

Over the years the Department has joined a number of international
networks and developed extensive contacts worldwide. Many distinguished
scholars have visited the Department and stayed here for shorter or longer
periods of time. Some of these scholars have contributed to the present
volume, and we are pleased to be able to include essays by Harumi Befu
(UCLA), Wendy Larson (University of Oregon), and Graham Young (University of New England).

One of the most significant features of the Department in the early 1990s
is the emergence of a group of promising young scholars and Ph.D. students.
Their ongoing work is an indication of the future of the Department, and we
are happy to present five essays by the young generation of scholars associated with the Department: Susanne Juhl, Gunner Mikkelsen, Greg Kulander,
Marie Roesgaard and Mette Halskov Hansen.

The general framework of the present volume has allowed us to draw
together essays by a number of the scholars who have helped shape the Department of East Asian Studies over the years, although certainly not everyone. The framework of *cultural encounters* has been employed in a very open
sense, but it is a framework nevertheless. The essays are organized into four
main groupings: premodern, artistic, social and political encounters.

In the first group of essays, placed under the heading of *Premodern
encounters*, Knud Lundbæk takes us back to the early years of the 19th century. He presents the work of five pioneer sinologists, whose efforts are seen
as part of a process leading up to the moment in Paris on January 16, 1815,
when Abel Rémusat, at only 27 years of age, took up the first chair of Chinese
studies in Europe. Gunner Mikkelsen's analysis of the translation of the
Manichean texts into Chinese and his account of the Western recovery of the
Chinese manichaica in the early part of this century also includes an account
of the painstaking work of scholarship of one of Abel Rémusat's successors,
professor Paul Pelliot. Among those Westerners who helped introduce Japan
and the Japanese language in the West was the Swedish botanist Carl Peter
Thunberg, one of the extremely few Westerners to live in Japan during the
18th century. His constructed dialogue in Japanese, contained within his observations on the Japanese language, published in latin in 1794, is the focus
of Bjarke Frellesvig's essay. While these three articles all deal with aspects of
cultural encounters between East and West, mainly as seen from the West,
Susanne Juhl describes an early cultural encounter without Western elements,

i.e. the Buddhist influence in the Northern Liang, during the reign of the Xiongnu ruler, Juqu Mengxun, in the fifth century.

Vibeke Børdahl's essay on the still living oral tradition of Yangzhou story-telling begins the section on *Artistic encounters* and is concerned with an indigenious encounter within Chinese culture. Combining linguistic, phonolo-gical and literary analysis she discusses the encounter between high and low, and between oral and written communication in this unique art form. Roy Starrs and Anne Wedell-Wedellsborg are both concerned with the influence of one of the great Western literary movements in this century, i.e. moder-nism, on East Asian fiction. Roy Starrs looks at the traditional and modernist elements in the work of the great Japanese novelist Kawabata Yasunari, and Anne Wedell-Wedellsborg addresses the question of how the concepts of time and memory, so central to Western modernism, have been expressed in con-temporary Chinese fiction. Du Wenwei demonstrates how the traditional Chinese theatre was adapted to suit the American audience of the Broadway stages, notably by magnifying the theme of love. Wendy Larson on the other hand, in her essay on three of Zhang Yimou's films, analyses how this direc-tor, while often using an aesthetic code particular to the West, succeeds through his images of erotic play in producing a highly personal critique of Chinese national culture. This section on artistic encounters is concluded by an in-depth interview with the Chinese poet, Bei Dao, who lectured for two years at the Department, and who in his own person embodies the stimula-ting and painful experience of a cultural encounter between East and West.

Harumi Befu, an accomplished student of Japanese cultural identity, opens the section on *Social encounters* with a survey of Japan's changing self-images throughout the period of modern transformation from the late Tokugawa pe-riod to the present day, noting extreme swings between periods of strongly negative self-identity and periods of equally overwhelming positive self-identity. Stig Thøgersen's essay on the inspiration drawn from the Danish folk high schools by the prominent Chinese social reformer Liang Shuming in the 1930s is also related to cultural self-images in nation-building; Liang Shuming attempted 'cultural borrowing' from Denmark because the Danish folk high schools appeared to embody Liang's idea of a national consensus emerging from a network of village-based organizations fueled by mass education. Greg Kulander similarly focusses on Chinese uses of Western models and theories in his study of the dissemination of Western educational theories in con-temporary China, taking as his case study the Chinese reception of Prag-matism (John Dewey) and Structuralism (Jean Piaget and Jerome Bruner) during the initial reform period in China 1978-1984; Kulander examines the different levels of assimilation and discusses ideological constraints in the Chinese approach to Western educational theories. Marie Roesgaard's contribution is also within the field of education; her essay is a study of the concept of individuality in contemporary Japanese educational debates, highlighting the widely different usages of the concept by the various organizations and government institutions involved in the debates. Kirsten Refsing's study of intercultural communication in Japanese-Danish marriages is a study of a cultural encounter *par excellence*. The focus is more on discourse and perception than on the sociological features of intercultural marriages, and Kirsten Refsing concludes that 'when the discourse turns to the concrete reality of the spouses themselves, cultural differences become reduced to a minor factor of no serious consequence for their relationship.' Mette Halskov Hansen's study of ethnic consciousness among one of China's minority nationalities, the Naxi people in Southwest China, focusses on the interplay between traditional Naxi culture, Chinese concepts of ethnic identity, and internal stratification among the Naxi, succinctly demonstrating the paradoxes of ethnic consciousness in contemporary China.

The culture concept, even in its most open-ended sense, is perhaps less obvious in relation to politics and economics. However, the essays in the section on *Political encounters* all deal with the exchange and encounter of *ideas* related to politics and economics. Graham Young's study of the political ideology of Liu Shaoqi — Mao Zedong's second-in-command until the demise and condemnation of Liu during the Cultural Revolution — is seen as a case of 'Sinification of Leninism.' Flemming Christiansen likewise examines China's assimilation of ideas from abroad in his study of how Chinese economists have creatively borrowed the Western concept of 'dualism' in economic theory by subsuming it under dialectical materialism. Clemens Stubbe Østergaard examines EC–China relations in the early 1990s; his essay deals with a number of factors that continue to constrain EC-China ties, including conceptual and doctrinal factors. Concluding the political section, and the volume as well, Søren Clausen's study of how Chinese political culture is currently perceived by Western scholars reviews a number of studies and suggests a close linkage between current 'political culture' and 'civil society' debates among Western analysts.

Finally, a few words of thanks to some of the persons and institutions that made this volume possible. We wish to thank the *Aarhus University Research Foundation* as well as the *Daloon Foundation* and the *Tuborg Foundation* for generous financial support. Grateful thoughts also go to ever-patient *Tønnes Bekker-Nielsen* of *Aarhus University Press*. Finally, our most heartfelt thanks to the secretarial genius of Ms. *Ivy Mortensen*, the Department Secretary, who has once again found time to help in the work of organizing and editing a publication by the Department on top of all her other duties.

Aarhus, August 1994

Søren Clausen
Anne Wedell-Wedellsborg

The Establishment of European Sinology 1801–1815

Knud Lundbæk

Academic sinology was established in Paris on January 16, 1815, when Abel Rémusat gave his inaugural lecture at the College du Roi, but we should see this as it was seen at the time, namely as the culmination of a process that began in the year of 1801 with the publication of the *Explanation of the elementary characters of the Chinese* by Joseph Hager. This book caused a revival of the interest in the Chinese language which had lain dormant for half a century. The present paper aims to sketch in the drama of the establishment of European sinology in the first nearly twenty years of the 19th century. It will deal with the writings of Joseph Hager, Antonio Montucci, de Guignes Jr., Julius Klaproth and Abel Rémusat.

T.S. Bayer and Étienne Fourmont

Before we enter into the establishment period — 1801 to 1815 — we shall look briefly at the two scholars who had devoted their lives to the study of that language in the first part of the 18th century.

Theophilus (Gottlieb) Siegfried Bayer (1694-1738), a German scholar at the Academy of Sciences in St. Petersburg, published his *Museum Sinicum* in two volumes in 1730 — the first book about the Chinese language to be printed in Europe. In the following years he published a number of smaller but in portant works on Chinese, especially his article about the *Zi Hui* (字彙) dictionary.[1]

Étienne Fourmont (1683-1745), professor of Arabic in the College du Roi in Paris, had begun to study Chinese when he met Arcade Huang, a French-speaking Chinese attached to the Royal Library, in about 1703. He produced, with immense labour, his two large books, the *Meditationes Sinicae* (1737) and the *Linguae Sinarum mandarinicae-hieroglyphicae grammatica duplex..* (1742). On the way he had received Joseph de Prémare's excellent textbook of Chinese language and literature, but he could not use it — it was far above him. It was not published until 1831.[2]

Fourmont had taken two young persons in, André Deshauterayes, his nephew, and Joseph de Guignes, a friend of his, introducing them to Arabic, Syriac and Chinese.[3] Later in life de Guignes published his great *Histoire générale des Huns* (Paris 1756-58), while Deshauterayes edited de Mailla's *Histoire générale de la Chine* (Paris 1777-85).

In the period between 1742 and 1801 there appeared only one text about the Chinese language. The *Dictionnaire élémentaire ou Introduction à l'étude des sciences et des arts* (I-III) was published in 1767 in Paris by abbé Pétity. This pious work, which was obviously meant as a counterweight to Diderot's and d'Alembert's great *Dictionnaire*, contains twelve pieces about the twelve 'mother languages': Hebrew, Greek, Latin, Arabic... but also Chinese and Manchu. These two were written by André Deshauterayes, but his name is only mentioned in the acknowledgements. The article about the Chinese language is a long one from Jesuit sources, with the 214 radicals written by Deshauterayes himself. There is one interesting thing in it, a criticism of his uncle. He writes that the ideas of Étienne Fourmont about the old age and the metaphysical system of the 214 radicals are quite wrong.

However, an interest in China had been awakened in the last part of the century by the publication of the huge *Mémoires concernant l'histoire, les sciences, les arts, les moeurs, les usages etc. des chinois* — Volume 1-15 printed in Paris in 1776 to 1791, volume 16 in 1814. During the same years the *Histoire générale des chinois* — 13 volumes — had attracted the attention of European readers.

The Vatican Dictionary
We have to say also a few words about the publication of a Chinese-European dictionary. This was necessary for the emergence of the discipline of sinology.

By the treat of Tolentino (1798), after Napoleon's victories over the Allied forces in the first Italian campaign, it was decided that 'one hundred paintings, busts and vases, together with 500 manuscripts' should be taken from the Vatican and sent to Paris.

The events during the short-lived Republic of Rome (1798-99) made it possible for Danou (1761-1840), the great historian, to select these treasures. Among them was a Chinese-Latin dictionary, clearly the finest one among others in the Vatican Library. The fate of this dictionary, usually just called the Vatican Dictionary, is intimately connected with the rise of sinology in Europe.

It had been composed by Basilio Brollo from Gemona (1648-1703) a Franciscan missionary who had worked in China from 1680.[4] Its title was *Han Zi Xi Yi* (漢字西譯): Chinese-Western dictionary.

Once it came to the Imperial Library in Paris, it became the obsession of Napoleon to get it printed. The editing was entrusted first to Joseph Hager, then — for a moment — to Antonio Montucci, and finally to de Guignes Jr. who produced it in 1813 under the title of *Dictionnaire chinois-français et latin, publié d'apres l'ordre de Sa Majesté l'Empereur et Rois Napoleon le Grand; par M. de Guignes, résident de France à la Chine...*

Joseph Hager — A False Start

Joseph Hager (1757-1819) was born in a German family in Milan. He studied history and languages, first in Vienna, later on in Rome. He lived for two years in the Imperial Embassy in Constantinople, where he learned Arabic. Afterwards — a wealthy man — he travelled in Italy, France, Spain, Germany and Holland, visiting the great libraries there. At a certain time he got involved in Chinese matters.

In 1800 he published a short article in a London magazine, *Literary and Philosophical Intelligence*, with a prospectus about a Chinese dictionary:

A dictionary will be published, now ready for print; performed in China, composed and improved with the best MSS dictionaries existing in that country, etc. Proposals for publishing by subscription a dictionary of the chin. Lang. By Dr. Hager. London 1800.

Subscriptions would be received — at a price of ten guineas — at one of five addresses in London, in Hamburg, Leipzig, Vienna and Paris.

It appears that the dictionary would contain the 10,000 most common characters, arranged alphabetically. He made himself ridiculous by adding that they would be followed by 'all the characters in three Chinese dictionaries, including the *Hai Bian*' — with its 80,000 characters!

He sent this article to A. L. Millin (1759-1818), conservator of the Museum of Antiquities in the Bibliothèque Nationale, who published a translation of it in his fine *Magasin encyclopedique* (Paris, Année VI, tome 2, 1800).

Hager had sent Millin a letter with this article, asking him for information about Chinese dictionaries in the Bibliothèque Imperiale. Millin turned to L.Langlès of the Department of Oriental Manuscripts about it, and he wrote a piece about them which Millin had printed after Hager's article.[5] It is a ten page description of thirteen Chinese-European or European-Chinese dictionaries, including a long chapter about Basilio de Gemona's dictionary — one of the many magnificent manuscripts which 'came by our victories in Italy from the Vatican to Paris'.

However, not enough subscribers came forward — what would he have done if they had come forward?

In 1801 he published his first China book: *An explanation of the elementary characters of the Chinese, with an analysis of their ancient symbols and hieroglyphs* (London 1801). This announcement and the publication of this book caused a sensation. In 1802 he was called to Paris to work in the Bibliothèque Imperiale and to produce a Chinese dictionary.

An explanation of the elementary characters of the Chinese...
This book, which opened the field of Chinese studies in the 19th century, is a slender folio of 119 pages, sumptuously printed with large type. The Chinese characters are far from being elegant, nor quite correctly drawn, but easily recognizable.

Essentially the book contains the 214 radicals with transliteration and one meaning — all of it taken from Fourmont's *Meditationes Sinicae*. This fills 43 pages. It is preceded by a 76 page foreword.

Hager begins by wondering about the strange fact that, since T. S. Bayer and Fourmont published their works in the 1730-40s, nobody has written about the Chinese language. What he now wants is to fill out that lacuna.

It is true, he says, that in the last years of the 18th century the ex-Jesuits of Peking, Amiot and Cibot, did deal with and presented many 'ancient' characters in the *Mémoires concernant l'histoire etc. des chinois*, but this did not help the reader to understand the Chinese script..

Today, he says, Fourmont's books are very rare and his *Meditationes Sinicae*, 'besides being written in Latin, is so embarrassed by verbosity as to exhaust the patience of every inquirer... Then again, the engraved characters in T. S. Bayer's *Museum Sinicum* are so wretchedly expressed as to offer but little advantage'.

Now Hager is offering his *Elementary explanation*, intending to revive the study of Chinese characters. He refers to his announcement about a Chinese-English dictionary, saying that 'the present volume is intended to precede it', but as an introduction to a forthcoming dictionary it is not very useful.

It begins with the 'knotted cords' used in China before the invention of characters. Then follows a note on the trigrams and the hexagrams, 'the first script', including a section on the abacus and the similarity between Chinese and Roman numerals. Then the author mentions the poem about the city of Mukden, composed by the Qian Long emperor and published in 32 kinds of 'ancient' characters — he knows that there is a copy of that work in the Bibliothèque Nationale in Paris.[6] From there he proceeds to a long section on 'ancient' scripts as shown in the Japanese Encyclopedia, lately brought to Europe by Mr. Titsingh.[7] He shows not less than 45 such characters, quite fancy, as an introduction to a dictionary. Moreover, he prints on a vast folding sheet the famous Inscription of Yu, also from the Japanese encyclopedia. (See p. 47)

The author then changes to a short discussion about the issue — yet again — of the possible origin of the Chinese from the Egyptians, but soon gives up. Then he tries to present the four tones of the Chinese language by descriptions and by musical notes — quite wrongly.

The last ten pages, however, contain some useful hints on how to identify the radicals in a character. It includes a general criticism of the 214 radical system — 'as was pointed out long ago by T. S. Bayer'. Here we also find a note on Fourmont who had affirmed brashly that if one only knew the meaning of each of the radicals, it would always be possible to understand any character in which this radical occurs. This postulate is demolished by one example.

Hager boasts of having access to two Chinese dictionaries, the *Zi Hui* (1609) and the *Zheng Zi Tong* (1671), but he only used them to look up a few things on the first pages of these works.[8]

All in all it is a light and superficial book, with a number of errors though written in an entertaining style.

Le Monument de Yu

Joseph Hager's second publication was *Le Monument de Yu ou la plus ancienne inscription de la Chine* (Paris 1802). It is a large folio with 12 pages of introduction and the 72 'characters' of the inscription shown very large, four per page. As we have seen he had included the monument text from Titsingh's Japanese encyclopedia in his *An Explanation of the elementary characters...*

Once in Paris he found in the Bibliothèque Nationale a manuscript by Amiot, the court Jesuit (1718-93), containing a copy of the strange inscription together with a transliteration of it by 'Chinese antiquarians', and Amiot's French translation of it. He decided at once to publish this work.

This monument had been found on a mountain top at some time. From there, in 1666, it had been brought to Xian where it was placed as number one among very many ancient monuments.

Hager expressed himself cautiously about the veracity of this monument: 'whether it really dates back to the time of the Great Yu — 4000 years ago — or whether it was put up at a later time by some of his successors in memory of the hero'. He also expressed his doubts about the 'antiquaries' who had been able to transliterate this text, written with characters completely different from any Chinese, old or new.

The story about a large inscription on a mountain top is, of course, but one of the hundreds of tales about the life and deeds of the great cultural hero.

Descriptions des médailles chinoises du cabinet imperiale de France, précédée d'un essai de numismatique chinoise (Paris 1805)

His next book, printed in the Imprimerie Imperiale three years after he came to Paris, deals with the Chinese medals and coins in the Cabinet de Médailles in Paris and with Chinese numismatics in general. In the Preface to this work he takes pains to inform his reader that he has not forgotten his task: to produce a dictionary.

Speaking about Fourmont's many wooden characters, he says that he had seen them only recently — 86,417 pieces in 236 boxes. They were in a state of confusion and his first job was to arrange them according to the 214 radicals. 'After working on that for several months most of them are now in their proper order... the printing of the dictionary is about to start at once...'

However, he was dismissed the following year.

This book is interesting because of the source of his numismatic information. He says that he has taken most of his many illustrations from a Chinese work called *San Cai Tu Hui*, but some of them are also to be found in Duhalde's book.[9] He had seen one copy of *San Cai Tu Hui* in the Bibliothèque Imperiale, it came there after Fourmont's time and is therefore not in the catalogue of Chinese books in the *Linguae Sinarum... grammatica duplex*. There is, however, he adds, another copy of this work in Paris, namely in the private collection of Abbé Tersan — we shall hear more about that man and that copy presently.

The *San Cai Tu Hui* (Collected Illustrations of the Three Powers) composed by Wang Qi and his son Wang Siyi (Preface 1607) is a great encyclopedia. It is essentially a number of pictures, maps and tables, accompanied by short texts. It contains pictures of all the Chinese emperors, and pictures of cloths, tools, buildings, precious stones and coins, kinds of script, plants and flowers, animals and parts of the human body. There is a large section on more than one hundred peoples from foreign countries, mostly imaginary such as one-legged people, headless people, etc. — and in most cases taken from illustrated editions of the *Shan Hai Jing*.

San Cai Tu Hui is a very unusual kind of Chinese book, something in between an ordinary encyclopedia and the small popular encyclopedias for semi-literate users, the so-called *Wan Bao* books.[10] It is mentioned in the *Si Ku Quan Shu* (四庫全書) that speaks about its numerous pictures. The *Si Ku Quan Shu* says that it is acceptable to be told that Cang Jie is said to have had four eyes but ridiculous to be shown a picture of him with his four eyes. At the end the *Si Ku Quan Shu* says that the *San Cai Tu Hui* is 'childlike'.

Hager describes this extraordinary work and prints its title in Chinese: 三才 圖會. It is the first description of it in Western literature. 'This work deals in 88 juan [actually there are 106] with all kinds of things, from the cedar to the hyssop, from the stars to the insects. Two 'envelopes' deal with ancient coins and medals.'

There are about 200 pictures of coins from the oldest times to the beginning of the Song period, the oldest said to date from the time of the Great Yu, shown as a circle surrounded by a square. Hager says, however, that according to the Kangxi dictionary such coins were not introduced until during the Zhou dynasty.

Hager discusses the coins in the Cabinet de Médailles, among others the so-called 'Knife-coins' which are very old but of uncertain date.

He translates a few passages from the *San Cai* work and inserts many digressions about ancient Greek coins.

Panthéon chinois, ou parallele entre le culte religieux des Grecs et celle des Chinois, avec des nouvelles preuves que la Chine a été connue des Grecs, et que les Sérés ont été des Chinois (Paris 1806).
This is the last of Hager's Parisian works, but it was not printed in the Imprimerie Imperiale and on the title page he calls himself 'professeur public des langues orientales de Pavie'. The dedication is to 'His Imperial Highness Eugène-Napoleon de France, Viceroy de l'Italie, etc.' He expresses his gratitude because the Viceroy has helped him to a chair in the 'first university in Italy'.

In his preface he reminds his reader of the last chapter in his *Description des médailes... et numismatique chinoise*, which had the title 'La Chine connue des Grecs'. Now he devotes a whole book to that problem.

Speaking about the connections between the Greeks and the Chinese, he says that the Greeks had travelled to China to buy silk, the Greek sacrificial vessels were admired in China, Jason's 'golden fleece' was a piece of silk, the wisdom of Thales and Pythagoras was similar to that of Lao Zi and Confucius, etc., etc...

However, there is something of interest in the Preface — the last pages of it contain a kind of self-portrait and self-defence. 'Before ending this Preface I have to give an account to the Republic of Letters about a work which I announced already in the year 1800, in England, and which has still not been published.'

He explains that at a certain time he had resolved to compose a Chinese dictionary. For that purpose he went to Berlin (1799) and worked for two months there with Diaz's dictionary and that of Dr. Mentzel.

Afterwards he went to London and inspected the various manuscripts in the British Museum, the Royal Society and Mr. Titsingh's collection: 'Then I was able to produce my first dissertation: *An explanation of the elementary characters of the Chinese*'.

In Paris, he says, he wanted to work, not only with the language but also with Chinese literature and the Chinese antiquities 'that still need so much research'. He immediately published his *Monument de Yu* from a manuscript in the Bibliothéque Imperiale. Next he composed an exact index, still to be printed, of all the Chinese books that had come to the Library after Fourmont's time... And then his next two books!

In conclusion he says: 'My chief, the minister of the interior, has expressed his satisfaction with the way I have employed my time and several persons, distinguished by their knowledge and their dignity, have assured me that nobody could blame me for not having carried out what I had solemnly promised to Europe, which has cost me several expensive voyages and which nobody more than myself wants to see finished'. This was probably as close as he could get to an angry protest against his dismissal.

He stayed in Pavia till his death in 1819, publishing some small works on Chinese matters.

Antonio Montucci, the man who loved the Chinese language

Antonio Montucci was born in 1762 in Siena. Having lost his father at the age of five, he was brought up in a college. With a bursary for the university he obtained the degree of Doctor in Law. At the same time he had studied several modern languages and was made a professor of English in the Collegio de Tolomei in Siena at the age of 23 years.

Four years later, in Florence, he became friends with Josiah Wedgwood (1730-95), the famous English manufacturer of pottery, who was in Italy at the time. Wedgwood took the young man with him to England where he lived in the colony named 'New Etruria' in Staffordshire, teaching Italian to his large family.

He had already begun to study Chinese from Fourmont's books in 1789, when — in 1792 — he heard of the four young Chinese missionaries who had been fetched from Naples to take part in Macartney's embassy to China.[11] He wrote them a letter in Chinese and afterwards got very friendly with them. They gave him a copy of the *Zheng Zi Tong* dictionary. From that moment he never gave up his passionate interest in the Chinese language.

Living in Germany from 1806 to 1828, publishing books on Italian literature, writing librettos to Italian operas, and giving Italian lectures at the courts of Berlin and Dresden, he continued his Chinese studies, having many thousands of fine Chinese characters engraved, and buying many expensive handwritten Chinese-Latin dictionaries. In 1828, after more than forty years, he returned to his native Siena. He went to Rome and there sold his books and his many Chinese-European manuscripts and 27,000 Chinese characters to the Vatican for 1,000 Zecchini.[12] He died the following year, 1829.

We are going to deal with three of his most important works, beginning with his *Letters on Chinese Literature*.

Letters on Chinese literature
These are four letters printed in the *Universal Magazine*, London, signed Sinologus Berolinensis, but actually written by Antonio Montucci. They deal with 'the Dr. Hager and Dr. Montucci controversy...'.

In 1801 Montucci had published a small article in an English newspaper on a Chinese manuscript in the British Museum. For that he had been criticized in another newspaper by one of 'Dr. Hager's advocates'. Now Sinologus Berolinensis took up that matter in a series of letters to the *Universal Magazine* (1804).

They were lectures, adorned with a number of Chinese characters on the hexagrams, the six kinds of characters according to the *Shuo Wen Jie Zi*,[13] and the various kinds of Chinese script, from the Tadpole script to our days'

Chinese characters, revealing his profound knowledge of the Jesuit books about Chinese matters. This is mixed up with the most violent attack on Joseph Hager's *An Explanation of the elementary characters of the Chinese* (1801). In particular he is enraged about one page — page XX — of this book which shows the trigrams surrounded by the hexagrams that pertain to them.

Hager intimates that he has taken them from a Chinese edition of the *Yi Jing*, but Montucci says that he has inspected dozens of different editions of this book where this particular structure does not occur. It does occur, however, slightly modified, in volume 2 of the *Mémoires... des chinois..*![14] To conceal his plagiarism Hager had altered 27 of the small hexagrams surrounding the trigrams. Montucci speaks about his 'most infamous plagiarism', his 'artful and maliciously contrived disguise of its baseness'. He also ridiculied Hager's *Prospectus for a Chinese Dictionary*, which 'discloses his stupidity and profound ignorance of the Chinese language'.

Undoubtedly, Montucci's style must have delighted Julius Klaproth (more on whom below), when he came to see these letters!

Remarques philologiques sur les voyages en Chine de M. De Guignes.
The *Remarques philologiques* was published on November 12, 1808 'at the expense of the author'. In the postscript he says that he had taken great pains to obtain a copy of de Guignes Jr.'s book (more on that work below), getting it only on June 9 — he had to finish his *Remarques philologiques* in six months!

The book begins oddly with a long letter in German from Sinologus Beronlinensis to Antonio Montucci, in which the merits of Montucci are enumerated in detail while his enemies are scorched.

In the book itself Sinologus Berolinensis begins by saying that the appointment of de Guignes Jr. came as a great surprise to all European orientalists when it was advertised in all the newspapers — 'the son of a great scholar, famous for his knowledge of Chinese literature, and a man who sojourned for 14 years in China'. His engagement came just after he had published his *Voyages de Peking*...

The writer goes on to say:

Today Chinese literature has found support from the French government... I believe that I have to reveal to the noble ministers the merit of that language, revealing also the falsehood that de Guignes has advanced against it. Also just to mention my fear that in choosing him they may have settled again on the wrong person. If, unfortunately, time is going to justify my predictions, these ministers may at least have their eyes on another person who knows better how to accomplish such a task...

It looks as if he is trying, at the very last moment, to turn the tide and get into the Bibliothèque Nationale where de Guignes had already begun his dictionary work!

The text itself begins with a very detailed criticism of the Chinese emperors' names — 29 of them are wrong! Then follow 70 pages about the history of the Chinese script, some of it rather confused, especially in his discussion of the famous six kinds of characters. On the way he comes to recommend a dictionary system of 'less than 100 radicals' for the use of European students.

After that there are a few pages about de Guignes' remarks on Chinese grammar and style — quite wrong most of the way. Here he inserts a section about the origin of the Chinese language:

'Who can deny that it came from God himself? The Chinese have existed since the great FIAT of the Eternal. Our children, don't they speak Chinese before getting their first tooth? How could it be that at the beginning there were alphabets, later to be followed by symbols and hieroglyphs? I recommend to my readers the excellent book by Mr. Webb.'

This surprising reference — in a 19th century book — is to the work of the learned 17th century architect John Webb, entitled *A historical essay endeavouring the probability that the language of the Empire of China is the primitive language* (London 1669).

Urh-chih-tsze-teen-se-yin-pe-keaou, being a parallel drawn between the two intended Chinese dictionaries by the Rev. Robert Morrison and Antonio Montucci, LL.D. London 1817 (二帙字典西譯比較).

Montucci was roused to action again at the sight of the first fascicle of Robert Morrison's *A Dictionary of the Chinese Language* which had just come out from Macao in 1815.

This dictionary, which was to become of immense importance to the establishment of sinology, was published in 6 large volumes during the years 1815-23 (Macao and London). Its full title is *A Dictionary of the Chinese Language in three parts. Part the first containing Chinese and English, arranged according to the radicals. Part the second, Chinese and English, arranged alphabetically. Part three, English and Chinese.*

The first part of it is based on the Kangxi dictionary. The first fascicle, which Montucci saw, contains an introduction, a table of the 214 radicals, and the characters from radical 1 to 40.

The *Urh-Chih Tsze...* is a stately quarto, beautifully 'printed for the author', with many fine Chinese characters. It cannot have been seen by many, and can only have been understood by very few, a handful of persons around Abel Rémusat. Rémusat surprisingly does not mention it in his several articles about the Morrison dictionary.

Klaproth mentions the book in Montucci's obituary but without giving its title or the place and time of its publication. 'Montucci had printed in English a parallel between Morrison's work and the one he was about to produce. But this book does not explain the superiority of his system as against the one adopted by Morrison.' He does not intimate what Montucci's 'system' consisted of.

It is a very personal, nearly private kind of work, often taking the form of a letter, a fine and carefully constructed text, very different from the hasty notes of the *Remarques philologiques*, and practically without defamatory expressions.

Montucci begins with some — polite — comments on the Preface to Morrison's dictionary. He dwells on the characters in the Kangxi emperor's Preface to his dictionary. They are reproduced as the emperor wrote them, i.e., in the *manuscript style* in contradistinction to the text of the dictionary itself which is in the *printed style*, the Song Ban. He comments on a number of characters which are completely different in the two styles, such as 朼 (此), the first not to be found in any dictionary.

Then, and many times after, he speaks about the twenty-two manuscripts of Chinese-European dictionaries in his possession, especially two old ones, composed by missionaries before the publication of the *Zi Hui* dictionary with its 214 radicals (1615). One of them has 306 radicals!

He says that he agrees with Mr. Morrison that the 214 radical system is the most convenient — if he alludes to the natives of China, or to the European already in possession of the most essential part of the language. 'But for *beginners* I look upon it as the very first desponding steps, I courageously maintain, that to obtain a sufficient number of scholars persevering in the study of this language amongst us, something must be contrived, in the publication of a dictionary for them, to facilitate the research of characters, otherwise many will try, but very few will persevere'. Mr. Morrison himself observed: 'The Imperial dictionary was intended for natives, not for foreigners' (p. 31)

Then he proceeds to explain his new plan for a Chinese dictionary for beginners:

New radicals should be constructed, being the *most conspicuous* parts of the characters, and the position of the radical in the character ought to be *unequivocally ascertained* by a very short and easy proceeding. Nine series of radicals are proposed, in which the radical is placed at the top, at the left side, at the right side, at the bottom, extending over the top and the left side, etc.

Just to mention one case, the characters having ⼚, ⼴ or ⼢ are all to be placed in the last of the examples just mentioned. As to the number of radicals he now proposes to 'double or treble' their number! Such a system, strictly logical-geometrical, avoiding all the 'allegories' of the traditional radical system, would make it easy for the beginner to find the character he is looking for.... The 'proceeding' is, however, neither short nor easy since the explanation of it covers 24 pages!

Thinking of his own 'first desponding steps', Montucci forgets, however, that things have happened since 1793. At that time he was alone, with nobody to help him. Now there are *teachers* who have themselves overcome the difficulties inherent in an analogous system and who can help their pupils get accustomed to its peculiarities.[15]
He says that

to this day my Chinese characters amount to twenty thousand — all the way to the syllable 'pang' — which is about three quarters of the whole.

The appearance of Mr. Morrison's first part of a Chinese dictionary now redoubles my ardour, and in about two years I hope to see the end of my engravings... then I shall be able to put to press a Latin translation of Morrison's invaluable Lexicon on the plan and with the improvement above stated.

But I begin to get old [he was 55]. If I don't live long enough to complete my work, let those account for it, who were deaf to my solicitations... but too late, I am afraid. For the present, it is sufficient for me to have proved by the above and the following observations that much is left to be done to introduce the European Tyro to the knowledge of the most essential elementary mechanisms of the Chinese characters...

The rest of the book — half of it — is taken up by discussions (with many examples) of the minute differences between the manuscript style and the Song Ban.

At the end of the book he reprints Robert Morrison's translation of the well-known children's book, the *Three Character Classic (San Zi Jing)* (三字經), together with the Chinese text *in the manuscript style.*

Before we turn to de Guignes Jr. let us look at what Montucci wrote at the
end of his *Remarques philologiques*:

'Another quality required to publish a Chinese dictionary, and which Mr.
de Guignes lacks completely, is ENTHUSIASM (sic)'.

'We have a grammar and other excellent works by Étienne Fourmont, and
that is because he was going into raptures over the genius of that language
and was struck by astonishment at the composition of the Chinese characters.
We hear him exclaiming: 'Lingua philosophica!' Lingua divina! He gave up
all the other oriental languages which he knew, to devote himself entirely to
the Chinese language for thirty years.... De Guignes always speaks coldly,
without passion and without interest... Would he devote fourteen or fifteen
hours a day for ten years to publish the Vatican dictionary? Fourteen or
fifteen hours a day, what is that to a man passionately engaged in a study?
They will pass like the days and nights of idle persons at balls or at games!'

De Guignes Jr. — The Practical Man

Chrétien Louis Joseph de Guignes (1759-1845) was the son of the famous
orientalist Joseph de Guignes (1721-1800) of the Académie des Inscriptions et
Belles-Lettres, the author of the great *Histoire générale des Huns* (1756-58),
editor of the translation of the *Shu Jing* and the *Éloge de Moukden* (1770), also
of the important *Notices et extraits des manuscripts de la Bibliothèque du Roy*.

De Guignes Sr. taught the elements of Arabic and Chinese to his son and
in 1783 arranged for him to be attached to the French consulate in Canton.
The young de Guignes stayed there and in Macao for fourteen years. In 1794-
95 he followed the Dutch embassy to the imperial court in Peking.

In 1801 he was back in Paris, starting to work on his voyages in the East.
It took him seven years to finish the *Voyages à Peking, Manille et l'Ile de France,
faits dans l'intervalle des années 1784 à 1801* (Paris 1808). It is a three volume
work with a large 'atlas' containing pictures of bridges, pagodas, scenes from
daily life in China, etc.

The book contains a long history of ancient China from Jesuit sources, a
diary-like description of his uneventful voyage as the 'secretary' to Titsingh,
the Dutch ambassador to the emperor of China, and of his trips to the Philippines and to the Ile de France. Besides, there are long chapters called 'Observations sur les chinois' — on their homes, meals, habits and general character.
They are said to be laborious and good at business, but also to be lying, de-
ceiving and cruel, and to love games and debauchery.

In the same year — 1808 — the year when he had published his *Voyages* — de Guignes was asked to work in the Bibliothèque Imperiale and to edit Basilio Brollo's manuscript Chinese-Latin Dictionary, the Vatican Dictionary. He worked hard at it, changing its alphabetical order to that of the 214 radicals, and having it printed with Fourmont's large characters, engraved between 1715 and 1742 but still preserved in the Bibliothèque Imperiale. In 1813, after five years of work, he published a big folio entitled *Dictionnaire Chinois-Français et Latin, publié d'apres l'ordre de Sa Majesté l'Empereur et Roi Napoleon le grand par M. de Guignes, resident de France en Chine...*

It was a bad mistake not to have put the name of Basilio Brollo on the title page. In his Preface de Guignes just said that he had been given 'de Glemona's dictionary as a model and then started to compose the new dictionary'. Actually de Guignes' dictionary is a copy of Basilio Brollo's, and this fact would soon be disclosed.

De Guignes knew that he had an enemy — Antonio Montucci — but he probably did not regard him as dangerous. He did not know that he would have to face two other persons, far more redoubtable — Julius Klaproth and Abel Rémusat.

The Dictionnaire is a thick folio of 1,181 pages with a small introduction and long preface about the history of China and of the Chinese script, taken from Jesuit sources. It contains 13,619 characters, transliterated and translated into Latin and French. At the end there is a complete 'Dictionnaire par tons', with all the words arranged alphabetically (pp. 981-1106).

This dictionary was severely criticized by Abel Rémusat in his anonymous preface to Julius Klaproth's *Supplement*. It was printed in 1819, but Abel Rémusat's preface might have been written between 1813 and 1815 (see p. 44). De Guignes was a practical man. He says himself in his Introduction that he 'does not dare to call himself an erudite'. He lived to the age of 85 and never reacted to Klaproth's and Abel Rémusat's criticism. However, a printed Chinese-European dictionary was there, de Guignes had prepared it, it was indispensable and Abel Rémusat recommended it to his students in his inaugural lecture in 1815.

We shall discuss the arrangement of the dictionary together with that of Klaproth's *Supplement* to it and Rémusats *Examen critique* of it (see p. 48).

Julius Klaproth — The Irascible Orientalist

Julius Klaproth was born in Berlin in 1783, five years before Abel Rémusat. He died in Paris in 1835, three years after Rémusat. He was the son of a famous chemist who wanted him to become a natural scientist. He began to study chemistry, mineralogy and botany, but after a few years he turned his attention to oriental languages.

He began his Chinese studies with Bayer's *Museum Sinicum* and visits to the Royal Library in Berlin where he saw Francisco Diaz's fine dictionary, the *Vocabulario de Letra China* and the correspondance between the old court physician Christian Mentzel and the China Jesuit Phillip Couplet. At the same time he started to read Hebrew, Arabic, Turkish and Persian.

At the age of nineteen he published a journal called *Asiatisches Magazin* which appeared in Weimar in 1802. In Berlin in 1804 he met the Polish count Jean Potocki who was going to be his protector for many years.[16] The count arranged for him to go to St. Petersburg as an adjunct in oriental languages and literature. From there he went, with the count, on the unsuccessful Golowkin embassy to China in 1805. He travelled alone through Siberia to Irkutsk, visiting on his way many peoples and tribes, living with them and collecting vocabularies of their languages. The rest of the embassy arrived in Irkutsk late in 1805 and they all crossed the Baikal Sea to Kiachta. In the following months he studied Mongol, Manchu and Chinese and acquired many books — Chinese, Manchu, Mongol and Tibetan.

After the failure of the embassy — in Urga (Ulanbator) Golowkin refused to follow the tributory ceremony in front of the Chinese governor of Mongolia (February 1, 1806) — Klaproth rode back through Southern Siberia, again staying with various tribes, returning to St. Petersburg after nearly two years of absence. Accepted with acclamation by the Academy he was made extraordinary member and was sent on a new expedition, this time to the Causacus, where he collected further language specimens. He left Russia in 1811 and in the following year he tendered his resignation.

In 1811 he published his *Inschrift des Yü*, and during the following war years he tried to get three books about his Caucasian experiences printed— they did not appear until 1814.

He must have seen Abel Rémusat's *Essai sur la langue et la litterature chinoises* (1811), at the same time as Rémusat must have seen his *Inschrift des Yü*, published the same year. A correspondence sprung up, but unfortunately none of the letters seem to have been preserved.

In 1814 he went to Elba to offer his services to Napoleon who received him kindly. After the Hundred Days he came to Paris late in 1815 where he met the newly nominated professor Rémusat. Here, upon the recommendation of Alexander von Humbolt, King Friedrich-Wilhelm III of Prussia made him professor of Asian languages and literatures with permission to stay in Paris. And here he lived for the rest of his life, publishing a great number of books and articles, printed at the expense of the Prussian king.

Klaproth was an orientalist, studying many eastern languages. He published hundreds of works about Afghan, Uigur, Georgian and Caucasian languages. His main work, the *Asia polyglotta* (Paris 1823), contains vocabularies of about 70 Asian languages, among them 14 Samoyedic, from his long voyages in Siberia and the Caucasus or — many of them — from Messerschmidt.[17] The words of these languages are 'compared' with words in German, Latin, Finnish, Breton, Albanian, Irish, Malay, Persian, Assyrian, Armenian, Tibetan etc.etc. He distinguishes, but inconsequently, between antediluvian and postdiluvian languages.[18]

This took most of his time, but his heart was with the Chinese language — he said in 1819 that he had studied that language unremittingly since 1794. He gave examples of his Chinese learning already in his *Asiatisches Magazin* in 1802. He showed his knowledge of Chinese matters in his translation of the Monument of Yu in 1811, and quite especially he demonstrated his great familiarity with the language in his *Supplement* to the Gemona dictionary (1819). The last of his contributions to sinology was his notes to Abel Rémusat's *Föe Koue Ki*, printed after both of them had died, in 1836.

Klaproth was notorious for his bad language. Most of his articles and books contain virulent attacks on one or more scholars. Moreover, besides his research works, he delighted in violent personal diatribes against other orientalists, often published under pseudonyms and often with more or less absurd titles, such as *Leichenstein auf dem Grabe der chinesischen Gelehrsamkeit des H. Joseph Hager* (Berlin 1811), or *Grande exécution d'automne* (Paris 1815), against Stephen Weston (1749-1830), a British amateur sinologist. Everybody knew, however, that the author was Julius Klaproth from the extremely offensive manner of his writing.

He seems to have infected Abel Rémusat with this style in the first years of his sinological career. However, J.B.B. Eyriès (1767-1846), a geographer who collaborated with Klaproth at one time, speaks kindly about him.[19] He was feared, he says, because of the harsh style of his polemics. But people who sought his advise and help were surprised to find him so kind and polite. He adds that he was not at all a solitary erudite, bent over his books. On the contrary he appreciated the pleasures of high society and enjoyed a fine and elegant style of life.

Asiatisches Magazin

In 1802, when he was nineteen years old, Klaproth published at Weimar his *Asiatisches Magazin, verfasst von einer Gesellschaft Gelehrten und herausgeben von Julius Klaproth*, two volumes. It contains more than 50 large or small texts, many of them translated from English translations of Sanskrit or Persian texts, such as a section of the *Bagavad-gita*.

There is also a long article by Joseph Hager on recently discovered Babylonian inscriptions, filled with quotations in Hebrew and Arabic, and with some very critical remarks by Klaproth about some Chinese allusions in it. [20]

Klaproth contributed two long articles, the one about the conquest of China by the Manchus, mainly from Martini, the other on old Chinese literature, taken from various Jesuit sources. This text ends with a chapter on the *Yi Jing*, containing a translation of the text of the 15th hexagram, called 'Humility'. Klaproth declares (p. 553): 'I have taken the explanation of this hexagram from the edition of the Kangxi emperor, where it is much longer. I have contented myself with extracting the marrow of it'.

He does not say that the *Yi Jing* and especially its 15th hexagram was well known in Europe at the time. At the end of de Guignes' (Sr.) *Le Chou-King, un des livres sacrés des chinois* (Paris 1770) there is a 'Notice du livre chinois nommé Y-King', written in 1728 by Claude de Visdelou (1656-1737). This long article, covering 35 quarto pages, contains a translation of the texts of the 15th hexagram, *verbatim* as in Klaproth's *Asiatisches Magazin*, and with the same words about taking it from the Kangxi edition, the 'marrow', etc.

There are small chapters by Langlès and by Silvestre de Sacy. There are also some small notes, excerpts from 'Briefe von Kopenhagen'. One of them is on Chinese music and theatre, another on the customs of the Buddhist monks, which did not please the author. The third is on Cornelius de Pauw's *Recherches philosophiques sur les Egyptiens et les Chinois* (Berlin 1774), directed against Joseph de Guignes who had argued that the Chinese were an Egyptian colony, but also generally against the China picture of the Jesuits. It was widely read at the time.

These letters are anonymous but one of them is signed 'P.F.M'. They are by a Dane by the name of P.P.F. Mourier (1746-1837), who had been supercargo in the Danish Indian Company from 1770 to 1785, and who had used his time to study Chinese, first with a missionary, then with a Chinese.[21]

Inschrift des Yü
In 1811, after he had come home from Russia to Germany, and before he had handed in his resignation to the St. Petersburg Academy, Klaproth published his *Inschrift des Yü, übersetzt und erklärt von Julius von Klaproth* (Berlin 1811), with a dedication to Sergei von Uwarow, honorary member of the Academy.

In this 63 page quarto he first deprecates the work of Joseph Hager (Paris 1802), which is described as incorrect and of no importance. He says that on his voyage to the frontier of China — in 1805 — he had acquired a number of Chinese works that have helped him to explain the text of the Monument of Yu, in particular the *Zhuan Shu Yuan Qi* (篆書緣起), 'On the origin of ancient characters', printed in Peking in 1749. This work with its 32 'ancient' Chinese characters served as an introduction to the Qian Long emperor's great 'Eulogy of Mukden'.

He reproduces the text of the inscription and goes through all of its 77 'characters', to find some similarities to seal characters, the characters in his *Zhuan Shu Yuan Qi* or other dictionaries. Most of them are quite unconvincing and all in all this juvenile exercise must be regarded as a meaningless tour de force. However, it was highly esteemed at the time, because it seemed to demonstrate that he was able to translate several Chinese texts.

Supplement au Dictionaire Chinois-Latin
In 1819, six years after de Guignes' *Dictionnaire Chinois-Français et Latin* came out, Klaproth published his *Supplement au Dictionnaire Chinois-Latin du P. Basile de Glemona, imprimé, en 1813 par les soins de M. de Guignes*. It is a 168 page folio, including an 'Examen critique de l'édition du dictionnaire Chinois-Latin..' — anonymous, but written by Abel Rémusat. It was printed in the Imprimerie royale in Paris, but it has an extra litographed sheet after the title page, containing a dedication to Friedrich Wilhelm III, king of Prussia, signed 'fidèle serviteur et sujet'.

In his short Preface Klaproth gives a history of the vicissitudes of the production of a Chinese-European dictionary in France:

'France had promised the publication of a Chinese dictionary since the time of Louis XIV... but it was only in the year 1800 that the French government accepted the proposition made to it of publishing such a work. How-

ever, the task was entrusted to a man who had not sufficiently proved that
he knew Chinese... After four years he was dismissed and the plans for publication were shelved.'

'In 1808 Mr. Antonio Montucci of Siena was proposed to the Ministry of
the Interior to carry out the work; but all of a sudden it was felt that the glory
of the name of France would be jeopardized if a foreigner was called to publish it. Then Mr. de Guignes was approached, the son of the famous author
of the *Histoire des Huns*, who had lived for a long time in Canton. Scholars
who knew only his *Voyages à Peking*..., published in 1808, doubted his insights
into the Chinese language, but it was believed that he would be able to do
what the French government had entrusted him with: not to compose a new
dictionary, but just to publish that of P. Basile de Glemona which had belonged to the Vatican Library.'

'The critical examination of this work which we have placed after this
Preface, composed by Mr. ***, will show that Mr. de Guignes has deceived the
hopes of those who had proposed him for the task and that by the methods
he has chosen the dictionary of P. de Glemona has lost much of its utility.'

Klaproth says furthermore that he is publishing the Supplement to make
it possible for students of Chinese to use with profit the dictionary of Basile
de Glemona. He does not mention that it is a supplement only to the first 61
of the 214 radicals, probably because he intended to finish it some time later.
There is no endpaper.

We shall discuss the Dictionary and the Supplement together.

The Dictionary with its more than 13,000 characters has a number of
examples of them, in combinations or as parts of short sentences. However,
these examples are given only in transliteration. The reason was that in Paris
at the time there were only Fourmont's large characters.

Abel Rémusat says in his 'Examen critique...' (p. 29) that one could have
shown all the characters of the examples if one had suppressed the numerous
blank spaces in the great folio, and had omitted the unnecessary French translations. This, however, with the big characters of Fourmont, would have
swelled the book to much more than a thousand pages.

Most of the characters in the Dictionary are annotated in one way or
another in the Supplement. They are shown by their numbers in the Dictionary, but there are some extra characters, marked 'bis' or 'tert', which are
shown in Chinese characters.

Most of Klaproth's additions give other pronunciations or supplementary
meanings. Often he says: 'This character can mean many different things as

will appear clearly from the following examples.' Often — more than once per page — we find: 'Delete de Guignes' translation and substitute for it... so and so.'

Many times we read that 'x is used also for y' and there are many references to ancient or vulgar forms. There is much useful grammatical and syntactical information in the individual sections. There are a great many geographical and historical names, such as '.... the name of a town of the third order during the Han dynasty'. Klaproth now and then quotes from Abel Rémusat, Robert Morrison or de Guignes Sr.

He refers to several Chinese dictionaries but only once to the famous old Han dynasty dictionary, the *Shuo Wen Jie Zi*. This is under the very common character Ye (也), and Klaproth tell us — correctly — that in that dictionary the old form of the character is 'shown and means' the female external genital organs.

One feature that seems superfluous in a Chinese-Latin dictionary is the many translations into Manchu written with Manchu letters. Klaproth also sometimes includes remarks about the sound in Cantonese, Japanese or Korean, and there are a few words written in Hebrew, Arabic, Persian, Sanskrit or Tibetan script.

To understand the arrangement of the Dictionary and the Supplement we may look at the first page of both works. The Dictionary has on its first page:

一. Unity, priority. perfection: one, perfect.

This is followed by five two-word examples:

Ty-x, number one. X-ta, Heaven. X-seng, throughout life. X-sin, with all my heart. X-x, by itself (第一, 一大, 一生, 一心 and 一一) but a knowledge of Chinese is required to get at the right result.

In the Supplement to the Dictionary the characters are noted by their numbers in the Dictionary. Thus 一 is called 1.

On page one this is followed by a number of examples in which the character is denoted by x, as in the Dictionary.

The first three examples are as follows:

1. x-jé: (x-1790), i.e. 一夜 'all night.'

2. x-meng: (x-9031), i.e. 一萌 'at once it started to grow.'

3. x-kiao x tao (x 1116 x 777), i.e. 一叫一到 'as soon as he was called he came.'

There are 16 examples under 一.

As we see, Klaproth does not try to guess the characters for the transliterated words of the Dictionary but supplies his own from his many years of Chinese studies.

After 1819 he published many articles and books on oriental problems, but none on the Chinese language. He died alone in his vast library on August 27, 1835 from a ruptured aneurysm of the aorta.

Professor Abel Rémusat

Abel Rémusat, who was to become professor of Chinese language and litera- ture in the College du Roi in 1815, at the age of 27 — the first in Europe — was born i Paris in 1788. His father, who was a surgeon attached to the royal household, died in 1805. The son lived with his mother until her death in 1831. He died one year later, during the great cholera epidemic, but not of cholera.

The colleges being closed during the revolution, Abel's father took it upon himself to teach his son Latin. Aged 19 at the death of his father, he started to read medicine to be able to support his mother. In 1813 he defended his doctoral thesis, entitled *Dissertatio de glossosemeiotica*, dealing with the signs of diseases to be observed by inspection of the tongue — 'especially among the Chinese'. This small work was based on a Chinese textbook of medicine, translated by Michael Boym, a China Jesuit (1615-59). It shows young Rému- sat balancing between medicine and sinology!

Already as a medical student he had decided to learn Chinese. After his father's death, in 1806, he paid a first visit to the vast collections of curious, old and strange books belonging to the abbé Tersan, which were on display in several rooms in the Abbaye-aux-Boix in Paris.[22]

Here, according to legend, the abbé showed him a Chinese work on plants and teased the medical student because he could not identify the pharma- ceutical plants on the plates of the work. We know, however, that the Chinese work he showed him was the vast encyclopedia called *San Cai Tu Hui* (men- tioned above). At that time or shortly afterwards, he must have lent this work to Abel Rémusat.

We also know from his letters to his friend Jeandet that already in that same year, 1806, he began to work on problems concerning Chinese. In 1808, at the age of 20, he composed a small Chinese dictionary for himself. He tried to get access to the Chinese-European dictionaries in the Bibliothèque Impe- riale, but without success. Between the years 1808 ad 1813, as we know, de

Guignes was editing the great dictionary of Basilio Brollo de Gemona, and nobody else was allowed in! In spite of that Rémusat continued his studies, and in 1811 he published a small but remarkable book entitled *Essai sur la langue et la litterature chinoises*.

The next year he wrote three articles, one on the study of foreign languages among the Chinese, one on translations of the Bible and one on the so-called Monument of Yu. The following year he published an interesting article in a provincial newspaper, dealing with a jade tablet with inscriptions in strange kinds of Chinese characters.

This surprising output from the hands of a young medical student caught the attention of several older scholars, especially Silvestre de Sacy (1758-1838), professor of Arabic in the College Imperiale and powerful administrator of many academic institutes in Paris, who helped Rémusat to obtain Chinese books from Berlin and St. Petersburg.

When the great dictionary mentioned above came out in 1813 it was clear to his protectors that the right moment had come to establish a chair of Chinese for Abel Rémusat. In 1814 he was nominated professor of Chinese and Manchu languages and literature, on the recommendation of Silvestre de Sacy. He gave his inaugural lecture on January 16, 1815.

Then, finally, he was admitted to the treasures of the Royal Library — the Chinese books and the manuscripts of the missionaries — being charged with cataloguing it all. Most importantly, he discovered here the manuscript of a work that was going to be of the greatest importance for his studies and teaching in the following years, the *Notitia Linguae Sinicae*, written about 1729 by the French China Jesuit Joseph de Prémare (1666-1736). Rémusat made a copy of it for himself and several other copies were made by his pupils.[23]

At first this advanced textbook of Chinese language and literature, based on profound studies during more than 30 years, must have been over the head of teacher as well as pupils, but they learned by it. Some years later, when Rémusat published his own *Elemens de la grammaire chinoise* (Paris 1822) it was obvious to his pupils that it was based to a large degree on the *Notitia Linguae Sinicae*.

We are going to deal with each of Abel Rémusat's youthful works, from his little *Dictionnaire chinois* (1808) to his inaugural lecture in 1815. But before beginning to do so, let us look at a remarkable correspondence between Abel Rémusat and his friend François Jeandet, or rather at only one side of it, for we do not have Jeandet's responses to Abel Rémusat's letters. They have been noticed but not analysed.[24]

Letters from Abel Rémusat to François Jeandet

There is in the Bibliothèque Nationale of Paris a series of letters from Abel Rémusat to François Jeandet, his friend and cousin of the same age (1788-1860), dated from 1806 to 1828. (Fr. nouv. acq. 6518)

In these letters we can follow Rémusat's endeavours with the Chinese language from the first day till the day when he gave his Inaugural Lecture as professor of Chinese and Manchu languages and literature in the Collège Royale.

In the first letter of September 19, 1806, written when he was 18 years old, he tells his friend that he had found in ancient Chinese books clear evidence of a belief in the Holy Trinity. He also quotes a sentence in Chinese (書不盡言, 言不盡意): *Libri non exhauriunt verba, Verba non exhauriunt ideas.*

He adds: 'Look at the proverb I am sending you here — in Chinese so that you can see its excellent sense. I doubt that I have seen anything finer than these words. I am sure you will find it beautiful, even if you do not understand the characters'.

He does not tell his friend that he simply took the information about a triune God in China and the 'proverb' from the first volume of the great *Mémoires concernant l'histoire... des chinois (pp. 101 and 323),* (Paris 1770). He must have started his Chinese studies in 1806 with this great work — he writes in 1811 that he has studied the Chinese language for five years.

In a letter dated August 26, 1807 he writes: 'While you were away I have learned the Chinese language rather well, but I still cannot read a Chinese book'. He says that he has begun to read Confucius, quoting in Chinese a sentence from the *Analects* (Vol.II, 11) about revering the old and learning new things.

We know that the next year, in 1808, he composed his first Chinese dictionary, and on July 26, 1809 he refers to a letter (not in the collection) where he had written a sentence in Manchu.

The letters from 1811 — the year he published his *Essai sur la langue et le litterature chinoise* — contain three interesting pieces of information. On August 21 he tells his friend about a very important thing that had happened to him. 'Julius, eruditissimus Berolinensis' — Klaproth — must have read his *Essai.* Now he informs him about a Chinese-Latin manuscript dictionary for sale (in Berlin). This 'much desired work' contains 1,300 Chinese characters translated into Latin. 'The price is enormous, really more than I can afford, but I must do what I can to obtain it'. Shortly after, on October 4, he tells him that one of the books of Confucius is going to be printed in Paris—'in Chinese with my Latin version and a French translation' — 'it will cost me nothing!' (*L'invariable Milleu* (Paris 1817)). Finally, on November 12. he is sending him Saint-Martin's enthusiastic review of his *Essai*, printed in the *Magasin encyclopedique*.

January 27, 1813 he writes that he has just received Klaproth's *Mémoire sur la langue et l'ecriture des Ouigours* (Berlin 1812) 'together with my box (?) and my new dictionary'. It is not clear if this is the dictionary mentioned above.

On July 11, 1813 he writes: 'The *Lettre de Lintz* has been finished and is now deposited in the hands of the 'Maha-gourou' — this is the anonymous *Lettre écrite de Lintz par un orientaliste allemand*, published at Strasbourg in 1814, and the Maha-gourou can only be Klaproth. Its harsh criticism of Langlès is in Klaproth's style.

Finally there is a jubilant letter of December 8, 1814.

I am telling you now, my dear friend, that by a decree of November 29th his Majesty the King has created two new chairs in the Royal College, one for Chinese language and literature, and one for Sanskrit, and that he has nominated Abel Rémusat and Chezy to them. I am now in the midst of visits and preparations for my installation... I received the official appointment only two days ago. You see that the king has given me much more than I had asked for, much more than I had dared to strive for, and even more than I deserve... Mr. Langlés said yesterday to somebody that I might apply for a chair in Chinese, as Chezy had done for one in Sanskrit, but that Mr. de Guignes, who has lived for fourteen years in China and who has produced the dictionary, would be preferred. The poor man still does not know that lightning has struck, crushing him together with his unlucky protegé (de Guignes).

My salary will be 6,000 Francs from January 1, 1815.

Dictionnaire chinois

The long title of Abel Rémusat's handwritten Chinese dictionary is *Dictionnaire chinoise, contenant les caractères plus usités et leur prononciation, leur tons et leur signification en français, augmenté de deux tables des caractères chinois seulement disposés suivant leurs clefs, et l'autre des vocables ou mots avec leur renvoi au dictionnaire*.

Underneath the title he put the Chinese name he had chosen: Ming Kezi 明可子.[25]

Abel Rémusat had collected Chinese words since 1806, and now, on December 27, 1808 he finished his *Dictionnaire chinois* — 275 large pages with about 1500 characters.

He says that he has not followed the 214 radical system because he does not understand it completely.

I have decided to arrange the 1,500 characters which make up this dictionary in 20 classes according to the number of strokes in them. In the 20th class I have put characters with 20 or more strokes — they are not many.

Furthermore I have divided each class into five sections. The first section comprises the simple or primitive characters, in the second I have put characters that can be divided in a natural way into an upper and a lower part. In the third section I have put those which can be divided just as naturally into a left and a right part. In the fourth class I have put characters containing one part which is covered or enclosed by another. Finally, in the fifth class I have arranged all characters that did not fit into any of the first four ones...

This method is arbitrary and has not been used by anybody before me, but it seems to me to be as simple and as elementary as possible.

As to orthography, he sticks to a slight modification of the French way, giving also the Portuguese pronunciation. At the end of his dictionary he has arranged all the 1,500 characters alphabetically with reference to the radicals and the extra strokes in Chinese dictionaries. He mentions that he has not put in a number of familiar expressions or proverbs as they are found in Kircher's *China... illustrata*. 'My dictionary does not attempt to teach the ordinary spoken Chinese, but just to help in the reading of the historical and moral works of the Chinese'.

The dictionary is written with bold strokes and there are a number of grass script characters added. The tones are always noted carefully according to the Jesuit system and sometimes they are shown with small circles in one of the four corners in the Chinese way. In most cases no source is given, but there are about one hundred referring to Fourmont's *Lingua sinarum... grammatica duplex*, with indications of page numbers. There are less than ten referring to Bayer's *Museum sinicum*, but some more to Intorcetta's Goa edition of the *Life of Confucius* and the *Doctrine of the Mean*. There are nearly twenty references to the Lord's Prayer.

There are about 200 characters marked 'Deshauterayes'. They have a radical and a pronunciation but no signification. Rémusat must have found them among the papers of Deshauterayes which were and still are in the Bibliothèque Nationale. He must have wished to fill them in later.

Finally there are about twenty references to the *San Cai Tu Hui*. Nearly all of them are references to the three page section on the legendary emperors of China. He must have worked hard with these pages, he cannot possibly have understood them.[26]

Essai sur la language et la litterature chinoises
In 1811 Abel Rémusat, aged 23 years, made his first appearance on the scene of sinology by publishing a small book, the full title of which is *Essai sur la language et la littérature chinoises, avec cinq planches, contenant les textes chinois, accompagnés de traductions, de remarques et d'un commentaire littéraire et grammatical, suivi de notes et d'un table alphabetique des mots en chinois.*

There is a Chinese title page where the book is called *Han wen jian yao* (漢文簡要) or A summary of the Chinese language, the author calling himself 'A Bo Er,(阿伯而) student'. The time of impression is given in Chinese as the winter of the year 1810.

In his preface Rémusat took his point of departure in a report to Napoleon, printed in the same year, about historical and literary studies in the last twenty years. In this there is a general complaint about the diminishing numbers of philological studies in France.[27] 'I have felt obliged to use this occasion to publish my first work on the Chinese language.'

'I have used', he says, 'nearly five years on the study of Chinese — as much as my other occupations (his medical studies) allowed me'.

'Bayer and Fourmont had access to Chinese-European dictionaries. I have not been allowed to use any of the 16 or 18 Chinese-European dictionaries of the Bibliothèque Nationale. Circumstances have prevented me from doing so. [The 'circumstances' was the simple fact that de Guignes was working in the Library with his dictionary project. Of course a young medical student, curious about Chinese, would not have been allowed in.]'

'I have not had in my hand a Chinese-European dictionary, I have never even seen one!'

All that he had done was produced with the help of a dictionary he had composed for himself and with a few fascicles of the *Zheng Zi Tong* and a Manchu dictionary which 'Mr. Langlès has been kind enough to let me use'.

'Sinologists will understand the problems I have had with translating a Chinese text with only a Chinese-Chinese dictionary — after looking for a character I was not sure that I understood, I often arrived at characters I did not know at all.

'Such difficulties may have driven away a person who is not, as I am, in love with the beauties of the Chinese language... Only I had to spend ten times as much effort on each problem as I would have had to do if I had had a dictionary.'

Then follows the expected quotation from Confucius about doing a thing in one day, in a hundred days or in a thousand days.

He insists that he does not offer information already available in the Jesuits' books or in the works of T. S. Bayer or Fourmont, only what he has found in Chinese sources. He gives a list of the very few Chinese books that he owned—the *Shu Jing*, the *Four Books*, a small Christian treatise called *Wan Wu Zhen Yuan*, 'The true origin of all things' by Julio Aleni (1582-1649), a China Jesuit, and *San Cai Tu Hui*. He says about the Jesuit book that it is written in such an easy style, far from the style of the Classics, that one can read it and understand it in a matter of six months.

He writes only a few lines about the *San Cai Tu Hui* — just that it is an encyclopedia that deals with everything. 'It has been very useful to me and I intend to give an analysis of it, extracting some pieces from it...' — he never did so. Having seen only few Chinese books, he was unable to recognize its strangeness.

That is all. We have to imagine young Abel Rémusat sitting at his writing table in his mother's apartment with only these four works before him—among them the fantastic *San Cai Tu Hui* work. But in the text of the book there are many more Chinese books quoted — he could examine Chinese books in the Bibliothèque Imperiale as long as he kept away from the rooms where de Guignes worked.

In the text of the book he deals with the trigrams and hexagrams — 'never meant to be a script' — the 214 radicals, obviously without knowing about the history of the radical system. He then gives examples of Chinese characters to show how by the addition of certain elements they are changed in a rational way to other meanings.

He mentions the six kinds of characters according to the *Shuo Wen Jie Zi*, but without going into details. He deals with the three kinds of script — the seal script, the Li script and the grass script, referring to several pages in the *San Cai Tu Hui* work which he had before him. He explains the technique of *fanqie* (反切), referring to T.S. Bayer's *Lexicon Cu Guei* (1738) and the four corner system for the indication of tones.

One of the most intriguing sections is the presentation of the traditional explanation of the eight parts of the character Yong 永, Eternity, shown on one of the folding tables of the work.

The last 15 pages of the text deal with the arrangement of dictionaries. He speaks about other radical systems until the final 214 radical system adopted in 1615. He also mentions the system invented by Bayer without going into details, although there is some similarity with his own system in his *Dictionnaire chinois*.

Speaking about combinations of words (characters) in a Chinese-European dictionary, he says that one has to find under each character the combinations or phrases where it occurs, always in Chinese characters, not in European letters. If not, one will be caught in a veritable chaos because each Chinese word — written with European letters — may stand for up to 160 characters. This is remarkable, because that was exactly what was going to happen with the *Dictionnaire chinois-francais et latin*, two years after! (see p. 30)

The last part of the *Essai* is taken up by annotated examples of Chinese texts.

The engraved characters are printed on four folding tables, with the pronunciation beside each of them. The 'Explication des planches' (43 pages) gives an explanation of each of the citations in transliteration with tone marks and indication of the radical number and the number of extra strokes. There are also several comments on grammatical and literary matters. Most of the quotations deal with metaphysical or moral problems, there are no scientific or technical terms.

There are long sections, such as from the *Zhong Yong* 中庸, the *Shu Jing* 書 經 and the *Li Ji* 禮記. The first example is from the Great Appendix to the *Yi Jing* 易經, about the Tai Ji (he took it from the *San Cai Tu Hui*) and another from the Treaty of Remarks on the Trigrams and several commentaries to this work.

There are citations from Luo Bi (蘿泌), but there are also quite short pieces such as the title of the *San Cai* work. The passage also includes some didactic pieces such as 21 characters shown with their appropriate tone marks as small circles in one of the four corners. His scoop was when he found a piece in his *San Cai* work which stated definitely that there are *five tones* in Chinese![28]

There are many notes, and at the end of the book there is a complete alphabetical list of the 500 Chinese words occuring in the text (20 pages).

Abel Rémusat himself says that since there are so few Chinese texts available, his book may be used by students as their first textbook.

All in all, this little book offers a surprising wealth of information, taking in consideration the time it was printed.

De l'etude des langues étrangères chez les chinois

This article, published in Millin's elegant *Magasin encyclopédique*, (vol. 5, 1811), may perhaps have contributed more than any other to his advancement. It shows that, in contradiction to the general opinion in Europe, Chinese scholars occupied themselves with studies of foreign languages.

It deals with works written in Mongol by Chinese scholars, but in particular with a great 16 volume book, eight of them containing vocabularies in Chinese, Manchu, Mongol, Tibetan and Uighur, the eight others being texts written in the respective languages. They pretended to have been letters written by foreign rulers to the Chinese emperor.

The China Jesuit Jean Joseph Marie Amiot (1716-93) had sent this work to the Bibliothèque Royale in Paris. He had added translations into Latin of the Chinese parts of it. Moreover he had written a very long article about the work which had been printed in the *Mémoires concernant... des chinois*, Tome XIV, 1789.

Rémusat had seen this work in the Bibliothèque Imperial and gives a detailed analysis of it.

The first of the vocabularies and the piece connected with it was Persian, written with Arabic letters. Rémusat says that he has shown them to several people in Paris who know Persian — they assured him that the language was correct. Amiot had not been able to decipher the Chinese translations of the many Persian-speaking countries, but Abel Rémusat reads them as Egypt, Samarkand, Mecca, Damascus, etc. He adds that he has seen a much better book on Muslims in China and that he intends to publish extracts from it — nobody has heard of Muslim books in China!

The second volume is called Si Fan, and is in Tibetan written with a corrupt form of Sanskrit. The third section is in Uighur, the fourth in Mintian, a dialect of southern Burma. The fifth section is about Si Tian languages, i.e., on the languages of India. This is perhaps the most surprising part of the book. It is Sanskrit and written with navanagari letters. Amiot had assumed that the text belonging to this section was a vocabulary, but Rémusat assures the reader that it is a period from the Sanskrit poem called *Purana*. He acknowledges the help he has obtained for this identification from his friend, the learned translator from the Persian of the *Medjnoun and Leila*—Antoine de Chezy.

Indian religion or language is often referred to in Chinese as 'fan', and Rémusat refers to the section on coins in the *San Cai Tu Hui*, giving page numbers for pictures or descriptions of foreign coins, some of them marked 'fan', which in these texts actually means Sanskrit.

He also thanks 'the famous French orientalist, M. Silvestre de Sacy, for his explanations of some Turkish words'. He says that the Chinese dictionaries often carry words in Sanskrit, written in Chinese transliteration, and he discusses at length a Chinese-Manchu-Tibetan dictionary!

This was a new picture of Chinese scholarship.

Translation of the Bible

A Protestant mission had begun shortly before 1810 in Canton and especially among the Chinese in Malacca. The great goal was to produce a Chinese translation of the Bible.

In 1811 Abel Rémusat wrote a short article — 'Sur la traduction de la Bible en langue chinoise' — about a translation of the Gospel according to St. Mark, published in Serampore by the Methodist missionary J. Marshman.[29]

It deals mostly with the new terms invented — after much agony of soul — by the Protestants to supplant those used for two centuries by the Catholic missionaries. First of all the Protestants used the word Shen 神, a spirit or a spiritual entity, for God, instead of the Tianzhu 天主 of the Catholics, or even Shangdi 上帝, suspected by many.

The purpose was first of all, of course, to find new terms different from those used by the arch-enemies, the Popish missionaries. Rémusat gives many reasons for rejecting 'Shen', but he does not enter into a discussion of the arguments of the Protestants. This discussion has been going on ever since.

The jade tablet in Grenoble

In the *Journal du Departement de l'Isère*, No. 6, 1812, there is an article by Abel de Rémusat (sic) entitled 'Explication d'une inscription en caracteres chinois et mandchous, gravée sur une plaque de jade qui appartient au Cabinet des Antiques de la Bibliothèque de Grenoble'. It deals with a jade tablet with Chinese and Manchu inscriptions, which the author had seen in the museum of Grenoble, the principal town in the department of Isère.

It measures 15 by 10 cm and carries an inscription of 17 Chinese characters arranged in three lines, separated by another kind of characters. He gives the characters in transcription and translates them as follows:

A Tablet from a musical instrument, in the Pavillion of Happiness, in the apartment of the August Empress who subjugates desire and whose heart is like the phoenix.

He discusses his own translation and tells why he thinks that this empress is one of the Qian Long emperor's wives. The reason is that the interpolated script is the same or just like one of the 'old Manchu scripts' invented for the Qiang Long emperor's poem called 'Eulogy of the city of Mukden'. This huge and monstrous work contains the poem of the emperor, printed with 32 'ancient Chinese characters', and with 32 Manchu letters made to resemble the Chinese ones. At the end the young scholar wonders how this piece came to rest in the museum of Grenoble.

This small article is of interest because it shows that Abel Rémusat had access to the Department of Oriental Manuscripts, at the time when he was prevented from entering the rooms where the Chinese-European dictionaries were kept.

Plan d'un dictionnaire chinois avec des notices de plusieurs dictionnaires chinois manuscrits, et des réflections sur les travaux exécutés jusqu'a ce jour par les européens, pour faciliter l'étude de la langue chinoise.
This is a 70 page article, printed in the *Mélanges asiatiques* II, Paris 1826, but Rémusat writes in a note on the first page that it had been printed already in 1814. Most of the edition having been destroyed at the printing office, he has now decided to print it again here.

Except for a two line note on p.96 added in 1826 it does not mention the *Dictionnaire chinois-français et latin* of de Guignes.

Rémusat begins with thanking Julius Klaproth profusely for helping him to obtain the means he needed for his Chinese studies. It was with his assistance that he became able to buy two precious manuscript Chinese-European dictionaries. There is a long chapter on European works dealing with the Chinese language, missionaries and others: Magaillans, Semedo, T.S. Bayer and Étienne Fourmont.

He then comes to Joseph Hager who arrived in Paris after he had published his *An Explanation of the Elementary Characters of the Chinese...* When 'considerations independent of his will' (?) retarded his dictionary work, he took to 'composing other works of considerable erudition, but not related to Chinese matters' (sic). He was dismissed and de Guignes took his place...

Montucci attacked Hager 'as another Aretino', later on treating de Guignes in the same way. He had an excellent knowledge of the Chinese language, but recently we have heard that he has abandoned his studies, to the regret of all the true friends of the Chinese language.

In a long chapter on manuscript dictionaries Rémusat praised Basilio de

Gemona's dictionary — it is undoubtedly the best one available. But he deplores that the double expressions and the examples are given only in Latin, not in Chinese characters, this 'diminishes the value of the work'. Actually nine tenths of it is useless, unless one knows Chinese beforehand.

He mentions several other manuscript dictionaries, especially one Chinese-Spanish that has all the examples in Chinese. However, it is written in the running hand style.

After a presentation of the Jinzhao 'dialect' — the language of Fujian and the Chinese in the Philippines, he embarks upon his grandiose plan for a Chinese dictionary: One had to start from one of the Chinese dictionaries, such as the *Zheng Zi Tong* or the *Kangxi Zidian*, taking from them 30,000 or 40,000 characters. Each character is going to be shown in its oldest form — we have books here about ancient Chinese characters, which could be used for that purpose. 'One could use as a model for that Klaproth's 'Monument of Yu'.

Then the many variants should be noted, perhaps with the help of the *Hai Pian* (海篇) dictionary, followed by the pronunciation in French, not only of the Mandarin Chinese but also of all the dialects (patois). One should also add information about ancient pronunciations, taken for example from the *Book of Odes*.

After that one should add synonyms and opposite words, and then at least one example for each character, in Chinese and in French. The Chinese have the bad habit of referring to a work simply as for example 'Mencius'. We have to look up book, chapter and article in each case, and to indicate which edition we are quoting from.

Arrived thus far in his musings, Rémusat admits that it may take more than one life to produce such a Thesaurus Linguae Sinicae. Before beginning to do so, one has to reread, 'pen and brush in hand', all the Classics of the first and second order, the philosophers of all schools, the historical works, the novels and the encyclopedias....

And still such a work may be insufficient. Rémusat says that Klaproth has suggested that one should acquire one hundred copies of the *Zi Hui* dictionary from Canton — they are very cheap — and give them away together with the Chinese-European dictionary. More than one hundred copies would not be required.

Finally he comes to the cost of such a work. It would be enormous if each of the characters had to be produced one by one. Perhaps, however, one could engrave them on copperplates and print only the pronunciation, significance, etc. — i.e., in principle as he had done in his little *Essai sur la langue et la litterature chinoises.*[30]

He wrote all of this in 1814, and it may perhaps seem strange that he repeated it in 1826....

The last part of the article deals chiefly with Rémusat's discovery of the 'plagiate' of Fourmont. He had taken whole sections from Varo's *Arte de lengua mandarina.* Rémusat is shocked by this discovery and it has been repeated ever since. As a matter of fact Fourmont sat down with Varo's book which contains no Chinese characters, and tried to find out what they were. He supposed that he was the only person in Europe who was able to do so.

Examen critique

Klaproth's *Supplement au Dictionnaire chinois-latin du P. Basile de Glemona* was published in 1819, but he says in his Preface that he had started printing it in 1815. We know that he sent sheets of it to Montucci in 1817. When it was published in 1819, Klaproth had put into it an 'Examen critique' of the dictionary ('admis à la tête de son ouvrage'), without Rémusat's name, just calling him 'by ***'. The 'Examen critique de l'edition du dictionnaire chinois du P. Balise de Glemona' fills 29 folio pages. It is a devastating criticism, attacking everything from the parts de Guignes ought to have included — the many tables — to the numerous errors he had committed.

Rémusat begins his article in a spectacular way by telling a standard story about a literary theft in China in the 17th century:

Zhang Zilie (張自烈), a poor scholar, had worked for many years in a library, composing a great dictionary which he gave the title *Zheng Zi Tong.* The head librarian, Liao Wenying (廖文英) who strove for fame but shunned work, persuaded the poor scholar to sell him his manuscript for one hundred ounces of gold. Shortly after, when Zhang Zilie died without leaving heirs, Liao Wenying published the dictionary under his own name (1671). However, as soon as the first edition was out, the fraud was exposed by other scholars who recognized the style of Zhang Zilie. A new edition was published with the names of these men, giving evidence that Zhang Zilie was the author of the *Zheng Zi Tong* dictionary, and since then this dictionary has always been called Mr. Zhang's dictionary.

From there Rémusat goes on directly to the work of the poor Franciscan, Basile de Glemona, who had composed the *Han Zi Xi Yi,* published now by de Guignes without de Glemona's name on the title page. Actually the only thing in de Guignes' dictionary that is not from Glemona is an Introduction and a Preface; both of them had nothing to do with the dictionary, and all of it was taken from earlier Jesuit authors — with many errors.

The 'Examen critique' is unusually sharp and contains several personal, defaming remarks about de Guignes.

It seems as if Abel Rémusat was surprised and perhaps shocked at seeing the 'Examen critique' printed anonymiously in Klaproth's *Supplement* in 1819. He probably had written this text shortly after the publication of de Guignes' dictionary in 1813 — perhaps before he got his chair.

In the same year he wrote a review of Klaproth's work entitled 'Sur le supplement au dictionnaire chinois-latin du P. Balise, redigé par M. Klaproth' in which he admitted to be the author of the 'Examen critique' (Melanges Asiatique, II, p. 220-22). There are some odd pages in this review:
'Mr. Klaproth has composed a supplement to the de Glemona dictionary, the first part of which has just been published. I have been called to present this work by a foreign scholar... At the same time I wish to express my opinion about an esteemed voyager, a compatriot, whose name is so honorable and so dear to all the friends of literature and sound erudition... I want to pay tribute to the editor of this eminently useful book, for his zeal, his patience and for his exactitude....' He adds that in his 'Examen critique' he has expressed himself with a severity that some readers may have regarded as excessive....

Inaugural lecture
Finally we shall look briefly at Abel Rémusat's inaugural lecture, the *Programme du Cours de langue et de litterature chinoises et de Tartare-Mandchou; précédé du discours prononcé à la première Séance de ce cours, dans l'une des salles du Collège Royal de France, le 16 janvier 1815, par M. Abel Rémusat, Docteur en Médicine de la Faculté de Paris, Lecteur et Professeur royal.* This marked the establishment of European academic sinology.

The 'programme du cours' — four pages — is proceeded by a 23 page text on the origin, the progress and the utility of Chinese culture in Europe. It is an eulogy of the Chinese language and a defence against its detractors. He speaks of the 'ridicule' which used to be attached to the very name of the people whose language we are going to study. He makes a point, all the way, of emphasizing the great role of French scholars in the advancement of knowledge about Chinese matters, and he does not mention Montucci or Klaproth. He speaks of Silvestre de Sacy as 'le prince des orientalistes de notre siècle'.

The Programme lists, point by point, the chapters on the spoken language, the written language from the Gua of Fuxi to our day's written style. It mentions by name the six kinds of characters according to the *Shuo Wen Jie Zi*, then phraseology and grammar. He says that he will read with his students the Nestorian Stele text, Prémare's translation of the 'Orphelin de la famille de Tchao', the 'second book of Confucius', fragments of the *Xiao Shu*, chapters from the *Shu Jing* and the *Shi Jing* and also something about foreign countries from Ma Duanlin. There is a short piece about Manchu, a great help in the study of Chinese.

Finally there is a list of the books which the students must use when following his course:

The two works by Étienne Fourmont and de Gemona's great dictionary. Useful are also two long articles by Pierre Martial Cibot in vol. VIII and IX of the *Memoires concernant... des chinois*[31], a letter from de Mailla placed at the end of the *Chou-King*, a dissertation on the radicals by Deshauterayes, printed in the *Encyclopedie élémentaire* and his own *Essai sur la langue et la litterature chinoises*, with its texts and translations.

In a note appended at the end he speaks about his 'Plan d'un dictionnaire chinoise' which was published in 1814 but only in a very few copies.

He says that the Chinese Grammar he is working on for the moment is not, as some people think, a purely imaginary project, nor is his plan for a great *Thesaurus Linguae Sinicae*. 'It will be carried out, if only some diligent persons would come along and help me with it.'

Consolidation

In 1822 Abel Rémusat published his *Elemèns de la grammaire chinoise ou principes généraux du Kou-Wen ou style antique, et du Kouan-Hoa, c'est a dire, de la langue commune généralement usitée dans l'Empire Chinois*. It was used by generations of students of Chinese in France and outside France, being reprinted unchanged but in a more stately form, in 1858.[32]

We are not going to analyze this work here. It suffices to say that it is a fine and elegantly written introduction to the Chinese language. It was based to a large extent on the *Notitia Linguae Sinicae*, written by Joseph de Prémare, S.J. in 1728 and sent by him to Étienne Fourmont in Paris. As we have heard already, Abel Rémusat had discovered the manuscript when he got access to the Chinese collections of the Bibliothèque Nationale in 1815. It had not been published in 1822, and Rémusat thought that it would never be possible to publish it. It was, however, printed in Malacca in 1831 at the expense of Lord Kingsborough.[33] This edition was again reprinted in Hong Kong in 1893.

Rémusat taught three times a week in the College du Roi, and he made his appearance regularly in the Académie des Inscriptions et Belles-Lettres, giving many lectures. There he was seen and heard by Henri Beyle — Stendhal — who admired him and called him the most learned man in France (*Oeuvr. compl.* vols. 47-48).

However, the most important event was the foundation of the Societé asiatique in 1822, the same year that Rémusat published his Chinese grammar. Its protector was the Duc d'Orléans, the later king Louis Philippe, its president was Silvestre de Sacy. It was dominated by Abel Rémusat, his friend Antoine Saint-Martin (1791-1832) the armenianist, and Julius Klaproth, who had many articles printed in its *Journal asiatique*.

All in all Rémusat published more than 30 papers and books, most printed in his *Mélanges asiatique, I-II*, (1825-26) and *Nouveaux Mélanges asiatiques I-II*, (1829), followed by *Melanges posthumes* in 1843. He wrote about Confucianism, Daoism, Buddhism, Lamaism, on the geography of Asia and on the Manchu language. He also made a translation of a Chinese novel, but all that belongs to a book about the life and work of Abel Rémusat.[34]

Abel Rémusat died of a cancer of the stomach or the pancreas on June 2, 1832, aged 44 years. He was succeeded by his most brilliant pupil, Stanislaf Julien (1797-1873), who dominated European sinology for the next forty years.

Notes

1. Knud Lundbæk: *T. S. Bayer (1694-1738) — Pioneer Sinologist.* London: Curzon Press 1986.
2. Knud Lundbæk: *Joseph de Prémare (1666-1736) S.J. — Chinese Philology and Figurism.* Aarhus: Aarhus University Press 1991.
3. Cécile Leung-Hanh-King: The Language of the 'Other': — Étienne Fourmont (1683-1745). Chinese, Hebrew and Arabic in Pre-enlightenment France. Doctoral dissertation University of Chicago, 1993.
4. At the time he was always called de Glemona. We shall call him de Gemona except when quoting.
5. Louis Mathieu Langlès (1763-1824), French orientalist. He pretended to know Arabic, Persian and Manchu and published an enormous amount of orientalist books, all of them translated from English or German. At the end of the century, director of the Department of Oriental Manuscripts in the Bibliothèque Nationale, Abel Rémusat, who hated him because he would not let him get access to the Chinese-European dictionaries in the Bibliothèque Nationale, published anony-

mously a devastating diatribe against him entitled *Lettre ècrite de Lintz par un orientaliste allemand*, Strasbourg 1814.

6. The Qian Long emperor (ruled 1736-95) paid a visit in 1743 to the graves of his ancestors in Mukden in Manchuria and wrote a poem which he had printed privately in 64 huge volumes (juan), 32 in 'ancient' Chinese characters and 32 in 32 Manchu letters, made to resemble the 32 Chinese characters.

   J. J. M. Aimot (1718-93), a Jesuit at the Imperial Court in Peking, acquired a copy of this work and translated it into French. He sent the work together with his translation to the Bibliothèque nationale in Paris where it was published in 1770 under the title *Éloge de la ville de Moukden et ses environs*, together with a great many general notes and notes on the 32 'ancient' Chinese characters.

7. Isaac Titsingh (1740/44-1812), for more than 20 years head of the Dutch Indian Company's factory in Nagasaki, Japan. He brought many curios and books with him when he came back to Europe in 1809. Among them was a Japanese encyclopedia which fascinated the scholars of the time. It contained a section with fancy 'old' Chinese characters, among them a 'facsimile' of the text of the Yu monument believed to have been carved on a mountain top in the Hunan province by Yu the Great (2207-2198 BC) and dealing with his exploits in draining off the Great Flood.

   Nowadays it is rejected with reference to the great Ming-Qing scholar *Yang Shen* who declared it to be a forgery. Hager and Klaproth accepted its veracity. Rémusat made a reservation calling it 'attribué à l'Empereur Iu'.

8. *Zi Hui*: Published in 1615. It was the first dictionary to use the 214 radical system. Zheng Zi Tong was a greatly enlarged edition of the *Zi Hui*. It was followed by the *Kangxi Zidian* of 1715, an expurgated edition of the *Zheng Zi Tong*, which became the standard dictionary since then.

9. *San Cai Tu Hui*: 'Collected Illustrations of the Three Powers'. There is a modern 6 volume edition of this work from Taiwan (Chengwen Chubanshe, 1970).

10. *Wan Bao* books: See Knud Lundbæk: *The Traditional History of the Chinese Script, from a seventeenth century Jesuit manuscript*, Aarhus 1988.

11. Macartney, before his embassy to Peking (1792-93), had sought everywhere for a person who knew Chinese. Finally he found four young missionaries in the Collegio Cinese in Naples and had them sent to London. They never arrived in China, deserting the ships in Goa.

12. Hartmut Walravens: *Antonio Montucci (1762-1829), Lektor der intalienische Sprache, Jurist und gelehrter Sinologe. Joseph Hager (1757-1819): Orientalist un Chinakundiger*. Berlin 1992. Very detailed bibliographies, including a 17-page catalogue of the many manuscripts Montucci sold to the Vatican.

13. *Shuo Wen Jie Zi* composed by Xu Shen about AD 100.

14. *Mémoires concernant l'histoire, les sciences, les arts, les moeurs, les usages etc. des chinois*. 1-17, Paris 1776-1814.

15. He mentions Rémusat, Klaproth and 'a professor in the Hertford College', the college of the East India Compagny, by the name James Summers.

16. Count Jean Potocki (1761-1815). Polish scholar and novelist. Called to St. Petersburg by Catherine II, he was sent as second ambassador in Golowkin's unsucessful embassy to Peking, together with Julius Klaproth. Afterwards he

travelled widely in Europe, Siberia and North Africa. He published twenty works about the peoples of Russia. In the last part of his life he worked on a vast and fantastic novel, consisting of a great many interlocking stories in various styles — roman noir, fairy tale, ghost story, astrological and philosophical discourse. It was printed only partly at the time. After having been rediscovered in 1958 by Roger Caillois, the surrealist, this marvellous book was finally published under the title of *Manuscrit trouvé à Saragosse* (Paris: José Corti 1989).

17. Daniel Gottlieb Messerschmidt (1685-1735), German explorer, who travelled in Siberia on the instructions of Peter I from 1720 to 1727. He studied the local peoples, their language, literary records, and ancient monuments. His 10 volume *Survey of Siberia* had not been published at Klaproth's time, but the manuscript was available to scholars in St. Petersburg.

18. Landresse, a pupil of Abel Rémusat, says in a long note on Klaproth, printed in the *Nouveaux Journal Asiatique* (XVI, 1835), the year of his death, that the *Asia polyglotta* and similar works were old-fashioned the moment they were published because of their 'comparison' of syllables. Klaproth was aware of the criticism. He says in the Preface to the *Asia polyglotta* that 'Die Wurzeln und Wörter sind der Stoff der Sprachen... Dennoch ist es meine Absicht nicht, die grammatische Vergleichung als ganz unnütz zu verwerfen' — still he never uses grammatical comparisons.

19. Eyriès in *Biographie universelle*.

20. 'Ueber die vor kurzem entdeckten Babylonischen Inscriften'.

21. Mourier was the son of a Swiss pastor in the Reformerte Kirke in Copenhagen. When he came to Canton at the age of 24 he decided to learn Chinese. In the Royal Library of Copenhagen there are three Chinese-European dictionaries which he had copied, among them the *Han Zi Xi Yi*. There is also an exercise book that shows how hard he worked with the language. When he came back to Copenhagen in 1785 there was absolutely no interest in the Chinese language. In 1801 to 1804, when he was 55-58 years old, he received letters from Julius Klaproth, then 19 years old, who was preparing his *Asiatisches Magazin*. Mourier sent a number of Chinese works to the young German, and lent him his copy of the *Han Zi Xi Yi*. He wrote to Klaproth several times to get it back, but without success. His copy of Mourier's copy is now in the British Museum (Add. 11709). It has been shown that it is based on Mourier's copy. See Knud Lundbæk: 'Kinesisk con amore. Danskeren P. F. Mouriers sinologiske studier i det 18. århundrede', in *Fund og Forskning i det kongelige Biblioteks samlinger*, Vol. XI, 1964 (with an English summary).

22. Abbé Tersan: Charles Philippe Campion de Tersan (1736-1819), French antiquarian. A wealthy man, he formed a large collection of antiquities, medals and books, some of them Chinese, the largest and finest collection in Paris at the time. It was said of him that he was not only a collector but had a deep knowledge of the kind of things he collected.

23. See note 1.

24. L. Feer: 'Papier d'Abel Rémusat', *Journal asiatique*, 9'serie, tome IV, p. 550, 1894.

25. In a letter to Jeandet of April 6, 1808 he writes: »In spite of your sarcasms I continue to sign myself 'Lumiere'. Look at 'Ming' as the initial of the word 'Ming

Ko Tseu'. I apply a seal showing it.« In his *Dictionnaire chinoise* of 1808 'ke' or 'ko' is said to mean 'convenable, digne'.

26. Pp. 560-61 in the modern Taiwan edition.
27. *Rapport historique sur le progrès de l'histoire... depuis 1789...* redigé par M. Dacier. Paris 1810 (given in 1808).
28. It is on page 1649 in the modern edition.
29. Mélanges asiatiques, I, pp. 1-14, 1825.
30. It is impossible not to compare these lines to the *Catalogue des ouvrages de Monsieur Fourmont l'aisné*, published anonymously in 1732, but such that everybody could see who was the author.

    In this strange work Fourmont speaks about his many Chinese dictionaries, especially of one which he called *Dictionnaire historique, chronologique et geographique de l'Emprie de la Chine*, four volumes in folio. He sent this book to Joseph de Prémare in Macao who responded with an angry letter: 'If we had fifty missionaries here, all of them good at Chinese, working together on something like your Chinese *Moreri*, I am sure they would never be able to accomplish such a work. How can you imagine that you alone, and in Europe, could do what so many missionaries could not do?'

    Rémusat never mentions Fourmont's *Catalogue des ouvrages de Monsieur Fourmont l'áisnè* and maybe he did not know it. In 1826, however, when he repeated his megalomaniac propositions, he must have known Prémare's reply, for Klaproth had found it and got it printed in the *Magasin encyclopedique* in 1817.
31. These articles show clearly that Cibot was a fervent China Figurist. Rémusat never mentions that problem. See Knud Lundbæk: 'Pierre Martial Cibot — the last China Figurist', in *Sino-Western Cultural Relations Journal*, XV, 1993.
32. In the 'avertissement' to the second edition it is stated that a cousin of the author 'has resolved to have a new edition of the *Elemens de la Grammaire chinoise* printed, completely as the first edition of the Imprimerie Imperiale, in 1822' — perhaps François Jeandot, he died in the year 1860.
33. Lord Kingsborough (1795-1837), the rich English nobleman who was publishing his enormous *Antiquities of Mexico*, nine volumes in Royal Folio (1830).
34. Knud Lundbæk: 'Notes on Abel Rémusat and the beginning of academic sinology in Europe', in the *Actes du VIIe Colloque international de Sinologie*, Institut Ricci, Paris 1992. Ibid.: *Abel Rémusat (1788-1832): The Beginning of Academic Sinology in Europe* (in preparation).

Cultural Exchange in Northern Liang (397-439)

Susanne Juhl

In Chinese history, the period between the Han and Tang dynasties is generally described as politically very confused. Kingdoms often rapidly appeared and disappeared. Chinese culture, as expressed in literature and art in Southern Chinese dynasties, was only handed down on a small scale from Northwestern China. However, during this period, intense Buddhist activity influenced Northwestern China, in particular the Liangzhou region located in present-day Gansu.

It is generally believed that the Liangzhou region, in this period, was relatively wealthy and prosperous. Due to its geographical location, the economy of the region was based on trade, especially profits from the caravan routes passing from China through the Liangzhou region to the Central Asian kingdoms and to India. Since the Han Dynasty trade had been centrally controlled and largely used as a means of political pressure on nomads. Many of the trade routes, mainly dominated by merchants of Iranian origin, were situated in areas connected with the newly established nomadic states that were in a position to control the trade.

Buddhism, first noted in China in the first century of our era, in this period underwent a wide propagation, and in some small kingdoms in the Liangzhou region Buddhism was supported by the central authorities. Caravan routes, being an important factor in the spread of religion, were travelled by Chinese pilgrims on journeys to the Central Asian kingdoms and to India, and by monks from these kingdoms on journeys to China to propagate the Buddhist faith.

This paper will discuss some of the historical accounts and the archaeological materials that can elucidate cultural and religious currents, especially those affecting the Northern Liang kingdom (397-439) ruled by the Xiongnu clan Juqu.[1]

A Short History of Liangzhou

Since the second century BC the Liang region had been mainly occupied by branches of the Xiongnu tribe, which had, at that time, expelled the Indo-European Scythian tribe *Yuezhi*.

During the Han Dynasty, the Liang region and large territories, all located northwest of China and inhabited by nomadic tribes, were annexed by the Chinese state.

One of the means employed by the Chinese government to secure stability in the region was forced resettlement of Han-Chinese. Many nomadic tribes living outside the newly annexed territories were likewise forced to become farmers and settle inside the new borders. At the same time these nomads were forced to defend the Chinese borders under the general policy 'using barbarians to fight barbarians'.

The Chinese government also donated substantial tributes to the nomads, mainly in the form of grain and silk, as well as establishing marriage relations with the rebellious tribes. In 317, under heavy pressure from nomadic tribes, the Chinese government and imperial family of the Western Jin Dynasty (265-313) escaped and established a new kingdom south of the Yangze River. In the next two centuries China was split up into various dynasties and small kingdoms. A part of this period is, for the northern territories of China, named 'The Sixteen Kingdoms', and 'The Invasion of the Five Barbarian Tribes' (317-440).

Fu Jian (r. 357-385), emperor of Former Qin, had during his reign united the various branches of the Xianbei tribe mainly occupying the east of northern China, and branches of the Xiongnu and Tibetan tribes mainly occupying the northern and northwestern parts of China, and incorporated them into a central state covering the whole of northern China.

One of Fu Jian's aims was to gain full control of the profitable trade with the Central Asian kingdoms, and in 383 he dispatched General Lü Guang[2] with a force of 70,000 men to secure the allegiance of these small kingdoms. On this expedition Lü Guang secured the submission of more than 30 kingdoms, which formerly had acknowledged the suzerainty of the Central Asian kingdom of Kucha.

Fu Jian had political as well as economic reasons for these actions, but he might also have had some ambitions of a more religious nature, as described by Hui Jiao in the biography of the great Buddhist monk Kumarajiva in *Gao seng zhuan (Lives of Famous Buddhist Monks)*:

After Kumarajiva's teaching had flowed through the Western Regions, his reputation spread to the Eastern Streams. At the time Fu Jian had usurped the imperial title in Guan-zhong (Changan)... In the thirteenth year of Fu Jian's reign period *jian-yuan*, the year *ding-chou* (377), in the first month, the Grand Astrologer reported to the throne: 'A star has appeared in the portion of the zodiac corresponding to the foreign kingdoms. There will be a wise man of great moral power coming in to assist the Middle Kingdom.' Jian replied: 'We have heard that in the Western Regions there is one, Kumarajiva. In Xiangyang (in northern Hubei) there is the *sramana* Shi Daoan. Would it not be one of these?' Whereupon he sent a messenger to [Daoan] to inquire of him... On the eve of [Lü Guang's] departure Jian gave a farewell banquet to Guang in the *Jian-guang* Palace, on which occasion he said: 'Emperors and kings rule in compliance with Heaven, rooting themselves in the love of all creatures as their own sons. It is unthinkable that we should make a punitive expedition against them out of covetousness for their territory. On the contrary it is precisely for the sake of those who cherish the Way that we do so. We have heard that in the Western Regions there is one, Kumarajiva, who profoundly understands the *dharmas* and their manifestations (*fa xiang*), and is well versed in the Positive and Negative Principles (*yin yang*), and is the admiration of all his disciples. We long for him intensely. The worthy and wise are a kingdom's greatest treasure. If you should conquer Qiu-ci [i.e. Kucha, the dominant power in Turkestan at the time], then send back Kumarajiva by mounted courier.' (translation by Mather, 1959:4-5)[3]

When Lü Guang returned from his expedition, however, Fu Jian had lost control of the empire and Former Qin had fallen apart. Over the next years, Former Qin was fragmented into a number of small states, most of them ruled by non-Chinese chieftains.

Lü Guang participated in this anarchy, in 389 styling himself king (*wang*), and in 396 Heavenly Appointed King of the Great Liang (*tianwang daliang*). Historically his state is named Later Liang. The territory of Later Liang covered the area around Gaochang, present-day Turpan, in Xinjiang, to Guangwu, present-day Yongdeng in Gansu.

There is reason to believe that the population in the Liangzhou region in the late fourth century formed a mixture of Han-Chinese and non-Chinese groups, but the nature of this assimilation is very hard to deduce from written information.

The History of Juqu Mengxun

The very first information divulged in the biography of Juqu Mengxun is that he belonged to the Zhangye, Linsong, Lushui *Hu*. This firstly informs us he belonged to the Xiongnu tribe (*hu*). The branch of the Xiongnu tribe named the Zhangye, Lushui *Hu* was scattered over an area covering the Zhangye and Linsong commanderies in central Later Liang, approximately the area around present-day Zhangyexian, and further south to the Luxishui River, west of present-day Xining in Qinghai[4].

The next information given is that Mengxun's family for generations had held the leading position as Left *Juqu*[5] of the Xiongnu tribe. The *Songshu* traces the family back to Mengxun's great-great grandfather and great grandfather who both were vigorous, had a reputation and had applied the title as their family name. His grandfather was enfeoffed as prince of the *Di* Land, and his father, who had inherited that title, had been appointed Military Protector of Zhongtian. It is obvious from this information that for a long period the Juqu clan must have been able to maintain a relatively high degree of tribal organization.

The biography has a vivid description of a man with some remarkable characteristics: we are told Mengxun was well versed in Chinese histories, which not only indicates that he knew the Chinese language but also that he was familiar with Chinese culture. He had some knowledge of astrology, was brave, heroic, and eminent in strategy; moreover, we are told, he was humorous and good at adapting to circumstances.

The king of Later Liang, Lü Guang, decided in 397 to attack Western Qin, and two of Mengxun's uncles were sent to participate in the battle. Lü Guang was severely defeated, losing his territory south of the Yellow River, and his brother was killed in the battle. Lü Guang then accused Mengxun's two uncles of the death of his brother and ordered their execution. Mengxun took this opportunity to start an uprising, and at the funeral of his uncles he was able to gather more than 10,000 members of their clan, who all swore rebellion and organized an army. They captured the Linsong commandery, and then encamped at Jinshan, northeast of Linsong.

Mengxun and his cousin Nancheng put forward the governor of the Jiankang commandery[6], Duan Ye, as Governor of the Liangzhou region and enfeoffed him as Duke of Jiankang. Moreover, they altered the Later Liang era name to the first year of *shen-xi* (the Divine seal, 397-399). In 399 Duan Ye arrogated to himself the title King (*wang*) of Liang and appointed Mengxun to a high position. Why Mengxun and his fellow tribesmen chose, as leader of the rebellion, a person who was not a member of their clan, can only be guessed. In the biography of Mengxun, Duan Ye is characterized as a person well versed in the history and good at writing letters. He had some reputation among the nobilities, but he could not carry out severe injunctions and his underlings arrogated authority. Furthermore he believed in divination by stalks, prophesies by diagrams, witches and wizards, and omens, and therefore he was easily misled. (translation by Mather, 1959.)

In fact, after waiting until the new state was consolidated, in 401 Mengxun plotted an intrigue in which he had his cousin Nancheng killed. Mengxun then deliberately accused Duan Ye of the misdeed and planned to have him killed too.

One more time Mengxun was able to gather a host of more than 10,000 people who, weeping angry tears, followed him. In a couple of months Mengxun captured Duan Ye and, in spite of his pleading, had him decapitated. Mengxun then, among other titles, declared himself Governor of the Liang Region and Duke of Zhangye, and he altered the era name to *Yong-an* (Eternal Peace, 401-412).

Meanwhile Lü Guang's power was declining, and in 401 the king of Later Qin, Yao Xing[7], dispatched one of his generals to attack Lü Guang in the capital, Guzang. Two month later Lü Guang finally surrendered and the surrounding states, Western, Northern, and Southern Liang, all hurried to send tributes to the conqueror, who transferred Lü Guang, as well as the Buddhist monk Kumarajiva, to the capital Changan.

The Tufa clan, a western branch of the *Xianbei* tribe, participated in the struggle for supremacy in the region. The clan had from the third century occupied parts of the Liang region, and the chieftain Wugu had in 397 declared himself king of Xiping. In history the state is known as Southern Liang (397-414).

The first appearance of the Tufa clan in the biography of Mengxun is in 399, when Duan Ye requested assistance from the clan to attack Lü Guang. During the following years there were countless alliances and attacks involving Tufa Nutan[8], Juqu Mengxun and various tribes in the region. However, under heavy pressure from Mengxun, in 405 Nutan gave up his independence and surrendered to Yao Xing, who then appointed him Prefect of Liang Region to defend Guzang. Later on, however, Nutan again declared his independence, with the political situation again becoming very unstable.

Mengxun entered the former capital Guzang in 412. Styling himself 'King West of the River' (*Hexi wang*), he proclaimed a general amnesty within the realm, altered the era name to *Xuan-shi (the Profound Beginning, 412-28)*, and appointed his officials. In 414 Qipan, the king of Western Qin, entered

Nutan's capital. Nutan was forced to retreat, and two years later, when he died, Southern Liang ended.

If we go back to the year 401, we meet the Governor of Dunhuang, Li Gao (Li Haisheng), who, in that year, had mobilized and declared his independence. Li Gao established Western Liang, including the northern part of the newly conquered realm of Mengxun, and he applied to the year the cyclical designation (geng-zi).[9]

Dunhuang was Western Liang's centre until 405 when Li Gao established the capital in Jiuquan, located in the southern part of the realm. Li Gao died in 417 and was succeeded by his son Li Xin (Li Shiye)[10]. During Li Xin's reign Western and Northern Liang were involved in a number of battles. However, in 412 Mengxun directed an attack on Jiuquan and Li Xin was killed. The *Jinshu* then continues: 'the inhabitants of Jiuquan continued to dwell in peace and Mengxun's troops treated them in an impartial manner. Mengxun appointed his son as governor of Jiuquan, and the old officials of Western Liang were selected according to their talent.'

This is about the last information on Mengxun's life given in *Jinshu*. The historical information about the last part of Northern Liang is primarily recorded in *Songshu*. This record continues that a brother to the king of the Western Liang established a fortification in the Dunhuang commandery and declared himself Grand General. Mengxun personally directed an attack on Dunhuang and built dikes to flood the town. After two month had passed the officials in Dunhuang surrendered, the king's brother killed his wife and children and committed suicide, and for the time being the Li clan lost influence.

Now Juqu Mengxun had enlarged his territory to the edge of the desert and had gained access to the main trade routes crossing the desert on the way to India and further west. In consequence the king of Shanshan went to the court in Guzang to pay his respects and the 36 kingdoms of the Western Regions all acknowledged the suzerainty of Mengxun and hurried to send tribute. During this period the king of the southern Chinese Liu Song dynasty also established a closer relationship to Mengxun. He conferred upon him a number of titles, among them the title of Regional Inspector of the Liang Region, and Duke of Zhangye.

According to the information we are given in *Songshu* it seems that Mengxun, after the subjugation of Western Liang, had lost his previous great desire for expanding his territory and instead was more engaged in intellectual occupations. In 426 Mengxun dispatched his son to the Song capital, Nanjing, in order to make a request for the Book of Changes (*Yijing*) and a collection of the works of early philosophers, and it is recorded that he was presented with a collection of 475 scrolls.

After a reign of more than 30 years Juqu Mengxun died in 433 at the age of 66 and was succeeded by one of his sons. Four years later, the new king of Northern Liang sent a return present to the Song court including a library of 21 different works in 154 scrolls. According to Soper, some of these return gifts were clearly local products, others were historical or Confucian books going back to the Han, which must have been preserved in Gansu libraries for many generations.[11]

The expanding Northern Wei (386-532) in 439 occupied the territory of Northern Liang. The king and his family as well as 300,000 households and 3000 Buddhist monks were transferred to the Wei capital Pingcheng and subsequently, during a period of intense Buddhist persecution, most of these people were executed.

Buddhism in Liangzhou

Buddhism, introduced to China in the first century of our era, was following the old commercial routes traversing the Liang region, stretching south of the Yellow River to the new centers of Chinese civilization in the Southern Dynasties.

In the period of the Sixteen Kingdoms, the Dunhuang commandery, established by Emperor Wudi of the Former Han (206 BC-25 AD), had for centuries been an important station on the Silk Route, and Buddhist religious activity naturally took place in this area. Dunhuang commandery had since its establishment possessed an important strategic position, and, although located at the edge of the desert, it commanded a populated area. In the biography of Li Xuansheng it is recorded that Fu Jian, king of Former Qin, transferred several tens of thousands of households to Dunhuang, and during Later Liang thousands of households from the Wuwei and Zhangye commanderies escaped to the Dunhuang and Jinchang commanderies (*JS*,87:2263).

The wide distribution of the Buddhist faith during the period of the Sixteen Kingdoms is demonstrated by historical accounts as well as by archaeological materials. The Chinese Buddhist monk Faxian travelled in the period 400-14, from China to the Ganges Plain in order to obtain holy Buddhist scriptures. After his return to China he wrote down the account of his journey in the autobiography *Gaoseng Faxian Zhuan*. Faxian records how in 399, due to the imperfect state of Buddhist scripts available in China, he decided to go to India in the company of a like-minded group. They started out from Changan, crossed the Long region and arrived at the court of Western Qin where they spent the summer. They continued their journey and arrived at the court of Nutan in the Southern Liang state. They then crossed the Yangloushan Mountains (present Qilianshan Mountains) and arrived in Zhangye (the first capital of Northern Liang). At this time Zhangye was in a state of rebellion, the highways were impassable, and the king, Duan Ye, in order to protect them, invited them to stay. Then Faxian and his companions spent the summer in Zhangye where they formed friendships with a group of local monks among whom one is recorded as a being from Liangzhou and one as a being from Western Liang. At the end of the summer they continued their journey to Dunhuang, staying there for more than a month. Then Faxian and his five companions took leave of the new acquaintances they had met in Zhangye to continue the journey. Before their departure into the desert they were provided for by the governor of Dunhuang, Li Gao (who later the same year declared himself king of Western Liang).

Dunhuang was the center of Western Liang before Li Gao, in 405, moved the capital to Jiuquan. Some of the cultural activities taking place during his reign are mentioned in his biography (JS, 87:2259) but no information about Buddhist activity is noted. We are told he established a seat for discussing state affairs and military undertakings 'Jinggong Tang' (The Hall of Tranquility and Reverence), he erected a temple for 500 illustrious scholars, and behind his park he erected a hall for the study of the annals 'Jia'na Gong' (The Hall of Excellence and Giving).

However, the account of the Kashmiri monk Dharmamitra (Tanmo Miduo) can contribute some clarification concerning the Western Liang ruler's attitude towards Buddhism. It is recorded in his biography (Gao seng zhuan T.50:342-343)[12] that he arrived in Dunhuang from Kucha. The account does not mention the date of his arrival but continues:

He established a monastery on an unoccupied site, he planted a thousand trees and cultivated a garden on one hundred mu. The houses, pavillions, ponds, and trees all were majestic.

Later Dharmamitra travelled to Liangzhou (Guzang) and the account continues:

He repaired the old government halls and pavillions, his disiples were numerous and the practise of contemplation was earnestly pursued.

The account then continues how Dharmamitra in 424 arrived at the court of Liu Song in Nanjing, and later arrived at a monastery where he established a hall of contemplation.
From this information it can be deduced that Dharmamitra arrived in Dun-huang during the reign of Western Liang. In 421 Western Liang was occupied by Northern Liang, and it is unrealistic to believe that in only three years Dharmamitra would have been able to carry out all these enterprises and completed his travels from Guzang to Nanjing.

The account of the Buddhist monk Kumarajiva provides the most detailed information on any Buddhist monk of the period. Kumarajiva, who has a biography in the Standard History (JS, 95:2499-2502), was one of the most influential and venerated Buddhist monks in China. He was born in Kucha to Indian immigrants and was later trained in Kashmir. As already noted, he was brought to China at the request of King Fu Jian of Former Qin. In Lü Guang's biography (JS, 122:3056) we are told that when he departed from Kucha he was accompanied by Kumarajiva as well as:

more than 20,000 camels loaded with precious goods from the foreign kingdoms, a thousand expert entertainers, marvellous actors, exotic birds, bizarre animals, and over ten thousand swift horses.'(translation by Mather, 1959:35)

Kumarajiva stayed in Guzang, the capital of Later Liang, from 386 until 401, serving as a court prognosticator, rather than officially practising the Buddhist faith.

In 401, just before Mengxun entered the capital, Kumarajiva was brought to Changan, the capital of Later Qin, and for the rest of his life he was patronized by the king, Yao Xing, himself a dedicated Buddhist. Yao Xing's biography continues: (JS, 117:2984-85)

Once Xing had been converted to the Buddhist Way, the nobility and lesser folk naturally wished to follow his example. The *sramanas* who came thither from foreign parts numbered over five thousand. A pagoda was erected in *Yong Gui* and a Prajna Terrace was raised in the Middle Palace. A thousand monks and more were continually in meditation. Conversion was carried out in the provinces [to such an extent] that nine of every ten families were Buddhists. (Translation by Soper, 1959:89).

Kumarajiva, esteemed as one of the best translators of Buddhist scripts, mastered the Chinese language to the extent that he did not need a Chinese translator, only a copyist who wrote down dictation. Kumarajiva and Yao Xing developed a friendship, and for the first time in Chinese history the translation of the Buddhist scriptures became a matter for the central authorities instead of a private affair of the monasteries.

The translation sessions took place in Changan in a big auditorium named The Garden of Leisure *(Xiaoyao yuan)*. Kumarajiva discussed here, in collaboration with a large group of monks, the difficult passages of the texts and translated more than one hundred important works of the Buddhist canon.

The translation sessions were often carried out before an audience of several hundred monks. We are told of one special occasion when Kumarajiva translated the *Fanwang jing (The Sutra of the Brahma's Net)*; he had an audience of more than 300 collaboraters and 3000 students.

The account of the Kashmiri monk Buddhayasas (Fotuo Yeshe) contributes also to the picture of Buddhism during the period. In his biography *(Gao seng zhuan, T.50:333-34)* it is recorded how Buddhayasas was already highly esteemed when he stayed at the royal house of Kashgar. When Kumarajiva arrived at the court the two monks developed a friendship and Kumarajiva studied under the guidance of Buddhayasas.

At this time Lü Guang was sent to the Western Regions and had orders to bring back Kumarajiva to Changan. Ten years later Buddhayasas arrived in Kucha and Kumarajiva hurried to send him an invitation to come to Guzang. Buddhayasas did not get permission to leave; however, on a later occasion he took an opportunity to escape from Kucha. When finally he arrived in Guzang, it was only to find that Kumarajiva had already been transferred to Changan.

The biography of Buddhayasas does not record the exact period he stayed in Guzang, but this must have been during the reign of Mengxun.

When Kumarajiva began his translation activities he asked permission for Buddhayasas to assist him. Yao Xing, who in the first place had denied the request, finally agreed, and an envoy was dispatched to Guzang with an invitation. At first he refused to go to Changan because of rumours that Kumarajiva had been forced to have intimate contact with women, and afraid of similar treatment he refused to leave. Finally, after a second request, Buddhayasas consented and went to Changan, where he was greatly admired and took part in the intensive translation activities.

The Standard Histories have hardly any information concerning Buddhist activities relating to Juqu Mengxun.

The single piece of information found in the dynastic histories, revealing Mengxun's dedication to the Buddhist faith, is found in *Wei Shu*, 114:3032, *'Treatise on Buddhism and Daoism (Shilaozhi)'*:

Before this, when Juqu Mengxun was in Liangzhou, he also loved Buddha's law. There was a Jibin sramana, Tanmo-chen [Dharmaksema], who conned scriptures and treatises. In Guzang, with the sramana Zhisong and others, he translated the *Nirvana* and other scriptures, more than ten in number. He was also wise in fortune-telling and the casting of spells. He spoke one after another of the fortunes of other countries, and many of his words proved right. Mengxun always consulted him on affairs of state.

During *Shen-jia* [428-32] the Emperor commanded Mengxun to send [Tanmo]Chen to the Capital, but grudging this he did not send him. Later, fearing the reproaches of Wei, he sent a man to kill Chen. On the day of his death Chen spoke to his disciples, saying, 'Soon now there will be a guest coming. Let us eat early and await him.' When they had finished eating, an express rider arrived. The men of that time said that Chen knew what was fated.

Liangzhou had from Zhang Gui onward for generations believed in Buddhism. Dunhuang touches upon the Western Regions, and the clergy and laity both acquired the old fashions. The villages, one after the other, had many reliquaries and temples.

During *Tai-yan* [439] Liangzhou was pacified and the people of the country moved to the capital. The *sramanas* and Buddhist practices both went east, and both the images and the doctrine prospered more and more. Then, since the *sramanas* were numerous, an Imperial edict ordered that those of age under fifty be unfrocked. (translation by Hurvitz, 1956:57-61).

Detailed information on religious activities during the reign of Juqu Mengxun comes chiefly from *Gao seng zhuan (Biographies of Famous Buddhist Monks)* compiled by the Liang dynasty monk Hui Zhao (497-554) (T.50:322-423), and *Xu gao seng zhuan (Continuation to the Biographies of Famous Buddhist Monks)* compiled by the Tang historian Dao Xuan (596-667) (T.50:425-707).

Mengxun was, according to these sources, a keen patronizer of the Buddhist faith. There are references to nine monks who, during his reign, stayed in the capital and translated 82 works from Sanskrit all in all, more than 311 scrolls. Moreover, records refer to ten famous Chinese monks who, in the same period, travelled West in search of holy scripts. Mengxun's cousin

Juqu Jingshen was also among these travellers; as a young man he went to Khotan to study under an Indian monk, and later he brought back to Liangzhou Buddhist scriptures for translation (Tang Yongtong, 1991:391).

The Buddhist monk Dharmaksema (Tanwuchan, 385-433) was the most influential Buddhist during the reign of Mengxun.

According to Dharmaksema's biography (*Gao seng zhuan* T.50:335-57) he was originally from Central India; as a child he had studied the Hinayana school of Buddhism but, after seeing the *Mahaparinirvana Sutra (Niepan jing)*, converted to the Mahayana school and at the age of twenty mastered the classics from both schools as well as 200 more scriptures of more than 200,000 words. He went to Kashmir and later to Kucha. However, the inhabitants in both these countries were believers of the Hinayana school, and Dharmaksema continued his journey to Dunhuang where he stayed for several years.

When Mengxun in around 420 conquered Western Liang, Dharmaksema moved to the capital Guzang. During his stay he became one of the most prominent Buddhist translators of the time. A library of Buddhist scriptures was established, and he acted as the superintendent for more than one hundred monks, with whom he discussed problems of translation.

In the biography a number of supernatural events are described which provide vivid examples of the current beliefs.

After a short stay in Kucha Dharmaksema planned to travel to Guzang. During his journey, we are told, he made a halt at a post station. Afraid of thieves, at night he placed his manuscripts under his head as a pillow. In the night a voice in the dark asked him why he was hiding the texts of redemption; Dharmaksema then very ashamedly, the next night, placed the scripts on an open platform. As expected, thieves attempted to steal the scripts, but they were so heavy that no one was able to carry them. The next morning, realizing Dharmaksema was able to carry the texts without problem, the people all respectfully gathered around him.

The account then continues to relate how Mengxun, having established himself in Northern Liang, learned of Dharmaksema's reputation; he received him at court and supported him generously. Mengxun, who was very interested in the Buddhist faith, urged Dharmaksema to publish his scripts. However, Dharmaksema, unfamiliar with the Chinese language, studied the language for three years, then translated the first ten scrolls of the *Mahapanirvana sutra*. After the publication of these scrolls his reputation reached the highly esteemed *sramanas* Huisong and Daolang. The clergy and the laymen, numbering more than one hundred, discussed the difficult parts of the text under the guidance of Dharmaksema, who in a very eloquent manner explained the difficult passages. Huisong and Daolang encouraged Dharmaksema to proceed with the publication of his Buddhist scripts, and within the next years Dharmaksema published texts containing more than 600,000 words. In 414 Dharmaksema began the translation of the next part of the *Mahapanirvana sutra*, and the translation of the complete sutra counting 33 scrolls was finished in 421.[13]

Another incident is recorded in which Dharmaksema displayed his supernatural power:

Once Dharmaksema told Mengxun epidemic and calamities would occur because demons had gathered in the city. Mengxun, having a very suspicious nature, wanted to see the demons for himself. Accordingly, Dharmaksema cast a spell on Mengxun who then saw the demons. Dharmaksema then fasted for three days reciting the *Dharani* Spell sutra in order to drive off the demons. When three days had passed he told Mengxun the demons were driven off. People, who had seen the demons in the city, now declared they had seen hundreds of demons assemble and escape. Thanks to Dharmaksema peace again prevailed inside the borders, and Mengxun now respected Dharmaksema even more than before.

In the second year of the *Cheng-xuan* period (429), Mengxun crossed the Yellow River in order to attack the king of Western Qin. The heir Xingguo, whom Mengxun had sent in advance, was captured by the enemy and eventually killed. This incident caused Mengxun to get so angry that he accused the Buddha of the misdeed and ordered all *sramanas* under fifty to return to lay life.

On a previous occasion Mengxun had had a sixteen-foot stone image made on behalf of his deceased mother. This statue now wept sadly and, after much persuasion by Dharmaksema, Mengxun finally cancelled the order.

Later, the fame of Dharmaksema reached the Toba Dao (Emperor Taiwu of Northern Wei) who, on the threat of war, ordered Mengxun to send Dharmaksema to the Northern Wei capital. However, Mengxun refused, and still refused when the Toba king once more sent an envoy showering Mengxun with titles. In 433, when Dharmaksema applied for permisson to travel westward in search of the last part of the *Nirvana sutra*, Mengxun, being very suspicious eventually had him killed.

Buddhist Manifestations

Archaeological evidence of Buddhist activity during the period of the Sixteen Kingdoms is provided by cave temples established along commercial routes extending from northern to southern Gansu. These cave temples possess great importance, as they represent the initial stages of the Chinese Buddhist art fully developed later in the famous cave temples at Yungang near Datong and Longmen near Luoyang. As the Hexi corridor in the western part of Gansu was the most important region for long-distance trade, quite naturally the greatest number of cave temples are found here.

Based on archaeological excavations and the relevant historical material, Su Bai published in 1986 in *Kaogu xuebao* a detailed study on the subject, Huang Wenkun contributed a short summary on the subject in *Wenwu* 1992, and Zhang Xuerong in 1993 summarized and discussed some of the problems concerning the identification of the cave temples in *Dunhuang yanjiu*.

The most important cave sites dating from the earliest cave construction period are the Mogao cave site near Dunhuang, the Yulin cave site near Anxi, the Changma cave site near Yumen, the Wenshushan cave site near Jiuquan, the Jintasi, Matisi, and Qianfodong caves near Zhangye, and the Tiantishan caves near Wuwei, all situated in the foothills of the Qilianshan Mountains in the Hexi corridor. In the southern part of Gansu close to the trade-routes are found the Binglingsi cave complex near Yongjingxian, and the Maijishan complex near Tianshui and the Wei River.

Based on studies of the relevant historical material, and analysis of the caves, sculptures, and the paintings found in the caves, the majority of the earliest dated caves are considered to belong to the Former, Later, and Western Qin kingdoms, and to the Northern Liang kingdom. However, due to the scarce written evidence, there are various opinions regarding classification of these cave sites to the period of Northern Liang.

Some of the probable cave sites related to Northern Liang are the Matisi cave complex located about 60 kilometers southeast of Zhangye, the Wenshushan cave site located about 15 kilometers southwest of Jiuquan, and the Tiantishan cave site located about 60 kilometers south of Wuwei.

The Matisi complex comprises the northern and southern Matisi stupa cave group, the two Jintasi stupa caves, the Qianfodong stupa caves and the Guanyin stupa caves.[14]

The caves are carved into precipices in the Qilianshan Mountains, the distance between the groups varies from two to ten kilometers. Because the material of the cliffs is a kind of coarse red sandstone the majority of the figures are modelled in stucco. The earliest caves at this site all have a number of characteristic elements indicating they where constructed during the Sixteen Kingdoms. (Su Bai, 86:440).

Briefly, the two Jintasi stupa caves are cut into the steep precipices about seven kilometers east of the Matisi cave group. The caves are composed of two almost identical caves named the Eastern and Western Caves. The two rectangular caves contain a square central pillar extending from floor to ceiling. The Eastern Cave, which is the largest, is 9.70 meters by 7.65 meters, and the height to the ceiling is 6.05 meters. The central pillar is 4.50 meters on the side, divided into three tiers. The front wall is collapsed, and the pillar is badly damaged as well. Carved decorations are found on the central pillar but not on the walls.

On the bottom tier three faces of the pillar are carved with large arched niches each containing a cross-legged Buddha sitting on a lotus throne flanked by standing bodhisattvas, and on the northern face are placed the images of two *Bhiksus*. On each side of the niche's lintel are placed six to eight large- size flying *apsaras*. Small images of Thousand Buddhas are placed in blank spots outside the niches. All four faces of the middle tier are carved with three arched niches placed in due succession. Each niche has an image of a Buddha wearing a robe with a bare right shoulder. On the western face the Buddha is sitting with his ankles crossed, on the other faces the Buddha is sitting crossed-legged. The space between each niche contains an image of a bodhisattva, and the northern face has between the niches the images of the Thousand Buddhas. The top tier has on three faces images of the sitting Buddha. Behind the Buddha is placed the half body of bodhisattvas, between the Buddhas are the images of Thousand Buddhas, botthisattvas, and flying *Apsaras*. On the western face are placed only two images of flying *Apsaras*. The three preserved walls have paintings in three sections. The majority of the paintings are very blurred, but some of the paintings can be interpreted as images of Thousand Buddhas.

The Western Cave is a bit smaller. Each of the four faces of the pillar in the western cave is also divided into three tiers containing carved niches. The bottom tier has, on all four faces, carved large central niches each containing a cross-legged Buddha flanked by images of warriors. The middle tier has on the southern and eastern face images of a sitting Buddha wearing a long robe; central on the western face is a meditating bodhisattva. On the eastern, western, and southern faces are on each side placed four images of a sitting bodhisattva. The top tier has on all four faces images of Thousand Buddhas and bodhisattvas. The walls in this cave have rather blurred paintings in three sections, some of which can be interpreted as images of Thousand Buddhas.[15] A great many of the sculptures made on the central pillar in the two caves have undergone a number of restorations through the ages, but some of them are still untouched and so represent very good examples of the belief and art of the period in which they were made. (*Wenwu* 1965:3)

The Tiantishan site still has 13 caves extant. Among them Cave 1, Cave 4, and Cave 18 are characterized as having a 'northern dynasty style'. A large stupa cave ruined in an earthquake in 1927 is supposed to have belonged to Juqu Mengxun.

Due to the establishing of a new water reservoir in 1959 the majority of the statues and paintings were transferred to the Gansu Provincial Museum. During the removal were found paintings having an earlier dating than the early dated paintings in the Dunhuang caves. This has put in question the dating of these to the Northern Liang period [16]. However, no reports about the paintings have been published.

Cave 1 forms almost a square. It is 4.78 meters wide and deep, the height to the ceiling is 5.15 meters, and the square central pillar is 2.27 meters on the side. The pillar is on all four faces divided into three tiers, the bottom and the middle tier have on all four faces a large niche containing a Buddha, the top tier has on all four faces carved two niches; all of them have undergone many restorations. Cave 4 is almost identical.

According to copies preserved by Dunhuang Institute for Cultural Relics the images of bodhisattvas painted on the bottom tier on the wall in Cave 1 have some points of resemblance to the sacrificing bodhisattvas carved on the stone pillars found in Jiuquan, Dunhuang, and Turpan. Some of the similar stylistic features are the free and unrestrained attitude of the bodhisattvas, their hair worn in a bun, and the form and shape of their robes and personal ornament. (Su Bai, 86:438).

The Wenshushan cave complex is one of the most important cave sites in the Hexi region. The remaining caves, grouped on two steep cliffs, number about ten. Most of them are badly damaged, only the Thousand-Buddha Cave and the Ten thousand-buddha Cave are relatively well preserved. The Thousand-Buddha Cave forms almost a square between 3.80 and 3.94 meters deep and wide and the height is 3.60 meters. The cave contains a square central pillar extending from floor to ceiling measuring two meters on the side. An antechamber is placed in front of the cave. The square pillar is divided into two almost identical tiers. On all four faces of the bottom tier is carved one arched niche containing a sitting Buddha flanked by an image of a bodhisattva. The cave opening is placed in the middle of the front wall.

Paintings are still preserved on the northern and western wall of the cave. The paintings on the northern wall are divided into two parts. The top part has painted images of Thousand Buddhas wearing long skirts and bare torsos, the bottom part has painted 10 standing Buddhas, some have bare torsos and wear long skirts, and some wear long dresses with a bare right shoulder. Central on the western wall are painted images of Amitabha Buddha, Avalokitesvara, Mahasthamaprapta, as well as two bodhisattvas. On both sides of the image of the Amitabha Buddha are at the top painted images of Thousand Buddhas, and at the bottom are painted images of donors standing in a row. On the ceiling round the central pillar is painted a number of flying *apsaras* and Deva-dancers.

A number of small stone pillars date the Northern Liang dynasty. Six pieces were found in Wenshushan, Jiuquan, four pieces in Dunhuang, and two pieces were found in Turpan (Su Bai, 86:438-39). The shape of the pillars is approximately similar, the size varying from 36 to 96 centimeters. Six of the pieces have a legible dating covering the period 426 to 436. The earliest dated have engraved the name Bei Liang as well as a corresponding era name. The two latest dated (434 and 436), however, have engraved the name Bei Liang, but instead of the corresponding era name these pillars have engraved the era name applied by the Northern Wei dynasty, indicating Northern Liang at this time was declining.

Some of the pillars are described by Soper:

The earlier of the dated pillars is a piece 41 centimeters high and 21 in circumference, lacking both top and pedestal. An upper tier shows three miniature niches, each with a figure in high relief. Around the bottom runs an incised frieze of standing deities, holding lotus offerings. Between each pair of heads is engraved one of the eight trigrams of the 'Book of Changes.' Thus, although the report mentions only that six such offering figures remain, it is clear that the pillar was originally octagonal. The intermediate zone is filled with a carefully written *sutra* passage, in the clerkly hand, which terminates in the name of the donor — one Tian Hong — a prayer on behalf of his deceased parents and his ruler; and a date fixed by both the reign era, the second year of *Cheng-xuan*, and by cyclical characters, the former being equivalent to AD 429 and the latter to 428. (Translation by Soper, 58:131-33).

The second stone pillar has an inscription speaking of the 'Late great Juqu Mengxun of the Liang' (i.e. Juqu Mengxun, who died in the fourth month of 433), and gives a cyclical combination equivalent to 434. Among numerous miswritten or obliterated characters, a prayer stands out for rebirth in the presence of Maitreya. (Translation by Soper).

Of the four remaining stone pillars from the Wenshushan site two pieces have the datings 426 and 436, and two pieces have illegible dating.
The dating of the Dunhuang pillars is based on stylistic features, the dating being illegible.

One of the stone pillars near Turpan was found by the French explorer A. von Le Coq during his expedition in 1902-5. The two stone pillars show some minor differences from the Wenshushan pillars. However, one of the Turpan pillars has the same inscription engraved as found on the Wenshushan pillar dating 436 (Su Bai, 86:439). There is reason to belive the Turpan pillars were produced during the 440's and 450's when a part of Mengxun's family, in order to continue Northern Liang, escaped to Gaochang (Turpan).

Elements found in the Tiantishan Caves 1, 4, and 18, the Eastern and Western Jintasi Cave, the two caves at Wenshushan, and elements found on the stone pillars from Jiuquan, Dunhuang, and Turpan, all share some common features characterized by Su Bai as a special 'Liangzhou type' of Buddhism (Su Bai,86:441). Some of these elements are: 1. The establishing of largely sized Buddhist cave shrines. The majority are rectangular or square stupa caves with a central pillar extending from floor to ceiling. The pillar is broader at the top and narrower at the bottom. Some of the rectangular caves have an antechamber like the Thousand Buddha Cave at Wenshushan. 2.The images are primarily Sakyamuni Buddha, and Maitreya bodhisattva sitting cross-ankled. Secondly are found the images of Maitreya Buddha and the meditating bodhisattva. From the Wenshushan site are found the group of ten Buddha images, and the images of three Amitabha Buddhas. Except for the group of ten standing Buddhas all the Buddha images are in a sitting-position. 3. The majority of the paintings have images of Thousand Buddhas. In the Jiuquan Thousand-Buddha Cave are paintings of Amitabha Buddha and pictures of donors. 4. The Buddha images as well as the bodhisattva images all have round faces, narrow, long, and deep-set eyes, high bridged noses, and they all have robust torsos. The bothisattvas and flying *Devatas* have a variety of vivid postures. Moreover, the flying *Apsaras* are made in large size.

The Binglingsi cave site possesses some valuable information on   the development taking place in the period. The cave building activity at this site began in Western Qin and continued to the Ming period, and the site has more than 195 niches and caves still intact. In Cave 169 Niche 6 is found an inscription in ink of Western Qin dating 420. This is the earliest dating found in any cave in the Liangzhou region. Moreover, some of the sculptures found in Cave 1 and Cave 169 all have stylistic features relating to the sculptures found in the Liangzhou caves. However, the construction of caves here seems to have followed another pattern. There was no practice of building deep caves, and the statues and paintings were made nearest to or directly on the rock face either in natural rock shelters or in shallowly cut rectangular niches with the opening in front of them. Each niche is an independent unit in arrangement of images and has no connection with the rest (Su Bai, 86:446).

The Binglingsi Caves are related to Northern Liang in the historical material also. The biography of the famous Buddhist monk Xuangao records that after having served as royal advisor at the court of Western Qin, he moved to the court of Juqu Mengxun who paid him great honours.

Historical Material

A number of literary sources include references to cave building in Liangzhou during the period. However, the identification of any of the cave temples by the information in the texts is complicated by the fact that no references later than Tang are found.

As already mentioned we are told in the biography of the Buddhist monk Dharmaksema how Mengxun in 429 accused Buddha for the death of his son and ordered all monks to return to lay-life. Previously he had had a sixteen-foot stone image made on behalf of his deceased mother, and this now began to weep profusely. This fact, as well as Dharmaksema's strong persuasion, caused Mengxun finally to cancel his orders.

The same story, described in more detail, is found in a text by the Early Tang monk-historian Daoshi in *Fayuan Zhulin* (The Forest of Collections of Buddha's Law), (*T*.53:212). Daoshi describes how Mengxun, after the death of his son, abolished Buddhism and ordered the destruction of all Buddhist temples. When Mengxun, on a later occasion, travelled to Yangshushan, a great number of Buddhist monks were standing along the roadside. On seeing the monks, Mengxun became so furious that he decapitated several of them. At that time generals and petty officials went to the temple for a religious ceremony, and they all became terrified when they saw the image crying with tears squirting out like a fountain. When Mengxun was told the story, he wanted to see for himself what was happening. Arriving at the entrance of the temple his body was trembling with fear as if somebody was attacking him. He shouted out and was supported and sheltered as he went into the cave. When he had entered the cave and saw the tears of the image, he bowed his head to the ground and accused himself of the misdeed. Subsequently he made a statement at a large gathering. Mengxun's belief was now even stronger than before, and the monks were all allowed to return to their previous religious occupation.

An almost identical story also regarding cave building activity is found in *Ji Shenzhou Sanbao Gantonglu (Buddhist Miracles in China)*.[17] This text has three entries on Northern Liang; one entry records the story of the weeping image, and one entry records the story about 'the moulded auspicious images in the Liangzhou cliffs' (*T*.52:418):

A hundred *Li* to the south of his city there is a line of cliffs that runs a great distance east and west. There he excavated caves and installed the holy likenesses; some being of stone and others moulded in clay, in so infinite a variety of forms, that those who worship are amazed and dazzled in mind and eye. Among these there are certain saintly monks made of clay that seem just like men who must continually walk about because they have as yet no place of repose. Seen from afar they move; it is [only] when inspected closely [that they are revealed as] immobile; even the expressions on their faces [suggest that] they are moving. Sometimes dirt has been spread on the ground so as to keep watch on their movements; for when no one is near they actually do set foot on the earth, and they make the moist footprints of men going and coming without a halt. This phenomenon has continued for over a century now, or so the people thereabouts say. (Translation by Soper, 1959:92).

No specific dates are referred to in the text, and a number of identifications of these 'moulded auspicious images made in the Liangzhou cliffs' have been proposed. The main issue in the discussion is whether Mengxun had the cave temples established before or after he moved the capital to Guzang in 412. Some scholars argue that the cave temples Matisi, Jintasi, and Qianfodong were established by Mengxun when he had the capital in Zhangye, and the earliest dated of the Tiantishan caves were established by Mengxun after the removal to Guzang; Liangzhou included Hexi as a part of the Liangzhou Region, and the cave temples Matisi, Jintasi, and Qianfodong are all located about one hundred *Li* south of Zhangye, which in this connection is referred to as Liangzhou. In addition, the fact that the Chinese monk Faxian in 400 stayed in Zhangye, where he met some local Buddhist monk with whom he spent the summer, proves that Zhangye, at this time, already was an active center for Buddhism.

However, a more convincing theory is provided among others by Su Bai and Zhang Xuerong who both argue that only the earliest caves at Tiantishan can be identified as the caves constructed by Mengxun. They base their arguments on the fact that Dao Xuan as well as Dao Shi, who wrote the accounts of the cave temples, both based their geographical information on Tang administrative geography. Guzang was in the Tang period a part of Liangzhou, which did not include Zhangye, and the cave site at Tiantishan is in fact located one hundred *Li* south of Guzang.

Another argument is that the establishing of cave temples was an enterprise requiring stable economic and political conditions. When Mengxun had his capital in Zhangye he was surrounded by enemies, the political situation was very unstable and during 12 years he was engaged in more than 20 great battles. When Mengxun in 421 had conquered Western Liang and seized Dunhuang commandery the economic and political situation was more stabilized. We are told of the Buddhist monk Dharmaksema who arrived in Guzang in this period and who was met with appreciation by Mengxun; moreover, *'The Palace for Pleasurable Ease' (Xianyu Gong)* was established. Here Dharmaksema, as well as more than one hundred monks, were engaged in the translation of Buddhist scripts, among them also Mengxun's cousin Juqu Jingshen and a number of highly esteemed Buddhist monks.

Still, an argument is that in the Tiantishan caves are found sculptures cut in stone as well as modelled in clay as referred to in the accounts. Moreover, the earliest dated caves are all stupa caves retaining a square central pillar, which is a significant feature for the earliest cave temples in this part of China.

Cultural Traditions and Religious Belief

The present study has only touched on some of the effects produced by the cultural encounters taking place in this period of Chinese history.
From the above discussion it is evident that the non-Chinese Northern Liang kingdom, as well as the surrounding small non-Chinese kingdoms of the period, all were in varying degrees influenced by traditional Chinese culture as well as Buddhism.

Evidence of traditional Chinese culture carried on in this period is provided especially by information in the Standard Histories. The archaeological material is relatively scarce: only a few burials reveal in paintings, artifacts, and scripts the actual continuation of traditional Chinese culture.

One of the most significant tombs is Dingjiazha Tomb No 5 located eight kilometers northwest of Jiuquan.[18] The tomb has two chambers connected by a passage. The tomb chamber measures 3.36 by 3.32 by 3.22 meters, the base lies 12 meters below earth surface and has a sloping passage 33 meters long. The tomb has been previously robbed, leaving only a small amount of artifacts such as some bronzes, one stone ink-slab, two ancient iron mirrors, lacquer fragments and 63 brass coins.

The antechamber has paintings on the faces of all four walls as well as on the ceiling. The upper part of the walls have among other motifs paintings of the sun, moon, and *Dongwanggong* (Royal Lord of the East) and *Xiwangmu* (Royal Lady of the West), both of these belonging to traditional Chinese mythology.

The remaining part of the walls have paintings depicting scenes of daily life of the deceased. One scene depicts the deceased having dinner while he is watching a dance performance to the accompaniment of music. Another picture contains a procession depicting the tomb occupant, carriages, servants, and guards. Still another picture has scenes of farming, sericulture, animal husbandry, and cooking.

No written evidence is found in the tomb, but according to the excavation report the burial might belong to the period between 386 and 441.[19]

The various scenes in the paintings prove the dominant part still possessed by traditional Chinese culture. The clothing, offices, and rites as well as the various occupations like farming and sericulture are all typically Chinese features.

An interesting feature in the painting is that while the tomb owner and his attendants all are dressed in traditional Chinese style, the labouring people are all dressed in non-Chinese style, some of them having high-bridged noses and deep-set eyes. This phenomenon does not, according to the excavation report, indicate the upper-layer of the society belonged to the Han-Chinese, but instead that the upper-layer belonging to the tribal groups had adapted Chinese institutions.

However, the dating of the tomb has a great significance for this kind of interpretation. If the tomb belongs to the period of Western Liang (400-421) the tomb occupant might very well have continued traditional Chinese culture, as we know the upper stratum of the Western Liang society felt very dependant on Chinese culture. If the grave can be dated to Northern Liang, it may provide information on the Xiongnu tribe's adoption of Chinese culture.

A more exact dating is necessary for any interpretation of this phenomenon. Also important is the fact that Buddhism might not have been supported by all members of the upper stratum of society. (Wu Rengxiang 1990:17)

At Turpan are excavated a cemetery of fifty-one tombs, among which eleven are dated to the period of the Sixteen Kingdoms. The graves have been previously robbed, and only a small amount of grave goods have been found. Besides paintings on the walls in some of the graves, depicting the life of the deceased, these graves also contained written material. 102 documents have been found, all written in Chinese, with era names from Western Liang, Northern Liang, Xia, and two unidentified ones.

The Western Liang documents are all responses for a *xiucai* examination held in 408. The questions have not survived but on of the responses concerns an attack by Jin, Han and Wei against Zhao in the Warring States period.

By far the greatest amount of documents are dated to Northern Liang. The majority deal with military affairs, and provide some new information on military organization: one is a receipt for wine received by some troops, and some deal with punishment for deserters and excuses to avoid service. In addition, some documents deal with monks, fugitive slaves, substitutes for military service and remission of military service.[20]

The historical information given in the biographies of the Standard Histories, however, due to the nature of Chinese historiography, primarily deal with political and military affairs. Questions dealing with the actual standard of living of these non-Chinese groups are hardly ever touched upon. Information on the subsistence, cultural values, habits and religious activities are only given in scattered glimpses. It is difficult to deduce any cultural values related to the nomadic traditions that might have continued to influence the societies in question.

Historical information on cultural exchange in this period consists entirely of accounts of traditional Chinese culture persistently penetrating all levels of the non-Chinese societies. However, a few accounts in the *Jinshu* biography of Juqu Mengxun directly provide some personal information on his life. We are told how Mengxun in 414 became a victim of an attempted murder. On one occasion when he was resting in 'The New Tower' he was stabbed by an eunuch and his foot was injured. Mengxun's wife organized the eunuch's capture and he, as well as his family, were executed.

We are also provided with examples that point to Mengxun's deep affection for his mother: In the same year, 414, that his mother became seriously ill, Mengxun was obviously deeply moved and went to 'The Southern Illuminated Gate' in order to offer coins to the common people. Thereupon he issued a summons and declared his heavy dependence on the spirits of the ancestral temple; quoting various passages from the *Yijing* he avowed his great desire to support the common people and handed down a general amnesty for those sentenced to capital punishment. Nevertheless, within a short period of time his mother died.

In the biography of the Buddhist *sramana* Dharmaksema, as well as in the two Tang accounts, we are told Mengxun had a sixteen- foot stone image made on behalf of his deceased mother which began to cry when he abolished Buddhism because of the death of his son.

According to the traditional practice in Chinese historiography, religious activity is hardly ever touched upon. However, in the *Jinshu* biography of Mengxun one notice occurs with some information on his religious behaviour. In 418, we are told, Mengxun travelled in a western direction to go to some salt marshes to carry out a sacrifice in 'The Temple of the Western Mother'(*Xiwangmu si*). Inside the temple was 'The Black Stone Divine Plan' (*Xuanshi shentu*) and Mengxun ordered one of his officials to compose a poem which was engraved on a tablet in front of the temple. This incident only appears in the *Jinshu* biography; information on the temple of the goddess, the black stone deity, or on the locality for this temple are not to be found.

The establishing of cave temples proves the influence of Buddhism during the period. The earliest cave temples, described in this article, are all located along the existing trade routes naturally, as Buddhist monks travelled along the same routes as merchants and caravans. Along the routes were facilities needed for a traveller such as lodging and protection from bandits etc. Besides carrying religious influences the routes also carried commercial and cultural influences. For example, in 1955 was found within the old city of Turpan a coffer containing ten Persian Sassanian silver coins dating from the period between 310 to 388.

The style of the Buddhist art in the cave temples in this first phase of Buddhist art in China is quite naturally deeply influenced by the Buddhist art deriving from more mature Buddhist regions. Features in the style of the sculptures both in their ornament, clothing and figures, can all be traced especially to the Buddhist art predominent in the small kingdoms located along the great Taklamakan Desert. Sutra passages inscribed on the stone pillars found in the Qilianshan Mountains prove the influence of Buddhism during the reign of Mengxun. However, on the same pillars are engraved inscriptions of the eight diagrams from *Yijing*. These phenomena all prove the mixture of religious belief and traditional Chinese values under the 'barbarian reign' of Juqu Mengxun.

References

Abe, Stanley K. (1990): 'Art and Practice in a Fifth-century Chinese Buddhist Cave Temple', *Ars Orientalis*, XX. vol. 20, pp. 1-20.

Dien, Albert E. (et al., eds.) 1985 Chinese Archaeological Abstracts, (Monumenta Archaeologica, vols. 9-11), ed. by Jeffrey K. Riegel, and Nancy T. Price. Los Angeles: Institute of Archaeology, University of California.

Fuchs, Walther: 'Zur Technischen Organisation der Übersetzungen Buddhistischer Schriften ins Chinesische', *Asia Major*, MCMXXX, pp. 84-103.

Gansu Provincial Bureau of Culture, Archaeology Team (1965): 'Matisi, Wenshushan, Changma zhu shiku diaocha dianbao' (A brief Report of the Investigation of the Matisi, Wenshushan, and the Changma Cave Temples) *Wenwu* (Cultural Relics), vol. 3, pp. 13-23.

Gao seng zhuan, (Biographies of Famous Buddhist Monks). Compiled by Hui Jiao, Liang Dynasty (AD. 502-57). Tripitaka Vol. 50, pp. 322-423.

Hong Liangji, [1746-1809], *Shiliu guo Jiangyu zhi* (Treatise on the Border Areas of the Sixteen Kingdoms [317-439], Gouxue jiben Congshu, 2 vol. Taipei: Commercial Press.

Huang Wenkun,(1992): 'Shiliuguo de shiku yu Dunhuang Shiku Yishu' (Grottoes of the Sixteen Kingdom Period and the art of the Dunhuang Grottoes), *Wenwu*, vol. 5, pp. 44-49.

Ji Shenzhou Sanbao Gantonglu, (Buddhist Miracles in China). Compiled by Daoxuan (AD. 596-667). Tripitaka Vol. 52, pp. 404-35.

Jinshu, (1991): (The History of the Jin Dynasty [265-419 AD] by Fang Xuanling, 578-648), critical ed., 10 vols. Beijing: Zhonghua Shuju 1991.

Mather, R.B. (1959): *Biography of Lü Kuang*, Translated and Annotated. Chinese Dynastic Histories Translations no. 7, East Asia Studies. Institute of International Studies, Berkeley and Los Angeles: University of California Press.

Qian Hanshu, (1962): (The History of the Former Han Dynasty [206 BC-AD 23.] by Ban Gu 32-92), critical ed., 12 vols. Beijing: Zhonghua Shuju.

Shih, R. (1968): *Biographies Des Moines Eminents (Kao Seng Tchouan) De Houei-Kiao*. Bibliotheque Du Museon, vol. 54. Louvain.

Songshu, (1987): (The History of the Song Dynasty [420-29] by Shen Yue 441-513). Critical ed., 8 vols. Beijing: Zhonghua Shuju.

Soper, A.C. (1958): 'Northern Liang and Northern Wei in Kansu', *Artibus Asiae*, vol. 21, no. 2, pp. 131-44.

Soper, A. C. (1959): *Literary Evidence for Early Buddhist Art in China*, Switzerland: Artibus Asiae Publishers.

Su Bai, (1986): 'Liangzhou Shiku yiji he 'Liangzhou Moshi' (The Liangzhou Cave Temple and the 'Liangzhou Type'.) *Kaogu xuebao* ('Acta archaeologia Sinica'), vol. 4, pp. 435-446.

Tang, Yongtong (1927): *Han Wei Liangjin Nanbeichao Foshi* (Buddhist History from the Han to the Southern and Northern Dynasties). Reprint Shanghai 1991.

Tsukamoto Zenryu (1956), *Wei Shou, Treatise on Buddhism and Taoism*, tr. Leon Hurvitz, Kyoto.

Weishu, (1987): (Documents of the Wei Dynasty [386-550] by Wei Shou 506-72). Critical ed., 8 vols. Beijing:Zhonghua Shuju.

Wu Rengxiang, (1989): *Jiuquan shiliuguo mubihua (Wall Paintings of the Sixteen Kingdoms Tomb at Jiuquan)*. Beijing: Wenwu chubanshe.

Zhang Xuerong, (1993): 'Liangzhou shiku ji youguan wenti' (the Liangzhou Grottoes and some Problems concerned), *Dunhuang Yanjiu* ('Dunhuang Studies'), vol 4, pp. 47-60.

Zhongguo Lishi Ditu ji (The Historical Atlas of China), vol. VI. Sponsor: Chinese Academy of Social Science. Chief Editor Tan Qixiang. China Cartographic Publishing House.

Zizhi Tongjian (1991): (Mirror as an Aid to Government [403 BC- 960 AD] by Sima Guang 1019-1086) 2 vols. Shanghai: Guji Chubanshi.

Notes

This article is based on the first part of a Ph.D. dissertation concerning aspects of cultural and social relations in the Northern Liang with special emphasis on the interaction between nomads and a sedentary population.

1. By far the most detailed information on the life of the first ruler of Northern Liang, Juqu Mengxun, appears in one of the 30 chronicles (*zaiji*) which are appended to the Standard History of the Jin Dynasty, *Jinshu*, 129:3189-3201 hereafter *JS*.
2. Lü Guang was the first ruler of Later Liang (r. 386-399). His biography appears in *JS*, 122:3053-3064, and in *Weishu*, 95:2085-06.
3. The biography of Kumarajiva is translated by Robert Shih, tr., *Biographies des moines eminents (Kao seng tchouan) de Houei-kiao*, Louvain, 1968:60-82, and by Johannes Nobel, 'Kumarajiva', *Sitzungsberichte det Preussischen Akademie der Wissenschaften*, Berlin 1927:206-33.

4. Information on administrative geography is found in Hong Liangji [1746-1809], *Shiliu guo jiangyu zhi (Treatise on the Border Areas of the Sixteen Kingdoms* [317-439], hereafter SLGJYZ.

   Information on political geography is found in Tan Qixiang chief.ed. *Zhongguo lishi dituji (The Historical Atlas of China)* vol 4.

5. The designation Juqu as a title of the Xiongnu tribe appears for the first time in *Qian Hanshu (History of the Former Han)*, 96:3928.

6. Jiankang Commandery was located in the northern part of Later Liang (later situated in Western Liang) *SLGJYZ*, 8:327 and 9.339.

7. Yao Xing, a member of the *Rong* tribe, was ruling Later Qin (399-416). At this time Yao Xing had absorbed Western Qin into his domain. His biography appears in *JS*, 117, 118:2975-3004, *Weishu*, 95:2082-2085, and in *Beishi*, 93:3076-77.

8. The biography of Tufa Nutan appears in *JS*, 126:3147-3161, and in *Weishu*, 99:2201-2202.

9. The biography of Li Gao appears in *JS*, 87:2257-68.

   Li Gao was descended from an old Chinese family, which might have been the reason he felt dependent on the Chinese Southern Jin Dynasty, never actually declaring a new era name but instead applying to the year the cyclical designation *geng-zi*. According to information in *Xin Tangshu* the first emperor of the Tang Dynasty, Li Yuan (565-635) was a seventh generation descendant of Li Gao. More fanciful is the information that Li Gao was a descendant of the Daoist philosopher Laozi.

10. The biography of Li Xin appears in *JS*, 87:2268-2273.

11. Refering to *Songshu* and *Weishu*, Soper records how Mengxun on seizing the Western Liang began by confiscating several thousand manuscripts from a library belonging to one of the scholars in Dunhuang. Later, however, Mengxun paid his respect to this scholar and appointed him guardian and senior prime minister to the heir apparent. Another scholar of the Western Liang court served, during the reign of Li Gao, as the director of the Confucian college, and later became Mengxun's privy librarian, heading a staff of several hundred literati. For more information see Alexander C. Soper, 1958:131-144.

12. *T* is an abbrevation of the Buddhist Canon Taisho Daizokyo.

13. The exact year for Dharmaksema's move to Guzang is unclear; according to his biography he moved to Guzang between the period when Mengxun established himself in Guzang in 412, and the subjugation of Western Liang in 420-21. According to a number of other records he moved to Guzang only after the fall of Western Liang (see Tang Yongtong, 1991:392).

14. According S. Abe 1990:5, the ritual of circumambulation was commonly associated with the central pillar, insofar as the pillar is understood as a form of the Indian stupa or Chinese pagoda, although extant Chinese Buddhist sutras and biographies of monks from the fifth century contain surprisingly few references to circumambulation practices. This suggests that circumambulation may have been only one of the rituals involved with central pillars in the fifth century'. See S. Abe's article for a detailed discussion of the function of and practise in this kind of cave temple.

15. A far more detailed description of the cave site is to be found in *Wenwu*, no. 3, 1965, pp. 13-23.

16. The historical texts have no references to any cave building or similar activity in the Dunhuang area during the reign of Mengxun. Archaeological investigations give no final conclusion on the dating of the earliest caves. Both Northern Liang and Northern Wei have been suggested. However, the opening of cave temples was a matter for the central authorities, and it is unlikely caves were opened in Dunhuang during the reign of Mengxun. During the conquest of Western Liang, Dunhuang had been badly damaged, and was located too far from the center of power.(Huang Wenkun, 92:44).

17. *Ji Shenzhou Sanbao Gantonglu (Buddhist Miracles in China)*, comp. by Daoxuan (596-667). T. 52, pp. 404-435. An almost identical story is found as a postscript to Cui Hong (d.ca. 525), *Shiliuguo Chunqiu (Annals of the Sixteen Kingdoms)*, Ch. 94, 'Bei Liang Lu', and in Daoshi, *Fayuan Zhulin*, Ch. 21, 'Jingfo Bian'.

18. For a report of the excavation see Wu Rengxiang, (1989) *Jiuquan shiliuguo mubihua (Wall Paintings of the Sixteen Kingdoms Tomb at Jiuquan)*. Beijing: Wenwu chubanshe.

19. The form and construction of Tomb No 5 at Dingjiazha is very close to a number of large brick-chamber tombs found in the same area. The dating of these tombs range from the Western Jin dynasty to the period of the Sixteen Kingdoms. One of the arguments provided in the report for assigning Tomb No 5 to exactly the period within Later Liang and Northern Liang (386-441) is based on a rather groundless supposition. On one of the mureals in the tomb are depicted a setting of a group of musicians one of which plays a waist-drum. The waist-drum is known as a common instrument in the Western Regions and according to the excavation report this picture is the earliest example found in China. Further the argument is based on an information in a chapter on barbarian music in the Song encyclopedia *Cifu Yuangui* (1013): When Lü Guang of Later Liang had conquered Qui-ci [i.e. Kucha] he brought back their music. However, another picture of a waist-drum has been found in a tomb in Anak, Korea. This tomb, belonging to the Chinese official Dong Shou, is dated to 357 on the basis of some inscriptions excavated from the tomb. (See Finsterbusch, K. (1991): Darstellung von musikern auf Relief und Wandmalereien in Gräbern der Han- bis Sui Zeit. *Chinablätter*, vol. 18 Nov. 1991:15-17.)

20. For an English abstract of the excavation report see Dien, Albert E. 1985:1566-67.

Skilfully Planting the Trees of Light:
The Chinese Manichaica, their Central Asian Counterparts, and some Observations on the Translation of Manichaeism into Chinese

Gunner B. Mikkelsen

A major breakthrough was granted the study of Manichaean ecclesiastical history and doctrine, when, during the first two decades of this century, substantial remains of genuine Manichaean texts were unearthed in the Turfan region of Chinese Turkestan (present-day Xinjiang), chiefly from the ruins of the former Uighur capital Qocho (Gaochang 高昌), and the startling discovery of the library treasure-trove at the Mogao 莫高 Caves of Thousand Buddhas, some 25 kilometres southeast of Dunhuang (in Gansu), was made. On these locations, numerous Manichaean manuscripts and fragments were recovered, dug up or purchased, by British, German, French and Russian archaeological expeditions, and were by these — together with great quantities of texts belonging to other religions once actively present in Central Asia and China, *e.g.* Buddhist, Daoist, and Nestorian Christian scriptures, and documents on secular matters — subsequently carried to Oriental institutes, libraries and museums in the West. A few fragments of Manichaean texts were, in addition, collected in the same context by expeditions mounted by the Reverend Count Ootani Kozui, and were along with several hundreds of manuscripts carried eastward to Japan; this before the Chinese authorities, around 1910, succeeded in curbing most of the archaeological ventures undertaken by 'foreign devils' in Chinese Turkestan, hampering especially the large-scale manuscript take-away enterprise involved.

Among the more active foreign parties in the Eastern regions of Chinese Turkestan were the German archaeological expeditions. The successful recovery of Manichaean fragmentary texts in Middle Iranian and Old Turkish at four different sites in Qocho by the first German expedition to Turfan (November 1902 – April 1903), headed by Albert Grünwedel, director of the Indian Department of the Museum für Völkerkunde in Berlin, and the

ensuing publication of a major part of the texts in Middle Persian and
Parthian by the iranologist F.W.K. Müller in 1904 (*HR ii*) must have
encouraged the dispatch of a second German expedition to the region
(September 1904 – December 1905), now enjoying royal support. This first
Königlich-Preussischen Turfan-Ekspedition was led by Albert von Le Coq, an
employee at the Museum, who a few years earlier (in 1900) had commenced
studies of Oriental languages in Berlin. The main objective of the second
expedition was the further recovery of manuscript-remains in the Turfan
ruins (cf. Le Coq, 1913: Vorwort); it was therefore most satisfactory when a
considerable number of manuscripts were found at *inter alia* the Qocho ruin
complexes 'K' and 'α', many of which soon were to be identified as
Manichaean. Also the third (December 1905 – June 1907) and fourth (January
1913 – February 1914) German expeditions to the Turfan region successfully
recovered Manichaean fragments. After four remunerative visits to the
sand-buried ruins of Central Asia, the Berlin Turfan-Sammlung possessed a
large amount of Manichaean texts, most in a fragmentary state of preservation
(cf. Boyce, 1960: 1ff.), and primarily written in a highly distinctive script akin
to Syriac Estrangela and in Sogdian script in three Middle Iranian languages
— Middle Persian, Parthian, Sogdian — and in New Persian. The Sammlung
furthermore counted a number of fragments of Manichaean texts in Old
Turkish, of which a major part were studied, translated and published by Le
Coq himself shortly after the arrival of these at Berlin. Not surprisingly, the
rich Iranian Manichaean material has been the object of much scholarly
attention ever since its collection. This contrasts with the Manichaean
fragments in Chinese, of which photos and annotated translations just
recently have reached a broader scholarly audience thanks to the Berlin
sinologist Thomas Thilo (Ch 174, = T II 1917, and Ch 258, = T II T 1319; Thilo,
1991: 161-70, Tafel XX-XXIII). Interesting links between these two text-bits and
other texts found in Central Asia have been established by the iranologist
Werner Sundermann, who has identified two parallels in Parthian and
Sogdian (M 8287; = T III D 280, and 10 200/1 (5); Sundermann, 1991: 171-74)
to one of the texts (Ch 258), and by Inokuchi Taijun and Thilo who have
observed similar versions of the texts in some of the Manichaean hymns
found at Dunhuang (Thilo, 1991: 165ff.).

Among the loads of scriptural evidence removed by Western expeditions
from the library cache of Mogao cave no. 17 during the years 1906-9 were
three scrolls containing Manichaean texts in Chinese. Two of these were
obtained by the famous Hungarian-British orientalist and explorer Aurel Stein

on his visit at the site in spring 1907: firstly, a long scroll (7,5 m) entitled *Monijiao xiabu zan* 摩尼教下部讚 'Lower Section of Manichaean Hymns', and containing a collection of more than twenty hymns and prayers, and secondly, a small scroll, in an excellent state of preservation, constituting the first part of a Manichaean catechism entitled *Moni guangfo jiaofa yilüe* 摩尼光佛教法儀略, 'Compendium of the teachings of Mani the Buddha of Light'. The two manuscripts, commonly referred to as the *Hymnscroll* and the *Compendium*, were deposited in the British Museum (today in the India Office Library and Records, British Library), and here catalogued by the 'Stein numbers' S 2659 and S 3969. The two scrolls were catalogued together with 8100 other Dunhuang texts by Lionel Giles, who registered them as nos. 7053 and 7054 respectively (Giles, 1957: 228-29). The German orientalists Ernst Waldschmidt and Wolfgang Lentz were the first to produce translations (in German) of some of the hymns of the *Hymnscroll*; these formed part of their celebrated studies on the role of Jesus in Manichaeism, published in 1926 (*W.-L. i* 119-20 (cols. 360-63 and 368-71), 123-24 (cols. 387-400; photo appended), *et passim*), and Manichaean dogmatics, published in 1933 (*W.-L. ii* 485-91 (cols. 120-53 and 164-75; annotations pp. 491-545)). Waldschmidt and Lentz were able to recognize parallel versions of the short phonetically transcribed invocations included in the Chinese *Hymnscroll* among the Middle Iranian texts from Turfan (Waldschmidt/Lentz, 1926a: 119-22, 298-99). They succeeded in identifying parallel (or original?) passages to the Chinese transcription of an invocation of Jesus (cols. 176-183) in two texts in Parthian (M 259c and M 529), and in one in Sogdian (TM 351). These passages have more recently been examined in detail by Enrico Morano (Morano, 1982: 9-34), while parallel passages in Old Turkish have been studied by James Hamilton (Hamilton, 1986: 37-56). Yoshida Yutaka has pointed to a possible 'Aramaic' basis of the transcriptions (Yoshida, 1983: 326-31). Moreover, Waldschmidt and Lentz attempted identification of Middle Iranian parallels to the two other phonetically transcribed invocations of the *Hymnscroll* (cols. 1-5 and 154-58).

As noted by Peter Bryder, who has carried out in-depth studies of the *Hymnscroll*, not least of the 'Middle Iranian hymns transcribed in Chinese characters' (Bryder, 1985: 47-62), the 'phenomenon of Iranian hymns transcribed into Chinese characters shows the eagerness of the missionaries to hold to the original' (*idem* 62). The same point is inferred by Yoshida's work. As we shall see, the importance of a *verbatim et litteratim* transmission of the textual message is on more than one occasion stressed in the Chinese Manichaean texts; the injunction laid down for the missionaries to adhere strictly to the original word when translating the text into Chinese is explicitly stated in the very texts they subjected to translation. In a postscript, the translator of the *Hymnscroll*, named Daoming 道明, informs us that the hymns have been translated from select passages of 'three thousand passages in Sanskrit (*fan* 梵, *i.e.* Middle Persian and Parthian) books', and that they are 'uniformly based' on these works. He admonishes 'anyone who wishes to learn' to study the texts in great detail so that he/she will know 'the right order any time they are shown to him/her', and impresses the scribe to 'collate them carefully, and arrange them according to the right method'. The chanter must first go to the enlightened teacher, and learn 'the mistakes and differences', presumably for the sake of exact recitation of the phonetically transcribed stanzas (cols. 416-20; cf. the English translation of the full *Hymnscroll* by the Chinese buddhologist Tsui Chi, 1943: 215). Among other plausible explanations of the translator's preference for phonetical renderings of the Iranian refrains — in addition to the one of considering a verbatim transmission — one may point, as Samuel N. C. Lieu does, to the importance of enabling the Chinese converts unable to read Iranian languages to join in chanting with their Sogdian priests (Lieu, 1992: 245), and also to the transmitters' deference to the sacred value and meaning of 'original' liturgical formulas.

The Manichaean teachers did not, however, produce exact duplicate translations of the Iranian originals into Chinese. In Central Asia and China — like anywhere else the Manichaean Church established new mission stations — the translation work was carried out in strict accordance with the principles of universalism and conscious syncretism as formulated and practised by Mani himself. A sinicized version of these basic principles is outlined in the *Compendium*, where Mani is equated with Buddha Śākyamuni and Laozi in a Manichaean interpretation of the important Chinese *sanjiao* 三教 theory: 'how, on the basis of their inborn spirituality, should the Three Saints (*sansheng* 三聖) be different, since, by the maintenance of their perfected Nature, they all apprehended the Truth.' (cols. 14-15).

How and to what extent the texts in the process of translation were adapted to the target or recipient milieu of Tang China may be estimated from the translation from Parthian into Chinese of one lengthy eulogy in the *Hymnscroll*, the 'Praise of the World of Light' (*Tan mingjie wen* 歎明界文; cols. 261-338), as this is strongly reminiscent of the first canto of the Parthian hymn-cycle *Huyadagmān* (formerly read as *Huwīdagmān*, 'Fortunate for us'), a text which has been partly reconstructed from a large number of fragments found at Turfan (the first canto is also attested in several Sogdian fragments, see esp. Sundermann, 1990: 23f.). As pointed out by W. B. Henning (*apud* Tsui Chi, 1943: 217-19), Mary Boyce (text and ann. transl. of *Huyadagmān* I; Boyce, 1954: 66-77; add. and corr.: Boyce, 1956, 314-22), and, in particular, by Bryder (1985: 63-74), several of the verse-lines in the first canto of the Parthian hymn-cycle are parallel to the Chinese version of the hymn to such an extent that one must assume that a Parthian version may have served as the original version on which the Chinese translation was based. However, the Manichaean principle of translation *qua* approximation — by one later Chinese Buddhist critic termed *xiangsi dao* 相似道 'the doctrine of approximation' of a religion which considered itself to be *shangshang cheng* 上上乘 'the superior vehicle' (*Da Song sengshi lüe* 大宋僧史略, xia; *TD*, LIV, p. 253c17-18) — is clearly manifested in the Chinese eulogy, as the depiction of the Light World here, in contrast to its Parthian counterpart, is heavily tinged with the Buddhist notion of Sukhāvatī, i.e. Amitābha's Western paradise. At the time of the introduction of Manichaean texts in the Chinese language into Northern China, a process which presumably went on from the early eighth century to the late ninth, the World of Light was from a Manichaean missionary point of view most effectively presented to the Chinese through the adoption of imagery and terminology associated with Buddhist *sukhāvatī* paradises, or, in Chinese, *jingtu* 淨土 'pure lands'. The actual widespread popularity enjoyed by the *buddhaksetra* of Amitābha in China offered an attractive, a 'fashionable', and — one may add — a 'natural' clothing to the depiction of the Manichaean notion of Heaven, which was readily borrowed by the Manichaean translators. The 'Praise of the Light World', which due to its status as the only Chinese hymn with extant Parthian parallels (to more than just a minor part) is of greatest importance to the study of Manichaean translation techniques, depicts the Light World as a 'world of perfect bliss' (*jile shijie* 極樂世界; cols. 328 and 332), 'where everything is light, and no place is dark; where all the buddhas (*fo* 佛) and envoys of Light (*mingshi* 明使) live', and 'everything is clean and pure, eternally happy (*changle* 常樂), calm and quiet, undisturbed and unhindered; one receives happiness and has no worry or affliction' (cols. 265-66; Tsui Chi, 1943: 199). While, as mentioned, the *Huyadagmān* contains no specific references to 'pure lands' of buddhas, the term 'buddha-land' (*burxanlar uluši*; Skt. *buddhabhūmi*) occurs in the Turkish 'Great Hymn to Mani' (T III D 260 (53) and (164), *TTT iii* 188-89, 200-1), and, as we shall see, the Light-World is in fact termed 'pure land' in at least one other Parthian text.

    In March 1908, a third Manichaean manuscript in Chinese was discovered in the Mogao 'bibliothèque médiévale' by Paul Pelliot, then Professor of Chinese at the École Française d'Extrême-Orient at Hanoi. The French expedition to Central Asia greatly benefited from the philological capacity of its young *conducteur* — Pelliot's multi-linguistic training enabled him to read and identify on location most of the documents stored in the cache. Pelliot was, furthermore, an expert on Eastern Manichaeism. He had, a few years before the outset of his mission to Chinese Turkestan, studied and published a compilation of a number of Chinese sources on Manichaean missionary activity in China, including an interesting reference to a Manichaean version of the popular *Laozi huahu jing* 老子化胡經, 'Scripture on Laozi's Conversion of the Barbarians' (Pelliot, 1903: 318-27). In his long letter composed at Dunhuang on March 26th 1908, and sent to Émile Senart, director of the Committee in charge of the mission, Pelliot briefly surveys some of the sources mentioned in his earlier study before moving on to make a report on a 'fragment manichéen' which he had just discovered among the more than 15,000 manuscripts in the library cache (Pelliot, 1908: 516-18). The fragment, he states, contains the concluding lines of a paragraph (4) which apparently concerns 'l'exposition des cadavres', followed by two paragraphs (5-6), one which enumerates the chambers of a temple and the titles of three community superiors, and one which concerns the initiation of monks (*idem* 518). A few years later, the fragment (Bibliothèque Nationale: Don 4502, Pelliot 3884), commonly referred to as *Fragment Pelliot*, was translated into French by Edouard Chavannes and Pelliot himself, and published with a photographic reproduction in *Journal Asiatique* (*Traité II*: 105-16, Pl. I). This was however not the first publication of the *Fragment*. In *ultimo* 1909, a facsimile edition by Jiang Fu had appeared in Luo Zhenyu's *Dunhuang shishi yishu* 敦煌石室遺書 ('Lost Books from a Stone Chamber of Dunhuang'; 2287-89), and, in 1910, photos of the manuscript were published by Luo in his *Shishi bibao* 石室秘寶 ('Rare Treasures from a Stone Chamber'; MS. (11): 'Monijiao jing canjuan' 摩尼 教經殘卷).

It was not until the mid-1920's that Pelliot, probably inspired by the work of two Japanese scholars, Ishida Mikinosuke and Yabuki Keiki (cf. Lin, 1988: 89-90), realized that his fragment in fact formed an uninterrupted continuation of Stein's *Compendium* (Pelliot, 1925). He commenced work on a translation of the Stein part but was not granted enough time to finish his project. Now, more than half a century later, this partial translation, with Paul Demiéville's completing translation and commentary, has been published as an appendix to a new annotated French translation of the full *Compendium* by

Nahal Tajadod (Tajadod, 1990: 255-70). The earliest translation of the *Compendium* to appear was produced by G. Haloun and W. B. Henning but this was somewhat surprisingly published without the *Fragment Pelliot* (Haloun/Henning, 1952: 188-93, incl. photographs).

Although no Iranian parallels to the *Compendium* have been detected among the Turfan fragments, the text, or surely parts of it, must have been compiled on the basis of texts in Middle Persian or Parthian. Thus, several key terms, titles of books of Mani's Canon, the five grades of the community, and titles of important clerical ranks, listed in the text, are given as transcriptions of Middle Iranian *termini technici*.[1] These are, however, followed by Chinese translations, and/or definitions in Chinese. As stated in the preface of the text, the *Compendium* was compiled as a response to an imperial request forwarded on July 16th, 731. This fact explains adequately why the catechism includes quotations of Buddhist and Daoist scriptures which were familiar to most Chinese at the time but certainly were not the result of translations from Iranian originals (cols. 33-40). Evidently, the first paragraph of the text has been reformulated and elaborated with the purpose of converting the Chinese emperor to Manichaeism or convincing him, as well as influential Buddhist and Daoist clergy, about the historical importance of the religion, its relevance and good intentions in China. The Manichaean missionaries were strong exponents of the strategy so characteristic of the history of foreign proselytising religions in China: they attempted to safeguard their mission by conversion 'from the top down'.

The Manichaean missionary legations that arrived at Chang'an during the eighth and ninth centuries were mainly teachers and merchants of Sogdian extraction — a people who had distinguished themselves in Central Asia as experts on marketing, influential agents in politics, and as in every respect experienced in various aspects and implications of cultural encounter; this was manifested by their principal role as intermediaries in the exchange of not only saleable commodities but also of cultural goods. As they thus were mobile, polyglottal and well-acquainted with local religious ideas and religico-philosophical currents, the Sogdians were ideally suited to act as conveyors of the Manichaean religion from the cultural melting pot of the Tarim Basin into the not less variegated religious scene of Tang China. When the Manichaean missionaries passed through the Jade Gate borderpost not far from Dunhuang, and travelled down through the Hexi Corridor towards the capital, their objective — reflecting both missionary and mercantilist attitudes and ambitions — was single and clear-cut but at the same time involved dual considerations: they wished first and foremost to make an impact, that is to convert, but in order to achieve this goal they at the same time concentrated on accommodating themselves and their message to the new situation. Their missionary ambition and task was to 'translate' (in the broadest sense of the word) the teachings of Mani to the new situation, but without allowing any 'transformation' of the original essence of these to take place in the process. The Manichaeans seem to have been highly aware of the multiple problems and pitfalls related to the process of translating texts and doctrines to new contexts without essentially transforming them. Thus the issue of missionary and translation techniques holds a prime position in one of the most important texts of their Church, the fourth and last Chinese Manichaean manuscript to be discovered at Mogao.

At the Mogao cache Pelliot collected no less than six thousand manuscripts, mostly sinica but a fair amount of tibetica as well. His collection was based on a critical selection which, according to his letter, was based on a quick examination of every single scroll and fragment in the library. How he was able to carry out and complete this huge project within the limitation set by an extremely tight time schedule, he describes in his letter with an enthusiasm that was to give rise to much criticism and debate among colleagues and scholars back in France:

Mon parti fut vite pris. L'examen au moins sommaire de toute la bibliothèque s'imposait, où qu'il dût me mener. De dérouler d'un bout à l'autre les quelque 15.000 à 20.000 rouleaux qui se trouvaient là, il n'y fallait pas songer; je n'en eusse pas vu la fin en six mois. Mais je devais au moins tout ouvrir, reconnaître la nature de chaque texte, et quelles chances il offrait d'être nouveau pour nous; puis faire deux parts, l'une de crème, de gratin, de ce qu'il fallait se faire céder à tout prix, et l'autre qu'on tâcherait d'obtenir (*viz.* from the Daoist abbot in charge of the cave complex), tout en se résignant, le cas échéant, à la laisser échapper.

Malgré que j'aie fait diligence, ce départ m'a pris plus de trois semaines. Les dix premiers jours, j'abattais près de 1000 rouleaux par jour, ce qui doit être un record: le 100 à l'heure accroupi dans une niche, allure d'automobile à l'usage des philologues. J'ai ralenti ensuite. D'abord j'étais un peu fatigué, la poussière des liasses m'avait pris à la gorge; et aussi mes négociations d'achat m'incitaient à gagner du temps, autrement dit à en perdre. Un travail aussi hâtif ne va naturellement pas sans quelque aléa; des pièces ont pu m'échapper, qu'à plus mûr examen j'aurais aimé m'annexer. Toutefois, je ne pense pas avoir rien négligé d'essentiel. Il n'est pas seulement un rouleau, mais un chiffon de papier, — et Dieu sait s'il y avait de ces loques, — qui ne m'ait passé par les mains, et je n'ai rien écarté qui ne m'ait paru sortir du cadre que je m'étais tracé. (Pelliot, 1908: 505-6)

His methods being scientifically justifiable or not, one can only congratulate Paul Pelliot on his accomplishment of a task of stupendous proportions, single-handedly and under very difficult working conditions. Not only did he work his way through thousands of fragile and dusty scrolls, pothis, booklets, fragments etc., written in various South, Central and East Asian languages and scripts, handling almost two per minute (!), but Pelliot spent three long weeks uncomfortably crouching in a dark cave, leafing through and studying intensively the manuscripts by the light of a candle, the only space for work being the minimal space resulting from the removal of Stein's great haul. With his stated conviction of having checked the identity of every single scrap of paper in the cave, and his priority system as well as his special interest in Manichaeism *in mente*, one may however be slightly surprised to learn that one very long (6,21 m), very well-preserved and very important Manichaean text in Chinese had escaped him. This text, a treatise on cosmo-theogony, soteriology, and missionarycommunity life, was among the manuscript left-overs which in 1909 were transported to Beijing to be deposited at the Jingshi Tushuguan 京師圖書官 (*yu* 宇 56; now in the new Beijing Library on Baishiqiao Road, registered as bei 北 8470).

Being the longest Manichaean text known at that time, its discovery caused great excitement among scholars in East and West alike. In 1911, a hand-written copy of the text was published by Luo Zhenyu in his journal *Guoxue congkan* 國學 叢 刊 ('Collection of National Learning'; fasc. 2). A hand-copy of the text was at some point sent to Paris, and its text was within a short period of time translated into French by Chavannes and Pelliot. Their translation, accompanied by extensive commentaries and a copy of the Chinese text, appeared as 'Un traité manichéen retrouvé en Chine' in *Journal Asiatique* later that same year (*Traité I*). Parts of the opening lines of the original text, including the title, were/are missing (the only lacunae), and, because Luo had not been able to determine whether the text was a Nestorian, a Zoroastrian or a Manichaean treatise, he had provided it with the provisional title *Bosijiao canjing* 波斯教殘經 'Fragmentary Scripture of a Persian Religion'. Carrying this title, the treatise was in the late 1920's, alongside the other Chinese Manichaean texts and some Nestorian, included in the Japanese printed edition of the Chinese Buddhist Canon, the *Taishoo shinshuu daizookyoo* (*TD*, LIV, no. 2141 B, pp. 1281a-86a)[2]. The recently published German translations of the Chinese manichaica by Helwig Schmidt-Glintzer are to some extent based on the *Taishoo* prints (Schmidt-Glintzer, 1987b: 11ff.; *Taishoo* editions are appended and references interspersed in the translated text). The decision to downgrade a critical reading of the original manuscripts is, however, an unfortunate one, as the *Taishoo* editions — especially in the case of the *Hymnscroll* and the *Traité* — contain several copyist errors. Likewise, the basis on which Chavannes and Pelliot prepared their pioneering edition was a rather fragile one, as Luo's hand-written text-copy, on several points, does not remain faithful to the original. This is most unfortunate as the French *savants* were very attentive to palaeographical problems when translating the text and commenting on its contents[3]. The printed edition of the text by Chen Yuan, published in 1923, gives a more accurate copy of the original text, but this, too, contains some copyist errors, incorrect interpretations of variant characters, and unwarranted emendations (Chen, 1923: 531-44; text republished with some changes in Chen, 1980: 375-92; for examinations of the variants in the manuscript, see Aurousseau, 1912: 55-63, and Mikkelsen, 1992). Photos of the manuscript have been included in the *Dunhuang baozang* ('The Treasure-Store of Dunhuang'; Huang, 1984: 418-26) and in Lin Wushu's *Monijiao ji qi dongjian* ('Manichaeism and its Eastward Spread'; Lin, 1987: plates 1-18) .

Although Pelliot was not the discoverer of the scroll, the text has in later Western studies often been referred to as *Traité* or *Traktat Pelliot*. This occasions a return to the intriguing question of why Pelliot, whilst working at Mogao, failed to recognise the text as Manichaean. The answer to this may be quite simple: Pelliot was not only oppressed by difficult working conditions and tight time schedules, he was actually, in addition, confronted with a text which at first sight appeared to be a Buddhist *sūtra*. The prologue in fact follows the pattern of famous Buddhist treatises, like the Diamond *sūtra* and the Lotus *sūtra* — both abundantly represented in the same library. As observed by Herbert Giles, the Manichaean treatise 'not only (...) is like in form to a Buddhist *sûtra*, but it is tinged here and there with traces of Buddhist thought', and the dialogue between Mani and his disciple, Atuo 阿 駞 (Adda(s)?), which forms the opening of Mani's treatise, strongly resembles the common Buddhist *sūtra*-style of master-disciple dialogue, as Mani, after having listened to the question of Atuo, »began his reply by the very words of Buddha in the Diamond *Sûtra*, the Chinese characters being the same in both cases, 'Good indeed! Good indeed! In order to benefit the innumerable crowds of living beings, you have addressed to me this query, profound and mysterious. You thus show yourself as a good friend to all those living beings of the world who have blindly gone astray, and I will now explain the matter to you in detail, so that the net of doubt in which you are ensnared may be broken for ever without recall'« (Giles, 1915: 190-91; cols. 5-8). Giles states, that 'we do not possess the opening words of this treatise, and cannot therefore say if they coincide with the conventional words with which a Buddhist *sûtra* begins; but we may fairly well infer that such was the case, partly from the remarkable imitation of Buddhist phraseology throughout, and also from the closing sentence, the Chinese text of which, *mutatis mutandis*, might well be interchanged with that of the Diamond *Sûtra*':

Diamond Sûtra	*Manichaean Treatise*
When the Buddha had delivered this *sûtra*, all the monks and nuns, lay-brothers and lay-sisters, together with all the *dêvas* and demons in the universe, having heard Buddha's words, rejoiced with one accord, and accepting them with faith, proceeded to put them into practice.	Then, all the members of the great assembly, having heard this *sûtra*, accepted it with faith and rejoicing, and proceeded to put into practice.
	(Giles, 1915: 194-95)

So, even if Pelliot, in order to identify the text, had gone further than to unroll the scroll slightly to read just the opening sentences, his eyes would have met a text with a framework and a phraseological style that was so similar to that of a Buddhist *sûtra* that it would have been more than easy for him, or for that matter anyone else, erroneously to take it for being exactly such. But precisely this type of reaction to the textual presentation, *i.e.* the reaction of initial misidentification of the text as Buddhist, does in actual fact form an important part of the Manichaean missionary strategy as formulated in the Chinese manichaica — and most explicitly in the *Traité* itself.

Quite analogous to the christianization and zoroastrianization of the presentations of Mani's *gnosis* witnessed in the Roman and Persian empires, and attested in extant Coptic and Syriac texts and Middle Iranian texts respectively, the Manichaean missionaries, when entering the vast missionary field of the Chinese Tang-empire, attempted an accommodation to important local religious terminologies. But when reaching this dominant empire situated at the far eastern end of their missionary route — comerging with the vital so-called 'silk route' named after the most important Chinese commodity transported along it — way beyond the oasis towns of the Tarim where many creeds and convictions coexisted at relative peace with each other, the translators of the Manichaean texts were compelled to adopt a position of utmost alertness in relation to the high-cultural weight of the 'locale' encountered. This was particularly true because of the strong capability and tendency of the Chinese world to 'contain' or assimilate incoming ideas, implying indigenization of foreign belief systems, religious concepts etc. Therefore, the Manichaean teachers, when translating their texts into Chinese, did not blindly attempt an approximation to the Chinese textual tradition; they were cautioned to pay great attention to the risks of altering their holy texts and terminologies beyond recognition as this might easily cause distinct original meanings of Manichaean concepts and ideas eventually to become obliterated and distorted, and then absorbed by native or naturalized (viz. Buddhist or Buddhist-Daoist tinged) beliefs. In their work, the Manichaean missionaries faced the same sort of problems as propagators of other foreign religions in China did or had done: they were forced to overcome the dilemma of translating their holy message into Chinese by means of 'established' terminology tainted with indigenous, or previously introduced, ideas and doctrines, thereby inevitably causing the loss of important facets of original doctrine, *and* at the same time translating with the ambition of expressing their ideas in words familiar and appealing to most Chinese. *In summa*, the Manichaeans as advocates of an inherently syncretistic and eclectic religion, which placed itself above all religions of the world and at the same time regarded itself as a 'container' of these, and as a consequence encouraged its propagators legitimately to incorporate other-religious concepts and terms to strengthen its case, had to tread very cautiously when introducing their Gospel into the Chinese religious environment, as this environment — not least during the Tang period — was characterized by a strong endemic penchant for religious and philosophical harmonization.

In the *Traité*, Mani treats at great length (as a reply to Adda's initial question on 'expedient means' for the liberation of the Light-Nature; cols. 1-4) on missionary strategies, and the implementation of these by the *diannawu* 電那勿 (M.Pe. *dyn'wr*; i.e. the 'virtuous ones') on the basis of their attainment of the right missionary attitude and divine qualities. Mani instructs the Elects to bring their missionary quest on earth into accord with the actions of the gods in the 'mythical' scenario. While they, in fact, are urged to 'internalize' the spirit of the cosmic drama, the teachers must in their capacity as earthly apostles of the Light identify themselves with the godly protagonists of this drama and consequently 'imitate' their ingenious acts. Thus, the treatise encourages them to employ combat devices like the usage of 'baits' with the object of 'captivating' or 'seducing' their audiences and luring their demon-besieged minds to cling unto the Words of Light like 'flies sticking to honey, like a bird caught on lime, like a fish which has swallowed the hook' (cols. 10-11). The powers of Darkness, expressing themselves as negative human character traits which poison or darken the originally enlightened mind of man, must be defeated by 'means of expediency' or 'skilful means', *(shanqiao) fangbian* 善巧方便 (corresponding to Mahāyāna Buddhist Skt. *upāya kauśalya*), *i.e.* by the same means as those employed by the agents of the Father of Greatness, and in particular by the Light-Nous, in the mythical micro-macrocosmic struggle. The Light-messengers on earth must let the Light-Nous endow them with the mental qualities and the stratagems necessary for a propagation of the Words of Light expediently suited to the different levels of perception or degrees of 'poisoning' of their audiences, and in that way provide the right stimuli for these to awaken and attain liberating enlightenment. From Mani's treatise can be deduced that the Light-gods' cosmic struggle with the demons of Darkness (referred to as *anmo* 暗魔 or *mo* 魔, equivalent to Buddhist Skt. *māra*) and the missionary campaign on earth are integrated: the latter, as a microcosmic (*xiao shijie* 小世界; col. 30) struggle in the mind/body of man and as a macrocosmic (*da shijie* 大世界; col. 23) one in expanding missionary territories on earth, forms 'part' of the former. The Manichaean teachers must therefore undertake their liberation quest in the dark territories armed with the 'hatchet of Wisdom' (*zhifu* 智斧; cols. 54 and 170), and as 'skilful (*shanqiao*) agricultural labourers (*tianren* 田人, 'field-workers'?) of the Light-Nous (*huiming* 惠明 [4])' (col. 147) they must cut down the 'poisonous trees' (*dushu* 毒樹) of Death, and clear the ground so that 'precious trees' (*baoshu* 寶樹) of Light can be planted in their place, and a new 'princely hall' can be built and a new 'throne-platform' erected (cols. 147-51; cf. cols. 169ff.). The plantation of light trees and the construction of palaces and thrones signifies the establishment of Manichaean communities in new missionary fields, platforms for preaching the Law, as well as the implantation of light qualities in the mind of man, implying enlightenment or conversion and the ability to enlighten — vital aspects of the Nous (*huiming xiang* 惠明相; cols. 220-316). One of the five light trees planted as a replacement for one of the five dark trees represents important qualities of the perfect Nous-inspired teacher:

Then he planted the Tree of Reasoning; the root of this tree is Wisdom; its trunk is the Complete Understanding of the Meaning of the Two Principles; its branches are Skill in Discussing the Radiant Law; its leaves are Familiarity with the Arguments in a manner appropriate to the circumstances, Ability to Crush Heterodox Doctrines, Honouring and Affirming the True Law; its fruits are Skill at Questioning and Replying, and Excellence at Speaking by Using Appropriate Arguments; its taste is Excellence at Using Parables which make men understand well; its colour is the Agreeable Expressions which make that which one expounds pleasing to the multitude. (cols. 179-83; tr. Lieu/Mikkelsen, 1993)

Although the complete liberation of the light-particles imprisoned in man was of paramount importance to the Manichaean Church, this did not permit the translators to abstract freely from the terminology and phraseology of the original text. This important point is signified by the implantation of the third 'sign' of the Tree of Faith:

Concerning the holy scriptures, they do not allow themselves to add or subtract a single word or sentence. (col. 273; tr. Lieu/Mikkelsen, 1993)

How the translators were able to balance their obligations towards the practice of *fangbian* on one side and the instruction of not to tamper with the original texts on the other, is exemplified in the translation of the *Traité* itself from Parthian into Chinese. Several fragments of Parthian and Sogdian versions of the *Sermon of the Light-Nous* (*mnwhmyd rwšn wyfr's*) containing passages parallel to sections of the *Traité* have been identified among the Turfan manuscripts housed in the Staatsbibliothek Preussischer Kulturbesitz at Berlin, forty in Parthian and seven in Sogdian, and, in addition, two Parthian fragments of parallels have been discovered in the Ootani Collection of Ryukoku University in Kyoto. After the positive identification of a few parallel versions of parts of the *Traité* in Parthian by Waldschmidt and Lentz in 1926 (*W.-L. i* 44), and the publication of some lists found among the Sogdian fragments enumerating the various 'parts' of the trees described in the *Traité* by W.B. Henning (Henning, 1940: 3-5), several more Middle Iranian parallels were identified among the Turfan fragments by Boyce and listed in her catalogue as belonging to texts of a 'Traité-type' or as texts 'similar to the Traité' (Boyce, 1960: 148, 15.-16.). All fragments listed as versions of or as similar to the Chinese text, together with several more Parthian and Sogdian parallels, have been compiled in Werner Sundermann's recently published work — including text in transcribed and photographical form, translations, commentaries and wordlists — on the *Sermon of the Light-Nous* (*SLN*; cf. Sundermann, 1983: 231-42). As observed by Sundermann, the reconstituted Parthian *Sermon* cannot have served as the original version from which the Chinese treatise was translated; this and the *Traité* might more likely have been translated from the same Parthian 'Urtext' (*SLN* 11-13). Nevertheless, it is possible that some of the fragments, written by several different scribes, recovered by more than one expedition on various locations in the Turfan region, actually formed part of the version from which the *Traité* was translated. It is noteworthy that Mani's treatise on the Light-Nous apparently enjoyed great popularity everywhere as the text is the most copied and circulated of all Manichaean texts — or, at least, it is the one text of the Manichaean religion which has survived in most copies or versions in most languages. Thus, fragments of the text, quite parallel to sections of the *Traité*, were furthermore identified among the Turkish material by Le Coq, who published half a dozen treatise fragments about which he remarked that they (too) were 'von verschiedenen unserer Expeditionen an verschiedenen Fundstellen in Chotscho ausgegraben', and that they belonged to four different books (*TMC iii* 15-22; retranslated and published with Chinese parallels by H.-J. Klimkeit and Schmidt-Glintzer, 1984: 82-117 (*TPT*)). To one of these books belonged a fragment (T. M. 423d, presented in the same edition by Le Coq; *TMC iii* 23-24) which appears to come from a Turkish version of the canonized *Book of the Giants*. As a double-fragment in Middle Persian, deposited at the Institute Vostokovedenija in St. Petersburg, has been found (by Sundermann, 1984: 491-505, esp. 498ff; cf. *SLN* 15-17) to contain on its first page a part of the *Book of the Giants*, and on the other, passages quite similar to passages of the *Traité*, stronger support is lent to the supposition of a close connection between the two works. Among other versions parallel or closely related to the Chinese treatise we find the Coptic *kephalaion* 38 on 'the Light-Nous, the Apostles and the Holy Ones' (*Keph.* 1.part: 90,20-99,17; cf. *SLN* 13-15), the *kephalaia* 39 and 4 (cf. *SLN* 18-19), the Sogdian text of fragment M 133 (cf. *SLN* 17f., 128-30) and sections of a Sogdian book of confessions (Henning, 1936: 37).

Synopsis I: *Traité* (1) and Middle Iranian and Old Turkish parallels (2)

(1)	(2)
cols. **(1)-25**	*SLN* §§ 1-8 (Pth.)
(*TD*, LIV, 1281(a22)-b22)	
cols. **36-67**	*SLN* §§ 9-17 (Pth.)
(*TD* 1281c6-82a17)	
cols. **80-99**	*SLN* §§ 18-23 (Pth.)
(*TD* 1282b6-c3)	
cols. **146-(197)**	*SLN* §§ 24-38 (Pth.)
(*TD* 1283a29-(84a6))	
cols. **202-279**	*SLN* §§ 39-77 (Pth. & Sogd.)
(*TD* 1284a13-85a28)	
cols. **(301)-(303)**	*SLN* §§ 78-79 (Pth.)
(*TD* 1285(b29)-(c3))	
cols. **175-183 (157-183)**	T ii(oyoq)(Sogd.); Henning, 1940: Fr I (II: T i)
(*TD* 1283c8-c17 (83b13-c17))	
cols. **28-192** (*partim*)	M 133 (Sogd.); *SLN* 128-30
(*TD* 1281b25-83c29)	
cols. **157-183** (*partim*)	S I ^{0}/120 II *recto-verso* (M.Pe.); Sundermann,
(*TD* 1283b13-c17)	1984: Fr. L/II, 502-4
cols. **72-80**	T II D 119 *recto-verso* (Turk.); *TMC iii*: 16-17;
(*TD* 1282a25-b7)	*TPT* 86-87
cols. **(98)-100**	T M 300 *recto* (Turk.); *TMC iii*: 17; *TPT* 89
(*TD* 1282(c1)-c3)	
cols. **103-105**	T M *verso* (Turk.); *TMC iii*: 17-18; *TPT* 89
(*TD* 1282(c7)-c8)	
cols. **209-(229)**	T M 423 c & b (Turk.); *TMC iii*: 18-20;
(*TD* 1284a23-(b20))	*TPT* 90-91
cols. **230-236**	T M 423 e (Turk.); *TMC iii*: 20-21; *TPT* 93-94
(*TD* 1284b21-c1)	
cols. **260-263**	T I α 2 *recto* (Turk.); *TMC iii*: 21; *TPT* 94-95
(*TD* 1285a5-a9)	
cols. **267-269**	T I α 2 *verso* (Turk.); *TMC iii*: 21; *TPT*: 95
(*TD* 1285a14-a15)	

cols. **300-310**   T M 423 a (Turk.); *TMC iii*: 22; *TPT*: 96-97
  (*TD* 1285b28-c11)

The existence of such a wealth of text passages parallel to the Chinese text
offers the modern student of Manichaean missiology a rare opportunity to
gain a clearer understanding of how the Manichaean translators handled the
transmission of the message into new contexts and, in particular, how they
overcame the pronounced Chinese challenge. Subjected to a more thorough
comparative examination these texts may shed much light on the Manichaean
translation techniques in the East and thus sharpen and balance our view of
the Manichaean text-based missionary action as a worldwide enterprise. Only
a few observations, though, on the relationship between the extant passages
of the Parthian and Sogdian *Sermon of the Light-Nous* and the Chinese *Traité*
can be made here[5].

The vocabulary of the *Traité* appears on the whole to be less buddhisized
than that of the Chinese Manichaean hymns and the catechism. Obviously the
close-knit structure of sections of the text (cf. Alfaric, 1919: 99-103), involving
rather tedious enumerations of parts of trees and anthropological features, has
facilitated an exact 'transplantation' of much of the original terminology and
wording, in contrast to the poetic liberties taken by Daoming in his translation
into Chinese of the hymns and prayers. The Manichaean *interpretatio buddhica*
as concerns terminology and imagery is not entirely a Chinese — or an
Uighur Turkish (see Tongerloo, 1984: 243-52; Klimkeit, 1987: 65-69) — affair.
Not an inconsiderable number of instances of Indian and Buddhist terminology has been attested in Manichaean texts in Middle Iranian languages, in
particular in the texts in Sogdian and Parthian (see Asmussen, 1965: 135ff.;
Sundermann, 1982: 99-113; Sims-Williams, 1983: 132-41; Klimkeit, 1987: 58-65).
As a natural consequence of the influences issuing from Buddhist centres in
neighbouring regions, terms and concepts of Buddhist and Indian derivation
must, already centuries before the Manichaean apostle Mār Ammō 'entered
the gateway of the East', have been incorporated into the Parthian language,
which was — despite being essentially Western Iranian as the state language
of the Arsacid dynasty — widely used in the Eastern regions of Iran, where
it eventually gained position as the principal liturgical language of the
Manichaean Church[6].

Significantly, the fragments of the Parthian *Sermon* do not only contain
quite a few Buddhist terms transcribed or derived from Sanskrit, e.g. *b'š'h*

'hymn' (< Skt. *bhāṣā*; *SLN* §§ (66), 97), *cxš'byd* 'moral precept' (< Skt. *śiksapāda*; *SLN* §§ (58), (70)), *mrn* 'death' — *mrnyn* 'deadly' (< Skt. *maraṇa*; *SLN* §§ 27, 28, 29, (30), (31), [32], 84, 91a), *zmbwdyg* 'world' (< Skt. *jambudvīpa*; *SLN* §§ (6), (8)), but several Buddhist terms employed in the Chinese version, and elsewhere attested in Parthian manichaica, are absent, e.g. *mwxš* 'salvation' (< Skt. *mokṣa*; *Traité*: *jietuo*), *bwt* 'buddha' (*Traité*: *fo*), *krm* 'karma' (*Traité*: *ye, yexing*) (all references listed in Synopsis II below). The *Traité* does, however, follow the *Sermon* in parts of its text, but very rarely a term of closest relation, that is of the same Buddhist derivation as the Parthian, is employed in the exact corresponding passages of the treatise. The different relationships to Buddhism held by the peoples living in Eastern Iran and in China during the early medieval period explain partly, for one set of instances, the translation into Chinese of the 'original' Manichaean idea of pure earths and fertile soils in opposition to soiled earths and broken soils, attested in the Parthian *Sermon*, by means of Buddhist *sukhāvatī* terminology. The Chinese Buddhist terms *jingtu* 'pure land', *i.e.* the blessed *buddhakṣetras*, and *huitu* 'impure land', *i.e.* the present *sahā* world, are employed in the *Traité* in non-parallel passages but do convey the essential meaning of the Parthian Manichaean concepts (for these and other terms of this category, see Synopsis II). The motifs of trees of life and death hold strong positions in Manichaean imagery, in art and text alike (in both Western and Eastern sources; cf. Arnold-Döben, 1978: 7-44, 1980: 9-29), and they are employed in the Parthian as well as the Chinese versions of the treatise. But an approximation of the Light-world to the Buddhist paradise of the West seems far more obvious in the *Traité* where a strong association to the 'bliss and joy' and 'preciousness' of this paradise is established; terms like *anle* 'peace and happiness', *anle chu* 'region of peace and happiness', *changle* 'eternal happiness', *wuliang le* 'utmost happiness', *baoshu* 'precious, jewel trees' and *baohua* 'precious, jewel flowers' are used here, though not in the *Sermon*.

On the other hand, it is notable that the Chinese translator did not on every occasion seek the *interpretatio buddhica*. In the *Traité*, transcriptions from Parthian and Middle Persian (!) terms (mainly Zoroastrian-Manichaean 'share-ware') are in several instances preferred to translations of names and titles: e.g. *moheluosaben* 摩訶羅薩本 (col. 79; M.Pe. *mhr'spnd'*, i.e. the Light Elements imprisoned in matter), *yiliueryunni* 嶷嚕而云曋 (col. 63; Pth. *grywjywndg*, i.e. the Living Self), *Hulushede* 呼盧瑟德 (cols. 18, 74, 76, 207; Pth. *xrwštg* 'Call'),

Poluhuode 哱嚧嚩德 (cols. 18, 74-75, 76, 207; Pth. *pdw'xtg* 'Answer'), *Sulushaluoyi* 窣路沙羅夷 (cols. 18, 20, 43, 80-81, 122, 206; M.Pe. *srwš'hr'y*; i.e. the Column of Glory, Pth. *b'm 'stwn*). While the last of these names has undergone some buddhicisation on its last mentioning in the *Traité*, where in the concluding eulogy this important soteriological figure is referred to as the 'precious column of diamond' *jingang baozhu* (Synopsis II; cf. Hymnscroll col. 365: *jingang xiangzhu* 金剛相柱 'radiance column of diamond'), the first term listed exemplifies how the translator has decided on rendering the sounds of the original Middle Persian term instead of adopting the available Chinese Buddhist term *fojia* 佛家 'buddha family', as found in one of the Chinese hymns (col. 234), possibly with reference to Sogdian texts (*pwt'ny kwt'r*; < Skt. *buddhagotra*) (cf. Klimkeit, 1987: 65)[7].

Finally, the faithful transmission of manichaeanized Indian cosmology from the *Sermon* to the *Traité* deserves mentioning. The idea adopted in Buddhist Cakravāla single-world cosmology of Mount Sumeru as an *axis mundi*, surrounded by seas and ranges of smaller mountains, four iron walls, three ditches, three clothings, two vehicles (*i.e.* the sun and the moon), one sphere, ten skies and eight earths, is solidly integrated into Mani's sermon in both its Parthian (*SLN* §§ 4 & 8) and Chinese versions (cols. 14-16 & 24-25). The two vehicles in the Parthian version (*dw wrdy(w)[n]*; *SLN* (4) & [12]?) are in the Chinese version referred to as 'two light ships' (*er mingchuan*), which carry the souls across the 'sea of birth and death' (*shengsi hai*), or as 'palaces of the sun and the moon' (*riyue gong*). Both notions undeniably parallel Buddhist ideas of man's journey to *nirvāṇa* but, in fact, conceptions of liberating palaces and ships moving across the sky are firmly established in the Manichaean world of thought and are well-attested, even in Western sources (e.g. in the Coptic Psalm-book and Kephalaia, and in the Syriac text of Theodor bar Konai; cf. Arnold-Döben, 1978: 165-69; furthermore, the description of the macrocosm in f.ex. *Keph.* 169,29-170,20 resembles in part the description in the *Traité*). The elaborated Chinese version of Mani's treatise does typically, though, paint a picture of the road to the safe harbour of Heaven which is more easily understandable to the Buddhist reader than the Parthian is; no references, for example, to a sea of birth and death, or to the escape from the miserable 'earth-prison' (*diyu*), are made in the *Sermon*.

Synopsis II: Some Buddhist terms in the Chinese *Traité*, with equivalents attested in the Parthian and Sogdian *Sermon*

yuan 緣 'concurrent, incidental occasion' (< Skt. *pratyaya, karma*) 1

jietuo 解脫 'salvation, liberation' 'redeem, release' (< Skt. *vimokṣa, mokṣa*) (1), 52, 60, 61 (*SLN* § (15) (Pth.): *'z'd kryd* 'make free'), 72, 200, 255, 327

roushen 肉身 'body of flesh' (< Skt. *māṁsa-kāya*) 2, 23, 29, 47 (*SLN* § 11 (Pth.): *tnb'r* 'body'), 66, 71, 112, 168, 305

fangbian 方便 'skilful means' (< Skt. *upāya kauśalya*) 3, 14 (*SLN* § 7 (Pth.): *[h](wyd)gyft nyzwm'n* 'skilfully and [well]made creation'), 71, 243 (~ *SLN* § 52b (Sogd.): *[wy](δδ)b'γ 'ty prβ'r* '[prea]ching and explanation'), 289, 295

anle 安樂 'peace and happiness', (< Skt. *sukhāvatī*) 3, 49, 175 (*SLN* § 35 (Pth.): *hwnsnd-* 'glad, joyful'); *anle chu* 安樂處 'region of peace and happiness' 315-16

shanzai 善哉 'excellent!' (< Skt. *sādhu*) 5

shan zhishi 善知識 'good friend' 'friend of knowledge, experience' (< Skt. *kalyāna-mitra*) 7

yiwang 疑網 'net of doubts' (< Skt. *vicikitsājāla*) 7

yelun 業輪 'wheel of retribution' (< Skt. *karma-cakra, saṁsāra*) 14 (*SLN* § 4 (Pth.): *['spyr]* 'sphere'), 24

riyue gong 日月宮 'palaces of the sun and moon' 14 (*SLN* § 4 (Pth.): *dw wrdy(w)[n]* 'two vehicles'); *riyue guangming gongdian* 日月光明宮殿 'light-palaces of the sun and moon' 120; *rigong* 日宮 'sun-palace' 211

san lun 三輪 'three wheels' 15 (*SLN* §4 (Pth.): *[hry cxr]* '[three wheels]')

san *zai 三災 'three *calamities'[8] 15, 24 (*SLN* §§ 4 & 8 (Pth.): *[hry] p'rgyn* '[three] ditches')

tiewei si yuan 鐵圍四院 'four surrounding iron walls' (< Skt. *cakravāla*) 15, (24) (*SLN* §§ 4 & 8 (Pth.): *c(f)'r pry(s)[p]* 'four walls of fortification')

Weilao jufu shan 未勞俱孚山 'Mount (Su-)meru' 15 (*SLN* § 4 (Pth.): *myrw(?) kwf* 'Mount Meru')

mo 魔 'evil and destructive one, devil' (< Skt. *māra*) 12 (*SLN* § 2 (*et al.*) (Pth.): *'hrmyng'n* 'diabolical'), 13, 16, 19, 28, 29, 40, 47, 49, 70, 83, 89, 94, 98, 103, 110, 113, 114, 138, 201, 217, 218, 219, 274; *tanmo* 貪魔 'demon of greed' (< Skt. *rāgamāra*) 21 (*SLN* § 7 (*et al.*) (Pth.): *"z* 'Greed'), 31, 34, (61), 68, 82-83, 138, 169, 213; *jimo* 飢魔 'hungry demon' 64 (*SLN* § 16 (Pth.): *'hr(m)[yn]* 'devil')

tanyu 貪慾 'desire' 'greed and concupiscence' (< Skt. *ragā*) 23, 42 (*SLN* § 10 (Pth.): *"z 'wd 'wrjwg* 'greed and covetousness') 61, 152, 161 (*SLN* § 28 (Pth.): *"zbryft* 'desire, greed'), 301

tandu 貪毒 'poison of desire' 29

xiang 相 'characteristic mark/sign' (< Skt. *lakṣaṇa, nimitta*) 'radiance, aeon'[9] 31 (*SLN* § 9 (Pth.): *[b'm]* 'brilliance'), 36, 50, 70, 72, 83, 84, 85, 87, 115, 116, 118, 119, 122,

153, 157, 172, 203, 204, 209, 211, 220, 223, 227, 311, 323, 334; *xianghao* 相好 '(larger and smaller) signs' (< Skt. *lakṣaṇa-vyañjana*) 339-40

mingchuan 明船 'light boat' 48 (*SLN* § 12 (Pth.): [*rwšn*] *my(hr)* 'light ship'), 50-51

shengsi hai 生死海 'sea of birth and death' (< Skt. *saṁsāramahāsamudra*) 48; *shengsi* 生死 'birth and death' (< Skt. *saṁsāra*) 315

shanzi 善子 'good children, people' 49, 314

diyu 地獄 'earth-prison, hell' (< Skt. *naraka*) 51 (*SLN* § 13 (Pth.): *dwjx* 'hell'), 130

lunhui 輪迴 'transmigration' (< Skt. *saṁsāra*) 51

wu qu 五趣 'five destinations' (< Skt. *pañcagati*) 51

miaofa 妙法 'wonderful law' (< Skt. *saddharma*) 53 (*SLN* § 14 (Pth.): *'ndrz* 'law'), 340

shenzhou 神咒 'magical spell' (< Skt. *ṛddhi-mantra, dhāraṇī*) 53, 333

dizang mingshi 地藏明使 'Envoy of Light who is in the womb of the earth' (< Skt. Kṣitigarbha) 110-111

gongde 功德 'meritorious virtue, commendable acts' (< Skt. puṇya) 136, 186, 193, 197, 222, 287, 288, 298, 328

baozhu 寶珠 'precious pearl' (< Skt. *maṇi*) 141, 142, 190

baoshu 寶樹 'jewel trees, precious trees' 150, 155 (*SLN* § 26 (Pth.): *d'lwg'n 'f(r)ydg'n* 'blessed trees'), 171, 310, 314, 331

ganlu 甘露 'sweet dew, ambrosia' (< Skt. *amṛta*); *ganlu shui* 甘露水 'water of sweet dew' 171; *ganlu dahai* 甘露大海 'great sea of sweet dew' 324; *ganshu* 甘樹 'sweet trees' 'trees of immortality' 184

jingtu 淨土 'pure land' (< Skt. *sukhāvatī; buddhakṣetra*) 199; *qingjing zhuchu* 清淨住處 'place of purity' 292; *qingjing baodi* 清淨寶地 'precious earth of purity' 154 (*SLN* § 26 (Pth.): *'spnd'rmyd pw'g* 'pure land, soil'; also *SLN* § 83 (Pth.): *z[my]g pw'gyft* 'land of purity')

mingwang 明王 'light king' (< Skt. *rāja*) 204 (*SLN* § 40a (Pth): *qnyg* 'virgin'), 310

huitu 穢土 'impure land' 205 (*SLN* § 25 (Pth.): [*z*]*myg* ('z)*wštg* 'perverse earth'; also *SLN* § 91a (Pth.): (*z*)*myg p(dn)gynyft* 'land of impurity')

baohua 寶花 'precious flower' 228

fo 佛 'buddha' 228 (*SLN* §§ 13 & 15 (Pth.): *yzd* 'god')

yexing 業行 'karmic action, conduct' 242; *ye* 業 'act, work, deed' (< Skt. karma) 107, 163, 260

jingang 金剛 'diamond' (< Skt. *vajra*); *jingang baozhu* 金剛寶柱 'precious column of diamond' 325

rulai 如來 'the thus-come' (< Skt. *tathāgata*) 328

References

Alfaric, P. (1919): *Les écritures manichéennes*, II: Étude analytique. Paris: E. Nourry.

Arnold-Döben, V. (1978): *Die Bildersprache des Manichäismus*, Arbeitsmaterialen zur Religionsgeschichte, Religionswissenschaftliches Seminar der Universität Bonn. Köln: E. J. Brill (comm.).

Arnold-Döben, V. (1980): 'Die Symbolik des Baumes im Manichäismus', *Symbolon, Jahrbuch für Symbolforschung*, N.F., V, pp. 9-29.

Aurousseau, L. (1912): 'Ed. Chavannes et P. Pelliot, – Un traité manichéen retrouvé en Chine, – Journal Asiatique, 1911, II, p. 499-617 (compte rendu)', *Bulletin de l'École Française d'Extrême-Orient* XII, 9, pp. 53-63.

Asmussen, J. P. (1965): *X^uāstvānīft; Studies in Manichaeism*. Copenhagen: Munksgaard.

Bang, W. & A. von Gabain (1930): 'Türkische Turfan-Texte, III', *Sitzungsberichte der Preussischen Akademie der Wissenschaften in Berlin, phil.-hist. Kl.*, pp. 183-211. (*TTT iii*)

Boyce, M. (1954): *The Manichaean Hymn-Cycles in Parthian*; London Oriental Series III. London: Oxford University Press.

Boyce, M. (1956): 'Some remarks on the present state of the Iranian Manichaean MSS. from Turfan, together with additions and corrections to 'Manichaean Hymn-Cycles in Parthian'', *Mitteilungen des Instituts für Orientforschung* IV, 1956, pp. 314-22.

Boyce, M. (1960): *A Catalogue of the Iranian Manuscripts in Manichean Script in the German Turfan Collection*. Berlin: Akademie Verlag.

Bryder, P. (1985): *The Chinese Transformation of Manichaeism; A Study of Chinese Manichaean Terminology*. Löberöd: Plus Ultra.

Chavannes, E. & P. Pelliot (1911): 'Un traité manichéen retrouvé en Chine', *Journal Asiatique*, pp. 499-617. (*Traité I*)

Chavannes, E. & P. Pelliot (1913): 'Un traité manichéen retrouvé en Chine; deuxième partie', *Journal Asiatique*, pp. 99-199, 261-394. (*Traité II*)

Chen Yuan 陳垣 (1923): 'Monijiao canjing yi' — 'Monijiao canjing er' 摩尼教殘經一二 ('Manichaean Fragmentary Scripture, 1-2'), *Guoxue jikan* 國學季刊 I, 2, pp. 531-46.

Chen Yuan (1980): 'Monijiao canjing yi' — 'Monijiao canjing er', in *Chen Yuan xueshu lunwen ji* 陳垣學術論文集, Vol. I, Beijing: Zhonghua shuju, pp. 375-97.

Giles, H. A. (1915): *Confucianism and its Rivals*. London: Williams & Norgate.

Giles, L. (1957): *Descriptive Catalogue of the Chinese Manuscripts from Tun-huang in the British Museum*. London: The Trustees of the British Museum.

Haloun, G. & W.B. Henning (1952): 'The Compendium of the Doctrines and Styles of the Teaching of Mani, the Buddha of Light', *Asia Major*, N.S., III, pp. 184-212.

Hamilton, J. (1986): *Manuscrits ouïgours du ixe - xe siècle de Touen-houang*, tome I. Paris: Peeters.

Henning, W.B. (1936): *Ein manichäisches Bet- und Beichtbuch*, Abhandlungen der königlichen preussischen Akademie der Wissenschaften, phil.-hist. Kl., Nr.10. Berlin: Verlag der Akademie der Wissenschaften.

Henning, W.B. (1940): *Sogdica*, James G. Forlong Fund, Vol. XXI. London.

Huang Yongwu 黃永武 (ed.) (1984): *Dunhuang baozang* 敦煌寶藏 *(The Treasure- Store of Dunhuang)*. Vol. CX. Taibei: Xinwen feng chu chuban gongsi, pp. 418-26.

Jiang Fu 蔣斧 (1909): 'Moni jing canjuan' 摩尼經殘卷 ('Fragment of a Manichaean

Book') in Luo Zhenyu (ed.) 羅振玉 *Dunhuang shishi yishu* 敦煌石室遺書, Shanghai, pp. 2287-2304.

Klimkeit, H.-J. & H. Schmidt-Glintzer (1984): 'Die türkischen Parallelen zum chinesisch-manichäischen Traktat', *Zentralasiatische Studien* XVII, pp. 82-117. (*TPT*)

Klimkeit, H.-J. (1987): 'Buddhistische Übernahmen im iranischen und türkischen Manichäismus', in Heissig W. & H. J. Klimkeit (eds.) *Synkretismus in den Religionen Zentralasiens*, Ergebnisse eines Kolloquiums vom 25. bis 26. Mai 1983 in St. Augustin bei Bonn, Studies in Oriental Religions XIII. Wiesbaden: Otto Harrassowitz, pp. 58-75.

Le Coq, A. von (1913): *Chotscho. Facsimile-Wiedergaben der wichtigeren Funde der ersten königlich preussischen Expedition nach Turfan in Ost-Turkestan.* Berlin. (repr. Graz: Akademische Druck- u. Verlagsanstalt, 1979)

Le Coq, A. von (1922): *Türkische Manichaica aus Chotscho,* III, Abhandlungen der Preussischen Akademie der Wissenschaften, phil.-hist. Klasse, Nr. 2. Berlin: Verlag der Akademie der Wissenschaften. (*TMC iii*)

Lieu, S.N.C. (1992): *Manichaeism in the Later Roman Empire and Medieval China;* Wissenchaftliche Untersuchungen zum Neuen Testament LXIII. Tübingen: J. C. B. Mohr.

Lieu, S.N.C. & G.B. Mikkelsen (1993): *Traktat Pelliot* (preliminary translation; forthcoming).

Lin Wushu 林悟殊 (1987): *Monijiao ji qi dong jian* 摩尼教及其東漸 (*Manichaeism and its Eastward Spread*) Beijing: Zhonghua shuju chuban.

Lin Wushu (1988): 'On the joining between the two fragments of the 'Compendium of the Teaching of Mani, the Buddha of Light" in Bryder P. (ed.) *Manichaean Studies;* Proceedings of the First International Conference on Manichaeism; Lund Studies in African and Asian Religions I, Lund: Plus Ultra, pp. 89-93.

Mikkelsen, G.B. (1992): 'Towards a new orthographical reading of the *Bosijiao canjing'*, paper read at the *Third International Symposium of Manichaean Studies*, London, 13-15 July 1992. (forthcoming)

Morano, E. (1982): 'The Sogdian Hymns of *Stellung Jesu'*, *East and West* XXXII, pp. 9-43.

Müller, F.W.K. (1904): *Handschriften-Reste in Estangelo-Schrift aus Turfan, Chinesisch-Turkestan, II. Teil*, Abhandlungen der Preussischen Akademie der Wissenschaften, phil.-hist. Kl., Anhang Nr. 2. Berlin: Verlag der Akademie der Wissenschaften. (*HR ii*)

Pelliot, P. (1903): 'Les Mo-ni et le Houa-hou-king', *Bulletin de l'École Française d'Extrême-Orient* III, pp. 318-27.

Pelliot, P. (1908): 'Une bibliothèque médiévale retrouvée au Kan-sou', *Bulletin de l'École Française d'Extrême-Orient* VIII, pp. 501-29.

Pelliot, P. (1925): 'Two new Manichaean Manuscripts from Tun-huang', *Journal of the Royal Asiatic Society*, p. 113.

Puech, H.-C. (1949): 'Un catéchisme manichéen chinois inédit' in *Actes du XXIe Congrès International des Orientalistes*, Paris, 23-31 Juillet 1948, Paris, pp. 350-54.

Schmidt, C.G., H.J. Polotsky & A. Böhlig (1940): *Kephalaia*; I. Hälfte (Lieferung 1-10), Manichäische Handschriften der staatlichen Museen Berlin, Band I, Stuttgart: C. Kohlhammer. (**Keph.**)

Schmidt-Glintzer, H. (1987a): 'Das buddhistische Gewand des Manichäismus: Zur buddhistischen Terminologie in den chinesischen Manichaica' in Heissig W. & H. -J. Klimkeit (eds.): *Synkretismus in den Religionen Zentralasiens*; Ergebnisse eines Kolloquiums vom 25. bis 26. Mai 1983 in St. Augustin bei Bonn, Studies in Oriental Religions XIII. Wiesbaden: Otto Harrassowitz, pp. 76-90.

Schmidt-Glintzer, H. (1987b): *Chinesische Manichaica; Mit textkritischen Anmerkungen und einem Glossar*. Wiesbaden: Otto Harrassowitz.

Sims-Williams, N. (1983): 'Indian Elements in Parthian and Sogdian', in Röhrborn K. & W. Veenker (eds.) *Sprachen des Buddhismus in Zentralasien*; Vorträge des Hamburger Symposions vom 2. Juli bis 5. Juli 1981. Wiesbaden: Otto Harrassowitz, pp. 132-41.

Sundermann, W. (1982): 'Die Bedeutung des Parthischen für die Verbreitung buddhistischer Wörter buddhistischer Wörter indischer Herkunft', *Altorientalische Forschungen* IX, pp. 99-113.

Sundermann, W. (1983): 'Der chinesische Traité Manicheén und der parthische Sermon vom Lichtnous', *Altorientalische Forschungen* X, 2, pp. 231-42.

Sundermann, W. (1984): 'Ein weiteres Fragment aus Manis Gigantenbuch' in *Orientalia J.Duchesne-Guillemin emerito oblata*, Acta Iranica XXIII, Hommages et opera minora IX, Téhéran-Liège: Bibliothèque pahlavi. Leiden: E.J. Brill, pp. 491-505.

Sundermann, W. (1990): *The Manichaean Hymncycles Huyadagmān and Angād Rōšnān in Parthian and Sogdian*. Corpus Inscriptionum Iranicarum; suppl. series vol. II; Photo edition, transcription and translation of hitherto unpublished texts, with critical remarks. London: School of Oriental and African Studies.

Sundermann, W. (1991): 'Anmerkungen zu: Th. Thilo, Einige Bemerkungen zu zwei chinesisch-manichäischen Textfragmenten der Berliner Turfan-Sammlung' in Klengel H. & W. Sundermann (eds.) *Ägypten, Vorderasien, Turfan; Probleme der Edition und Bearbeitung altorientalischer Handschriften*, Schriften zur Geschichte und Kultur des Alten Orients XXIII, Berlin: Akademie Verlag, pp. 171-74.

Sundermann, W. (1992): *Der Sermon vom Licht-Nous: eine Lehrschrift des östlichen Manichäismus; Edition der parthischen und soghdischen Version*, Berliner Turfantexte XVII. Berlin: Akademie Verlag. (**SLN**)

Taishoo shinshuu daizookyoo 大正新修大藏經 (1924-32), 85 vols. Takakusu J. & K. Watanabe (eds.). Tokyo: Taishoo Issaikyoo Kankookai (**TD**)

Tajadod, N. (1990): *Mani le Bouddha de Lumière; Catéchisme manichéen chinois*; Sources Gnostiques et Manichéennes 3. Paris: Cerf.

Thilo, T. (1991): 'Einige Bemerkungen zu zwei chinesisch-manichäischen Textfragmenten der Berliner Turfan-Sammlung' in Klengel H. & W. Sundermann (eds.) *Ägypten, Vorderasien, Turfan; Probleme der Edition und Bearbeitung alt-*

orientalischer Handschriften, Schriften zur Geschichte und Kultur des Alten Orients XXIII, Berlin: Akademie Verlag, pp. 161-70.

Tongerloo, A. van (1984): 'Buddhist Indian Terminology in the Manichaean Uygur and Middle Iranian Texts' in Skalmowski W. and A. van Tongerloo (eds.) *Middle Iranian Studies*; Proceedings of the International Symposium organized by the Katholieke Universiteit Leuven from the 17th to the 20th of May 1982, Leuven: Peeters, pp. 243-52.

Tsui Chi (1943): »Mo Ni Chiao Hsia Pu Tsan; 'The Lower (Second?) Section of the Manichaean Hymns'«, *Bulletin of the School of Oriental and African Studies* XI, 1, pp. 174-219.

Waldschmidt, E. & W. Lentz (1926a): 'A Chinese Manichæan Hymnal from Tun-Huang; Preliminary note', *Journal of the Royal Asiatic Society*, pp. 116-22; *ibid.* 'Additions and Corrections', pp. 298-99.

Waldschmidt, E. & W. Lentz (1926b): *Die Stellung Jesu im Manichäismus*, Abhandlungen der preussischen Akademie der Wissenschaften, phil.-hist.Kl., Nr. 4. Berlin: Verlag der Akademie der Wissenschaften. (*W.-L. i*)

Waldschmidt, E. & W. Lentz (1933): 'Manichäische Dogmatik aus chinesischen und iranischen Texten', *Sitzungsberichte der Preussischen Akademie der Wissenschaften in Berlin*, pp. 480-607. (*W.-L. ii*)

Yoshida Yutaka (1983): 'Manichaean Aramaic in the Chinese Hymnscroll', *Bulletin of the School of African and Oriental Studies* XLVI, 2, pp. 326-31.

Notes

1. The terms have by some scholars been assumed to be of Aramaic origin; see e.g. Puech, 1948: 351.
2. In the same volume: *Monijiao xiabu zan* (no. 2140; pp. 1270b21-79c10) and *Moni guangfo jiaofa yilüe* (no. 2141 A; pp. 1279c16-81a11).
3. It should be noted, though, that Chavannes and Pelliot did manage to correct most of the miscopies in Luo's text, partly thanks to L. Aurousseau, whose review of their translation (Aurousseau, 1912) was based on a careful examination of the original manuscript in Beijing; cf. e.g. *Notes additionelles* in *Traité* II 378-82).
4. The manuscript reads *huiming* 惠明 'beneficent light', but simple textual and palaeographical observations suggest that the character *hui* 惠 is a variant of or rather a recognised substitute to the character *hui* 慧 (cf. *Hanyu da cidian* 漢語大辭典 IV, 2309f (12)). The character *hui* 慧 is only once employed in the *Traité*, in the compound *shanhui* 善慧, 'excellent wisdom' (col. 311); on all other incidences the character *hui* 惠 replaces *hui* 慧, even in *zhihui* 智惠 'knowledge'. There is therefore reason to believe that *huiming* 惠明 should be read huiming 慧明 'light of wisdom', 'gnostic light' or 'Light-Nous'. The Parthian terms *mnwhmyd rwšn*, 'light of knowledge, Light-Nous', and *mnwhmyd rwšn dyn frh*, 'glory of the religion of the Light-Nous' correspond to the terms *huiming* 惠明 (col. 76 *et passim*), and *huiming faxiang* 惠明法相, 'thought of law of the Light-Nous' (col. 115).

5. For further investigations of the Manichaean adoption of Buddhist terms in principle and practice, see Schmidt-Glintzer, 1987a: 76-90, and my M.A. thesis *Manikæismens introduktion i Kina; et studium af den manikæiske missionsmetode i aktion-reaktionsperspektiv (The Introduction of Manichaeism into China; a Study of the Manichaean Missionary Method in Action-Reaction Perspective)* submitted in 1993 to the Department of East Asian Studies here celebrated.

6. Buddhist terminology was from the beginning employed by Mār Ammō, cf. Klimkeit, 1987: 59-62.

7. The more advanced buddhicisation of the Chinese hymns may suggest a later date of translation than the *Traité*. Palaeographical observations lend further support to this assumption.

8. In the *Hymnscroll* (col. 337), in the Chinese Turfan-fragment Ch 258 (cf. Thilo, 1991: 166-67) as well as in the *Traité*, the character used is *zai* 灾, which in Dunhuang manuscripts is a common variant of *zai* 災. As suggested by Chavannes and Pelliot (*Traité I* 518-19) the original character may well have been *xue* 穴 — meaning 'underground cave' or 'ditch' and thus corresponding well to the Parthian term — which then at an early stage has been confused with the character *zai* 災 of the Buddhist cosmological-eschatological concept *san zai* 三 災, 'three calamities (of fire, water and wind)'. For a comparison of the Chinese and Parthian terms, cf. Sundermann, 1991: 173, and *SLN* 80.

9. For the special Manichaean meaning of the term, see Bryder, 1985: 128-34.

A Cultured Encounter:
Dr Thunberg meets Mr Matsuhiro[1]

Bjarke Frellesvig

This paper concerns a Japanese dialogue of 40 lines which may be found in C.P. Thunberg's 'Observationes in Linguam Japonicam' from 1792. Following a general introduction (section 1), section 2 quotes and translates line by line the relevant part of 'Observationes' into English. Section 3 discusses the establishment of the extract as a coherent text, and suggests that this text may be seen as part of the discourse within which the European image of Japan was formed in the late 18th century.

Introduction

In the course of his extensive travels, the Swedish botanist Carl Peter Thunberg stayed in Japan for well over a year during 1775-6.[2] His experiences in Japan are related in volumes 3 and 4 of his *Resa uti Europa, Africa, Asia, förrättad åren 1770-1779* (henceforth: 'Resa'), published 1788-93 in Uppsala.[3] Another well known result of Thunberg's stay in Japan is his *Flora Japonica* (1784, Leipzig). In fact, it was with the purpose of doing botanical research in Japan that Thunberg, who was a student of Linné's, embarked on his long voyage which took him through various parts of the world.

This was, of course, during the period of *sakoku* ('closed country', 1639-1853) in Japan when the only Westerners allowed were the Dutch, who were confined to Deshima (*Dejima* in Japanese) off Nagasaki. It was therefore necessary for Thunberg to learn Dutch (which he did in South Africa during 1772-5 before going to Japan; see Forbes 1986) and to enter into Dutch service. Although Thunberg was stationed on Deshima, he was allowed some access to Nagasaki and surrounding areas where he collected botanical specimens. He also made friends among the Japanese, both interpreters (who knew Dutch) and various scholars.[4] In the first half of 1776 he accompanied the Dutch envoy to Edo (Tokyo); they spent approximately 4 months on the trip,

PREMODERN ENCOUNTERS

visiting both Kyoto and Osaka on the way back.[5] All in all, Thunberg enjoyed a freedom of movement and intercourse with the native population which was quite extraordinary during *sakoku*.[6] He thus had the opportunity to observe and describe in some detail the country, its people, customs, etc. Thunberg was an intelligent and acute observer and *Resa* makes fascinating, informative reading.[7]

Thunberg made an effort to become acquainted with the Japanese language and became quite proficient,[8] mainly with the aid of local informants; he also had a Latin-Portuguese-Japanese dictionary at his disposal (*Resa*:41f, 295).[9] *Resa*:294-354 deals with '*Japanska Språkat*', the Japanese language, and consists mainly of a Swedish-Japanese dictionary. To supplement this, Thunberg in 1792 published a short (16 pp.) article in Latin, 'Observationes in Linguam Japonicam' (henceforth 'Observationes'), in which he reports on the grammar of the Japanese language.[10]

'Observationes' is quite valuable for the historical and dialectal study of Japanese (as noted by Sugimoto (1989:113), more so for the data it presents than for the description it gives), but unfortunately a thorough study of the Japanese in 'Observationes' is still pending.[11] The language represented in 'Observationes' clearly exhibits dialectal traits (e.g. the -*ka* ending of adjectives stereotypical of Kyushu Japanese); however, it also gives the impression of being dialectally (/sociolectally) and to some extent historically heterogeneous and it would be wrong simply to identify it with contemporary Nagasaki Japanese. In the main, it should probably be thought of as an educated Common Japanese coloured by the local dialect; see further Sugimoto 1955:109 about this.

The final section of 'Observationes' (pp. 269-73) gives 'some examples which show usage, first of all of the verbs, and their conjugations',[12] in the form of Latin utterances which are given Japanese equivalents. As may be expected, the examples largely consist of short utterances, such as (p. 269):

Do, *wataks jaru* ('I give')
dedi, *wataks jatta* ('I have given')
heri dabo, *wataks mionitji jarrimassu* ('I shall give tomorrow')[13]

On closer inspection, however, it turns out that the final 40 example utterances — i.e. the last 4 lines of p. 271 and pp. 272-3 — may be read as a coherent *text*, although it is not indicated in 'Observationes' that they form a text. This text has hitherto not been reported upon in the scholarly literature.

In the remainder of this paper, I quote line by line the example utterances in question and propose a translation of them into English, accompanied by a few notes (section 2); in section 3, I discuss the establishment of these forty lines as a coherent text.

Quotation and translation

(1)-(40) in the following present *a*) the Latin text, *b*) the Japanese text, *c*) my translation into English and *d*) the modern Japanese form (se below) for each of the final 40 example utterances in 'Observationes'. The translation follows the Japanese where its meaning differs from the Latin; in a few cases (viz. (2), (18), and (23)), however, the meaning of a Japanese word is not clear and it has been necessary to rely solely on the Latin. Students of older Japanese or of Japanese dialectology will recognize features in the Japanese part of the example utterances which are characteristic of older Japanese and/or of Kyushu Japanese. As, however, my foremost concern here is with the text made up by (1)-(40) as such, and not with the Japanese language depicted in 'Observationes', I shall not go into this in any detail.[14]

For this reason, notes are kept to a minimum; instead, I give [enclosed in square brackets] for each example utterance the words of which the Japanese text may be thought to consist *in their modern Japanese form*.[15] As the Japanese part of 'Observationes' is larded with misprints, mistakes in morpheme segmentation, and inconsistencies in transcription, this identification of words/morphemes should make it easier to follow and check the translation into English.

In addition to misprints and mistakes on Thunberg's part, there are two possible sources of differences between the Japanese in 'Observationes' and modern Japanese: difference in dialect and difference in historical stage. Two such differences are conspicuous and may distract if not mentioned here: (a) the very frequently used /-r/ stem verbs *kudasaru*, *nasaru*, *gozaru*, and *degozaru*, which are slightly irregular in modern Japanese, retain the stem final /r/ in the forms that drop it in modern Japanese, cf. (1-6, 8, 10, 12-19, 23-25, 27, 29, 31, 33, 35-37, 39). (b) The nonpast of the suffix *-masu* 'polite' appears in two shapes (each in various transcriptional guises): *-masu* in (3-6, 14, 15, 16, 18, 19, 21-23, 38) and *-masuru* in (10, 11, 17, 24, 35, 36, 39); these two shapes reflect the difference (which has merged in modern Japanese) between the *shuushikee* and *rentaikee* forms of verbs, but the distribution of the two forms is here totally haphazard (*pace* Steenstrup 1978:25).

(1)   *a*) Ostende mihi domum Domini Matufiro, si placet,
             b) *Matufiro samma no ie o osite kadassari.*

             c) 'please tell/show me Mr Matsuhiro's house'
             d) [*Matsuhiro-sama no ie o oshiete kudasai*]

(2)   Vides ne illam scalam?
             Ano gimba jo minoserri?

             'please see that ladder'
             [*ano gimba yoku mi-nasai*].

The meaning of *gimba* is not clear: in *Resa*, Thunberg gives *Fakko fassigo* and *fassigo* as translations of Swedish *Trappa* 'staircase' (p. 346) and *Fassigo* as the translation of *Stega, en stega* 'ladder' (p. 341); it would therefore seem that *gimba* is meant to translate some other meaning of Latin *scala*, but I have no good suggestions and therefore use 'ladder'. The '?' in the Japanese is probably a misprint or mistake; as reflected in the translation, the Japanese verb is in the imperative.

(3)   utique,
             ai, jo guserrimassu.

             'yes, I do'
             [*hai, yoku gozaimasu*].

While the Japanese in both (2) and (3) are reasonable translations of the Latin, there is no discoursive coherence between the Japanese of (2) and (3), suggesting a line by line translation from Latin into Japanese.

(4)   domus proxima est,
             aska no torrari de guserrimassu.

             'it is next to there'
             [*asoko no tonari degozaimasu*]. *torrari*: misprint for *tonari*.

(5)   gratias ago,
             kadeski no guserrimassu.

'thank you'
[*katajike no gozaimasu*]

(6)   est ne Dominus Matufiro domi?
         Matufiro samma ie de gusarrimassuka?

         'is Mr Matsuhiro at home?'
         [*Matsuhiro-sama ie degozaimasu ka*].

ie 'house, home' is here used as a locative adverb ('at home') and *degozaru* 'copula' as an existential verb, suggesting a literal (and wrong) translation from Latin (or Swedish) into Japanese (cf. *domi esse, vara hemma* 'to be home').

(7)   Nuper exiit,
         tata jma dererrimasta.

         'he just went out; he is out right now'
         [*tadaima deraremashita*].

Thunberg occasionally uses the honorific (passive) to mark 3.prs., also where it would not be used in Japanese, as here.

(8)   ubinam ivit?
         doki osi de naserrimastaka?

         'where did he go?'
         [*doko ni oide nasaimashita ka*].

I take *doki* to be a fused form of *doko* 'where?' + *ni* (or *e*) 'allative'. *osi de*: misprint for *oide*.

(9)   in vicinia,
         kensjo ni.

         'in the neighbourhood'
         [*kinjo ni*]

(10)   numne cito rediet?
         fajo okajiri na jerrimassurka? Nasarri massuriru?

'will he return soon?'
[*hayaku o-kaeri-nasaimasu ka*].

For some reason, Thunberg provides alternative versions (also spelt differently) of the final part of the Japanese sentence.

(11)   hoc quidem credo,
         wataks no so omemassuru.

         'I think so'
         [*watakushi no soo omoimasu*]

(12)   placet ne tibi sedere?
         osuwari na serrimassinka?

         'won't you sit down?'
         [*o-suwari-nasaimasen ka*]

(13)   intra cameram interiorem,
         nando ni oidena serrimasse.

         'please come into the living room'
         [*nando ni oide nasaimase*]

(14)   Estne Dominus Matufiro?
         Matufiro samma de guserrimaska?

         'is it Mr Matsuhiro?; are you Mr Matsuhiro?'
         [*Matsuhiro-sama degozaimasu ka*]

(15)   Est ille,
         anata de guserrimassu.

         'it is he; yes, I am'
         [*anata degozaimasu*].

Thunberg here uses *anata* to translate Latin ille; that is to say, in its earlier meaning of distal (and 3rd prs.) pronoun (here equivalent to *ano hito* 'that (distal demonstrative) person'); in (18, 20, 37) he uses *anata* in its later (and presentday) meaning 'you', i.e. 2.prs. pronoun. As noted by Sugimoto

(1955:104) (based, however, on an examination of that part of *Voyages* dealing with the Japanese language, cf. note 11 above, not primarily on 'Observationes'), Thunberg's publications on Japanese are an important source for dating the shift in meaning of *anata* to 2.prs. pronoun. It is interesting to find that Thunberg was not consistent in this regard; this suggests that Thunberg translated the text from Latin into Japanese based on notes he had gathered in Japan from different sources, probably after his return to Sweden.

(16)   quomodo vales?
         gokigin jo guserrimaska?

         'you are well?'
         [*gokigen yoku gozaimasu ka*]

(17)   optime,
         jo guserrimassur.

         'I am fine'
         [*yoku gozaimasu*]

(18)   aliguid abs te rogandum habeo,
         ana ta ni kota sugika guserrimassu.

         'I have something to ask you'
         [*anata ni kota sugika gozaimasu*].

The meaning of *kota sugika* is unclear.

(19)   cujus nomine?
         dari kara de guserrimaska?

         'from whom is it?'
         [*dare kara degozaimasu ka*]

(20)   nomine cujusdam tuorum amicorum in Osaka,
         anatano Osaka no fabaikara.

         'from a friend of yours in Osaka'
         [*anata no Oosaka no hoobai kara*]

(21)   quodnam ejus nomen?
            nawa do musmaska?

            'what's his name?'
            [*na wa doo mooshimasu ka*]

(22)   nominatur Gorobe,
            Gorobe to Mosimassu.

            'his name is Gorobei'
            [*Gorobee to mooshimasu*]

(23)   valet ne bene?
            mada sagassu guserrimaska?

            'is he all right?'
            [*mada sagashiku gozaimasu ka*].

sagashii usually means 'steep' or 'dangerous'; its meaning here is unclear.

(24)   litteræ hæ tibi dicent hoc,
            kono tsio ni kaite guserrimassuru.

            'it is written in this letter'
            [*kono sho ni kaite gozaimasu*]

(25)   quando huc accessisti?
            kokini itsu ootski naserrimastaka?

            'when did you arrive here?'
            [*koko ni itsu o-tsuki-nasaimashita ka*]

(26)   heri vesperi,
            jasin.

            'in the middle of the night; late last night'
            [*yashin*]

(27)   quando Osakam reliquisti?
            Osakka its otastsi naserrimastaka?

'when did you leave Osaka?'
[*Oosaka itsu o-tachi-nasaimashita ka*]

(28)   primo hujus mensis,
         kono tsi tassini.

         'on the 1st of this month'
         [*kono tsuitachi ni*]

(29)   festinanter accessisti,
         fajo gotjakf naserrimasta.

         'you arrived fast'
         [*hayaku go-chaku-nasaimashita*]

(30)   intra septem dies,
         nanka no utsini.

         'in seven days'
         [*nanoka no uchi ni*]

(31)   nullum no infortunium habuisti?
         na nimo fusiu na koto wagurrimassinka?

         'there is nothing bad/ill-omened, I hope?'
         [*nani-mo fusyoo na koto wa gozaimasen ka*].

wagurrimassinka: misprint for *wa guserrimassinka*

(32)   non,
         inne.

         'no'
         [*ina*].

As the question in (31) may be given the modal interpretation reflected in the translation, the use of *inne* 'no' corresponds to modern usage concerning answers to negatively phrased questions.

(33)   quid heic agendum tibi est?
         koki nanni sini oide naserrimasta?

'what have you come here to do?'
[*koko ni nani shi-ni-oide nasaimashita*]; *koki*: cf. (8).

(34)   Provinciam visurus venio,
         kuni wo mini kimasta.

         'I've come to see the province'
         [*kuni o mi-ni-kimashita*]

(35)   quid dicis de Nagasaki?
         Nagasaki wa do guserrimassurka?

         'how is Nagasaki?; how do you find Nagasaki?'
         [*Nagasaki wa doo degozaimasu ka*].

do guserrimassurka: *de* of the copula probably left out due to a misprint.

(36)   amoenus est locus,
         kekkono tokoro deguserrimassur.

         'it is a beautiful place'
         [*kekkoo no tokoro degozaimasu*]

(37)   manebis ne heic per aliquod tempus?
         anata wa kokoni fisassu torio na serrimassinka?

         'won't you stay here long?'
         [*anata wa koko ni hisashiku tooryuu (o) nasaimasen ka*].

Whether *torio* is to be interpreted as a rendition of *tooryuu* 'stay' or as representing the dialect form *toori* 'do.' + *o* 'accusative' is an open question.

(38)   usque in sequentem mensem heic commorabor,
         Lai gits made torio itassimasju.

         'I'll stay until next month'
         [*raigetsu made tooryuu (o) itashimasu*]; cf. (37).

(39)   ubinam deinde abibis?
         soste kara doki oide naserrimassurka?

'where will you go then?'
[*soshite kara doko ni oide nasaimasu ka*]; *doki*: cf. (8).

(40)   Ad Fisen & inde ad Siguisen,
         Fiseni, saste Siquiseni.

         'to Hizen and then to Chikuzen'
         [*Hizen ni, soshite Chikuzen ni*]

Establishing the text

(1)-(40) make up the final part of 'Observationes' and thus its conclusion. However, (1)-(40) are not typographically or otherwise set off from the preceding 68 example utterances; it is, in other words, not indicated that they are intended to form a text.[16] It is the fact that they cohere meaningfully as a text which allows us to read (1)-(40) as a text.

It will be appreciated that (1)-(40) are spoken lines and that the text they constitute is in the form of a dialogue. We are given no narrative frame (i.e. who, where, etc.) other than that provided by deictic clues within the dialogue. They are, briefly: (a) one of the speakers is a Mr Matsuhiro (cf. (1), (6), and especially (14) and (15)); (b) part of the dialogue takes place in Mr Matsuhiro's living room (cf. (13) onwards) and part of it outside within viewing distance of Mr Matsuhiro's house (cf. (1)-(4)); (c) Mr Matsuhiro lives in Nagasaki (cf. (35)).

Based on this and on the content in general, I have (a) divided the text into three parts ((1-5), (6-13), (14-40)) and supplied settings for each part, and (b) identified the number of participants (four), assigned specific lines to each participant, given descriptive labels to the minor *personae*, and fixed the main character as Thunberg. The result of this (and of adjusting the translation a little) is (41).

A certain amount of evidence for the internal structure of the text, and thus for the arrangement in (41), may be found in the use of capitalization in the Latin part of the text: the first word spoken by a newly introduced participant is capitalized, cf. (1), (2), (7), (15); this is one factor in interpreting (13) as spoken by 'servant' rather than 'Matsuhiro'.[17]

Clearly, the text translated as (41) is not a transcribed record of an actual Japanese dialogue. Rather, the text was composed by Thunberg; as indicated in the notes in (3), (6), (7), and (15), it seems likely that Thunberg composed the text in (Swedish or) Latin and translated it into Japanese based on his notes and command of the language, probably after returning to Sweden.

(41) is thus a piece of *fiction*. While certainly drawing on Thunberg's own experiences, (41) is in no way autobiographical: for example, it took Thunberg more than two weeks to travel from Osaka to Nagasaki (*Resa*:257f) and not the seven days of our main character (cf. (30)). More significantly, Thunberg was — for all practical purposes — confined to Deshima and Nagasaki, he was no visitor who had 'come to see the province' (cf. (34)) or who would have entertained plans about travelling in Japan again after his return from Edo (which was the only occasion on which he travelled from Osaka to Nagasaki), although the course of travel (Nagasaki — Hizen — Chikuzen, cf. (40)) is the one he followed himself on his way to Edo (*Resa*:116ff). In fact, it was hardly the right of anyone in Japan at the time to indulge in the kind of free travel and sightseeing proposed by Thunberg in this text.

(41)
[*In the street in Nagasaki*]
Thunberg:	'Please tell me the way to Mr Matsuhiro's house.'
Passer-by:	'Do you see that ladder?'
Thunberg:	'Yes, I do.'
Passer-by:	'Mr Matsuhiro's house is right next to that.'
Thunberg:	'Thank you.'

[*At Mr Matsuhiro's house*]
Thunberg:	'Is Mr Matsuhiro in?'
Servant:	'He is out just now.'
Thunberg:	'Where did he go?'
Servant:	'Somewhere in the neighbourhood.'
Thunberg:	'Will he return soon?'
Servant:	'I think so. Won't you sit down?'

[*a little later*]
Servant:	'Please come into the living room.'

[*In the living room*]
Thunberg:	'Are you Mr Matsuhiro?'
Matsuhiro:	'Yes, I am.'
Thunberg:	'How are you?'
Matsuhiro:	'I am fine.'
Thunberg:	'I have something to ask you.'

Matsuhiro:	'From whom?'
Thunberg:	'From a friend of yours in Osaka.'
Matsuhiro:	'What's his name?'
Thunberg:	'His name is Gorobei.'
Matsuhiro:	'Is he all right?'
Thunberg:	'It's written in this letter.'
Matsuhiro:	'When did you arrive here?'
Thunberg:	'Late last night.'
Matsuhiro:	'When did you leave Osaka?'
Thunberg:	'On the 1st of this month.'
Matsuhiro:	'That was fast.'
Thunberg:	'Seven days.'
Matsuhiro:	'Nothing unpleasant happened on your way, I hope.'
Thunberg:	'No.'
Matsuhiro:	'What have you come here to do?'
Thunberg:	'I've come to see the region.'
Matsuhiro:	'What do you think of Nagasaki?'
Thunberg:	'It's a beautiful place.'
Matsuhiro:	'Won't you stay here long?'
Thunberg:	'I'll stay until next month.'
Matsuhiro:	'Where will you go then?'
Thunberg:	'To Hizen and then to Chikuzen.'

Now, the overt purpose of the Japanese text is to exemplify the Japanese language and its usage; as such, the dialogue also represents Thunberg's perception, or rather portrayal, of what constituted socially wellformed intercourse in a Japanese context.[18] (41) thus forms part of Thunberg's presentation of Japan and Japanese society to learned Europe, and is part of the Japan-related discourse of the time. Future research may fruitfully incorporate (41) in a further evaluation of Thunberg's presentation of Japan (as mentioned earlier, Steenstrup remarks that Thunberg idealized certain parts of Japanese society to fit 'his own political preconceptions' (1979:25f)), and in a general evaluation of the formation of the image of Japan in Europe during the late 18th and early 19th centuries.

I shall not go further into this here, though, as the main purpose of this paper has been to establish the dialogue as a text — in the form of (41) — and to draw the attention of the scholarly community to its existence. It may be remarked, however, that what is depicted in (41) is an encounter between *equals*. There is no hint of either condescension or awe. What we find represented here is *interpersonal* rather than (the allegedly difficult or even impossible) *intercultural* intercourse. Hence the title of this paper.

References

Engberg, Jonas (1990): *Observationes in Linguam Japonicam — Observations on the Japanese Language — by Carl Peter Thunberg*, Occasional Paper 9, Center for Pacific Asia Studies, University of Stockholm (Stockholm); [Introduction + facsimile reproduction of *Thunberg 1792* + translation into English of the Latin part thereof].

Forbes, V. S. (ed.) (1986): *Carl Peter Thunberg Travels at the Cape of Good Hope 1772-1775*, Second Series no. 17, Van Riebeck Society (Cape Town); [prefaces + modern English version of those parts of *Thunberg 1788-93* dealing with the Cape of Good Hope; based on the original English translation of Thunberg 1788-93].

Societas Jesu (ed.) (1595): *Dictionarium Latino Lusitanicum ac Japonicam* [Latin-Portuguese-Japanese Dictionary], (Amakusa).

Steenstrup, Carl (1978): 'A Japanese Grammar Published in Sweden in 1792', in *Newsletter of the Scandinavian Institute of Asian Studies* XI/XII:22-9.

Steenstrup, Carl (1979): 'A Gustavian Swede in Tanuma Okitsugu's Japan: marginal notes to Carl Peter Thunberg's travelogue', in *The Journal of Intercultural Studies* 6:20-43.

Sugimoto, Tutomu (1955): 'Tsunberugu no nihongo kansatsu' [Thunberg's observations on the Japanese language], in *Kokugogaku* 21:98-111.

Sugimoto, Tutomu (1989): *Seeyoojin no nihongo hakken. Gaikokujin no nihongokenkyuushi 1549-1868* [The discovery of the Japanese language by western people. A historical survey of learning and study of Japanese], Sootakusha (Tokyo).

Thunberg, Carl Peter (1784) *Flora Japonica*, (Leipzig).

Thunberg, Carl Peter (1788-93): *Resa uti Europa, Africa, Asia, förrättad åren 1770-1779* [Travels in Europe, Africa, Asia in the years 1770-9], Vols. 1-4, (Upsala).

Thunberg, Carl Peter (1792): 'Observationes in Linguam Japonicam' [Observations on the Japanese Language], in *Nova Acta Regiae Societatis Scientiarum Upsaliensis* 5:358-74.

Thunberg, Carl Peter (1796): *Voyages de C. P. Thunberg, au Japon, par le Cap de Bonne-Espérance, les Isles de la Sonde, etc*, (Paris); [translated and annotated by L. Langlés and J. B. Lamarck].

Thunberg, Carl Peter (1980): *Resa til och uti Kejsaredömet Japan åren 1775 och 1776* [Travels to and in the Japanese empire, 1775-6], Rediviva (Stockholm); [facsimile reproduction of volume 3 and those parts of volume 4 dealing with Japan of *Thunberg 1788-93*].

Yoshimachi, Yoshio (1933): 'Observationes in Linguam Japonicam a Car. Petr. Thunberg. Hyakurokujuunen-mae no nagasaki hoogen shiryoo' ['Observations on the Japanese language' by Car. Petr. Thunberg. Data on the Nagasaki dialect of 150 years ago], in *Hoogen* 3/9:18-36; [introduction + facsimile reproduction of *Thunberg 1792*].

Notes

1. In the preparation of this paper I benefitted from discussions with Olof Lidin; thanks are also due to the staff of the library of the Japan Foundation Japanese Language Institute, Saitama, and to Bent Lindblad of the Royal Danish Embassy in Tokyo.
2. Thunberg arrived in Nagasaki on 14 August 1775 and left on 23 November 1776. A brief biographical sketch of Thunberg can be found in the prefaces in Forbes 1986 (which may also be consulted for references concerning Thunberg's life; further, Steenstrup 1979 contains a wealth of references on Thunberg).
3. At the time, translations appeared in English, German, and French; see Forbes 1986: xxiii-xxiv and Steenstrup 1979:24 for details. Those parts of Thunberg's *Resa* which concern Japan (volume 3 and parts of volume 4) were issued in a facsimile reproduction in 1980. Page references to *Resa* are throughout to volume 3 which was published in 1791.
4. He even reports corresponding with some of his Japanese friends after his return to Sweden, exchanging both letters and presents (*Resa*:232).
5. They left Deshima on 4 March 1776, arrived on 27 April in Edo where they stayed until 25 May, and returned to Deshima on 30 June; *Resa*:116-258 relates the journey forth and back and the visit to Edo.
6. This was a period during *sakoku* when even official interest in science was high, whence restrictions on contact with foreigners were not too strictly enforced (Steenstrup 1979:29, Sugimoto 1989:113).
7. Note, however, Steenstrup's remarks that 'in matters of politics and what we would today term cultural anthropology, Thunberg was *not* an objective observer. He idealized the entire Japanese polity, because it fitted his own political preconceptions' (1979:25f).
8. In *Resa*:245, Thunberg proudly notes that, in the course of a conversation conducted through an interpreter, he surprised his Japanese visitor by writing the name of certain herb in Japanese letters.
9. It is clear from the description in *Resa*:41f that this was the *Dictionarium Latino Lusitanicum ac Japonicam*, published by the Jesuit Society in 1595 in Amakusa (Societas Jesu 1595).
10. 'Observationes' was published in the *Nova Acta Regiae Societatis Scientiarium Upsaliensis* 5:358-74; it is more readily available in a facsimile reproduction in *Hoogen* 3/9:18-36, prefaced by a short introduction by Yoshio Yoshimachi (Yoshimachi 1933). After finalizing this paper, my attention was brought to Engberg 1990 which contains a facsimile reproduction of 'Observationes' and a translation into English of the Latin part of the text, thus making 'Observationes' easily accessible to interested scholars.
11. Steenstrup 1978 is a brief and at best superficial discussion of a few aspects of the language in 'Observationes'. The 1976 French edition *Resa* (viz. *Voyages de C.P. Thunberg, au Japon, par le Cap de Bonne-Espérance, les Isles de la Sonde, etc* translated

and annotated by L. Langlés and J.B. Lamarck, henceforth 'Voyages'), in addition
to a French-Japanese version of the Swedish-Japanese dictionary given in *Resa*,
comprises a reworking of 'Observationes'. The part of *Voyages* dealing with the
Japanese language is examined in Sugimoto 1955. Sugimoto takes *Voyages* to
represent a *refinement* of 'Observationes', most likely done by Thunberg himself
(1955:99), whereas it strikes me rather as a *corruption* (whether done by Thunberg
or not); I shall not go further into that matter here, though, but see below (note 13)
for a single example.

12. 'Exempla quædam, quæ demonstrant usum, imprimis verborum, eorumque
    conjugationes' ('Observationes':269).

13. This line contains, what seems to be a curious lapse on Thunberg's part:
    apparently he mistook Latin *heri* 'yesterday' for *cras* 'tomorrow'; however, *dabo* is
    the future tense ('I shall give') and Japanese *mionitji* means 'tomorrow', so the
    meaning is clear enough. Interestingly this lapse further seems to have been given
    rise to a misunderstanding in *Voyages* where the French equivalent of *vataks
    mionitchi jarrimarou* is given as *je donnai hier* (*Voyages* 2:190), i.e. 'I gave yesterday'.

14. Also, that would entail a detailed examination of the language in 'Observationes'
    in its totality, a task quite beyond the spatial limitations of this paper.

15. It should be emphasized that this is no translation into modern Japanese; indeed,
    the resulting strings of words often read very poorly as modern Japanese
    sentences. In the transcription of modern Japanese, I follow the slightly modified
    version of the Hepburn system (with double vowels rather than diacritical markers
    to write long vowels) used throughout this volume; further I use hyphens
    occasionally to indicate morpheme boundaries where I have thought it helpful.

16. Apart from the use of capitalization (cf. below) which will be seen, however, to
    bear rather on the internal structure of the text than on the delimitation of it.

17. This leaves unexplained the use of capitals in (14), (34), and (40) (but note that (40)
    is the final line of 'Observationes' and that in (14) both horizontal ((14): ...
    Dominus Matsuhiro) and vertical ((15): Est) assimilation may be at play); however,
    viewing 'Observationes' in its totality capitalization is not employed all that
    systematically.

18. It is amusing (at least to me) that (41) reads much like a lesson from many a
    modern Japanese language textbook. It is an interesting question whether this says
    more about Thunberg or about the language textbooks.

Three Bowls and You Cannot Cross the Ridge: Orality and Literacy in Yangzhou Storytelling

Vibeke Børdahl

The art of Yangzhou storytelling has existed and flourished as an oral tradition for more than three hundred years in a society deeply imbued with writing and written literature. This has important implications for our understanding of the social and literary functions of the art. If storytelling was intended for the illiterate and poor, it was also always a highly esteemed art for the learned connoisseurs. It is very unlikely that the art was ever considered merely a substitute for those who could not read. What kind of encounters and exchange between the Chinese worlds of high and low literature, of oral and written communication, do we find in the storytellers' tales?

An oral art

Yangzhou storytelling (*Yangzhou pinghua* 扬州评话) has survived as an oral tradition of epic narration from Ming times to the present day. The storytellers' art of language was — and is — not only *orally* performed/communicated, but also orally transmitted from master to disciple, and largely orally composed and recomposed. However, the structure of the spoken texts bears witness to the extreme imbrication and contagion between the oral and the written word (Alleton 1980) that characterize Chinese popular literature.

In the narrative structure we find traces of the mutual exchange between the *written vernacular* genres of novel/short story and the oral storytelling. The style and language are interlaced with elements belonging to the non-vernacular vocabulary of *literary Chinese* (*wenyan* 文言), and whole passages are taken over from written sources or created in the style of written sources. During performance there is a constant shifting between different 'styles of mouth' (*shuokou* 说口) correlated to high and low style, implying *literary* versus *vernacular* colouring of style, grammar and phonology — down to the linguistic building blocks of the morphemes, where the Yangzhou dialect has remnants of the phenomenon of 'split pronunciations' (*wen bai yi du* 文白异

读）, i.e. different *literary* and *colloquial* pronunciation of the same morpheme. For our understanding of the interaction between orality and literacy in Chinese culture, the exploration of the storytelling arts is therefore a case in point.

Orality and literacy

In the West the 'Homeric question' has incited an avalanche of studies of what 'orality' and 'literacy' meant for ancient Greece and for the early 20th century Yugoslav poets known from the Parry-Lord collections (Lord, 1960, Thomas, 1992). These pathbreaking studies are important also for our understanding of Chinese literature, especially when we want to explore the so-called 'oral' traditions (Foley 1985:70, Goody 1987:262 ff, Finnegan 1992:5 ff). In Chinese storytelling, including *Yangzhou pinghua*, we find parallel features, but also conspicuous differences when comparing the basic setting with that of the Homeric era:

1) *Yangzhou pinghua* is a living tradition. In competition with radio, television and a new life style, it may be on the brink of extinction, but we can still listen to performances by masters, educated according to the age-old customs. There is also still an audience, albeit dwindling, of regular customers in the storyteller's houses. We have the possibility to know or inquire about many things that one can only guess or theorize about in the Greek tradition.

2) Historical sources on this specific storytelling tradition go back only 3-400 years. It belongs to a very much older culture of rich literary and oral traditions, and there has been a constant diffusion (both ways) of ideas, styles and formulas between the written and oral genres. This is different from the case of the Homeric poems which were supposedly created in a society without writing (or with very little use of writing) and written down later as some of the earliest documents of Greek literature.

3) *Yangzhou pinghua* is a prose tradition, not a tradition bound to metre and rhyme. The improvisatory aspects seem more pronounced, and the role of formula less obvious than in the practice of the Yugoslav bards, as reported by Parry and Lord.

It has long been debated whether the storyteller's art is 'genuinely oral' or only 'pseudo-oral', i.e. artistic performance of written texts learned by heart.[1] These categories fit the situation of Chinese oral narrative badly, the first being too 'pure' and 'pristine' for most oral traditions in China, the second too far away from the orality aspect of these traditions. Rather we have to acknowledge the specific conditions of every oral tradition: 'Orality must be culturally specific, its manifestations largely if not entirely formed — like literacy — by the specific nature of the society in question' (Thomas 1992:107).

Entering the study of oral versus literary features of a certain genre of art and its verbal manifestations, we may soon find ourselves entangled in a series of related, but far from synonymous, concepts, e.g. *written, literary, high style* versus *oral, vernacular, low style*. The naive coupling of these three pairs of interrelated concepts can be highly misleading for the understanding of the complex linguistic and cultural structures beneath them. We shall try to ferret out the specific application of these terms vis-à-vis the tradition and language of our target: Chinese storytelling from the town of Yangzhou.

Masters and schools

The renowned storyteller Liu Jingting 柳敬亭 (1587-c. 1670), who came from a town in the vicinity of Yangzhou, made the art famous outside of the local milieu, and since his time we have historical sources on the activities of storytellers from Yangzhou (Sun Longfu 1962, Hu Shiying 1980:373-381, 614 ff, Wei Ren & Wei Minghua 1985). The repertoires are mainly drawn from the fount of historical and legendary themes, popular all over China in a wide range of oral and written genres. Specializing in one or the other of the great epics of SAN GUO 三国 (Three Kingdoms), SHUIHU 水浒 (Water Margin), YUE ZHUAN 岳传 (Yue Fei) etc.,[2] different schools of Yangzhou storytelling formed and developed. By word of mouth generation after generation of storytellers have brought down the tradition from their masters, polishing and reworking the stories, creating their own versions. The unrivaled master of this century, Wang Shaotang 王少堂 (1889-1968), belonged to one of the old storyteller families of Yangzhou. He specialized in the tradition of SHUIHU, the legendary tales of a band of outlaws roaming in Shandong province during the Song dynasty. Told in the Yangzhou dialect (*Yangzhou fangyan* 扬州方言, shortened: Y.), one of the North Chinese dialects (*Bei* 北) pertaining to the River dialects around the Yangzi (*Jianghuai fangyan* 江淮方言), the art of Wang Shaotang, nevertheless, became so famous that he was ranked among the greatest artists of China:

> In opera you have to see Mei Lanfang,
> in storytelling you have to hear Wang Shaotang!

Today his son, Wang Xiaotang 王筱堂, and granddaughter, Wang Litang 王丽堂, are still practicing the art of their forefathers alongside with a handful of disciples who were received by the old master in the late fifties and early sixties. This article is based on a corpus of spoken tales from *Yangzhou pinghua*, told by these descendants of Wang Shaotang, recorded in Yangzhou 1986-1992.

'Fighting the Tiger'

The SHUIHU tale 'Wu Song Fights the Tiger' (*Wu Song da hu* 武松打虎 /U3 Son1 da3 hu3/,[3] shortened *Da hu* 打虎 'Fighting the Tiger') is chosen as sample text for close analysis. This tale constitutes the opening session from the first 'round' or chapter (*hui* 回) of the story-cycle 'Ten Chapters on Wu Song' (*Wu shi hui* 武十回). In the Wang-school repertoire, which comprises four such story-cycles around four of the famous heroes of the marshes, this tale is arranged as the first. Moreover, it is the first story that disciples of the Wang-school have had to study as their initial education in the art. It has served as their ABC of storytelling (Wang Shaotang 1979:289, Wang Xiaotang 1992:31, Fan Fu 1979).

The tale is here studied mainly in the spoken version told by Wang Xiaotang (b. 1918), the oldest representative of the Wang-school. For comparative purposes other recorded versions, by Li Xintang 李信堂 (b.1935), Ren Jitang 任继堂 (b.1942) and Chen Yintang 陈荫堂 (b.1951) are also considered.[4]

Synopsis of the story
The Wang Xiaotang version of the '*Da hu*' episode can be divided into the following subdivisions:

1) THE INN 1:1-15:13. Wu Song arrives at the inn of Jingyang town and gets drunk after emptying 30 bowls of the strong wine called 'Three bowls and you cannot cross the ridge'. He leaves the inn and continues in spite of his drunkenness.

2) THE QUARREL 15:14-25-14. The waiter Xiao'er and the young innkeeper quarrel about the silver that Wu Song has left for Xiao'er as a tip. Xiao'er runs after Wu Song to tell him about the tiger, but Wu Song doesn't believe him and beats him.

3) THE PROCLAMATION 25:15-28:14. On his way he discovers the administration's

proclamation about the tiger on Jingyang ridge; he begins to worry about his behaviour towards Xiao'er.

4) THE ROCK 28:15-30:14. Nevertheless, he climbs the mountain ridge and goes to sleep on a big flat rock.

5) THE TIGER'S LOVE STORY 30:15-32:6.While he is asleep, the tiger appears: storyteller's digression about the unfortunate love story of this particular tiger.

6) THE PREY OF THE TIGER 32:7-36:6. The tiger's majestic air: storyteller's digression on the tiger's hunting methods and the reaction of the various animals that are attacked.

7) THE WIND AND THE STENCH 36:7-42:14. A sudden gust of wind, followed by a bad smell, wakes Wu Song from his slumber. The tiger attacks.

8) THE FIGHTING 42:15-48:4. Whenever the tiger attacks, Wu Song dodges, until he gets his chance and kicks both of its eyes blind and breaks its tail. But he is at a loss how to kill it!

9) THE KILLING 48:5-51:5. He suddenly realizes that a tiger must have a 'death point' just like man, and then he beats it on the temples. The tiger dies. The deed is praised by later generations.

10) ANOTHER TWO TIGERS TURN UP! 51:6-52:13. Completely exhausted Wu Song is about to return to the flat rock to get some sleep, when he becomes aware of two tigers more hiding in the bushes...

The first episode of THE INN of the 'Da hu' tale relates how the main protagonist, Wu Song, is traveling through a mountainous region on his way home to see his elder brother. One afternoon he arrives in a small town and enters the local inn which advertises a wine called 'Three bowls and you cannot cross the ridge'....

For the purpose of the present article I shall mainly refer to examples taken from this introductory passage, which is appended in English translation and in Chinese character version.[5]

Composition, transmission and communication

In my analysis of the amalgamation of oral and literary elements I shall distinguish between three kinds of activity that are generally found to differ in their relation to writing and society: composition, transmission and communication/performance (Finnegan 1977:16-24, Thomas 1992:27). This division of the description seems just as relevant for our Chinese subject matter as it has proven elsewhere, but it is equally obvious that the three activities have a transitory relationship and the point where one activity ends and the other begins is often blurred.

Composition

Who has composed the version of *'Da hu'* selected for analysis, and how has this happened? In an 'oral' fashion or in a 'literary' fashion? We shall consider this question from a synchronic as well as from a diachronic angle.

From the synchronic perspective, the uniqueness of each contemporary performance is an obvious characteristic. Every storyteller tells the tale differently from the others, although they have all learned from the same master. Even when a storyteller tells the same tale several times, it turns out differently each time.[6] Thus during performance the storytellers do not deliver literal declamations, learned by heart, of a finalized text (spoken or written), attributed to some authoritative source (the alleged author), but we may consider the individual storyteller, if not the author, then the composer of his performance. This view is sustained by the way Yangzhou storytellers express themselves about learning by heart from books. They have several terms of jargon to describe this:[7]

shuo kong shu 说空书
'empty storytelling', about a storyteller who has not received the basic training in the tradition from master to disciple (*zhen chuan* 真传), but simply relies on the written novels, and only has learned 'the story line' (*shu luzi* 书路子). His choice of words is therefore of poor workmanship and his improvisations arbitrary.

Shuo si shu 说死书
'dead storytelling', storytelling based on learning written texts by heart, performance of low standard.

However, the many features of similarity between the various versions, i.e. the basic layout of the story, the nearly identical sequences, the set pieces of poems, proverbs and other fixed passages, the recurrent use of certain expressions etc., point to the common origin (the word of the master) which is the basis for the composition in performance.

Comparing our sample text (WANG) with the versions of Li Xintang (LI), Ren Jitang (REN) and Chen Yintang (CHEN), we find the following patterns of word-by-word identical or near identical passages:

Three of the four versions are introduced by the seven-syllabic couplet of the title (Wang 1:1-2), only REN starts head-on with the story, without any presentation. The initial passage from the title to the proverb 'Wave upon wave...' (Wang 1:1-15) is very similar in the versions of WANG, REN and CHEN. In the LI version, only the first part until the 'Three /   / characters of Jingyang Town' is near identical. The adjective used to describe the 'three characters' varies in the different versions. WANG has 'Three /hollow/ characters', REN and CHEN have /large/ and LI has /red/. For this particular version LI has chosen to skip the whole passage in the inn, and continue with what happens after Wu Song has drunk the wine and decided to climb the mountain in spite of the innkeeper's warnings.

The poem in praise of the wine (Wang 1:25-30) is near identical in WANG, REN and CHEN.

The name of the wine 'Three bowls and you cannot cross the ridge' (Wang 1:12 ff) is identical in all four versions.

After the proverb 'Wave upon wave...' (Wang 1:15), we find that WANG, REN and CHEN move forward with the same sequence of passages: Wu Song enters the inn, asks for good wine, is served by the waiter Xiao'er, the waiter tries to speak northern dialect, serves Wu Song a weak wine and explains to him why he cannot drink the strong wine 'Three bowls and you cannot cross the ridge'. LI only summarizes the fact that Wu Song becomes drunk from the strong wine. The wordings of WANG, REN and CHEN are sometimes word-by-word identical, but most of the sentences are in a free form, individual to each storyteller, though the contents are very much the same.

The difference between the various versions is getting more marked as the story progresses.

Thus, the composition of the individual storyteller's version of a tale, common to his tradition, involves both conservative elements of literal memorization, and creative elements of individual improvisation. But written materials or writing have no immediate function during the process of composition in which the individual storyteller engages before and during performance.

From a diachronic perspective, it is the *multi-authorship* of the tradition that leaps to the eye. In this historical process written materials, foremost the Ming novel *Shuihu zhuan*, attributed to Shi Nai'an (and/or Luo Guanzhong), as well as drama, are generally considered to have deeply influenced the art (Dars 1978:CXIV).

According to the dominant view, the exchange between oral and literary traditions in the development of the present *pinghua* tradition of SHUIHU is seen as a movement from original oral form (folktales, various oral narrative arts) —> to written form (drama, novel) —> to new oral form (folktales, oral arts including *Yangzhou pinghua*) (Duan Baolin 1992:74). The origin of the Wang-school repertoire, it is agreed, must be traced back to the 'original work' (*yuanzuo* 原作):[8] the unified whole of the present four cycles of stories from SHUIHU in *Yangzhou pinghua* would be unthinkable without the ingenious creative work of the mastermind of *Shuihu zhuan*. The influence of the *written novel* on the formation of the later oral storytelling art is of major importance, since the framework of the novel is largely similar to the framework of the oral tradition. These studies tend to see the development of the SHUIHU tradition of *Yangzhou pinghua* as a succession of brilliant artisans chasing out and swelling the masterpiece of *Shuihu zhuan*, so that their oral expoundings have become longer and longer, better and better (Chen Wulou 1992).

In some studies the credit given to *Shuihu zhuan* is more modified. This view holds that the oral traditions have had their own life from the beginning until our time, resulting at times in various written materials (*huaben*, drama, novel, new *huaben* etc.) (Ruhlmann 1974:60). Apart from some simple *huaben*, that have apparently served as *aide-mémoire* for storytellers, most of the *huaben* literature as well as drama and various novel editions have circulated as popular reading materials (or theatre stagings) with undeniable back-feeding to the storytelling traditions, but without implying a kind of absolute turning point around the creation of the novel (Hu Shiying 1980:615). The main source for the present day oral storytelling is therefore earlier storytelling. The existence since Ming times of *Shuihu zhuan* has been still another source of inspiration, but not *the* origin for the later storytelling. The common framework for the SHUIHU of *Yangzhou pinghua* and the *Shuihu zhuan* is, according to this theory, the result of 1) a common source for both, i.e. the pre-Ming storytelling and drama tradition, and 2) a certain adaptation of the oral tradition to the layout of the novel.

A chronological list of the major names of 'authors' in the multi-authorship of the SHUIHU of *Yangzhou pinghua* contains:

Shi Nai'an (early Ming) (often mentioned together with **Luo Guanzhong**), the supposed editor-author(s) of *Shuihu zhuan*.

Liu Jingting (1587-ca.1670), the first storyteller from the area of Yangzhou, about whom we know that he had SHUIHU stories in his repertoire, and that he probably told his stories in Yangzhou dialect, recognized as the 'father of storytelling' of China.

Wang Shaotang (1889-1968), the famous storyteller from this century, who developed the repertoire of his forefathers to more than double length during his lifetime, considered the greatest recreator of the Wang-school tradition.

Between Liu Jingting and Wang Shaotang historical sources mention many other names of Yangzhou storytellers telling the SHUIHU tales. Usually the descriptions are centered around the specific style of performance and next to nothing is said about the elaboration and recreation of the repertoire. Even about the immediate forefathers of Wang Shaotang, little is known of their individual contribution to the development of the tradition.

Transmission

There is no doubt that a good *memory* is a very important factor for the storytellers, endeavoring to transmit the word of their masters. The question is *what* the disciples of the art were supposed to remember? The repertoires in which the storytellers of different schools excel are of enormous dimensions. The SHUIHU repertoire of the Wang-school is estimated to encompass a volume of words more than ten times the length of the novel *Shuihu zhuan*.[9] How were the artists ever able to come to grips with story cycles of such incredible length? To what degree are the spoken texts formulaic and in what sense? What role did written materials play in education and preparation of performances? Again we may get an impression from some of the storytellers' slang:

kou chuan xin shou 口传心授
'transmit by mouth and teach from the heart', the teaching method generally used by the storytellers, i.e. teaching orally sentence by sentence, while guiding the student by one's own experience and the whole range of performance technique on the stage.

kou, shou, shen, bu, shen 口手身步神
'mouth, hand, body, step, expression', five basic elements of storytelling: 'mouth', i.e. the art of telling; 'hand', i.e. gesture; 'body', i.e. body movements; 'step', i.e. movements of the legs; 'expression', i.e. expression of the face and eyes.

shu luzi 书路子
'story line', the organization of the sequence of events. The first thing a storyteller must make himself familiar with and remember.

These three expressions give us a key to the pedagogical praxis:

1) teaching by doing: letting the student imitate at first short passages, then longer and longer sequences
2) the secret of memory to be closely connected with the intimate combination of words with the movements of hands, feet, body and face
3) teaching the framework (story line) of the stories and the style of telling them, formulary expressions and set pieces, leaving the rest to individual improvisation.

The storyteller of our sample text, Wang Xiaotang, is the son of Wang Shaotang's brother. His grandfather and grandfather's brother, his father, uncle and brother were all storytellers. As a child he was adopted by his uncle, Wang Shaotang, who had no son, and he was brought up in the family tradition as a storyteller. Both Wang Shaotang and Wang Xiaotang have *told* their personal memoirs about their life and education with a view to publication (it is noteworthy that none of them have written anything).

Wang Xiaotang tells in detail about his efforts as a child to learn the art. His daily routine consisted in listening to his stepfather's performances both in public and at home, 'eating them down in his stomach' (*chixia du* 吃下肚), i.e. trying to remember them, and then 'returning the text' (*huan shu* 还书), i.e. reciting passages for his stepfather who corrected and often spanked him, if he could not do it well enough. He would sit alone for hours, practising his 'scene-abilities' (*taigong* 台功), pondering and acting out the passages and scenes he was supposed to 'return' the next day. He did go to school and received the basic education of classical works, but we never hear that any written material was used for his education as a storyteller (Wang Xiaotang 1992:30-34). However, after being severely punished one day for not being able to remember a certain expression, he began to make his own notes of the most difficult expressions and fixed poems (Wang Xiaotang 1992:34-37). This seems to be an individual solution, not a common practice.

In Wang Shaotang's memoirs there is no mention of written materials in the transmission and education of the art. On the contrary, it is told how Wang Shaotang's father once took in a blind disciple and educated him in the SHUIHU tradition. The blind child was exceptionally gifted to memorize the words and diction, but he had a hard time learning to imitate the movements and facial expressions (Wang Shaotang 1979:287-88). There is no indication that his inability to read would impede him in the least.

Thus writing and written materials are hardly mentioned, and therefore if not non-existent, are at least of very little practical use in the transmission of the Wang-school in the generation of Wang Xiaotang and his predecessors. In the fifties Wang Shaotang's performances were taken down in notational editions (Wang Shaotang 1959, 1985). These books are currently being used to teach storytelling in classroom at Yangzhou Drama School, but the post-Cultural Revolution generation of storyteller novices are not yet fully educated, and it is too early to evaluate the influence of written material on their style of performance.

As for the now middle-aged generation of storytellers, who were educated by Wang Shaotang and Wang Xiaotang, including Wang Litang, daughter of Wang Xiaotang, they all seem to have received the old-style education, relying very little on written materials, if at all .[10] This is also the impression that one would get from comparing their versions. If they had based themselves on learning by heart the printed version of Wang Shaotang's *Wu Song*, one would expect a much more uniform performance of the '*Da hu*' episode.

Although written materials have been peripheral to the transmission of the SHUIHU in the Wang-school, we should not draw the conclusion that such materials have been absolutely banned in *Yangzhou pinghua* at large. The storytellers do mention the existence of 'scripts':

jiaoben 脚本
'script', storyteller's written copy of his text. In former times only a few storytellers with a relatively high education were in possession of such a 'script'. There were generally speaking two kinds of 'script': One kind consisted only in a short summary of the story line, the important episodes and the dialogue of the major characters. The other kind was a more detailed notation of the story as told on stage.

This definition is parallel to our understanding of the two-fold function of *huaben*: 1) as a storyteller's aide-mémoire; 2) as a more or less complete and reworked notation of the storyteller's performance, mainly prepared for the purpose of commercial distribution. The sources on Yangzhou storytellers' *jiaoben* and other kinds of handed-down manuscripts are not easily accessible and await further study.[11]

Communication

The situation of performance

Yangzhou pinghua is performed without any reliance on written materials. Before the performance the artist will usually prepare himself for some time in silent meditation, in storytellers' jargon called:

wu shu 悟书
'warming up the story'; before ascending the stage, the storyteller will ponder in silence the story line for the day's performance.

During the performance of the present version of '*Da hu*' Wang Xiaotang had in front of him only the requisites traditionally used during the cold season: his storyteller's stick, the so-called 'talk-stopper' (*zhiyu* 止语), and his handkerchief.[12] The requisites are handled in a studied and artful way, characteristic of the whole accompaniment of gestures and mime. The application of these items to represent certain objects of importance to the tale, i.e. the handkerchief symbolizing the tray of Xiao'er, the beating of the 'talk-stopper' at certain points of the tale, the 'choreography' of movements, seems to work as much as a 'formulary' support to bind the memory as do the linguistic units of formulary character.

The spoken text
Much research on 'oral' literature has been conducted on the basis of written editions, never meant to reflect very precisely the original oral form. This is also the case with most studies on *Yangzhou pinghua* that are based on the 'corrected' and revised editions of the great masters of this century. It is one of the fundamental premises for the present study that it should be based on spoken texts, recorded on tape and taken down in notation in the most faithful way. The sample text of '*Da hu*' is therefore presented and analysed according to this principle.

The text as a whole manifests a uniform style of performance and language. Nevertheless, beneath the uniform over-all appearence, we find a mosaic of elements and structures which are more or less akin to 'literacy' or 'orality', more or less attached to 'high' or 'low' style. These structures are interlocked in 'Chinese nest of boxes' systems:

In Chinese literature, as in many other world literatures, there is a general appreciation of certain genres of literature as *high literature* (*wen* 文) versus other genres deemed *low literature* (*xiaoshuo* 小说). In this picture *Yangzhou pinghua* will traditionally be ranked as *low literature* by virtue of being dialectal, oral, fictional and popular. Here the idea of *low literature* comes near to the concept of *vernacular literature* (*baihua wenxue* 白话文学), i.e. literature written in a medium reminiscent of spoken language. The novel of *Shuihu zhuan*, being written in a medium close to the spoken language of Early Northern Chinese and presumably incorporating a number of standard phrases of the storytellers of that time, was traditionally considered *low literature*, no matter how ingenious and in spite of the far-reaching reworking by the literati editor-authors of its mature forms.

If we look at *Yangzhou pinghua* as a genre, we find that the different schools of storytelling are divided into the 'major texts' (*da shu* 大书) and the 'minor texts' (*xiao shu* 小书), and this division implies the idea that the major texts are mainly in *high style* (*fangkou shu* 方口书) while the minor texts are mainly in *low style* (*yuankou shu* 圆口书). SHUIHU belongs to the major texts and is thus mainly in high style. In this sense all of our sample tale is *high style*.

But when we come still closer and analyse the performance of a tale, we find a mixing of *fangkou* and *yuankou*, a playing with *high* and *low* style in the impersonation not only of different dramatis personae, but in the variation between overt dialogue and covert inner monologue, and further in the differentiation between the storyteller's voice in detached summary and description versus involved and intimate commentary. And if we venture even further down into the layer of morphology, we find an interplay between high and low forms of 'split pronunciations' (*wen bai yi du* 文白异读).

To sum up: In the big box of Chinese literature (high and low) our text belongs to a genre considered *low literature*. This genre comprises schools of *high style* and *low style*, and our text belongs to the *high style* schools. In the performance of texts of high style, both *high* and *low* style passages are combined, and on this level our text is *mixed high and low*. In *low* style passages we find specific morphemes with colloquial form, marking *low* style, but in both *high* and *low* style we find lots of morphemes in literary form, with no implication of high style.

Focusing once more on the first few minutes of the performance, the introductory incident of Wu Song's stay in the inn of Jingyang Town, we shall take a look at some examples of these intricate patterns on the levels of phonology, grammar, style and narration.

Phonological and grammatical features

On the phonological level the difference between high and low style is manifested by the speaking styles of 'square mouth' (*fang kou* 方口) and 'round mouth' (*yuan kou* 圆口) (Børdahl 1977 and 1991a).

fangkou 方口

'square mouth', a forceful, over-distinct, steady diction, with a regular sentence pattern, often using four- and six-character phrases, and performed with dignified modulation, giving less room for improvisation.

yuankou 圆口

'round mouth', a smooth, quick and continuous diction, nearer to everyday speech, incorporating earthy localisms (*tuyu* 土语) and open to all kinds of improvisation.

'Square mouth' and 'round mouth' are not antagonistic opposites. In stories told in 'square mouth style' one may find passages of 'round mouth' interpolated, and in 'round mouth' stories one can often find short passages of 'square mouth'.

Wang Shaotang was known as the best storyteller in the *fangkou* style of his time, basing himself on a mixture of *fangkou* and *yuankou* (*Yangzhou pinghua xuan* 1962:383). The present version by Wang Xiaotang is also told in a mixed style, with some passages tending more towards *fangkou*, some tending more towards *yuankou*.

From the phonological point of view, Wang Xiaotang in *fangkou* passages observes fairly consequently some phonemic distinctions found in the northern varieties of the North Chinese dialects, but not in the Yangzhou dialect (Y.).[13] While his pronunciation is generally according to the system of Y. phonology, the most important deviations are: distinguishing the /l/n/r/ initials that are assimilated into only one phoneme /l/ in ordinary Y., diphthongal pronunciation of finals in emphatic position that in Y. have monophthongal manifestation etc. (Børdahl 1991a:139-141). Wang Xiaotang's *fangkou* style is applied in narrative summaries and descriptions. It is characterized by a slow and distinguished pace, giving his performance a special aristocratic atmosphere.

Another variant of *fangkou* style is found in Wang Xiaotang's impersonation of the dialogue of Wu Song. Here he imitates the phonology of 'northern language' (*Beifang hua* 北方话), also called 'language of the Capital' (*Jinghua* 京话), changing most of the sounds, including the tonal system, in the direction of Modern Standard Chinese. This pronunciation is also found in the first few sentences of greeting that Xiao'er has taught himself in order to ingratiate himself with the many foreigners coming to the inn. The poem describing the wine is also recited by Xiao'er in *Beifang hua*. Wu Song is characterized as a hero and a man of the world by his imposing *fangkou* diction and *Beifang hua* pronunciation. Although he is far from being a man of letters, his status as a 'personage' (*renwu* 人物) entitles him to a position among the high and mighty, and as a consequence his language is in high style. With Xiao'er it is a different matter: He is only a 'small person' (*xiao renwu*), and speaks usually in broad dialect in *yuankou* style. When he uses *Beifang hua* it is to show off and speak a kind of foreign language in order to make himself understood with the travelers on the road. His recitation of the poem in this style implies, however, the overtones of high style and literary refinement.

In *yuankou* passages the pronunciation of Wang Xiaotang follows ordinary Y. phonology, with some exceptions, e.g. morphemes such as 耳 'ear', 儿 'son', 二 'two', which in Modern Standard Chinese are pronounced: *er* (+ 2,3,4 tone, respectively) are always (both in *fangkou* and *yuankou*) pronounced in a similar way /er/ or /ar/ (+ 2,3,4 tone) while ordinary Y. pronunciation is /a/ (+ tone)(Børdahl 1991a:143). In emphatic position there is a tendency even in *yuankou* to distinguish /l/n/r/ and diphthongize, but the whole sound spectre is closer to ordinary Y. This style is characterized by a more sloppy and slurred diction, often in a quicker pace. It is used for storyteller's commentary and summary, for the impersonation of dialogue by 'small persons', such as Xiao'er in the sample text, and for the inner monologue of Wu Song. It conveys an atmosphere of intimacy and homeliness, sometimes bordering on the rustic and ridiculous, clearly a mark of low style.

Elsewhere I have tried to demonstrate the interesting correlation between the phenomenon of 'split pronunciations', *wen bai yi du*, literary (LIT) versus colloquial (COL) pronounciation of certain morphemes, and the *shuokou* of *Yangzhou pinghua* (Børdahl 1990 and 1993a).

In the present sample text, we find for instance the morpheme 家 *pinyin*

(P.): *jia1*) with two different pronounciations in the Yangzhou dialect (Y.):
LIT:/zia1/ and COL:/ga1/. It occurs 15 times in the sample text (p.1-2 of the
character version), 10 times in LIT pronunciation and 5 times in COL pronunciation. The cases of COL pronunciation are marked with a square in the character text.

The COL forms of 家 are found in two passages where our storyteller
impersonates the inner thought of Wu Song (Wang 1:34-35 and 2:16), and in
another passage where he impersonates the ordinary speech of Xiao'er. In
every case the use of the COL form adds to the flavour of homely, everyday
chatting. For instance, in the case of Wu Song there is a clear change of
modulation between his dialogue passages in forceful *Beifang hua, fangkou*
style, and his inner deliberations in ordinary Y. dialect, *yuankou* style. A
humoristic effect is created by the contrast between the imposing outward
behaviour and the more 'human size' inner life of the hero.

While the use of COL forms marks a given passage as colloquial Y., the
use of LIT forms is more neutral, since LIT forms are widespread in both low
and high style. The LIT form is not necessarily 'literary' or 'bookish'. It is
found in many daily words and constructions with no flavour of 'high'
language at all. However, in passages of *literary Chinese (wenyan)* flavour in
grammar and vocabulary, only the LIT forms of the affected morphemes are
used (Børdahl 1993a).

On the morphological and syntactical level of analysis, we find that our
text is sprinkled with forms typical for Y. grammar, while of more restricted
usage or non-existent in MSC, e.g.:

The more frequent occurrence of nouns etc. suffixed with— 子Y./zø/ (forms not
found in MSC) (Børdahl 1991b:175-176). Examples:

鸡子 /zi1-zø/ egg (MSC: 鸡蛋 *jidan*), (Wang 1:19)
尾子 /ue3-zø/ tail (MSC: 尾巴 *weiba*) (Wang 2:11)
这么子/ 'ze'-mo-zø/ this way (MSC: 这样 *zheiyang*)   (Wang 2:26)

The existence of two kinds of disjunctive questions, V 不V ? /V be' V ?/ and 可V?
/kw V ?/ (in this text we even find the form 可V 不V ? /kw V be' V ?/)
(Børdahl 1991b:195). Examples:

...可有好酒
Therefore even before he had entered the inn, he would first ask *whether they had
good wine.*' (Wang 1:23)

...可好不好?
'*Don't you think* the wine of that inn *was good?*' (Wang 1:35-36)
Negation of the verb of existence 有/iw3/ in the forms 没得 /me' de'/ and 不
得/be' de'/ (Børdahl 1991b: 186-188) Examples:

...不得好酒....
'He was afraid that they *did not have* any good wine in this inn.' (Wang 1:22)

一个酒客都不得.
'*There was not* one single customer.' (Wang 2:2)

一点个口力都没得.
'(That mouthful) *didn't have* the least strength.' (Wang 2:19)

Grammatical forms of non-standard usage, but belonging to ordinary
Yangzhou dialect usage, as demonstrated in the examples above, have a
relatively higher frequency in passages of *yuankou* style than in *fangkou*
passages. But also in *fangkou* style we find a certain density of Y. grammar
and lexicon. In Wu Song's dialogue in *Beifang hua* no trace of Y. grammar is
found, however. It seems obvious that the higher the density of Y. grammar
in the text, the more the text is characterized as low style.

Forms of overt *wenyan* grammar are not frequent, but we find them
typically in four-syllabic phrases (Wang 1:4, 1:22), which are more widespread
in *fangkou*, cf. below. *Wenyan* vocabulary and compactness of expression is
further found in the title (Wang 1:1-2), the poem (Wang 1:25-33) and proverb
(Wang 1:15-16) of our sample text, all *fangkou* passages.

Stylistic features

In another study I have analysed the stylistic features of *prosody, parallelism*
and *repetition* in a '*Da hu*' version by Li Xintang (Børdahl 1993b). Here I shall
only point to a few examples of these stylistic features and discuss how far
they may be correlated to the idea of high and low style discussed above
(*fangkou/yuankou*) and to the more general question of orality/literacy.

In our sample text we can find some *prosodic* phenomena that seem correlated to the *fangkou/yuankou* dichotomy. The poem (Wang 1:25-33) and verse-
like passages (Wang 1:1-2, 1:15-16) are all in *fangkou* diction, and this
observation holds true also for verse passages later in our text. The density
of four-syllable phrases, i.e. the rhythmical entity of phrases of four syllables,

including four-syllable expressions (*sizige chengyu* 四字格成语) as well as proverbs and ad hoc constructions, is higher in *fangkou* summary and description than in *yuankou* (but not in *fangkou* dialogue, e.g. Wu Song's utterances).

Verse and four-syllable phrases belong to the stable part of the performance, constituting formulary expressions and passages that are memorized and repeated in the tradition. Examples of formulary four-syllable phrases from the first summary and description part in *fangkou* of our sample text:

非止一日 /fe1 zø3 ie' le'/ '(He) was not just one day (on the road)' (Wang 1:4). Also found in identical form in LI, REN and CHEN.

腹中饥馁，意欲打尖 /fo' zon1 zi1 lue4 , i4 io' da3 zien1/ '(He) felt hungry in his stomach and wanted to take a rest' (Wang 1:6). Also in identical form in LI and CHEN.

The poems and verse-like passages of our text are generally short, two to eight stanzas (cf.Wang 1:1-2, 1:15-16, 1:25-33), and these passages are repeted almost word-by-word identical in the other versions where they occur (sometimes a word or two are exchanged with another word of similar meaning). The '*Da hu*' text includes, however, a somewhat longer prose-poem (*fu* 赋) of 25 stanzas (Wang 9:5-10) and here the various versions show a greater variation.

How are we to interpret the poetry of *Yangzhou pinghua* vis-à-vis the question of orality/literacy? The grammar of the poems found in our corpus is in *literary Chinese* (*wenyan*), marked as such either by overt grammatical form or by the compact structure and bookish (*shumian*) vocabulary. The prosodic form is cast in the style of Tang regulated poetry and other classical verse forms. However, this kind of poetry has always had both an oral and a written creative tradition, so tightly intertwined that it evades classification (Alleton 1980:219). They are often part of the introductory or concluding passages. They may be inserted at moments of high suspense to prolong the time of expectancy, or at sequences of lyrical description. They constitute a special kind of storyteller's comment in high-strung rhetorical declamation. In a contemporary performance of *Yangzhou pinghua*, these poems — in spite of their literary flavour — stand out as symbols of the *oral* storytelling situation.

Phrases and sentences of varying length, characterized by grammatical *parallelism* with other phrases in the near environment, are irregularly distributed all over the text, with apparently no correlation to either *fangkou* or *yuankou*. But parallel passages definitely belong to the formulary part of the language material. Example:

柜台里头坐了个小老板
/gue4-tæ2 li3-tw zo4-le gw4 siå3 lå3-bæn4/ ......
　N　L-suff. V-suff. M　A　N
'Behind the counter sat a young innkeeper, ...
柜台外头站了个店小二
/gue4-tæ2 uæ4-tw zæn4-le gw4 dien4 siå3-er4/
　N　L-suff. V-suff. M　N　Nr
In front of the counter stood a young waiter, Xiao'er,'
(Wang 1:14-15).
With slight variation this passage is found also in REN and CHEN.

In the long introductory *fangkou* passage of our sample text there is a famous passage of marked *repetitive* style (in Chinese stylistics called 顶针 *dingzhen*, 'thimble' linking). It comes just after Wu Song has entered the city gate and arrived at the inn, a 'brand-new thatched cottage' (Wang 1:10-14):

The adjective 'brand-new' is repeated ten times, at first in *dingzhen* linking constructions, where the end of one sentence is repeated in the beginning of the next, building up to a climax in the announcement of the wine-flag: 'Three bowls and you cannot cross the ridge!'. Then going on with repetitions in accelerating tempo in short, staccato phrases, called 'sprinkling mouth' (*pokou* 泼口 using a special breathing technique), finally ending with a drawn out: 'brand-new-people'. The passage is found in near identical form in REN and CHEN.

While the *dingzhen* linking is generally considered an elegant figure of Chinese stylistics, mainly adorning written specimens of various genres, the repetitive pattern is here exaggerated to the point of comical farce. The humour of the passage is, however, heavily dependent on the modulation of diction, *pokou*, which cannot be rendered in the character version. This kind of farcical repetition is therefore strictly connected with the *oral* performance, and in written form it may, to the contrary, convey a tedious, long-drawn impression.

Repetition of syllables is the most common form of onomatopoeia in Chinese. We find an example, describing the sound of Wu Song's feet, marching eagerly towards the gate of Jingyang Town: /da-da-da-da-da-da..../

(Wang 1:7). The liberal distribution of a variety of onomatopoeia is clearly a feature of the orality of storytelling.

Different figures of repetition on morphological, syntactical and macro-syntactical levels of analysis can be found all over the text, but a correlation to *fangkou/yuankou* style seems doubtful. The above examples occur in a *fangkou* passage of high style, but both have typical *oral* features and clownish connotations, usually played on in *yuankou* style.

Narrative features

In the written legacy of the Ming and Qing vernacular novels and short stories, where elements from both literary and oral models were absorbed, the narrative mode generally reflects the storytelling communication situation. The narrative voice is invariably simulating the rhetoric of the storyteller (Wang D.T. 1983:133 ff.). This feature is manifested most obviously in the form of narrator's comment and in the application of a set of storyteller's stock phrases. The character of these two devices clearly places them as *oral* in origin. However, after being absorbed by the long and short genres of vernacular fiction, they became a *literary convention* for *written* fiction.

In the living oral tradition of *Yangzhou pinghua* we find that the convention of narrator's comment is still very important, while the convention of stock phrases of introduction, connection and conclusion is absent.

The oral character of the narrator's comment is reflected most clearly in the frequent occurrence of *simulated dialogue* with the audience (*zi wen zi da* 自问自答). In our text the first instance of narrator's comment and simulated dialogue occurs after the *dingzhen* passage, mentioned above. Our storyteller draws a deep breath after the strain of the previous *pokou* passage, and asks:

Why? In this world things can be 'new'; can people also be 'new'? Yes! Behind the counter sat a young innkeeper, altogether twenty-one or twenty-two this year. In front of the counter stood a young waiter, Xiao'er, not yet twenty years old. The proverb says:
  Wave upon wave the Yangzi-river flows,
  New people overtake the elder generation...   (Wang 1:14-16)

A little later in the passage, when Wu Song asks for good wine, we find the second instance of comment and simulated dialogue:

Oh, that was strange! Even before Wu Song entered the inn, he asked for good wine, how come? People of former times in their daily life had four words of importance to them: wine, sex, wealth and vigour. But Wu Song only cared for two things: He was fond of drinking and he used his strength on behalf of innocent people. He saw that the town was small and the inn was small, too, so he was afraid that they did not have any good wine in this inn. Therefore even before he had entered the inn, he would first ask whether they had good wine. (Wang 1:20-23)

It is evident that such questions are rhetorical adornments, not real invitations to a conversation with the public. Even if they enter in a genuinely oral communication situation, they function as symbols of orality, rather than symptoms. They belong to the style of the 'eternal storyteller' in China, but they do *not* actually presuppose the response of an active audience. Nevertheless they are instrumental in creating the intimate atmosphere of mutual understanding typical of the narrative mode of Chinese storytelling.

In the novel *Shuihu zhuan* chapters are regularly introduced by the storyteller's stock phrase: *hua shuo* 话说, 'The story tells...' or 'It is related...' and concluded by: ....*zheng shi shen ren, qie ting xia hui fenjie* ... 正是甚人, 且听下回分解. '(If you want to know) who was ......please listen to the explanation of the next session'. Paragraphs are connected by the phrases: *hua fen liang tou* 话分两头 'we'll divide our story in two ...', *qie shuo* 且说, 'meanwhile let's tell...', *que shuo* 却说, 'let us talk rather of...' etc. Ellipses are marked by: *hua zhong bu shuo* .....*zhi shuo* 话中不说... 只说, 'we'll talk not of...but rather of...', *hua xiu xu fan* 话休絮烦 'but enough of petty details, ...' etc. Paragraphs are concluded by phrases such as: *bu zai hua xia* 不在话下, 'of that we'll say no more', etc.

In Chinese literature these expressions signal that the discourse belongs to the genre of traditional fiction in the storyteller's mode, just as our expression 'Once upon a time ...' signals the genre of fairy-tale. Again it is a pertinent feature that these expressions are characterized as *oral* (they all play on the oral communication situation of 'telling' and 'listening'), but they have developed into a *literary convention* for a certain genre of *written* literature: vernacular long and short fiction.

In my corpus of spoken *Yangzhou pinghua* these conventional phrases are never used. They are not part of MSC usage and neither of modern Yangzhou dialect. But we might have expected some dialectal or modernized variations of these phrases to have replaced the old stock phrases. However, in my collection of spoken texts, both from the Wang-school and from other schools of *Yangzhou pinghua*, this kind of fixed introductory, conclusive and combinatory phrases are absent. Nevertheless, we do find some expressions of relatively frequent usage, suggestive of the former storyteller's stock phrases: *na xiaode* 哪晓得/la3 siå3-de'/, 'who would have imagined that....' is often used to introduce a new turn of events (but it is also part of simulated dialogue discussed above), *...bu V bian ba, zhe yi* V..., 不V 便罢, 这一 V /...be' V bien4 ba4, ze' ie' V.../, 'if ...had not...that would have been the end (of the story), but now that he ...'(Børdahl 1993b:141). Since there is no instance of such phrases in our sample text, the above examples are taken from a passage occurring later in our text and from the LI version.

It is puzzling that the former stock phrases, seemingly representing some of the most evident features of orality in the written tradition of vernacular literature, have left no trace in present day storytelling from Yangzhou. One may wonder if these expressions were ever part of the oral tradition, or rather a *literary convention* of simulated storytelling from the very beginning?

'Three bowls and you cannot cross the ridge'
The plot of the '*Da hu*' episode as related in *Shuihu zhuan* and as told by the storytellers of the Wang-school of my corpus, is surely very much alike in the larger framework, but differs radically in the actualization of the subplots and even more in the working out of every single situation. If it were true that Yangzhou storytellers essentially built their tradition on the written novel, why did they use so little from it? For example: when Wu Song against the advice of the waiter, Xiao'er, stubbornly begins to climb the mountain where the tiger lives, he is warned once more by the proclamation on the temple at the roadside. This proclamation is written in officialese style in *Shuihu zhuan*. It is also rendered in highly officialese style by the storytellers of the Wang-school, but they have their own version. Why haven't they taken over this documentary piece as a set piece directly from *Shuihu zhuan*? *Shuihu zhuan* has about the same frequency of four-syllable phrases as found in the versions of the Wang-school. Why are these more or less fixed expressions not taken over by the oral artisans of *Yangzhou pinghua*? They are not. They have found or stuck to their own variations. Actually, in the whole chapter of the '*Da hu*' episode, the only fixed expressions that are common to *Shuihu zhuan* and the Wang-school texts are: 1) the name of Wu Song, 2) the title couplet, and 3) the name of the wine: *San wan bu guo gang* 三碗不过岗 /sæn1 uon3 be' go4 gan1/, 'three bowls and you cannot cross the ridge'.

Conclusion

From the above discussion it appears that the concepts of *orality* and *literacy*, when applied to a storytelling tradition of China, such as Yangzhou storytelling, are just as chameleonic and evasive as they have proved in studies from other cultures.

From the point of view of composition and transmission, the *oral* aspects of education and composition-in-performance are fairly easy to determine. The diachronic influence of *written* sources such as *Shuihu zhuan* is generally recognized, but our materials lead us to question the idea of massive loan from the novel to the modern storytelling tradition: the link seems to be tight on account of the common framework of plot and development, but the fact that actually so little of the 'filling' is carried over from the novel to the oral tradition makes us suspicious about the closeness of the connection.

The situation of performance is clearly *oral*, but when we begin to scrutinize what the storyteller actually says, his spoken text, the contagion of the written and spoken word, of *literacy* and *orality* on a scale of different levels of analysis, becomes apparent. We find that in most cases, we have to arrange the *oral* and *literary* features in a hierarchical 'Chinese nest of boxes', where something that is *oral* on one level may be *literary* on the subsequent level and then vice versa on the next level, etc. We get a most complicated, but not less interesting, mosaic of linguistic, narrative and genre-related features.

Within the 'folksy', and therefore, low-style genre of *Yangzhou pinghua*, the Wang-school of SHUIHU represents the 'major texts' of 'square mouth' style (*fangkou* shu), i.e. *high* style. The performance of Wang Xiaotang of our sample text is characterized as a whole by a *high-brow* attitude, reflected in phonology, grammar and style. However, we can observe how he plays with the encounter between *high* and *low* language in the mouths of the various dramatis personae: Dialogue of Wu Song (*high*), of Xiao'er (mostly *low*), inner monologue of protagonists (*low*), storyteller's voice in summary and description (*high*), storyteller's voice in commentary (*low*), in verse-passage commentary (*high*). Within this mixture of *high* and *low* style passages, we find that linguistic entities of *literary Chinese* (*wenyan*) flavour are almost exclusively found in *high* style passages, but in general the language used is plain *dialectal vernacular Chinese*, also in these high style passages. In *low* style passages we find expressions of special *colloquial* pronunciation, which are very rare in high style passages. But the corresponding so-called *literary* pronunciations are equally frequent in *low* style, since they seem to be *neutral* in their stylistic impact.

The oral art of storytelling has been able to co-exist for centuries along with the written and printed word. The challenge from the highly orally oriented media of radio and television seems to represent a much greater threat to the old traditions.

References

Alleton, V. (1980): 'En Chine: La contagion de l'ecrit' *Critique*, No. 384, pp. 217-27.

Børdahl, V. (1977): 'The Phonemes and the Phonological Structure of the Yangzhou Dialect', *Acta Orientalia*, Copenhagen, No.38, pp. 251-320.

Børdahl, V. (1990): 'Literary and Colloquial Forms in a Yangzhou Storyteller's Tale', *East Asian Institute Occasional Papers*, Copenhagen, No. 6, pp. 77-87.

Børdahl, V. (1991a): »'Square Mouth' and 'Round Mouth' in Yangzhou Storytelling«, *Acta Orientalia*, Copenhagen, No.52, pp. 135-47.

Børdahl, V. (1991b): 'Grammatical Gleanings from a Yangzhou Storyteller's Tale', *Cahiers linguistique asie orientale*, Paris, Vol. XX, No. 2, pp. 169-217.

Børdahl, V. (1993a): '*WEN BAI YI DU*: Literary and Colloquial Forms in Yangzhou Storytelling', *CHINOPERL Papers*, Harvard, No. 16.

Børdahl, V. (1993b): »'Wu Song Fights the Tiger' in Yangzhou Storytelling«, *Acta Orientalia*, Copenhagen, No. 54, pp. 126-49.

Chen Ruheng (1985): *Chen Ruheng quyi wen xuan*, Beijing: Zuojia chubanshe.

CHINOPERL News (1974), Harvard, No. 4.

Dars, J. (1978): *Shi Nai-an Luo-Guan-zhong: Au bord de l'eau*, I, II, Paris: Pléiade.

Fan Fu (1979): 'Yan shi gao tu, ye jing yu qin. Ji Yangzhou pinghua yanyuan Wang Litang', *Quyi*, No. 6, pp. 41-42.

Finnegan, R. (1977): *Oral Poetry. Its Nature, Significance and Social Content*, Cambridge.

Foley, J. M. (1985): *Oral-formulaic Theory and Research*, New York.

Goody, J. (1987): *The Interface between the Written and the Oral*, Cambridge: Cambridge University Press.

Hu Shiying (1980): *Huaben xiaoshuo gailun*, shang, xia, Beijing: Zhonghua shuju.

Lord, A. (1960): *The Singer of Tales*, New York: Harvard University Press.

Li Xintang (1992): »Shuole sishi nian 'Wu Song' reng wei ding gao«, *Quyi xinxi*, No. 29, p. 4.

Ruhlmann, R. (1974): 'The Wu Sung story in Yangchow p'ing-hua', *CHINOPERL News*, No. 4, pp. 59-64.

Shi Nai'an: *Shuihu*, Renmin wenxue chubanshe, Beijing 1972, shang, xia, 862 pp.

Sun Longfu (1962): 'Yangzhou pinghua de lishi fazhan', *Yangzhou shiyuan xuebao*, No. 16, pp. 20-32.

Thomas, R. (1992): *Literacy and Orality in Ancient Greece*, Cambridge: Cambridge University Press.

Wangpai Shuihu pinglun ji (1990) (Collected articles on 'Water Margin' of the Wang-school), Beijing: Zhongguo quyi chubanshe.

Wang Litang (1989): *Wu Song*, Beijing: Zhongguo quyi chubanshe, shang, xia.

Wang Shaotang (1959): *Wu Song*, Huaiyin: Jiangsu renmin chubanshe, shang, xia, reprinted 1984.

Wang Shaotang (1979): 'Wo de xueyi jingguo he biaoyan jingyan' (My artistic career and experience of performing) in *Shuo xin shu*, Shanghai: Shanghai wenyi chubanshe, No. 2 pp. 286-310. (First published in *Yangzhou pingtan*, neibu ziliao, Yangzhou: Yangzhoushi wenhuachu, 1961, pp. 58-89.)

Wang Shaotang (1985): *Song Jiang*, Huaiyin: Jiangsu renmin chubanshe, shang, zhong, xia.

Wang Xiaotang (1992): *Yi hai ku hang lu* (Recollections of difficult navigation on the sea of art), Zhenjiang: Jiangsu wen shi ziliao bianjibu.

Wei Ren & Wei Minghua (1985): *Yangzhou quyi shihua*, Beijing: Zhongguo quyi chubanshe.

Wivell, C. (1975): 'The Chinese Oral and Pseudo-oral Narrative Traditions', *CHINOPERL Papers*, No. 5, pp. 117-25.

Yangzhou pinghua xuan (1962), Shanghai: Shanghai wenyi chubanshe.

Notes

1. For a short but lively discussion of the question of influence between written and oral literature, cf. *CHINOPERL News*, (1974) No. 4, pp. 53-58, 'Proceedings at the fourth meeting of the Conference'. Wivell 1975 considers the better part of the Chinese storytelling traditions of *tanci* 弹词 and *pinghua* (selecting most of his examples from *Yangzhou pinghua*) to belong to 'pseudo-oral' traditions rather than 'genuine oral tradition'. The definition of the 'pseudo-oral' performer is taken from Scholes and Kellogg 1966:30: 'A new kind of professional entertainer, one who merely memorizes written texts and goes about reciting them, can begin to compete with the genuine singer. When the term 'oral tradition' is misapplied by literary scholars, it usually refers to this kind of oral recitation of a fixed literary text which has been composed in the modern way with pen and paper. The method of composition, not the mode of presentation, distinguishes the genuine oral tradition from the written.' As we shall see in the following, *Yangzhou pinghua* certainly does not belong to Scholes and Kellogg's category of 'pseudo-oral' literature.

2. Capital letters are used to indicate that I am speaking about an *oral tradition*, in contrast to the *written* novels of — more or less — the same names, i.e. *Shuihu zhuan* 水浒传, pointing to the Ming *novel* attributed to Shi Nai'an.

3. Pronunciation in Yangzhou dialect (Y.) is rendered within brackets. The transcription follows the phonemic system in Børdahl 1977: 284-88, except for the

four long tones, largely correlated to the four tones of MSC, here written with numbers. The short *ru* tone is written /'/.

4. Disciples of Wang Shaotang all were bestowed an artist's name with the syllable *tang* 堂. Ren and Chen in daily life use their former names: Ren Dekun 任 德坤 and Chen Shiyong 陈 世 勇. The version by Li Xintang was recorded in November 1986 (40 min.), Ren Jitang in May 1989 (30 min.) and (continued) November 1992 (45 min.), Chen Yintang in May 1989 (20 min.) and Wang Xiaotang in November 1992 (90 min.).

5. The performance was arranged in the home of Wang Xiaotang in Zhenjiang, on November 19, 1992. It was a private performance, with only a small audience of five persons, including myself. The session lasted for one and a half hour, almost the length of a public performance. The introductory passage rendered here lasts ca. 12 min.

6. My corpus comprises several versions of the '*Da hu*' tale by Li Xintang, 1986 and 1989, by Wang Xiaotang 1989 and 1992.

7. Cf. 'A list of Yangzhou storytellers' jargon and technical terms', appendix to Børdahl, V.: *The Oral Tradition of Yangzhou Storytelling* (to appear). The explanations are translated from definitions given by my informants among Yangzhou storytellers, mainly by Mr. Fei Li, former storyteller of the SAN GUO tradition, presently researcher of *Yangzhou tanci* and *pinghua*.

8. The extremely complicated textual history of *Shuihu zhuan* (the existence of several lines of structurally quite different editions, the obscurity of the authorship of an 'original work', if any) suggests the possibility of correlation between the *Yangzhou pinghua* SHUIHU story cycles to some parts of the *Shuihu zhuan* sources rather than to other parts. This question seems to await further study.

9. The estimate is based on the oral performances of Wang Shaotang in the 1950s. Two of the four cycles of his SHUIHU repertoire have been recorded in notational editions, i.e. Wu Song 1959, 1131 pp. (ca. 800,000 characters), and Song Jiang 1985, 1440 pp. (ca. 1,000,000 characters). These versions are thoroughly 'corrected', revised and considerably shortened. The seventy chapter standard edition of Shuihu zhuan (1644 edition) comprises ca. 500,000 characters (English translation ca.1600 pp.).

10. Biographical information on Wang Litang is found in Fan Fu 1979, and in the preface to Wang Litang 1989. As for her contemporaries, Li Xintang, Ren Dekun and the somewhat younger Chen Shiyong, we have some few reminiscences by Li Xintang, who was born into a storyteller family and taught by his father, only later studying the art of Wang Shaotang (Li Xintang 1992). Ren Dekun and Chen Shiyong were admitted to a special class by Wang Shaotang 1962-66.

11. My informants among Yangzhou storytellers agree that before the large scale publication of notational editions of *Yangzhou pinghua* after 1950, *jiaoben* were very scarce. Ordinary storytellers would not have the leisure to sit and write down the millions of characters of their performances. At best they would only have some

sketchy jottings of set pieces, poems and bits of dialogue, more or less the kind of notes Wang Xiaotang made for himself as a child.

12. During the hot season the fan is obligatory, and nowadays many storytellers apply the fan as a versatile prop both summer and winter. Often the storyteller has a teapot and a cup of tea at hand, too.

13. According to Wang Shaotang 1979:301 and Wang Xiaotang 1992:38 this pronunciation is rooted in the old northern *koiné*, *Zhongzhouyun* 中州韵, the basis of drama-dialogue in both Beijing opera (*Jingju* 京剧) and the *Kunqu* (昆曲) drama.

Appendix

Wu Song Fights the Tiger

Told by Wang Xiaotang

(*fangkou passage*; yuankou passage; <u>Beifang hua</u> passage)

Chai Jin accomodates guests in Henghai County
Wu Song fights a tiger on Jingyang Ridge.

When Second Brother Wu Song from Guankou had in Henghai County received news from his elder brother, he bade farewell to his lord, and went off to Yanggu District in Shandong to find his brother. He was not only one day on the road, he had marched for more than twenty days, and today he had reached the boundary of Yanggu District in Shandong. There was still more than twenty li to the city along the highway. It was in the middle of the tenth month, and now the sun was slanting towards the west.

Our hero felt hungry in his stomach and wanted to take a rest. The moment he looked up, he saw in front of him a pitch-black town. He shouldered his bundle and went in big strides: 'Ta-ta-ta-ta.....' forwards to the gate of the town, and there he stopped on his two feet. When he raised his head and looked up, he saw the wall piled up with flat bricks all the way to the roof. Here was the round city gate. Above it there was a whitewashed stone. On the whitewashed stone there was engraved three hollow characters: 'Jingyang Town'. As our hero forked his legs and entered the city gate, he saw a broad alley, neatly lined with shops on both sides. He passed by the fronts of more than ten shops, and then in the next place there was an inn, a brand-new thatched cottage with three wings. In the doorway of the shop a brand-new green bamboo-pole was stuck in, and on the green bamboo-pole a brand-new blue wine-banner was hanging. On the blue wine-banner a piece of brand-new pink paper was glued. On the pink paper were written five big brand-new characters: 'Three bowls and you cannot cross the ridge!'. When our hero glanced inside the inn, he saw a brand-new kitchenrange, a brand-new chopping-board, brand-new tables and stools, a brand-new counter and brand-new people.

Why? In this world <u>things</u> can be 'new'; can people also be 'new'? Yes! Behind the counter sat a young innkeeper, all together twenty-one or twenty-two this year. *In front of the counter stood a young waiter, Xiao'er, not yet twenty years old. The proverb says:*

Wave upon wave the Yangzi-river flows,
New people overtake the elder generation.

Just as Wu Song prepared to enter the inn, that waiter of the inn, Xiao'er, — who would have imagined it — was so eager to try out the tricks of the trade that he came forward to the door, all smiles, lifted both of his hands in salutation and looked at Wu Song:

'Oh! Yes, Sir! Do you want to take a rest in our humble inn? Millet gruel, sorghum, chicken, pancakes, steamed rolls, the food is fine and the prices are reasonable. Please, come in and have a seat, Sir!'

   'Xiao'er!'
   'Yes, Sir!'
   'Do you also have good wine in this inn?'

Oh, that was strange! Even before Wu Song entered the inn, he asked for good wine, how come? *People of former times in their daily life had four words of importance to them: wine, sex, wealth and vigour. But Wu Song only cared for two things: He was fond of drinking and he used his force on behalf of innocent people. He saw that the town was small and the inn was small, too, so he was afraid that they did not have any good wine in this inn. Therefore even before he had entered the inn, he would first ask whether they had good wine.*

'Oh! Sure, Sir! In our humble inn, we wouldn't boast about other things, but the quality of the wine is amazingly good. People from afar have given our humble inn eight verselines in praise.'

   'What eight lines?'
   'It is like jade nectar and rosy clouds, its sweet bouquet and wonderful taste is worth boasting. When a wine jug is opened, the flavour will make people tipsy three houses away. Bypassing guests will pull up their carts and rein in their horses. Lu Dongbin once payed with his famous sword, Li Bai, he pawned his black gauze hat, the immortal loved the wine so much he never went home-.'
   'Where did he go then?'
   'Drunken he tumbled into that West River embracing the moon!'
   'Good wine!'

Oh, gee! Wu Song was comforted in his heart. The wine of that inn must be extremely good. When they opened a jug, the flavour of the wine would make people tipsy three houses away. Those people wouldn't even drink the wine, just by smelling the flavour of the wine they would become drunk. Don't you think the wine of that inn was good? The immortals loved the wine so much, one lost his famous sword as a pledge, one pawned away his black gauze hat. Oh, that wine must be good. Wu Song followed Xiao'er into the inn. *They went through the front wing, passed the half-door, and came to the next wing. Oh, the roof of the hall was thatched. The tables and stools of the hall were neatly arranged, the whole place fresh and cool. But there was not one single customer. Quite right, it was already long past the lunch time rush. Wu Song took down his bundle, placed it on a bench beside him, and seated himself at a table right in the middle. Xiao'er wrought out a hot napkin for Wu Song to wipe hands and face, and brewed a pot of tea for him. Then Xiao'er stepped over besides Wu Song:*

'Master, what do you want to eat with the wine?'
'Bring me some good wine and good food, and be sure there is enough, too!'
'Ow! — Yes!'

Xiao'er turned round and off he ran.

Strange! Didn't that waiter turn out a fine Beijing accent a moment ago at the gate? Why does he afterwards begin to speak in local dialect? Oh, that was just because his inn was situated in the area of Shandong. Because there was a lot of traffic in front of the gate, people traveling from south to north, people speaking in all the southern and northern idioms. Suppose you were standing at the gate of the inn, then if you were speaking the local dialect and wanted to do some business, then some people would not be able to understand. Therefore he had studied a few sentences of Beijing accent, he had studied af few Beijing dialect sentences. But he had only learned these few sentences. If you asked him to continue speaking, he couldn't turn any more out. In that moment his fox-tail would show and he would betray himself.

Xiao'er went out in front to cut some beef, put steamed rolls on a plate, poured wine and at the same time arranged cup and chopsticks on a tray, and then carried it back to the rear wing. When he stepped into the rear wing, he placed the tray on a table beside Wu Song. Then he arranged the wine and food on the table in front of Wu Song and took away the tray. Then Xiao'er took up a position ready to serve his guest.

When Wu Song saw that the wine and food had arrived, he placed the wine cup in front of him, lifted the wine mug and: 'Sh-sh-sh...' poured himself a cup. Then he put down the wine mug, while he gave some clicks of dissatisfaction and shaked his head. 'According to Xiao'er, that wine of his inn should be very good. But I think that when I poured it down, it's colour didn't look right and it didn't have any flavour. Hm, perhaps it is no use to look at it, maybe one absolutely has to taste it. Let me try and have a sip!' Our hero lifted the wine cup. My! When he had a mouthful, it didn't have the least strength. 'Oh, that must be a joke! I must ask that waiter, Xiao'er, about it.'

> *'Xiao'er!'*
> 'Yes, Master!'
> *'Is this the good wine of your inn?'*
> 'Oh, no, no, no! This is only a medium good wine of our inn!'
> *'Don't you serve me the good wine?'*
> 'Master, if Your Honour actually wants to drink our good wine, then that is the one called 'Three bowls and you cannot cross the ridge'.
> *'Fine!'*

Oh, my! Wu Song became glad at heart. No wonder that before he entered the inn, he had seen those five characters on the wine banner of the inn: 'Three bowls and you cannot cross the ridge'. But he did not understand the meaning.

> *'What does it mean: 'Three bowls and you cannot cross the ridge'?'*
> 'Oh, Master, that is because the wine of our humble inn is very good! So if you have drunk three cups, then you will not be able to climb that ridge on the other side of our town, that ridge seven <u>li</u> from our town along the highway, called Jingyang Ridge — you will not be able to cross Jingyang Ridge, because you will be drunk from the wine. And that's why people have given this name to our inn: 'Three bowls and you cannot cross the ridge''.

武松打虎
（扬州评话《水浒·武松》选段）

王筱堂　口述

横海郡柴进留宾
景阳岗武松打虎

　　灌口二郎武松在横海郡得著哥哥消息，辞别王驾，赶奔山东阳谷县寻兄。在路非止一日，走了有二十余天，今日已抵山东阳谷县地界，离城还有二十余里大路。其时在十月中旬天气，太阳大偏西。

　　英雄腹中饥馁，意欲打尖。抬头一望，一看看见迎面是乌酣酣的一座镇市。他背著包裹，大踏步，"踏踏踏踏……"到了镇门口，两脚站定。再把头抬起来一望，只看见扁砖直砌到顶，是圆圈镇门，上头有一块白矾石，白矾石上头錾了三个凹字："景阳镇"。英雄又步进了镇门，看见街道宽阔，两边店面整齐。走了总在十几家门面，就在下首有一家酒店，三间簇崭新的草房，就在店门口敁了一根簇崭新青竹竿，青竹竿上头挑了一方簇崭新蓝布酒旗，蓝布酒旗上贴了一张簇崭新梅红纸，梅红纸上写了簇崭新五个大字："三碗不过岗"。英雄再朝店里头望了一望，只看见簇崭新锅灶，簇崭新案板，簇崭新桌凳，簇崭新柜台，簇崭新的人。啊，天下东西有新的，人还有新的吗？有的。柜台里头坐了个小老板，今年总在二十一二岁，柜台外头站了个店小二，不满二十岁，俗语云："长江后浪催前浪，世上新人赶旧人"。

　　武松才预备进店，哪晓得这个店小二做生意的门儿是一绝，笑嘻嘻地走到店门口，双手一抬，就望著武松："啊唷，是，爷，就在小店打尖吧，粟黍、高粱、鸡子、薄饼、馒首，东西又好，价钱又巧，爷请家来坐。""小二！""是，爷。""你店中还有好酒？"咦，奇怪啦，武松还没有进店咧，先问一声好酒做事呢？古时候的人呐，平生都有四个大字：酒、色、财、气。但是武松只好两个，他好贪杯，好动无辜之气。他看见镇市又小，酒店又小，怕他家家里头不得好酒吃，所以未曾进店先问一声可有好酒。"啊唷，是，爷，小店旁的东西不敢讲高，酒的身份是怪好，外人送小店八句。""哪八句？"

　　　　　　　　　"造成玉液流霞，
　　　　　　　　　香甜美味堪夸，
　　　　　　　　　开坛隔壁醉三家，
　　　　　　　　　过客停车住马。
　　　　　　　　　洞宾曾留宝剑，
　　　　　　　　　太白他当过乌纱，
　　　　　　　　　神仙爱酒都不归家，"

"他上哪儿去啦？"

　　　　　　　　　"醉倒那西江月下。"

　　"好酒！"啊唷喂，武松心里头舒服呢。他家这个酒是好极了，开坛子，这个酒香把隔壁就醉倒了三家，人家没有吃酒，闻到这个酒香就醉倒了。你说他家这个酒可好不好？神仙爱酒把个宝剑都押掉了，把乌纱都当掉了。唔，这个酒好呢。武松就跟随著小二进了店门，走前进，进腰门，到了第二进。啊，是一座草厅。厅上的桌子、板凳倒是整整齐齐，清清爽爽。一个酒客都不得。不错，已经过了中饭市了。武松把包裹朝下一抹，就朝旁边座上一放，人就朝正当中桌上一坐。小二就打了一把手巾，把武松擦擦手脸，泡了一碗茶。小二到了武松的旁边："爷驾，你吃什么酒肴？""拿好酒好肴，多拿这么一点儿。""嗄——哎！"小二掉脸就跑。奇怪罗，店小二在店门口不是玩的二八京腔吗，为什么到了后头又说土语的呢？嗳，就因为他这一片店哪，就并在个山东的地界，因为他店门口来来往往啊，都是南来北往的，南蛮北侉的人都有，你要说是如果站在店门口，就说是地方上的土语来招揽买卖，有的人就不懂，所以他呐就学了这么几句京味儿，学了几句京话，但是只学了这么几句，你叫他到后头再说呐，玩不起来了，那一来狐狸尾子就 [四] 下来了，就现相了。

小二到了前头就切了一点牛肉，装了馒首，打了酒，接逗就拿了杯筷，一托盘，就托到后进。到了后进，就把托盘朝武松旁边桌上一放，把酒肴就朝武松的桌子上一放。他把托盘收掉了。小二就站在旁边伺候。

武松看见酒肴到了，把酒杯子朝面前一拿，酒壶一起，"沙——"斟了一杯，酒壶朝下一放。武松就咂嘴摇头。照小二说起来：他 [家] 酒好得很，我看斟下来这个颜色就不对，而且香味也全无。唔，照常不中看哪，抑样中吃呐，吃吃看。英雄把酒杯子朝起一端。唉喂，"口——""咂咂咂"，唉喂，吃到嘴里头啊，一点个口力都没得。嗳，笑话笑话。我倒要来问问这个小二呢。"小二！""嗳，爷驾。""这就是你店中的好酒？""噎，噎不不不，这是我们店里的中等酒。""你不拿好酒给爷吃吗？""爷驾，你老人 [家] 要如果再要吃好酒的话，就叫'三碗不过岗'。""好！"啊唷喂，武松心里头高兴。怪不道没有进店的时候啊，就看见他家酒旗上头的五个大字"三碗不过岗"，不晓得怎么讲法。"怎么叫'三碗不过岗'？""噢噢，爷驾，因为我们小店里头酒呐，太好了，你要说是吃了三杯下去啊，我们这个镇外头啊，离镇七里大路有一座岗，叫景阳岗，你就不能跑过景阳岗了，你就吃醉了，所以这么子嘛，人家家里起了个名子，就叫'三碗不过岗'。"

Modernism and Tradition in Kawabata's Art of Fiction

Roy Starrs

Among Japanese writers from the Meiji period down to the early part of Shoowa, much drama was created out of the conflict between native tradition and Western or modern influence. Of course, to borrow a phrase from Tolstoy, each unhappy writer was unhappy in his own way, and each responded to the problem with a different level of intensity, from Oogai's Apollonian detachment to Akutagawa's neurotic obsession. As a writer who came to maturity in early Shoowa, Kawabata could learn from the experience of his elders and at first did not seem at all preoccupied with this issue. Nevertheless, when we view his career now as a whole and place it in its proper historical context, we discover that he too was not immune to this typical problem of his age; rather he embodied it in a new and somewhat more subtle and complex way. First of all, because the modern Western influence of his time took a more aggressive form — the various post-World War 1 avant-garde movements and innovations we now describe generally as modernism. Secondly, and quite surprisingly, because Kawabata managed somehow to effect a harmonious synthesis between this radical new Western modernism and certain key elements of the Japanese aesthetic and literary tradition.

Kawabata is often and quite rightly perceived as one of those modern Japanese writers who were most deeply rooted in the native literary tradition. His exquisitely imagistic or impressionistic style reminds many of *haiku*. The associative leaps in his narrative structures are frequently said to resemble those of the medieval poetic form of *renga* or linked verse. The very images which recur as symbolic or thematic motifs throughout his major works often seem quite stereotypically traditional: cherry blossoms, geisha, Mount Fuji, tea bowls, Noh masks.... The general mood of these novels too seems redolent of a traditional elegiac pathos, a *mono no aware* nostalgia. Kawabata himself encouraged this impression, especially in the wake of Japan's defeat in the

Pacific War, which, according to him, only deepened his elegiac mood and his single-minded dedication to the native tradition: 'The realization that I wrote in a Japanese style, and the determination to continue the traditions of Japanese beauty were not new for me, but perhaps I had to see the mountains and rivers of my country after it had been defeated before everything else could disappear' (Keene, 1984: 825).

No doubt he was also well aware, as his Nobel Prize acceptance speech suggests, that it was his 'traditionalism' which gave his work such great appeal to Western readers, who were, of course, delighted to find a writer who seemed so splendidly representative of the Japanese tradition and who were also, perhaps, equally delighted not to be confronted by yet another Japanese clone of Kafka or Camus. Conversely, Kawabata's sometimes stereo-typical 'Japaneseness' also accounts for his surprising (to us) unpopularity among large segments of the Japanese themselves, especially among the younger generation of *kokubungakusha* (scholars of Japanese literature). Per-haps Mishima Yukio, though an admirer of Kawabata, put his finger on the key objection when he claimed that Kawabata was totally lacking that *sine qua non* of the serious modern Japanese writer, a 'will to interpret the world' or, in the language preferred by the really serious-minded, a *Weltanschauung* (Miyoshi, 1974: 95). What this really means, of course, is not that Kawabata was totally innocent of all philosophy but that, again like a good traditional writer and unlike Mishima himself, he was never, except in a few early stories such as 'Lyric Poem', overly obvious or explicit in giving expression to his philosophy, whether in his narrative passages or by making his characters serve as mouthpieces.

While the general recognition of Kawabata's traditionalism is well-founded, then, the mistake often made is the concomitant assumption that this precludes his modernism. Since he seems such a dyed-in-the-wool tra-ditionalist, his experiments with modernist writing in the 1920's and early '30's are often regarded as a mere flirtation, an anomalous episode which had no lasting impact on the main body of his work. This seems to be the pre-ferred view of some of his Western interpreters: Donald Keene, for instance, claims that: 'For Tanizaki or Kawabata Modernism was only a passing phase in careers devoted to more traditional literature; to treat them as Modernists would be misleading, if only because their best works are not in this vein' (Keene, 1984: 631). Similarly, Gwenn Petersen categorically states that the 'true sources of Kawabata's delicate prose' are in the 'classical literature of Japan' rather than in 'supposed links with individual French writers or

European movements, or the Scandinavian literature he is said to have read in high school' (Petersen, 1979: 126). Both these statements, it seems to me, are based on a misconception and consequently underestimate the depth and persistence of Kawabata's modernism. The misconception is that modernism and traditionalism are necessarily mutually exclusive: a writer must be essentially either a traditionalist or a modernist. I would argue that, in the context of Japanese literature in particular, in which many of the 'innovations' of the modernists seem to have been broadly anticipated by traditional writers (as Kawabata himself recognized),[1] modernism and traditionalism are often mutually supportive. Thus it is sometimes difficult to discriminate between modernist and traditional elements in a given work of modern Japanese literature. Are Kawabata's freely associative interior monologues, for instance, in the tradition of the modernist writer James Joyce or of the medieval *renga* poet Soogi and random essayist Kenkoo? In a work of Kawabata's 'modernist period' such as *Crystal Fantasies* (*Suishoo gensoo*, 1931), they seem quite obviously Joycean. In a work such as *Snow Country* (*Yukiguni*, 1935-37), written just a few years later in his 'traditionalist period', they seem to belong more to the native tradition. And yet, can we assume that the fact that Kawabata experimented at one point with Joycean stream of consciousness had no relation whatsoever to the fact that, in writing *Snow Country* just a few years later, he developed his own form of this narrative technique, albeit in a more subtle and traditional way? This seems to me an extremely unconvincing assumption. What seems far more likely is that Kawabata did learn some lasting lessons from his encounter with modernism, but that, after a short period of raw influence, these lessons were adapted and absorbed into that native tradition which still survived within him in much the same way as, on a larger historical scale, foreign influences have always been absorbed and adapted by the Japanese.

Furthermore, if, as Keene argues, Kawabata's modernism was merely a 'passing phase' and his 'best works are not in this vein', why did he continue to write the often very modernistic or surrealistic prose poems called 'palm-sized stories' (*tanagokoro shoosetsu*) for the rest of his career, works which Kawabata felt, as Keene himself notes, represented the very 'essence of his art'? (Keene, 1984: 802) Certainly, by modernist standards, they are works of extremely high quality; though called 'stories' many are, in fact, haunting surrealistic prose poems of the highest order, comparable to anything produced by Breton, Reverdy or Michaux. Then again, if his modernism were merely a passing phase, we might ask why, very late in his career, Kawabata

returned to an equally surrealist or modernist mode with works such as
Sleeping Beauties (*Nemureru bijo*, 1961), 'One Arm' (*Kata ude*, 1965) and
Dandelions (*Tanpopo*, 1972)? Are not these among his 'best works?' Certainly
they are among his most interesting, and any reader with a taste for
modernist writing would be loathe to rank them any lower than the more
'traditional' works.

Kawabata began his career at a very early age in a very traditional mode:
as a writer of autobiographical fiction or *shi-shoosetsu*. These works center
largely on the sorrows of his childhood, when all the members of his immediate family died off one after the other, and on his struggles to overcome the
'orphan psychology' which resulted from this. In some ways this apprentice-
ship as a traditional 'I-novelist' may be said to have predisposed him towards
the European modernism of the 1920's. One of the main features of the modernist novel, after all, and certainly one of the features which distinguish it
from the nineteenth-century European novel, is its extreme subjectivity,
whether achieved by a Joycean stream-of-consciousness narrative or by the
author simply focusing primarily on the contents of his own psyche. In other
words, many of the Western novelists of this period also wrote 'I-novels' or
'lyrical novels', as they've been called, whose central characters could be
closely identified with the authors themselves: Joyce, Proust, Gide, Lawrence,
Woolf, Fitzgerald, Hemingway, to name just a few of the major examples.[2]

The Twenties of this century, which were also Kawabata's twenties (he
was born in 1899), were an exciting time for a young writer to be exploring
the possibilities of his art, in Japan as in the West. It was an age conspicuous
for its adventurous, experimental spirit, when all the old moral and aesthetic
values seemed discredited and a new aesthetic movement or 'ism' seemed to
be inaugurated almost every day: among the more lasting ones, Dadaism,
Surrealism, Expressionism, Futurism and Proletarianism. All these 'movements' had Japanese exponents, in literature as in the visual arts. Whereas in
the West it was primarily the cataclysm of the First World War which had
caused such a total and radical break with the past, in Japan the devastation
wrought by the Great Kantoo Earthquake of 1923 seemed to accomplish much
the same purpose or, at least, to make the younger writers more receptive to
the Western avant-garde. As Odagiri Susumu points out, expanding upon a
suggestion first made by Akutagawa Ryuunosuke, a new radicalism arose in
the Japanese literary world after the earthquake, as if a cultural upheaval had
followed the geological one (Odagiri, 1965: 23 et passim). This 'radicalism'
formed itself naturally into two main streams, one political, the Marxist-

oriented 'Proletarian Literature' movement, and the other aesthetic, the Modernism of the *'shin kankaku ha'* or 'Neo-sensory School', to which Kawabata belonged.

Besides the immediate 'stimulus' of the earthquake, however, there is another, more long-term historical factor which should be taken into account. Kawabata's generation, those writers born around the turn of the century and who came to maturity in the Twenties, were the 'third generation' of modern Japanese novelists — that is, novelists who wrote, to some extent, under the influence of Western literature. Writers of this 'generation of 1900', compared to previous generations, were much less conversant with the Chinese classics and much more familiar with the full range of Western literature, if only by way of the many translations which had by then appeared. It is also true, of course, that by their time the general 'Westernization' or 'modernization' of Japanese culture had progressed apace, so that cultural products of the West were bound to seem less alien to them than they had seemed to earlier gene-rations. Thus they were able to absorb Western influences more naturally, with less tension, than earlier writers, and also to turn these influences more self-confidently to their own purposes, even to the extent of adapting them more to native tastes.

Where does Kawabata himself fit within this overall context? In many ways he is typical of his generation. Indeed, he soon became one of its principal spokesmen: as a literary theorist and critic, writing manifestoes to justify the new techniques and new vision of himself and his fellow 'Neo-sensory' writers. In 1924 he was one of the founding members of the magazine, *Bungei jidai* (*Literary Age*). Indeed, he chose its name, optimistically hoping to signify by it that the world was now passing from a 'religious age to a literary age', and that literature would now serve as an instrument of salvation as religion had done in the past, in this agreeing with Mathew Arnold's prediction of the previous century. In January of the following year, 1925, he wrote a Neo-sensory School manifesto for the same magazine, entit-ling it, quite grandly: 'An Explication of the New Tendencies of the Avant-Garde Writers', in which, calling for a new immediacy of expression in the language of novels, he draws for support on dadaist theories of free associa-tion (psychic automatism) and German expressionist theories of the primacy of the artist's subjectivity.

In the second half of the Twenties, he continued in his critical role as apologist of modernism. This was the period in which Japanese readers were introduced to the really substantial achievements of the European avant-garde, as opposed to the many eccentric 'isms' of the immediate post-war years. After the demise of the *Bungei jidai* in 1927, Kawabata, besides writing a long series of reviews of current literature for the *Bungei shunjuu* (*Literary Chronicle*), served on the editorial board of a new literary magazine, *Bungaku* (*Literature*, 1929-), which published translations of Proust, Joyce, Breton, Mann and other contemporary European authors.

The novella *Crystal Fantasies* is generally regarded as the most notable creative product of Kawabata's 'modernist' or 'experimental' period. Indeed, Japanese literary historians have emphasized the work's general historical importance as a uniquely successful adaptation of a Western modernist technique — Joyce's 'stream-of-consciousness' — by a Japanese writer of the 'experimental' age of the late Twenties and early Thirties. Nakamura Shinichiroo, for instance, claims that, of all the many 'experimental' works which were produced by young Japanese writers under the influence of the post-World War One Western avant-garde, *Crystal Fantasies* is the only one which survives today as a kind of 'memorial' of that movement (Nakamura, 1974: 118). Similarly, Isogai Hideo claims that *Crystal Fantasies* remains as *the* representative work written under the influence of the so-called 'New Psychologism', though the movement itself was initiated largely by Itoo Sei, one of the early translators of Joyce and a well-known novelist in his own right (Isogai, 1969: 112). Despite the vast amount of time and energy he expended in trying to become the Japanese Joyce, Itoo himself was never able to develope, as Donald Keene says, a 'valid Modernist idiom' (Keene, 1984: 667). This was accomplished, with apparently much less effort, by his friend Kawabata.

Despite its occasional awkwardnesses and its incompleteness (Kawabata never finished it), *Crystal Fantasies* is indeed remarkably successful in using a freely associative stream-of-consciousness technique to reveal a woman's psychology in depth and to portray the problematic nature of male/female relations. Kawabata's presentation of the goings-on in the wife's mind, the memories, thoughts and reactions which reveal her personal history and her inner nature, is not as unremittingly direct as Joyce's presentation of Molly Bloom's mental activity in the long interior monologue which concludes *Ulysses*. To some extent this is merely a difference in scale, but also, by intermingling passages of pure stream-of-consciousness with passages of more conventional third-person narrative and dialogue, Kawabata is able to more objectively present certain external stimuli which set in motion the interior monologues. There are mainly four of these: a mirror, a dog, her husband and a young lady visitor, each of which takes on a particular symbolic significance in the woman's mind. The story is thus structured in an almost fugue-like manner as a contrapuntal interplay between external stimuli and interior monologue.

In the first of the story's three 'scenes' or 'movements', the mirror is the main stimulus both of the wife's thoughts and of her dialogue with her husband. It is the 'crystal' reflecting her thoughts and fantasies, a true 'mirror of the heart', and it also protects her against reality, especially reality in the form of her husband since, as we are told, she talks only to his reflection in the mirror, not to the 'real man'. Indeed, what is reflected in the mirror is also the major topic of their conversation to begin with. The mirror has three sides, and the left-hand side reflects the glass roof of a cage for small animals used for experiments by her husband, an embryologist. Their dialogue begins with the wife's claim that their 'extravagant' purchase of the mirror is justified because it will enable her to be 'forever looking at the garden's sperms and eggs' (i.e., in the embryological cage), implying that this might help her to become fertile. The narrator comments on the 'tragedy bottled up within these words', betraying a Freudian influence on Kawabata here: the idea that even in our jokes we unconsciously reveal our deepest anxieties. Freudian theory was, of course, very much a part of the intellectual background of modernism, and *Crystal Fantasies* is one of Kawabata's most obviously 'Freudian' stories. At any rate, through the agency of the mirror, we are quickly introduced to this couple's 'tragedy', the main irritant and alienating force between them: their infertility.

The narrator then tells us that the wife was 'unaware of the slight strangeness of her words' because she had become absorbed in another reflection in the mirror: that of the blue sky. This beautiful reflection precipitates her first stream-of-consciousness:

Small birds falling like silver stones through the blue sky. Sailing vessels fleeing like silver arrows freed from the sea. Fish darting like silver needles through a lake. (Kawabata, 1975: 328)

This rather *renga*-like stream of images may first seem to have no relation whatever to the previously mentioned 'tragedy', but on closer inspection one notices that each one of these images suggests the sudden, darting movement of ejaculated sperm. Kawabata, following Freud, shows how even a seemingly random stream of images arising spontaneously from the depths of the woman's mind betrays what troubles and obsesses her. Thus, the narrator tells us, the images make her feel 'cold' and 'lonely' because, of course, they remind her of her childlessness and of her consequent alienation from her husband.

Though the wife may have desired the mirror as an 'extravagant' indulgence of her narcissism, it turns out, then, to function also as a kind of Freudian 'reality principle', reflecting certain uncomfortable truths about her condition, especially her infertility and estrangement from her husband. Her infertility is given ironic emphasis by the fact that she is an embryologist's wife and a gynecologist's daughter. Indeed, there is actually a causal relationship here: as the story evolves it turns out that her infertility is both caused by and symbolical of the life-destroying sterility of modern science and technology, as embodied in both her husband and her father.

Towards the story's end she even suggests to her husband that, since she wants nothing more to do with 'pipettes' — that is, with artificial insemination he might try 'ectogenesis' (using the Aristotelian term) or, to use the modern term, a test-tube baby. He might thus be able to produce a child entirely from his own sperm, a modern scientific version of the mythical 'virgin birth', what she calls 'this dream of being able to produce, in chastity, a child of the father's without any admixture of the mother's blood'. Science here seems to create an ultimate expression of narcissism and alienation.

Unlike many of Kawabata's later and more traditional works, *Crystal Fantasies* does not end with any comforting monistic resolution, such as an experience of mystical union with nature. It remains an uncompromising and highly sophisticated study of the psychology of alienation. Alienation, of course, was probably the modernist theme *par excellence*, and readers by now may be tired of hearing of it. But in this work Kawabata handles the theme already in his own distinctive manner, with his own considerable delicacy of touch. The skill and subtlety with which the painful interactions of husband and wife are depicted, with all the complex nuances of their mutual dislikes, the powerfully convincing evocation of the wife's psychic turmoil, and the brilliant interplay of a whole range of still-urgent contemporary themes — scientific, psychological, philosophical and even religious — which touch upon the central theme of alienation, make this relatively short work seem a marvel of compressed modernist writing at its best.

Looking back, then, over this 'modernist phase' of Kawabata's career, one's first reaction might well be one of wonder that this supposedly very traditional writer was so successful in his modernist experiments — as if, indeed, he were a 'born modernist'. *Crystal Fantasies* is both impressively modernist in technique and also startlingly up-to-date in its imagery and themes. Indeed, it almost seems to belong more to our own time than to the early 1930's, dealing, in its brief compass, with topics such as artificial insemination, test-tube babies, the dehumanization of life by science and even, less directly, male oppression and exploitation of women. Looking back at it from our present perspective, the work seems to take on an almost prophetic air.

Given the fact that Kawabata made such a very good showing as a modernist, then, one's second reaction might well be regret that he soon (by the mid-Thirties) apparently 'retreated', so to speak, back to more traditional methods and themes, no longer confronted with such originality and vigor the challenges and problems of the contemporary world, but seemed to retire into the comforting cocoon of the Japanese past, with its long-established themes and conventions and its general mood of nature-loving serenity. In literary terms, this could be described as a 'retreat' from modernist realism back to a traditional romanticism which some may regard as sheer escapism. From this perspective, the dilettante Shimamura, the hero of *Snow Country*, the first major work of this new 'conservative' period, might be seen as an apt symbol of such retreat and escapism: the snow country itself is a kind of idyllic dream world where traditional aesthetics still prevail, in contrast to the modernist urban nightmare of the Tokyo from whence he comes. If one were politically or historically minded, one might even see Kawabata's 'retreat' as part of the general conservative nationalism, the anti-foreign 'back to Japan' movement, of the late Thirties.

But before we express too much regret, perhaps we should consider two questions: firstly, did Kawabata really abandon everything he had learned from modernism when he embarked on a more traditional phase of writing? Secondly, what did he gain by this return to tradition?

Kawabata's period of writing in a more traditional vein would last for about twenty years, from the mid 1930's to the mid 1950's — in other words, the period of his ripe maturity, his 'golden age', during which he produced those works generally regarded as his masterpieces, works of the calibre of *Snow Country*, *Thousand Cranes* (*Sembazuru*, 1952) and *The Sound of the Mountain* (*Yama no oto*, 1954).

In what sense are these works 'traditional'? Apart from the obvious, surface level of the frequent use of a traditional poetic imagery, his famous 'haiku style', some critics have professed to find a deeper, structural affinity between these novels and certain genres of traditional Japanese literature, especially *renga* or linked verse.

Both Japanese and Western critics have noted certain *renga*-like features in Kawabata's narrative art. The most prominent translator of his works into English, Edward Seidensticker, has written about *Snow Country*:

It is quite obvious that Kawabata cannot have known where he was going when he started to write, any more than a group of poets know where they are going when they sit down to compose a *renga* sequence. The first chapter was intended to be a short story, and the last chapter is based on an actual event that had not yet happened when the writing was begun.

The narrative element in *Snow Country* is slight at best, having to do with an affair between a Tokyo dilettante and a hot-spring geisha, and at one point Kawabata breaks it off completely to give us an extended prose lyric about silk weaving (Seidensticker, 1979: 119).

Yamamoto Kenkichi similarly has pointed out that Kawabata's habit of writing a novel as it was being serialized, chapter by chapter, in various literary magazines, so that each chapter was semi-independent, may also account for the *renga*-like structure of the work as a whole, since *renga* poets also write verse by verse. Just as each verse in a *renga* sequence may be enjoyed either on its own or in relation to either the preceding or succeeding verse, so each chapter of a Kawabata novel may either stand alone as a kind of short story or be related to the whole group of such 'stories' or chapters which comprise the entire novel (Yamamoto, 1957: 318). Nakamura Mitsuo goes even one step further than this, claiming that the structure of a Kawabata novel is as divisible as that of an earthworm: you may cut it up into any number of parts and each part will be able to survive on its own — a graphic albeit not a very flattering analogy (Nakamura, 1978: 189).

Interesting as they are, these comments are all made merely 'in passing' and relate only in a very general way to the structure of Kawabata's narratives. Can there really be any deep affinity between two such apparently disparate forms of literary art, which seem as remote from each other in intention as they are in time, a modern fictional narrative and a classical poetic tradition of highly formal, even rigid conventions? Earl Miner describes *renga* as 'plotless narrative', but this seems to beg the question: one understands why a series of random images should be called 'plotless' but in what sense does it form a narrative? (Miner, 1979: 5) There do seem to be some narrative elements in the overall structure of *renga*: for example, a basic *jo-ha-kyuu* structure as in *noo*, and a rhythmic pacing of highpoints and lowpoints, but this is a highly artificial, impersonal structure, externally imposed and governed by a great number of inflexible rules; it is not, like the narrative structure of a modern novel, the personal creation of an individual artist which grows organically from his peculiar world-view. It is a purely formal rather than a thematic or narrative structure in the true sense.

Are we to say, then, that there is absolutely no relation between narrative and *renga*? This does not seem quite true either. Why is there an explicit prohibition in the rules of *renga* against any direct continuity of meaning beyond two verses of the series (usually a hundred verses)? Is it not for the very reason that *renga* aims to frustrate the natural narrative tendency of the human mind, the tendency to develop images or ideas in a logical, linear series or, in the specific *renga* context, the natural tendency of one poet to continue developing the nascent story or thought of the previous poet? Thus *renga* does have a definite relation with narrative but it is an adversary one; it may be characterized properly not as 'plotless narrative' but as 'anti-narrative'. If one were to look for a philosophical basis for this seemingly unique and 'modernistic' stance of *renga*, one need look no further than the Zen Buddhism which was a dominant cultural influence in the age which gave rise to this art. By cutting off rational, linear thinking, and its concomitant sense of the continuity of an individual ego through a continuum of time, *renga*, like Zen, sought to realize the moment-to-moment enjoyment of the unbound consciousness. Or, to put this in more strictly literary terms, by turning the reader's attention away from narrative development, *renga* is able to focus it on the random flow of poetic imagery which, as Konishi Jin'ichi asserts, constitutes its principal beauty (Konishi, 1975: 29-61). Konishi describes *renga* as a 'symphony of images' (Konishi, 1975: 45) and goes on to say that: 'Each verse taken either singly, or as linked with either the preceding or succeeding verse, has its specific semantic value, and these values are part of the pleasure of *renga*. But the essence of *renga* is the essentially *meaningless* pattern of images.' Furthermore: 'It is in the orchestration of simple images that the beauty of *renga* lies' (Konishi, 1975: 47).

There are some obvious general parallels here with the art of Kawabata, any of whose novels might also be well described as a 'symphony of images', but underlying this surface level of imagery a philosophic affinity can also be found. One critic, Katoo Shuuichi, has described the metaphysics implicit in Kawabata's style as *setsunashugi*, a term difficult to render in English (ephemeralism?) but implying a consciousness that human existence is only moment to moment and is lacking in any continuous identity (Katoo, 1976: 190). Thus Kawabata's works are redolent with the traditional aesthetic sentiment of *mono no aware*, but it arises not only from a sense of the transitoriness of perceived objects but also of the perceiving subject. Just as, in *renga*, there is no sustained continuity of narrative voice but rather what Donald Keene has called 'a multiple stream of consciousness' (Keene, 1955: 315), so in Kawabata what I would call the moments of 'narrative stasis' have the effect of a sudden break in the ego-centered consciousness of the central character. A striking example of this occurs, for instance, in the final, climactic scene of *Snow Country*, in which Shimamura loses all sense of self and is described as being filled with and overwhelmed by the Milky Way.

Perhaps the point could be made more graphic by a reference to the Japanese theatrical arts, for anti-narrative 'resistance to time' is by no means confined to *renga* alone in traditional Japanese culture. One finds it, for instance, in *noo* and even in the popular art-form of *kabuki*: most conspicuously, in both the *noo kata* and the *kabuki mie* there is a sudden stoppage of the narrative flow as the actor assumes a motionless pose. As with Kawabata's moments of narrative stasis, such theatrical moments give a sense of timelessness and also a strong intuition of a kind of Zen-style 'emptiness': the sudden arrest of the action reveals the illusory nature of all that is happening on the stage. (In Kawabata's case, of course, the 'action' is not so much external and physical, as on the stage, but within the mind of the viewpoint character: it is the linear flow of his thoughts that is suddenly cut off, giving a sense of the illusory nature of his ego's continuity.)

As suggested by the example already given from *Snow Country*, however, these moments of stasis also have their positive side: as the sense of the presence of man as an individual identity lessens, the sense of the presence of objects, especially of natural and aesthetic objects, greatly increases. It is as if, once a vacuum is created within man, it is filled immediately by the presence of nature or, to a lesser extent, by the presence of art. This parallels the aspect of *renga* already mentioned: with the cutting off of narrative progression comes an increased awareness of the random flow of images. Interestingly enough, one also finds a similar trade-off in the *chosisme* of the *nouveaux romanciers* of the 1950's and '60's: by reducing the presence of man — that is, by explicitly refusing to create well-rounded characters in the traditional sense — they too sought to increase the presence of objects, and the 'new objectivity' which resulted was one of their most often-avowed goals (see Robbe-Grillet, 1963, and Baque, 1972).

Objects, both natural and artificial, do loom unusually large in Kawabata's works, and the more so as we approach his last writings. By the time of the brilliant, slightly pornographic story, *Sleeping Beauties*, even human beings have become objects: the drugged girls whom Eguchi, the old man, spends the night with, exist only as physical presences for him; given the state they are in, they are not even allowed the possibility of individual identity. In the surrealistic fantasy, 'One Arm', which could be regarded as a kind of companion piece to *Sleeping Beauties*, woman's body is so objectified that her limbs may be detached at will, as if she were no more than a doll. Again, Kawabata's interest in pornography as an extreme form of the objectification of human beings is also shared by *nouveaux romanciers* such as Robbe-Grillet, whose *Maison de rendez-vous*, for instance, has some obvious affinities with *Sleeping Beauties*.

But, of course, unlike *renga*, Kawabata's works are not simply a 'symphony of images'. They are novels of a sort, and so they do, in the end, have stories to tell. And, paradoxical as this may seem, even their so-called 'anti-narrative' elements contribute ultimately to the telling of these stories. Or perhaps we might say that Kawabata's stories are structured upon the tension between narrative and anti-narrative elements, between the oppressive everyday sequential time of the conventional novel and the freedom and timelessness of lyric poetry.

It is a dialectic which would be easily recognizable to many European modernists — Proust in particular. For the anti-narrative impulse is by no means unknown in the modernist novel; in fact, as Joseph Frank pointed out long ago, it is one of its defining characteristics. In his seminal essay of 1945, Frank traced what he called 'the spatialization of form in the modern novel' back to the country fair scene of *Madame Bovary*, in which Flaubert, working against the chronological order of the narrative, tried to attain effects of simultaneity by juxtaposing words and sounds heard in several different places at the same time. As Flaubert himself said: 'Everything should sound simultaneously; one should hear the bellowing of the cattle, the whisperings of the lovers and the rhetoric of the officials all at the same time' (Frank, 1952: 43). Of course, given the sequential nature of language, this is a practical impossibility, but Flaubert attempts at least to approach this effect by interrupting the time-flow of the narrative and juxtaposing simultaneous events. The method depends, as Frank says, on the 'continual reference and cross-reference of images and symbols which must be referred to each other spatially throughout the time-act of reading' (Frank, 1952: 54).

Frank goes on to demonstrate how this method was taken up later by modernist writers, both poets and novelists, who were also interested in overcoming the limitations of chronological narrative. Joyce, for instance, applied it on a massive scale in *Ulysses* to try to represent all the simultaneous goings-on in a single Dublin day. Proust, however, offers the closest parallel to Kawabata, because he found the perfect theme to fit this innovative form: like many of Kawabata's central characters, Marcel is obsessed with a longing somehow to transcend everyday chronological time, to escape into the timeless realm with its promise of complete spiritual freedom.

It hardly seems coincidental, then, that shortly after being exposed to these European modernists, and making his own quite successful versions of modernist writing, Kawabata should continue to use the same techniques of juxtaposition and spatial form even in his more 'traditional' novels. The famous train window scene which opens *Snow Country* is a perfect symbol of this very method: Yoko's eye reflected in the train window superimposed on a fire in the passing landscape, and Komako's image superimposed on Yoko's (that is, memories of the past superimposed on experiences of the present). To take another major example from the plot structure of the whole novel: Shimamura visits the snow country three times over the course of a couple of years, and each time he notices that Komako has aged slightly. It is mainly by the juxtaposition of the images of these three 'different' Komakos that Shimamura and the reader is made to feel the *mono no aware* pathos of the young geisha's gradual aging. Proust uses exactly the same technique to express his own obsession with passing time.

One might also note that these spatializing techniques meant to achieve effects of anti-narrative or supra-narrative simultaneity: juxtaposition, super-imposition, montage, etc., are characteristically cinematic, and, of course, the new art of cinema was another major influence on modernist writing. Kawabata too undoubtedly felt this influence, as his work clearly shows. Indeed, during his modernist twenties, he even wrote the scenario of a surrealistic film called *A Mad Page* (*Kurutta ichi pêji*, 1926) which depicts the delusions of mental patients — a theme he would return to many years later in his very last work, *Dandelions*. *A Mad Page* itself is now celebrated as Japan's first avant-garde film and is all the more significant because it was not only scripted by Kawabata but directed by Kinugasa Teinosuke (1896-

1982), a leading figure of the Japanese cinema, at the beginning of his long career (see Satoo, 1982: 8, 57).

Finally, the question might arise: given Kawabata's remarkable success in harmonizing traditional and modern elements in his work, should we conclude, then, that he did not suffer at all, like earlier Japanese writers, from any sense of cultural conflict, that there was no dialectical tension in his life and work between the modern and the traditional or the Western and the Eastern? Not quite. Although modernity and tradition were not always polar opposites for Kawabata, and often seemed quite complementary, nevertheless there is a significant overall difference in tone or mood between his modernist and his more traditional works. This becomes obvious if we compare works such as *Crystal Fantasies* and 'One Arm' with works such as *Snow Country* and *The Sound of the Mountain*. A significant hint as to the meaning of this difference may be taken from Kawabata's Nobel Prize acceptance speech. At the very end of the speech, after having evoked at length the paradisal, monistic vision of traditional Japanese poetry and Zen, he says: 'We have here the emptiness, the nothingness, of the Orient. My own works have often been described as works of emptiness, but it is not to be taken for the nihilism of the West. The spiritual foundation would seem to be quite different' (Kawabata, 1968: 41). And, earlier in the same speech, he defines this 'Oriental emptiness' in his favorite monistic terms: 'This is not the nothingness or the emptiness of the West. It is rather the reverse, a universe of the spirit in which everything communicates freely with everything, transcending bounds, limitless' (Kawabata, 1968: 56). Like Sôseki before him, Kawabata believed that modern Western civilization led ultimately to alienation and nihilism, whereas Eastern tradition encouraged a paradisal monistic ideal of union between man and man and man and nature. Sôseki ended his life preaching a return to the tradition of *sokuten kyoshi* (follow Heaven and forsake the self). What about Kawabata? Despite what he said in his Nobel speech, not all his works present a comforting vision of Oriental spirituality. As already indicated, a modernist work such as *Crystal Fantasies* presents rather a bleak nihilistic vision of irredeemable alienation. This is perhaps the deepest reason why, to return to an earlier question, Kawabata turned away from modernism in his middle age — it was not just an aesthetic nor certainly just a political choice. And in his middle age he seems to have gained as much psychologically as aesthetically from this return to tradition. His old age, though, was not a happy one. Suffering from severe insomnia, addicted to that ultimate symbol of modern alienation, the sleeping pill, it seems that the consolations of the traditional culture were no longer enough for him. Thus his powerful return to modernism and to a bleak nihilistic vision in his final stories. It was a nihilism every bit as unrelieved as Mishima's. And, though he condemned Mishima's suicide in 1970, tragically he followed his protégé in this too just two years later.

References

Baque, Francois (1972): *Le nouveau roman*. Paris: Bordas.

Frank, Joseph (1952): 'Spatial Form in the Modern Novel', in Aldridge, John W., *Critiques and Essays on Modern Fiction 1920-51*. New York: Ronald Press.

Isogai Hideo (1969): 'Suishoo gensoo', in Hasegawa, Izumi, *Kawabata Yasunari sakuhin kenkyuu* (*Studies of the Work of Kawabata Yasunari*). Tokyo: Yagi Shoten.

Katoo Shuuichi (1976): 'Saraba Kawabata Yasunari' (Farewell, Kawabata Yasunari), in *Gendai no naka no rekishi* (History in Modern Times). Tokyo: Shinchoosha.

Kawabata Yasunari (1968): *Utsukushii Nippon no watakushi* (Japan the Beautiful and Myself), translated by Edward G. Seidensticker. Tokyo: Kodansha.

Kawabata Yasunari (1975): *Suishoo gensoo* (Crystal Fantasies), in *Kawabata Yasunari shuu* (Selected Works of Kawabata Yasunari), pp. 328-47. Tokyo: Chikuma Shoboo.

Keene, Donald (1955): *Anthology of Japanese Literature*. New York: Grove Press.

Keene, Donald (1984): *Dawn to the West. Japanese Literature in the Modern Era. Fiction*. New York: Holt, Rinehart and Winston.

Konishi Jin'ichi (1975): 'The Art of Renga' in *Journal of Japanese Studies*, Autumn, pp.29-61.

Miner, Earl (1979): *Japanese Linked Poetry*. Princeton: Princeton University Press.

Miyoshi Masao (1974): *Accomplices of Silence: The Modern Japanese Novel*. Berkeley: University of California Press.

Nakamura Mitsuo (1978): *Kawabata Yasunari*. Tokyo: Chikuma Shoboo.

Nakamura Shin'ichiroo (1974): *Kono hyakunen no shoosetsu* (Novels of the Past Century). Tokyo: Shinchoosha.

Odagiri Susumu (1965): *Shoowa bungaku no seiritsu* (The formation of Shoowa literature). Tokyo: Keisoo Shoboo.

Petersen, Gwenn Boardman (1979): *The Moon in the Water. Understanding Tanizaki, Kawabata, and Mishima*. Honolulu: The University Press of Hawaii.

Robbe-Grillet, Alain (1963): *Pour un nouveau roman*. Paris: Les Editions de Minuit.

Satoo Tadao (1982): *Currents in Japanese Cinema*. Tokyo: Kodansha.

Seidensticker, Edward (1979). *This Country, Japan*. Tokyo: Kodansha International.

Takeda Katsuhiko (1981): 'Yasunari no sotsugyoo rombun' (Yasunari's Graduation Thesis), in *Koei no aishuu* (The Sorrow of the Shadow of Loneliness), vol. 10 of *Kawabata Yasunari kenkyuu soosho* (Library of Kawabata Yasunari Research). Tokyo: Kyooiku Shuppan Sentaa.

Yamamoto Kenkichi (1957): 'Kaisetsu' (Commentary), in Kawabata, Yasunari, *Yama no oto* (The Sound of the Mountain). Tokyo: Shinchoosha.

Notes

1. As early as 1924, in the thesis he wrote to graduate in Japanese literature from Tokyo Imperial University, *A Short Essay on the History of the Japanese Novel* (*Nihon shoosetsu-shi shooron*), Kawabata already found precedents for the subjective focus of the modern novel in such classical Japanese prose genres as the *monogatari* (tale), *nikki* (diary) and *zuihitsu* (essay). See Takeda 1981:7-26.
2. See Ralph Freedman, *The Lyrical Novel* (Princeton University Press, 1963).

Confronting Time: Aspects of Temporality in some Recent Chinese Prose

Anne Wedell-Wedellsborg

> When one has thus
> perfected oneself in
> the art of forgetting
> and the art of remembering,
> then one is able to play
> shuttlecock with the
> whole of existence.
> (Kierkegaard: *Either/Or*.
> The Aesthetician.)

As Chinese literature is moving fast into the mid-nineties, splitting into many layers and directions, increasingly influenced by commercialization and with a small avant-garde group of writers and critics trying to keep up with contemporary international currents of postmodernism, it may be time to consider some of the fiction written in the 1980s, when Western modernism was the main item on the literary agenda. Already in the 1920s and 1930s, modernism was introduced into China, but for various social and historical reasons it never caught on. It was not until the mid-eighties that the broad encounter and confrontation between Chinese writers and 20th century masters such as Kafka, Virginia Woolf, Proust, Joyce, Faulkner, etc., took place. Unfortunately the encounter was in some cases only indirect, and a result of the symbiotic relationship that exists between writers and critics in the literary milieu. Western works, creative and theoretical, would be swallowed haphazardly in big chunks by eager young critics, only to be thrown up undigested by aspiring writers. However, to a number of the best writers of the recent decade, the encounter with the narrative techniques and spiritual content of Western modernist literature has opened up new and original ways of coming to terms with the predicament of modernity. This essay addresses the question of how memory and the concept of time, so central to Western modernist writing, has been expressed in China in some of the fiction of the 1980s.[1]

1.

If we look back on what is perceived as aesthetic modernity in the West, epitomized in high modernism, the emergence of a new time-concept was of central importance. Speaking in very broad terms we may say that already by the mid 19th century something had happened to the historical momentum and sense of coherence so that the linear time-complex, predominant since the renaissance, had begun to be disrupted. At the turn of the century the conception of a single, universal and chronologically progressing linear time was further undermined by theories of William James, Henri Bergson and Freud which all, from different perspectives, emphasized the subjective dimension of the time experience. By then an irreversible split had already occurred between the perception of modernity as a stage in the historical progress of Western civilization, and modernity as an aesthetic concept. In the modernist art movement this split turned into downright hostility and the textual subversion of exterior linear time became one of the basic tenets of literary modernism.[2]

It was especially the idea of time as a state of consciousness, expounded by Henri Bergson, which deeply influenced many writers.[3] In Bergson's analysis there are two temporal modes: the exterior, or abstract time which is that of convention, of history and the social dimension, that which the 'I' has in common with others. That kind of time is negatively valorized, whereas interior or concrete time, in Bergson's view, is the original, real time. This is 'duration' (la durée) in which memory exerts the crucial function of tying together past, present and future in a continuous flow. Therefore time as actually experienced is characterized by internal difference — the repetition of something can never be the same because one has always 'lived in the meantime' (vecu dans l'intervalle).

The basic dichotomy of the modern time experience and its textual representation has been recognized by many later philosophers and theorists and explored from highly sophisticated angles.[4] But in terms of influence on creative writing, none of these have had the direct impact that Bergson had in the early part of the 20th century. In the literary movement of modernism it was also reflected in the paradoxical duplicity of its time-concept: on the one hand Western modernist literature is characterized by its insistence on being always up-to-date, involved in the ever changing present. On the other hand it, more than any previous literary 'ism', recognizes the constant presence of the subjective past in the mind of each person. As is well known, this new notion of time and memory was accompanied by drastic changes in narrative technique and textual structure. Most evidently in the technique of stream-of-consciousness, which, in its imitation of the inner flow of impressions and reminiscences, demonstrates how the individual's response to every new event is at the same time conditioned by the private past. The strong subjectivity of Western modernist fiction (and poetry) thus privileges private memory over the larger cultural/historical, either by simply excluding the latter or by viewing it solely through the filter of individual consciousness.[5]

In early modern Chinese literature the problematic connection between temporal and psychological issues was circumscribed by the specific social conditions in which this literature arose, and therefore much more closely linked to the larger issues of nation/culture/politics than its Western counterpart.[6] As Leo Oufan Lee has shown, the early Chinese concept of modernity was defined as a mode of consciousness in which time and history move together in unilinear progress. This dynamism, influenced by Darwinian evolutionary thought, was manifested among May Fourth and post-May Fourth intellectuals in their view of the ego's active fusion with the forward tide of — history.[7] This sense of time has strong resemblance to the post-renaissance view in the West. Leo Lee argues that the crucial point of difference between China and the West was that the Chinese writers in the early part of this century, 'did not choose to separate the two domains of historical and aesthetic modernity in their pursuit of a modern mode of consciousness and modern forms of literature'.[8]

Interestingly, Bergson was actually well-known in China in the 1920s and exerted quite a strong influence on philosophers like Li Shicen, Carsun Chang and Zhang Dongsun. But it seems that he was mainly interpreted as an evolutionist thinker, stressing the concept of a unilinear forward flow of time from past through the present to the future. Bergson's ideas about concrete, interior time, as opposed to abstract, exterior time, did not catch on the way they did in the West.[9]

2.

Although the privileging of interior subjective time in the narrative is certainly found in works by writers such as Lu Xun and Yu Dafu, Shen Congwen and others, as well as in those of the 'new perceptionists' (xin ganjuepai) Shi Zhecun, Liu Na'ou, Mu Shiying and others, who have recently received renewed interest both in China and abroad, the main trend of Chinese literature in the twentieth century is of a different vein.[10] With the embracing of realism and later social realism most Chinese writers readily acknowledged the primacy of the exterior time concept. After 1949 this tendency became even more prominent and it is hard to imagine anything more linear and more adhering to a social, exterior time structure than for example the land reform novels of the 1950s, 1960s and 1970s.

By contrast, the 1980s rural novels by Mo Yan and others, while mostly adhering to the linear progress of temporal events, nevertheless, through the subjectivity of the narrative voice and the manipulation of individual memories, manage to demonstrate the force of the individual time concept. And this brings me to my main argument: the temporal dichotomy emblematic of Western modernity is also to be found in Chinese fiction of the last 10-15 years. But in the best of contemporary Chinese fiction it seems to be primarily conceived of as a split between private and collective memories. The conflict between interior subjective time and exterior social time, rather than being expressed as a dilemma of temporality in the present, is often explicitly played out in the mental realm and structural framework of remembrance.

Thus it would seem that in the literature of the last fifteen years we have been witnessing a tremendous movement towards a recuperation of the private past. In a vast number of novels and short stories published through the 1980s, the unique memory of the individual character stands out as a prominent feature governing the thematic content, and/or acting as a structural principle on the textual level. Across the diversity of stylistic approaches, from imitations of stream-of-consciousness to the semi-historical fiction of the late 1980s, the retrieval of the private past has functioned as one of the primary means of constituting identity. This process towards regaining subjectivity has, however, been going on simultaneously with, and in interaction with, a radical re-evaluation of what may be termed the larger, collective memory of China, whether in the form of inquiry into the national culture, or in the form of re-examinations of the recent political past. It is the complicated relationship between these two 'types' of memory, the 'big' one and the 'small' one, which is the underlying — and unresolved — issue in some of the more interesting fiction of the recent period.

The specific interaction involved in the recuperation of the private memory and the rewriting of the collective one, has been approached from highly differing angles. At the one end of the spectrum we find writers whose primary concern is to incorporate the individual memory into another, larger context — however different this may be from the official vision of history/culture — thus attempting to merge the individual and the common space of remembrance. These are the majority. At the other end are those (few) who seem to reject anything outside the private memory as inauthentic and unreliable, focusing on the exploration of the past from a purely subjectivist angle. For instance, it would seem that two such disparate trends as the 'shanghen wenxue' (scar literature) of the late 1970s and the 'xungen wenxue' (root-searching literature) of the mid 1980s could both be interpreted in terms of their efforts to negotiate a new relationship between personal memories and a redefined conception of national memory. By contrast, I find in Bei Dao´s prose (from about the same time as scar literature) one of the few consistent commitments to the solitary individual remembrance as the only valid one.[11]

The introduction of memory — or shall we say the *construction* of fictional memory (since we are dealing with fiction) — as a narrative device obviously serves to build up the identity of a character in its temporal and psychological dimensions. But the process of remembering can also function as a structural principle governing the lay-out of the text — as we see, for example, in some works by Su Tong and Mo Yan. To name but a few examples: In his novella 'Yi jiu san si nian de taowang' (The Diaspora of 1934) Su Tong presents the story as a kind of imaginary memory extending into the historical past.[12] In works such as 'Hong gaoliang jiazu' (Red Sorghum Clan) and even more in 'Tiantang suantai zhi ge' (Paradise Garlic Song) Mo Yan skillfully manipulates the interaction of different individual memories in his depiction of the local history of rural China.[13] Written in a very different vein, most of Ge Fei's stories manifest themselves as arduous reconstructions of memory. The narrator's subject position is anchored in the past, specifically in the moment when he remembers and registers the fragmentary flashes of his personal past.[14] In Liu Suola's novella 'Xunzhao gewang' (Searching the King of Singers) the I-narrator's memory (of her search for the king of singers together with her boyfriend) is juxtaposed with impressions of the moment and acts as an alternative present, which is now rejected now embraced, as she tries to gain control of herself in the flux of modern life.[15]

The extreme complexity of the relationship between the private memory and the common one, as well as the profound ambiguity of the time-experience, is enacted in a very particular way in Can Xue's writings, especially her short texts from the years 1985-88. Dreams and their surrealist images are specific forms of intensely personal memory, or memory distorted. And the dream seems to be the paradigm for many of these stories. In others she utilizes memory as scraps of past which pop up in the consciousness of the narrator, to whom they appear undifferentiated from the chaos of the present.[16]

Despite the almost total lack of narrative movement, time is constantly present. But it is interior time, not linear clock time. It is there in the changing of day into night, night into day-break, sun and moon and stars sometimes present on the sky simultaneously, in the growth, greenness and withering of plants, and in the sudden transformations of people: their cheeks disappear, teeth fall out, their faces or body rot away, they die. And there is the alarm clock ringing constantly or at sudden intervals, or the pocket watch on the wall. Actually a lot of Can Xue's narrative refers to processes, especially the decay of the human body, but these descriptions occur as random impressions, sabotaging rather than adding any dynamic progress to the text. Instead they effect a complex experience continuum which belies a sequential self. Time, then, does not exist as the string that binds together various experiences, that orders and collects them, and that serves to unite life under one coherent horizon. Instead the narrative discourse works to subvert, replay or even pervert the normal passages of time.

The impression gained from several of her texts is one in which the narrative voice seems to be trying to 'master' time by transforming it into symbols or metaphors of temporality — which are then confronted simply as spatial objects. But time operates unpredictably and constantly shows itself to be beyond the control of the narrator. Thus the overall effect is one in which, on the one hand, there seems to be no exterior objective common time, since everything in the text is subordinated to the subjective voice of the narrator/protagonist. On the other hand an uncontaminated interior, individual time cannot exist either: it is constantly being broken, intruded upon, split and scattered.

Thematically, therefore, I read her stories as demonstrating the impossibility of separating not only the two notions of time, but also the individual and the common memory. The fervent desire to transgress time remains, and is manifested in the efforts to rescue memories: the re-membrance of the past is always attempted, yet invariably disturbed.[17]

The female literary critic Ji Hongzhen in a recent reading of Can Xue's breakthrough story 'Shanshang de xiaowu' (The Mountain Hut, 1985) has interpreted that text as yet another allegory of the perpetual circle of Chinese existence (reminiscent of Lu Xun's view, only substituting the iron house by a wooden cabin).[18] One might add that on the level of textuality it is also a temporal circle in which the individual memory is never allowed to unfold undisturbed, and in which the future is conspicuously absent as a point beyond the circle. Can Xue's recent short story 'Guitu' (The Road Back, 1993) is structurally more linear than her early work, but thematically it is about the interior break-down of individual time and the dissolution of memory into total blackness.[19]

While most Chinese writers of the last decade testify to the importance of memory by actually displaying it in their texts as a thematic or structural element, Yu Hua's approach is radically different. He addresses the predicament of memory in contemporary China by way of its conspicuous absence.[20] As I read his fiction from the 1980s, especially 'Xianshi yizhong' (A Kind of Reality) and 'Yijiubaliu nian' (Nineteen eighty-six), the issue of remembrance is of central concern.[21] One of the most chilling aspects of the characters in these works is their lack of reflective memory.[22] But what is more, and what ultimately generates disaster, is the fact that they do not have recourse to any collective memories either. While the former explains the immediate absence of morality and feelings, it is the non-existence of a common cultural framework of remembrance which allows for the extremes of death and revenge in 'Xianshi yizhong'. The characters live in a sort of perpetual present which may well be seen as a fictional reflection of the human condition under a totalitarian regime which willfully obliterates the historical past.[23]

'Yijiubaliu nian' is the story of a school-teacher who went insane as a result of the cultural revolution, disappeared for twenty years, and now returns to his hometown as a sado-masochist wreck, unrecognized by his former family. Here past (the madman) and present (his wife and daughter) have been sealed off from one another. The madman has no present, is nothing but congealed past concentrated in the trauma of his cultural revolution experience, which can now be expressed only in terms of the torture he inflicts upon himself and imagines he inflicts upon others. His family, on the other hand, live entirely in the little moments of the present.

On a psycho-allegorical level this is not a story about memory erased, but a fable about memory repressed and consequently doomed to reappear in distorted form.

3.

The return of the mad school-teacher to his hometown ironically echoes what I would call a special sub-genre within the modern Chinese short-story — the homecoming story, i.e., the story in which the urbanized intellectual returns to visit his old home in the countryside. This narrative theme, so deeply embedded in some of the fundamental issues in Chinese culture and society — and indeed one of the major themes in classical poetry — is one that obviously begs for reflections on the questions of time and memory and their implications for identity and subjectivity. New dimensions were added to the theme in some of the 'zhiqing xiaoshuo' through the figure of the young student who had been 'sent down' during the cultural revolution. Generally these stories tend to affirm the country as the locus of memory, as opposed to the city phenomenon of time. The confrontation with landscapes and people left behind serves to reactivate in the protagonist, often a first person narrator, forgotten memories, and thus becomes a confrontation with the self.

The prototype of the homecoming-story is of course Lu Xun's 'Guxiang' (Hometown 1921). In Lu Xun's story the narrator's golden memories of his childhood friendship with the peasant boy Runtu are starkly contrasted by the unbridgeable gap so manifestedly existing between his 'present' self and the dull and servile grown-up Runtu. But it is not simply that the nostalgic fascination with the past is revealed as an illusion. Rather it is problematized and complicated by a modern awareness of the instability of even the very act of remembrance. In the process of remembering a sense of vulnerability is generated, and by means of various textual devices a kind of subversive effect, ironically undercutting the progress of time, is achieved. Seen from the point of view of the subjective consciousness of the protagonist (in this case the narrator, calling himself Lu Xun), the past is merely something that reappears in the narrative present, as the wonderful image of Runtu as a child which he recalls: 'a round, golden moon suspended in a deep blue sky and under it the sandy verge of the sea, on which was planted an endless succession of jade-green watermelons. In their midst was a boy of eleven or twelve, wearing a silver ring around his neck and grasping an iron pitchfork in his hands'.[24] But as it turns out, the overall impact of the text is one in which the past ends up restricted by the present, thereby losing its original meaning, at the same time as the present has been disturbed and imperceptibly changed by the encounter with the past.[25]

In Mo Yan's 1985 story 'Baigou qiuqianjia' (White Dog and the Swing) the narrator, like Lu Xun's, filled with a mixture of apprehension and nostalgia, reluctantly returns to his home village.[26] Memories of his childhood and youth are evoked as he meets his former playmate, the one-eyed woman, whose misfortune was in part due to his own carelessness. His backward—extending recollection of what happened earlier is juxtaposed with the reality of the present as he gradually learns of the woman's later fate. She married a mute and bore three mute sons. But in this case the narrator is not allowed to leave, consoling his half-guilty conscience with self-deluding rationalizations on past, present and future, the way Lu Xun could leave Runtu sixty-four years earlier. In Mo Yan's contemporary scenario the narrator's memories take on their own life and claim him in a highly physical manner: the woman demands that he make love to her so that she can bear one child who can speak.

While the two temporal levels of past and present are here clearly separated in the mind of the main character, Ge Fei in his homecoming story 'Mizhou' (The Lost Boat, 1987) weaves together time and consciousness in a highly intriguing way.[27] The critic Zhang Fu has called Ge Fei's writing-technique a kind of 'memory research',[28] and the text can certainly be read as a meditation on memory as constitutive of individual subjectivity and as generating the motivational structure of human action.

The text is told by an omniscient narrator in seemingly realist mode and set up as follows: A short preamble states that on the 21 of March 1928 Commander Xiao disappeared mysteriously as the region was being taken over by the northern expedition army. Then follows the actual story which is divided into eight sections, entitled 'prologue', 'day one', 'day two', etc., until 'day seven' (the end). The plot is very simple: Xiao, accompanied by his bodyguard, returns to his native village to attend his father's funeral. He spends the night with the girl he was attracted to in his youth. Her husband finds out and mutilates her, she is sent back to her parents in Yuguan. Xiao goes to Yuguan and upon his return is shot by his bodyguard, suspected of treason. The exterior textual structure is thus set in the framework of an ordinarily progressing linear time. However, this outer, objective time-concept is steadily undermined in a kind of reverse movement, as Xiao moves further and further into the labyrinth of subjective time created by his memories. The river Lianshui, which he crosses to go to his hometown, is like a boundary of time, and once he has passed it he enters a different realm, in which the reality of the approaching battle no longer exists for him. The resurgence of previous odours and sentiments plunges him into a chaos that cannot be disentangled. This military commander now becomes like the lost boat of the title, drifting on the waves of remembrance without being able to navigate, led by the subcurrents towards his own destruction. The name of the girl, Xing, is synonymous with the word for sexuality/gender. Since she never appears in the story as a character in her own right, it is possible to see her as merely a symbol or signifier for the existence of desire. But it is a desire born out of or activated by memory. In the words of the Chinese scholar Zhang Xudong: 'Xing is nothing but a briefly blossoming flower of time inside memory and illusion'.[29]

Underneath the psychological time which dominates Xiao's immediate consciousness we may perceive a deeper, at first unrecognized, level of time. This level of time or temporal mode is connected to his father. We are told that his father was a warrior, a survivor of the Small Sword Society, who also constantly kept with him one book of poetry — i.e., a man of both 'wen' and 'wu'. As the story progresses, this more ancient level of time, which is simultaneously related to the private and to the common heritage of Chinese culture, gradually emerges from the depths of Xiao's consciousness. Finally, before deciding to go on his fatal trip to Yuguan, he 'accidentially' enters his father's dark and dusty room, and here the three levels of time converge in his mind for the first time. His death at the end is, in fact, meaningless from a logical point of view: the bodyguard explains that he was supposed to shoot him if he tried to go to Yuguan (where the enemy is). Yet now he shoots him after he has been there. On the symbolic level we may therefore interpret the almost silent figure of the bodyguard as representing the shadow of the present time which, though hardly noticed by Xiao during the seven days of his stay in his hometown, has always been at his side. The spatial enclosure of the rivers and mountains, demarcating the mental realm of remembrance, in the final scene narrows down to the courtyard of his old home, where he meets his death. He is prevented from escape because his mother just happened to have closed the gate. Time and space coalesce into a black hole, 'the unfathomable deep muzzle of the gun' and 'all sorts of scenes from his past flashed in front of his eyes, like so many petals scattered on the river, moving past and then vanishing'(100).

Han Shaogong's 'Guiqulai' (Going back, 1985) can be read as yet another, rather special, exposition of the homecoming theme, with the question of individual memory at the very heart of the plot.[30] The 'I', a young man by name of Huang Zhixian, goes to a village deep in the mountains. Though he is quite sure he has never been there before, he has a strange feeling of déja vu. The villagers recognize him as Ma Yanjing (Spectacles Ma) a 'zhiqing' who was sent there during the cultural revolution, and left the place ten years ago. This Ma is well remembered in the village, where it seems he killed a local villain, experienced both hardship and friendship, and left a girl who died later. Images of darkness and blackness permeate the text and seem to act as spatial metaphors of the mental state of the 'I'-narrator. At the beginning of the story, when the 'I' is approaching the village he notices that 'a few circles of motionless black shadows rise above the small pools beside the road '. What looks at first like rocks turns out to be small water-buffaloes, 'old at birth' . The walls of the blockhouse guarding the entrance to the village are as dark as if they have 'congealed the black of many nights', etc. The narrator's blurred perception of these scattered pieces of dark objects, which only upon closer examination reveal their features, functions as a metaphorical flashforward of his later temporal and psychological predicament: his reluctant acceptance of the pieces of seemingly strange information about his own identity that the villagers offer him. As the narration progresses, Huang gradually takes on the identity of Ma, including fragments of his memory, before he ends up fleeing the place. At the end of the story he is in a nearby inn, in a state of complete identity confusion. It never becomes quite clear to the reader whether he actually is Ma, suffering from amnesia, or not.[31] Thus this short text explicitly deals with memory and its function in the identity formation process.[32]

Time and space are shown to be tightly interlaced. The moment the narrator enters the enclosed space of the mountain village, he also enters a different temporal realm. Significantly, at no point does the 'I' convincingly try to counteract the 'enforced' identity by way of reference to his 'actual' life in the city of the present. It is not just that this is pushed into the background by his experience in the village, it is more as if it is simply blotted out by the overwhelming forces of the past. The few traces of the world outside that are found in the village — a dilapidated textbook with crumbled yellow pages of marxist theory of peasant movements, bits of agricultural terms and an article on the 1911 revolution, a rusty barbell, an almost erased slogan on a wall — are emblematic of not only the passage of time, but also the utter irrelevance of the political aspects of the 'zhiqing' presence in the countryside. Those are all objects which originally, during the cultural revolution, were invested with a highly charged symbolic value as tokens of the new society. But in the textual framework of Han Shaogong's story they take on a completely different meaning: they become allegorical images, in the modern sense as defined by Walter Benjamin, signalling precisely the absence of any genuine and stable point of reference.[33]

In fact the text, like Ge Fei's story discussed above, contains not two but three levels of time or temporal modes — i.e., underneath the narrative present and the immediate past of the cultural revolution ten years ago, a deeper level of something ancient or even timeless is lurking. For example the villagers speak in a semi-archaic dialect and their customs seem to have remained unchanged throughout, 'probably they ate in the same manner thousands of years ago'. (33)

There are obvious intertextual references not only to Zhuangzi and Lu Xun's 'Guxiang',[34] but also to the regional literary ancestry of West Hunan, the 'Chu Ci' and most blatantly Tao Yuanming from whom Han Shaogong borrowed the title. The reader will also be reminded of Shen Congwen's 'Recollections of West Hunan', although Han Shaogong's vision of the mystery and uniqueness of the landscape and people is more ominous and ambiguous than Shen's.[35] David Wang has recently argued that in Shen Congwen's writings memories of the past are 'reinvented' so as to constitute a kind of 'imaginary nostalgia'.[36] In that sense, Han Shaogong's story can be read as a sort of countertext, in which memories are indeed invented, but not by the subjective consciousness of the narrator. Instead they are shown to be manipulated by forces outside the individual. Read in that perspective 'Guiqulai' may therefore be interpreted as an allegory on the deprivation of the private memory in a culture of oppressive collectivity. The implications of this are spelled out at the end, when the narrator's final words reveal his utter identity confusion: 'I was tired, never would I be able to escape this immense me (ju da de wo). Mama!'[37] As can be seen, the predicament of the 'I' is conceived not just as the difficulty of choosing between two identities, or as a problem of remembrance and forgetting, but as the inability to separate/distinguish a private, individually defined self (a xiaowo) from the collective, overwhelming big self (dawo) enforced by the surrounding culture. The mountain village is depicted as a spatial and temporal enclosure, separated from high Han-culture and from ordinary contemporary society. As such it could represent the offer of an alternative memory/identity, which might be accepted or rejected. But in the textual universe of Han Shaogong's story the ultimate problem of the relationship between the individual and the larger cultural memory remains unresolved.

Looking back on the diversity of preservation, construction and reinventing of memory in some Chinese fiction of the recent decade, it would seem that the fascination with the problematics of time remains inextricably entangled with this issue. In Western high modernism individual memory was recognized as a constant living force, participating in the shaping of the flux of the present, and as a constituent part of subjective time. As such it could exist independently of, though not of course separated from, history.[38] By contrast, it seems that to many Chinese writers subjective memory is not enough in itself. Though positively valorized, searched for and privileged over its collective counterpart it constantly seeks to come to terms with the larger, common memory and time concept. Whether by interacting with it or by reacting against it. While the stories discussed above all testify to an increased, or reawakened, textual awareness of the self and its dilemmas and ambiguities vis á vis modernity, it would hardly be appropriate to describe them as simply Chinese versions of modernism. Although the very heterogeneity of what we call the modernist literary movement in the West would seem to allow room for ample variety, in the Chinese case such a generalized categorization would look more like yet another expression of the idea of literary development as consisting of a fixed series of stages that all literatures have to go through. An idea that beset Chinese intellectuals from the turn of the century on, and which still was widely accepted in the 1980s.[39] A vague sense of a separation between an aesthetic and a historical concept of modernity did seem to exist among some Chinese writers by the mid 1980s, but it was never a mainstream and was soon eroded by the spread of commercialization.

References

Benjamin, Walter (1925): *Ursprung des deutschen Trauerspiels*. Reprinted, Frankfurt a.M. 1974.

Brown, Dennis (1989): *The Modernist Self in Twentieth Century English Literature*. London: Macmillan.

Calinescu, Matei (1977): *Faces of modernity: Avant-Garde, Decadence, Kitch*. Bloomington, Ind.: Indiana University Press.

Can Xue (1988): *Tiantang li de duihua* Beijing: Zuojia chubanshe.

Can Xue (1993): 'Guitu' *Shanghai Wenxue* 1993, 11.

Dolezelova-Velingerova, Milena (ed.) (1980): *The Chinese Novel at the Turn of the Century*, Toronto, University of Toronto Press.

Duke, Michael S. (1993): 'Past, Present and Future in Mo Yan's Fiction of the 1980s' in Ellen Widmer and David Der-wei Wang (eds.): *From May Fourth to June Fourth. Fiction and Film in Twentieth Century China*. Cambridge, Mass.: Harvard University Press.

Ge Fei (1987): 'Mizhou' in *Shouhuo* 1987, 6.

Han Shaogong (1985): 'Guiqulai' in *Shanghai Wenxue* 1985, 6.

Huters, Theodore (1993): 'Ideologies of Realism in Modern China: The Hard Imperatives of Imported Theory' in Liu Kang and Xiaobing Tang eds. *Politics, Ideology, and Literary Discourse in Modern China*. Durham, N.C.: Duke University Press.

Ji Hongzhen (1994): 'Bei qiujin de linghun' *Dangdai zuojia pinglun* 1994, 1.

Kinkley, Jeffrey (1993): 'Shen Congwen's Legacy in Chinese Literature of the 1980s' in Ellen Widmer and David Der-wei Wang (eds.): *From May Fourth to June Fourth. Fiction and Film in Twentieth Century China*. Cambridge, Mass.: Harvard University Press.

Lee, Leo Ou-fan (1990): 'In Search of Modernity' in Paul A. Cohen and Merle Goldman ed. *Ideas Across Cultures*. Cambridge, Mass.: Harvard University Press.

Lee, Leo Ou-fan (1990): 'Modernity and its Discontents. The Cultural Agenda of the May Fourth Movement' in *Perspectives on Modern China. Four Anniversaries*. New York, M.E. Sharpe.

Lee, Leo Ou-fan (1991): 'On the Margins of Chinese Discourse: Some Personal Thoughts on the Cultural Meaning of Periphery' in *Dædalus* vol. 120 no. 2.

Li Oufan (1986): »Man tan Zhongguo wenxue zhong de 'tuifei'« *Jintian* 1993, 4.

Liu Kang and Xiaobing Tang eds. (1993): *Politics, Ideology, and Literary Discourse in Modern China*. Durham, N.C.: Duke University Press.

Liu Suola (1986): 'Xunzhao gewang' in *Ni bie wu xuanze* Beijing: Zuojia chubanshe.

Lu Xun Quanji (1981) Renmin Wenxue chubanshe, Beijing.

Mo Yan (1987): *Hong gaoliang jiazu* Beijing: Jiefangjun wenyi chubanshe.

Mo Yan (1988): *Tiantang suantai zhi ge* Beijing: Zuojia chubanshe.

Mo Yan (1987): *Touming de hong luobo*. Beijing Zuojia chubanshe, 1986.

Plaks, Andrew H.:'Towards a Critical Theory of Chinese Narrative´ in Plaks, A.H. ed. *Chinese Narrative. Critical and Theoretocal Essays*, Princeton, N.J. Princeton University Press 1977

Quinones, Ricardo J. (1985): *Mapping Literary Modernism. Time and Development*. Princeton, N.J.: Princeton University Press.

Su Tong (1990): *Qiqie cheng qun* Taibei. Yuanliu.

Tang, Xiaobing (1992): 'The Mirror as History and History as Spectacle: Reflections on Hsiao Yeh and Su T'ung' *Modern Chinese Literature* vol. 6 nos 1&2.

Wang Jing (1993): 'The Mirage of 'Chinese Postmodernism': Ge Fei, Self-Positioning, and the Avant-Garde Showcase' in *Positions* vol. 1 no. 2.

Wedell-Wedellsborg, Anne (1995): 'Self-identity and Allegory in the Fiction of Yu Hua' in Lisbeth Littrup ed.: *Identity in Asian Literature*. London: Curzon Press (in press).

Widmer, Ellen and David Der-wei Wang (eds.) (1993): *From May Fourth to June Fourth. Fiction and Film in Twentieth Century China*. Cambridge, Mass.: Harvard University Press.

Xue Yi (1993): 'Yuyan de dansheng' *Shanghai Wenxue* 1993, 2.

Yu Hua (1989): *Shiba sui chu men yuan xing* Beijing: Zuojia chubanshe.

Zhang Xudong (1990): 'Ge Fei yu dangdai wenxue huayu de jige muti' in *Jintian* 1990, 2.

Zhang Fu (1992): *Zuojia de bairimeng*. Guangdong Huacheng chubanshe. 1992.

Notes

1. Parts of this essay were first published in 'The Past in the Present: Remembrance and Forgetting in Recent Chinese Fiction' Joakim Enwall ed., *Outstretched Leaves on his Bamboo Staff*, Studies in Honour of Göran Malmqvist on his 70th Birthday. Stockholm, The Association of Oriental Studies, 1994.
2. Matei Calinescu: 1977. As ref. by Leo Oufan Lee 1990:124.
3. Bergson's theories were especially influential between 1900 and 1921, when he lectured at the College de France. In 1928 he was awarded the Nobel prize in literature.
4. To mention but a few: Borges, Sartre, Paul Ricoeur, George Poulet. The dichotomy has been largely approached by way of various binary poles such as, e.g., transcendent versus immanent; diachronic versus synchronic; irreversible versus structural; self-time versus social time; prescriptive time versus innovative time.
5. For a discussion of time and literary modernism see for example: Ricardo J. Quinones, Princeton, N.J.: 1985. Also Dennis Brown: 1989
6. See especially Leo Ou-fan Lee (1991): 'Modernity and its Discontents. The Cultural Agenda of the May Fourth Movement' in *Perspectives on Modern China. Four Anniversaries*. New York. M.E. Sharpe.
7. Op.cit. p. 164
8. Op.cit. p. 167
9. Leo Oufan Lee 1990: 117-120.
10. As studies by Plaks (1977) and Dolezelova-Velingerova (1980) have shown, traditional vernacular fiction was characterized by linearity of plot (though not in the same 'focused' way as in the West) except for the occasional use of flashback in the form of 'yuanlai....' Wu Woyao seems to have been the first well-known vernacular writer to use the limited point of view and he was also the first to experience with time-inversion.
11. See, for example, the novel 'Bodong' (1981)
12. Su Tong 1990: 13-78 1992.
13. *Hong gaoliang jiazu* Beijing: Jiefangjun wenyi chubanshe, 1987. *Tiantang suantai zhi ge* Beijing: Zuojia chubanshe 1988. For a close analysis of this story see Michael S. Duke: 1993
14. For a discussion of Ge Fei's use of memory see Jing Wang: 1993

15. Liu Suola 1986: 130-86.
16. See for instance the stories collected in *Tiantang li de duihua* Beijing: Zuojia chubanshe 1988.
17. In reading Can Xue one is often reminded of Walter Benjamin's reflections on 'Erinnerung' as opposed to 'Gedächtnis'. In contrast to the latter which is tied to consciousness, to the actual recalling of a reality that once was, 'Erinnerung' is related to the sensations and the unconscious, it arbitrarily fragments and combines the flow of time, and can have a destructive effect on what appears as the given reality preserved by memory.
18. See Ji Hongzhen: 'Bei qiujin de linghun' *Dangdai zuojia pinglun* 1994,1 pp. 64-65.
19. Can Xue: 'Guitu' *Shanghai Wenxue* 1993,11.
20. I am not here concerned with those stories by Yu Hua which explicitly deal with the paradox of time, such as ' Siyue sanri shijian' and 'Wangshi yu xingfa'.
21. Both of these novellas are to be found in *Shiba sui chu men yuan xing* Beijing: Zuojia chubanshe, 1989
22. For a detailed analysis of the concept of self in Yu Hua's fiction see Anne Wedell-Wedellsborg: 1995 (in press).
23. See also Jing Wang 1993.
24. *Lu Xun Quanji Renmin Wenxue chubanshe*, Beijing 1981 p. 477. Here quoted from Theodore Huters 1993: 163.
25. See also Li Oufan 1993: 30-31.
26. In Mo Yan 1986.
27. Ge Fei: 'Mizhou' in *Shouhuo* 1987,6. Translated into English in Henry Zhao ed. *The Lost Boat'* London Wellsweep Press, 1993.
28. See Zhang Fu 1992: 231.
29. See Zhang Xudong 1990: 76-84. Zhang also describes Xiao´s relationship with Xing as 'a rite in the search for the past', and compares her to a siren pulling Xiao towards his final fate, her cries when tortured by her husband as irresistible as the songs of the sirens. My reading of the story is much inspired by Zhang Xudong's.
30. *Shanghai Wenxue* 1985,6.
31. Leo Ou-fan Lee (1991) reads the story as a search for an 'Other', not just another persona, but an alternative realm outside the officially defined. To Joseph Lau it is the story about a victim of the cultural revolution fated to spend the rest of his days wondering who he actually is. Joseph S.M. Lau: 'Visitation of the Past in Han Shaogong's Post-1985 Fiction' in Ellen Widmer and David Der-wei Wang (1993). To Jeffrey Kinkley (1993) it is a story in the Western modernist tradition about Ma whose journey home invests him with an identity truer than his apparent one.
32. This is how I choose to view the text in the context of the present short essay. However, as indicated in the previous note, it can certainly be read from other angles as well, most obviously in the context of Han Shaogong's famous manifesto on root searching, which was published just a few months before this story.
33. Walter Benjamin 1925.
34. Especially in the protagonist's self-deluding attitude to the sister of the girl he left, and his unconvincing use of the cliché of 'roads are trod by people' originating from the end of 'Guxiang'.
35. See Jeffrey Kinkley 1993.

36. David Der-wei Wang 1993.
37. Han Shaogong 1985: 37.
38. See for example Dennis Brown 1989. My description here is of course vastly generalized.
39. In this essay I have not touched upon the lengthy discussions on the concept of modernism and its possibilities in China, which took place in literary periodicals from early to late 1980s. Up to around 1984 the debate had strong political and nationalistic connotations.

Traditional Chinese Theatre on Broadway

Wenwei Du

As its title suggests, this essay deals with the issue of East-West cultural encounters from a theatrical perspective. It concentrates on American adaptations of traditional Chinese drama and theatre on the Broadway stage.

Traditional Chinese theatre has been presented to the American audience through three channels: 1) classical performances in Chinese theatres in Chinatowns, 2) theatrical tours to U.S. cities by first-class troupes from China, and 3) American adaptations of classic Chinese plays. The first two have served as influential sources for the latter.

As early as the middle of the last century, Americans began to see Chinese theatre in the Chinese communities in major U.S. cities such as San Francisco and New York. Though primarily catering to the entertainment of the Chinese, these theatres also drew the attention of non-Chinese audiences which included local residents, tourists from other cities in the U.S., and well-known playwrights and theatre critics of the time. The Chinese theatrical groups were very active until the early 1920s when American moving pictures reached Chinese communities and began to dominate the entertainment world. But theatrical activities never ceased in the Chinese communities. America's contact with the Chinese theatre reached its peak when Mei Lanfang, one of the greatest actors of the twentieth century, made his theatrical tour to the U.S. in 1930. All that was involved in Mei Lanfang's American tour — his reputation as the foremost of Chinese actors, his perfection of acting, his universal acclaim, and the expositions and comments by critics on the aesthetics of his art — set a milestone in the American audience's awareness of the existence of a higher level of Chinese acting. Since Mei Lanfang's performance, other theatrical troupes from China have visited New York stages from time to time. Of these troupes the best known include the Chinese Cultural Theatre Group from Shanghai which performed on Broadway in 1939 and 1947; the Foo Hsing Theatre Company from Taiwan between November, 1962 and January, 1963; and the Peking Opera Troupe from Beijing in 1980. While theatre companies from China have regularly performed in America, the theatrical troupes or actors based in Chinatowns have also been invited to perform or demonstrate on university campuses and in theatrical workshops. Meanwhile, scholarly publications in English on the Chinese drama and theatre have made a rich tradition of diversified dramatic genres known to an ever-growing readership. In short, the American stage has never lost touch with the traditional Chinese theatre since Chinese immigrants first arrived in America.

Furnished with scholarly knowledge and exposed to live Chinese theatrical performances, twentieth-century American theatre people have staged their own Chinese plays. Those produced on the Broadway stage have been more influential than those produced elsewhere because Broadway is the American theatrical Establishment and has had the most powerful capacity to make the production of any play known to the American public. An analysis of the adaptations on Broadway will reveal the Chinese thematic and theatrical elements 'encountered' and interpreted on the American stage. First, I will supply a brief chronicle of the adaptations. Second, I will highlight a Broadway trend of altering the original Chinese sentiments to the American taste on a thematic level. Third, I will comment on the significance of these adaptations on a theatrical level.

Since the beginning of this century, there have been several attempts to stage traditional Chinese plays. The first play adapted for the American stage was *The Flower of the Palace of Han* by Charles Rann Kennedy on March 19, 1912, at the Little Theatre in New York, based on Louis Laloy's French dramatization of the Yuan *zaju* play *Hangong qiu (Autumn in Han Palace)* by Ma Zhiyuan.[1] It was overshadowed by the much more successful production in the same year of *The Yellow Jacket* conceived by J. Harry Benrimo and George C. Hazelton with a resemblance to the Yuan *zaju* play *Zhaoshi gu'er (The Orphan of Zhao)* by Ji Junxiang. The play was produced under the direction of Benrimo at the Fulton Theatre on November 4, 1912. The first run lasted ten weeks. It succeeded in following years both in New York (1916, 1921, 1928 and 1929) and in a number of other cities. It was also staged on various university campuses. Internationally, the play claimed more success, touring countries in Europe. The adaptation of another Yuan *zaju* play entitled *Huilan ji (The Story of the Chalk Circle)* by Li Qianfu first appeared on stage in 1925 in Moshe Leib Halpern's version; I. S. Richter's version of the same play was staged in 1930 and 1933; James Laver's version was presented in 1941, 1947 and 1950.[2] These three versions in the name of *The Chalk Circle* or *The Circle of Chalk* were from the same German adaptation by Klabund (Alfred

Henschke).[3] Also among the best known adaptations was the 1936 *Lady Precious Stream* by S. I. Hsiung from the *luotan* (regional operas) sources, especially the Peking Opera, concerning the love story of Xue Pinggui and Wang Baochuan.[4] With a successful first run of 105 performances at the Booth Theatre on January 27, 1936, it was later produced by different American theatrical troupes at various places over the next twenty years or so. *Lute Song*, adapted in the late 1920s by Sidney Howard and Bill Irwin from the Chinese *chuanqi* classic *Pipa ji (The Story of the Lute)* by Gao Ming, was produced as a Broadway musical at the Plymouth Theatre on February 6, 1946. It ran for about five months for a respectable 142 performances. It went on tour to other cities and was revived at the City Center Theatre in New York in 1959.[5] Since 1960 more Chinese plays have been adapted and produced off Broadway. They include A. C. Scott's *The Butterfly Dream* (1961, 1966) for the Institute for Advanced Studies in the Theatre Arts, and Tisa Chang's *The Return of the Phoenix* (1973) and *The Orphan of Chao* (1976) at La Mama Experimental Theatre Club. This period saw more and more productions of Chinese plays on university campuses outside New York City.

A reading of the scripts of some major adaptations in comparison with their respective Chinese versions will reveal a strong tendency on Broadway of altering Chinese themes to Western tastes. The first major production was *The Yellow Jacket*. Its plot concerns revenge within a royal family. Wu Sin Yin ('Great Sound Language'), the Great, has two wives.[6] The second and favorite one, Due Jung Fah ('Fuchsia Flower'), is very jealous of the first wife Chee Moo ('Kind Mother') and by witchcraft arranges for her rival's child to become a cripple. Displeased by the crippled child, Wu the Great wants to put the first wife to death and raise the second wife to the first position. He commands Lee Sin, a farmer and the husband of the first wife's maid, to kill the first wife. Loyal to the princess, Lee Sin accomplishes a false execution and helps the first wife and her baby flee from the palace. On her way, she is greeted by the soul of the child's ancestor, who encourages her to abandon the baby to the protection of the gods. She bites her finger and uses the blood to write the background on the baby's jacket. Thereafter she dies from loss of blood and goes to heaven. For fear that Wu the Great might see through the facts about the execution, Lee Sin and his wife run away too. On their way, they find the baby on the ground and decide to rear him as their own. Twenty years later, the baby child has grown into manhood. Named Wu Hoo Git ('Young Hero'), he is now a man of brawn, no longer crippled. Meanwhile, Wu the Great has died; the second wife's son named Daffodil sits on the thrown. After his real ancestry has been revealed to him, Wu Hoo Git sets out to get revenge. On his way to the palace, the hero overcomes a series of obstacles: lofty mountain peaks, monsters, rivers, thunderstorms, a spider-web of evil, tigers, a snow-storm — all set up supernaturally by Daffodil. Wu Hoo Git overcomes one obstacle after another and finally wins back his throne.

Such a plot demonstrates that *The Yellow Jacket* has its Chinese root in *Zhaoshi gu'er*.[7] The resemblance of *The Yellow Jacket* to *Zhaoshi gu'er* is striking in the framework of the plot. Wu Hoo Git is Zhao Wu: both are orphans. The mother of each dies for saving her only child in order to get revenge later. The farmer Lee Sin in *The Yellow Jacket* corresponds to Cheng Ying in *Zhaoshi gu'er*, each being the hero's foster parent. As a Chinese saying goes, 'ten years are not too long for a gentleman to wait for revenge.' Not by coincidence, both plays set the revenge twenty years later. In the end both villains Daffodil and Tu'an Gu are punished and the heroes are honored. Yet the authenticity of *The Yellow Jacket* as a Chinese play lies only in the framework of the revenge plot with its belief that revenge must be carried out by the offspring of the victim, that the mother should sacrifice for her son, and that the servant should be loyal to his master. Within this general framework, the underlying principle for the revenge and the execution of the revenge deviate far from the true Chinese spirit.

In any Chinese play with such a beginning as that of *The Yellow Jacket*, the theme would focus on the revenge by the young hero upon his foe as in *Zhaoshi gu'er*. The revenge or doing justice would be the sole motive for the young hero to drive his foe off the throne. Significantly different from the way of carrying out a true Chinese revenge theme, *The Yellow Jacket* executes the revenge in a romantic way centering on love connections. Act II of the play is solely devoted to the episodes in the Land of Perfumed Pleasure and on the Flowery Sea of Sin. In these two episodes the hero Wu Hoo Git encounters different women. His experiences with women are intended to purify his soul through tempering his body. Interestingly enough, in these two episodes, the young hero does not object to the temptation of the flowery girls. He is allowed to know sensual excitement for the first time, he enjoys it for most of the episodes, and he is willing to pay for his pleasure. He is given a chance to taste physical pleasures and to exhaust his physical energy. To summarize the two episodes, the Chorus recites: 'All men approach the god-like realms of thoughtful sufficiency after the bodily attainments wane' (Hazelton and Benrimo, 1913: 142). Such an experience could not be permitted in a young hero with the noble cause of avenging his family in traditional Chinese literature. His involvement with women would be disapproved by his foster parents as a diversion from or hindrance to his quest for revenge. Similar experiences of encountering seductive flowery girls would only occur to a young Chinese scholar who indulges himself in sexuality and temporarily forgets his academic study on his way to the imperial examination, as is seen in the genre of *caizi jiaren* (gifted-scholar-and-beautiful-lady) plays. Even in such cases, involvement with women is always regarded as a source of ruin for one's cause. In no way is it considered a necessary step toward wisdom. Therefore, the sexual indulgence of the young hero is not justified in the revenge-setting if the play were to follow authentic Chinese conventions.

Finally, the hero falls in love with the virtuous lady Plum Blossom. On his way to win back his legitimate throne, the young hero has three symbolic tokens with him: the old Philosopher accompanying him on the journey, the baby jacket with his heritage written on it, and his sweetheart Plum Blossom's slipper. The Philosopher stands for wisdom as he always gives advice to the young hero before the latter challenges an obstacle. He represents, in Benrimo's words, sophistication with 'Chinese aphorisms which we [the authors] readily found in translations of philosophy' (Benrimo, 1928). The baby jacket always reminds the young hero of the throne and through it he communicates with his mother's spirit in Heaven. It symbolizes supernatural power from the ancestors. The slipper symbolizes love which provides the young hero with unconquerable inner force. Though these three forces supplement one another, the force generated by love is the dominant one. It is the young hero's love for Plum Blossom that leads him from one victory to another. When challenged by Loy Gong, the God of Thunder, the hero declares:

But I fear you not. My wisdom buds with courage, impregnable to gods and man, and teaches me that every word-might or heavenly power has one still higher before whom it quails — called love.

Loy Gong asks: 'And what is love?' The hero proudly replies: 'For me, Plum Blossom' (Hazelton and Benrimo, 1913: 153). Later, when the hero is entangled by the Spider's web of evil and almost dies, he shakes the slipper and Plum Blossom's disembodied soul is summoned to defeat the Spider on the battle field. The symbolic meaning of the slipper is clearly stated: his love for Plum Blossom is an unconquerable power. In a traditional Chinese context, a young hero's love affair would, more often than not, harm his quest for revenge. But in *The Yellow Jacket*, love is the decisive factor. Therefore, from a thematic point of view, *The Yellow Jacket* is a blend of the Chinese and the American with the latter superseding the former. The dramatization of various adventures in *The Yellow Jacket* aims at testifying to the invincible power of the hero's love for his sweetheart. Thus Wu Hoo Git becomes a Western medieval knight whose heroic actions are guided by his love for a certain noble lady. Such a departure from the Chinese dramatic tradition results from a fantasized treatment of a love theme in the revenge plot of *The Yellow Jacket*.

Not only were 'Chinese' plays conceived or imagined by American authors pregnant with romantic fantasies and exaggerated exoticism, but plays adapted from acknowledged Chinese sources also reflect a tendency toward fantasized alteration. The case of *The Chalk Circle* was typical. Although a more or less faithful translation of the play appeared as early as 1832 in Stanislas Julien's French version and Ethel Van der Veer's faithful English version was published in 1933, all the adaptations in New York favored Klabund's German version and catered for a thematic change. In the original Chinese version, Zhang Haitang, who has been a prostitute, is purchased and married to Lord Ma as his concubine. She gives birth to a son. Mrs. Ma, the first wife, becomes jealous and plans a murder with her paramour. One day, Haitang's brother comes to beg from his rich brother-in-law's family. Mrs. Ma instructs Haitang to give him some robes and a head ornament, and then, on the evidence of their loss, accuses Haitang, to Lord Ma, of having a lover. Lord Ma beats Haitang; Mrs. Ma puts poison in his soup and Lord Ma dies; then Mrs. Ma accuses Haitang of murdering her husband and claims Haitang's son as her own in order to claim the inheritance. Mrs. Ma bribes a corrupt judge who imprisons Haitang. The law suit is later brought up to Judge Bao, who orders the two 'mothers' to pull the child out of a chalk circle drawn around him on the floor, both at the same time. Haitang, the real mother, does not pull the child because she is unwilling to hurt the child while Mrs. Ma grabs the child's arm forcefully and pulls him out of the circle. This way Judge Bao is certain that Haitang is the real mother. Then the correct judgment follows and justice is finally done. But in Klabund's version, one significant modification is made: a character entitled 'prince' is introduced. Before Haitang is married to Lord Ma, the prince meets her in a high-class brothel and fails to outbid Lord Ma in purchasing her. But he manages to make love to her on the first night of her marriage. By the end of the story, it is the prince, who now becomes the emperor, that conducts the final trial. Finally, after Haitang is set free, the emperor and Haitang are united. Haitang becomes the empress and the emperor turns out to be the real father of the child.

In order to suit Western taste, the New York versions followed Klabund's love theme which is not in the Chinese original. To make this 'love-interest' legitimate in plot, the Western concept of romantic love guides the portrayal of characters. Haitang is a virgin when she is sold into the brothel by her destitute mother. On her first day in the brothel, the prince is attracted by her beautiful songs: 'I was led here by the song of a nightingale' (Laver, 1929: 14).[8] They fall in love at first sight. One clever device Klabund used is that he took liberties with the concept of the chalk circle itself and used the circle as a dramatic motif to connect the different acts of the play. When the two first meet in the brothel, Haitang draws a chalk circle to symbolize a mirror of the fate of the two lovers:

PO [the prince]. The circle is the symbol of the bowl of heaven; the circle is the symbol of the ring which husband and wife exchange, linking heart to heart. (Laver, 1929: 19)

She further draws in the chalk circle four magic lines which reflect the face of the prince. When she asks the prince how she has caught his likeness reflected in the circle, he answers romantically: 'You have hit me, with an arrow, to the heart!' The image of Cupid is thus secured; yet it is an utterly Western concept. To the face in the 'mirror,' she recites with passion:

> I would this were my friend indeed....
> The glances of his eyes are birds that fly
> To join the eagles in the upper sky.
> His lashes are the willow-trees that seem
> Beside a quiet lake to droop and dream.
> His hands are thin, and pale like snow
> Too many memories have made them so.
> His small, red lips are pressed together tight,
> As if they had forgotten quite
> To smile, and kiss aright.
> Alas, they are a two-edged sword of fire,
> Sweeping athwart the sleepless night of my desire! (Laver, 1929: 21)

Although the prince is unable to offer the owner of the brothel more money than Lord Ma does to purchase Haitang (which is itself an improbability in a Chinese context), he romantically climbs into her bedroom on her bridal night and enjoys her while she dreams of him. Here, the Chinese prince is portrayed as a Western gallant knight. This has legitimately paved the way for the dramatic denouement: the emperor's proclamation of Haitang as his wife and his acceptance of her child as his own son. Haitang attributes the rehabilitation of her reputation to the power of love :

> The secret truth love made to appear,
> The darkness was through love made clear.
> Love confounds the lying tongue,
> Love is triumphant over wrong,
> Love is like the sun in heaven,
> Love is the calm that falls at even,
> Love will cheat death of his prey,
> And never, never pass away. (Laver, 1929: 105)

Within such a framework of love, the family's inner strife of jealousy and greed is developed. The insertion of a romance involving a prince who fails to save his beloved at the beginning would be unconvincing to Chinese opinion. This love theme is forced upon a Chinese story to suit Western taste. Accordingly it appealed to Broadway audiences.

Furthermore, the creation of an atmosphere for romantic love in the adaptations results in a modification or elimination of the ruthlessness that exists in the original. In the Chinese version, the corrupt judge, Mrs. Ma and her paramour are all severely punished in the end: the corrupt judge is deposed from office; Mrs. Ma and her accomplice are cut into a hundred and twenty pieces. These punishments are historically true in a Chinese moral context. In the adaptations, however, the bloodshed is totally avoided. The emperor allows Haitang to pass 'the judgment on these three from [her] own clear heart':

> HI-TANG [Haitang]. ..... Chu [the corrupt judge] and Chow [Mrs. Ma's paramour and accomplice] are unworthy of their office and must lose it. Otherwise they are free to go where they will. Mrs. Ma also shall be free, although I cannot forgive her for putting poison in Mr. Ma's tea. Go. Make yourself tea I leave you to your conscience. (Laver, 1929: 102-3)

Thus Western humanitarianism substitutes for Chinese legal morality. Haitang's tolerance makes her a noble lady much needed in a romantic love story. The moral importance and urgency of ruthless vindication in the original would have tainted the 'clear hearts' of the true lovers.

As the Chinese idiom *'wu du you ou'* points out, things do not come singly but in pairs. The drastic change from brutality into civility is also distinctly reflected in *Lady Precious Stream*. It tells the widely-known Chinese story of Wang Baochuan (Precious Stream), the third daughter of a Prime Minister, and Xue Pinggui, first a poor gardener and later the king of the Western Region of China during the Tang period. Precious Stream is driven out of her rich family by her own father because of her love for a poor man. After marriage, the couple live in a cave. Later Xue's heroic act in taming an unbridled horse makes him an army officer. He is ordered to lead an army to fight against the Kingdom of the Western Region. Betrayed by Precious Stream's brother-in-law, he is captured by and married to the Princess of the Western Region. By inheritance he becomes the king of the region. Meanwhile, Precious Stream lives in poverty at home and waits for Xue's return. Her fidelity to her husband makes her suffer for eighteen years in waiting. Finally, she wins her husband back by writing a blood letter to Xue. The theme is the test of one of traditional Chinese women's fundamental virtues — chastity. Although the plot in the adaptation follows the pattern of the original, bloodshed is totally avoided. In the different Chinese versions of the Wang Baochuan story, either her father, a usurper of the throne and a ruthless father, or Wei Hu, her brother-in-law who has attempted to murder Xue, is killed in the end. Yet, the adaptation saves their lives by the virtues of all the female characters who decide the judgment instead of those men in power.

Since the original story overlaps a love theme, the adaptation does not have to sacrifice much to accommodate the story to the taste of the American audience. Even so, faithful love between Xue Pinggui and Precious Stream is still highlighted so that the marriage between Xue Pinggui and the Princess of the Western Region is not permitted in the adaptation. In the end, the relation between Xue and the Princess becomes that of brother and sister, paving the way for the reunion between Xue and his original wife. Humorously to a Western audience yet absurdly to a Chinese audience, the adaptation ends with a scene where the Princess of the Western Region is wooed in a Western style by the Minister of Foreign Affair of the Chinese kingdom who 'must have had many 'affairs' in foreign countries' (Hsiung,

1935: 168). Here, people from the Western Region are considered as foreigners to the Han Chinese. In the scene, the Chinese minister 'kisses her outstretched hand' while 'she takes his arm and looks at him lovingly' (Hsiung, 1935: 168). They both act in 'charming manners,' with a tinge of Western romanticism. Finally, Lady Precious Stream, who is supposed to be the paragon of the traditional Chinese lady, is left alone on the stage, fantasizing about herself in the same romantic situation:

> Precious Stream. (imitating the tones and actions of the Minister and Princess). 'My sincere welcome and respects to you, Your Highness!' (She kisses her own hand.) 'Oh, thank you!' (She offers her arm.) 'Will Your Highness come with me?' (She takes the offered arm.) 'With pleasure!'
> (She retires on the invisible gallant's arm.) (Hsiung, 1935: 168-9)

Such an ending reflects a penetration of the Western concept of romanticism into a story about a Chinese lady who remains chaste through a long duration of suffering. In the original version, one sees a story more of chastity than of true love in the character of Lady Precious Stream while, in the adaptation, one sees true love in the couple. The tolerance toward the villains, the imitation of Western manners and, above all, the change from the ending of one husband with two wives to that of one husband with one wife contribute to the thematic alteration in *Lady Precious Stream*.

Like *Lady Precious Stream*, the adaptation of *Lute Song* does not permit a Chinese ending of one husband with two wives, either. In the original *Pipa ji*, Cai Yong (Tsai-Yong) leaves his newly-wed wife, Zhao Wuniang (Tchao-Ou-Niang), and departs for the capital to sit for the imperial civil service examinations.[9] In the absence of her husband, Zhao Wuniang lovingly takes care of her parents-in-law for three years with the help of a good neighbor named Zhang Guangcai (Honorable Tchang). Though she sacrifices everything trying to protect them when famine breaks out, the parents do not survive. Zhao Wuniang sets out to seek her husband from whom there has been neither news nor help. Meanwhile, in the capital, having received top honors and become imperial counselor, Cai Yong is compelled by the emperor's decree and the prime minister's wish to marry the latter's daughter, Niu Ji (Nieou-Chi or Princess). Zhao Wuniang arrives in the capital and meets Niu Ji. The two reveal their identities to each other. Moved by Zhao Wuniang's filial piety, Niu Ji nobly accepts her as elder sister and first wife. Finally, the husband and the two wives go to Cai's hometown to mourn for the dead parents. The dominant theme of the Chinese *Pipa ji* is *xiao*, filial piety. Yet the American *Lute Song* changes this ending by having Cai Yong choose between the two. As a result, Niu Ji retreats; Cai Yong and Zhao Wuniang are absorbed in their mutual love.

The return from polygamy to monogamy at the end of *Lute Song* was partly prompted by the actress Mary Martin and her husband-manager, Richard Halliday. The reason is that 'sharing a man was unworthy of a star of Mary's magnitude' (Houseman, 1979: 168). The producer Myerberg yielded to this demand. Therefore, as a result, the women are treated as equals to men. In the original, their actions are subject to the norms of a male-dominant society. In *Lute Song*, one senses in both women a kind of dignity revealed by their decisions about their respective relations with Cai Yong. Specifically, Zhao Wuniang in *Pipa ji* is a dependent of Cai Yong. Whether or not he still loves her does not interfere with her decision to seek her husband and reunite with him. Her belief, like that of most Chinese traditional women, is simply that 'where husband leads, wife follows' and 'the hen must fly with the rooster' (Mulligan, 1980: 222).[10] Yet *Lute Song* tries to portray her as an equal to Cai Yong, so faithfulness in love is valid for them. Niu Ji is portrayed as a liberated woman in that she can choose to stay with or leave her husband, whereas in the original, she is only a noble woman in whose characterization the author makes her bow to the virtue of Zhao Wuniang — a reconfirmation of traditional filial piety.

The ending of one husband with one wife is quite natural in a romantic setting which determines the alterations in theme and characterization. When Cai Yong parts from Zhao Wuniang, the couple in the Chinese *Pipa ji* sing a long aria. The moods expressed are sadness, anxiety and insecurity. Their primary concern in the parting song is filial piety. When the parting song is adapted into the American *Lute Song*, the theme centers only on the relation between the husband and his wife. Zhao Wuniang sings:

> If you need me I will be nearby
> Mountain high,
> Valley low,
> My love follows you 'til the last
> ...

Cai Yong sings in reply:

> I'll be with you 'though our fortunes sway.
> ...
> When your hair turns snow white,
> You will find me by your side.
> (Irwin and Howard, 1955: 7)

The general mood of the parting song is optimistic about mutual love: there is no fear and insecurity on the part of the wife. The couple vow their love to each other. What is more significant, the song is repeated throughout the play, sometimes in words and sometimes in music, so that it becomes a motif or a theme to the degree that the whole play is developed out of it.

While the Chinese *Pipa ji* uses hardships (such as pawning personal belongings for food, eating husks, and selling hair) to portray Zhao Wuniang's virtue as a foil for her husband's moral lapse — his inability to take care of his parents personally — the American *Lute Song* treats the same hardships as tests to display Zhao Wuniang's unquestionable faith in her husband. In *Pipa ji*, Zhao Wuniang serves her parents-in-law in her husband's stead with devotion and without complaints in public, but privately she gives vent to her bitterness and sadness since her separation from her husband. In the American *Lute Song*, instead of her ambivalence toward her husband, Zhao Wuniang shows her firm belief in her love for her husband. Zhao Wuniang's love is so passionate that she even challenges her father-in-law and breaks his staff which is meant as a tool to beat Cai Yong if he ever returns. Zhao Wuniang rejects the idea and exclaims:

The gods will give me strength to break [the staff], for love is stronger than doubt or anger! (Irwin and Howard, 1955: 60)

In a true Chinese context, disobedience to one's parent, especially on his deathbed, such as Zhao Wuniang's challenge to her father-in-law's decision of beating the son, would be a violation of filial piety; Zhao Wuniang's breaking of the staff at this point would undo all her filial deeds. The same is true with the characterization of Cai Yong when he challenges the emperor by saying the following words at the court:

I defy the Emperor and the gods themselves! (Irwin and Howard, 1955: 38)

No one except rebels would say these words in traditional China. Here one senses an exhibition of the traditional American challenge to all authority. As a result, one sees in Cai Yong a brave and rebellious young American lover who believes in the proposition 'all for love and the world well lost' rather than a traditional timid and humble Chinese scholar who should be at once a loyal subject, a dutiful husband and a filial son.

Most critics of *Lute Song* failed even to mention filial piety when they retold the story in their reviews. The appreciation of the change of theme from filial piety to love is reflected in the critic George Jean Nathan's review of the play's premiere on Broadway. With his background knowledge about *Pipa ji*, Nathan was the only critic who noticed the shift in theme at the time. 'This,' said he, 'is not only thoroughly legitimate... but even an improvement, at least in the case of the Western stage. The filial piety idea in the original is overly extended in treatment... the counterpoint story of the young husband [and wife] is the stronger dramatic thread, and the adapters have in the main done well with it' (Nathan, 1956: 588). What Nathan complained about is *Lute Song*'s allusion to filial piety carried over from the Chinese original which, he thinks, 'at times...intrudes' (Nathan, 1946: 588). What Nathan observed simply means that the love story, rather than the story of filial piety, accords with the Western mentality.

Being the products of American hands, *The Yellow Jacket*, *The Chalk Circle* and *Lute Song* reflected a Broadway tendency to present traditional Chinese subjects in a fantasized or romanticized way. Though *Lady Precious Stream* was adapted by a Chinese expatriate scholar, it was also influenced by such a romantic trend. Though claimed by their authors to be the representation of the Chinese spirit, these plays were substantially influenced by the love theme indispensable in a Broadway play. The Chinese loving attachments, if any, were treated according to the American ideal that love conquers all. Hence the message was this: exotic as they are, the Chinese share the same values as the Americans. What was presented as different from the American remains theatrical (in the manner of rich colorful costumes, stage conventions and acting style), linguistic (in the manner of flowery language full of aphorisms) and superficially cultural (in the manner of visible behavior).

While exoticism was the main focus or attraction of such a group of plays when Broadway's imagination turned to traditional China, the experience of producing Chinese plays has borne fruit in presenting Chinese staging techniques on the American stage. An analysis of the theatrical aspects of some influential adaptations will illustrate the point.

It can be safely said that the production of *The Yellow Jacket* practices with all-round Chinese staging techniques for the first time in history on the Western stage. As a protest against the theatrical realism entrenched on the American stage, J. Harry Benrimo conceived the idea of doing *The Yellow Jacket*. He found in George Hazelton the first sympathetic reaction to the idea of a play in non-realistic mode. The popularity of *The Yellow Jacket* was largely secured by its Chinese theatricality. The play was reviewed and commented on mostly because of its stage techniques. It is true that the play was 'done in a Chinese manner' as the authors declared on the title page of the published text (Hazelton and Benrimo, 1913: i). Its theatrical origin was purely in the Chinese theatre in Chinatown. Benrimo was brought up in California. His familiarity with the Chinese theatre dated from his early youth. He spent many hours in the old Jackson Street and the old Washington Street Chinese theatres in San Francisco, watching the ubiquitous property man set the stage, listening to the actors in an attempt to fathom the meaning of their falsetto sing-song and conventionalized gestures, and getting Chinese friends to explain to him the action (Chu, 1936: 284). Later, as an actor and director, he employed what he had learned about Chinese staging (Benrimo, 1928). It was made clear on the play bill of the first production that 'the Scene Represents the Stage of a Chinese Theatre, Modeled After the Old Jackson Street Theatre, San Francisco' (Hazelton and Benrimo, 1913: xi). A review of the stage directions in the published text and of the photos of various stage scenes reveals the employment of the following Chinese techniques.

The stage of *The Yellow Jacket* is a Western proscenium modified into a traditional Chinese stage:

Curtains part, revealing a set in dull orange with green and gold trimmings. There are two doors, one stage left for entrance and one stage right for exit. In the center at the back is an oval opening surrounded by a grill, within which the musicians sit. (Hazelton and Benrimo, 1913: 4)

The properties are basic: chairs and tables. Within the decorative framework that carries the imagination into realms of fancy, there is no scenery in the performing area, which is the essence of the traditional Chinese stage.

On the modified bare stage, the different scenes are created by the basic properties of a symbolic nature with the help of the property man and his assistants; the changes of scenes are effected by the entrances and exits of characters and the narration of the Chorus and characters.[11] By arranging chairs and stools in different patterns, many scenes are created symbolically. As on a Chinese stage, a whip is used to stand for a horse and two wheel banners are carried by two assistant property men to form a chariot. With these and other simple props the actors are challenged in a more difficult way to effect the symbolism and the audience is more engaged in creative imagination.

The Chinese property man is deliberately overwrought to 'reflect the spirit rather than the substance' (Hazelton and Benrimo, 1913: vii), so he is treated as a non-dramatic character on the stage. Present on the stage all the time, he sets the symbolic settings by arranging tables, chairs and stools with the help of his assistants, gives to characters such properties as sword, whip, etc., signals the Chorus to explain imaginary settings, and does his own business such as reading a Chinese newspaper, smoking and eating while he is not required in the development of the plot. The audience has been reminded earlier by the Chorus that the 'property man is to your eyes intensely invisible' (Hazelton and Benrimo, 1913: 4). Yet, here and elsewhere, the Property Man is 'intensely' visible since he is performing on the stage. The Property Man is magnified to let the American audience see clearly what is going on on a typical Chinese stage such as the author-director Benrimo had witnessed in the Chinese theatres in Chinatown.

According to the stage directions, actors were to use pantomimic gestures and body movements to symbolize the actions of riding a horse, entering and exiting from doors, closing windows, etc. In the episodes of the hero's adventures, a kind of acrobatics seems to be choreographed into various fighting scenes. The costumes are very rich in color and exotic to the American audience. Standard artificial beards are worn by some characters as well. Wu the Great wears a black beard and the Philosopher a white beard. The 'painted face' convention is applied to some of the evil characters. The second wife's father is modeled upon the role of painted face as his name Fah Min (the Cantonese term for *hualian*) suggests. Although the play does not involve any singing, music is used in a modified way. Chinese-style percussion music is employed to accompany the movement of the characters. Musicians are seated in the center at the back, modeled upon the Chinese stage as Benrimo saw it in Chinatown.[12]

Overall, *The Yellow Jacket* was staged in a Chinese way. The Chinese Ambassador in London, who saw the performance for several times when it was later produced there, said: 'It is sufficiently Chinese to make me homesick.'[13] A.E. Zucker, author of *The Chinese Theatre* (1925), one of the few

Western books on the subject at the time, commented when the play was revived in 1928: 'Present-day Americans who wish to get the spirit of the Chinese theatre had best turn to *The Yellow Jacket*' (Zucker, 1929: 18; 74).

The significance of introducing these Chinese theatrical practices to the American stage lies in three historical factors. First, the play was produced around the time when serious American dramatists, playwrights and players began to struggle against the dominance of physical realism and spiritual emptiness in the theatre; second, such an all-round introduction of Chinese theatrical practices by Western actors was the first in the history of Western theatre; third, the play was widely seen through its many revivals in New York and other cities. One of the critics expressed his point brilliantly about its stagecraft at the time of the play's first revival on Broadway:

Mr. Hazelton and Mr. Benrimo... had translated into concrete terms the new, abstract ideas that were already tingling in the minds of such men as Reinhardt and Stanislavsky... Nothing in the theatre could seem credible except what was transmuted into truth by the active imagination of the audience. Many centuries from now, when the history of the 'new stagecraft' comes ultimately to be written, this superbly imaginative play by Hazelton and Benrimo will be referred to as a marking milestone in the progress of the drama from the imitation of the actual to the adoration of the real.[14]

The significance of *The Yellow Jacket* was not limited to America; its influence was international. The play was performed in many cities in Europe. People who staged the play included such world masters as Reinhardt, Stanislavsky, Tairov and Benavente.[15] Although its impact upon the Western theatre masters could not be compared to that of Mei Lanfang's American and Russian tours in the 1930s, *The Yellow Jacket* served as the first bridge between Chinese and Western theatricality. In other words, it exported Chinatown theatre to the world in an American version.

Unlike *The Yellow Jacket* which applied Chinese practices to all its theatrical components, *Lute Song* adopted a few Chinese conventions which were combined with features of the Broadway musical. Its theatrical aspects reminiscent of Chinese practices include the color symbolism of the back drop curtains and hangings, the visibility of the 'invisible' property men, conventional pantomime, and the employment of the Stage Manager/ character role.

The casting of one actor in two roles such as the stage manager and one character in the play follows the convention of *fumo kaichang*: the opening of the show by the Stage Manager's remarks on the nature of the play in a summarizing fashion in the Chinese *chuanqi* plays. This presumed stage manager is always in the role of an old man and often performs one or more secondary old male characters. Based on Bazin's faithful translation that reflects this stage convention, *Lute Song* engages one actor in the roles of the Stage Manager and Zhang Guangcai, the venerable old neighbor. By doing so, *Lute Song* introduced to the American stage, for the first time, the existence of a Stage-Manager figure who also plays other roles in Chinese drama. Different roles assumed by the same actor make the drama much more theatrical. When the narrative function of the Manager is combined with the illusionary function of a dramatic character, the drama develops between the realm of illusion and the realm of reality:

MANAGER: [after he introduces the theme of the play and listens to the opening monologue of Tsai Yong in his study] Now I assume my part in the playthat of the Honorable Tchang, an old friend of the family and counselor to them and the whole village.

(During this speech the FIRST PROPERTY MAN enters R, carrying a hat. He removes the MANAGER's robe, exchanges the hats and withdraws R. The SECOND PROPERTY MAN enters L, carrying a stool which he places D R C, and withdraws L. The MANAGER speaks to the audience.)

TCHANG: Nine families have I advised in the last three days and now comes the affair of this obstinate young scholar! (Goes up steps right of platform and knocks on imaginary door. In similar pantomime, TSAI-YONG pushes aside books, rises, opens imaginary door.... TCHANG... enters.) Tsai-Yong, why do you linger here? The Emperor of the Middle Kingdom summons all young scholars to the capital to prove by examination their right to be exalted in the Imperial Service. (Irwin and Howard, 1955: 12)

Then the two engage in a dialogue. In this way, the Manager walks into and out of the drama smoothly with the property men's assistance. The function of the Manager in *Lute Song* is different from that of the Chorus in *The Yellow Jacket*, that of the Mistress of Ceremonies of Mei Lanfang's performances in New York, and that of the Honorable Reader in *Lady Precious Stream*: the latter is created on the Western stage to explain the Chinese conventions to Western audiences while the former is inherent in the dramatic structure of the Chinese *chuanqi* play. Such a structure, when realized on stage, was a revealing theatrical technique to those who sought for non-realistic methods. Among Western theatrical innovators, Thornton Wilder was the first to make this structure vital to his own dramaturgy.[16]

If *The Yellow Jacket* was directly influenced by the Chinese theatres in America, then *Lute Song* resulted from both direct contacts with live Chinese performances and scholarly translations. These two productions represented two forms of influences. A third form of influence was theatrical direction and actor training by Chinese experts.

The first event in the third category was the Broadway production of *Lady Precious Stream*. Under Hsiung's direction, the production employed conventions of the Peking Opera stage. Noticeable to the critics are the same techniques employed in *The Yellow Jacket*. Judging from the stage photos, the costumes were of an authentic style, much more faithful to the Chinese original than those used in *The Yellow Jacket* and *Lute Song*. The experiment was much appreciated by the theatre public because the production offered a fairly good example of an American performance of a Chinese play under the direction of a Chinese expert. Based upon a scholarly translation and approached with expertise in taste and discernment, the production of *Lady Precious Stream* on Broadway and beyond started a new trend in staging Chinese plays on the American stage.

The next effective event was A.C. Scott's production of the Peking Opera play *The Butterfly Dream (Hudie meng* or *Da pi guan)* under the auspice of the Institute for Advanced Studies in Theatre Arts (IASTA).[17] Scott's English translation of the play, like his other translations in his three volumes of *Traditional Chinese Plays*, provides more theatricality than any other translations in that his copious stage directions give detailed description of the character's movements — a landmark in the history of English translations of Chinese plays. The significance lies in the fact that the production of *The Butterfly Dream* emphasized authentic body movements and exact stylized gestures, the first of its kind in the American history of staging Chinese plays. To impart to a cast of American, British and Canadian actors the knowledge and skill of Chinese stage movements — walking, running, symbolic gesture, complex sleeve movement, facial expression, hair movement, beard movement, and acrobatic fighting, Scott invited two Peking Opera performers, Hu Hung-yen and Hu Yung-fang from Hong Kong, to coach the Western actors. The six weeks of rehearsal mainly centered on body training. What was attempted in the production was to develop the actor's practical understanding and application of traditional Chinese methods in staging a play. The play deals with the fickleness of woman. Although the literary value of such a work is slight, 'its entire value lies in the experience generated on stage and in the auditorium by clearly defined and artistically rendered stylization' (Pronko, 1967: 49). From a theatrical point of view, the production of *The Butterfly Dream* was a big step forward from that of *Lady Precious Stream*. The staging of a Chinese play no longer stayed at the superficial level of imitation. The production aimed at the true spirit of acting.

Since the 1960s, performances of Chinese plays done by American actors in a Chinese manner under the direction of a Chinese expert have sprung up at various university campuses and theatrical research institutions. To name a few noted in various publications, *Hong luan xi (Twice a Bride)*, was performed in 1963 at the University of Hawaii and then in 1967 at Hanover College, Indiana; *Meilong zhen (The Price of Wine)* was produced at Grinnell College in 1963 and later staged at the State University of Iowa; *Jiugeng tian (One Missing Head)* was presented at the University of North Carolina at Greensboro in 1967; *Wulong yuan (Black Dragon Residence)* was played at the University of Colorado; *The White Snake* was presented as theatrical demonstration at the Asia Society in New York in 1972. The 1980s witnessed further development in staging Chinese plays. On February 14, 1985, the Peking Opera play *Feng huan chao (The Phoenix Returns to Her Nest)* was staged with singing in an English version accompanied by authentic tunes at the University of Hawaii. All the above productions were either directed or coached by Chinese professors in theatre or Chinese professional actors. The staging of Chinese plays in America has become ever more authentic.

The rich Chinese theatricalities revealed by scholars and exhibited by live Chinese performances have been in one way or another practiced by American theatre people. The most practiced on the American stage are the appearance of the property men in full view of the audience, the concept of a bare stage, the narrative mode, the symbolic properties, the imaginary pantomime, and the Stage Manager's multi-role. The imitative and innovative uses of these Chinese techniques have been part of the conscious effort of American playwrights, directors and performers to break away from the realistic mode traditionally dominating the American stage. Like other Asian theatrical traditions, Chinese conventions have been digested in various American innovations leading to new ways of presenting life and will become indispensable to the search for a total theatre.

To sum up, when the American theatre people presented classic Chinese plays in their adaptations on stage, particularly on the Broadway stage, they had two main concerns. Thematically, they tended to magnify the love seed between man and woman from the original and worked it into a full-blown romance or fantasy. In traditional Chinese culture, expressions of love have always been very much a private matter. Marital love or love between male and female tends to be regarded as a sexual matter. The characters in classical plays would openly sing about the gratifications of their love, but those gratifications have to yield to the glory of fulfilling social and familial duties such as duties of being loyal to the superior, doing justice, getting revenge and exemplifying filial piety. Due to the private and sexual nature of love in the Chinese context, love between couples is most often suppressed as a negative thing whenever it conflicts with the couple's respective duty in the family and society. Love, if present at all, is not depicted in plays with major themes of revenge, chastity, and filial piety as romantic and spiritually ideal, as in the American adaptations. Duty and obligation come first and love between couples is always secondary. The adapters bypassed these subtleties and highly romanticized the love between male and female. In the seed of love in the original they tend to see a confirmation of the Western idea that love is universal and love conquers all.

Theatrically, Chinese staging techniques have been consciously explored, adapted and employed in order to break down the dominance of realistic theatricality and to create new theatrical modes that serve the dramatic purposes of expressing political meanings, elevating social life to the level of a higher significance, probing into psychological reality, and revealing symbolic implications. George Kernodle and Portia Kernodle, in their *Invitation to the Theatre*, comment on the present-day American stage in its relation to the Chinese theatre: 'Authors write monologues and direct addresses to the audience. Scenery is changed, often in full light, before the eyes of the audience; the use of masks, symbolic properties, and fragments of settings is acceptable to the theatregoers. Time and space can be made completely flexible' (Kernodle, 1978: 162). These features that seem commonplace nowadays are all reminiscent of Chinese techniques.

In short, in the process of this theatrical encounter, the American stage condescendingly remolded Chinese cultural images with Western values while respectfully studying the Chinese theatricalities and absorbing them into a system of non-realistic stagecraft.

References

Benrimo, J. Harry (1913): London's Play In The Chinese Way: Mr. Henry Benrimo Explains 'The Yellow Jacket.' *London Weekly Bugle*, April 16.

Benrimo. J. Harry (1928): The Facts About 'The Yellow Jacket.' *The New York Times*, November 4.

Chu, Peter, et al. (1936): *Chinese Theatre In America*. Bureau of Research, Region of the West, Federal Theatre Project (Division of W.P.A.).

Hazelton, George C. and J. Harry Benrimo (1913): *The Yellow Jacket*. Indianapolis: Bobbs-Merrill Publishers.

Houseman, John (1979): *Front and Center*. New York: Simon and Schuster.

Hsiung, S. I. (1935): *Lady Precious Stream*. New York: Liveright.

Irwin, Will and Sidney Howard, trans. & adapt. (1955): *Lute Song*. By Kao-Tong-Kia. Chicago: Dramatic Publishing Company.

Kernodle, George and Portia Kernodle (1978): *Invitation to the Theatre*. Brief 2nd ed. New York: Harcourt Brace Jovanovich.

Laver, James (1929): *The Circle of Chalk*. London: Heinemann.

Mulligan, Jean, trans. (1980): *The Lute: Kao Ming's P'i-p'a chi*. New York: Columbia University Press.

Nathan, George Jean (1946): 'The Theatre: the Lute, the Trombone and Criticism.' *American Mercury*, 62 (May), pp. 587-90.

Pronko, Leonard Cabell (1967): *Theater East and West: Perspective Toward A Total Theatre*. Berkeley: University of California Press.

White, Sidney Howard (1977): *Sidney Howard*. Boston: Twayne.

Zucker, A.E. (1929): »How 'Chinese' Is Our Chinese Drama?« *Theatre Magazine*, 49 (January), 18, pp. 74.

Notes

1. Louis Laloy's French dramatization entitled *Le Chagrin dans le Palais de Han* was first produced at the Théâtre des Arts, Paris on June 2, 1911.
2. Moshe Leib Halpern's version was directed by Maurice Schwartz and produced by the Yiddish Art Theatre Players at the Bayes Theatre on December 22, 1925. I. S. Richter's version was staged by himself on December 29, 1930, at the American theatre by Adrienne La Champ on August 22, 1993 at the Playmillers Theatre. James Laver's version was presented by the Dramatic Workshop of the New school at its Studio Theatre, directed by James Light under the supervision of Erwin Piscator on March 25, 1941; this production was revived in 1947 for the United Nations Festival and in 1950 at the President Theatre. Some of these productions were off-Broadway.
3. The story of the chalk circle was also an inspiration for Bertolt Brecht's *The Caucasian Chalk Circle*, whose world première was at Carlton College, Northfield, Minnesota, in the spring of 1948. Its first Broadway production was at the Vivian

Beaumont Theatre on March 24, 1966, under the direction of Jules Irving in Eric Bently's English version.

4. There are different titles for the Chinese versions of the story. *Hongzong liema (Redhaired Stud)* and *Wang Baochuan* are two well-known titles for the complete version of the story. S.I. Hsiung was a Chinese expatriate scholar living in England and his adaptation was first produced with success in London.

5. Based on the French translation by Antoine P.L. Bazin, Howard and Irwin adapted the Chinese *Pipa ji* into *Lute Song* in the late twenties. On September 1, 1930, they had their adaptation tried out at the Berkshire Playhouse, Stockbridge, Massachusetts, under the direction of Alexander Kirkland (White, 1977: 155, n. 1). The play had waited for almost fifteen years before it appeared on a Broadway stage. The Broadway première was directed by John Houseman, with Mary Martin and Yul Brynner (his debut on Broadway) as the heroine and hero.

6. The spellings of characters' names with their English meanings in parentheses are from the published script (Hazelton and Benrimo, 1913). The transliterations are obviously based on the Cantonese dialect.

7. *Zhaoshi gu'er* was the first Chinese play ever translated into a Western language. The French Jesuit J. Prémare rendered it as *Tchao-chi-cou-eulh, ou l'orphelin de la maison de Tchao, tragédie chinoise* in 1735 and Voltaire adapted it for the French stage as *L'Orphelin de la Chine* in 1755. The first English version appeared in William Hatchett's *The Chinese Orphan: a Historical Tragedy, Alter'd from a Specimen of Chinese Tragedy in Du Halde's History of China, Interspers'd with Songs* in 1741. Five more English versions followed in the eighteenth century. It is highly likely that Benrimo had read the play, or that as a theatre goer in Chinatown, he had seen one or more performances of the play in San Francisco, since it has been part of the permanent repertoire of traditional Chinese theatres including the Cantonese Opera, the main genre in the Chinatowns of American cities.

8. In discussion, I use Laver's English version which is translated directly from Klabund's version.

9. The different spellings of the names in parentheses are used in *Lute Song*.

10. Mulligan's translation is a faithful version of the original.

11. The one-man Chorus is created to help explain the Chinese stage conventions to the American audience.

12. Some photos of the New York Chinatown stages taken around the turn of the century show the same location of the musicians.

13. Quoted from the Yellow Jacket Scrapbook, MWNZ + n.c. 4328, pp. 110-11, the Billy Rose Theatre Collection, the New York Public Library at the Lincoln Center for the Performing Arts.

14. Quoted from an unidentified newspaper clipping in the Yellow Jacket Scrapbook, MWNZ + n.c. 4328, pp. 110-11, the Billy Rose Theatre Collection, the New York Public Library at the Lincoln Center for the Performing Arts.

15. The play first went to London where it was performed at the Duke of York's Theatre for almost two hundred nights. Then the play was translated into German and produced in Berlin by Max Reinhardt. He presented the play all over central Europe, initiating innumerable actors and stage managers into the subtleties of Chinese acting via Benrimo's expertise. This version was subsequently acted in

other German cities. It was exported to Vienna, which led to Magyar version in Budapest, Hungary. In Russia, the play was produced under the name of *Jeltaya Kofta*. Under Stanislavsky, Meyerhold and Tairov attentively studied the production. Tairov himself later produced the play with his wife Alice Koonen, the best known interpreter of tairov's ideas, playing the role of Plum Blossom. The performance of the play quickened the interset of Russian stage directors in the Oriental theatre. Having had an interest in the Oriental platform stage before. Meyerhold was stimulated by *Jeltaya Kofta* and turned his attention specifically to the Chinese and then to the Japanese theatre. The French version was prepared during World War I and later produced in Paris after the War. In Spain, the play was translated by Jacinto Benavente, the greatest living dramatist at the time. It was produced in Madrid with great success and toured Spanish speaking cities in South America. The information on the productions in Europe comes from three sources: 1) Chu, *The Chinese Theatre*, 1935: 289-92; 2) an unidentified critic's review of the revival of the play in America in the late 1920s, in the Yellow Jacket Scrapbook, MWNZ + n.c. 4328, the Billy Rose Theatre Collection, the New York Public Library at the Lincoln Center for the Performing Arts; and 3) the Coburn's promotion leaflets for the play's revival on November 7, 1928, in the file of 'The Yellow Jacket MWEZ + n.c. 12354,' the Billy Rose Theatre Collection, the New York Public Library at the Lincoln Center for the Performing Arts.

16. In Wilder's famous play *Our Town*, the Stage Manager introduces the play and the background of each character, plays some secondary characters such as the drugstore owner, the minister of the church, etc., and arranges the stage properties in the full view of the audience. It is highly likely that Wilder had read Bazin's French translation of the *Pipa ji* or seen the earlier regional production of Howard and Irwin's English version before he wrote his own play.

17. The play was first produced at the auditorium of the Library of Congress on November 27 and 28, 1961, and at the IASTA for 10 performances beginning on December 1, 1961. In 1966, the IASTA staged it at the Greenwich Mews Theatre in New York. The IASTA was founded by Dr. and Mrs. John D. Mitchell for young professionals to become familiar with foreign theatrical traditions under the direction of masters of those traditions.

Zhang Yimou:
Inter/National Aesthetics and Erotics

Wendy Larson

Three of Zhang Yimou's internationally known films all show a similar structure in which eroticization both indicates national strength and points toward
an international aesthetic perspective. In *Red Sorghum* (1987), for example, the
character Jiu'er becomes the fulcrum through which male power is directed
toward national salvation. Through her active participation in erotic play and
the organization of power through erotics, Jiu'er arranges a group of male
workers into productive order and galvanizes them toward sacrifice for the
nation in a battle with the Japanese. In *Judou* (1989) the lead female character,
Judou, similarly tries to use erotics to motivate Tianqing, yet they are
struggling on behalf of their own happiness against a hegemonic system.
Although Judou is also implicitly working against feudal organization for the
good of the Chinese nation/culture, she is not as successful as is Jiu'er. In
Raise High the Red Lanterns (1991), Songlian feebly attempts to eroticize and
empower her master's son, but because he is afraid of women he cannot re-
spond and throw off the bonds of this evil traditional household.

The narrative movement in each film is remarkably similar. The female
character played by Gong Li is positioned between two men, one an older
man who is diseased, perverted, or cruel, and who marries her through an
arranged agreement for economic reasons, and the other a younger man who
has a relatively healthy body and is attracted to her erotically. The first two
films also have a son based on the union of the woman and the younger man.
In *Red Sorghum*, the younger man transfers his creative power to the son and
then on to the narrating grandson, but in *Ju Dou* the son denies his biological
father, instead recognizing the older man and insisting on social orthodoxy
through correct nomination. In *Raise High the Red Lantern*, the young man
makes only a fleeting entrance and there is no offspring. Arranged in a chart
the relationships look like this:

	Red Sorghum	*Judou*	*Raise Lanterns*
WOMAN:	Jiu'er	Judou	Songlian
OLD MAN:	leper	Jinshan	Master
YOUNG MAN:	Grandpa Tianqing	Master's son	
CHILD:	Douguan	Tianbai	--------

In all three cases, a woman becomes the point through which a young male character can fight for modernity, progress, and Chinese national culture. She must catalyse through erotics, and in the end she is destroyed. As Zhang Yimou continues his experiment, we see that this female character's power becomes progressively weaker and the young male character loses the ability to fight, indicating that Zhang is losing faith in the formula of hinging cultural modernity on masculine re-empowerment through feminine erotic engagement. The power of the traditional order, in every case symbolized by an old man who wishes to harness the female character's eroticism not for progress but to bolster his own ageing and weakness, gets stronger as Zhang continues through the films. In *Red Sorghum* this power, as represented by the leper, is virtually unseen and easily destroyed. In *Judou* the old husband Jinshan puts up a good fight by utilizing the discursive system of kinship and family definition to capture the son's voice and identify himself as father, but he eventually dies. In *Red Lanterns* the master is abstracted beyond our direct vision (we never see his face) and is strong throughout.

While the old man gains in strength as we go chronologically through the films, the young man loses power. *Red Sorghum*'s Grandpa murders Jiu'er's leperous husband and establishes himself as head of the household and winery, and goes on to lead the fight against the Japanese. Tianqing of *Judou* consummates a sexual relationship with Judou but cannot bring himself to kill Jinshan and take the patriarch's place. The son in *Red Lanterns* recognizes Songlian's erotic desire toward him but professes fear of women and, through symbolic play with a flute, identifies himself as homosexual.

The erotics and the aesthetics of Zhang's films often attract attention in the west, where critics define them as 'powerful' and Gong Li as 'the most beautiful woman in the world.'[1] Some critics were disappointed with Zhang's latest film, *Qiuju Goes to Court* (1993), because Zhang has somewhat altered his direction and Gong Li is allowed only brief display of sexuality. In adapting novels for the screen, Zhang Yimou makes choices that further this investigation of erotics and power. This paper analyses his techniques and discusses the cultural meaning of his filmic investigation, showing how Zhang relies on an erotic enactment of masculinity and femininity through tropes familiar to Hollywood film.

Erotics and aesthetics cannot be clearly separated in Zhang's work, but intertwine to produce different meanings for different viewers. Whereas the erotics of Zhang's films do not shock the western viewer, but lend themselves to analysis within notions of repression and individual desire, they are more significant to the Chinese viewer, and critique national culture as a kind of personal and collective repression. For the western viewer, it is the violent aesthetics that appear shocking and seem to be speaking directly about Chinese life. Just as erotics provide the thematic and aesthetic fulcrum between Chinese society and international films and film audience, the woman is situated at the crux of transference, and uses her erotic power to propel the positive male character toward a viable national future. However, Zhang loses faith in this formula by the time he directs *Red Lanterns*, and depicts the remasculination of the Chinese cultural body as a myth.

Red Sorghum

In terms of erotics and aesthetics, *Red Sorghum* possesses great ideological clarity, which comes from Zhang's decision to highlight one aspect of Mo Yan's novel *Honggaoliang jiazu* and disregard the rest. In focusing on the Japanese invasion of China as it is played out in a small village, Zhang delineates an historical and cultural enemy that is easily recognized by all.

Critics have pointed out Zhang Yimou's shocking use — in terms of pre-Fifth Generation cinema — of the semi-naked male body in initial scenes with the sedan bearers, in Grandpa's many appearances, and in wine-making and wine-drinking episodes. In 'Ideology of the Body in *Red Sorghum*: National Allegory, National Roots, and Third Cinema,' Yingjin Zhang discusses the 'sweat and dirt' and the 'sheer presence of muscles' that foreground the [male] human body and privilege it, 'with all its undaunted violence and vitality, over the repressive tradition of the Chinese (patriarchal) society' (39-40). Zhang believes that *Red Sorghum* can be viewed as an attempt, in a way described in the research of Mikhail Bakhtin, 'to return the human body from its now private and psychological status to its original public domain' (41). Thus sweating and urinating, supposedly intimate acts, are performed publicly and define *Red Sorghum* as 'a reunion of the private and the public' (42) that coelesces into a 'powerful unifying force' (43).[2]

It may be difficult to construct a case for a privatized and psychologized body that is now 'returning' to some kind of originary public power, but Yingjin Zhang's analysis brings out the physicality and violence of *Red Sorghum* and allows us to consider the way these elements function aesthetically to startle and disarm Chinese viewers. At the same time these forms assure the western viewer that this indeed is serious cinema that 'knows' about the conventions of modernity — in particular those of Hollywood.

On the second issue, Yuejin Wang has analysed how in the context of cinema, Fredric Jameson's theory of national allegory and third world texts is difficult to totally deny.[3] While Wang dislikes the theory because it turns Chinese film into nothing but the 'cinematic grunts and frets of a society under colonial tyranny,' he admits that 'the attempt to wrest oneself from the overwhelming dominance of the colonizing metropolitan countries is a cultural given one can hardly ignore' (33). This is because the 'structure of the film industry is a capitalist construct' (33) and indeed the 'traditional' aesthetics of Chinese film are nothing more than 'the theatrical consciousness cast into the grammatical mold of classical Hollywood, motivated by traditional didactic desires and later by Soviet dogmatism' (36). *Red Sorghum*, with its action, violence, naked male bodies, and relatively overt sexuality, flies in the face of this formula.

Red Sorghum marks itself as Fifth Generation film that refuses to focus its critique on the historical past, postulating that something far more basic is wrong with the state, the culture, the people and their social interactions. Through the equivalence of the leperous body with the cultural and national body, *Red Sorghum* implies that 'ours [i.e. the Chinese] is a diseased body' (Wang, 35). However, a new, vigorous, male body has emerged and can carry the modernizing burden.

Wang also provides an answer to the first question — that is, how does the film appeal to western viewers, by showing how *Red Sorghum*'s search for an alternative other to Chinese civilization — a search common to Fifth Generation films — is interpreted by western viewers as simply national allegory, a Chinese film about China. Yet there is also another way in which the film situates itself as world cinema: by its interpretation and representation of national and cultural crises as problems for which solutions gendered through familiar tropes of masculinity and femininity can be proposed.

Since the early days of the feminist movement, American scholars have been interested in the construction of masculinity in literature, film, sports, television, and psychology, and its meaning for women as well as men.[4] Film critics have noted that while the 1960s and 1970s roles for women are limited to '[w]hores, quasi-whores, jilted mistresses, emotional cripples, drunks... [d]affy ingenues, Lolitas, kooks, sex-starved spinsters, psychotics....[i]cebers, zombies, and ballbreakers,' the 'film protagonist who is sensitive, or alienated, or baffled, or idealistic, or triumphant is invariably male' (3-4).[5] More recently, in an article about William Holden and the spectacle of masculinity in 1950s film, Steven Cohen shows how in the film *Picnic* the muscular, clean-shaven (even on the chest) male not only gazes at the female, but himself becomes the target of the erotic female gaze. Cohen argues against the interpretation of this female gaze as empowerment of the woman, however, because 'all of this visual attention to Hal keeps turning the film's narrative around the problem of his masculinity, which gets played out at the site of his body, and not Madge's sexuality... Madge therefore does not dominate the film's focalization or discourse...' (208).[6]

The shot-reverse-shot gaze scene in *Red Sorghum* also specularizes the male body and shows Jiu'er gazing with open desire at the working, muscular body of Grandpa, at that time one of the sedan bearers.[7] Although Jiu'er's feet are fetishized and made the object of Grandpa's desire, she by contrast is fully clothed, even when she lies down on the sorghum with her arms and legs spread out waiting to be ravished. Yet as in *Picnic*, the visual attention that Grandpa gets does not truly empower the woman or center her as the dominant interest of the discourse. In the first half of the film Zhang Yimou continues to play upon Grandpa's muscular strength, deviating from the novel by showing him physically pick up Jiu'er and carry her into the house as he establishes himself as the household head.

Grandpa's physical strength and renegade mentality are used up in symbolically meaningless manual labor until he is activated by Jiu'er's erotic gaze. After he chases/runs after her into the sorghum and rapes/makes love to her, Grandpa kills off her leper husband and his son and signs on as a laborer at her winery. After a few drunken antics in which he is thoroughly humiliated by Jiu'er and her workers, Grandpa makes claim to his offspring growing inside Jiu'er, sullies (and consequently improves) the wine with masculine fluids, and in an act of sheer mental bravado and physical power carries Jiu'er into her own home. He thus replaces Jiu'er's rightful husband and his son with himself and his own son.

In the second half of the film, Jiu'er's ability to erotically catalyse Grandpa becomes the need to galvanize Grandpa and the other laborers toward national salvation.[8] It is Jiu'er who demands that the men drink wine to prove that they are men, and go out to fight the Japanese. Viewers cringe as they watch the most terrifying scene of the film, the flaying, but this too refers back to a Hollywood convention. Yvonne Tasker, writing on masculinity and the body in the late 1980s and early 1990s, comments that Hollywood's obsession with the male body as spectacle and masculinity as performance plays on 'images of power and powerlessness at the center of which is the male hero' and that 'suffering — torture, in particular — operates as both a set of narrative hurdles to be overcome, tests that the hero must survive, and as a set of aestheticized images to be lovingly dwelt on' (230).[9] While it may be impossible to consider the flaying episode as something to be lovingly dwelt on and the person flayed does not survive, the male body is empowered through its muscularity and its ability to withstand torture; at the same time, violence is aestheticized through a number of close-up shots of blood, ripping flesh, and agonized looks.

Jiu'er successfully empowers Grandpa and the other men, and this strength is passed on in a directly male lineage in which she has no part outside of that of catalyst and vessel. Whereas this subsidiary role is traditional, the empowerment of the male for national salvation through erotic engagement is not, nor is the muscular specularization of the male body. When the enemy and the trajectory of struggle are clear, the film presents a direct line of action toward national fulfillment through specifically gendered and eroticized roles that are tropes of power in Hollywood film.[10] In his next film, Zhang Yimou questions the validity of this structure.

Judou

In a telling move, Zhang Yimou chooses an actor in his forties to play the role of Tianqing, who in Liu Heng's novel *Fuxi fuxi* is twenty to Judou's twenty-four when they begin their affair.[11] This transformation marks the beginning of the loss of male physical and cultural power and of the eroticized female catalyst as an alternative to a deadening social orthodoxy. Whereas *Red Sorghum* contains an aestheticized male body that can be eroticized and put into motion through a shot of desire from a woman, *Judou* shows an older, less muscular, more timid male body that also receives and projects desire but is unable to move toward decisive action. The power in Grandpa's body and totally absent from Jiu'er's leperous husband is split more evenly between the two men in *Judou*, with Jinshan initially possessing enough physical strength to kill two wives and beat Judou black and blue, and eventually able to transform physical strength, which he loses progressively as the film goes on, into social and hierarchichal power and into a truly terrifying reproduction of both physical and social force in the child Tianbai. In contrast, Tianqing loses any kind of power through the progress of the story.

As in *Red Sorghum*, Judou is married to Jinshan to gain economic benefit for her family. The novel carries the story well up into the 1950s and later, tracing the way in which Jinshan's exchange of land for Judou ironically saved him from classification as a landlord in the Communist era. Zhang's film, however, places the narrative 'sometime in the 1920s' in a small unidentified village, furthering the ahistorical critique for which Fifth Generation directors are well-known. The existence of an interiority of doubts, warmth, and musing in both Jinshan and Tianbai that becomes clear throughout the novel is missing completely in the film, highlighting Zhang's decision to turn both characters into symbolic forces of the past and the future.[12]

The aesthetic presentation of environment typical of *Red Sorghum* is continued in *Judou*, but the focus is brought inward and fixed on the colorful dye bolts, an invention not in the novel at all. Judou's body takes the center, upstaging Tianqing's aging male body. In contrast to *Red Sorghum*, Zhang Yimou shoots many shots of Judou scantily clad, with breasts clearly visible through thin material, and even nearly naked. It is through presentation of her naked body to the peeping Tianqing that Judou hopes to attain the dual goal of erotically stimulating him and getting him to fight against Jinshan's control over her.[13]

Thus the erotic empowerment of the male so unproblematically presented in *Red Sorghum* as unified — both an individual fulfilment and a national trajectory — shatters when the enemy is situated with the Chinese cultural body itself. As a character with a psychology, Tianqing appears almost perverted. Repressed and hesitant, he is unable to carry out any logical and direct plan of action, such as that put into effect many times by *Red Sorghum*'s Grandpa. Unafraid to be the buffoon on his way to his goals, Grandpa throws himself into attempt after attempt, and eventually it is he and his offspring who hold the revitalized future in their hands. While Tianqing represents a symbolic way out (through commerce) for the family, he cannot solidify his position and stands as a failed masculine vision.

As the possibility of an embodied masculinity that can energize the nation fades, the woman character gains more representational space. The world of *Red Sorghum* is virtually completely male, with a number of men working under only one substantial female character. *Judou* also has only one substantial female character, but the number of male characters has diminished and Judou, both in terms of her body and her on-camera time, is more prominent. Judou desperately tries to get Tianqing to take his 'proper' masculine role, overthrow the corrupt patriarch, and be a father to Tianbai. She is more highly eroticized than Jiu'er and is more physically represented. This increased representational space seems to draw away from the male ability to overthrow the old and move toward the new, and in Zhang's next film this possibility vanishes.

Raise High the Red Lanterns

Raise High the Red Lanterns is Zhang Yimou's third 'red' film; as in the other two, the young woman — in this case Songlian — marries into the Master's family through an economic transaction. The Master, however, has three wives still living, and the film revolves around interactions between the women. The Master himself is a shadowy creature who never comes into full view of the camera, and the young male position occupied by his homosexual son is also barely present.

The Master in *Red Lanterns* is abstracted as a virtually non-physical, timeless force. Unlike the leper, whose disease and frailty damns him from the beginning, or Jinshan, whose age and sickness impoverish and weaken him, this patriarch is strong and unplagued by the body and its ills. Although the viewers eventually discover the man's cruelty and his intolerance of infidelity on the part of his wives, he hardly exists as a visual material body. His violence against women is carried out by others on his orders. Zhang Yimou's sublimating of the older patriarchal male into the confining architecture of the buildings — a move initiated in *Judou* — turns the master into a kind of sheer, deadly, pure power of the kind one may imagine would exist in Tianbai's mind when he became an adult. The Master is a force with the ability to whimsically choose and reject women as part of an aesthetic game, as indicated by the red lanterns, and as a form of erotic play. His power is not just ideology, but deeply subsumed into material life, including its most formidable and limiting structures.

Songlian quickly discovers that she must play this game to gain the Master's attention and sympathy. Songlian also tries the trick of pregnancy, that which temporarily gained better treatment for Judou and yet eventually worked against her as a never-ending fear; since she is only pretending, however, Songlian's ruse fails. In this narrative the cold and artistically organized patriarch is so bereft of life-giving force that he cannot father a son other than his adult child, a progeny who fears women and thus cannot carry on the line. The power assignment has shifted radically, with all energy invested in the father, none in the son, and Songlian totally disabled in her quest to find an eroticized escape.

Zhang Yimou continues to grant increasing representational space to the women characters and to take away the possibility that the young man will be able to fight against the old order. In *Red Lanterns*, Zhang shows exactly what kind of power it is that women have within his scheme of the past and present. When they are able to use their 'erotic essence' to catalyze men, women can actualize themselves in the best possible way, changing a meaningless male energy into a purposeful masculine force. While they enable the male to go forward in the struggle, the women must perish when their role has been acted out. Should this role be blocked by a too powerful conservatism, however, women flail about as nothing more than pawns in an aesthetic game, unable to take any direct action on their own. Within this schemata, the woman's death is glorious; the alternative is not life, but eternal insanity such as that which Songlian endures, and mere replacement by another woman.

The man's world of *Red Sorghum* — a place of direction, earth, and power — has been replaced by the woman's world of *Red Lanterns* — a place of games, rooms, and form. The vast countryside has shrunk through *Judou*'s single village into a simple complex of rooms, and the markers of the outside world and the progression of historical time have almost disappeared. Through Grandpa, Tianqing, and the phantom homosexual lover, the alternative possibility of remasculinization through a strong body and a firm mind diminishes, while the conservative, orthodox power of the past increases. The woman's ability to use her erotic being to tip the power scales in favor of the alternative other also disappears.

In terms of the male and female body, both *Red Sorghum* (for the male body) and *Judou* (for the female body) are more transgressive than *Red*

Lanterns. Songlian's female form is sillouetted against the sky and we see her, at various times, looking directly at the camera, as if to beg for recognition of her as a beauty. Yet neither male nor female appear naked in *Red Lanterns*, and the film corresponds much more to the aesthetic formula that Yuejin Wang identifies as specific to Chinese film than do the other Zhang Yimou films. These characteristics include 'understatement in the emotional rhetoric; the exploration of emotional subtlety; the indulgence in the situation of 'faintly sadness' [sic]; the 'distracted' narrative structure; and the conscious evocation of familiar lyrical motives by tapping the traditional Chinese poetic repertoire' ('The Cinematic Other' 37-38). The overt violence of the earlier films, including blood, fire, torture, and pain, is diffused into the narrative structure of submission and the mandatory aesthetic game. Songlian seems to go crazy of her own accord, from mere knowledge of this reality; surely nobody beats her. In this sense Zhang Yimou confirms what Yuejin Wang suspects: that Chinese directors now believe the traditional aesthetics of restraint is actually a hidden historical tendency to circumscribe action and fulfilment (39).

The title of this paper, *Inter/National Aesthetics and Erotics*, implies that Zhang's films use an aesthetic code particular to the west to be appealing to international viewers while also utilizing the widely accepted notion that Maoism 'repressed' sexual expression in order to frame the films as critiquing the confining past and aimed toward a future freedom and true revolutionary change, now embodied in individual erotic fulfilment. I believe that Zhang makes use of a highly aestheticized and clearly gendered erotics in order to convey a sense of modernity, both thematically in terms of cultural choices for Chinese society, and filmically in a presentation that will appeal to a wide range of international viewers because it plays off images and relationships which they understand. Ultimately, however, Zhang weakens and eventually rejects this form, showing how enacted within China, it results in an excessively aesthetic culture without power for the present or direction toward the future, a culture that superficially represents women but is controlled by a shadowy masculine figure who lives off their manipulation. The positive engagement with the future that Zhang theorizes in *Red Sorghum* turns into a series of difficulties in *Judou* and finally ends in *Red Lantern*.

Notes

1. This phrase is found on many posters and advertisements promoting Zhang's films in the United States.
2. Zhang's article is in *East-West Film Journal*, 4.2 (June 1990), 38-53. See also 'Cultural and Economic Dislocations: Filmic Phantasies of Chines Women in the 1980s,' Esther C.M. Yau, *Wide Angle* 11.2 (1989) 6-21, especially 17-20. Yau analyses *Red Sorghum*'s presentation of male virility and national strength, showing that the viril male body is an attempt to re-empower those politically emasculated during the Maoist Years.
3. See 'The Cinematic Other and the Cultural Self?: De-centering the Cultural Identity on Cinema,' *Wide Angle*, 11.2 (1989), 32-39.
4. See *Screening the Male: Exploring masculinities in Hollywood cinema*, ed. Steven Cohan and Ina Rae Hark, New York: Routledge, 1993; also *Male Trouble*, ed. Constance Penley and Sharon Willis, Minneapolis: University of Minnesota Press, 1993.
5. See *Women Enter the Wilderness: Male Bonding and the American Novel of the 1980s*, Donald J. Greiner, Columbia: University of South Carolina Press, 1991. The list of female film roles is quoted by Greiner from *From Reverance to Rape: The Treatment of Women in the Movies*, Mary Haskell, Baltimore: Penguin, 1985.
6. 'Masquerading As the American Male in the Fifties: Picnic, William Holden and the Spectacle of Masculinity in Hollywood Film,' in Penley and Willis, ibid., 203-32.
7. In 'Red Sorghum: Mixing Memory and Desire,' Yuejin Wang discusses the 1980s Chinese interest in masculinity as a reaction to the portrayals of 'tough guys' that were common in western and Japanese cinema, and the newly awakened sense that China 'lacked' these figures (85). Wang also analyses the traditional use of wine to bring on masculine activities, and the implication that masculinity is a deluded state of mind that does not exist when one is sober (87). The transgressive nature of Jiu'er's direct expression of sexuality is a breaking of moral as well as gender codes (94-95). See *Perspectives on Chinese Cinema*, ed. Chris Berry, London: BFI Publishing, 1991.
8. Yuejin Wang's analysis grants more unifying power to the female character than does mine, claiming that 'it is through a feminine vision of totality that the masculine past is reconstructed and obtains coherence and meaning' and Jiu'er's death 'means the loss of perception, consciousness and meaning, since she has hiterto been the pivot around which the cinematic universe evolves' (98).
   Whereas I agree that it is Jiu'er's eroticized desire and vision that activate a seemingly inert but potentially powerful masculinity, and that the child's crying out at the end of the film does indicate a loss the meaningful transference of power thorugh male lines is sustained and expanded. Furthermore, Jiu'er does not in herself have any way to actualize her vision outside of male activity. see Berry, ed., ibid.
9. See 'Dumb Movies for Dumb People: Masculinity, the body, and the voice in contemporary action cinema,' in Cohan and Hark, ibid., 230-44.
10. See *Male Subjectivity at the Margins*, Kaja Silverman, New York: Routledge, 1992.
11. For an analysis of Liu Heng's novel *Fuxi fuxi* that details the structural symbolic unity of the narrative and its use of the myth of Fuxi and Nuwa, see 'Liu Heng's *Fuxi Fuxi*: What about Nuwa?,' Marie-Claire Huot, *Gender and Sexuality in*

Twentieth-Century Chinese Literature and Society, ed. Tonglin Lu, New York: State University of New York Press, 1993, 85-105. Whereas Huot believes that Liu's work is a phallic critique, she sees Zhang Yimou as working 'with a Hollywoodian benevolent attitude toward women' (85).

12. See *Fuxi fuxi*, Liu Heng, Beijing: Zhongguo wenxue chubanshe, 1991; also 'The Obsessed,' in *The Obsessed*, tr. David Kwan, Beijing: Panda Books, 1991, 16-125.

13. W.A. Callahan analyses this scene only as Judou's attempt to gain Tianqing's political cooperation and recapture the control of her own body; the move there is 'not gratuitous sex or soft porn but part of a struggle of empowerment for Ju Dou' (56). I maintain that Judou's empowerment comes from erotic engagement, both of Tianqing and of the viewer. See 'Gender, Ideology, Nation: *Ju Dou* in the Cultural Politics of China,' *East-West Film Journal*, 7.1 (January, 1993), 52-80.

Secrecy And Truth
An Interview by Anne Wedell-Wedellsborg

Bei Dao

Bei Dao is a Chinese poet, born in Beijing in 1949. His real name is Zhao Zhenkai. In December, 1978, he and a few of his friends founded the unofficial periodical *Jintian* (Today), the first to introduce 'underground literature' to a wider audience. Even though *Jintian* was soon closed by the authorities, it came to have a decisive impact on the literary renewal of the coming years. By chance Bei Dao was abroad during the massacre on the Square of Heavenly Peace in June, 1989, and has since been persona non grata in China, among other things because of his role in initiating an open letter on freeing political prisoners. In 1990, he reopened *Jintian*, which is now published in the West and quickly has become the most important Chinese-language literature periodical published outside China. Bei Dao lived in Denmark between 1990 and 1992, lecturing in Chinese at the Institute of East Asian Studies, University of Aarhus. At the moment he is living in the United States.

A Personal History

I often think about why I write, and why I started. It is difficult to answer, there may be many reasons, but to me it is primarily a way of com-municating. If not for the Cultural Revolution, I might very well have found other ways of communicating, I might have studied, become a real intellectual, and so not have had this need. But more importantly and more personally, I think it has to do with the fact that I found it difficult to communicate directly with others. I have always felt inhibited, but I did not discover until I was a teenager that it was a problem. When I think back on it now, it may have a connection with my experiences as a child - for instance, I had big fights with my father, we were often at war with each other.

But I liked to read from the time I was a child, and we had a lot of books at home. My father had put some authorized and innocent books on the shelves in the living room, but he also had many others that he hid in the attic of a shed we had, a place where children normally could not get at them. I soon discovered that these were the interesting books, and always found a way to get my hands on them. There were all kinds of different books, but among others there were works of 18th and 19th century literature from the West. My father was not a real intellectual — because of the war against the Japanese, the civil war and the chaos in society, he had never received any real education — but he always bought many books. The family comes from the South and is originally a kind of noble family which has continually slid downhill, a little like the family described in the great novel, *The Dream of the Red Chamber* (Hong lou meng, 1760).

Where you therefore expected to become engaged in literature?
No, on the contrary, my father always opposed this because it was too dangerous. Since 1949, all ideological campaigns and such have included literature and writers. My father was terrified the first time he saw my poems. In one of them I had written: 'the green sunlight streams through the tree's crown'. The sun was a symbol of Mao, who was the red sun in all Chinese hearts. Calling the sunlight green was life-threatening, so my father tore up the poem.

And if we add to this the custom in the Chinese cultural tradition of expressing oneself in poetry?
Well, the whole question about tradition is very complex, but when we are talking about working against tradition, then my parents were for me really representatives of tradition. My father was a traditional Chinese father, he was the head of the family and put a lot of pressure on me. That may have helped to create my introversion. When I became a teenager, I realized that I could not easily open up to anyone, except maybe to a very few friends. I had difficulties communicating and establishing close friendships. I still have this problem. I feel a strong inhibition or constraint when I am together with others.

Could that not also be connected to different ways of relating to others in the West and in China?
No, actually Chinese society is very open to communication, and great stress is laid on the social dimension. In China, loneliness does not exist, you can not be really alone, simply because of the structure of society. Only when I

came to the West did I experience loneliness in the social sense. Here you are isolated — I think that is a price I have paid. Loneliness in China is different because relationships between people are different. If, for instance, in China you are thinking: now I will begin working on a poem, then without doubt friends or readers will immediately knock on your door to come in and have something to eat. You should be pleased with this because you must have someone around you. Another thing is that loneliness in a deeper sense is a basic human condition which many do not dare face. Really you can say that the exile situation is an extreme clarification of every poet's situation. By writing poetry you challenge the dominating culture and language, therefore you are never really at home anywhere — you could almost say that poetry and exile in that sense are synonymous concepts. But to me it is evident that I have an introvert soul.

Has this linking of poetry and loneliness also to do with the special situation at the time you started writing — I am thinking of the Cultural Revolution?
In 1968, when Mao sent young people to the mountains and the countryside, I was lucky and became a construction worker far away from Beijing. When I think back, it was really a wonderful period of my life. The isolated life and the beautiful natural surroundings enhanced the experience of loneliness, and this blended with the total emptiness that the Cultural Revolution left behind, that complete absence of something to believe and have faith in. After work, I often wandered about among streams, rocks and collapsed temples, and some detached chaotic threads of thought suddenly formed into sentences. I wrote them down, and they became poems, which — even though they were very immature — brought me a particular joy and satisfaction. None of us young people had learned anything, and at one point we started thinking about our future, you had to develop a talent, learn something. Some taught themselves to paint, play music or sing. I also tried these things but was not any good at them, and so in the end I chose the most useless: writing. It was a dangerous occupation that would not bring any good, only mortal danger. There were actually people at that time who were caught and executed for what they wrote. But to a young person it is often the dangerous which holds the greatest attraction. The police were constantly searching for those kinds of documents and you faced a lot of trouble, so the readers were mostly your good friends. During the Cultural Revolution the demand was not just for social realism: you could only write that which praised Mao and the Party. I was in a circle of friends who wrote, we often disagreed, challenged each

other, fought and inspired each other. Later we started *Jintian*, our own unofficial periodical, when politics became a little more liberal. So ten years had passed between the time I started writing until I published my own periodical.

At that time you also wrote prose along with poetry, and your novel Waves (Bodong) and the short stories from 1978-80 were, with their modernist composition technique, regarded by many as the artistically best created in the People's Republic and as a decisive new break in the post-Maoist literature of fiction. Why did you stop writing prose?
I based *Waves* on a strong personal experience, and was, by the way, inspired by the script for the movie *Casablanca*, which was circulating at the time! But I lost faith in my own abilities as a writer of prose as more and more good writers emerged.

Keeping a Secret

You have said that poetry is a way of keeping a secret, but at the same time the poet must also tell the truth. That is, the secrecy must be maintained but the truth must be told. Is there not a contradiction in this?
Yes, at least there is a kind of barrier. Very often this problem about telling or not telling arises. It is something fundamentally human that there is a limit.

The secret belongs to the personal, the truth to the public, but still both are present in your poetry as a kind of loop...
Of course, because in my opinion there is no 'truth', at the most some kind of counter-truth or several counter-truths. Because of tradition and the communist ideology there was in China a public truth that everyone had to recognize, something that was pressed down upon us, which we could react against. And this official truth was intimately connected with the language. It was difficult to exist as an individual, you could not express individual emotions — even in love poems you had to mention the Party and socialism. At that time we talked a lot about fighting tradition, but I actually discovered that my language could not be separated from tradition. In the West the struggle against tradition has been gradual, so it is difficult for people here to understand the suddenness of the upheaval in China. It was not until the beginning of this century that it really began in China, so my generation and

I have grown up in a cultural chaos. In the beginning there was something concrete to break with — feudal customs, for instance — but very quickly it became confused and chaotic, and you did not know what you were breaking with.

The word 'tradition' is very broad — what do you really understand it to be? When you use the word tradition, it seems as if you are talking about something contemporary and negative.
Chinese intellectuals' struggle with tradition for the past hundred years has in one way or another to do with the way we have turned around the relationship between the individual and society. Like when you write on Chinese envelopes: first the country, then the city, then the address and last the individual. And the family name comes before the personal name. The humanist traditions in China are very different from the West. In the West everyone is equal before God, but in the East, where there is no God, humanism has been put into a social context. Every man has his place in the family and in society, and this place is predetermined. So the lack of equality is not just a political phenomenon. It has deep roots in history and the cultural tradition. It is therefore difficult for a Chinese writer to know what he should be working against or protecting. It is a dilemma history has put us in. I started searching in my origins — not for any truth, but for a moral guideline, some principles to live by. I think that it is most important to make the starting point the individual human being, and I believe that no one can escape the necessity of pain, that is the first step in the intellectual history of the individual. Christian culture does not evade pain but recognizes its significance in human life. This is completely different from Eastern culture. But it applies to all intellectuals and writers that if you do not know suffering and soul-searching and do not recognize the absurdity of existence, then it is much too easy to become a victim of any ideological system.

But to me personally — and a little more concretely — what I understand by tradition has to do with language. That is, the rebellion becomes a linguistic rebellion. From the time I was little I was constrained by an official language, a linguistic harness which we did not know how to get out of, because we had never known anything else.

How, then, did you find your individual poetic language?
It has been there all the time, but it was not until later that I became conscious of it. It has come from the outside and is at the same time

something deeply personal, which is connected with my hatred of centralism. I found out that when you use the same language as a despot, it affects you, it is something that comes from the outside in. Then you try to struggle free from this foreign body. But personally, after my discovery, it happened that during this process I gradually realized that the darkness did not come from the outside but from the inside, it was my own darkness.

Since the official language was so pervasive, how can you explain the strength with which the new lyric poetry broke forth already from the end of the 1970s?
If I should say what enabled the new lyric poetry and prose to spring up in the mid-1970s as underground literature — that is, when I myself started writing in this political climate, where 'literature' consisted of pieces of propaganda — then it was to a high degree those translations of Western modern literature we had access to. The chaos of the Cultural Revolution allowed the circulation of an internal translation series published from 1962 onwards, a systematic introduction of Western modernism and thaw-literature from the Soviet Union. It was meant for limited circulation among cadres above a certain rank and had yellow bindings — therefore they were never called anything but 'huangpishu', yellow bound books. Here were Kafka, Camus, Sartre, Salinger, Kerouac, Beckett, Ehrenburg and others. It is not too much to say that these books had revolutionary significance, and it was not just because of the contents. Just think: in the linguistically politicized cliché-atmosphere which ruled, where language was violated daily in the official rhetoric, the use alone of the Chinese language which we met in the translations was an inspiration and a revelation. That these things were so splendidly translated is probably due to the fact that many of China's best writers had to stop their own creative activity after 1949, and especially after the purges in 1957, and instead devoted themselves to translations. But because these books only existed in limited supply, and for the most part only around Beijing, they were in great demand in the literary salons. This meant that a salon could have a book for a couple of days before it circulated on. People lined up, forgot about eating and sleeping and read day and night. It was around this time that the underground literature began to really flourish.

Have you then experienced Western literature differently after coming to the West?
The starting point will always be important. My starting point was Western modernist literature, and only afterwards did I come to the West. But that was a big leap in time. The West that I arrived in was no longer this West of

modernism — that was already over — but instead an extremely commercialized West. So I am willing to admit that in these years I have felt somewhat lost. It is as if I am sitting in a modernist train, but what I am looking at is a post-modernist landscape. This difference in time has been a great shock to me. Another problem for me is that I experience the West's propaganda media, the circulation of the means of communication, etc. as a big pressure. You cannot escape from them. I feel that in a way they pose a much larger danger to the secrecy of poetry than the Chinese media. Therefore I usually say no to interviews. They always twist what you say and turn you into propaganda for something...

It must also have been a shock for you to find out how concepts like secrecy and individuality have been distorted in much of the new literature here? How do you for instance perceive this mixture of different languages, including media language, in a poet like John Ashbery, whom you have recently interviewed for your periodical? To use a fashionable expression, you could say that he uses a deconstructive method by mixing all these things. Everyone has his own special way of writing, and John Ashbery, who lives in such a news and communication society, has no possibility of fleeing it, but uses this method to escape: he attacks the poison with poison, drives away evil with evil....

So maybe one can after all write poetry without defending the concepts we have talked about, secrecy, truth, individuality?
No, I do not think so, I think that Ashbery preserves the secret character of the English language exactly through that special method he uses. He knows that there are some things that have value, and succeeds in preserving them and their secret character in his poems. But, of course, the secrecy we are talking about is not what is normally understood by keeping a secret. It is the secrecy of language. He creates a language, and through this process of creation, in which language comes into existence, a new secrecy of language arises. You can see that the way he uses language is unusual. His language is not transparent. It is not a language that you can use to exchange information — on the contrary, it cannot conform to or be used for anything social. It is not social, not common.

The Most Important Things are Inexpressible

Turning to your own poems, one could say that they are not to any high degree experienced as central lyric poetry — especially not the later ones. It is first and foremost pictorially strong lyric poetry, put together by different elements. How does the individual make itself heard in your poetry?

I often use 'I' in my poems, but this 'I' rarely has anything to do with the real me. Whatever personal pronoun — I, you, he — you use has no connection with whom you are talking about. They are a kind of mask. I think that one of the reasons that I use so many images is that the Chinese written language is pictographic; that is, the characters in their form and structure are still a kind of picture. A character is not a word, but neither is it just a syllable, as in the Western languages. It has its own independent meaning.

Also, the stories I read as a child had a strong metaphorical character — things were very rarely said straight out. And, for instance, in Tang poetry it is always images that are the mainstay. Earlier, images had to be appropriate or correct and correspond to the specific things they were symbolizing. Traditionally there were exact formulas for what symbolized what — moon, chrysanthemum, melancholy, longing, etc. That has changed; we have broken this code system. And this is not to mention the way the Communist Party controlled the language and symbols, as we discussed earlier. For instance, the poet Mang Ke wrote in 1972 a poem with the lines: 'The sun rises/the bloody shield', and thereby rescued the image of 'the sun' from the clutches of the state. But it is only since I have come to the West, and especially since I have come to know surrealism, that I have realized how important it is to break the images, to turn the symbols around and to destroy the system of rules.

There are things in your work that ressemble surrealism — the dreams and the collision of images, but also the ellipsis, the omissions, etc.

Surrealism is directed against reason, it arose against the background of Western society which builds on reason. Therefore it has had a great value of rebellion here. I think there are some common features between surrealism and Eastern thought, and in a certain sense surrealism has to me been one of the keys to understanding my own culture. In Eastern culture there are many things that cannot or should not be said directly — actually this is a fundamental premise in most of Eastern philosophy. But also Western philosophers, such as Wittgenstein and Heidegger, think that the most important things are inexpressible — truth, for instance.

Were you not criticized in China for exactly this irrational trait?
Yes, of course, any propaganda or political power will try to use so-called rational arguments or reason to oppress people. What happened in the beginning of the 1980s, when so many started writing, was also a kind of escape by opacity; that is to say, you created a space that the official criticism could not enter. Part of the secrecy is also to create a culture, which others cannot enter.

But could you not also say that this secrecy is very open, that it consists of what you want to read into it? In that sense your own poems are very open.
It is very complicated and there are different elements. One thing is that secrecy which lies in the national cultural experience, another is the secrecy of language itself, and finally there is the individual's own secrecy. In reality it invites anyone who feels like it to come in and take part in this secrecy.

There is no interpretation that can claim the truth?
No.

In one of your poems it says: 'I return to my starting point'. Does that have a concrete source, so that you know your background better now?
In the strictest sense I do not think that anybody can ever return to their starting point. Thus that is a paradox, since all attempts to return are doomed to fail - 'the meaning returns' it also says; that is, we are looking for a meaning in life, but it folds into itself and returns. So there is a contradiction in art: man has always dreamt of returning, but if you try, you discover that the whole foundation has gone. For instance, many Chinese writers now wish to return to the good tradition, but we discover that it is just a dream, an illusion. Tradition is nothing but a ruin, but we belong to that ruin, we are ourselves part of it.

Poetry is Not Speaking in your Sleep

Let us talk about the process of writing. What for instance gets you started when you are writing a poem?
That is different. Sometimes it is just a very small thing — an expression, a sentence, a discovery or a picture — that can be stimulating, and sometimes there is no reason at all, you sit down and start playing with words. There can often be three or four months when I do not write anything, but then it

comes in a mighty wave. I recharge. I also have certain writing seasons —
earlier it was very pronounced, from the end of fall until spring, but after
coming to the West this has been turned around. Usually I write in the
evening because it is the most quiet, or I get up very early. I still have a kind
of jet-lag. The difference is also that when you are a writer in exile, the
language you write in is another than that which is spoken around you —
that is to say, there is always a background noise to the language you create
in. It is the mother tongue that experiences loneliness. But the mother tongue
is at the same time your wealth, your only capital which you have to protect.

Do you work with notes, or do you write poems down right away?
I often make notes, sometimes only in my head. When I write I am often in
a kind of sleeplike condition, a false sleep which gets my imagination started.
Sometimes the images arise from a misunderstanding of Western things or
Western words and sentences.

Does it have any resemblance to the surrealists' automatic writing?
No, not at all, I do not believe in that kind of thing at all — actually that is
what takes the longest time to adjust and change. Poetry is a kind of order in
chaos: if this order is not there, then poetry does not exist either. If we look
back on surrealism and the writers who used automatic writing, I do not
think that any truly great writers have come out of it. It is not real poetry,
because poetry is not speaking in your sleep, or at least should not be. On the
contrary, it has to be utmost consciousness.

Does the unconscious dreamlike come first and conscious logic follow?
Does one use reason to adjust and put things in order? It is also too simple
to say that. The process of ordering and adjusting is also very complicated,
you cannot separate the two. It is a little like a process of clarification or
settling, like when things come to rest again quietly after a storm.

How do you know when a poem is finished?
That takes a long time, because sometimes you are very satisfied just when
you have written something, but then after a while it changes. And
sometimes it is also the case that what you do not like yourself, others like a
lot. There are poems I never change, but you always want to make changes.
It is like looking at paintings: because the light is different at different times,
the effect of the picture is also different. It is often so that because of the

different experiences of life, you view the pictures you have made at various stages of your life differently. At a later time, the same pictures can give you a whole new feeling. But normally I think poets like best what they have written recently.

Earlier you wrote in longhand, now you write on a computer. Has that changed anything?
I feel a little uncomfortable admitting that I write on a computer. Actually one ought to be opposed to computers.... Sometimes I write notes by hand first, but most of the time I write directly on a PC. But of course I do know that the computer is a tool to oppress humanity — I think that post-modernism and the computer are closely connected. So I do write with great pleasure on a tool I really should hate.

But you have said earlier that you think that the computer has made you more aware of the characteristics of the Chinese language and made you better able to use them.
Yes, because the computer makes it very easy to play with the words, to change them about. Because the Chinese language is such that you can replace one character with another just like that — without then having to change all the other words, as you would in Western languages with cases, tenses, endings, etc. — so in Chinese you can still keep the rhythm. Sometimes I feel that putting words together in poetry is multiplication rather than addition. Inserting one or more characters some place, or taking one out does not just mean that something is added or taken away, but maybe that the poem is multiplied to become so much better or something quite different. Or, if you wish, divided into an essence. That is one thing. Another is that I like the pure, the visually clear. So earlier when I wrote on paper, I had to copy and rewrite all the time to make the poem stand clearly before I could assess it at all. Now I see it in a finished form right away.

Existence is the Moment

Except for 'Daydream' (Bairimeng from 1986) all of your poems are short, some even very short. In China there is no tradition of epic poetry, but in the West a lot of poets have in recent years published long poems. One could mention Brodsky and Walcott for example.
Personally I think that poems should express the moment, therein lies their beauty; only in that way can their wonder, their secrecy appear. I actually do

not think that epic poetry is a living tradition, and after the appearance of the novel it became obsolete. It is very difficult to avoid it becoming a sort of prose or essay. It is true that I have written 'Daydream', which is a long poem, but in reality it is a suite of poems, consisting of a row of short poems. By the way, I do not think that it is very successful.

In that case you must reject a lot of Western poetry — Wallace Stevens, Derek Walcott, Brodsky...
Yes, then I must do that. I do not like Brodsky very much. But it must be said that what I have read are not the originals, but Chinese translations. Walcott I have not read yet.

On the other hand, there is a poet like T.S. Eliot, but I feel that his importance is not so much in his poetry as such, as in the changes he brought to lyric poetry in general, the break he created in literary history. I feel that his poetry has too much cultural stuffing. Considered as poetry, I think it is a misunderstanding.

Pain, loneliness and isolation are recurring themes with you. Is that also something that belongs to the concentrated?
Yes, on this point I will say that I am against time, against the past and the future. Existence is the moment. When the mood of melancholy is more prominent with me, it has to do with my actual existence, nothing else. I certainly do not deny that happiness and love can be contained in poetry, but here there is also a danger: if it is spoken about too obviously or directly, it clashes with the artistic and very easily becomes hollow and superficial.

Hemingway also spoke of the fear of big words in the Western mind, and now they may have become so eroded that they simply do not have any meaning?
I should actually not criticize the West, but I feel that the big problem is that there is no dream here — maybe precisely after all these things have been eroded. The Chinese thinker, Li Zehou, has said that intellectuals must also have a dream; if they do not, there is no use for them. Maybe that is the reason I have felt very disappointed with the Western poetry of the recent years: there is no dream, everything has been undermined or become a game. I am very afraid that this will happen in China too, now that it is also becoming a commercialized commodity society. Actually it is already happening. Of course there are many fine poets here in the West who both write well and have dreams, but broadly speaking I think poetry is at a low

point. Recently an anthology of new French lyric poetry was translated into Chinese, and it was deeply disappointing to see how empty and hollow and trivial it was, when you think about how many outstanding poets France has fostered. But again, I have not read the originals.

The American sinologist, Stephen Owen recently, in a much discussed article, criticized the new Chinese lyric poetry — among others yours — for being too international, without the historical and national ballast which he thinks is the trademark of Chinese poetry. What do you think of this criticism?
Stephen Owen is a classical sinologist, a specialist in classical Chinese literature, and he criticizes modern poets from a classical point of view. But he is right on one point, and he describes something which is a common condition: the communication and commodity system has made the possibility very real that humanity will become more and more alike, the different characteristics becoming blurred. From that point of view he is right. But in reality you cannot speak abstractly about the West and the East or any other country; it is an extremely complicated process, which in practice cannot be simplified and summarized. Each writer is different from others in his secret place, his experiences, his history. You can in very general terms talk about how a dilution is happening, but in reality that is no good when we come down to the individual, because every writer has a very strong individuality, his own precise and private way of writing. Maybe you can say, as the Chinese critic Huang Ziping has, that there is a great common musical theme, but each presents it in his own way. Owen's article, which we have translated in *Jintian*, has started a discussion and a reflection, and strengthened the awareness that you must have something to offer as a poet in an international context.

You, and many other controversial Chinese writers, have repeatedly emphasized the necessity of pure literature. But at the same time your poems have had great political significance, and you are considered by the regime in Beijing as a political figure. How do you explain that contradiction?
I often think back on the years (1978-80) where we posted *Jintian* on the Democracy Wall. We discussed again and again whether we should maintain the purely literary course at that time, in the midst of the torrent of the democracy movement, and we did waver for a while. But retrospectively I think that our function as linguistic overthrowers was far more important than our role as advocates for democracy in relation to a weakening and de-

struction of the power apparatus. Today the singer Cui Jian and the writer Wang Shuo each in their own way have great influence on the undermining of the public consciousness, and this has a much bigger effect than political declarations.

But the most important function of poetry is to preserve the living language. Many of the poets of the older generation have of course attacked politics, but they have done this in the language of politics. That is why we have emphasized pure literature — the most important thing is to keep one's distance from power.

The Chinese cultural tradition has always been that 'literature communicates the right way', and recent history has been about 'saving the nation'. This, together with the Chinese intellectuals' ideal conception about the great harmony, explains why the May Fourth Movement (1919) never gained a foothold. It had hardly started before it became a tool for the revolution. This tendency was further reinforced after the 1930s, and later literature gradually lost its independence. Only a very few writers tried from a position on the periphery of society to create real literature, but after the Communist take-over in 1949 they also disappeared.

I have often admitted the perplexity I feel as a poet, and I think many other writers have the same experience Czeslaw Milosz has described as the contradiction between being and acting; that is, the contradiction between art and the involvement in your countrymen's fate: art demands a distance which at the same time is a kind of moral treachery.

Notes

This interview was originally published in *Den Blå Port*, vol. 25-26, Copenhagen 1993. In parts of the conversation, which took place in the fall of 1992, Niels Frank participated as co-interviewer.

Translated from the Danish by Camilla Østeraa and Chris Kieliger

Swings of Japan's Identity

Harumi Befu

Introduction[1]

The contemporary discourse on Japan's national, cultural identity takes place in the genre of Nihonjinron, otherwise called Nihonron, Nihon bunkaron, and the like. In this discourse, Japan's uniqueness is argued and demonstrated by Nihonjinron writers, at least to their own satisfaction, in terms of the whole gamut of Japan's traditional cultural repository, including values, language, social institutions, and mental disposition. According to Nihonjinron writers, these characteristics are not only what makes Japan unique, but what makes up or is responsible for Japan's cultural sophistication, such as in art and literature, and also what constitutes the 'cultural infrastructure' for Japan's economic success. For example, decision by consensus, hierarchical organization, and group-orientation are but a few of the characteristics which constitute the contents of this identity.

The nature of this identity, however, has not been the same throughout the history of Japan. In this paper I wish to deal with the complexity of these differing identities in different periods by examining what comprised Japan's national identity in the past and how it has changed. This brief review of the vicissitudes of Japan's identity discourse is attempted, not so much for the intrinsic interest in the history of Japan's identity discourse as such, but to ask what external factors have affected changing definitions of national identity. For it is my thesis that national identity is a creature living very much in adaptation to its external environment. A historical review with an eye to these factors is instructive in appreciating the process and change in the character of Japan's identity, especially with respect to such factors as Japan's 'Other,' Japan's geopolitics and geoeconomics, the nature of self-evaluation, its sponsorship, and popular support, as we shall see. Strictly speaking what I present in this paper is not a history in the proper sense of the term, but rather an analytical account of identity politics and the factors surrounding its development in different periods of Japanese history.[2]

How far back in the history of Japan can we trace Japanese concern for their identity? In short, when did discourse on Japan's identity begin? Granted that this discourse may not have always been called Nihonjinron, we are referring to the self-reflective discourse, systematic or otherwise, on who the Japanese thought they were. In that ethnic identity of a people is a process accompanying its awareness of others who are not part of their ethnic group, it is a process of defining itself in comparison and in contrast with other ethnic groups or nations. Understanding contemporary Nihonjinron and its historical lineage takes us back at least to the beginning of the late eighteenth and early nineteenth century, or the late Tokugawa, feudal period.

Nascent nativism in the Late Tokugawa period

In the late Tokugawa period, we already find clear and definite discussion of self-identity of the Japanese. We see budding Nihonjinron, though it was not called that in those days, in the so-called kokugaku or 'national learning' school of scholarship.

Kokugaku arose in reaction against the received sinology emphasizing neo-Confucianism of the time, which heavily influenced the shogunate and daimiate feudal governments in formulating the official political and moral philosophy. To contrast with the official learning, kokugaku emphasized and lauded virtues of what kokugaku scholars, such as Kamo no Mabuchi (1697-1769) and Motoori Norinaga (1730-1801) considered to be pure, indigenous Japanese characteristics, including the Japanese imperial institution and Japan's aesthetic values, such as mono no aware. In Shoiko, Mabuchi openly criticized the effeminate China and in contrast raved about Japanese masculinity (masurao). When Norinaga pointed to fragrant cherry blossoms seen against the rising sun as the essence of the ethos of Japan (yamato-gokoro), juxtaposed with kara-gokoro (the ethos of China), he was definitely staking a claim of a Japan totally different from China and of the superiority of Japanese culture over Chinese culture. Norinaga also declared in Kenkyoojin that the sun goddess, Amaterasu, stood at the pinnacle of the world.

It is important that Norinaga originally studied neo-Confucianism, and his specialization in kokugaku was in personal reaction to neo-Confucianism, in response to his dissatisfaction with it.[3] In attempting to demonstrate the superiority of Japanese culture over its referent culture — China — kokugaku scholars already manifested some of the same characteristics of modern Nihonjinron, which tries to prove Japan's superiority over the West.[4]

The fundamental fault of the Tokugawa regime, as far as the National Learning School was concerned, was that the shogun displaced the emperor as the rightful sovereign ruler of the country. For the imperial system was a primordial institution indigenous to Japan. There was no way to rectify this situation except by toppling the Tokugawa regime and replacing it with the emperor system. For the National Learning school, Japan's highest virtues were to be sought in traditional Japan, unencumbered by any Chinese influence whatsoever. It made its mark by scoffing at and denigrating Chinese civilization and all that it represented. Hegemony of neo-Confucianism in Japanese polity was an unfortunate as well as erroneous twist in history from which Japan had to be rescued by putting back indigenous institutions and values in the center stage where they once were and where they rightfully belong. Kokugaku thus provided a crucial ideological impetus for the political movement to topple the Tokugawa feudal regime and replace it with a government which held the emperor as its sovereign.

It is important to note here that Japan's alternative cultural identity—alternative to the hegemonic Confucian - based identity — was being formulated at this time in the guise of kokugaku, a learning whose raison d'etre was derived from rejecting Chinese philosophy precisely because China was for Japan the most significant reference point. Kokugaku, then, was a nascent Nihonjinron which arose to compete with the dominant identity discourse based on Confucianism.

Western civilization was known to the Japanese predominantly through the presence of Westerners in Nagasaki, the only port open for foreign trade, where the Portuguese and the Dutch, along with the Chinese, were alone given permission to trade. Thus, isolated individuals did contrast Japan with Europe, which they could not see because of the ban on foreign travel, but knew only through readings (Minami 1980:13-14). However, these individuals' views had little impact in those feudal days of seclusion, even among the ruling samurai elite, let alone the vast majority of peasants and townspeople.

To generalize, then, discourse on national identity is directed at the foreign culture which is perceived to be the most significant for Japan for the moment, whether in military, political, or economic terms. In the Tokugawa period, this foreign culture was China, as it had given Japan much of the 'high culture,' such as Buddhism, artistic and architectural styles, and a writing system. In post-Tokugawa Japan, it has been the West. Thus the post-Tokugawa national discourse on Japan's identity has had to contrast Japan with the West. Japan's relation to China in this regard became secondary and less relevant.

But this was not a sudden shift. From the end of the eighteenth century, black ships of Western powers, one after another, began to appear off the coast of Japan, demanding that Japan open its ports for trading, thus initiating what one might call 'gunboat diplomacy.' Hard as Japan tried to ward off the 'hairy barbarians', the guns on the black ships, symbolizing Western military might, proved too much for the very best swords of Japan, or even the tane-gashima firearms which the Japanese obtained from the Portuguese in the sixteenth century. As a result, Japan had to experience the humiliation of being forced to give up its self-imposed seclusion and sign treaties with terms unfavorable to itself. The shame of this 'symbolic rape' was too much for Japanese political leaders to endure. It was indelibly imprinted on them, and defined Japanese attitudes toward the West for the next one hundred forty years.

It is this geopolitics of shame which led the impatient shishi, the 'samurai with purpose' of a National Learning persuasion, to take a competing stance against the shogunate and to challenge its legitimacy by proclaiming the legitimacy of the, for all intents and purposes deposed, emperor on the basis of the latter's primordial legacy.

The late Tokugawa period was then characterized by these competing two forces, one propounding neo-confucianism and interpreting Japan in its light, neglecting the role of the emperor in the process, and the other placing the emperor on the center stage, and regarding neo-confucianism as inauthentic and the shogunate supported by it as illegitimate.

In the end kokugaku's basic tenets held sway and successfully led to the collapse of the regime which was supported by and supported a rival ideology of neo-Confucianism. The new Meiji regime, however, did not do away with Confucianism, but combined it with central elements of kokugaku, in creating a new imperial institution.

This phenomenon of Japan imbued with overwhelmingly positive valuation and negative 'Other' (China, in the Tokugawa period) was to be repeated in Japanese history. The late Meiji was one example and from around 1930 to the end of WWII was another. Most recently, the last fifteen to twenty years is a third.

Auto-orientalism of the Meiji period

To come to terms with the military and technological gap with the West which Japan was forced to recognize, Meiji leaders ushered in a frenzied period of catch-up through borrowing and adaptation of Western technology and institutions in an effort to bring not only its military strength but political, economic, educational and other institutions up to par with the West.

This situation necessitated that Japan develop a new definition of itself vis-à-vis the West. China was no longer a nation to contend with. The question of 'Who are the Japanese?' became one of 'What is different about Japan from the West?' Japan turned literally 180 degrees from facing west toward China to facing east toward the United States and Europe. Now Japan's identity had to contain elements to distinguish it from the West.

Fukuzawa Yukichi, Nishi Amane and other intellectuals wrote in the second half of the last century comparing Japan with the West and argued the pros and cons of Japanese culture. In a pseudonymously authored article, Fukuzawa contrasted Japanese character with Western character and listed those character traits in which Westerners were supposedly superior and those in which Westerners were inferior (Minami 1980: 116-17). Among the former were the sense of independence, cooperation, perseverance, ability to take care of assets swiftly, and valuing of trust. And among the latter were excessive pitying of women leading to excessive respect of them, arrogance of women, forgetting one's station in life, and neglect of ethical considerations because of desire for accumulation of wealth. These may also be seen as what Fukuzawa perceived to be the flip side of the Japanese character traits.

Fukuzawa was rather radical in advocating changes to the Japanese character, which would supposedly lead to changes in lifestyle. In particular, he despised what he regarded as an outmoded 'feudal' mentality among the Japanese. This view of basically denigrating the Japanese character by upholding European character and contrasting it with the Japanese, was supported by a number of other intellectuals who belonged to a progressive organization called Meirokusha. Many others took Japanese traditional values and institutions to task, and some even advocated mixed marriage with Europeans as a way of infusing Caucasian blood to improve the Japanese race, according to Minami (1980:25).

The overwhelming mood of the time was that Japanese technology and social institutions were hopelessly outmoded and needed to be replaced by the more advanced Western technology and institutions. The zeal with which the Japanese absorbed Western civilization was phenomenal. It went far beyond guns and boats. Western costume was declared to be the official attire for government employees. Things of Western origin, whether food, shelter, or clothing, enjoyed high prestige. This infatuation with Western civilization ushered in the so-called 'Rokumeikan period,' so-called because of a Western style 'society' building called Rokumeikan in the middle of Tokyo, where the members of high society competed in displaying how completely Westernized they were, showing off their Western clothes and their skills in Western social manners and ballroom dancing.

The Japanese language, that sacrosanct store of the essence of Japanese spirit according to National Learning scholars, lost its raison d'etre for some of the Meiji thinkers. According to Minami (1980: 110-11), Nishi Amane, one of the foremost thinkers of the time, was one with an unfavorable opinion of the Japanese, believing the oppressive feudal political system of the past two hundred and fifty years under the Tokugawa regime had given the Japanese a subservient character, which was convenient for the new Meiji government. He even advocated in 1874 using the English alphabet (yooji) to record Japanese (wago), prescienting Mori Arinori's similar but more extreme proposal only a few years later. Mori Arinori, one of the intellectual leaders of the Meiji period and a one-time minister of education suggested abolishing Japanese and replacing it with English.[5]

The Japanese did not arrive at this conclusion by themselves. Most Westerners who came to Japan to teach Japanese Western technology and to help build institutions modelled after those in the West, such as banking, the military, and education, assumed that Japan was a backward country needing the enlightenment of the West. Western scientists, engineers, and scholars came to Japan in droves, taking high-paying salaries no Japanese of equivalent position could possibly earn, and showed Japanese how to become modernized.[6] Some, like Edward Morse and Lafcadio Hearn, were among the small minority who showed great appreciation of things Japanese. Western cultural emulation during the Meiji, in the end, was rather superficial in many respects, costume parties at Rokumeikan being a metaphor for the super-ficiality of the Western cultural cloak which Meiji socialites and elites wore, as Uchida Roan wrote in 1916 assessing the so-called Rokumeikan period (Uchida 1968).

I propose to call this process 'auto-Orientalism.' It is a process of accepting the 'orientalism' of the West (Said 1978) by the very people who are being orientalized. Psychologically a masochistic process, it signifies internalization by the orientalized people of the observation and judgement of the West toward it. Said, of course, focused on the Middle East as the orientalized people, but a similar orientalizing process took place in other parts of the world, including Japan (Kang 1988; Minear 1980; Mouer 1983). It is a process whereby the Japanese accepted the Western-centric scheme of the universe, and believed in Westerners' value judgements about the backwardness of Japan.

However, as far as basic human substance was concerned, the Japanese then — as now — believed they had what it took spiritually to transform Japan into a modern nation. Wakon yoosai, meaning 'Japanese spirit, Western know-how,' was the motto of the day, appropriately modified from the older motto, wakon kansai, meaning 'Japanese spirit, Chinese know-how.' China was no longer the role model for Japan, and was replaced by the West.

But one cannot say that the discourse on national identity of the day had a mass following in the way Nihonjinron has now. Concern with Japan's identity vis-à-vis the West was a minor issue for the Japanese population as a whole, even though, to be sure, it was the few economically powerful men and women — those who made the difference for Japan's future — who, though small in number, concerned themselves with the issue of who the Japanese were. Historians of Nihonjinron, in discussing Nihonjinron before 1945, necessarily take up the small number of well-known writers and analyze their views. But the vast majority of Japanese, living in rural hinterlands, were conducting life not much different from the feudal days, and the question of national identity occurred to them only when Japan engaged in wars, such as with Russia and China. Of course, a sense of national identity was taught in schools then, and newspapers carried articles about Japan's role in international affairs. But for most rural peasants, the question of who they were vis-à-vis Europeans was not an issue that occupied their minds.

We should not lose sight of the contrast in numbers and proportions of those engaged, actively or passively, in this identity discourse then and now. It is only after the Second World War that identity discourse became a concern of the masses. Until then, a relatively small, though increasing number of people was involved in this discourse.

It is important that from the beginning of Meiji, the West was permanently established as Japan's reference group, as the possessor of good things to emulate. The feeling of inferiority was firmly implanted as a result of the gun-boat diplomacy in the last years of the Tokugawa period. Love and admiration of things Western was induced later. The term hakurai, meaning coming from abroad, but more specifically from the West, had a prestige value of its own, like the English term 'imported' the in American consumer market, only much more. The slogan of the day, bummei kaika, meaning 'flowering of civilization,' referred to adopting Western civilization as a means of developing Japan. Love and admiration of the West continued as the manifest modus vivendi, as one can see in the writings of Fukuzawa Yukichi and others. Fukuzawa was particularly harsh on Japan, and criticized it while lauding the West. For these individuals Western culture was all-powerful, and Japanese culture represented backwardness to be abandoned and forgotten.

Return of positive identity

Yet one should not conclude that during the Meiji period the intellectual outlook was totally oriented towards degrading Japan. Far from it, as demonstrated in the volume edited by Sakata Yoshio (1958) on Japan's nationalism in the early and middle — but mostly middle — Meiji period. Perhaps partly in reaction to excessive Western devotion, in mid-Meiji, periodicals like Nihon (1889-) and Nihonjin (1888-), whose mission was to reawaken Japanese to uniquely Japanese characteristics and thereby bolster the feeling of national pride and extol virtues of Japan, began to appear.

This position received a major boost when the Imperial Rescript on Education was promulgated in 1890, which officially defined the mythologically founded emperor system and outlined the fundamental principles which were to govern the Japanese educational system for the next 55 years — until the defeat of Japan in the Pacific war. Promulgation of the Imperial Rescript on Education also officially crystallized the pro-Japan positive discourse on Japanese identity. What is contained in this imperial message is a curious mixture of traditional Japanese virtues and Confucian moral values. While the centrality of the imperial institution was affirmed, at the same time, the Confucian five relations were also given a position of importance in the education of the Japanese. In it, the Japanese family system was presented as the embodiment of virtues and the foundation of the Japanese nation. The emperor was the father figure for the subjects. Social values such as on (one's indebtedness to others) and filial piety were said to be what created a social order unequalled around the world. This imperial message unquestionably remained the most influential document for propagation of the hegemonic ideology of the time and for officially defining Japanese identity.

As Winston Davis has analyzed, (Davis 1976) Inoue Tetsujiroo, a Tokyo University Professor, wrote commentaries on the Imperial Rescript, propounded on the national morality as derived from Shinto — the indigenous religion translated as 'the way of gods' — and tied it in with the imperial institution and the concept of national polity (Inoue 1891). Although an army of others also wrote commentaries on the Imperial Rescript, Inoue was one of the most influential of the time. He successfully exploited his prestigious academic position to spread his ideas.

Inoue was one of the most ardent nationalists of the mid-Meiji. When the controversy erupted as to whether foreigners should or should not be allowed to live in Japan in intermingled residence with Japanese, he was moved to write from Berlin to voice his opinion against the idea. He feared racial contamination, which, according to him, would result in loss of the ability of the Japanese to work together, in physiological alterations in the Japanese and possibly in extinction of the Japanese race (Minamoto 1958:179-180). This contrasts sharply with the early Meiji view of advocating mixed marriage for the eugenic purpose of improving the Japanese race mentioned earlier.

The Imperial Rescript on Education and also a good deal of Nihonjinron of the time contained many Confucian-derived ideas, such as the 'five principles' of human ethics. The Confucian analects were taught in schools, too, and assiduously memorized by schoolchildren. This amalgam of indigenous Japanese and Confucian values may seem contradictory, if Nihonjinron were to identify Japanese values in contradistinction to any foreign value. What is important to remember, however, is that in Meiji the significant Other was no longer China, but overwhelmingly the West. Thus the incorporation of Chinese or Confucian values, especially as nativized by Japanese neo-Confucian scholars, was not seen as a problem in defining what constituted Japaneseness. After all, at this point, distinguishing Japan from the West was all that mattered. Whether in the process Chinese elements were mingled in the definition of Japaneseness was of little consequence.

To regard neo-Confucianism as an element of traditional Japanese culture does no violence insofar as the 'Other' to be contrasted with is the West.[7] Had the 'Other' been China, as it was during the Tokugawa period, then this would have posed a serious problem. By the same token, it would be difficult in contemporary Nihonjinron to talk about automobiles or Western dress, no matter how Japanized, as something expressing Japanese cultural essence vis-à-vis the West. Certain adaptations of them are undeniably Japanese, yet this argument becomes too subtle for popular consumption, for which Nihonjinron is designed (Befu 1990).

By the late Meiji, as Japan's industrialization proceeded successfully, and as Japan was slowly able to gain a stronger position vis-à-vis the West in diplomacy, trade issues, and military matters, the affirmative view of Japan began to hold sway. Japan was beginning its imperialist expansion into the continent and fighting back incursion by Western powers into East Asia. To rationalize Japan's action and to bolster Japanese morale, it was imperative to develop a national identity which made Japanese people feel proud of themselves. With the successive victories in the Sino-Japanese war of 1894-1895 and the Russo-Japanese war of 1904-1905, Japanese people were in a mood to accept such a self-definition. In spite of the fact that these wars crippled Japan's economy, the victories vastly enhanced Japan's international position. Thus, the improving self-image of Japan and the ascendancy of positive Nihonjinron should be seen in this geopolitical light.

As one might surmise, Nihonjinron of this time was imbued with nationalism. In fact the two were not separable. To laud and praise the ethnic essence of Japan was to sacralize the emperor and the nation. There was no better way of accomplishing this objective than to coopt the indigenous folk Shinto and upgrade it to state Shintoism by placing the imperial institution at the center of this primordial, quintessentially Japanese religion, and formally organizing hithertofore private Shinto shrines into a hierarchy of state Shinto ecclesia. Creation of State Shintoism (Hardacre 1989; Holtom 1963), in short, was achieved by embracing, encompassing and comprehending folk Shinto — so integral to essentialized 'Japanliness' — under the state umbrella. As folk Shinto constituted an underpinning of Nihonjinron, appropriation of this Nihonjinron-in-private-sector for state purposes was a strategic move.

Shiga Shigekata, a political economist who contributed much to the magazine Nihonjin on Japan's economic policy, also wrote on uniquely Japanese characteristics (Iijima 1958: 229-232). In creating his version of Nihonjinron, Shiga (1976, originally 1894) wrote a piece claiming Japan's natural scenery to be the most beautiful in the world, deriving from it a positively characterized Japanese personality. Miyake Setsurei (1977, originally 1891) was more even-handed in his view of the Japanese, enumerating both their ugly, seamy side and their laudable side. Miyake criticized Japan's 'feudal class structure' and certain other facets, but this did not lead him to advocate wholesale adoption of Western culture. Rather, he also lauded Japan's traditional culture. Miyake's efforts were in reaction to the excessive Westernization of Japan, and were supported by the ground-swelling movement to ameliorate the unequal treaties Japan had to sign with Western powers. It is no surprise that both Shiga and Miyake were some of the principal contributors to the afore-mentioned magazine Nihonjin, which often featured right-wing nationalism (kokusui shugi) of the time (Motoyama 1958).

By the late Meiji, intellectuals expressing positive views of Japan were legion. Oomachi Keigetsu wrote a good deal on the incomparable virtues of Japan. In the area of esthetics, one might mention Kitamura Tookoku, who elaborated in 1891 on the plebeian aesthetic concept of iki, having to do with the aesthetic value of the plebeian culture which developed in the Tokugawa period, in his review of Ozaki Kooyoo's Kyara Makura, anticipating Kuki's classic study (Kuki 1930) of the same concept (Minami 1980: 90). These views of Japan expressed by intellectuals are consonant with the manifest ideology which crystallized in the late Meiji. (Gluck 1985; Pyle 1969) This late Meiji period, in fact, is what Kamishima calls 'the first phase' of the Japanese concern with national identity (Kamishima 1990: 1).

Taisho Interlude

During the so-called Taisho democracy, liberal thinking pervaded Japan. There were some like Tanaka Yoshitau (1924), who wrote a very successful nationalistic book, reprinted six times in three years, on 'national morality.' His writings are reminiscent of the afore-mentioned Inoue Tetsujiroo's in that the Imperial Rescript on Education is the center piece of his argument about 'human conduct,' which according to Tanaka, has to do with Shinto, bushidoo (the code of the warrior), familism, and loyalty to the nation.

But basically the Taisho period did not promise, promote or encourage strong continuation of Nihonjinron. Virtually all of the thousands of foreign engineers, technicians and scholars, brought over to create a Westernized Meiji, had been sent back by the end of Meiji. This was a time of relative peace in Japan. The liberalism of the Taisho period, though of course rooted in Western thought, was no longer obsessed with wholesale and uncritical absorption of Western culture, but was more reflective and selective, mirroring assessment and evaluation of things Western before importing. Western thought, in fact, began to take root now, rather than being merely a facade floating in the appearance of enlightenment and progressivism, as in the Meiji period. Thus there was little room for staunchly nationalistic Nihonjinron to hold sway. Kamishima's periodicization of Nihonjinron — though he does not call it that — in fact skips the whole of Taisho era, and begins the second phase in the early Showa (Kamishima 1990: 1).

Ultra-nationalism of the thirties to 1945

It is in the nineteen-thirties that we see the resurgence of patriotic Nihon-jinron of the basic variety we saw in the late Meiji period. As Gluck says, Meiji ideologues laid the foundation of political thinking which was to continue until 1945. Rhetoric familiar from the late Meiji was repeated ever more fervently at this time: the emperor as father figure for Japan's subjects, the Japanese family system as embodiment of virtues and the foundation of the Japanese nation. Social values such as on and giri were what created social order unequaled around the world. This self-praise, often in the form of unqualified ethnocentrism, increased in the 1930's when frenzied claims began to be made of the superiority of the Japanese in comparison with Europeans and Americans.

It was in the early Showa that Watsuji wrote his *Fuudo*, a classic in Nihonjinron which sees an inextricable relationship between Japan's environment and its culture. As Minami (1980) notes, this publication was precipitated by the rise of Marxism. It was to be an answer to Marxism to demonstrate the impossibility of accounting for Japanese culture in the framework of historical materialism. About the same time, Kuki (1930), resuscitating Kitamura Tookoku's argument but further enhancing it, wrote his wellknown treatise on the aesthetic concept of iki as representing the quintessential aesthetic value of the plebeian Japanese. It is significant that Kuki's writing came after a decade of study in France, as Watusji's came after his sojourn in Germany (Minami 1980: 94-95). Shirayanagi Shuuko (1938), in his treatise on the Japanese people and nature, also argued the role of the environment in creating Japanese culture. Japanese environment, according to him, was the best and most desirable in the world, and was even responsible for creating uniquely Japanese genetic lineage (ketto) at the confluence of the continental culture and the oceanic culture. Note here the conflation of environment, culture, and biology. As Watsuji did in his treatises on ethics, Shirayanagi devoted much space to the mythological creation of the Japanese nation and founding of the emperor system.

If the Imperial Rescript on Education was the most canonical of all canons of Nihonjinron before 1945, Kokutai no Hongi (The Japanese Polity), issued by the Ministry of Education in 1937 and distributed in large qualities, was at least one of the most canonical of the warperiod Nihonjinron documents. This work elaborated on the centrality of the imperial institution in Japan and also argued how Japan was the best in the world in terms of its history and culture. While there was no explicit comparison with other nations, the intent was clearly to demonstrate the superiority of Japan over its real and imagined enemies in Asia and the West and to convince the Japanese people that therefore Japan was destined to win the war and rule the world. Numerous versions of its commentary were published and reprinted to meet the high demand.

Even Hasegawa Nyozekan, that spokesman of Taisho liberalism, in 1938 wrote Nihon-teki Seikaku (The 'Japanly' Character), extolling what he argued to be specifically 'Japanly' virtues. His argument is reminiscent of Watsuji's ecological theory, starting with the supposed impact of the geography of Japan upon its culture and extending into lifestyle, human relations and art. Japanese art, according to him, is not isolated and divorced from nature, as Western art — like a framed painting in a museum — supposedly is. Instead it is an integral part of nature, as seen in the Japanese garden and home. Hasegawa spoke of the refined sensitivity of the Japanese mind.

Suzuki Daisetz' Zen to Nihon Bunka (Zen and Japanese Culture, 1940) also appeared about this time, in wartime Japan, with endorsement by none other than Nishida Kitaroo, arguably the foremost philosopher of the Kyoto school. Suzuki reviewed the influence of Zen in Japanese art, the ethics of warriors, Japanese Confucianism, tea ceremony, and haiku, the seventeen-syllable poetry. It may seem odd to bring in Zen Buddhism in the discussion of a uniquely Japanese culture, since Zen Buddhism originated in China. As I indicated earlier, however, at this time in history, Japan was concerned with defining its identity by distinguishing itself from the West, not from China. In that context, marshalling forth an Eastern religion was not seen as odd. Besides, Suzuki's point was to demonstrate the uniqueness of Japanese arts and esthetics as influenced by Zen.

Kooyama Iwao, writing in 1941, developed a theory of cultural taxonomy to place Japan in a theoretical system of classification which is quite reminiscent of the climatic classification in Watsuji's Fuudo. Kooyama speaks of the delicate natural environment in which Japanese culture has been nurtured, and attributes Japanese love of nature, appreciation of subtle colors, and delicate disposition to the physical environment. His Nihonjinron is almost a replica of Watsuji's in many respects, deriving from the environment Japanese personal character, aesthetics, and patriotism. Of course, Kooyama did not forget to single out the emperor system as the hallmark of Japanese polity and claim it to be unique in the world, calling Japan a divine nation.

It was the uniquely superior character of the Japanese that was going to bring about the inevitable victory of Japan.

One of the greatest Japanese Christians, Uchimura Kanzoo, was also moved to discuss the essence of Japaneseness through certain well-chosen 'representative' Japanese (Uchimura 1941). This work is a timely translation of a book originally published in English as Representative Men of Japan in 1894 — timely, in that Japan was to enter the Pacific War in a few months, and demonstration of 'Japanliness' to the Japanese people was needed more urgently than ever. But its timelessness is also demonstrated by the fact that, at least until 1973, the book was reprinted on the average of once a year.

Uchimura chose to represent the best qualities of the Japanese, Saigoo Takamori, a tragic hero of the Meiji Restoration, who was forced to rebel against the government and commit suicide, Uesugi Kenzan, a feudal lord who ruled his domain with skill and benevolence in the eighteenth and the nineteenth century, Ninomiya Sontoku, the agrarian philosopher/administrator of the same period, Nakae Tooju, a country Confucian teacher of the seventeenth century whose fame pervaded the country, and Nichiren of the thirteenth century, who founded the nationalistic Nichiren sect. It is highly instructive that Uchimura, a Christian, did not hesitate to include a Buddhist priest to demonstrate what it takes to be a Japanese. It goes to show the 'Japanization' of Christianity in Uchimura. This fact is relevant when Nihonjinron is regarded as Japan's civil religion (Befu 1993).

Nihonjinron in one form or another became part of official ideology in the period from the Meiji Restoration to the end of the Second World War. It was part of the war propaganda of the government and was preached, broadcast and forced upon people. The government used every means possible to propagate this world view, including educational institutions and newspapers. It used secret police to almost totally shut out alternative and rival views, notably Marxism. This effort reached a crescendo scale during World War II. And the bloated view that Japan in every respect was superior to the rest of the world continued until it busted in August, 1945.

It may have looked as though all of Japan was spouting some version of Nihonjinron during the frenetic period of wartime — though no doubt in varying degrees of conviction or disbelief, some being true believers, some simply riding the pragmatic tide without conviction, and still others being forced to take the position through coercion from the police and other authorities.

But the view of Japan as backward, behind the West, and needing infusion of ideas from the West never completely died from early Meiji. Even at the height of government thought control, some like Sakada Ango were able openly to deny significance to Japanese tradition in the March 1942 issue of Gendai Bungaku, according to Ikumatsu (1963: 21-22). Sakada maintained what was important in life is convenience. If chairs and tables proved to be more convenient, so be it; one need not apologize for adopting Western conveniences. I recall my own middle school principal publicly praising the Allied leaders — Roosevelt, Churchill, Stalin and Chiang Kai-shek — for staying in office throughout the war to provide consistent leadership while criticizing the Japanese government for the frequent change-over of its leadership.

One may also venture the suggestion that Japan maintained inferiority-superiority complex: the Japanese were, on the one hand, convinced of their inferiority to the West, which they desperately needed to overcome, and at the same time claimed spiritual superiority, and tried to compensate technological shortcomings with what they perceived to be their spiritual advantage. In the postwar years, too, Japan has maintained the same inferiority-superiority complex. Japan's postwar history has been in fact one of striving to reverse its techno-economic inferiority with the West. Before August 1945 Japan tried to achieve this end by conquest, colonization, and war; since the war it has done so through economic means.

Postwar auto-orientalism

In the immediate postwar era, disastrous defeat in the Pacific war meant not only military defeat but total devaluation of Japanese cultural values. For at least a decade, perhaps two decades after 1945, Japan entered a period of depressing soul-searching. With the nation vanquished, the idealized Nihonjinron valorizing traditional values now seemed worthless. For if it were worth anything, why did Japan lose the war? Japanese people were promised victory by virtue of Japan's superior culture. The culture which was supposed to lead Japan to victory and conquest of the world fell flat on its face and utterly failed to accomplish its mission. Traditional Japanese values and institutions, which were mobilized for fighting the war, were now all objects of criticism. 'Feudalistic,' 'pre-modern,' 'outmoded,' and 'backward' were some of the epithets constantly thrown at whatever represented old and traditional Japan.

Indeed, even legitimacy of the emperor system was now in doubt (Befu

1992). After all, the emperor himself was summoned to the headquarters of the Supreme Commander of the Allied Powers, and had to pay homage to General Douglas MacArthur, rather than summoning MacArthur to the imperial palace for an audience. Newspapers carried in the front page a huge picture of the emperor side by side with MacArthur, the diminutive emperor dwarfed by the six-foot-tall leader of the Occupation force, who was now often referred to as Japan's new emperor. The Japanese now had no choice but to admit their emperor no longer was the king pin of the Japanese polity. The imperial institution with its mythic foundation, national ideology and symbolism, all of which were marshalled forth for the war effort and constituted the core of Nihonjinron, well nigh lost their venerable and revered status.

The Japanese family system, for one, was now to be condemned for its 'feudal' character, as argued in the influential writings of Kawashima Takeyoshi (1950, 1957), as will be elaborated later. The normative values of on and giri likewise were given negative scores. Japan's traditional virtues all were cast as vices. Before and during the war, wartime propagandists contrasted democracy and individualism with Japanese values, and denigrated the former as worthless simply because they contrasted with what Japan had and valued. But with the military reversal, democracy was in and whatever contrasted with democracy was out because the latter was by definition the cause of the defeat, according to the now fashionable post-war interpretation.

Even the Japanese language, the supposed storehouse of Japanese values and virtues according to war-time and prewar Nihonjinron advocates from Motoori Norinaga on, could not remain free from attack: Japanese affords no logical discourse, according to its critics, as European languages presumably do. It enables only discourse in feeling and emotion. Shiga Naoya, a well-known writer who was called 'a god of fiction' for his literary facility, in 1946 even went so far as to resuscitate Mori Arinori's suggestion fifty years earlier to abolish Japanese and replace it with another language like French (Miller 1982: 109-10). It was one thing for the Occupation to declare the inutility of Japanese, as they were wont to do. It was totally another for a notable Japanese intellectual who made his living with his pen to concur with such an Orientalizing remark. The wholesale castigation of traditional values was about as thorough as the total praise of them during the war.

In this situation, discourse on Japan's identity of the late nineteen forties and the nineteen fifties became one of comparing Japan with the West as Japan's way of convincing itself how wrong it was — a way of providing a rationale — for the lost status of the wartime ideology. The West was upheld as the model and the ideal, and whatever the West had and Japan did not have was the reason for the defeat of the war and for criticizing Japan, be it its cultural traits, social institutions, or personality. The example was set by Ruth Benedict, who in The Chrysanthemum and the Sword, pronounced the death of Japanese culture, according to Douglas Lummis (1982). The Chrysanthemum and the Sword, since it was authored by an American, is not in itself an example of discourse on self-identity. However, the book was read in translation by millions of Japanese almost as a revelatory Truth about themselves. Legions of other Western observers, including MacArthur (who claimed that the Japanese had the mentality of a twelve-year-old), saw and analyzed Japan against the mirror of their own social values, and in their free and unencumbered, naive ethnocentrism denigrated everything Japanese. Japanese intellectuals, in the postwar skeptical mood, were delighted to have their new-found conviction confirmed by observers from countries which represented a superior civilization and the new model for Japan.

To illustrate how pervasive this self-castigation was, let us take issues of one of the most popular magazines — Chuuoo Kooron ('Central Review') — for just one year — 1947. In the January issue, Ishiwata Sadao, Hani Goroo, Inoue Kiyoshi and Ishimoda Tadashi — leading scholars of the time — held a round-table discussion whose purpose was 'to discuss in concrete terms backward and feudalistic elements woven into the fabric of Japanese society as reactionary factors preventing Japan's democratic revolution.' (Ishiwata et al. 1947) Among these factors, Inoue suggested that the emperor system so unique to Japan was born as a result of the fact that the 'Meiji Restoration did not solve [the problems of] the feudal system thoroughly.' Hani squarely placed the blame of the criminal war of invasion into China and the Pacific war on the emperor system. Hani also spoke of 'the backwardness of Japanese society.'

In the March issue, Katoo Hyooji (1947) blamed the failure of contemporary politics on 'forces of the feudalistic bureaucracy.' In the April issue, Ishiwata Sadao (1947), a member of the round-table discussion featured in the January issue, blamed 'the semi-feudalism of Japanese landlords' for the high rent for tenancy. In May, Kawashima Takeyoshi (1947) argued on the 'Asiatic characteristics of Japanese feudalism,' and regarded the adoption system, in which a person, usually a man, is adopted for the purpose of taking over the family name and the family enterprise, as a form of slavery.

In June, Hoashi Kei (1947) advocated getting rid of the 'semi-feudalistic, reactionary fascist forces which parasitically have lived on Japan's giant monopoly capitalism.' In the August issue, Prince Takamatsu (Chuuoo Kooron Editors 1947) held an interview with editors of the magazine, in which he alluded to the need to destroy the 'feudality' of the Japanese family system and democratize it. In November, Tokyo University sociologist Fukutake Tadashi spoke of 'the survival of the familistic atmosphere' in northeastern rural communities, in which the main household in a doozoku system held a powerful position vis-à-vis its local branches. In all these writings, terms like 'feudalism' and 'familism' are of course used as derogatory epithets. Such examples can be multiplied. But the forgoing makes it abundantly clear that indictment of Japan's traditional past was a widely accepted and even fashionable mode of defining Japan's identity.

Such auto-Orientalism was, of course, rampant in other fora of writing than Chuuoo Kooron. A few examples will suffice. Tanigawa Tetsuzoo, who taught at Hoosei University and was associate director of a national museum at the time of writing, criticized the Japanese national character in Bunkaron (1947) on several grounds. For one, in contrast to Christianity, which seeks salvation of the soul, Japanese mythology emphasizes hierarchical human relations and merely teaches obedience before authority. Secondly, this same mythology was responsible for the tendencyof placing the interest of the nation-state above the interest of the individual. Third, the Japanese do not know how to use freedom correctly. Fourth, the Japanese do not know how to respect the individual. In short, he criticized the Japanese for not possessing values commonly accepted as Western.

Kawashima Takeyoshi, sociologist of law, was even more critical of the Japanese family institution in his Ideorogii to shite no Kazoku Seido (The family system as an ideology) (1957) and Nihon Shakai no Kazoku-teki Koosei (Familistic structure of the Japanese society) (1950). In the former, for example, he singles out the concept of filial piety, relates it to the feudatory lord-vassal relationship among the samurai, claims that it is supported by Confucianism brought over from China and implies that it was not an indigenous Japanese concept. He concludes that the defeat of the war, first of all, destroyed the power structure which supported the old ideology and, second, removed the obstacle for the growth of a modern family morality which was in the process of developing among the populace. It was the Occupation policy which assisted this growth, and the new constitution which helped stabilize it. This is the historic meaning of the defeat and the new constitution, according to Kawashima. Finally he notes current efforts being made to revive the ideology of filial piety; but to teach filial piety, which was originally not their own value but was imported from China, would mean turning the gear of history backward—a quixotic act (Kawashima 1957: 125).

In 1951, with a grant from UNESCO, Japanese social scientists conducted a series of field researches on social tension. In the concluding round-table discussion, a sociologist at Tokyo Metropolitan University, Suzuki Jiroo, who investigated the burakumin outcast minority, blamed the Tokugawa 'feudal' system for the formation of the burakumin system. (Nihon Jimbun Kagakkai ed. 1953: 464). Toyota Takeshi, professor at Tohoku University, suggested in the same report that social tension occurs when 'feudal' society makes the transition into modern society.

This self-castigation — blaming Japan's tradition for Japan's misery — went hand in hand with the Occupation's pronouncement that virtually everything in Japan was anti-democratic, outmoded, and had to be reformed. The Japanese accepted the Occupation's judgement that, in essence, the West was best and Japan was its opposite. The Occupation's zeal to create a democracy from the ashes of the war and to prevent the resurgence of an enemy of the Allied Powers of course did not stop at mere pronouncements. Reforms proceeded on practically all fronts of social life, from adoption of a new constitution and land reform to educational reform and dissolution of the zaibatsu. As the West was represented almost solely, and mightily, by the military might of the Allied Powers, notably the United States, it was almost inevitable that the attitude of the Japanese toward the West echoed that of a hundred years before, when the Japanese were overwhelmed by Western military power, and later by the glitter of Western civilization. They agreed with Western observers and were convinced that Japanese culture and social institutions were fundamentally flawed, and desperately needed an overhaul. Thus, for the second time in history, Japan went through a major period of auto-Orientalism.

It is in this context that we can comprehend the publication of one of the strangest science fictions, Kachikujin Yapuu, subtitled 'Yapoo, the Domesticated Cattle,' which was originally serialized in Kidan Kurabu starting in 1961 and authored by a certain Numa Shoozoo (1991a, 1991b), a pseudonym presumably for Kurata Takuji, a judge. This highly complex science fiction takes place in the twenty-first century, when the white race finally conquers the universe and establishes an inter-galactic empire, in which sex roles are completely reversed. Blacks in this story are reduced to slaves to serve their white masters — but with some human rights.

The white race obliterates all the yellow races, except the Yapoo — the name being presumably derived from 'Japanese' — who are allowed to live, but only as a subhuman species whose only purpose of living and reproducing is to serve the white race in myriad ways. Surgery is performed for example on Yapoo to make their mouth elongated and thus more able to swallow the urine and feces of their white masters or to elongate their tongues in order to provide maximum sexual stimulation for their female masters. The Yapoo considered this diet the most delectable, and thanked God for the privilege. Genetic engineering is executed to create a whole variety of subspecies of Yapoo which serve different purposes, such as carrying their white masters on their back, squatting to become a living chair for the white master, etc. One subspecies is created to provide the most delicious meat for the white race.

The story is probably the ultimate in auto-Orientalism among Japanese intellectuals. It was borne of the author's reaction to Japan's defeat: he was ashamed of his country which had surrendered unconditionally, and ashamed of the ugly view of the emperor standing with General MacArthur in the photograph published in the newspaper in January, 1946 (Numa 1991b: 654). This sense of shame then was expressed in creating a world in which the Japanese were totally subjugated by the white race and enthralled by their subjugated status. The sheer fact that a story of this sort could be published indicates the extent to which Japanese were under the auto-Orientalizing spell.

Ascendancy of cultural nationlism since the late nineteen-sixties

It was not until the late sixties that the balance began to tip and Japanese began to see themselves in a positive light more than in a negative light. By this time, the postwar 'allergy,' as this defeatist attitude of almost masochistic self-negation is sometimes called, slowly began to be out-weighed by a more self-confident, self-congratulatory identity.

The end of the Allied Occupation of Japan, the signing of the peace treaty with the U.S., the gradual economic recovery of the late nineteen fifties and the nineteen sixties all contributed toward the regaining of self confidence, or at least the lessening of the feeling of inferiority and psychological or spiritual defeat and loss. As the postwar economy began to 'takeoff' and enter the stage of rapid growth, the Nihonjinron too began to take a turn, and began to portray Japan in a more favorable light. The same social institutions and the same cultural values which were objects of condemnation in the immediate postwar years were now seen to have positive valence — if they were not any better than those of the West, at least they were just as good. The Japanese were now finally able to take the position of a cultural relativist, rather than accepting uncritically and in toto the victor's value judgments (Aoki 1989).

Slowly regaining self-confidence, the Japanese began to marvel at the phenomenal economic development and to see it as a result of or as fostered by Japan's unique social institutions, cultural values and personality rather than as resulting in spite of Japan's 'pre-modern' or 'feudalistic' institutions and values. The overwhelming majority of Nihonjinron literature now began to discuss the unique characteristics of Japan as its strength and the basis of Japan's global economic success.

In the most recent period, the definition of Japanese cultural and national identity has been imbued even with ethnocentrism, seeing positive values in Japanese culture while denigrating the West.

The nineteen sixties and seventies were still decades in which negative Japan and positive Japan co-existed as uneasy bedfellows. 'Critical' (or negative) Nihonjinron held sway early in this period, but it was slowly taken over by a more positive Nihonjinron. From the late seventies on, the vast majority of Nihonjinron literature began to discuss the unique characteristics of Japan as its strength and as the basis of its economic success, and even propounded the Nihonjinron thesis as Japan's prime mover.

Conclusion

In the modern history of Japan, one can identify periods of overwhelming negative self-identity and also periods of equally overwhelming positive self-identity. The first period of positive identity came in the late eighteenth century and the first half of the nineteenth century with the Kokugaku nationalist movement. The self-confidence gained through valorization of indigenous institutions and values in this movement, however, was shattered by the overwhelming military and technological superiority of the West, forcibly thrust upon Japan through gunboat diplomacy.

Although not conquered or colonized by any Western power, Japan suffered humiliation, having to sign unequal trade treaties and pay indemnities to European nations for the 'wrongs' done to their citizens. As Japanese began to have more and more contact with the West — by traveling to Europe and America (e.g., the Iwakura Mission), by having Westerners come to Japan as consultants and university professors in the guise of the so-called oyatoi gaikokujin ('hired foreigners'), Japanese began increasingly to see themselves as inferior in all aspects of civilization vis-à-vis the West.

Another period of negative identity came after World War II. Again Japan experienced humiliation, this time by being totally vanquished by Western military powers. The military superiority of the West, especially the United States, impressed the Japanese even more when the Allies landed on the Japanese islands and demonstrated their materiel.

In both cases, Japan reacted with almost complete denigration and self-castigation of its own culture and with a corresponding admiration and almost adoration of Western culture in a process I term 'auto-Orientalism.' In both periods denigration was so complete that responsible individuals went so far as to propose doing away with the Japanese language. In both, the feeling of inferiority turned into adoration of the West, extending over the entire gamut of Western civilization including art and literature.

Positive self-evaluation in Nihonjinron has a longer and somewhat more continuous history but it was particularly pronounced in the late Meiji and just before and during World War II, especially since alternative, negative views of Japan were all but eliminated by the forces of the state. A few people murmured comments reflecting negative valuation of Japan but they were few indeed and they risked police repression and reprisal. A third period of positive self-evaluation is now, since the late sixties, as Japan's economic success around the world has become more and more firmly established as a permanent order of the world. In both periods positive evaluation is all-encompassing and not limited simply to Japan's military prowess or economic power. In pre-war days, Japan claimed superiority to Western civilization in spiritual power as well as in military might. Japan's unique aesthetic qualities and social institutions were not forgotten. The same may be said of Nihonjinron at the present time. Its contents run the whole gamut of the cultural catalogue from climate, creation myth and religion to social and political values.

What is different in the contemporary period from the war time situation is that there is no overt state suppression of contrary views, at least not the sort of suppression which secret police executed during World War II. Yet the sort of negative identity that prevailed in the immediate post-war era is well nigh gone. The Japanese who are embracing the view that 'Japan is Number One' because of its unique qualities are doing so without obvious coercion or state promotion. Forces of suasion are more subtle and indirect. In this respect, the contemporary positive evaluation of Japan may perhaps be a stronger, more firmly rooted affair than during the Second World War. For those who believe that contemporary Nihonjinron leads to narrow nationalism, conservatism, and rejection of a cosmopolitan outlook for the Japanese, this contemporary trend may be something to worry about.

Looking back at the vicissitudes of the varieties of Japanese self-identity from the beginning of the nineteenth century, and considering factors for its swings from positive to negative and back to positive, one can make several observations.

One is the nature of the reference group. Japan's self-identity is constructed in comparison with a civilization which is exerting predominant influence upon it. In the Tokugawa period, this referent was obviously China. By those who sought ideological independence from China, Japan had to be defined as non-China. Supposedly non-Chinese aspects of Japanese tradition then were enlisted to create this definition. In post-Meiji Restoration Japan, the referent was Europe and the United States. The definition of who the Japanese are was made in conscious comparison with the West. China was almost totally forgotten in this exercise.

Secondly, the relative strength of Japan vis-à-vis the referent is important in defining Japan in a positive or negative light. When Japan is strong militarily or economically, or at least when Japan perceives little or no threat, as was the case vis-à-vis China in the late Tokugawa period, Japan's self-definition is overwhelmingly positive.

Current Nihonjinron then must be seen against the background of Japan's strong economic position worldwide. How long the positive view of themselves will continue will depend on Japan's geoeconomic strength relative to world economic powers, notably the United States.

References

Aoki, Tamotsu (1989): 'Nihon bunkaron' no hen'yo 4,34 Sengo Nihon no bunka to aidentitii [Transformation of Nihonjinron: Culture and identity in postwar Japan]. Tokyo: Chuuoo Kooronsha.

Befu, Harumi (1990): Nihon bunka ron wa taishuu shoohi zai (Nihonjinron is a mass consumer product). In Ideorogii to shiteno Nihon bunkaron [Nihonjinron as ideology] by Harumi Befu. Pp. 54-67. Tokyo: Shisoo no kagakusha.

Befu, Harumi (1992): Symbols of nationalism and Nihonjinron. In Ideology and practice *in modern Japan.* Goodman, Roger and Refsing, Kirsten, eds., pp. 26-46. London: Routledge.

Befu, Harumi (1993): Civil religion in contemporary Japan: The secular theology of Nihon kyoo and Nihonjinron. *In* Acta Universitatis Temperensis Series B. 42 (Transient societies: Japanese and Korean studies in a transitional world). Jorma et al. Kiritö, eds. Pp. 18-50.

Benedict, Ruth (1946): *The chrysanthemum and the sword.* Boston: Houghton Mifflin.

Chuuoo Kooron Editors (1947): Takamatsunomiya to kataru-Kooshitsu no kazoku seido ni tsuite (Conversation with Prince Takamatsu: On the family system of the imperial household). *Chuuoo Kooron,* August, pp. 41-46.

Dale, Peter (1986): *The myth of Japanese uniqueness.* New York: St. Martin's.

Davis, Winston (1976): The civil theology of Inoue Tetsujiroo. *Japanese Journal of Religious Studies* 3(1), 5-40.

Fukutake, Tadashi (1947): Toohoku nooson no kazoku shugi (familism in northeastern villages). *Chuuoo Kooron,* November, pp. 36-41.

Gluck, Carol (1985): *Japan's modern myths: Ideology in the late Meiji period.* Princeton: Princeton University Press.

Haga, Yaichi (1977): Kokumin sei juu ron (Ten comments on national character). *In Nihonjin ron.* Ikumatsu Keizoo, ed. Pp. 125-263. Tokyo: Fuzanboo.

Hardacre, Helen (1989): *Shinto and the state, 1868-1988.* Princeton: Princeton University Press.

Hasegawa, Nyozekan (1938): *Nihonteki seikaku* [The Japanese character]. Tokyo: Iwanami Shoten.

Hoashi, Kei (1947): Kokumin sai kyooiku no shigoto [The task of reeducating the citizen]. *Chuuoo Kooron,* June, p. 23.

Holtom, Daniel (1963): *Modern Japan and shinto nationalism.* New York: Paragon.

Minear, Richard H. (1980): Orientalism and the study of Japan. *Journal of Asian Studies* 39(3), 507-17.

Iinuma, Jiroo (1958): Meiji nijuu-nendai no keizai shisoo (Economic thought in the twenties of the Meiji era). *In Meiji zenhanki no nashonarizumu* [Nationalism in the first half of the Meiji period]. Yoshio Sakata, ed. Pp. 213-60. Tokyo: Miraisha.

Ikumatsu, Keizoo (1963): Senzen no Nihon bunka ron, *Shisoo,* no. 463 (January) 12-23.

Inoue, Tetsujiroo (1891): *Chokugo engi* [Commentary on the Rescript]. Tokyo: Keigyoosha.

Ishiwata Sadao (1947): Roonoo-ha riron o hihansu (Critique of the Ronoha theory). *Chuuoo Kooron,* April, pp. 31-45.

Ishiwata Sadao (1947): Minshu kakumei to Nihon no shakai (Democratic revolution and the Japanese society). *Chuuoo Kooron,* January, pp. 39-54.

Kamishima, Jiroo (1990): Society convergence; an alternative for the homogeneity theory. *Japan Foundation Newsletter,* 17, 3, 1-6.

Kang, Sang-Choong (1988): 'Nihon teki orientarizumu no genzai-kokusai ka ni hisomu hizumi (The Japanese style Orientalism today: Hidden traps in internationalization). *Sekai*, December, pp. 133-39.

Katoo, Hyooji (1947): Kiro ni tatsu shakaitoo (The Socialist Party at a crossroad). *Chuuoo Kooron*, March, pp. 34-39.

Kawashima, Takeyoshi (1947): Nihon hooken sei no Ajia teki seishitsu (The Asiatic character of the Japanese feudalism), *Chuuoo Kooron*, May, pp. 6-19.

Kawashima, Takeyoshi (1957): *Ideorogii toshiteno kazoku seido* [The family institution as ideology]. Tokyo: Iwanami Shoten.

Kawashima, Takeyoshi (1950): *Nihon shakai no kazokuteki koosei* [The familistic structure of the Japanese society]. Tokyo: Nihon Hyooron Sha.

Kooyama, Iwao (1941): *Bunka ruikei gaku kenkyuu* [Taxonomical study of culture]. Tokyo: Koobundoo Shoboo.

Kuki, Shuuzoo (1930): *'Iki' no koozoo* [The structure of iki]. Tokyo: Iwanami Shoten.

Lummis, Douglas (1982): *A New look at the chrysanthemum and the sword*. Tokyo: Shohakusha.

Miyake Setsurei (1977): Shinzenbi Nihonjin (Truth, goodness and beauty in the Japanese) *and* Giakuki Nihonjin (Deception, evil and ugliness in the Japanese). *In Nihonjin ron*. Ikumatsu Keizoo, ed. Tokyo: Fuzanboo.

Miller, Roy Andrew (1982): *Japan's modern myth: The language and beyond*. New York: Weatherhill.

Minami, Hiroshi (1980): *Nihonjin ron no keifu* [History of Nihonjinron]. Tokyo: Koodansha.

Minamoto, Ryooen (1958): Kyooiku chokugo no kokka shugi teki kaishaku (Nationalistic interpretation of the Imperial Rescript for Education). *In Meiji zenhanki no nashonarizumu* [Nationalism in the first half of the Meiji period]. Yoshio Sakata, ed. pp. 165-212. Tokyo: Miraisha.

Motoyama, Yukihiko (1958): Meiji nijuunendai no seiron ni arawareta nashonarisumu (Nationalism manifested in political theories of the Meiji twenties). *In Meiji zenhanki no nashonarismu* [Nationalism in the first half of the Meiji period]. Yoshio Sakata, ed. Pp. 37-84. Tokyo: Miraisha.

Mouer, Ross E. (1983): 'Orientalism' as knowledge: lessons for Japanologists? *Keio Journal of Politics* 4:11-31.

Numa, Shoozoo (1991): *Kachikujin Yapuu* (Human cattle, Yapoo). Tokyo: Sukora.

Numa, Shoozoo (1991): *Kachikujin Yapuu. Kanketsu-hen* [Human cattle, Yapoo: The concluding volume]. Tokyo: Mirion Shuppan.

Pyle, Kemeth B. (1969): *The New generation in Meiji Japan: Problems of cultural identity: 1885-1895*. Stanford: Stanford University Press.

Said, Edward (1978): *Orientalism*. New York: Random House.

Sakata, Yoshio ed. (1958): *Meiji zenhanki no nashonarizumu* [Nationalism in the first half of the Meiji period]. Tokyo: Miraisha.

Nihon Jinbun Kagakkai, ed. (1953): *Shakaiteki kinchoo no kenkyuu* [A study of social tension]. Tokyo: Yuuhikaku.

Shiga, Shigetaka (1976): [1894] *Nihon fuukei ron* [Theory of Japanese landscape]. Tokyo: Iwanami Shoten.

Shirayanagi, Shuuko (1938): *Nihon minzoku to tennen* [The Japanese people and nature]. Tokyo: Chikura Shoboo.

Suzuki, Daisetz (1940): *Zen to Nihon bunka* [Zen and the Japanese culture]. Tokyo: Iwanami Shoten.

Tanaka, Yoshitau (1924): *Kokumin dootoku yooryoo koogi* [Lectures on the principles of national morality]. Tokyo: Nihon Gakujutsu Kenkyuukai.

Tanigawa, Tetsuzoo (1947): *Bunkaron* [On Culture]. Tokyo: Kinbundoo Shuppanbu.

Uchida, Roan (1968): Rokumeikan jidai (The Rokumeikan period). *In Gendai Nihon kiroku zenshuu* [Documentary compendium on modern Japan] vol. 4 Bunmei kaika [Civilization and enlightenment]. Shigeki Senuma, ed. Pp. 23-31. Tokyo: Chikuma Shoboo.

Uchimura, Kanzoo (1941): *Daihyoo teki Nihonjin* [Representative Japanese]. Tokyo: Iwanami Shoten.

Watsuji, Tetsuroo (1935): *Fuudo-Ningen gaku teki koosatsu* [The climate: Humanological considerations]. Tokyo: Iwanami Shoten.

Notes

1. This paper was written on the basis of the research conducted at East-West Center, Honolulu, Hawaii, where the author held a fellowship from September 1991 to March 1992. The Center's support is gratefully acknowledged. Also thanks are due Ms. Nancy Stalker for her excellent editorial work.

   Japanese personal names in the text are written in accordance with the Japanese convention of showing the family name first, followed by the given name.

2. For the history of Nihonjinron see Aoki (1989), Ikumatsu (1963), Minami (1980).

3. It reminds one of Watsuji Tetsuroo, who a hundred years later was to write Fuudo, after returning from his study of Western philosophy in Germany, in reaction to Western philosophers' theory of the relationship between nature and human being (Watsuji 1935).

4. Minami, in his history of Nihonjinron, points out (1980:84), however, that Norinaga had in mind a pan-human feeling when he spoke about mono no aware, rather than a uniquely Japanese quality. Just as Western scholars create what they consider to be universal concepts out of their own Western intellectual experience, Norinaga was doing the same.

5. See Miller (1982:107-9) for the circumstance surrounding this suggestion.

6. The fact that the Japanese government was willing to pay such high salaries to foreigners was in itself Japan's political leadership's self-admission of Japan's backwardness.

7. This is a point which Dale (1986: 59-60) misses in his critique of Nihonjinron.

Liang Shuming and the Danish Model

Stig Thøgersen

> During the last forty-fifty years, Denmark has become the best country in the
> world.... Not by defeating other nations, but by promoting education.
>
> Liang Shuming (1931b; 299)

Between 1931 and 1937 the Chinese philosopher and social reformer Liang
Shuming headed an experiment with rural reconstruction in Zouping County,
Shandong Province. This was one of the most important theoretical and
practical attempts at defining an alternative both to the revolutionary path of
the Chinese Communist Party and to the corrupt bureaucracy of the
Guomindang Nationalists, a Third Way designed to lead China peacefully
into the modern world while retaining the best of traditional mores and
values. Searching for organizational and ideological precedents both in
China's past and in the West, Liang was struck by the success of the Danish
peasantry's non-violent creation of a prosperous society on the ruins left after
Denmark's defeat by Prussia in 1864. He was particularly impressed by the
role played in this process by the folk high schools, and though he never
visited Denmark he became convinced, through the writings of representatives of the Danish folk high school movement and through personal
encounters, that the Danish model was as close to his own visions as anything
he could ever find abroad.

Liang's discussions of Denmark have received little attention in the
Western literature. Van Slyke mentions that: 'It is hard to conceive anything
better calculated to attract the attention of Liang Sou-ming'[1] than the Danish
co-operatives and folk high schools (Van Slyke, 1959; 467), but he does not
elaborate on their role in Liang's theory of rural reconstruction. Guy Alitto's
path-breaking biography, *The Last Confucian* (Alitto, 1986), which since its
appearance has been the major source of knowledge about Liang's life and
ideas in the West, and which includes a thorough discussion of Liang's interpretation of several Western philosophers, does not examine his 'Danish
connection' at all. Neither does Ma Yong's recent Chinese biography of Liang

(Ma 1992). In the following, I shall try to show that, although Liang Shuming's ideas on rural reconstruction and village education had already matured before he learned about Denmark, the Danish model did in fact play a quite important role for his argument by providing him with real-life illustrations of his most important points. In this sense, the case of Liang Shuming and Denmark is an interesting example of the role of foreign models in the shaping of Chinese responses to the trials of modernization, because it draws attention to 'the West' not as a uniform development pattern to be either rejected or 'slavishly' followed, but as a broad variety of experiences from which reform-minded Chinese intellectuals find arguments for highly diverse strategies.

I will first briefly describe the channels through which Liang learned about Denmark, and the situation he was facing at the time. I shall then turn to his interpretation of the Danish model and its implications for China, and finally analyze the role it played in his rural reconstruction theory and practice.

Liang's sources of knowledge about the Danish model

Liang Shuming first learned about the Danish folk high schools in detail from the Chinese translation of a book titled *The Folk High Schools of Denmark and the Development of a Farming Community* (Begtrup et al., 1926) written by three prominent folk high school principals, Holger Begtrup, Hans Lund and Peter Manniche. The translation appeared in January 1931 (Beituole, 1931) in the *Contemporary Educational Series* from Commercial Press which also included works by writers such as John Dewey and William Kilpatrick. In October that year Liang Shuming published a review of the book in *Village Government Monthly* (*Cunzhi yuekan*), a major platform for the rural reconstruction movement in general and Liang's own ideas in particular. As reflected in its title, *Danish Education and Our Education* (Liang, 1931a), this review, more than 15,000 characters long, developed into a significant exposition of Liang's own educational ideas, and it was later included first in an important compilation of his essays, *The Final Awakening of the Chinese People's Self-Salvation Movement* (Liang, 1932), and later in all major collections of his articles on education (Liang, 1935; Liang, 1987).[2]

In the beginning of the review, Liang wrote that he, because of his interest in rural economy, had long been aware of the importance of the Danish cooperatives and their relation to the folk high schools. Only after reading the book under review, however, had he realized what the folk high school idea was all about (Liang, 1931a, 654). This is supported by the fact that there are only few and brief references to Denmark in Liang's writings from before the time he read *The Folk High Schools*. In his preface from June 1930 to a book by Feng Tixia on cooperatism in China, he referred to Denmark as a country where cooperatives had developed from an ideology into a (social) system, and added that China would have to follow the same road (Liang, 1930a; 123). Danish cooperatives and rural education also received positive attention in at least one other text from 1930 (Liang, 1930b; 223, 230), but more thorough and detailed accounts of Denmark from Liang's pen are only found in his post-1930 writings, and they all seem to be based primarily on *The Folk High Schools*.

While working with rural reconstruction in Zouping, Liang received several Danish visitors who confirmed his positive view of the Danish model. In September 1934 two Danish folk high school teachers, Balslev and Juul Andersen, had two talks with Liang in Zouping, and in January 1936 they were followed by one of the authors of *The Folk High Schools*, Peter Manniche, who was the principal of the International People's College in Elsinore. As the outline of the Danish experience was generally quite well known among educational and rural reformers in China at the time, Liang probably learned about Denmark from other sources as well, but it is evident that his image of Denmark was primarily created by firm believers in, and promoters of, 'the Danish model'.[3]

What I here call 'the Danish model' had its roots in the agricultural cooperative movement and the folk high schools as they developed in the Danish countryside from the mid-nineteenth century onwards, with a social basis among farmers and smallholders and a political attachment to the Liberal (*Venstre*) and Social Liberal (*Radikale Venstre*) parties. By the 1930s, however, when Liang learned about Denmark, the industrial workers, politically committed to the Social Democrats, had taken up both the idea of cooperatives and of folk high schools. Peter Manniche, for example, was a Social Democrat with close connections to socialist politicians and union leaders in many European countries. In the early 1930s, a series of economic and social reforms were carried out in Denmark in relative harmony between Liberals, Social Liberals and Social Democrats, crowned by the 1933 Social Legislation Act which paved the way for the later development of the Welfare State. This caused considerable optimism and self-confidence among people in the folk high school movement, who believed that a model had been founded which could inspire other nations to enter a peaceful march towards economic and social progress for the whole people, a golden mean between Bolshevism and raw capitalism.

Thus, the folk high school leaders and activists from whom Liang received his information about Denmark were deeply engaged in promoting the 'Danish model' internationally. As we shall see below this led to a certain bias in the impressions he got.

Liang Shuming and rural reconstruction

When Liang Shuming read *The Folk High Schools* in 1931 he was just entering a crucial phase in his own life and career. Liang was born in Peking in 1893 and grew up in a family of scholar-officials.[4] His father, a reform-minded Confucian, sent him to a modern style school, where he even studied English from an early age, and up through his years in middle school (1906-11) he took much interest in Western ideas and reform politics. After the 1911 revolution, however, Liang was soon distressed by the meanness of political life, and this, together with his problematic relationship with his family, drove him into a state of mind which his biographer, Guy Alitto, describes as psychotic (Alitto, p.51). He turned from Western political ideas to Buddhism and lived in isolation from the world in his parents' home in Peking for a period of four years.

In 1916 Liang came out of his seclusion with the publication of a philosophical article which won him immediate fame in intellectual circles and gained him a position as lecturer of Indian philosophy at Peking University, an extraordinary honour for a man in his early twenties who had never received a college education (Liang, 1916; Alitto, 1986: 56-62). Liang did publish a book on Indian philosophy (Liang, 1919), but the work that really established his name was *Eastern and Western Cultures and Their Philosophies* (Liang, 1921; Alitto, 1986: 75-34). This book marked Liang's shift from Buddhism to his personal brand of Confucianism based on the belief that Chinese culture held the answers to the fundamental moral questions facing China and the entire world. He admitted that the Western spirit could solve mankind's material problems, but maintained that only the Chinese way of thought could solve the social and ethical ones and create personal and social harmony.

The fine qualities of Chinese civilization, however, had been destroyed by the Western invasion, so before it could play its global role, or even save itself, China had to be brought back to life. Liang saw education, particularly spiritual perfection, as the key to such a rebirth, and the villages as the only place where the dry but potentially rich roots of Chinese culture could still be found, so he spent the following years gradually developing his ideas on education and rural reconstruction. He resigned from his post at Peking University in 1924 and was subsequently offered high positions in the educational sector in Shandong and Canton, which he, however, only filled for short periods of time. In the late 1920s, when the attention of reform-minded Chinese intellectuals turned to the villages, Liang visited some of the most remarkable experiments with rural reconstruction and mass education at the time, such as one of Huang Yanpei's vocational education projects in Jiangsu, Tao Xingzhi's school complex in Xiaozhuang, James Yen's Ding County, and the more bureaucratic Shanxi programme initiated by the provincial governor Yan Xishan (Liang, 1929). For a short time he was with the Henan Village Government Academy, which was, however, soon closed by the Guomindang. Then, in 1931, the governor of Shandong, Han Fuqu, invited him to become leader of the Shandong Rural Reconstruction Institute which was set up in Zouping. While Liang already had considerable experience in different types of educational work, and a firm commitment to rural reconstruction, it was not until he came to Zouping that he had the opportunity to carry out a large scale implementation of his vision of a revitalized rural China. He must have read *The Folk High Schools* sometime between January and October, 1931, while he was busy establishing the Shandong Rural Reconstruction Institute and recruiting its first students, but before the efforts to transform the Zouping villages had really started.

Between 1931 and 1937 Liang Shuming succeeded in establishing in Zouping producers' cooperatives, particularly for cotton and silk, credit cooperatives as alternatives to usurious money lenders, an agricultural extension system, a militia to defend the villages against bandits and invaders, and improved health facilities. At the heart of his project were the village and township schools (*cunxue, xiangxue*), which were unique for Zouping and Liang's most original contribution to rural reconstruction. Zouping county was divided into townships which were again divided into villages. In each village there was to be a village school which should be an organ of self-government as well as serving as a link between the population and the county administration. These village schools were the living cells out of which Liang's new China should grow, the nuclei around which rural society would reemerge. When the people from the Institute came to a village, they would first make a careful investigation of the local conditions in order to find out how they could establish a village school. Based on this investigation they would find a group of people, seven or eight perhaps, who had a high status among the villagers. These people were then appointed by the county government to form the board of trustees (*xuedong*), and one of them was chosen as the director (*cun lishi*). The director would perform many of the same administrative tasks as the former village head, but in the name of education. Beside, or rather above, the director was the school principal (*xuezhang*), who should be a generally respected old gentleman of high morality. He should play the role of supervisor, mediator, and last court of appeal if there were any complaints against the director or the board. It was very important that the school principal never chose sides in a conflict, and always avoid open confrontations. Everyone else in the village, old and young, men and women, were named the 'students' (*xuezhong*). The final and crucial element was the teachers, the activists of the reconstruction movement, who did most of the actual teaching and communicated the policies and decisions of the county government to the villages.

The village schools organized a wide range of educational activities adapted to local needs. For the adults there were evening classes and winter schools offering literacy courses as well as courses in agriculture, singing, martial arts and contemporary affairs. The teachers of the village schools were given special training classes during the vacations. There were primary school courses for the school-aged children, and those children who were not enrolled in regular schools were taught in informal groups headed by school children of their own age, who used their lunch breaks for this purpose. Bad habits and old customs such as gambling, opium smoking and foot-binding were attacked with a combination of educational and administrative means. As even this brief description shows,[5] there were several similarities between Liang's approach and the folk high school idea.

Danish Education and Our Education

Liang's first extended discussion of the Danish model, his review of *The Folk High Schools*, was detailed, and interspersed with several quotations from the book. He first identified the 'essential spirit' of Danish education, and found that, contrary to his expectations from schools closely related to a rural cooperative movement, it consisted *neither* of subjects related to agriculture and cooperation, *nor* of traditional transmissions of book knowledge. Instead, it was primarily a spiritual awakening where '...the spirit of a minority inspired the spirit of the majority' (p. 655). This primacy of moral and spiritual education was fully in line with Liang's own ideals, and it set Denmark apart from 'the West' as he had described it in his earlier works. In 1922, for example, in an article titled *Differences in the Education of Easterners and Westerners*, he had claimed that Western education was characterized by the systematic transmission of knowledge about concrete matters, while Eastern education had its strong point in the teaching of ethics (Liang, 1922). In this respect, the folk high schools were obviously more 'East' than 'West'.

The dominance of spiritual training was absolutely essential to Liang, although in his educational writings and practice he always emphasized as well the importance of spreading modern technical knowledge to the rural population. This explains why, in the beginning of the review, he vehemently attacked the translator of the book, Meng Xiancheng, who was a notable educational reformer in his own right. In his preface to the translation, Meng had mentioned two important obstacles for the applicability of the Danish model in China, one of which directly concerned the question of spiritual vs. vocational training. He reminded the readers that the non-vocational nature of the folk high schools, far from reflecting negligence of practical subjects, originated in the fact that agricultural training in Denmark was the responsibility of another type of school, and that the poverty of the Chinese peasants furthermore forced Chinese educators to give higher priority to the teaching of basic agricultural techniques simply in order to keep the rural population from starving (Beituole, 1931: 1-2). These remarks, of course, would take the wind out of the sails of anyone trying to implement this aspect of the Danish model in China, and Liang retorted wryly, and without mentioning what Meng's points actually were:

Unfortunately, Mr Meng, when he translated the book, added some superfluous remarks in his translator's preface in the form of two points which are self-evident. They do not help the reader to pursue a comprehension of the deeper points, unavoidably detract from the beauty of the original book, and devalue his own work as a translator (Liang 1931a: 654).

Liang then went on to discuss three prominent figures whose biographies were included in the book: Nikolaj Frederik Severin Grundtvig (1783-1872), poet, priest, historian and politician, whose thoughts provided the foundation for the folk high school movement; Christen Kold (1816-1870), teacher and creator of the teaching style characteristic of the folk high schools; and Ludvig Schrøder (1836-1908), principal of Askov, the flagship of the folk high school movement. The book's initial description of Grundtvig's role had a tremendous appeal to Liang. In the original it proclaimed:

[The] aim and methods [of the folk high schools] are in every way determined by the life of the common people, from which they originated and which they are intended to serve. The idea which gave them birth was not conceived in the mind of a college professor; it was conceived in that of a prophet, a spiritual genius who understood the life and mind of his people throughout the ages, and who thereby had the vision of the special enlightenment that was needed to promote the well-being of his people. (Begtrup et al. 1926: 77).

Particularly the last phrase had a wonderful ring in Liang's ears, and he quoted it twice (Liang, 1931a; 656-57). Alitto has pointed to Liang's messianic vision of his own historical role (Alitto; 58-59), and though the 'spiritual genius' of the original had been toned down to 'leader' (lingxiu) in the Chinese translation, it is likely that Liang read these hagiographic remarks on Grundtvig as a description of his own role in China. The two men did, in fact, have much in common. They both went through serious psychological crises in their youth from which they emerged with powerful visions of their own historical missions. They both, at least temporarily, turned from promising careers in the intellectual establishment to work among the farmers, in whom they saw the future of their countries. Just as Grundtvig drew upon Norse mythology to create images that could spur national revival, Liang interpreted 'the life and mind of his people throughout the ages' in an idealized image of ancient Confucian thought and traditional social mores as they existed before they were corrupted by modernity. Just as Grundtvig attacked the use of Latin in the Danish school system, Liang opposed the the copying of foreign models in modern Chinese education.[6]

Liang mentions all these traits in Grundtvig's life and thoughts in the review, but what seems to have impressed him most is the way Grundtvig and his followers were described as exerting enormous influence on Danish political and economic life, while at the same time somehow standing above mundane political struggle. This was because, wrote Liang, the motivating force behind Grundtvig's activities was not just a wish to solve the immediate problems facing his people, but rather a philosophy of life and a religious faith (p. 659). Liang's own attitude to political power was ambivalent, and his respect for politicians limited, so Grundtvig's elevated role naturally appealed to him.

In Christen Kold, Liang found other qualities that matched his own ideals, first of all Kold's plain and simple life style: 'That is true! Only a simple outer appearance will contain the profound; outer glory is only proof of spiritual poverty', Liang commented (p. 661). This was a point he himself had repeatedly emphasized when addressing audiences of urban middle and upper class students. But also Kold's ability to inspire and communicate with his students was praised by Liang. As for Schrøder, Liang particularly noted his ability to combine down-to-earth practical work, like the improvement of crops and agricultural techniques, with the highest spiritual ideals. Again the relevance for Liang's project in Zouping was obvious.

After discussing the content of the courses in Danish, History, Music and Gymnastics which constituted the core curriculum of the folk high schools, Liang went on to sum up eight major lessons to be drawn from the Danish example (pp. 666-72): 1) The folk high schools were established by the local population on its own initiative, and they were not only places for teaching, but also the heart of the peasant organizations and of community life in general. 2) The students in these schools were not children, but young adults with a certain life experience, who had already completed at least primary education. 3) The schools were run by private people, and the students enrolled voluntarily, guaranteeing genuine enthusiasm among both teachers and students. 4) The state supported the schools financially but did not try to control their activities. 5) The social atmosphere of the schools was as in a family. 6) The relationship between students and teachers was one of friendship. This friendship influenced society at large, and it helped create the cooperatives, which again played a major role in promoting social and economic equality and preventing class conflicts. 7) The teaching method of the schools was one of discussions between teachers and students. 8) The schools had no fixed curriculum, but could set up courses in a flexible way.

Liang's review then turned to the later development of the folk high schools, where he noticed that they had integrated both natural and social sciences in the curriculum, and furthermore spread not only to the cities of Denmark but even to several other countries. He also mentioned that agricultural schools had been established as a supplement to the non-vocational high schools. It was essential to him, however, that spiritual awakening was the starting point of the movement and remained as its core value.

After this thorough survey of the Danish experience, Liang asked himself what lessons China could learn from it. He found that Chinese education was entering a transitional phase. After the Western invasion in the 19th century, China had emulated Western education, and as Western civilization was primarily urban, based on handicrafts and commerce, the imported educational system was also geared to meet urban needs. To catch up with the West, China had furthermore invested primarily in the training of a highly qualified indigenous elite which would transmit Western knowledge to their motherland. Since the late 1920s, however, many reformers had realized the inadequacy of this orientation towards the urban elite, and they were now, like Liang himself, emphasizing rural and mass education. This placed China in exactly the same position as Denmark had been in 80 years earlier, so that, although direct emulation of foreign models was never recommendable, China should use this historical coincidence to solicit from the Danish experience answers to two fundamental questions: 1) should education mainly focus on knowledge and skills or on how to live a life in righteousness? and 2) should it be run mainly by the state or left to private initiative? In both cases Denmark had chosen the latter option, whereas China during the preceding 30 years had chosen the first (p. 679), and in both cases China had, according to Liang, made the wrong choice.

As for the first point, China could not apply the knowledge and technologies studied abroad, because Chinese culture was like a dead tree upon which no new branches could be grafted. The Chinese, and particularly the peasants, the true bearers of Chinese culture, had to be brought back to life before anything else could be accomplished. All literacy campaigns and agricultural courses would be futile until 'a great educator with a deep faith and a strong will' would enlighten the people and lead it towards a fundamental psychological change (p. 681).

The question of private initiative was equally important. Modern education had been brought to China from abroad, wrote Liang, and, because society felt no real internal need for it at the time, the reform initiative had to come from the state. But, once the state takes over, education loses its vitality and becomes mechanical. Liang mentioned four reasons why state-run (*guanban*) education was a dead-end street: 1) State education is formalistic and without spirit. When the Chinese state ordered the counties to set up modern schools in the beginning of the 20th century, for example, all the local officials did was to put up signboards with the new name on, while the substance of the reform was ignored. 'Popular education' was now being treated in an equally formalistic way. 2) State schools are run in a uniform manner according to rules and regulations, while schools run by the local communities are free to experiment in a creative way. And experiments were badly needed in the desperate situation Chinese education was in. 3) The state imposes a type of education on society which is not adapted to society's needs and which is too far removed from social realities. 4) State education is wasteful; local communities can run schools much more economically.

The state should support and reward local schools financially and supplement local initiative when necessary, but it should not play a dominant role or even impede local efforts, as was now the case. This was the other main conclusion which Liang drew from the Danish experience.

Liang's other writings on the Danish model

Around the time of the publication of Liang's review of *The Danish Folk High Schools*, he gave a speech at the Rural Reconstruction Research Institute on the occasion of the so-called Manchurian Incident on 18 September 1931 which signalled Japan's invasion of Northeastern China. In the speech, which later appeared in the Tianjin-based newspaper *Da Gong Bao* (Liang 1931b),[7] he argued that the Japanese war-makers were merely responding to the challenge of the dominant Western civilization by imitating it. China, on the other hand, had for millennia proved her ability to peacefully absorb and transform foreign invaders through her high level of civilization, and should still fight back in this way by developing her *lixing*, which had been seriously weakened in the modern age. *Lixing* was a key term for Liang, the essence of China's contribution to the world, and it referred both to reason (which is the dictionary meaning of the word) and to the ability to enter into inter-personal relationships on the basis of high ethical principles.[8] In concrete terms Liang found that China's real problem was not a lack of military force but of social organization and *lixing*, and he mentioned two foreign pioneers of peaceful nation-building from whom China should learn: Gandhi in India and Grundtvig in Denmark. In this context he wrote:

The area [of Denmark] is small, but it is not surpassed in wealth by any other nation. Social conditions are extremely stable, there are no fights between workers and capitalists, and the country's riches are evenly distributed. How has this been achieved? Not by defeating other nations, but by promoting education. Denmark is an agricultural country, and their agriculture has been developed through cooperation. This civilization is the result of the efforts of an old educator, Grundtvig. He established a folk high school in a village so that young people between 18 and 30 years of age could receive education.... In the present era several countries imitate this kind of mass education. Grundtvig raised the level of the common people of Denmark, he made the citizens achieve *lixing*, and this was why the country started to flourish again (Liang 1931b: 299).

By using the term *lixing*, the hallmark of ideal Chineseness, about the spiritual quality generated by the Danish model, Liang went a long way towards establishing Denmark as his own private Utopia. Again it is obvious that he did not think of rural, agricultural and peaceful Denmark as belonging to urban, industrialized and aggressive Europe.

Liang's next extensive discussion of the Danish model is found in a 1934 text titled *The Essence of Spiritual Training* (Liang 1934a). This was originally a lecture given at the Rural Reconstruction Research Institute, and it was later printed in the Zouping periodical *Rural Reconstruction* (*Xiangcun jianshe*), and included in several collections of his essays. In *The Essence* Liang summed up many of the points he had already made in *Danish Education and Our Education*, with a special emphasis on the primacy of spiritual over vocational and practical training, but for the first time he also discussed the differences between Denmark and China. He held that the task of rebuilding the Chinese nation was much more demanding than was the case in Grundtvig's Denmark. In Denmark, the country's military defeat by Germany had been the most serious problem, and national revival had been brought about by men of the church who had relied on the latent religious feelings of the people. Such feelings could be aroused through literature, tales of national heroes, music, and songs. The Chinese were facing much more fundamental problems, and they were facing them in an era where the value systems not only of the Chinese but of people all over the world had been shaken in their foundations, so that a much more critical and sceptical attitude now prevailed. But first of all, Chinese culture was not religious but based on *lixing*. Therefore, it would take rational arguments and discussions of the most profound existential questions to mobilize the Chinese, not just a few good songs as in the case of the Danes (pp. 502-03). On the other hand, it would be this very ethical, reason-based attitude that would make it possible for the Chinese to overcome problems of a magnitude which the Danes would never have been able to handle.

In Liang's speeches and writings between 1934 and 1936 there are several other references to Danish people's high schools and agricultural cooperatives as alternatives to both the ways of 'the West' or 'Europe' and to Communism, but after the Japanese invasion put an end to the Zouping experiment in 1937 Denmark apparently lost its relevance for Liang, and he did not, to my knowledge, take up the Danish theme again.

Personal encounters

On at least two occasions Liang Shuming met personally with leading figures of the Danish folk high school movement. Contacts started in early 1934, when Peter Manniche came to China on a lecture tour which took him to several countries around the world.[9] In China he visited Hong Kong, Canton, Shanghai, Wuxi, Jinan, Tianjin, Peking and a number of rural districts. In Shanghai alone he gave 50 lectures over a period of six weeks, and he found that both government officials and intellectuals were extremely interested in what he had to say. He attributed this to the fact that the Chinese translation of *The Folk High Schools* had 'created quite a stir', sold 5,000 copies and was now to come out in a new edition. He even made an agreement with the Commercial Press about the publication of a sequel, which he planned to write on his way back to Denmark.

In Shandong Manniche was hosted by the provincial governor Han Fuqu, Liang Shuming's powerful patron, who had drummed up an audience of 2,000 military and civilian officials for Manniche's 7 a.m. lecture on Danish land policy. Manniche does not mention meeting Liang on this occasion, but in some way he was informed about the Zouping project. In his report to the Danish Ministry of Foreign Affairs he wrote that the best way to transplant the methods and aims of the folk high schools to Chinese soil would be through private schools sponsored by provincial governments, and he mentioned three particularly promising experiments of this type, one of which was 'Professor Liang's school in Chouping [Zouping], which is a beautiful modern representative of the system of the past, where scholars were in charge of administration as well as of economic life'.

During his stay in China, Manniche was asked to send over more folk high school experts, who could work as consultants for the Chinese. After his return, he chose two teachers from the Askov High School, S. Juul Andersen and J.U.S. Balslev. These two men visited Zouping in September 1934, probably on Manniche's suggestion, and their conversations with Liang Shuming on the 26th and 27th, later published in *Rural Reconstruction* (Liang

1934b), give a first-hand impression of the encounter between modernizing
Confucianism and the Danish model.

Liang opened the interview by stressing Denmark's unique status in
Europe and its similarity to China:

In China we often use the relationships between father and son and between
younger and elder brothers to describe also relationships outside the family, so that
officials and masters are called fathers and close friends are called brothers. This is,
according to what we have heard, very similar to the atmosphere in Danish folk
high schools and cooperatives. We often feel that there is too much competition
between Westerners and too little friendship, but now we have found in Denmark
a society where all are friends and there is no competition (p. 571).

Balslev answered that not only was there no competition between individuals,
but also class struggle and even political struggle were virtually unknown.
There was only little unemployment, and the farmers were always willing to
help workers in need. These two social groups also harmoniously shared the
political power between them. Thus reassured about the continued well-being
of his distant Utopia, Liang went on to expound his own views on
Confucianism and its role in Chinese culture. The two Danes were apparently
impressed with what they saw and heard, and both expressed the view that,
since they had come to China, they had found nothing so similar to Denmark
as the Zouping experiment (p. 574).

In late January 1936 it was Peter Manniche's turn to arrive in Zouping in
person.[10] The content of his talks with Liang was apparently not recorded,
but Manniche was a firm believer in the international relevance of the Danish
model, particularly for what was later to be called 'the developing countries',
as can be seen from his later publications (Manniche 1969), and there is no
doubt that he did his best to confirm Liang's positive view of Denmark.
Manniche's own notes from the trip show that he was duly impressed by his
host, even more impressed than he had been in Ding County, where he
agreed with those critics who felt that James Yen's model was too expensive
for China:

Much different from Tinghsien [Ding County] is the Chouping [Zouping] district.
This is China's own attempt of renewal.... Liang had carefully studied the Danish
folk high schools, and he was now trying to set up high schools to train leaders for
the rural districts, and particularly pioneers for the cooperative movement.... While
I talked to him in the large but old-fashioned Chinese courtyard where he lived,

some of the highest officials in the district, all disciples of him, were listening respectfully to his words.[11]

In these encounters both sides presented their ideal self-image, and the Confucian sage and the heralds of the Third Way obviously found pleasure in each other's company.

Presentation and perception of the Danish model

When analyzing cultural transfers from the West to China, we often focus on how the original idea or institution was perceived and implemented in China. In the case of the Danish model it is at least as relevant to look at the way it was presented to the Chinese. The historical experience of the Danish farmers from the mid-19th century onwards had already been turned into a national myth by the time Liang Shuming heard about it. It had become a crucial part of Danish national identity, and was now, in a carefully edited version, being sold to the rest of the world. When it reached China, Liang slightly re-wrote it for internal purposes and used it as evidence in the Chinese debate, but he did not have to alter much.

Liang was interested in Denmark during a period when China had given up wholesale import of foreign educational models and was trying to adapt ideas from abroad in a more eclectic way (Bastid, 1987). Many of the Chinese intellectuals advocating reforms inspired by the educational systems of Japan, the U.S.A., and the major European powers had had direct contacts with these systems through long periods of study abroad or through attending foreign-sponsored schools and universities inside China (Hayhoe and Bastid, 1987).

Such first-hand experiences were rare in the Danish case, though they did exist. A prominent Chinese visitor to Denmark was Mrs Yu Qingtang, a Columbia-trained educational reformer who ran an institute of education in Wuxi, Jiangsu, and who was almost as influential on the mass education scene as Liang, James Yen and Huang Yanpei. She was at Rødding High School in 1933 and also visited Manniche's International People's College in Elsinore, and she hosted him when he was in Wuxi. There are several references to Denmark in Yu's writings, and her evaluation of the folk high schools is as positive (though not as verbose) as Liang's (Yu 1992, 173-74, 178-80, 276-77, 300). Still she, like most other Chinese who visited folk high schools in Denmark, stayed only for a short period of time. As the schools run by Danish missionaries in China were not of the folk high school type,

Chinese understanding of the Danish model was therefore almost entirely based on Danish self-presentation. I shall not go into details with the national ideology built up in Denmark around Grundtvig and the people's high schools, but two issues which were essential to Liang, and which were presented to him in a somewhat biased way, deserve mentioning.

The first is the problem of class relations, which was, perhaps, the most fundamental issue of dispute between Liang and the Communists. Liang insisted that there were no antagonistic class contradictions in China, only different occupational groups, and that a violent revolution, therefore, would solve no problems. He used the Danish example not only to prove that peasants could gain political power without using violence, but also to show that schools could be instrumental in creating a social environment where such a peaceful transformation was possible. From what he could read in *The Folk High Schools* and from what he was told by his Danish visitors, he got the impression that social harmony prevailed in Denmark, and that equality and economic progress had been achieved in cooperation between all social strata in Danish society. This reflected the highly successful monopolization of the concept of 'the people' by the class of independent farmers, who had been the main social force behind Grundtvigianism, and who saw themselves as the only true representatives of the Danish people, as opposed to the urban bourgeoisie, the workers, the intellectual elite and the landless farm labourers (Østergaard, 1984).

Though Denmark never had a revolution, and though the political climate was generally more tolerant than in most other European countries, the social and political situation in Denmark from the mid-19th century till the 1930s was much less harmonious than Liang had learned from his sources. In the ten years between the publication of *The Folk High Schools* and Manniche's visit to Zouping, for example, there were continued bitter struggles particularly between the Liberals, representing the farmers, and the Social Democrats, representing the workers, and there were several major industrial strikes and lockouts. The political parties and their constituencies primarily saw themselves not as partners engaged in harmonious nation-building, but as competitors in the political and economic arenas. Denmark was also hit by the Great Depression, with the effect that the average unemployment rate among workers in 1932 and 1933 was around one third. All in all, the Danish way to capitalism had its unique features, but it was still a far cry from the rosy picture painted by the folk high school people, for whom the question of political power faded away, a question which Liang never really solved. He rejected the idea that China could follow the road of Western-style democracy, and seemed convinced that a national consensus would grow out of a network of village-based organizations. What he heard gave him reasons to believe that this was what had happened in Denmark, while it would be closer to the truth to say that the folk high schools had trained rural leaders to represent farmers' interests in a competitive political system, in explicit opposition to the large land-owners and the urban bourgeoisie.

The second question is more directly concerned with education. As we have seen above, one of the main lessons Liang drew from the Danish folk high schools was that education should be organized on private initiative and without any kind of coercion. A major difference between the situations of Grundtvig and Liang, however, was that the Danish peasantry was already literate well before the first folk high school was established, and that the students who attended these schools normally had studied seven years in ordinary primary schools. Compulsory education was introduced in Denmark by law already in 1814. The initiative came from above, and the law was enforced by the state against some opposition from parents and employers. If the Danish experience proved anything, it was rather that the state had to take the first initiative, backed up by formal legislation, while local society, on the basis of the general educational take-off brought about in this way, could later formulate demands for alternative types of schooling. In fact this was the other point of reservation towards the Danish model which Meng Xiancheng, the translator of *The Folk High Schools*, mentioned in the preface so scorned by Liang (Beituole, 1931: 2). The fact that the folk high schools operated on a basis of almost full popular literacy was not censured from the Danish materials, but it was certainly not emphasized either. Liang mentioned it in his review, but did not really calculate it into the conclusions he drew.

It is not surprising that the Danish visitors presented their model in what they felt was the most favourable light. Hubert Brown has noted, for example, that John Dewey had equally salutary words to say about American society when he was in China, in spite of his critical attitude at home (Brown 1987, 130-31). Furthermore, the idealized Danish self-conception coincided almost exactly with what Liang Shuming was looking for: a Third Way to modernity born out of rural society and delivered by a spiritual genius rooted in traditional culture. Neither he nor his informants had any interest in complicating the picture.

Did Denmark make a difference?

When Begtrup and Juul Andersen said that Zouping was much like Denmark, it was probably not just out of politeness towards their host. There was a striking similarity between Zouping and the Danish model, at least at the surface level: the close connection between education, economic organization and community-building in the villages, the broad, culture-oriented curriculum of the schools, and the basis in what the intellectual avant garde perceived as the best of national tradition. Even details like the morning talks (*zhaohua*) on moral and cultural questions, which Liang gave to his students, could in theory have been copied directly from Denmark.

In reality, however, a cultural borrowing of this sort was not what was going on in Zouping. First of all, Liang's project was in its general aims and methods similar to other experiments conducted simultaneously by reformers like Tao Xingzhi and James Yen (Hayford, 1990), who were not directly inspired by Denmark, so if the Danish model played any role at this general level, it was only as part of a much larger international movement for rural reconstruction and mass education. As for the unique features of Zouping, they can in most cases be traced back to ideas advocated or even practiced by Liang before he knew anything about Grundtvig and Kold. The morning talks are one such example.

The real importance of the Danish model for Liang seems to have been at another level. In the Chinese debate Liang was being attacked by the Communists for ignoring class struggle, and by some of the more Westernized reformers for being simply old-fashioned and anti-modern (Alitto, 1986: 269-72). The Danish example verified Liang's points in this debate: it could be used to show the Communists that peasants and workers could gain power without using violence; and it might convince the Westernized intellectuals that modernization and economic growth could be based on agriculture rather than on full-scale industrialization, that rural and backward were not identical concepts, and that indigenous cultural values were not obstacles but assets in the modernization struggle. In the more narrow debate on educational strategy, the folk high schools also supported Liang's arguments when he differed from other reformers, such as about the relative importance of cultural over vocational education. The Danish model did not give Liang many new ideas, perhaps, but it gave him substantial arguments for implementing the ideas he already had.

Cultural encounters and the need for Utopia

The most remarkable thing about Liang's use of the Danish model is the way he placed it outside the dichotomies which dominated his view on culture and politics. Culturally he described East and West as fundamentally different entities. In the political field, he talked about 'the two roads China cannot follow', one of which was the revolutionary road of the Soviet Union, the other the democratic model of the European countries. Obviously the Denmark of his description did not fit into these patterns. Only two other countries escaped, in different ways, the dualisms of Liang's thought: Japan, a country of the East which decided to beat the West with its own weapons, and India, which Liang saw as unique both in the cultural and the political sense. The Japanese model was lacking in ethical qualities, however, and India was not really a success story.

In any political or moral discourse, it is of crucial importance to underscore ideals and visions with real-life examples. Liang could draw on some traits in China's past, but Denmark provided him with an even better argument. It was a small country, far away, and without any reputation for imperialist behaviour in China. And it was a country which was more than willing to play the role of an alternative, a Utopia outside the maelstrom of urbanist, demoralizing and reifying modernization. Once Liang was ousted from his Lilliputian state in Zouping, he also lost interest in Denmark, and so did China, at least until the 1980s, when the reform wing of the CCP was looking for a middle road between planned economy and laissez-faire liberalism, and started to look more closely at the Scandinavian model.

References

Alitto, Guy S. (1986): *The Last Confucian. Liang Shu-ming and the Chinese Dilemma of Modernity*, Berkeley, Los Angeles, London: University of California Press, 2nd ed. (First ed. 1979)

Bailey, Paul J. (1990): *Reform the People. Changing attitudes towards popular education in early twentieth-century China*. Edinburgh: Edinburgh University Press.

Bastid, Marianne (1987): 'Servitude or Liberation? The Introduction of Foreign Educational Practices and Systems to China from 1840 to the Present', in Hayhoe and Bastid, 1987, pp. 3-20.

Begtrup, Holger, Hans Lund, Peter Manniche (1926): *The Folk High-Schools of Denmark and the Development of a Farming Community*, London: Oxford University Press.

Beituole, Lunte, Manniezhi (1931): *Danmai de minzhong xuexiao yu nongcun* (trans. by H. C. Meng), Shanghai: The Commercial Press.

Brown, Hubert O. (1987): 'American Progressivism in Chinese Education: The Case of Tao Xingzhi', in Hayhoe and Bastid, 1987, pp. 120-39.

Foght, Harold W. (1915): *Rural Denmark and its Schools*, New York: Macmillan.

Hayford, Charles W. (1990): *To The People. James Yen and Village China*, New York: Columbia University Press.

Hayhoe, Ruth and Marianne Bastid (eds.) (1987): *China's Education and the Industrialized World*, New York: M. E. Sharpe.

Liang Shuming (1916): 'Jiu-yuan jue-yi lun' [On tracing the origin and solving doubts], in *Liang Shuming quanji* [Collected works of Liang Shuming], vol. 1, Jinan: Shandong renmin chubanshe, 1989, pp. 1-22.

Liang Shuming (1919): *Yindu zhexue gailun* [An Introduction to Indian Philosophy], in *Liang Shuming quanji*, vol. 1, pp. 23-247.

Liang Shuming (1921): *Zhong-xi wenhua ji qi zhexue* [Eastern and Western cultures and their philosophies], in *Liang Shuming quanji*, vol. 1, pp. 319-547.

Liang Shuming (1922): 'Dong-xi-ren de jiaoyu zhi bu tong' [Differences in the education of Easterners and Westerners], in *Liang Shuming quanji*, vol. 4, Jinan: Shandong renmin chubanshe, 1991, pp. 655-59.

Liang Shuming (1929): 'Beiyou suo jian jilüe' [Record of what I saw during my travels to the North], in *Liang Shuming quanji*, vol. 4, pp. 874-904.

Liang Shuming (1930a): 'Feng zhu 'Cong hezuo-zhuyi yi chuangzao Zhongguo xin jingji zhidu' ti xu' [Preface to Feng's 'Creating a new economic system in China based on cooperatism"], in *Liang Shuming quanji*, vol. 5, Jinan: Shandong renmin chubanshe, 1992, pp. 122-23.

Liang Shuming (1930b): 'Shandong xiangcun jianshe yanjiuyuan sheli zhiqu ji banfa gaiyao' [Outline of purposes and methods for establishing the Shandong Rural Reconstruction Research Institute], in *Liang Shuming quanji*, vol. 5, pp. 222-39.

Liang Shuming (1931a): 'Danmai de jiaoyu yu women de jiaoyu' [Danish education and our education], in *Liang Shuming quanji*, vol. 7, Jinan: Shandong renmin chubanshe, 1993, pp. 653-84.

Liang Shuming (1931b): 'Dui Dong-sheng shijian zhi ganyan' [An expression of my feelings about the Manchurian incident], in *Liang Shuming quanji*, vol. 5, pp. 295-300.

Liang Shuming (1932): *Zhongguo minzu zijiu yundong zhi zuihou juewu* [The final awakening of the Chinese people's self-salvation movement], Beijing: Cunzhi yuekanshe.

Liang Shuming (1934a): 'Jingshen taolian yaozhi' [The Essence of Spiritual Training], in *Liang Shuming quanji*, vol. 5, pp. 492-519.

Liang Shuming (1934b): 'Yu Danmai de liang jiaoshou de tanhua' [Conversations with two Danish professors], in *Liang Shuming quanji*, vol. 5, pp. 571-576.

Liang Shuming (1934c): Liang Shuming: 'Cunxue xiangxue xu zhi' [What ought to be known about village and township schools], in *Liang Shuming quanji*, vol. 5, pp. 448-465.

Liang Shuming (1935): *Liang Shuming xiansheng jiaoyu wenlu* [Mr Liang Shuming's writings on education], Jinan and Zouping.

Liang Shuming (1987): *Liang Shuming jiaoyu wenji* [A collection of Liang Shuming's writings on education], ed. by Song Enrong, Jiangsu jiaoyu chubanshe.

Ma Yong (1992): *Liang Shuming pingzhuan* [A critical biography of Liang Shuming], Anhui renmin chubanshe.

Manniche, Peter (1969): *Rural Development and the Changing Countries of the World. A Study of Danish Rural Conditions and the Folk High School with its Relevance to the Developing Countries*, Oxford: Pergamon Press.

Thodberg, Christian and Anders Pontoppidan Thyssen (eds.) (1983): *N.F.S. Grundtvig. Tradition and Renewal*, Copenhagen: Det Danske Selskab.

Thøgersen, Stig (1994): 'Rural Society, Intellectuals and the State. Liang Shuming's Educational Reforms in Zouping 1931-1937', in Kjeld Erik Brødsgaard and David Strand, eds.: *Reconstructing Twentieth Century China: Discourses of State, Society and Nation*, New York: M. E. Sharpe (forthcoming).

Van Slyke, Lyman P. (1959): 'Liang Sou-ming and the Rural Reconstruction Movement', *The Journal of Asian Studies*, vol. 18, no. 4, pp. 457-474.

Yu Qingtang jiaoyu lunzhu xuan [Yu Qingtang's selected works on education], ed. by Mao Zhongyin and Chang Xiaochun (1992), Renmin jiaoyu chubanshe.

Østergaard, 1984: Uffe Østergaard: »Hvad er det 'danske' ved Danmark? Tanker om den 'danske vej' til kapitalismen, grundtvigianismen og 'dansk' mentalitet« [What's 'Danish' about Denmark? Thoughts on the 'Danish' way to capitalism, Grundtvigianism and 'Danish' mentality], *Den Jyske Historiker*, no. 29-30, pp. 85-137.

Notes

1. The second character in Liang's name had the traditional reading *sou*, but is now pronounced *shu*. The habitual English rendering has changed accordingly.

2. Articles on Danish folk high schools in the Chinese educational press can be found back to 1910, and the interest continued up through the 10s, 20s and 30s (Bailey 1990, 204, 221, note 147).

3. A very extensive and also highly positive book on Danish cooperatives and folk high schools (Foght, 1915) had earlier been translated into Chinese, but there are no indications that Liang ever saw it.

4. For Liang Shuming's life and philosophy, see Alitto, 1979.

5. For a more detailed discussion see Alitto, pp. 238-78. Liang's own plans for the village schools are described in Liang 1934c. I have discussed the outcome of Liang's reforms in Thøgersen 1994.

6. For an English-language account of Grundtvig's life and work, see Thodberg and Thyssen 1983, which presents the state of the art of Danish Grundtvig research.

7. Strangely enough the Chinese characters used for transcribing Grundtvig's name in this article are different from the ones used in the review and in all later writings by Liang. Judging from the time the speech was held and from its content it seems unlikely, however, that the source should not be *The Folk High School*.

8. For a more detailled discussion of this concept, see Alitto, pp. 183-86.
9. The information on Manniche's 1934 trip is from his report to the Danish Ministry of Foreign Affairs, dated 5 October, 1934, a copy of which is kept in Manniche's personal archive in the Danish National Archives.
10. A photo of Liang and Manniche together in Zouping is reproduced in front of the preface to *Liang Shuming quanji*, vol. 5.
11. From an unpublished manuscript in Peter Manniche's personal archive kept in the Danish National Archives.

The Chinese Filter: Assimilation of Western Educational Theories in the early 1980s

Greg Kulander

No education system in the modern world has been created and administered in isolation. Cross cultural influence continues to increase in tact with rapidly escalating international transactions of all kinds. In its development of a modern educational system, China has been profoundly impacted by developments in other countries. Japan, the former Soviet Union and the U.S.A. have all had their own periods of approbation; European educational ideas and techniques too have been influential at times. For the purposes of this study, the influence of two important Western theoretical frameworks will be dealt with, Pragmatism and Structuralism.

An analysis of the dissemination of the educational theories imbedded in these Western ideologies in China during the critical period from 1978 to 1984 will be used to expose some of the most significant factors affecting knowledge transfers across the cultural chasm between the West and China.

The working hypothesis upon which this paper is based is that successful transfer of educational theories is not only contingent upon specific historical circumstances and available channels of communication, but also the degree to which these theories 'fit' into the existing theoretical orientation of the host country educators. My thesis is that Chinese educational theorists have selectively borrowed from Western theories, sometimes ignoring the philosophical inconsistencies that arose, sometimes altering the theories to make them better 'fit' their pre-existing theoretical framework.

There are several reasons that this particular period has been chosen for this study. First, because it represents a real break with the past in terms of the inauguration of the Open Door policy: suddenly it became 'legal' to engage in research of foreign ideas. At the same time, the ideological mist permeating the educational sector began to dissipate and an acknowledgement that educational theories could be developed *independent* of communist political ideology gradually emerged. Finally, the actual number of qualified participants in the educational debate during this period was still a manageable size for such a study; in the latter part of the 1980s, interest and published research concerning Western education virtually exploded.

There are, of course, countless pitfalls such a study can fall into: the complexity involved in the transfer of educational ideas from culture to culture is enormous. The questions of why, what, and how, when applied to educational transfer, are not easily answered. In this analysis, I do not attempt to answer the question *why* the educational theories derived from Pragmatism and Structuralism were transferred (to some degree), nor do I make any concrete judgements as to *what* educational theories in fact were in the process of being transferred during the period: the theories of Pragmatism and Structuralism were chosen because it was my impression that they were among the most written about, and also because they represent Western schools of thought which have been influential worldwide. It is the question of *how* educational theories are transferred that lies behind the choice of analytical framework. Thus, not only will the treatment which the specific educational theories embodied in Structuralism and Pragmatism received be examined, but the channels through which foreign ideas such as these are conveyed to China will also receive a great deal of attention.

The study is organized as follows: first, the central terms are defined and a background for the methodology used in the analysis is presented. This is followed by a brief description of the political-social-economic context during the period under study and its relevance for the developments in the educational sector. A critical analysis of the different channels through which Western ideas reached China will illustrate the key role such channels play in cross culture transfer. A brief account of the reception of Pragmatism and Structuralism will then serve to exemplify the process through which Western theories met and were assimilated by Chinese educators. The paper will conclude with an evaluation of the various manners in which transfer of Western educational theories to China took place, including an analysis of the theoretical orientation which characterized Chinese educators and how this affected their response to Western educational theories.

Theoretical and Methodological Background

Educational theories are commonly divided into two types: general philosophically-oriented theories and more limited theories directly related to the teaching process. Hubert O. Brown (1982: 328-29) distinguishes the general theories as those which embody 'hard core' ideological concepts, and the limited theories as those which are based on 'intermediate' or 'auxiliary' hypotheses suggested by the hard core theories. The hard core ideological concepts are non-verifiable expressions of fundamental values, while intermediate and auxiliary hypotheses are verifiable results of empirical research.

General educational theories, unlike scientific theories, are thus not empirical and their conclusions can not be tested in the same way. They are practical, primarily prescriptive theories meant to be used by educators (professional or otherwise) in their educative efforts. General theories, according to Moore (1974: 12-13), are disposed towards what other educationalists might call educational philosophy: they are a set of recommendations for producing a certain type of person and/or society. They provide the philosophical platform upon which the limited theories are built. Indeed, general educational theories are often anchored in, or at least closely related to, ideologies which attempt to encompass a complete model of reality (Husén, 1979: 329).

The task here then is to explore the process in which Chinese educational theorists confronted two particular general educational theories together with their affiliated auxiliary hypotheses. How did the underlying assumptions of these theories about the nature of man, knowledge and society conflict/coincide with the Chinese philosophical outlook and how did this affect their reception and/or adoption by Chinese educational thinkers? What were the determining factors for genuine transfer of Western educational theories?

The feasibility of selective cultural borrowing in the form of transplantation of specific educational theories, techniques and/or institutions is an issue that has been relatively well-researched in the academic field of Comparative Education. Scholars such as Kandel, Hans, Sadler, Beredey, Noah and Eckstein, and Holmes have debated the relative merits of selectively importing the educational theories and practices of other cultures. Their work has provided us with an analytical framework in which certain tools for use in the study of the transfer of educational ideas have been generally agreed upon.

Most works written in the 18th and 19th century addressing foreign systems of education had as their purpose the utilitarian use of selected techniques/institutions in the reform of the writers' native educational system. The scope of their investigations did not include the general principles (or theories) underlying the development of these foreign systems. The first to present a more comprehensive view of educational systems was Michael

Sadler in his seminal work *How Far Can We Learn Anything of Practical Value from the Study of Foreign Systems of Education?* (1900).[1] In it he provides us with a perceptive allegory pointing out the difficulties of educational transfer:

'We cannot wander at pleasure among the educational systems of the world, like a child strolling through a garden, and pick off a flower from one bush and some leaves from another, and then expect that if we stick what we have gathered into the soil at home, we shall have a living plant. A national system of education is a living thing, the outcome of forgotten struggles and difficulties and battles long ago.' (Quoted in Hans, 1958: 3)

It is here that we find the roots of much of the comparative education work carried out in the 20th century. It is based upon a historical approach, where social, economic, political and cultural antecedents are investigated in depth in order to explain the origins of the educational principles and techniques used by a particular education system. '... the comparative approach demands first an appreciation of the intangible, impalpable spiritual and cultural forces which underlie an educational system; the factors and forces outside the school matter even more than what goes on inside it.' (I.L. Kandel in Hans, 1958: 3)

These various factors have been arranged into taxonomies of different types and levels of complexity (See for example: Hans, 1958). Noah and Eckstein (1969) then developed the model further and, through the use of statistical analysis, were able to postulate relationships between different educational variables. This breakthrough is important for the study of the transfer of educational ideas and practices, because suddenly it seemed possible to be able to predict the consequences of introducing a new pedagogical theory or convention. However, this increasing quantification and use of especially regression analysis to postulate relationships between different educational variables has provoked increasing criticism, the most vocal of which stems perhaps from Brian Holmes, long-time Professor of Comparative Education in the University of London Institute of Education. He represents a new group of social scientists who dispute the credibility of these positivistic cause and effect relationships.

Holmes has, in his two chief works (1965 & 1981), attempted to develop his own paradigm based on Dewey's 'problem-solving approach' and Popper's 'hypothetico-deductive method' for the conducting of Comparative Education research. He points out the impossibility of quantifying the so-called 'living spirit' of an educational system and the unavoidable bias collection of education data contains. He rightly criticizes the dangerous deficiencies a positivist-inductive theory of comparative education has, namely its disregard for the normative/ideological precepts researchers carry around as part of their intellectual baggage.

While Holmes is most concerned with developing a model for predicting outcomes of proposed educational policies, I would like to use some of his ideas to evaluate the receptiveness of educational thinkers and policy-makers in one cultural sphere — the Chinese — towards educational ideas and theories with their origin in another — the Western. The two aims are in reality quite similar to one another as the origins of many proposed educational policies today, especially in developing countries but certainly also in developed countries, lie precisely in other countries with a different cultural background.

Holmes advocates the establishment of an ideal-typical normative model in the spirit of Weberian sociology as an extremely useful means of providing a basis for dealing with otherwise incomparable (and naturally also unquantifiable) cultural phenomena, in this case the educational aims, norms and internalized attitudes influencing educational policy-making and policy execution.

He then goes on to analyze the actual *process* of policy formation, adoption and execution using the critical dualism of Popper. It asserts that there can be distinguished two types of law in any society — the normative and the sociological (Holmes, 1965: 50-51). Sociological laws apply to the functioning of social institutions and dictate relationships between different institutions, and are, according to Dewey, hypothetical policy solutions to identified problems (Holmes, 1981: 80). These laws are very suitable for sociological research, in part because they reflect sociological patterns in society, and in part due to their relative stable nature.

Normative laws lie one level deeper in man's consciousness, and as such, provide the context for which sociological laws (hypotheses) are to be understood and tested. The normative patterns of a culture can be drawn up by researching that culture's theories of knowledge (epistemology), individuality (psychology) and society (political science, sociology) (Holmes, 1981: 81). The assumption is, then, that these normative patterns are directly linked to the way institutions are organized and operate, and that research directed towards these patterns will yield a deeper understanding of the suppositions underlying the educational system of a particular culture.

The connection between the normative world and the social world is not always so clear however. Thus the relative significance of normative laws for educational systems is difficult to measure. However, the neglect of this area (often due to its 'unquantifiableness') ignores the great importance a culture's norms and values have for its educational system. Certainly, at the societal level at least, taking into account the *ruling* norms and values can provide an excellent basis for which to understand the educational debates taking place within that society. The topic of whether or not to introduce or adopt foreign educational theories, practices and institutions is often rather controversial precisely because they come potentially into conflict with the normative educational orientation of a given society. In the following analysis of the Chinese encounter of Pragmatism and Structuralism, I will investigate the extent to which the philosophical bases of these theories concur or conflict with the ruling normative educational orientation existing in China during the period 1978-1984.

Political-Social-Economic Context

1978 represents a turning point in Chinese educators' attitude toward Western non-Marxist educational theories. Ever since the turn of the century a debate had raged as to the feasibility of importing Western educational theories and practices. Before 1949, there evolved a general consensus that a necessary prerequisite to the modernization of the Chinese education system was the development of a new Chinese theoretical orientation capable of supporting modern educational institutions and ideas to replace the obsolete Confucian system of thought. After 1949, with the development and consolidation of the new ruling doctrine of Marxism-Leninism-Mao Zedong Thought, this new philosophical basis seemed to be in place. The official position regarding the adoption of Western theories followed the political seesaw over the correct interpretation of Marxism-Leninism, however, and the theories thus found themselves being castigated during one period and surreptitiously imitated in another.

It was first beginning in 1978 that the ideological dust had settled enough to permit the first fledgling attempts at more objective analysis of Western theories. This is not to say that these attempts were not weighed down with ideological baggage, on the contrary, and this is exactly the point, a strong unified theoretical orientation in the form of the Chinese interpretation of Marxist/Maoist educational theory continued to heavily influence the way in which Chinese educators perceived and addressed the Western educational theories during the period under study.

There were many significant developments during this early segment of the reform period of import for the educational realm. Politically, the period from 1978 to 1984 was marked by a distinct desire for stability after the ravages of the Cultural Revolution. Deng Xiaoping capitalized on people's growing political apathy and their anxiety towards chaos and turmoil to consolidate his power and introduce thoroughgoing economic reforms. His pragmatic emphasis of expertness over redness and of economic growth over political campaigns was strongly supported by the Third Plenum of the Eleventh Party Congress held in December, 1978.

Investment was poured into the building up of the Chinese industrial base and the need for specialized personnel rose proportionately. Scientific research was also stimulated in the hope that it could contribute to China's further development.

The focus of this reform movement was primarily the economic sector and its needs, and not so much the political arena where the new leaders clamped down hard on political dissidents, though some political reforms were attempted with mixed results. The old slogan 'Let a Hundred Flowers bloom, Let A Hundred Schools of Thought Contend' was again dusted off, but this time its connotation solely contained the inspiration of scientific innovation, not literary creativity or even worse political diversity (Taylor, 1981: 169). Political participants were to remain firmly within the bounds of the four fundamental principles: Dictatorship of the proletariat, party leadership, the socialist line, and Marxism-Leninism-Mao Zedong Thought. The so-called 'four freedoms' (to speak freely, to air one's views fully, to engage in great debates, and to write big-character posters) were deleted from the party constitution in 1982.

China's commitment to the Four Modernizations — of agriculture, industry, science and technology, and national defense — reflected the subordination of previous egalitarian social goals to the priorities of economic construction. The principal contradiction in Chinese society was no longer considered to be between the proletariat and the new bourgeoisie, but between 'the growing material and cultural needs of the people and the backwardness of social production' (Resolution, 1981: 76). The economic development necessary to resolve this contradiction presupposed the cooperation of the intellectuals and a dramatic expansion and quality enhancement of the educational sector. The social standing of intellectuals was raised notably, in part by redressing the gruesome wrongs perpetrated against them during the Cultural Revolution, in part by giving them status as members of the working class.[2] Similarly, the role of education in society changed in emphasis from the transmission of ideological values to the fulfilment of economic modernization needs.

Another important political policy change with far reaching repercussions for the educational sector was the commencement of the Open Door policy. This move away from the isolationism which had previously characterized Chinese foreign policy was precipitated for purely economic reasons however: China needed foreign capital and technology to achieve its economic modernization goals. Politically and indeed culturally, as shown by the recurrent campaigns against 'spiritual pollution' and 'cultural contamination' in the early and middle 1980s, the Chinese leaders were determined to retain control. This determination was not unanimous however: many, especially middle-level leaders, resisted this return to Cultural Revolution campaign tactics. Moreover, this resistance grew and spread with the increase in foreign contact via economic cooperation and the explosion in the numbers of Chinese students studying abroad.

The purposeful sending of students to study abroad was but one part of the extensive reforms carried out within the educational system. A return to the meritocratic system of the early 1960s was launched. Examinations were reintroduced as the means of determining access to and promotion within the education system. Resources were concentrated in key schools where the most promising students were assembled. Schools themselves were in addition often divided into 'fast' and 'slow' tracks. Academic knowledge was again heralded, at least indirectly, as examinations were based exclusively on theoretical knowledge. Moreover, the use of examinations as a selective mechanism had an enormous impact on curriculum planning: prestige (as well as allocation of resources) became attached to promotion rates. Middle schools, for example, concentrated almost all of their energies on the small minority of students with a chance of passing the national university entrance examinations.

Channels of Conveyance

Almost a century had passed since the pathbreaking translations of Yan Fu first introduced Western thought in any comprehensive manner to the Chinese intellectuals. Much had happened in the intervening period to change the way in which Western ideas reached the Chinese. The channels through which these ideas were conveyed have vital importance for the way in which they were received.

Three principal channels through which Western educational ideas and theories reached Chinese educational thinkers during the early 1980s can be identified: translations and descriptive introductions published primarily in educational journals; analytical studies carried out under the auspices of the newly established discipline Comparative Education and published likewise in educational journals; and direct Chinese-Western scholarly exchange primarily in the form of Chinese students and scholars going abroad for study and research.

Introductory materials dealing with Western educational theory were indeed decidedly few up to 1978.[3] Thereafter, concurrent with the rising openness towards and increasing contact with the West, more and more translations and descriptive presentations of foreign works began to be published. Educational journals containing articles on foreign education began cropping up already in 1979. The most prestigious — *Jiaoyu Yanjiu* (Educational Research)[4] - was published first as a bimonthly in 1979 and 1980 and thereafter as a monthly. Many of its articles referred to international developments in their analyses of contemporary or historical educational problems in China. In addition, there were, especially in this period, a multitude of outright descriptive accounts of foreign educational trends, issues and policies. More specialized in the area of foreign education study were the journals *Waiguo Jiaoyu* (Foreign Education), *Waiguo Jiaoyu Dongtai* (Developments in Foreign Education) and *Waiguo Jiaoyu Ziliao* (Materials on Foreign Education).[5] Here were to be found numerous translations of Western educational works, including the writings of such notable contemporary theorists as Jerome Bruner, Jean Piaget, and B.F. Skinner.

In addition, newspapers like the academically oriented, nationally distributed daily newspaper, *Guangming Ribao*, and the more specialized *Zhongguo Jiaoyu Bao* (Chinese Education Newspaper) also carried a great deal of general introductory articles about specific foreign educators or about the prevailing developments internationally within a specific educational field. Numerous monographs with titles like *A General Review of Foreign Education* (Zhang Weicheng, 1982) and *Contemporary Western Educational Philosophy* (Chen Yougong, 1982) were also published during this period. In addition, translations of entire introductory works by Western authors or of international educational compendiums were published. Finally, many foreign textbooks were directly imported in their original language, particularly in the early stages of the period.[6]

The great bulk of this material dealt with specific educational techniques or administrative structures. Following the instigations of the Chinese leadership to emphasize educational topics appropriate to the national goal of economic modernization, much attention was paid to effective methods of teaching scientific and technological subjects. In Xiao Cuilin's (1988) analysis of *Zhongguo Jiaoyu Bao* during the years 1985 to 1987 for example,[7] she found that of all articles concerning foreign education, there were six times more articles dealing with science and technology than there were concerning social sciences and humanities, a figure which becomes even more telling when it is disclosed that of those articles in the latter category, more than half dealt with the new field of 'management studies'.

The second channel through which Western educational theories made their way into the circles of Chinese educators was through the work of Chinese comparative educationalists. The first introductory accounts describing the academic discipline of Comparative Education as it is known in the West appeared in 1979 and 1980. It was not until 1981/1982 that articles and books dealing with the subject matter in depth and providing a Chinese analysis of the development of Comparative Education in the West and its potential use in China began to be published. The primary aim of Comparative Education, in the eyes of the Chinese authorities, was to help the educational leaders in their planning and policy-making (Jing & Zhou, 1985: 243).

The study of comparative education in China underwent very rapid development during the period under study. Methodological study of Western educational theories began to be promoted and better coordinated with the founding of the Chinese Comparative Education Society in 1979.[8] This society together with the various departments of foreign education at the major comprehensive and normal universities contained the core of Chinese educators specializing in foreign educational theories and practices. They were all proficient in at least one foreign language, many having studied abroad, and a large number had teaching experience at educational institutions (Jing & Zhou, 1985: 244). The most important of these institutions were: Beijing Normal University, East China Normal University, South China Normal University, Northeastern Normal University and Hebei University (Li Qilong, 1983: 15).

Starting in 1979, seven universities enrolled graduate students in the field of Comparative Education. The goals and content of the curriculum were concentrated around broadening students' horizons so that they could better understand China's educational situation, consolidating their problem-solving skills and knowledge of other social sciences and previously studied educational subjects, and encouraging the selective and critical use of foreign educational research results in the service of Chinese education (Zhang Weicheng, 1982: 66).

The first contemporary textbook dealing with methods of comparative education was published in 1982 (Wang Chengxu, 1982). Research results were published in the previously mentioned educational journals or in monographs. The People's Education Press published for example a series of books concerning foreign education: *Waiguo Jiaoyu Congshu*; more than 20 volumes had already been published by 1983.

Educators affiliated with the Comparative Education Society and/or the major universities' foreign education departments held a very key position in the information flow from West to East. A good indication of this is the fact that most of the sources for the following discussion of Western educational theories' reception in Chinese educational circles stem from these educators.

The final channel through which Western educational ideas and theories reached Chinese educators was through direct contact via study abroad, visits from guest scholars, and multi- and bilateral institutional cooperation.

The period up to 1978 was characterized by a high degree of isolation on the part of Chinese academics. Only during the decade of the 1950s when extensive contact was upheld with the Soviet Union have Chinese scholars had prolonged interaction with a foreign academic community. This self-imposed isolation contributed to the relative underdevelopment of Chinese scientific research. After 1978, concurrent with the implementation of the Open Door policy, an increasing desire on the part of Chinese political and educational authorities for educational contact with especially Western countries could be ascertained: the absolute numbers of Chinese studying or carrying out research abroad steadily increased, and the relative quality of educational interaction with the West also rose with more and more cooperative work taking place.

From 1978 to 1985 more than 36,000 Chinese students and scholars went abroad for study or research, and the large majority of this number, nearly 30,000, were government supported in some way, clearly indicating the seriousness of Chinese rhetoric during the period towards opening up to the Western world. By 1985, 16,500 of the students/scholars had already returned to China and taken up academic positions primarily at Chinese universities. Statistics show that around 80% of the Chinese students and scholars pursued studies in the pure and applied sciences while only 5% specialized in social sciences, and the remaining studied in the humanities.[9] This sustains Chinese policies emphasizing the achievement of the Four Modernizations via the improvement of scientific and technological research.

An important supplement to the direct exchange of students and scholars that evolved during the early eighties was the increasing amount of ever more sophisticated multilateral and bilateral cooperation between Chinese educational institutions and Western international organizations like the World Bank, UNESCO and UNDP as well as individual educational institutions. China became a member of the World Bank in 1980 and during the succeeding five years a total of eight major projects concerning post-secondary education in China were planned with implementation starting already in 1981. A total of U.S. 1 billion were to be invested in upgrading equipment and curricula, developing faculty resources and improving university management. The study abroad of thousands of Chinese scholars and graduate students were financed, as well as the visits of hundreds of Western experts.[10] In addition, literally hundreds of bilateral cooperative agreements were entered into by Chinese educational institutions during the early 1980s. The actual degree of interaction during this early gestative period is more uncertain, but at least some cooperative research projects were entered into and exchange of materials and personnel did in fact take place.[11]

The official aims of this increased Chinese study abroad were clear: 'The basic goals of [educational] interchange are to introduce modern science and technology to China, to serve teaching and scientific research, to train personnel, and to assist in China's modernization.'[12] To this should added the ideological limitation to this exchange as here stated by Deng Xiaoping himself:

We will unswervingly follow a policy of opening to the outside world and actively increase exchanges with foreign countries on the basis of mutual equality and benefit. At the same time we will keep a clear head, firmly resist corrosion by decadent ideas from abroad, and never permit the bourgeois way of life to spread in our country. (Quoted in Hayhoe, 1984b: 41)

The actual impact of increased Chinese contact with Western education and research institutions is less obvious. The Chinese leaders like to believe that study abroad is a means for exclusively transferring the technical and theoretical knowledge of the West, and that all other aspects of this intercultural experience can either be suppressed or ignored. In contrast, a leading Western sinologist, John N. Hawkins,[13] chairman of the department of education at UCLA and president of the Comparative and International Education Society, concluded in his study on the impact of educational exchanges on higher education reform in China:

However, initial evidence suggests that among the returned scholars there is an overt desire not only to transfer the techniques and technologies learned in the West but also to transform institutions and interpersonal relations in line with practices in the West and Japan. With respect to the United States, a desire to reform higher educational institutional relations can be seen, ranging from those involving student and faculty concerns, to administration and management, and finally to wholesale curriculum reform. Returned scholars have brought home with them not only knowledge of computers and plasma physics but also a whole range of administrative, management, and institutional forms that in their minds are closely associated with the knowledge thus obtained. (Hawkins, 1984: 30)

Strong barriers existed which effectively blocked the implementation of any educational reform along the lines of the West during this period however. Not only was there the aforementioned ideologically defined constraint, but equally important obstacles were the rigid administrative structures, personnel policies, and extreme academic compartmentalization at Chinese institutions of higher education and the lack of a free job market for academics.

Generally speaking, then, one could conclude that the period up to 1984 was really an incubative one in terms of the development of the concrete influence of the three channels through which Western educational theories reached China. Much energy in the beginning of the Open Door period was logically used to translate and introduce major Western works. Concurrently, a forum for systematic analysis of these Western educational theories was gradually created and nurtured under the sponsorship of the Comparative Education society. And finally, the explosive increase in direct contact between Chinese academics and Western educational institutions contained a great latent potential for future transfer of educational theories and practices. Many of those who had returned from abroad had already attained important positions, but the potential was as yet to be realized for political and historical reasons.

The Chinese Encounter with Pragmatism and Structuralism

This section will take up two of the most written about Western 'general' theories in China, Pragmatism (*Shiyongzhuyi*) and Structuralism (*Jiegouzhuyi*), and briefly describe their position among Chinese educational theorists in the early 1980s. No attempt is made to compare the influence of the two as they have completely different historical positions in China, Pragmatism being closely tied to the May Fourth movement and John Dewey's stay in China from 1919-1921, while Structuralism has not been involved in China's historical development in any way.

At the level of official ideology, all theories with Western origins were, apart from a few 'experimentally-based and scientifically grounded' psychological theories, arbitrarily relegated the Chinese ideological classification 'idealism' (*weixinzhuyi*), which effectively prevented any full-fledged officially sanctioned use of their ideas. They were accused of ignoring the vital relationship between education and the political economy.

The official aim of Chinese educational philosophy was to 'first and foremost ... study Marxism-Leninism-Mao Zedong Thought, and study those original works of the philosophy and political economy of dialectical materialism and historical materialism which apply to educational philosophy; and secondly, from the Marxist point of view, criticize and draw lessons from the scientifically valuable material to be found in Chinese and foreign educational philosophy works of the past and present' (Fu & Zhang, 1986: 14). This statement together with the often read '*Zhong xue wei ti, xi xue wei yong*' (Chinese learning as the essence, Western learning for its utility) perhaps best represented the attitude towards Western educational theories during this initial period of the Open-door Policy. They were only to be used parenthetically, in bits and pieces, and only in support of the ruling ideological framework of Marxism-Leninism-Mao Zedong Thought.

In scholarly accounts, however, a more nuanced interpretation of the two Western theories of Pragmatism and Structuralism was found and these interpretations will form the basis for my analysis.

Pragmatism and John Dewey (1859-1952)

John Dewey has not only been one of the most prolific educational writers of modern times, he has also been one of the most influential, not only in his homeland, U.S.A., but the world over, including China. Dewey spent two years in China from 1919 to 1921,[14] lecturing and teaching, and had enormous impact on especially educational theoreticians and policy-makers. His impact was enhanced greatly by the fact that several of the central Chinese figures during this period had received their education at Dewey's base in the U.S., Columbia Teacher's University. Through their articulate and enthusiastic translations (both oral and written) of his ideas, they generated a great deal of interest in Dewey's theories, especially those dealing with education.

These disciples of John Dewey did more than just translate however. In their capacity as leading educators and education administrators, they further spread the ideas of John Dewey. For example, Guo Bingwen, the first Chinese to receive a Doctorate of Education (1914) from Columbia Teachers University, was dean and president of Nanjing National Teachers College and systematically recruited graduates of Columbia Teacher's University for positions in his faculty of education, including such notable Deweyites as Tao Xingzhi, Chen Heqin, Zheng Zhonghai and Zhu Pinggui. The Deweyan faculty applied Dewey's ideas to their preparation of secondary and normal school teachers, who then in turn based their teachings on his thought.[15] School administrators were subject to the same influence in their training at Nanjing Teachers College. Jiang Menglin, the second Chinese to obtain his Doctorate at Columbia under Dewey, also possessed great influence in the educational sector, first in his position as Acting Chancellor and professor of education at Beijing National University and later as Minister of Education under the Nationalist regime.

Since its heyday during the 1920s, Dewey's educational philosophy has found itself thoroughly denounced during some periods and surreptitiously utilized in others. Though it never again was to play such a dominant role in national educational policy, it continued to set its mark on the educational debate right on up to through the 1980s.

The basic framework of his educational thought was his so-called 'pragmatic' theory of education, the central idea being the use of the scientific method to determine both the content and the method of education. Dewey's aim was the creation of modern, urban, democratic man (Moore, 1974: 42). He saw man as being an active, social, problem-solving animal, whose success is measured by the degree to which he is able to achieve a continual mastery of his environment. This interaction of man with his environment represents the core of education. Society, then, according to Dewey, is meant to provide an arena in which individuals can learn from each other.

Much of Dewey's thought can be seen as a reaction against the educational practices current in his day. Education was still largely conceived of as a process of formal instruction, the teacher presenting an ordered body of knowledge to the receptive and blank minds of his students. Dewey attacked the breaking up of knowledge into disciplines and was especially outraged by the pedagogical consequences of this conception of knowledge. He lamented the meaninglessness and lifelessness of traditional education and criticized especially the widespread use of strict one-way communication to transfer a (teacher) organized body of knowledge to passive students as advocated for example by Johan Herbart (1776-1841). In addition he rejected all of the traditional dualisms propounded in earlier theories of education: e.g. theory and practice, manual and intellectual work, labor and leisure, mind and matter, etc...

Knowledge for Dewey was the result of inquiry utilizing the scientific method. The individual attainment of this knowledge, then, is contingent upon that person's *active* and methodological search for it. Like Rousseau, Dewey favored a child-centered, activity-oriented process of education, but in contrast to Rousseau's protective learning environment for children, Dewey considered it essential that school and society become one. He stressed the need for developing creativity and openness in children in order that they be able to face and solve the changing problems of a developing society.

His epistemological assumptions are clearly portrayed in his seminal work *How We Think* (Boston, 1910). In it he states that we think when we are challenged and that this is carried out not by simply accepting what others have said previously but by critically involving ourselves in a process of inquiry. Man's greatest attribute is his plasticity, and this ability to learn should be collectively used to deal with the inevitable progressive changes within society.

In order to analyze the position of Pragmatism and John Dewey's educational thought in the Chinese educational debate during the 1980s, several types of sources have been examined: the education volume of a large encyclopedia (Hu Qiaomu, 1985), Chinese educational journals, and monographs dealing specifically with Western educational theories. A word of caution is necessary concerning the following analysis of the Chinese interpretation of Pragmatism: much of what is written about Pragmatism and Dewey in the early 1980s was heavily influenced by Dewey's prominent historical role in China, and as such subject to ideological colorations that Chinese accounts of other educational theories did not suffer from.

Under the entry of Pragmatism in the encyclopedia we find it described as an 'important school in Western modern capitalist educational thought' (pp. 328-30). Its central ideas are equated with those of Dewey, and indeed most of the entry concentrates on his work. He is termed an 'idealistic empiricist' because he considered experience to be the basic unit of the world, though it remains unclear (and unstated) precisely why he is labelled an idealist; his pragmatic emphasis on experience as the product of interaction between an organism and its environment and as the central criteria for knowledge make it difficult to understand this categorization. It might very well reflect an enmity towards the political turbulence of the Cultural Revolution and the need to dissociate new educational policies from those implemented during the Cultural Revolution.[16] One author attempted to explain why Dewey's thought was labelled idealistic: he stated that it is because Dewey 'brings the mind into the natural system, attaching great importance to the role of knowledge and regards the result as natural evolution.'[17] It is evidently Dewey's belief that the ultimate origin of knowledge lies within man himself and is dependent on his actions (based on his experience) which made his thought idealistic in Chinese eyes.

The entry goes on to cite some of Dewey's most prominent contributions to educational theory, namely his criticism of Herbart's formalistic, 'teacher-centered' educational thought and consequent emphasis on developing educational techniques and materials appropriate and relevant to a child's age and experience, his re-thinking of teacher-student relations with stress being placed on cooperation rather than confrontation, and finally his radically new conception of education's role in society — it was to be an instrument of social reform not the preserver of tradition. The entry concludes with a brief criticism of Dewey's attack on Marx's class-struggle theory and his advocacy of the use of the 'intelligence method' — that based on the experimental methods of natural sciences — to solve social problems as well. Under the entry entitled 'educational philosophy' (*jiaoyu zhexue*) Pragmatism is also criticized for failing to stress systematic pedagogy, which leads to a reduction in the leading function of teachers resulting in lower instructional quality and student knowledge levels (Hu Qiaomu, 1985: 185).

A common point made by all the authors was Dewey's close attachment not only to the United States as his homeland but also to the period of great economic and social change in which he wrote. They pointed out the importance of the immense progress made in industrialization and capital accumulation during this period as opposed to the continuing stagnancy of the educational sector. They considered Dewey's thought to be the logical reaction to this state of affairs. The schools were no longer fulfilling the needs of society (the capitalists), *ergo* reform was needed. Dewey's educational theories were seen as serving the interests of the ruling bourgeoisie. For example his emphasis on developing individuality in the child was regarded as antithetical to the nurturing of communist morality, but a necessary ingredient of a capitalist system based on mutual competition. Dewey was in fact attacked by several of the writers for attempting to conceal class differences and thus prevent class contradictions from becoming visible through a drowning diffusion of his concept of 'democracy'. By pitting individuals against each other on the economic market, and by giving them a false sense of political power, Dewey was accused of perpetuating the capitalist system and serving the interests of the oppressing class.

Another related criticism shared by the majority of the Chinese writers was that Dewey disregarded the importance of the productive forces in determining social and economic relations which in turn delimit social consciousness. Norms, values and even ideals of the people are, according to the Chinese Marxists, inescapably tied to the fundamental economic production forms of a given society. Dewey was accused of ignoring the existing socioeconomic context in which education takes place, making his 'social reform' in effect unattainable. In addition his learning theories themselves were criticized for not taking into account social relations within the classroom; these relations were called in Deweyan terms by the Chinese 'indirect experience'[18] and were considered an important part of a child's intellectual baggage.[19]

In general, Chinese educational theorists found Dewey's work concerning the psychologization of instructional materials and methods to make them suit the intellectual and experiential level of the students to be his greatest contribution. They considered it to be an important development away from the so-called 'traditional' school which stressed the rote learning of teacher organized material.

Interest in Dewey and Pragmatism was markedly on the rise during the period 1978-1984. A volume of selected essays was published in 1981 covering all of his major theoretical works (Wang & Zhao, 1981). Critical articles appeared acknowledging the political bias of previous material presenting the thought of Dewey and calling for a more objective and scientific debate on the merits and potential application of his ideas in service of the Four Modernizations. Renewed attention to one of Dewey's Chinese disciples in the 1920s, Tao Xingzhi, was also quite apparent.[20]

Structuralism: Piaget and Bruner

The entry 'structuralist philosophy' within the category of 'contemporary schools of Western educational philosophy' in the encyclopedia is only a brief one (Hu Qiaomu, 1985: 186-87). It states that it is a popular school of educational philosophy in contemporary Europe and America based on the belief that man's rationality contains a kind of innate structuring ability. Based on the work of Jerome S. Bruner, it became the guiding thought behind curriculum reform during the 1960s in the United States. The entry concludes with a brief statement basically dismissing its importance due to an 'excessive emphasis on the structure and degree of difficulty of knowledge ... divorcing itself from the realities of the students and increasing their burden' (Hu Qiaomu, 1985: 186-87). This simplistic account of Structuralism and its importance for education today requires additional supplementation before we can go further. It is in fact strikingly insufficient and downright misleading, though as we shall see below, it does foreshadow some of the Chinese criticism of Structuralism.

Jean Piaget, the famous Swiss psychologist and child development expert, is generally regarded as the founder of the Structuralist theory of cognitive development.[21] He developed a theory based on four concepts: schema, assimilation, accommodation and homeostasis. Man is born with an inherited 'schema', a structuralized subjective view of the world, which develops in response to outside stimuli. This development process is based on man's constant cognitive striving to reach a homeostatic equilibrium between himself and his environment. To achieve equilibrium two interrelated types of responses are available: assimilation and accommodation. New objects are assimilated into the existing schema as far as possible, and when this assimilation no longer is possible because of some fundamental conflict with that schema, accommodation takes place — the new information is incorporated into the schema and a new schema is created and equilibrium is once again achieved. It is in this way that experience induces learning. Learning is a process of developing more and more organized (and complicated) structures (schemas). Knowledge is consequently undergoing constant change.

A child's cognitive development is then made up of a continuum of equilibrations, which Piaget roughly divided into certain distinguishable stages: 1) the sensorimotor stage (0-2 years); 2) the preoperational stage (2-7 years); 3) the operational stage (7-12); and 4) the formal stage (12-15). He did not believe that this development can be speeded up by any appreciable degree (Lindauer, 1980: 43). He emphasized the importance of taking these stages (including their subordinate steps of development) into account in the field of education, thereby making teaching materials and methods appropriate to the specific stage of development in question.

Jerome Bruner further developed Piaget's ideas in the field of education.[22] His most influential book *The Process of Education* (1960) was used as the basis for extensive curricular reform in American primary and secondary schools during the 1960s.[23] Bruner stressed the uncovering and use of the 'basic structure' of a particular area of study for instructional purposes. This basic structure is a collection of the basic concepts, principles and laws applying to that particular area of study and is tightly bound to the methods used to 'discover' these fundamental ideas. In short Bruner advocated the teaching of these methods based on the existing knowledge/cognitive level of the students, and then allowing them to 'discover' the basic structure themselves through their own efforts. This entire process can (and should) take place at any educational level and Bruner postulated that any subject can be taught to any level of cognitive development if the appropriate methods are utilized.

The Chinese critique of Structuralist education theory was mixed. On the positive side, some Chinese education writers approved of its emphasis on the study and teaching of the basic structure of a subject area (Ding Zhiqi, 1979 and Zhang Huanting, 1979). They considered this an essential method of keeping up with the 'knowledge explosion' (*zhishi baozha*). The greatest contribution of Structuralist education in the eyes of these writers was its matching of children's cognitive (including psychological) development level with educational content and methods in a never ending spiral (Ding Zhiqi, 1979: 58-9). Its recognition of the importance of providing an educational environment which furnished children with stimuli appropriate to their level of knowledge and cognitive ability and the implications of this for curriculum planning was considered highly relevant to the Chinese situation. Bruner's Discovery Theory was also highlighted for its nurturing of independent thinking, an aspect, it was pointed out, it had in common with the Chinese *qifa* (elicitation) method of instruction (Ding Zhiqi, 1979: 71).[24] Finally the importance of children's cultural environment for their intellectual development as demonstrated particularly by Bruner was approvingly seen as a critical factor affecting the learning ability and knowledge level of children.

Three main areas of criticism towards Structuralism's philosophical base and educational concepts arose in the educational theory literature of the early 1980s. The first, and most damaging accusation in Chinese eyes, was that it has an idealistic philosophical base. This claim had two arguments: 1) Piaget's 'schema' is ultimately an innate one and can be regarded as having close association with the dualistic philosophy of Kant and its 'schema of a priori logic'. 2) In discussing the source of knowledge, Piaget emphasizes the interaction between the subject and the object, particularly the action/movement of the subject, thereby in effect reducing the object's status in the knowledge-making process. Knowledge becomes thus subjectively determined. Both of these arguments were refuted in the Chinese educational press but the charges continued to be raised in most descriptive and/or analytical articles dealing with Structuralist education.[25]

The second criticism was directed toward Structuralism's (especially Piaget's) neglect of the important role that social practice plays in children's intellectual development. This neglect generates the potential for this development to be underestimated (Zhu Zhixian, 1981: 4.22). It also leads to practical problems in the educational sector as the social realities of teachers and students can never live up to Piaget and Bruner's experimentally derived theories. The influence of the environment is greater than they suppose (Zhang Huanting, 1980: 60). Although they recognized the guiding role of teachers, they at the same time advocated the use of 'discovery' theory, which leads in effect to an undermining of this role by allowing for too much self-study and independent exploration without the inspiring leadership of the teacher's instruction (Luo Zhenghua, 1980: 39). They were also accused of overemphasizing the importance of the logical component of the cognitive structure at the expense of psychological and even spiritual elements in their development of instructional methods (Luo Zhenghua, 1980: 39 and Zhu Zhixian, 1981: 4.8).

Finally, the Chinese critics regarded Structuralist education methods to potentially be too child-oriented in a Deweyan fashion, leading to lower academic standards. Basing instructional activities on children's own basic impulses and attitudes and not externally determined materials, they maintained, would invariably result in lower standards. One harsh critic presented research results demonstrating the failure of the discovery method in practice (Tian Jie in Bulunei, 1983). He maintained that more than 1/2 of the middle school students had difficulties understanding the material and that their psyche was easily damaged as a result. He put the basic premise of Structuralism into doubt as well, stating that more and more experts did not believe a basic structure of knowledge existed in their field.

Much of the above criticism can of course be disaffirmed through closer analysis of Piaget and Bruner's works, especially as regards their conception of the teacher's role in the educational process and the importance of socio-cultural factors for intellectual development. In spite of the at times heavy criticism of Structuralist concepts, they were in fact used in Chinese research projects. For example a study of Chinese language instruction attempted to implement Bruner's theory of curriculum, including the discovery method (Chen Gang, 1981). One of the major research topics within the national plan was the development of cognitive processes among Chinese children, and Piaget's stage theory was used as the organizing framework.[26] The number and depth of available articles about the Structuralism school belie the occasional heavy criticism of its non-Marxist origins. Even Ding Zhiqi, one of it foremost critics had to admit that many of its ideas could be quite useful if the 'correct basic structure of knowledge could be found' (Ding Zhiqi, 1979: 57).

The Chinese Filter

Several components made up the Chinese filter through which Western educational theories and practices had to flow during the early 1980s: a political demand of the entire education sector to be of economic utility, a parallel charge made of students and scholars sent abroad to only study subjects relevant to the Chinese needs for economic modernization, and an overall dominant theoretical orientation of Marxism-Leninism-Mao Zedong Thought setting the ideological boundaries for academic research.

Specific government policies aimed at the economic and political sectors had a strong influence on developments in the educational sector, including the attitude toward and official theoretical view of Western educational ideas. A pragmatic emphasis on economic construction permeated all talk of educational reform, and on the surface at least, Western theories were to be carefully and critically evaluated in terms of their potential service to the Four Modernizations. Hence, the Chinese interest in teaching methods and educational theories which improved the learning capacities of children — both Dewey and Piaget/Bruner were praised for their work in the psychologization of instructional materials and the matching of children's cognitive levels with appropriate educational stimuli. The policy that education must serve the Four Modernizations had no doubt a great *agenda-setting* impact on the Chinese encounter with Western educational theories: it decided *which* theories were taken up in the Chinese debate, and only to a lesser extent, *how* they were potentially assimilated.

The economic construction criterion was similarly used to regulate the potentially most volatile channel of academic exchange — study abroad. Only subjects deemed important for economic development were to be studied, and this meant that the great majority of Chinese studying and conducting research abroad were natural and applied scientists. These subjects were not only considered of vital importance for the Chinese modernization drive, but also politically uncontroversial or 'safe'. This part of the Chinese filter was really very coarse, as it did not directly address educational theories and practices, and thereby allowed, as we saw above, a great deal of education-related ideas to rather inconspicuously enter the Chinese academic world. These ideas were not subjected to the same ideological rigour as theories which were presented in the official education press (as we shall see below), because they entered China indirectly, as part of the intellectual baggage of returned scholars and students.

Finally, the period under consideration was characterized by the existence of a strong central state with a ruling ideology at its disposal (albeit the actual omnipotence of this ideology was on the decline during the period). The absence of any significant political reforms meant that educational research continued to be under fairly tight control, and new initiatives lying outside the parameters of Marxism-Leninism-Mao Zedong Thought were to be throttled.

The importance of this ideological filter for academic investigations of Western educational theories should not be underestimated. It is necessary to briefly delineate the main principles of the official Chinese philosophic stance in education, including its historical antecedents, in order to fully comprehend the way in which Western educational theories were scrutinized in the Chinese context. The examples of the Chinese encounter with Western educational ideas cited above will then serve to illustrate how this filter actually functions.

If we begin by sketching out an ideal type of Marxist educational theory, we find many of the fundamental concepts present in Chinese educators' (official) philosophical outlook. Briefly the fundamental assumptions are as follows: Man is a product of social relationships which are in turn based on the economic foundation; Man is malleable and extremely receptive and responsive to environmental stimuli; Knowledge arises from the practical requirements of material life and develops out of the dialectic relationship between theory and practice. In essence, to paraphrase Marx himself, it is the mode of production which determines the social, political, and intellectual life processes in general.

Many of these basic tenets found fertile soil in the traditional Chinese ideology of Confucianism. For example, human relationships serve as the cornerstone in the ideal Confucian society too, and are governed by the central Confucian principle of *li* (proper conduct). Likewise, fundamental to the Confucian concept of man is the belief in his perfectibility. Man contains within himself innate variables that need only be released through either conscious effort (Xunzi) or the provision of the appropriate environment (Mencius). Man is thus always open for (positive) change; he is in effect malleable. And finally, similar to the Marxist materialistic view of knowledge, the basic Confucian criterion of knowledge is practical conduct. Objective facts outside of their social context are relatively less important.

To give an example of how the official theoretical orientation can shape policy statements, here is a statement from a leading Chinese educator prescribing the proper attitude to take towards Western educational concepts:

The system and experience of education in all countries are specific to their own conditions. It is necessary to apply the principles and methods of historical materialism to analyse their specific historical, political and economic factors so that comparisons can be made with the reality of our country; then we can discern what should be adapted and what should be abandoned. (Hao Keming, 1984: 153)

The statement above again reflects the prevalent attitude among Chinese political leaders that Western thought and technology can and must be sifted through an ideological filter before it can be adopted.

The Chinese criticisms of the educational theories espoused by Dewey's Pragmatism and Piaget and Bruner's Structuralism are perhaps now more understandable. Dewey's focus on the individual child, as illustrated by his child-centered instructional theories and his central concept of education - the interaction of man and the environment, is in direct contradiction with Chinese Marxist/Confucian theory, which demands that all education must be grounded in human relationships and the existing social environment. The epistemology of Dewey is also in conflict with the ruling Chinese ideology: knowledge for Dewey is a product of individual scientific inquiry, and can thus stand detached, while the Chinese Marxists insist that knowledge arises out of a dialectic between theory and practice and must be related to the practical requirements of material life.

The origin of the Chinese criticisms of Structuralism too has its roots in philosophical divergences. The seemingly idealistic epistemology of Piaget, and Bruner and his apparent neglect of the importance of social practice for intellectual development in children represent real threats to the Chinese ideological foundation.

A philosophical crack appeared in this ideological filter during the early eighties however. It concerned the existence of independent 'objective laws' (*keguan guilü*) governing educational developments. According to Chinese Marxists, education exists in a dialectical relationship with society, instructing the next generation in its cultural inheritance while at the same time being transformed in accordance with societal developments, particularly those concerning the mode of production. The question is whether this process of transformation occurs according to 'objective laws' independent of the economic structure. This was a very controversial issue during this period.[27] Indeed the very question of whether education should be considered as part of the economic base serving the productive forces or as part of the social and cultural superstructure built on top of the base was a matter for debate.[28]

If education could be shown to contain objective laws in its own right then it could rightfully be released from the ideological chains preventing scientifically based research. Furthermore this would open up possibilities for conducting investigations of foreign research as these basic 'objective laws' would of course have to exist in the same form abroad.[29] As of 1984 however no definitive conclusion had been reached and ideological control in the form of determining or influencing research topics and methods was still quite strict.[30] But as we will see below a gradual opening up towards Western theories did in fact occur in practice, perhaps as the result of an increasing decentralization of educational research.

Assimilation of Western Educational Theories

Assimilation of Western educational theories in the period 1978-1984 occurred in a complex and somewhat obscure manner. The complexity was due to the explosion of educational informations and research occurring abroad and the awesome size of the Chinese educational system (including the amount of educational research being carried out). The obscurity is a result of the

existence of a strong ruling ideology in China which often concealed the real
origin of educational ideas presented in China and the genuine opinions of
Chinese educators. In order to simplify and elucidate this process of
assimilation, it will be divided up into three levels: General theoretical,
limited theoretical and practical. Following our previous definitions of
'general' and 'limited' theories, these then represent the fundamental theories
of man, society and knowledge and their reflection in specific educational
principles/ideas respectively, while the 'practical' level refers to the existing
educational system including its curriculum, administration, institutional
organization etc.... Generally speaking assimilation takes place at all three
levels via the three main channels described earlier (translations and
descriptive introductions, analytical study and scholarly exchange), but as we
shall see below there is a certain pattern to this process.

At the general theoretical level, we saw no complete Western theory being
assimilated as was the case for example of Dewey's Pragmatism in the
1920s.[31] Rather it was the case of 'picking a flower here and there'. An
example would be the Chinese denial of the existence of an innate cognitive
structuring ability as postulated by Piaget while at the same time applauding
his structural theory of knowledge. There also exists a contradiction between
the Chinese approval of the Discovery method and its aim: a creative, independently thinking individual, and their basic view of the meaning of education: a planned, organized, practical activity, especially as regards to the
important guiding role of the teacher.[32]

The guiding philosophical outlook for this kind of theoretical borrowing
hinges on the discussion concerning 'objective laws'. If objective laws of
education exist then autonomous research of educational problems unrelated
to the economic base and political superstructure can indeed take place;
moreover foreign borrowings are thus vindicated. One author went so far as
to state that even educational ideas based on the theories of 'capitalist
educators who are politically reactionary and conservative and whose world
view is idealistically metaphysical' can 'score a lucky hit' (Jin Qiong, 1980: 28).
He based his reasoning on the philosophical stance that the 'difference
between idealism and materialism is basically their concept of the relationship
between thought and existence'. Thus if an educational theorist whose
thought is grounded in idealism only concerns himself with material phenomena, then his theories can include some positive elements potentially useful
for Chinese educators grounded in materialism. This leaves the door wide
open for selective borrowing of Western educational theories.

This acceptance of the selective appropriation of Western educational theories was echoed by many other writers and was indeed a part of official policy. The existence of the entire academic discipline of Comparative Education in China presupposed the possible grafting of selective foreign elements onto the Chinese educational system. Of course, this process should take place according to the fundamental principles of Marxism-Leninism-Mao Zedong Thought, but these principles in fact themselves contain one of the main criteria considered to be so essential by celebrated Comparative Educationalists like Hans and Schneider, namely the historical social-economic-cultural background for the education system in question. Perhaps this is one of the reasons that the science of Comparative Education achieved the degree of acknowledgement in China that it did. Certainly the emphasis of many Comparative Educators on the possibilities of quantifiably analyzing correlations between educational and societal variables across nation states perked the Chinese interest.[33] Deeper non-quantifiable cultural factors are easily overlooked by this methodology however, and this is without doubt one of the weaknesses of Chinese Comparative Education as carried out in the early 1980s. Nevertheless it does represent an assimilative method, albeit limited, used by Chinese educators.

A final method of assimilation at the general theory level was the re-evaluation and upgrading of Chinese educational theorists of the past who were strongly influenced by Western theories. The most conspicuous example of this was the case of Tao Xingzhi, the former disciple of John Dewey. A literal renaissance of interest in his work occurred in the late 1970s and early 1980s. Much energy was used to accentuate those parts of his theoretical and practical work which demonstrated his 'connection with the people' and recognition of the importance of social-economic forces for educational theory in order to make his educational theories more politically acceptable to Chinese educationalists.[34] Renewed interest in the whole May Fourth era was demonstrated by the large number of research projects carried out or planned which dealt with specific Chinese educational leaders from the period.[35]

The primary channels through which assimilation of Western ideas into general educational theories occurred were thus critical introductions and comparative education research. It is here we find that the necessary ideological flexibility was developed to allow a selective adaptation of Western ideas to the Chinese theoretical base.

At the limited theoretical level there were many isolated examples of consummate borrowing of Western educational theories and techniques. There were the previously mentioned examples of the use of Bruner's theory of curriculum in language instruction and the use of Piaget's stage theory of cognitive development as the organizing framework in a nationally sponsored research project concerning the cognitive development of Chinese children. In addition two large cooperative studies involving 15 institutions which were concerned with the development of mathematical concepts in children depended heavily on Piagetian techniques, constructs and tests; two other studies involving the development of language (10 institutions) and moral and personality development (14 institutions) were strongly influenced by Piagetian research designs (Brown, 1982: 339).

More subtle borrowing or incorporation was also quite prevalent. Under the guise of debating the relative merits of 'traditional' or 'modern' education, the 'modern' ideas and techniques of Western educators were often highlighted in a positive way.[36] Positive association with recognized Chinese educational concepts was another way Western ideas became covertly accepted. An example of this would be the numerous mentionings of the close similarities between Bruner's Discovery Method and the Chinese *Qifa* Method of instruction. Especially in the psychological sphere many Western concepts and methods were introduced *in toto* in the Chinese educational press; this was primarily because psychology had long been a neglected discipline in China and its methods were suitably 'quantifiable' and thus devoid of ideological content (this obviously does not include the theories and methods of Freud et.al. which were not acknowledged). Quantitative methods in general were in high fashion during this period as they fulfilled the Chinese requirements regarding 'objective laws'.

The most utilized channels through which assimilation of limited educational theories took place were then translations and descriptive introductions, and this accurately reflects the general stage of assimilation at which China found itself during this period. The source of the direct influence some Western theories had on Chinese educational research design, etc., is more difficult to pinpoint. It was probably a combination of the above introductions in scholarly journals and the impact of study abroad and/or cooperative research with foreign educators. It was too early for the results of Chinese efforts to build up a formal analytical apparatus of Comparative Education to be felt.

The final level of assimilation to be discussed is the practical one. The primary aim of this paper being to explore Chinese assimilation of Western educational *theories*, practical implementation of Western educational techniques and ideas into the Chinese educational system has not been investigated. Therefore only inferences made based on the section dealing with scholarly exchange between China and the West will be presented here.

A great potential for influence was imbedded in the large number of Chinese scholars having studied abroad but that potential was as of 1984 yet to be realized. In addition the type of influence was not limited to the scientific knowledge attained abroad or even the adoption of new methods, but went even deeper into the very conceptual framework of the Chinese researchers and affected their notions regarding the structure of academic institutions and their interrelations, curriculum reform, faculty development etc... including the very bedrock of their theory of knowledge.

It is however very difficult to ascertain how extensively this impact on the apex of the Chinese education system filtered downwards into lower levels. We have seen that the post-1978 reforms brought with them a very meritocratic bias in the educational structure and a pragmatic one in regard to the content of curriculum, but how much of this reflected Western influence and how much Chinese tradition or the serious demands of economic modernization is difficult to establish with any degree of certainty without further, comprehensive research.

Less difficult to substantiate would be that the channel through which this influence will in the future come to be felt is the direct contact of Chinese educators with Western institutions, be it in the form of their own study abroad or the arrival of an educational delegation from abroad or the systematic introduction of Western ideas as part of the work of an international organization in China. The other two channels (introductions in scholarly journals and systematic study in the form of the discipline of Comparative Education) are far more indirect and much more politically sensitive; they may in the long run be important for the development of *alternative* educational theories in China, but under the present political leadership, it would be difficult to imagine that free ideological reigns would be granted to Chinese educational theoreticians to develop non-Marxism-Leninism-Mao Zedong Thought based educational theories. Much more likely is the decentralized experimentation with or implementation of specific Western/Japanese educational ideas. In this way Western influence on the practical level may well impact the developments at the two theoretical levels. In any case the importance of direct contact with Western researchers and practitioners can not be overemphasized.

Further research is needed to answer the questions of why and what Western educational theories were and are being transferred to China. Likewise, a prerequisite to understanding the actual impact of these theories on education as carried out at the grass roots level would entail both micro and macro studies of Chinese educational practices set in relation to educational theoretical frameworks. Educational transfer is more than just picking 'off a flower from one bush and some leaves from another'.

Glossary of Chinese Terms

Guangming Ribao	光明日报
Jiaoyu Yanjiu	教育研究
Jiaoyu zhexue	教育哲学
Jiegouzhuyi	结构主义
Keguan guilü	客观规律
Li	礼
Qifa	启发
Shiyongzhuyi	实用主义
Waiguo Jiaoyu	外国教育
Waiguo Jiaoyu Congshu	外国教育丛书
Waiguo Jiaoyu Dongtai	外国教育动态
Waiguo Jiaoyu Ziliao	外国教育资料
Weixinzhuyi	唯心主义
Zhishi baozha	知识爆炸
Zhongguo Jiaoyu Bao	中国教育报
Zhong xue wei ti, xi xue wei yong	中学为体西学为用

References

Brown, Hubert O. (1982): 'Politics and the 'Peking Spring' of Educational Studies in China' *Comparative Education Review* Vol. 26, No. 3, pp. 329-51.

Brown, Hubert O. (1987): 'American Progressivism in Chinese Education: The Case of Tao Xingzhi' in *China's Education and the Industrialized World: Studies in Cultural Transfer* (Hayhoe, Ruth & Marianne Bastid, eds.), Armonk, New York: M. E. Sharpe, Inc.

Bulunei (1983): 'Bulunei 'zhishi jiegou' kecheng lilun shoudao piping' [Bruner's 'structure of knowledge' theory of curriculum is criticized], *Guangming Ribao* (26 August) p. 3.

Chen Gang (1981): 'Yuwen jiaoxue kexue tixi de chubu tantao' [A primitive study about the scientific system in Chinese language instruction], *Jiaoyu Yanjiu*, No. 6, pp. 56-59.

Chen Jingpan (1982): »'Duwei de daode jiaoyu sixiang pipan' de buchong«. [Supplementary remarks to 'Criticism of Dewey's Ideas of Moral Education'], *Jiaoyu Yanjiu*, No. 9, pp. 80-86.

Chen Yougong (1982) (ed.): *Dangdai Xifang Jiaoyu Zhexue* [Contemporary Western Educational Philosophy] Beijing: Jiaoyu kexue chubanshe.

Chen Yuanhui (1981): 'Jiaoyu kexue yanjiu de ruogan wenti' [Some problems in educational research], *Jiaoyu Yanjiu*, No. 2, pp. 15-18, 19, 20.

Cleverley, John (1985): *The Schooling of China: Tradition and Modernity in Education*. Sydney: George Allen & Unwin.

Dewey, John (1973): *Lectures in China 1919-1920*. Honolulu: The University Press of Hawaii.

Ding Zhiqi (1979): 'Bulunei de 'kecheng lun' chutan' [Bruner's 'theory of curriculum': a preliminary study], *Jiaoyu Yanjiu*, No. 5, pp. 55-59, 71.

Ding Zhiqi (1981): 'Bulunei de renshi fazhan lun jian jie' [A simple introduction to Bruner's theory of knowledge development], *Guangming Ribao*, 5 and 19 January, p. 4.

Fu Tongxian (1980): 'Shi lun Piyajie de fasheng renshi lun' [A modest study of Jean Piaget's Genetic Epistemology], *Jiaoyu Yanjiu*, No. 4, pp. 83-90.

Fu Tongxian and Zhang Wenyu (1986): *Jiaoyu Zhexue* [Educational Philosophy], Jinan: Shandong jiaoyu chubanshe.

Hans, Nicholas (1958): *Comparative Education: A Study of Educational Factors and Traditions*. London: Routledge and Kegan Paul.

Hao Keming (1984): 'Research on Higher Education in China Today', *Comparative Education* Vol. 20, No. 1, pp. 149-54.

Hawkins, John N. (1974): *Mao Tse-tung and Education: His Thoughts and Teachings*. Hamden, Conn.: The Shoe String Press.

Hawkins, John N. (1983): *Education and Social Change in the People's Republic of China*. New York: Praeger.

Hawkins, John N. (1984): 'Educational Exchanges and the Transformation of Higher Education in the People's Republic of China' in *Bridges to Knowledge: Foreign Students in Comparative Perspective* (Barber, Altbach & Myers, eds.), Chicago: University of Chicago Press.

Hayhoe, Ruth (1984a): 'Chinese-Western Scholarly Exchange: Implications for the Future of Chinese Education' in *Contemporary Chinese Education* (Ruth Hayhoe, ed.), London: Croom Helm, pp. 205-29.

Hayhoe, Ruth (1984b): 'A Comparative Analysis of Chinese Western Academic Exchange', *Comparative Education*, Vol. 20, No. 1, pp. 39-55.

Hayhoe, Ruth (1986a): 'China, Comparative Education and World Order Models Project', *Compare*, Vol. 16, No. 1, pp. 65-80.

Hayhoe, Ruth (1986b): 'Penetration or Mutuality? China's Educational Cooperation with Europe, Japan, and North America', *Comparative Education Review*, Vol. 30, No. 4, pp. 532-59.

Hayhoe, Ruth (1989): 'China's Universities and Western Academic Models' *Higher Education*, Vol. 18, pp. 49-85.

Hayhoe, Ruth and Zhan Ruiling (eds.) (1989): 'Educational Exchanges and the Open Door' *Chinese Education*, Vol. 21, No. 1.

Holmes, Brian (1965): *Problems in Education: A Comparative Approach*. London: Routledge and Kegan Paul Ltd.

Holmes, Brian (1981): *Comparative Education: Some Considerations of Method*. London: George Allen & Unwin.

Hu Qiaomu (1985) (main ed.): *Zhongguo Da Baike Quanshu: Jiaoyu* [The Complete Chinese Encyclopedia: Education], Beijing & Shanghai: Zhongguo dabaike quanshu chubanshe.

Huang Guixiang (1981): 'Tao Xingzhi bu tongyu Duwei' [The differences between Tao Xingzhi and Dewey], *Jiaoyu Yanjiu*, No. 9, pp. 78-80.

Huang Shiqi (1987): 'Contemporary Educational Relations with the Industrialized World: A Contemporary View' in *China's Education and the Industrialized World: Studies in Cultural Tranfer* (Ruth Hayhoe & Marianne Bastid, eds.). Armonk: M.E. Sharpe, pp. 225-51.

Husén, Torsten (1979): 'General Theories in Education: a Twenty-five Year Perspective', *International Review of Education*, Vol. 25, pp. 325-45.

Jin Qiong (1980): 'Waiguo jiaoyushi yanjiu zhong de ji ge lilun wenti' [Some theoretical problems confronted by research work in the history of education in foreign countries], *Jiaoyu Yanjiu*, No. 1, pp. 27-31, 5.

Jing Shi-bo and Zhou Nan-zhao (1985): 'Comparative Education in China', *Comparative Education Review*, Vol. 29, No. 2, pp. 240-50.

Keenan, Barry C. (1977): *The Dewey Experiment in China: Educational Reform and Political Power in the Early Republic*. Cambridge, Mass.: Harvard University Press.

Leng Ran (1979): 'Lun shi qifashi jiaoxue' [An attempt to discuss heurestic teaching methods], *Jiaoyu Yanjiu*, No. 2, pp. 49-53 (trans. in *Chinese Education*, Vol. 16, No. 2-3, pp. 183-96).

Li Kejing (1980): 'Is Education a Superstructure or a Productive Force? Major Differences appear in Discussion on the Essence of Education', *Social Sciences in China*, Vol. 1, No.3, pp. 195-214.

Li Qilong (1983): 'Woguo bijiao jiaoyu kexue de fazhan licheng' [The developmental course of the science of comparative education in China], *Waiguo Jiaoyu Ziliao*, No. 1, pp. 12-18.

Lindauer, Theodore (1980): 'The Education of Scientists in China — or Anywhere', *Eastern Horizon*, Vol. 19, No. 6, pp. 35-45.

Lu Jun (1980): 'Xinlixuejia Piyajie' [Psychologist Piaget], *Jiaoyu Yanjiu*, No. 4, pp. 90-94.

Lu Jun (1982): 'Piyajie lilun de jiaoyu hanyi' [The educational implications of Piaget's theory], *Guangming Ribao*, 12 and 26 February, p. 3.

Luo Zhenghua (1980): 'Bulunei jiaoxue sixiang shuping' [A review of Bruner's instructional thought], *Waiguo Jiaoyu*, No. 1, pp. 37-39.

Mae Chu-chang (1983): 'Research on Education in China' *Chinese Education*, Vol. 14, Nos. 2-3,4.

Meng Xiande (1985): 'Lun Duwei jiaoyu zhexue tixi zai jiaoyu shi shang de diwei' [A Discussion of the position in educational history of Dewey's system of educational philosophy] in *Duwei, He'erbate Jiaoyu Sixiang Yanyiu* [A Study of Dewey and Herbart's Educational Thought], Jinan: Shandong jiaoyu chubanshe, pp. 1-17.

Moore, T. W. (1974): *Educational Theory: An Introduction*. London: Routledge & Kegan Paul.

Noah, H. J. & M. A. Eckstein (1969): *Towards a Science of Comparative Education*. New York: Macmillan.

Ou, Tsuin-chen (1983): 'Dewey's Sojourn in China: His Lectures and His Influence on Chinese Thought and Education', *Chinese Culture* Vol. 24, No. 2, pp. 41-68.

Resolution (1981): 'Resolution on Certain Questions in the History of Our Party Since the Founding of the People's Republic of China', Adopted by the Sixth Plenary Session of the Eleventh Central Committee of the Communist Party of China on June 27, 1981, translated and published in *Resolution on CPC History (1949-1981)*. Beijing: Foreign Languages Press.

Taylor, Robert (1981): *China's Intellectual Dilemma: Politics and University Enrolment, 1949-1978*. Vancouver: University of British Columbia Press.

ter Weele, Alexander H. (1983): 'China/World Bank: University Development', *Prospects* Vol. 13, No. 4, pp. 493-501.

Thøgersen, Stig (1990): *Secondary Education in China after Mao: Reform and Social Conflict*. Aarhus: Aarhus University Press.

Wang Chengxu (1981): 'Yanjiu waiguo jiaoyu, zuida de kunnan shi quefa ziliao [The biggest problem in the research of foreign education is lack of materials], *Jiaoyu Yanjiu*, No. 2, pp. 37-38.

Wang Chengxu (1982), Zhu Bo & Gu Mingyuan, *Bijiao Jiaoyu* [Comparative Education], Beijing: Renmin jiaoyu chubanshe.

Wang Chengxu and Zhao Xianglin (1981): *Duwei Jiaoyu Lunzhu Xuan* [A Selection of Dewey's Educational Treatises] Shanghai: Huadong shida chubanshe.

Wang Shiqing (1980): 'Piyajie de fazhan lilun ji qi dui jiaoyu de yinxiang' [Piaget's development theory and its influence on education], *Renmin Jiaoyu*, No. 7, pp. 50-52.

Wu Yongshi (1984): 'Gaige jiaoxue, peiyang xuesheng de chuangzao nengli' [Carry out teaching reform to develop the creative ability of students], *Jiaoyu Yanjiu*, No. 5, pp. 8-14, 48.

Xiao, Cuilin (1988): 'China's Open-door Policy in Education: a content analysis of the Chinese Education Newspaper' *Compare*, Vol. 18, No. 2, pp. 163-72.

Yang Zhenning (1984): 'Yang Zhenning jiaoshou tan xuexi fangfa' [Professor Yang Zhenning talks about study methods] (1984), *Guangming Ribao*, 18 May, p. 3.

Zhang Fakun (1984): 'Lun dushu yu huodong, 'chuantong jiaoyu' yu 'xiandai jiaoyu'' [Reading vs. activity from the perspectives of 'traditional education' and 'modern education'], *Jiaoyu Yanjiu* No. 11, pp. 41-45.

Zhang Fakun (1985): ''Chuantong jiaoyu' yu 'xiandai jiaoyu' de yi zhi xing chu yi — Duwei, He'erbate jiaoyu sixiang de yi-tong' [A preliminary opinion about the singular nature of 'traditional education' and 'modern education' — differences and similarities in Dewey and Herbart's educational thought] in *Duwei, He'erbate Jiaoyu Sixiang Yanjiu* [A Study of Dewey and Herbart's Educational Thought], Jinan: Shandong jiaoyu chubanshe.

Zhang Huanting (1979): 'Lun 'jiegouzhuyi jiaoyu'' [A discussion of 'structuralist education'], *Jiaoyu Yanjiu*, No. 1, pp. 58-60.

Zhang Huanting (1980) (main ed.): *Xiandai Xifang Xichanjieji Jiaoyu Sixiang Liupai Lunzhu Xuan* [A Selection of Treatises from Modern Western Capitalist Schools of Educational Thought], Beijing: Renmin jiaoyu chubanshe.

Zhang Jian (1984) (main ed.): *Zhongguo Jiaoyu Nianjian 1949-1981* [Chinese Education Almanac 1949-81], Shanghai: Zhongguo dabaike quanshu chubanshe.

Zhang Weicheng (1982) (ed.): *Guowai Jiaoyu Xueke Fazhan Gai Shu* [A General Review of Foreign Education], Beijing: Jiaoyu kexue chubanshe.

Zhu Zhixian (1981): 'Piyajie xinlixue sixiang ji qi zai jiaoyu shang de yiyi' [Piaget's psychological thought and its meaning for education], *Guangming Ribao*, 8 and 22 April, p. 4.

Notes

1. A reprint of this work is available in *Comparative Education Review* Vol. 7 (Feb. 1964), 307-14.

2. Regarding intellectuals, Deng said at the National Science Conference in March, 1978 that 'generally speaking, the overwhelming majority of them are already intellectuals serving the working class and other working people. It can therefore be said that they are already part of the working class itself.... Everyone who works, whether with his hands or with his brain, is part of the working people in a socialist country.' (Quoted in Thøgersen, 1990: 37-8)

3. A severe lack of materials dealing with Western education hindered instruction at teacher's colleges in the subject. Professor Wang Chengxu (1981) of Hangzhou University attributes this quantitative lack of materials as being the number one impediment for competent research in this area. He sees a need for broad geographical and historical based research into the development of foreign educational theories and practices.

4. *Jiaoyu Yanjiu* is put out by the Central Institute of Educational Science (*Zhongyang Jiaoyu Kexue Yanjiusuo*), an affiliate of the Ministry of Education (now State Education Commission).

5. *Waiguo Jiaoyu* is a bimonthly put out jointly by the Foreign Education Dept. of the Central Institute for Educational Research (*Zhongyang Jiaoyu Kexue Yanjiusuo Waiguo Jiaoyu Yanjiushi*) and the Foreign Education Research Group of the Chinese Education Society (*Zhongguo Jiaoyu Xuehui Waiguo Jiaoyu Yanjiuhui*) and commenced publication in late 1979. *Waiguo Jiaoyu Dongtai* is a bimonthly put out by the Foreign Education Institute at Beijing Normal University (*Beijing Shifan Daxue*) and originally began circulation back in 1965. *Waiguo Jiaoyu Ziliao* is put out by the Foreign Education Institute at East China Normal University (*Huadong Shifan Daxue Waiguo Jiaoyu Yanjiushi*) and began publication in 1983.
6. More than 5000 volumes were imported from Britain, U.S.A., France, West Germany and Japan alone in 1978. *Chinese Education* Vol. 14, No. 4, p. 82.
7. I believe that these figures can safely be said to be representative for the years immediately antecedent to 1985 as well. Indeed the proportion may be even more lopsided.
8. The Chinese Comparative Education Society had 343 members, including institutional memberships, and had begun to branch out into provincial associations as of 1985. Four national meetings were held attended by some 50 to 120 participants in the period 1980 to 1984 (Jing & Zhou, 1985: 244-49).
9. Xiao Cuilin, 1988:165-66 and Zhang Jian, 1984: 668. See also Hayhoe, 1984b: 44-51.
10. For a detailed account of the World Bank projects see Huang Shiqi, 1987. See also Hayhoe, 1984a, Hayhoe, 1989, and ter Weele, 1983.
11. For example, Wuhan university, which traditionally has had close links with France, serves as the focal point for French academic transfers in China and represents a high degree of integrated cooperation between an institution of higher education in China and a Western country. French language is taught and used, French professors come regularly to teach, and a large number of both the Chinese staff and students go to France to improve their skills. See Hayhoe, 1986b:543-555.
12. He Dongchang, then Minister of Education, translated in Hayhoe and Zhan, 1988: 20-21 from *Renmin Ribao* (Sept. 21, 1984).
13. See his important monographs: Hawkins, 1974 and Hawkins, 1983.
14. See Keenan, 1977, and Dewey, 1973 for an analytical survey of Dewey's influence in China and a translation (back into English from the Chinese) of his lectures, respectively.
15. See Dewey, 1973:20-21, Ou, 1983:57-8, and Keenan, 1977:14.
16. The Minister of Education in 1975, Zhou Rongxin, charged Deweyan concepts like 'learning by doing' and 'child-centered education' with being used as the cornerstone for Cultural Revolution educational policies: he accused them of denying workers higher levels of education as well as preventing children from learning intellectual knowledge (Cleverley, 1985:211).
17. Meng Xiande, 1985:7. Meng also criticizes Dewey for ignoring the potential to change social relations and explaining social phenomena using biological inheritance and adaptability theories. See p. 9.
18. See for example Zhang Huanting, 1980:2: 'However, his one-sided emphasis on the 'direct experience' of children's lives leads to the ignoring of the position and role of indirect experience in the classroom which unavoidably lowers knowledge training standards and weakens basic knowledge.'

19. Some of the criticisms were merely an echo of the original attack on Dewey's theories during the 1950s. Chen Heqin, one of Dewey's former disciples, delivered two three-pronged attacks on Dewey: First his educational aims, curriculum and methodology were criticized; then the very philosophical platform on which he built his theories was attacked. See Dewey, 1973: 27-28 for a more complete presentation of Chen's critique.

20. A debate raged in the journal *Jiaoyu Yanjiu* from 1979 to 1981 discussing the true historical position and potential contemporary role of Tao Xingzhi. See issues 1979.3 pp. 52-57, 1980.1 pp. 75-81, 1980.6 pp. 80-84 and 1981.1 pp. 80-84. Numerous other articles dealing more descriptively with the life and thought of Tao Xingzhi also appeared in the above named journal as well as other educational journals and newspapers. His complete works were published in ten volumes in 1991.

21. For Chinese descriptive accounts of Piaget's thought, see: Fu Tongxian, 1980; Lu Jun, 1980; Lu Jun, 1982; Wang Shiqing, 1980; Zhang Huanting, 1980, pp. 349-51; and Zhu Zhixian, 1981.

22. For Chinese descriptions of Bruner's thought, see: Ding Zhiqi, 1979, Ding Zhiqi, 1981.1.5 and 1981.1.19; Fu & Zhang, 1986, pp. 374-81; Zhang Huanting, 1979. Some of Bruner's works have been translated in the Chinese educational press, including his seminal work *The Process of Education* (Shanghai People's Press, 1973).

23. Indeed it has been translated into at least 23 languages and has played an important role in curriculum development in many countries, especially in North America and Europe, but also in for example Japan (Ding Zhiqi 1979: 55).

24. For a discussion of the origins of the Chinese *qifa* method of teaching and its congruence with certain Western theories, including Bruner's, see Leng Ran, 1979.

25. See Fu Tongxian, 1980: 89-90. He bases his rebuttal on Piaget's own works, especially *Genetic Epistemology*. Ding Zhiqi, 1979 is perhaps the most critical work and also provides numerous citations in support of his contention that Structuralism is fundamentally an idealistic philosophy.

26. See Mae Chu-chang, 1983: ii. Two papers in Mae's collection are exclusively based on Piaget's theories. See pp. 101-23 and 124-39 for Chinese studies based on Piaget's concept of Conservation.

27. Zhang Jian, a leading educational policy-maker, in an article in *Jiaoyu Yanjiu* (1979.2), went so far as to say that Mao might possibly have been wrong when he held that education was 'an ideological reflection of the politics and economics of a given society' and that there existed scientifically based processes and laws, particularly in the so-called 'nonideological' subjects like natural science, mathematics, languages etc..., which were unchangeable and without class character (Brown, 1982:331-33).

28. See Li Kejing, 1980 for a review of the different opinions on this subject. He finds a graduated scale of five different schools.

29. Chen Yuanhui, 1981 maintains for example that instructional methods also are classless and thus can be exclusively developed using scientific methods. In general he stresses the need to find theoretical solutions in reality and practice as neither Marx, Lenin or Mao wrote a systematic work of educational theory, a point made by many of the writers.

30. Brown, 1982 presents the results of a study of official research topics which clearly illustrates a 'remarkable and genuine coincidence of interest between the educational needs of national economic policy and the aspirations of educational-ists...' (pp. 336-40).
31. For an excellent micro study of the subtleties of the transfer of Dewey's thought to Chinese educational thinkers during the 1920s, see Brown's (1987) analysis of Tao Xingzhi's assimilation of Dewey's ideas. Brown clearly exposes how these ideas were modified and even transformed by one of China's leading educational thinkers.
32. The qualities of creativeness and independent thinking were constantly being stressed in the Chinese educational press during this period. They seemingly recognized the importance of these qualities for research but did not fully comprehend their connection with teaching methods. For a report from a Chinese professor who does, see Yang Zhenning, 1984. See Wu Yongshi, 1984 for an analytic discussion of the problem.
33. Hayhoe, 1986a:66 provides a short description of the attractiveness of the positivist-inductive approach for contemporary Chinese educationalists.
34. See Huang Guixiang, 1981, passim for an example of this. He contrasts these positive qualities (in the eyes of Chinese Marxists) with those of Dewey.
35. 10 out of 60 historical studies planned or under way in 1979 concerned themselves with the May 4th period; in addition three studies took up the educational thought of John Dewey (Brown, 1982: 340). *Jiaoyu Yanjiu* also contained numerous articles dealing with Tao Xingzhi and the May Fourth era during this time period.
36. See for example Zhang Fakun, 1984, and Zhang Fakun, 1985.

The Concept of Individuality in Japanese Education

Marie Roesgaard

In Japan education and the reform of education has been the object of much discussion since the start of a national educational system in the 1880's. The government, conservatives and business have traditionally stood on the side of central control and an educational system suited primarily to national needs. In opposition has been teachers, who are quite well-organised compared to the general level of organisation across institutions in Japan, citizens' groups and academic groups. The discussion has been public and quite harsh. In the following I will describe the way the central concept of individuality has been defined by the different actors in the debate. To do this an introduction to the general ideas about individuality in Japan is necessary.

The concept of individuality and its meaning in a Japanese context is a subject which has received a huge amount of attention. As a concept originating in the Western philosophical and scientific tradition it has been taken up by the Japanese and fitted into their internal cultural debate, but it has not altogether remained the same as in the Western philosophical tradition.

When interpreting other cultures it has been common to emphasise the differences in order to prove a point. Thus, when Europeans or Americans have described Japan, the 'everything-is-opposite' model has been very popular. This typically included statements saying that the Japanese were group oriented rather than individualists or that they were emotional rather than rational. In other words, the opposite of our *ideal* selves. Individualism has been a cherished concept in Western culture and hence it has often been claimed by Westerners that non-Westerners — such as the Japanese — could not possibly possess this character trait, merely because they were 'opposite'. (Rosenberger 1992:2)

The Japanese on their side have also used this approach to affirm Japanese identity by using a systematic taxonomy of the 'Other' (China/the West). As a consequence, what is attributed to Japan must be denied the 'Other' and vice versa. (Dale 1990:39)

Edwin O. Reischauer, who has produced a lot of books on the Japanese and their history, describes in one of his later works this apparent oppositeness as a difference of *myths*. Americans and Europeans, he says, are likely to see themselves as independent individuals and as more free than facts would always warrant. The Japanese on the contrary are 'much more likely to operate in groups, or see themselves as operating this way'. (Reischauer 1990:128)

In the same work, he also touches upon the idea of the emotional Japanese versus the rational Westerner:

The Japanese have always seemed to lean more toward intuition rather than toward reason, to subtlety and sensitivity in expression rather than to clarity of analysis, to pragmatism rather than to theory, and to organisational skills rather than to great intellectual concepts. (Reischauer 1990:200)

Though somewhat cautious in his choice of words and emphasising that exceptions can always be found, his work clearly reflects the traditional binary way of describing a foreign culture, exoticising it by emphasising differences rather than similarities. In the earlier part of his career he was much more black-and-white in his analysis of East versus West, but apparently awareness of the budding criticism of this mode of interpretation prompted him to be more relativist in his wording though not necessarily in content. (Minear 1980:511-12)

The approach of seeing Japan as opposite an undefined 'West' — which is by the way usually the United States — is characterised by Peter Dale as being in danger of *exoticising prejudice* instead of creating an objective picture, because of its denial of homologies between otherwise similar situations. Additionally, Dale warns the focus on differences and the refusal by the Japanese to acknowledge the value of Western theories carries the danger of making the culture unable to understand its own human predicament, deprived as it is of the use of analogies and foreign experiences. (Dale 1990:7,40)

This approach is used in the literary genre called nihonjinron ('Theories of Japaneseness', further described by Befu in this volume) which among other things deals with the concept of individuality in a Japanese context. This genre has been criticised particularly strongly by Peter Dale (1990) and Mouer & Sugimoto (1986) for failing to take into account regional and class variations, the difference between voluntary and coerced behaviour and the role of conflict in its attempt to present Japan as a harmonious, homogeneous society.

Peter Dale, in a particularly acrimonious attack, calls nihonjinron 'an expression of an intense tradition of intellectual nationalism' which emerged around 1909-11 as a reaction to the crisis faced by the late Meiji leadership, and which is all the more menacing because it fervently denies having anything to do with ideology or politics. According to Dale, Nihonjinron describes a Japan as seen through the eyes of conscious nationalists out of touch with both reality and the principles of logic and method. (Dale 1990:9,38)

Despite the apparent unreasonableness and tendentiousness of the genre, one must take it into account when dealing with things like self and individual in Japan because nihonjinron is quite influential. Often the authors of such works are acknowledged scholars respected for their intellectual credentials and acting as spokesmen for the 'inarticulate soul of the national essence', though the inspiration for writing such works may often just have been the allure of money. Nihonjinron material is immensely popular in Japan and widely read, so its doctrines are well known to most Japanese and thus constitute common knowledge on the nature of the 'Japanese' as opposed to the rest of the world.

A Nomura Survey of publications on the theme of Japanese identity showed that from 1946 to 1978 approximately 700 titles were published on this subject, 25 percent of which were issued in the peak year period 1976 to 1978. (Dale 1990:14-5,17) For this reason, it becomes important to deal with the ideas expressed in nihonjinron in the attempt to analyze the nature of Japanese 'individuality'.

Well-known examples of the nihonjinron tradition are Nakane Chie, 1970, 'Japanese Society'; Doi Takeo, 1973, 'The Anatomy of Dependence' and Tsunoda Tadanobu, 1978, 'The Brain Structure of the Japanese'. Nakane Chie became the most famous, though by no means the only, advocate of the theories on the group orientation of the Japanese. These theories became so popular that her work was published by the Japanese Ministry of Foreign Affairs in an abbreviated form and distributed through Japanese embassies and government agencies[1]. Clearly it was seen as an ideal picture of Japanese culture, a picture to be presented to the world public. Statements such as the above by Reischauer have been supported by this supposedly 'native' and in effect semi-official way of interpreting Japanese society, though Reischauer's background for his statement on the group-oriented Japanese more probably stems from the 'opposite' model in which Western individualism was seen as opposed to Eastern groupism.

As for the Japanese version of individualism it has usually been charac-terised in terms of group orientation, as seeking identity through relationships with other people, and the perceived egotistic character of Western individua-lism has been distinguished from the relational individuality of the Japanese. (Rosenberger 1992:12-3)

The theory of group orientation has also been applied to schooling. Roger Goodman quotes an example from a school he visited. This school based itself on group action and claimed that 'success is not an individual success but that of the group.' (Goodman 1990:121)

The difference between Western and Japanese ideas of individualism is also revealed in the terminology applied by the Japanese. Japanese-type indivi-dualism is termed kosei whereas Western individualism is termed kojin shugi, which signals selfishness and immaturity. (Hendry 1992:56)

As Brian Moeran points out in his book 'Language and Popular Culture in Japan', the term kosei seems to consist of only the 'good' side of indivi-dualism, that is, individualism devoid of aspects such as selfishness and irre-sponsibility. The West is left with the entirely negatively evaluated term 'individualism' (kojin shugi). (Moeran 1989:70) This is a telling example of the way the 'opposite' model works. Kosei is attributed to the Japanese and hence the same characteristic is necessarily denied the 'Other', here the West. To make this distinction clear the terms are translated into 'individuality' for kosei and 'individualism' for kojin shugi respectively.

Takie Sugiyama Lebra in the article 'Self in Japanese Culture' deals with two types of 'self', two types of actors — whether capable of individual action or not is secondary to this distinction. One is the socially regulated self, which is more universal and cross-culturally accessible than the other, the inner self, which is a meaning-loaded self based on local culture and history. (Lebra, 1992) The term kosei clearly belongs in the inner self-sphere, as it is connected with local definitions and interpretations, but the problem is that because it is translated into 'individuality' it would seem at first glance to belong to a universally understandable self-sphere, which this special Japa-nese definition of individuality clearly does not, at least not in the Japanese interpretation.

Joy Hendry in an article on individualism and individuality emphasises:

...it is important to make a clear distinction between individualism, with its connotations of self-assertion and individual rights, and individuality, or the opportunity for an individual to develop his or her own particular talents or character. (Hendry 1992:56)

Hendry sees *individualism* as a strategy for survival in response to the increasing complexity of society, and *individuality* as existing in any society recognising individual differences and qualities. The latter would not necessarily presuppose the former. It follows then, that it is perfectly thinkable that a Japanese could possess individuality without being an individualist.

The emphasis on group life, for which Hendry traces the foundations back to early childhood, is thus not an obstacle to individuality in Japan. On the contrary, offering individual skills for the benefit of the group becomes an important part of group activities. Every group member can thus take advantage of the individual characteristics of the other members of the group. (Hendry 1992:60-1)

The role structure is supported by the traditional soto-uchi (outside-inside) distinction of public face and private self. Though the public face may be a rigidly defined role which has not been chosen by the individual, the fact that there exists this distinction makes it possible for the individual to have a completely different identity in the uchi/inside sphere, to be considerably more 'individual' than would be possible if the culture did not allow for this distinction. (Hendry 1992:63) Hence it would be wrong to say that the Japanese are incapable of being individualistic because of their rigid social customs. On the contrary, Hendry makes a case for saying that it is indeed *because* of the rigid social customs that a Japanese can sometimes be individualistic.

Brian Moeran explains the role of kosei-individuality in the traditional system of Japanese values by linking it to kokoro — 'heart' or 'mind'. Kokoro is one of the most popularly used words in advertising, in the press and when explaining the Japanese mind. It covers a wide range of aspects having to do with feelings, sensibilities, intimacy and spontaneous feeling (ninjoo, another traditional factor in the group model) and is an ingredient in what Harumi Befu has termed the 'social exchange model', a model based on the assumption that individual resources are exchanged for resources that he or she does not possess. The individual will maximise his opportunities by strategically allocating his resources. The social exchange model was created as an alternative to Nakane's group model, because the latter failed to account for behaviour going against group norms. (Befu 1980:179-80 in Moeran 1989:65)

Thus a concept seemingly alien to Japanese social structure such as individualism is transformed into individuality (kosei) and manifested as individual freedom of action within the bounds of the group, as described by Hendry and others, or as individual actions in a social exchange model, as described by Befu and Moeran.

An important characteristic of this particular brand of Japanese individuality is that it is not a threat to the established system, because it is firmly placed within the traditional social hierarchy. Though the concept of collective or interpersonal identity has often been criticised by Western-trained scholars, they also usually agree that Japanese conceptions of self are still embedded in interpersonal relationship (in the group model or the social exchange model), that growth toward individuality consists of aesthetic polishing toward a final unity of non-self, rather than individualism in a sense of essentialism and consistent identity. (Rosenberger 1992:13)

The interpretation of cultures by Western scholars ranges from relativist theories at one extreme, insisting on the uniqueness and the difference between cultures which would render any comparison useless, to a universalistic approach on the other extreme which tends to think that all things are really the same, that they are just different manifestations of the same basic human phenomena. The nihonjinron and much of the officially sponsored rhetoric on individuality in Japanese education is of the relativist persuasion, while the Japanese opposition's interpretation of individuality in education tends more towards the universalistic approach concentrating on universally applicable paroles such as peace on earth and human rights for children.

Reflecting these two completely different foundations the two main parties in the debate on individuality in Japanese education have argued heatedly against each other. Many problems arose from the choice of a word which signalled things which were never the intention. Though the government always used the Japanese term kosei, there was apparently no consensus as to what this term actually covered. The definitions made by people such as Joy Hendry, Harumi Befu and Brian Moeran apparently were not commonly accepted. Though both sides acknowledged that individuality had nothing to do with egotistic intentions it was clear that for the opposition kosei entailed individual choice of goals and freedom to act to a much greater extent than it did for the government.

Individuality as defined by the National Council on Educational Reform

The National Council on Educational Reform (NCER) was established in 1984 on the initiative of Prime Minister Nakasone Yasuhiro who had made educational reform one of the main topics of his preceeding election campaign.

The commisory of the NCER was to advise the Prime Minister on 'basic strategies for necessary reforms with regard to governmental policies and measures in various aspects, so as to secure such education as will be compatible with the social changes and cultural developments of our country'. (Rinkyooshin 1988:5)

Individuality was one of the things identified by NCER as a necessary requirement for future education in Japan.

Initially there was much discussion in NCER itself about how to express the idea of individuality properly in Japanese. It has consistently been translated into the English 'individuality', but in Japanese it was important to avoid expressions that would indicate any kind of egotism, which was difficult since this was what was very often associated with expressions denoting some kind of individuality or individual activities. In the beginning, NCER used the expression kosei shugi ('individualism'), but this was criticised at ensuing public hearings for smacking too much of ideology, probably because of the word shugi, which means something like '-ism' — indicating an inflexible approach to things — and it was further criticised for being too difficult to understand. (Interview with Minakami Tadashi, May 31, 1991)

So NCER changed its key expression to kosei no sonchoo ('respect for individuality') or kosei juushi ('attach importance to individuality'). The discussion on the respect for the individual was based on a broad idea of freedom or liberalisation (jiyuuka) in the educational system, which meant that the definition of individuality was actually much more broadly defined in Japanese usage than the English expression implied. NCER in an explanatory paragraph in its first report defined individuality as linked to the perception that 'each individual is a distinctive independent human being' and went on to say:

Individuality means not only the individuality of each person but also the individuality of each family, each school, each local community, each industrial firm, each nation, each culture etc. These individualities do not stand isolated from one another. Only those who really know their own individuality, develop it and fulfil their own responsibilities can fully respect and help develop the individuality of other people. (Rinkyooshin 1988:12)

Minakami Tadashi, a former NCER member, in an interview in May 1991 further elaborated on the relational character of this particular brand of Japanese individuality:

I believe the goal is the development of the individual's personality, not as an isolated individual but as an individual in a group. Man is a social being. If the personality is well developed, society, the country, the world will benefit.

The individual was firmly defined as existing within a group, within society, in the world. The main concern clearly was not with the individual as such but with its *relations* to other units of social organisation.
   Minakami further recollected that:

We [the NCER] did not think of the individual in particular. It was part of it, but we also emphasised that the families, the schools, Japanese culture, society and the country had to have their own peculiar characteristics. A very broad definition. (Interview with Minakami Tadashi, May 31, 1991)

Individuality was closely linked with freedom or liberalisation of education (jiyuuka), as was evident from the NCER report as well as from a remark made by Minakami, namely that 'freedom to make choices in education must be increased for the students, and this also goes for individuality. The schools have to change, to create a more varied curriculum — this is also what kosei juushi is about.'
   During their discussions NCER, according to Minakami, discussed several different 'freedoms'. For instance, was there to be freedom of method, freedom to choose whatever textbook one found to be best, freedom not to go to school at all? In the end NCER decided that doing away with standardisation and protecting the individual was to be considered real freedom. Teachers were to choose books and methods and be responsible for their choices, while staying inside the framework set up by the school boards. Only at university level could expressions of personal ideologies be tolerated, it was felt. Liberalisation and freedom of method and material apparently did not go well with basic education in NCER's view (Interview with Minakami Tadashi, May 31, 1991).
   The tendency to concentrate the efforts around liberalising schools and

structures rather than working on the way people judge and treat each other was evident. The emphasis was on institutional individuality from which individual individuality was expected to follow. As Professor Saitoo Taijun from University of the Air, a former employee of the Ministry of Education, saw NCER's attempts at individuality, they aimed at less control, a deregulation which would lead to more emphasis being placed on the individual. (Interview with Saitoo Taijun, May 17, 1991)

Freedom of choice and individuality were seen as possible by NCER only if schools were more differentiated in their offers. In a manner of speaking, students should, rather than choosing between different flavours of icecream, be given the choice between icecream and fruit. If schools became distinctly different, students would have a better background for choosing and for securing the perfect surroundings for the development of their individuality. (Interview with Minakami Tadashi, May 31, 1991)

In this way a close connection between conditions in education and society and the development of personality was established and this was part of the reasoning behind emphasising institutional individuality over individual individuality.

While analyzing the policies carried out under the heading 'respect for the individual', as well as the criticism of it, one should at all times keep the NCER definition of individuality in mind. At lot of problems arose from the fact that the interpretation of the word — whether it be 'individuality' or kosei juushi — differed considerably in NCER and in the groups who opposed to it. If the opposition expected kosei juushi to be primarily concerned with the individual, it was only to be expected that the measures taken by the government in this area would disappoint them.

The essence of the NCER individuality is institutional individuality and this was qualified later by a general director of the Ministry of Education, Satoo Jiroo, who, perhaps influenced by new reports issued by the NCER's follower 'Central Council on Education', stated that:

The task of Japanese education is to preserve quantity while enhancing quality - to adapt education to the different talents and needs of the individual. (Interview with Satoo Jiroo, June 6, 1991)

This adds a twist to institutional individuality — the institutions are to individualise their programs for the benefit of the individual, but evidently it is still the educational institutions which are the point of departure. In the call for adaptation to different talents we recognise the concept of diversification which has been on the agenda of the conservative government since the 1960's. Such ideas may well, as claimed by JTU, be a result of the desire to create elite education.

Why was more individuality necessary?

NCER's reason for emphasising individuality and putting it at the top of its priority list was the effect it was expected to have on a problem NCER had considered very seriously, namely the uniformity, rigidity and closedness of Japanese education, which were said to be 'deep-rooted defects' of the system. (Rinkyooshin 1988:278)

Minakami Tadashi, the former NCER member, saw two central problems in current Japanese education: lack of respect for children's personalities and lack of adjustment to society's evolution. These two factors he saw as causing most of the problems in education. (Interview with Minakami Tadashi, May 31, 1991) The problems mainly lay in lack of creativity and the so-called 'devastation' of education, the rising rates of truancy, violence and drop-outs. The conservative call for diversification originating in the 1960's had the same root: anticipation that the standardised educational system could not produce people who could be part of future development.

The proposed measure against the uniformity problem was the establishment in the educational system of such principles as dignity of the individual, respect for personality, freedom and self-discipline, and individual responsibility. Individualised educational institutions were also expected to be able to divert more students away from the traditionally much coveted universities:

certain Japanese universities — such as the universities of Tookyoo and Kyooto and Waseda for example — have too many applicants. They have long traditions and highly qualified teachers and students, which makes everyone crowd around these few universities and this makes the competition for entrance hard. But we have 500 universities. If every institution had distinctive characteristics I think this situation could get better. (Interview with Satoo Jiroo, June 6, 1991)

Reflecting on the history of Japanese education NCER pointed out that efficiency, continuity and stability had been emphasised in the educational system at the expense of respect for the individual and the fostering of free spirits. It went on to elaborate on the need to be able to cope 'flexibly with the social changes expected in the rest of this century and in the next', and emphasised that this necessitated the fostering of 'creativity, thinking ability and power of expression'. The purpose of it all was to produce 'more human resources with distinctive personality and creativity'. (Rinkyooshin,1988,278) Clearly, they were worried whether Japan would be able to turn out enough creative talent, whether Japan would be able to secure a vanguard position in global research and trade.

The close link between individuality and creativity and further on to manpower needs (human resources) in industry and research reflected the strong influence of the business world on NCER. The business world's requests for educational reform also ran along those lines of argument with statements like:

Creativity should be ranked as the most desirable qualification... The development of diversity, the antonym of uniformity, is hoped for in many areas in society. A combination of human resources each having a variety of unique characteristics is the source of strength for an enterprise, assuring flexibility in dealing with an uncertain future. (Keizai Dooyukai 1984:35)

The notion of individuality as something for the benefit of the individual and individual development was not absent from NCER's discourse, but it was not considered to be the core of the problem. Rather it seemed that NCER felt there was actually plenty of 'individual individuality', presumably in the sense of relational individuality kosei, as was clear from the following lines:' .. people's mental attitudes have been individualised and diversified, and their demand for freedom of choice have been increasing.' This development NCER wanted to support as 'a measure against standardisation in education', as they put it. (Rinkyooshin 1988:279) It would seem then, that NCER would like to have us believe that it was reacting on the impulse of popular demand, not on the impulse of worries over manpower supplies.

As NCER also proposed a review of contents and methods of teaching, educational structures and government policies in education, one can only assume that the lamented lack of creativity and power of expression was judged to be *caused* by the educational system, since NCER apparently saw no innate lack of individuality (kosei) in the people. The same belief in the beneficial effect deregulation and liberalisation in itself would have on education was aired by the business world.

The bottom line of it all, for NCER, apparently was that individuality was primarily a characteristic to be desired for developing society and industry and for staying among the economic superpowers. In the process the individual would of course be developed too, but this was not directly emphasised, and was never intended to be so, as Minakami pointed out. This influenced the measures taken in policy-making on the issue of individuality where the emphasis was on creating institutions of education with different characteristics.

Opposing views on individuality

In opposition to the idea of individualisation of institutions was the notion that individuality was primarily a question of free choice for the individual, along with less central control of the curriculum and the freedom to have and maintain different traits of character, according to the teacher organisation All Japan Teachers' Union (ATU). (Interview with Kawai Naoki, May 16, 1991)

The ATU (Zenkyoo in Japanese), when dealing with individuality, emphasised people's right to be different, to be given the chance of exploiting their particular strong points. Realising that at the bottom of the controversy with NCER were different interpretations of the expression 'individuality' (kosei), ATU explained that individuality in NCER terms was all about streaming and separation, that is, NCER was mainly concerned with providing elite and ordinary education, giving the not so clever pupils no more than elementary education. This claim they based on the NCER proposition of streaming in middle school and the emphasis on vocational secondary education, which in effect, they foresaw, would mean that less students would get academic high school education. (Interview with Kawai Naoki, May 16, 1991) Their claim was further supported by the likeness of the concept of 'individuality' to the already-mentioned conservative concept of 'diversification', which seemed to spell 'elitism'.

Individuality, for the teacher organisations, clearly implied, if not total abandonment of group activities, then at least a shift in emphasis away from them. Another teachers' union, the Japan Teachers' Union (JTU, Nikkyooso in Japanese), asserted that individuality certainly was part of the Japanese character, 'we just do not try to develop it in our education.' (Interview with Sakai Tomiko May 7, 1991) Further, the state of affairs in education was described by JTU as being characterised by too much irrelevant knowledge which had to be taught, by contempt for manual work and by a too rigid scale for evaluating people.

ATU, the more radical of the two teacher organisations, lived up to this label and went somewhat further away from the traditional emphasis on the group in its characterisation of individuality, claiming that 'every child has good and bad character traits and education must help them modify the bad traits.' Children should learn that people are not all alike - and indeed should not be — and that Man is not perfect but can be taught to emphasise his positive sides. How, ATU asked, can children possibly be expected to understand the diversity of Man if they themselves are treated alike? (Interview with Kawai Naoki May 16, 1991)

Both organisations agreed on the difficulties of treating a class of 40 to 45 students as individuals and on the danger of losing a substantial proportion of the class in the race for keeping up with the curriculum standards. In this connection ATU was particularly incensed by the efforts at streaming in middle school and the polarising effect this would have on the results of the middle school students.

In order to create real individuality, ATU asked for such measures as reducing class size to 20 pupils (it has only recently been reduced to 40) in order to make the individual more visible to the teacher in the class. If the teacher was unable to teach every child according to its abilities it would be impossible to instill in the children a sense of the value of each individual regardless of ability, ATU maintained. They saw it as the task of the adults, teachers and parents, to be good examples for the children, and the task of the government was to be only that of ensuring that the facilities would allow such behaviour. (Interview with Kawai Naoki, May 16, 1991).

In the guise of taking care of individual needs, ATU argued, the Ministry of Education just tried to separate the clever from the not so clever, and ensure that the latter would get only compulsory education and chose vocational careers at an earlier stage. Industrial needs as summed up by the ATU were as follows: 5 percent academics, 10 percent with intermediate education and the rest for peaceful obedient workers.

Though recognising that this was not actually spelled out in the NCER reports, ATU maintained that this was the hidden aim of the official efforts at individualisation in education, and they based this claim on the actual policies carried out after the NCER reports had been accepted as indicators of the course of the government's future educational policies.

Ideally, education should cater for the individual character traits of the child, not just be a means for separation and selection, and children should be taught to genuinely value the differences involved in individuality, not just see them as a means of selection, ATU felt. While for ATU teaching according to ability would be a means of helping all students reach the same level, the

NCER's version of teaching according to ability was criticised for being solely a means of selection and separation.

The Women's Democratic Council on Educational Reform (WDCER), an unofficial council consisting only of women, saw individuality in terms of human rights. Education in school should be conducted in such a way as to respect the human rights of every single child. This would include the child's right to be an individual with its own powers to grow and learn. As WDCER stated:

All children are individuals who cannot be compared with each other by one single standard. Education should be a common public enterprise, free of competition and bureaucracy, with children at the centre. It is wrong to think of education as something given by the state. (WDCER 1987:93)

WDCER was very concrete in its proposals for educational reform and one of its first and most urgent reform proposals was the abolition of the relative-standing evaluation system[2], which they felt did nothing but create losers as well as being unpedagogical and a mechanism prompting bullying. Also the naishinshoo, a secret report card to which students and their families have no access, which carries great importance at the time of high school admission, was attacked by WDCER as a source of discrimination. With the abolition of relative evaluation as well as the high school examination — the latter was also part of the WDCER proposal — the naishinshoo would be redundant. In the meantime WDCER suggested a new procedure for the preparation of the naishinshoo. In consequence only what they termed 'palpable reality' was to be evaluated and the secrecy of the evaluation was to be given up. (WDCER 1987:99)

Further proposals from WDCER were all equally concrete in their content, centring on securing the right to make choices, to file complaints and to change schools. Like ATU, WDCER also wanted class size to be reduced to 20-30 pupils to make more individualised and democratic teaching methods possible. As they said: 'With classes of 40 pupils it can only be done the hard way.' (Interview with Higuchi Keiko, June 27, 1991) WDCER clearly saw individuality as something closely related to the individual and not as a general feature applicable to institutions as well as persons, which was the way NCER had primarily defined it.

As mentioned earlier ATU was also inclined to interpret individuality more in terms of individual rights than as a general characteristic of persons and institutions. ATU chairman Mikami said on the subject:

We all have individuality (kosei), but not the kind of individuality that NCER deals with, which separates people into those who can and those who cannot. Our kind of individuality is the uniqueness of each and every human being. (....) Individuality is when you are loved by many people, not the way NCER has it. (Mikami 1989:34)

He further elaborated on this remark by pointing out that special traits of personality were often treated by the educational system as flaws to be corrected, rather than advantages inseparable from the personality. In Mikami's opinion the idea that there is one special foolproof recipe for getting particularly desirable results with children, the search for which he saw as lying behind many of the official reform attempts, was fallacious. Methods should be adapted to the needs of the individual child and should not be rigid regulations, he felt. (Mikami 1989:37)

More concretely ATU criticised the way they felt individuality was being hampered by the curriculum guidelines urging the teachers to introduce into the schools national(ist) symbols such as the Japanese flag and the Emperor song as well as to teach preschoolers to have a 'respectful heart'. This, in ATU's opinion, disregarded all concerns for the pupils' individual tastes and opinions as well as those of the teachers and the parents. (Zenkyoo 1990:17)

JTU, the other large teacher organisation, took the same side as ATU in this respect. The schools, in their opinion, were to be places where children could work according to their different interests, and schools were to provide a creative atmosphere where individuality (kosei) could prosper. (Nikkyooso 1991:9) They pointed out the flavour of commercial liberalism attached to NCER's use of the word freedom in education (jiyuuka), and the economic and materialistic connotations of this, and they doubted whether a 'liberalised' educational system would be able to secure social equality and equality of opportunities, because equality could not be expected to be profitable and hence it would not be interesting for private enterprisers.

Individuality, in JTU's view, was a thing which concerned the individual as such, just as ATU said, and while JTU definitely thought that individuality did exist innately in the Japanese, they accused such educational practises as rote learning and standing and walking in rows of making it bothersome for children to think for themselves and thus precluding manifestations of individuality. A recurrent theme for both teacher organisations consulted was the standardising effect Japanese education was seen to have on children. As the JTU representative put it, children were 'taught how to memorise, not how to think.' (Interview with Sakai Tomiko, May 7, 1991)

A grave concern for JTU was the effects streaming might have if it was effectuated in middle school as proposed by the Ministry of Education and NCER. Separating pupils according to ability would only aggravate the pressure of competition, they feared. On top of this the Ministry of Education introduced an even more compressed curriculum in 1989, while at the same time entertaining ideas of a five-day school week.

JTU was not opposed to the idea of a five-day week for schools, but without curriculum reductions it would have ominous consequences for the pupils, who would have even less time to learn the increasingly compressed curriculum, JTU maintained. Instead JTU wanted educational reforms to emphasise areas which could bring back elbowroom (yutori) in children's lives and be of use to them in the 21st century. Those were the universal things like peace, human rights, environment, development, training in the use and processing of information, in short what was needed to become world citizens and people capable of ruling themselves. They therefore saw Saturday as a day to be used for activities which would enhance the children's independence and autonomy. This meant that JTU discouraged school-club activities and cram school lessons on Saturdays and Sundays. (Nikkyooso 1991:3-4,18) So, while both the opposition and NCER were concerned with educating for the future, the central figure for the opposition was the individual whereas for NCER it seemed to be the national economy.

A common theme for most of the opposition was the fear that the liberalisation (jiyuuka) component of NCER's concept of individuality would mean privatisation of education. They were right to be afraid for the government made no secret of its desire for more private initiative, especially in elementary education. One of the major reasons for the worries of the opposition was that values such as equality of opportunity would be infinitely more difficult to uphold if part of the education was taken care of in private institutions where ulterior motives like money may matter more than they would in a publicly run system.

We here clearly see two different approaches to individuality. One is inspired by the traditional or official Japanese values of relational individuality, the other is based on a more 'Western' interpretation of the concept, putting the person at the centre, the individual in its own right, an individual existing as an entity in a system of social relations.

The use of the seemingly familiar word 'individuality' in the debate on Japanese educational reform has led to accusations not only from the Japanese opposition, who are aware of the difference in interpretations of the concept, but also from the West, where the Japanese are accused of saying things they do not mean. Whether this is attributed to enigmatic oriental behaviour or to the deviousness of the yellow race is largely a question of temperament and both interpretations are equally wrong.

The truth lies in the fact that the concept is re-defined for their special purposes by the official parties. It simply does not mean what we are accustomed to. This banal fact is muddled up by the fact that the opposition defines individuality much as we do in Western cultures. What we *can* derive from this is the realisation that the concept of individuality in Japanese education is infinite, open to interpretation, and not a finite concept. This is necessary knowledge if we want to understand the logic of action in the efforts at individualisation in Japanese education.

References

Dale, Peter (1990): *The Myth of Japanese Uniqueness*, London: Routledge.

Goodman, Roger (1990): *Japan's 'International' Youth*, Oxford: Clarendon Press.

Hendry, Joy (1989): 'An Interview with Chie Nakane' in *Current Anthropology*, 30, no.5, p. 643-9.

Hendry, Joy (1992): 'Individualism and Individuality: Entry into a Social World' in Goodman & Refsing (Eds) *Ideology and Practice in Modern Japan*, p. 55-71.

Higuchi, Keiko (1991): Critic, professor at Tookyoo Kasei Daigaku. Interview June 27.1991.

Kawai, Naoki (1991): Head of Department of Education and Culture, ATU (Zen Nippon Kyooshokuin Kumiai). Interview May 16, 1991.

Keizai Dooyukai (1984): 'A Proposition from Businessmen for Educational Reform' in Kawamura (ed.) *Discussions on Educational Reform in Japan*, p. 35-42.

Lebra, Takie Sugiyama (1992): 'Self in Japanese Culture' in Rosenberger (ed.) *Japanese Sense of Self*, p. 105-20.

Mikami, Mitsuru (1990): *Kyooiku ni Ai to Roman o*, Tookyoo: Kamogawa Shuppan.

Minakami, Tadashi (1991): Vice Managing Director, Museum of Edo-Tookyoo History. Interview May 31, 1991.

Minear, Richard H (1980): 'Orientalising the Study of Japan' *Journal of Asian Studies*, 39, no. 3, p. 507-17.

Moeran, Brian (1989): *Language and Popular Culture in Japan*, Manchester: Manchester University Press.

Mouer, R & Sugimoto Y (1986): *Images of Japanese Society*, London: KPI.

NCER (1985): *First Report on Educational Reform*. Government of Japan, Tookyoo.

Nikkyooso, (1991): *Kyooikukaikaku to shite no gakkoo istukasei*, Tookyoo.

Reischauer, E O (1990): *The Japanese Today - Change and Continuity*, Tookyoo: Tuttle.

Rinkyooshin, (Rinji Kyooiku Shingikai), (1988): *Kyooiku Kaikaku ni Kansuru Tooshin*, Tookyoo, Ookurashoo Insatsukyoku.

Rosenberger, Nancy R (ed.), (1992): *Japanese Sense of Self*, Cambridge: Cambridge University Press.

Saitoo, Taijun (1991): Professor, University of the Air. Interview May 17, 1991.

Sakai, Tomiko (1991): Head of Department for Education and Culture, JTU (Nihon Kyooshokuin Kumiai). Interview May 7, 1991.

Satoo, Jiroo (1991): Director General, Ministry of Education. Interview June 6, 1991.

WDCER (1987): *Oya no Kyooiku Sekinin wa 18sai Made*, Tookyoo.

Zenkyoo (1990): *Kodomo no Egao wa Watashi no Egao*, Tookyoo: Zenkyoo Fujinbu Hakkoo.

Notes

1. Nakane Chie, 1972. Human Relations in Japan, Ministry of Foreign Affairs, Tookyoo. Nakane's field of research is social anthropology and her work has mainly been about India, China and Tibet. She calls the group theory a by-product of her studies in India (Hendry, 1989, 645).
2. The relative standing evaluation system evaluates a student by comparison with the results of the rest of the class. A rank system is created in which there can be only one at the top.

The Discourse on Cultural Differences in Danish-Japanese marriages[1]

Kirsten Refsing

The fate of the earth depends on cross-cultural communication. Nations must reach agreements, and agreements are made by individual representatives of nations sitting down and talking to each other — public analogues of private conversations. The processes are the same, and so are the pitfalls. Only the possible consequences are more extreme. (Tannen, 1987:25)

Communication across cultures

An important ingredient in love relationships is the gradual revealing of oneself to one's partner. In endogamous marriages you reveal your personal tastes, sympathies and antipathies, small eccentricities, and details of the personal history of yourself, your family and your friends. The shared cultural background of the partners is intuitively and implicitly understood and accepted, even though the degree of attachment to that background may differ greatly between partners in an endogamous relationship.

In exogamous marriages you proceed to reveal the same things about yourself, but since in most cases your partner is ignorant of the broad cultural setting in which these qualities and experiences were acquired, every tiny revelation will either be accompanied by — or will in itself be perceived as — a general statement about culture and cultural history.

Cultural and national identity is negotiated and defined in a continuous dialogue with 'the other' — that which is different. Only in the confrontation with what you are not can you begin to perceive and verbalize what you are. Until that happens your cultural and national identity is more or less unconscious. Nowhere can the dialogue with 'the other' be more pervasive and relentless than in the cross-cultural marriage. In your mutual self-revelation no stone is left unturned in the exploration of cultural identity: one's own and that of the other. In order to reveal yourself to the foreigner you have come to love, you are forced to verbalize your 'unconscious culture'. As in all kinds of intercultural dialogue this easily becomes a dialectical process: what you are not defines what you are, and what you are defines what the other is not. Cultural opposites are easier to establish and understand than nuances, and especially the East-West cultural dialogue has been prone to easy definitions in terms of the dialectics of opposites.

Each cross-cultural partnership will have to explore its own definitions of the borderline between 'the cultural' and 'the personal'. If things go wrong and communication breaks down, the partners may agree — rightly or wrongly — that the blame should be attached to 'cultural differences'. Also, if one partner rejects a part of the other person's cultural heritage, it may well be perceived by that other person as a rejection of his or her personal identity, rather than of an aspect of the culture of origin.

The keen awareness on the part of the Japanese of being not only different from all other nationalities, but also generally misunderstood by the non-Japanese parts of the world, mirrors the widespread Western perception of Japan as 'oriental', exotic, and mysterious. The mutual expectations of problems with regard to understanding each other and communicating probably add to the difficulties experienced in cross-cultural marriages involving Japanese partners. Cultural explanations for intramarital problems are made readily available for such couples in all kinds of literature containing general descriptions of Japan and the Japanese. This paper will explore the discourse on Japanese-Danish cultural differences as it unfolds in interviews with cross-cultural couples living in Denmark.

Attitudes towards outmarriage

The generally positive attitude of the Japanese towards foreigners draws the line at marriage. Japanese parents rarely look upon a foreigner as a desirable marriage partner for their son or daughter. This may be partly a result of the xenophobia produced by Japan's long cultural isolation (1600-1853 and 1930-45), but it also has to do with the close-knit structure of Japanese society into which it is hard for a foreigner to fit. Foreigners in Japan are considered socially unstable, and if a Japanese chooses to marry such a person, 'love' has to be the only imaginable explanation, and 'love' alone is seen as a very flimsy basis for marriage in Japan. Traditionally marriage has been perceived as a practical arrangement in which two outwardly compatible persons with unambiguous role definitions enter into the socially well-defined project of establishing a family. In spite of the many changes that have taken place after

1945, this pragmatic view of marriage still holds a strong position. Of course adolescents (especially young girls) generally subscribe to a more romantic view of marriage, and also certain sectors of the media do their best to promote such a view, but when it comes to actually making serious decisions about marriage, romantic love is still considered a factor of secondary importance, if not an outright disturbing factor rendering otherwise sensible people momentarily incapacitated.

Although the view that love may influence the ability of people to make rational decisions is not unknown in Denmark, love is still seen as the central determinant for the establishment of marital bonds. Thus marriage may very well bring together partners of much less than optimal compatability, because love is supposed to 'conquer all', even language barriers and cultural differences. For a Dane, marriage to a foreigner is therefore not considered as something fundamentally different from marriage to a fellow Dane.

Marriage partners from the same linguistic, ethnic, cultural, and economical background are presumably well equipped to negotiate the terms of their shared lives, because the many things they already share can be left unsaid and unexplained. Divorce statistics show, however, that enough differences remain to make a large number of endogamous marriages fail. When, on top of the personal differences in endogamous marriages, the marital partners differ from the outset in race, culture, language, socialization, customs, religion, and lifestyle, the potential for conflict is multiplied enormously. Still, the difference in divorce rates between endogamous and exogamous marriages, e.g. in Denmark, is not as large as might be expected[2].

Japanese-Danish marriages

When the Japanese outmarry, the majority marry Koreans, Chinese, or Americans (Nitta, 1988), and when Danes outmarry, the preference is for other Europeans. The number of Japanese-Danish marriages is not large, less than ten such marriages are registered by the Danish authorities each year[3]. Danish men who marry a Japanese partner outnumber Danish women about two to one, and the number of divorces in proportion to the number of marriages is higher for marriages in which the woman is Danish and the man Japanese. The total numbers are too small to make this difference statistically significant, but it would not be too surprising if marriages between Danish men and Japanese women turned out to have a better chance of survival than marriages between Japanese men and Danish women. Traditional Japanese cultural virtues, such as reticence, circumspection, taciturnity, and *gaman* (endurance) are valued in both genders, but whereas, in the case of women, they reinforce the traditional female gender role of being quiet and unobtrusive, they may well be in conflict with some aspects of the traditional macho role of dominance and roughness. Contemporary Danish cultural values such as outspokenness, directness and honesty, on the contrary, fit well with the traditional gender role of men, but clash with that of women, which, as in Japan, is centered on mildness and holding back. So on the one hand we get a marriage between a Danish man and a Japanese woman, where both partners fit very well into the traditional male and female stereotypes of both cultures, and on the other a marriage between a Japanese man, who is too vague and feminine in the eyes of his Danish wife, and a Danish woman who is certainly too forward and domineering to suit the Japanese ideal of a wife[4].

The Danes and the Japanese who end up getting married to each other represent a varied segment of both populations, but a few common characteristics of such marriages may be discerned. Among the older generation we find a definite majority of marriages between Danish men and Japanese women, and many of these marriages came about as a result of the Danish man visiting Japan as a sailor or in connection with other kinds of work. In Japan he met a local girl, fell in love, and brought her back to Denmark. The background of the girl was often — but not always — lower class, and in some cases she was working in the world of entertainment or in a restaurant when she met her Danish husband. Younger Japanese people in Denmark tend to dismiss this whole generation of wives as *mizu shoobai*[5], but this image does not quite reflect reality. Some of the wives were ordinary middle class-girls who faced great opposition from their families when they decided to outmarry.

Among the older generation (age above 55) there are also a few cases of Japanese men who dropped out of university and went to Europe, where they ended up in Denmark in the late 1960's and stayed to enjoy the sexual freedom and the blonde girls, one of whom they eventually married. In general, mobility on the part of the male spouse seems to have been the rule — caused by work in the case of the Danish men, and adventure in the case of the Japanese men.

In the middle generation (age from 40 to 55) we find the same category of Japanese men, i.e. the discontented or adventurous youngsters who travel abroad, but there are also examples of more formalized types of 'study abroad' in this age group. Furthermore, female mobility is more pronounced,

and two of the Japanese wives among my interviewees in the middle generation were studying or working in Denmark when they met their Danish husbands[6]. They both give as a reason for staying on in Denmark that it is 'a
country where a woman can make it on her own'. In this way their giving up
Japan can be seen as parallel to the circumstances surrounding the Japanese
men in Denmark: Japanese society is seen as lacking in individual freedom
and as being too strictly controlled, with little possibility of making unortho-
dox choices for one's life.

Many of the Danes in this generation, male as well as female, went to
Japan as students on their own — i.e. not as part of any formal exchange
programme. In contrast to the sailors and other working men of the older
generation, the Japanese partners in these marriages mostly belong to the
middle or upper middle classes, and the marriages have generally had to
cope with stubborn opposition from the family of the Japanese partner.

In the younger generation (age under 40) 'study abroad' seems to have
been the dominant background for their marriages, either in the shape of
Danes studying in Japan or Japanese studying in Denmark. In my — so far
rather small — sample, the mobility appears to be shared equally between the
sexes. There is still a tendency, however, for the Japanese men I have
interviewed to be non-conformists, who leave Japan in the hope of avoiding
the *salariman* life style. A number of the Japanese men in all three generations
have had artistic ambitions, which could not unfold in Japan, and they have
started out as artists or artisans in Denmark. Some have made it, while others
have gotten by as dishwashers, Japanese restaurateurs or as interpreters and
tourist guides.

Conditions for the Japanese spouse in Denmark

The arrival of large numbers of foreign workers from Turkey, Pakistan and
Yugoslavia in the late 1960's and early 1970's presented the first real challenge
to the self-professed Danish tolerance in the post-war years. When unemployment figures went up, the foreign workers were blamed. The 1970's and 80's
have brought increasing numbers of refugees from faraway places, and the
enactment in the late 1970's of a law against making racist statements may be
a good indicator of how perceptions of foreigners had changed for the worse.

The Japanese, however, are perceived as 'good foreigners', and the general
image of Japan in Denmark is extremely positive — not least because
Denmark is one of the few countries that does not have serious trade frictions

with Japan. So the hostility towards foreigners rarely touches the Japanese. A few may have had the unpleasant experience of being mistaken for people from Denmark's former 'colony', Greenland, which means that they have been overlooked in shops or treated like retarded children. One elderly Japanese woman told me that she never carried bottles in a shopping bag without wrapping them first to prevent them from clinking, because she was afraid that she would be mistaken for an alcoholic Greenlander.

Generally a Japanese spouse is also received well in the Danish partner's family and circle of friends. Based on a widespread perception of romantic love as the best possible basis for marriage, marriage to a foreigner from the exotic East is seen as the apogee of romance. As one Danish husband put it:

People ask me where we met, whether I have been a sailor or been travelling around... It is as if they want to connect it to something exotic about having met in a wonderful place. They feel quite let down when they hear that we met in an ordinary restaurant... (Danish man in his early 40's)

But even though 'good foreigners' are treated with kindness in Denmark, they still may have a great deal of trouble fitting in. For a woman, being a housewife is no longer really an option in Denmark. Women are expected to work (or at least to draw unemployment benefit if they cannot find work), so both Japanese men and Japanese women who marry Danes and come to live in Denmark will have to learn Danish and to find a job. To a Japanese who has struggled in vain with English in school and has no specific interest in studying languages, learning Danish is an almost insurmountable barrier, and many never really get beyond the basics. This, of course, is a great handicap in the labor market, and even well-educated Japanese never get to use their education in Denmark, but stay in low-paid jobs where the language requirements are minimal. Of the Japanese among my informants so far, only two women have had what you might call 'ordinary Danish jobs'. One is a nursing assistant and the other a social worker. Two men are independent artists, but the rest are all employed in jobs where being Japanese is one of the main qualifications. Since job openings of this kind are not numerous there is an intense competition among the Japanese in Copenhagen for such jobs, and this again leads to a great deal of mutual slander and backbiting. Newcomers easily become victims of the widespread belief among Danes that 'there must be a need for people who can speak Japanese', so that instead of aiming for a competence that will eventually enable them to find a job on an equal footing with Danes, they keep trying to get by as part-time conversation teachers, tourist guides, waitresses in Japanese restaurants, salespersons in the big hotels in the summertime, etc.,etc. — in short, trying to make a living out of being born Japanese[7]. Of course, the inability of the immigrant Japanese spouses to find and fit into 'ordinary' jobs also reflects the intolerance of the Danes towards non-fluent speakers of Danish.

The psychological problems involved in adapting yourself to life in a foreign country are considerable. As I have already pointed out, few of my informants have met with anything but friendly acceptance, but some complained that this easy acceptance of them as 'just people' felt like a put-down. One woman said:

I wonder why the Danes have so little curiosity. They meet me and they know that I come from Japan, but they never ask me anything about myself or my background. It is as if I did not exist before I came here. (Japanese woman in her mid 50's)

The need to establish a new identity, because the old one does not count anymore, was mentioned by several informants as a problem they have had to overcome in various ways. To some it had meant a bad crisis, where they almost deserted their marriage and went back to Japan. Others had found comfort in Japanese friends in Denmark, or in going back to Japan for a short period to gather strength.

Under Danish law, foreigners with a permanent residence permit are eligible and can vote in local elections. Very few of my informants had ever exercised that right, and many were not even aware of its existence. There are no English-language dailies in Denmark, and because of the lack of competence in Danish many — especially in the older generation of women — have simply given up all interest in the world beyond their immediate family and friends. The men and the younger women circulate Japanese magazines, books, and newspapers among themselves, but since Denmark is rarely mentioned in the Japanese news, they remain unaware of the issues around them. Thus the Japanese spouses are generally characterized by a low degree of awareness of and participation in local issues, even after living in Denmark for decades.

Different religions of the spouses is often a major problem in cross-cultural marriages. Most Japanese are Buddhist and/or Shintoo believers, whereas Denmark has the Protestant variety of Christianity as its state religion. However, the majority of Danes are secularized to a degree where they almost never set foot in a church, and, although religion is very visible in Japanese society, the Japanese in general are very relaxed and tolerant towards different faiths. With one exception, all the couples I have spoken to have been married in a civil ceremony, and religion is not even remotely an area of conflict in their relationship. If religion enters into the picture at all, it is because both spouses have joined the same religion — be it a variety of Christianity or a variety of Buddhism — so when religion is a strong ingredient in the marriage, it works as a factor to keep the marriage together rather than the opposite.

Cultural differences

Some of my interview questions are designed to elicit responses concerning cultural differences between Japan and Denmark in general. Of course statements on this topic are often volunteered as well. In other questions I explore how these differences are perceived and dealt with in the relationship between the spouses. In general my informants see a lot of differences between Denmark and Japan and between Danes and Japanese, but in most cases they perceive of themselves as more or less unaffected by these differences. In the following I shall briefly present some of the differences most commonly pointed to, and after that I shall describe how the couples view their own relationship vis-à-vis these differences.

Society, Family and Gender Roles

In the Japanese media, Danish society is generally presented as a paradigm for social welfare, and many Japanese come to Denmark each year to study facilities for the elderly or for disabled persons. A few of my Japanese informants mention the high level of social welfare as a plus on the side of Denmark, but most focus on the many social problems and the lack of family cohesion as a contrast to Japan. In this their Danish spouses heartily agree. Among the social problems pointed to are drug abuse, crime, destroying public property, the abundance of single mothers, and the fact that people openly drink beer on the street. As one young Japanese wife put it:

I cannot understand why people destroy public property — telephone booths or parks. I think it is because everybody drinks alcohol over the weekend. I also don't like them urinating in the streets. Of course you may see that in Japan as well... But destroying things — that is disgusting. I don't drink alcohol myself, so when I see people in the street drinking from early morning I really feel uncomfortable. (Japanese woman in her early 30's)

Her husband chimes in:

You see, as a Dane it is quite normal to eat sausages and drink beer in public, but actually it annoys me to see especially a couple with a child between them come walking, each with a strong beer in one hand and the child in the other. I don't think that is right. Whether it is the influence I have received from Japan or just my petit-bourgeois morals, I don't know. (Danish man in his early 30's)

The informal dress codes of Denmark are also commented upon by many Japanese informants. One elderly Japanese wife describes her feelings the first time she had to go to a bank:

From Japan I was used to bank employees wearing uniforms, but here they wore blue jeans and old, worn shirts. And then they came up to serve me, and I just could not believe that they were bank employees. I was thunderstruck. (Japanese woman in her early 60's)

In contrast to Denmark, Japan is seen as a safe country with a low crime rate, a great deal of conformity and with tight and warm family and neighbour relations, which alleviate the need for social welfare. Among the older couples there is a tendency to idealize the three-generation family — one Danish man in his 60's even goes so far as to say that the presence of wise old grandmothers in the family prevents psychiatric problems among the family members. The younger generation is more aware of the potential problems involved in cohabitation with aged parents, but some of the young Japanese men still saw it as their responsibility to take care of their parents in old age, and they said that they would have to think carefully about going back — with or without their wives — should the need arise. Many stress that Japanese families have stronger ties to their roots and traditions, and that they are better at having a good time together. One young Danish wife puts it like this:

In Japan you care more about the old people, and you have duties towards your family. Here we have become totally free of duties, haven't we. I sometimes think that the Japanese have more fun. By having a culture where you always try to do your best, they also do their best to have fun. I find that a very positive trait. We

Danes have a disadvantage in this area. We can have fun spontaneously, but we may also end up being bored to death, and mostly it is our own fault. The Japanese seem to just decide to have fun, and then they have fun. They work hard at their social life, and I find that incredibly charming. They simply do not let you sit and brood — they work at it. (Danish woman in her early 30's)

The only aspect of Japanese family life which receives negative comment is the role of women. The woman in the family is seen as subordinate, isolated from the world, and dependent. This is stressed as one of the most negative things about Japan by both Danish and Japanese women of the younger generation. Danish women (and a few of the younger Japanese husbands) also mention that they perceive young Japanese women as incredibly childish and giggling all the time.

I think there is a fundamental difference between Japanese and Danish women. I wouldn't say that they are suppressed, but the overall pattern is so different. In the beginning I got very annoyed — e.g. the first time I visited Japan and saw women of my own age starting to giggle uninhibitedly because of something. And their movements — like they were all in knots. I do not think that it is because they are suppressed. Rather it is a cultural pattern which they are comfortable with. But I wouldn't be comfortable if I had to behave like that. (Danish woman in her early 30's)

The younger generation of Japanese and Danish men mostly keep silent on the subject of women's position, but older Danish men do not hesitate to revel in their good luck in marrying an oriental woman and thus not having to contend with a selfish, independent, and outspoken Danish wife. One of the sailor husbands of the 1960's says:

I think Japanese women know more about being a woman. Really. Danish women are more independent. They demand that their husbands do half of the housework. What kind of a marriage is that? I have never had that problem. (Danish man in his early 60's)

Work, Education, and Child Upbringing

In general the Danes are perceived as a laid-back people in contrast to the hard-working Japanese. A young Japanese husband says:

Now, I happen to be Japanese, so no matter what I do, the Japanese trait of putting work before everything else will come through. I try not to behave like that. I don't want to live for my work only or to have work as my highest goal in life. I can feel that because I am Japanese I easily fall into the trap of behaving in a very Japanese way. I prefer the Danish attitude, it is easier to live with, and I like it better than the Japanese. (Japanese man in his early 30's)

However, some Japanese women, who work with Danish colleagues every day, stress that they do not find individual Danes lazy at all. Instead they point out that Danes keep a much clearer segregation between work and leisure. One of them, a social worker, says:

I think the Danes work very hard. At least where I work. They are conscientious, and many of them are actually workhorses. Some of them even more than me, although they are the Danes and I am the Japanese. (Japanese woman in her mid 50's)

Another, who works in a hospital, says:

The difference between the Danes and the Japanese is that Danes work hard when they work, and in their free time they really relax. There is a clear segregation, and I really like that. (Japanese woman in her early 40's)

Another factor contributing to the relaxed feeling in the work place is the absence of authoritarianism. Bosses and ordinary workers are perceived as equal in the way they socialize, and human relations in general are seen as much less complicated and bothersome than in status-conscious Japan. This is pointed to as a good thing by most Japanese, men as well as women, but for some it is also very difficult to get used to. The social worker says:

It has to do with respect for authority. Respect for other people. This can be both good and bad. I really like that there isn't so much fuss about authority in Denmark. You call the boss by his first name. But some times it goes too far and becomes embarrassing. Anyway I have difficulty in doing it myself, and that makes me feel embarrassed. (Japanese woman in her mid 50's)

One of the younger Japanese wives has similar difficulties. She says:

In Denmark you express your own opinion — this is actually quite difficult for me to do, but I think it is a good thing. Denmark is not authoritarian. In Japan you must speak politely to older people and to teachers and such, and that may be very well, but on the other hand it is used in an authoritarian way. (Japanese woman in her late 20's)

Furthermore, the Japanese are seen as perfectionist and concerned with details, whereas the Danes supposedly pay less attention to detail and are more relaxed about results. A Japanese man expresses this as follows:

They succeed in the larger things, but many small things go wrong. That is typically Danish. I am Japanese, and according to Japanese thinking you cannot allow such small mistakes. (Japanese man in his early 40's)

To those of my informants who have children, their upbringing and education is a matter of great concern. Of course there is the question of language: Should they be taught Japanese and if so, how? This matter aside, there are also great differences in how children are viewed and brought up in the two countries. Most mothers say that they give little thought to whether they employ Danish or Japanese principles in the way they interact with their children. However, among the Danish wives there are two who work in kindergartens and one who is writing her Master's thesis on Japanese child-care, and they of course are more aware of the contrasts between Denmark and Japan in this area. They all speak highly of the close bonds between mother and child in Japan, but at the same time they all believe that it is important to confront the child directly when the child is misbehaving. One Danish mother puts it as follows:

I know that one tries to avoid conflicts with children in Japan. I find that hard to emulate, and I don't really know if I agree with doing that. I don't think I do. I think children should know when they have entered an area where I disagree, and where I don't want them to do something. I don't mind having conflicts with my children. I don't know if it is bad to avoid conflicts, but I can feel that to me it would be artificial. Setting up clear borderlines for the children is something which is deeply ingrained in me — to say 'No!' or 'Stop! You must not do that!' And saying that will of course bring about a conflict... (Danish woman in her early 40's)

The Japanese husbands rarely take an active part in the upbringing of their children, and if they do, they generally agree with the Danish mother. The Japanese mothers usually get more active participation from the Danish fathers of their children, and mostly they express appreciation of the rather 'free' Danish way of bringing up children as opposed to what they see as spoiling the child in Japan. Danish kindergartens and schools are also seen by all as 'free' and as places where the child can unfold his or her special abilities in a supportive environment. Still, some express a wish to have Danish schools approach the Japanese school system a little bit in matters such as discipline and respect for teachers. One Danish mother says:

I think it is an excellent thing to have respect for teachers. We lack that a little here in Denmark, where it becomes difficult to teach the children because there is no respect. (Danish woman in her early 40's)

A Japanese mother worries that Danish schools are so preoccupied with equality and with helping the slower children to get ahead that they end up holding the brighter children back, and her husband comments:

With regard to education I think that we have a much too lax attitude here in Denmark. I am not saying that the Japanese system is something to aim for — I have the impression that all they do is cramming a lot of knowledge into their heads, and they don't learn to use any of it. Take English: They study it for years, and you cannot exchange a sentence with them. At least the Danish system teaches you to use what you have learned, and it teaches you the independence needed to dare to make a mistake. In Japan you shut up rather than say something wrong. But the Danish system is too soft. Like you have to look up in your calender whether it is two weeks from now or only one until your child has homework again. That's too soft. A little Japanese discipline would go a long way. (Danish man in his mid 40's)

Personality Traits and Communicative Styles
As for personality traits, all my informants evaluate Danish independence and strong personal opinions as positive in opposition to Japanese reticence in expressing personal preferences. The Japanese are seen as vague, indirect, closed, and silent, whereas Danes are described as open, direct, clear, out-spoken, and talkative. A Danish husband put it this way:

I often say that the Japanese are chameleons. That's simply what they are. My wife always adjusts to the surroundings she is in. (Danish man in his early 30's)

And his wife adds:

The biggest difference between Danes and Japanese is that a Dane will say things right out where a Japanese will think, 'If I say that it will be too bad for that person'. We watch out, but in my experience the Danes are rather direct. It was difficult until I got used to it. But once you get used to it, it is actually easier to deal with. You clearly understand what is on a person's mind, whereas in Japan people will say something that sounds as if they agree with you, and you don't have the faintest idea what they are really thinking inside. Of course you may be shocked when people come right out and say something bad to you, but when you get used to it, you find that many things are easier that way. (Japanese woman in her late 20's)

This discrepancy in communicative styles may present some problems. One elderly Japanese wife said:

If you look at it from a purely Japanese point of view, people in this country are very outspoken. The Japanese are more vague — they do not answer clearly yes or no. This can lead to mutual annoyance. The Dane will think, 'What's the matter with her? Why can she never give a clear answer?' But the Japanese will think, 'Why must he always blurt out everything like that?' (Japanese woman in her late 50's)

However, the reverse side of the Danish outspokenness is seen as a lack of empathy and consideration for others, especially by some of the Danes themselves. One young Danish man said:

The Japanese are very considerate, and I like that a lot actually. Nobody acts in silly ways — like if you were living in this apartment you wouldn't dream of wearing wooden clogs, because it would disturb the downstairs neighbours. Well, this isn't obvious to a lot of Danes. Of course being considerate puts some restrictions on what you can do, but I think that it is a nice thing anyway. (Danish man in his early 30's)

Some Japanese pointed out that the Danes have trouble apologizing even when they know that they are in the wrong — instead they belligerently try to defend themselves. Many also viewed Danes as smug, egotistical, and self-sufficient, and therefore sadly lacking in curiosity as expressed by an older Japanese wife:

Sometimes I get angry about the Danish selfrighteousness and lack of curiosity. If you see something strange in the street, the Danes just walk by and never waste a glance. And when I meet a Dane for the first time, he never asks me anything. I feel as if I, too, have blond hair and blue eyes! Well, maybe they just accept me, or maybe they ignore that I am different, or maybe they are embarrassed to ask — but anyway, I believe that it is simply their lack of curiosity for new things. The Japanese aren't afraid of new things, they love them. And they include them in the Japanese culture and mix it in a Japanese way. That is what we have been doing all through history. I think there is a lot of energy in this feature of the Japanese. But here in Denmark people are afraid of foreign things, and everything changes very slowly. In Japan everything changes quickly. It is the Japanese curiosity in the face of everything new. New toys. (Japanese woman in her mid 50's)

Furthermore, Danes are seen as confrontational, whereas Japanese supposedly avoid conflict wherever possible. Mostly this is evaluated as a positive side of Danish culture. In the words of one Japanese man:

Danes sometimes get very excited. In the eyes of a Japanese they put themselves in a rather unbecoming position. But after all you reach a solution much quicker that way. We Japanese do not get excited, we do not say what we think, so you always have to guess what people actually mean. In Japanese culture you say things with few words and you get few words back. So you have to be clever at guessing the rest. Danish culture is about getting out your message as clearly and simply as possible. (Japanese man in his early 40's)

Many informants complain about what they see as a unique and particularly disgusting type of Danish humour, namely irony. One Japanese wife described how a visiting Japanese friend of hers had helped wrap a parcel to Japan. This was done very carefully with lots of knots in the right places, and when her Danish husband saw the result, he whistled and said, 'Is that the best you could do?' This was his way of saying that he was impressed, but both the wife and her friend took his words at face value and were laughed at accordingly. Another Japanese wife said:

Danes in general use ironical expressions a lot, and I hate it. When my children started to do that I became really crazy and mad. I tell them not to do it — they should say directly what they mean. But how can I make them do that, when my husband keeps using irony. (Japanese wife in her mid 50's)

The above are just a few examples from the topics most often touched upon in the discourse on cultural differences. Many more might have been presented, but these will suffice to give a general impression of the themes and comments which come up in connection with questions about 'what Danes and Japanese are like', respectively.

The role of cultural differences in the cross-cultural marriage

The statements made by my informants on Danish and Japanese cultural differences reflect many of the common assumptions about 'Japan versus the West'. Besides being based on their own observations, their comments must be assumed to be influenced by an on-going discourse in the milieu in which they live. Probably their statements are characterized by having been said and discussed many times in the company of other people in similar situations, Danish-Japanese friends, other compatriots visiting Denmark, etc. In order to investigate (among other things) to what degree my informants are influenced in their judgment by sources other than their own observations, I ask them all to fill in a questionnaire prepared by Harumi Befu and Kazufumi Manabe for use in their investigation on the extent to which *Nihonjinron*[8] myths are accepted among the Japanese (Befu and Manabe, 1987). For the Danish informants, I have translated the questionnaire into Danish, and the questions are changed so that they are about 'Danishness' instead. When all the questionnaires have come in, the answers will be analysed in cooperation with Befu and Manabe, so at this point it is too early to say anything about what they will show.

I furthermore use an adapted version of the 'role description checklist' presented by Dean C. Barnlund in an article from 1974 entitled 'The Public Self and the Private Self in Japan and the United States' (Barnlund, 1974)[9]. Barnlund uses this list to draw up a cultural profile of Japanese and Americans respectively, based upon a list of 34 adjectives distributed to 240 college students evenly divided between males and females, American and Japanese. The students were asked to check those terms which they felt best described the properties of Japanese and Americans. Thus it became both a description of oneself and of the other. Not surprisingly the Japanese scored high on qualities such as 'reserved, formal, silent, cautious, evasive, and serious', whereas the Americans scored high on 'self assertive, spontaneous, informal, talkative, humorous and frank' (Barnlund, 1974:52ff). When giving the list to my informants I ask them to check the qualities which they think describe their partner well, and on another list to check the qualities which they think describe themselves well. With the results from these questionnaires I intend to draw up a cultural profile of Japanese and Danes as seen by themselves and another as seen by their spouses. I furthermore divide the profiles according to gender. Eventually I shall compare the resulting profiles with the profiles resulting from Barnlund's analysis to see whether there are significant differences. The analysis is being done as the questionnaires come in, but as the number is still rather limited, no definite conclusions can be drawn yet. I shall just mention one rather interesting detail: Of the six Danish wives interviewed, four have put down 'talkative' as one of the features they think describe their Japanese husbands well. This does not fit with Barnlund's results, and it certainly does not fit the traditional image of Japanese men, as in the *Otoko wa damatte — Sapporo biiru* of the famous TV commercial featuring film actor Mifune Toshiro...[10]

Although the majority of my informants are convinced that cultural differences between Danes and Japanese are both numerous and significant, very few will say that cultural differences are a problem — or even an issue — in their own marriage, at least not as long as they are still married. In her book, *Interkulturelle Lebenswelten: Deutsch-japanische Ehen in Japan*, Irene Hardach-Pinke asserts that unhappy intermarriers are more apt to ascribe their problems to culture than people who are happily married. She says:

Glück wurde meist den Persönlichkeiten zugeschrieben, Unglück aber den kulturellen Unterschieden angelastet. (Hardach-Pinke, 1988:167)

My interviews with divorcees so far show no definite confirmation of Hardach-Pinke's assertion yet. But for people who are still married, cultural differences are clearly seen as a poor excuse for not making the marriage work. In the words of a young Japanese wife:

It's better if you do not think too much about each other as Danish and Japanese respectively. Danes are not all alike either. Rather you should think that your husband is such and such a person, and that is why he is like that. And I shouldn't explain my own behaviour by my being Japanese, but by my being me — such and such a person. Otherwise it easily turns into a war between nations. (Japanese woman in her late 20's)

And her husband adds:

There are differences all the time, and we all have that, but you shouldn't ascribe them to nationality. That is a way of disclaiming responsibility. There are no two couples alike, not Danish couples either. But it is so easy to say, 'That strangeness, that's because you are Japanese', or, 'You're acting silly, that's because you are Danish'. I think we have reached the point where my wife is simply my wife, and that's just the way she is. Of course there is something Japanese in it, but it is also because she is who she is. And I act the way I do because I am me. (Danish man in his early 30's)

A Japanese wife of the older generation says:

If problems arise I think it would be like running away if you explain them by our being from two different cultures, or if you say that it is because we are too different. It is a kind of escape. (Japanese woman in her mid 50's)

And her husband adds:

It is just too easy. (Danish man in his mid 50's)

Many Danes take pride in stressing that they are 'very Japanese', as may be seen from the following quotes from Danish wives:

I think I have adjusted well to say the least. After all it would be a pity for my husband if I had been a typical Danish wife. (Danish woman in her late 20's)

I think I am very much like a Japanese — I try not to be in the way and I wait politely for the master of the house to finish what he is doing, you know... (Danish woman in her late 30's)

A Danish husband of the older generation was telling me how his wife's friend had said to her that she had an easy time because her husband was indistinguishable from a Japanese husband, and his wife added:

I don't think he has any typical Danish traits at all. He is almost completely like a Japanese husband. He has gotten so used to it that the Danish part of him couldn't hang on. In the beginning he was different — considerate in a totally different way. He used to be so considerate that you would wonder whether he was really a man. (Japanese woman in her early 60's)

Interestingly enough the Japanese spouses never describe themselves as being 'very Danish' but rather as being 'un-Japanese'. This bias of everybody relating themselves to Japanese culture rather than to Danish culture is probably significant and may be interpreted as a sign of people's awareness of Japanese culture as a more clearly defined entity than Danish culture.

Final Remarks

The present project is not about how things are, but about how they are perceived and discussed by the people involved. Human beings do not become miniature editions of the cultures they grow up in even though popular opinion tends to define them as such. Perhaps this is what is reflected in the discourse in Japanese-Danish marriages on 'cultural differences': As long as the discourse deals with the abstract entities, 'Danes' and 'Japanese', the existence of cultural differences (and opposites) is readily acknowledged and propagated, but when the discourse turns to the concrete reality of the spouses themselves, cultural differences become reduced to a minor factor of no serious consequence for their relationship.

References

Barnlund, Dean C. C. (1974) 'The Public Self and the Private Self in Japan and the United States' in: Condon, C. & M. Saitoo (eds.) (1974) *Intercultural Encounters with Japan*, Tokyo: Simul Press.

Befu, Harumi (1987) *Ideorogii to shite no Nihon Bunkaron* [Cultural Theories of Japan as Ideology], Tokyo: Shisoo no kagaku.

Befu, Harumi and Kazufumi Manabe (1987) 'An Empirical Study of Nihonjinron: How the Myth' in: *Kwansei Gakuin University Annual Studies*, Vol. XXXIV, p. 97-111.

Hardach-Pinke, Irene (1988) *Interkulturelle Lebenswelten — Deutsch-Japanische Ehen in Japan*, Frankfurt: Campus.

Kokusai kekkon handobukku. Gaikokujin to kekkon shitara... (Handbook of International Marriages. If One Marries a Foreigner...) (1987), comp. by Kokusai kekkon o kangaeru kai, Tokyo: Meiseki shoten.

Mayer, Egon (1985) *Love and Tradition. Marriage between Jews and Christians*, New York: Plenum Press.

Mouer, Ross and Yoshio Sugimoto (1981) *Japanese Society: Stereotypes and Realities*, Melbourne: Japanese Studies Centre.

Nitta, Fumiteru (1988) 'Kokusai kekkon: Trends in Intercultural Marriage in Japan', *International Journal of Intercultural Relations*, 12, 205-32.

Oosawa, Chikako (1989) *Bairingaru Fuamirii — kokusai kekkon no tsumatachi* [Bilingual Family — the Wives of International Marriages], Tokyo: Chikuma shobo.

Refsing, Kirsten (1990a) 'Kæreste, hustru, moder' (Girlfriend, Wife, Mother), in: *Gode hustruer og vise mødre, facetter af kvindeliv i Japan* [Good Wives and Wise Mothers, Aspects of Female Life in Japan], Copenhagen: Rhodos, 116-33.

Setouchi, Harumi (ed.) (1989) *Kokusai kekkon no reimei. Jinbutsu kindai josei-shi* [The Dawn of International Marriages. Biographical History of Women in the Modern Period], Tokyo: Kodansha.

Tannen, Deborah (1987) *That's Not What I Meant*, New York: Ballantine.

Notes

1. This paper presents some preliminary results from my research project on intercultural communication in cross-cultural marriages between Japanese and Danes. The study is based on a series of semi-structured interviews with Japanese-Danish couples living in Denmark.

2. Endogamous Danish marriages: For each 100 marriages, 50 are dissolved. Marriages between Danish men and foreign women: For each 100 marriages, 52 are dissolved. Marriages between Danish women and foreign men: For each 100 marriages, 60 are dissolved (Abildgård:1991:24).

3. 1977: 10 (3), 1978: 7 (3), 1979: 7 (0), 1980: 10 (6), 1981: 10 (5), 1982: 4 (6), 1983: 4 (3), 1984: 4 (6), 1985: 4 (4), 1986: 6 (4), 1987: 4 (10), 1988: 6 (5), 1989: 4 (6), 1990: 5 (7), 1991: 9 (1). The numbers in brackets indicate the registered number of Danish-Japanese divorces of the same year.

4. I have dealt with this aspect of Japanese-Danish marriages in a paper entitled 'Gender Identity and Gender Role Patterns in Japanese-Danish Cross-cultural Marriages', which will be forthcoming in a conference volume from the Instituto Cultural de Macau.

5. The 'water trade': bars, entertainment, prostitution, etc.

6. The choice of Denmark rather than any other Western country has in quite a number of cases been decided by the possibility of attending one particular folk high school, namely 'The International High School' in Elsinore, which each year takes in a large number of Japanese students. If this school had not existed, the number of Danish-Japanese marriages might well have been considerably lower...

7. It should be noted in this connection that very few of the Japanese I have spoken to have elected to become Danish citizens even though they have been eligible for Danish citizenship for many years.

8. 'Theories of Japaneseness' — a rather nationalistically tinged, semi-scholarly discourse about what constitutes the professed uniqueness of the Japanese.

9. In: *Intercultural Encounters with Japan* (1974) Ed. by J. C. Condon and M. Saito, Tokyo: The Simul Press, p. 27-96. Later this article was elaborated into a book by Dean C. Barnlund entitled *The Public and the Private Self in Japan and the United States*.

10. 'Men keep silent — Sapporo Beer'.

'We are all Naxi in our hearts': Ethnic Consciousness among Intellectual Naxi[1]

Mette Halskov Hansen

Today we will take the initiative to control the progress of Naxi culture. We will create a new type of culture which roots in tradition but is on a higher level, which both contains our rich national characteristics as well as the spirit of this age. (The Society of Naxi Culture in Kunming, Guo Dalie, 1987: 24)

In recent years there has been a marked tendency among a number of China's minority nationalities to resume and revitalize religious and other cultural practices and customs. Ethnic consciousness, identity that focuses on ethnic affiliation, has in many cases assumed a rather dominant position over the other relational identities available (like gender, class, etc.). Several factors have, to various extent and in different local configurations, played a part in this process: international events like the break-up of the former Soviet Union, the more tolerant Chinese policy towards expressions of ethnic identity since the end of the 1970s, the general process of modernization of Chinese society, increased cross-border trade, promotion of tourism in minority regions, etc.

As the above quote clearly shows, members of the small Naxi minority in Southwest China have become spokesmen for a conscious formation of an ethnic identity: a Naxi identity, which would ideally encompass all individuals officially classified as Naxi, and thus consolidate and strengthen the Naxi as a communal, cultural group within the Chinese state. This essay, focusing on the Naxi's own perceptions of 'Naxiness', attempts to show how this project is formulated and worked out by intellectual Naxi in Kunming today.

During a five month stay at the Yunnan Nationalities Institute (from now: the Minority Institute) in Kunming, the capital of Yunnan province, in 1991, I conducted a study into the ethnic identity of members of especially the intellectual stratum of the Naxi minority.[2] Researchers of ethnicity in other areas of the world have pointed to the fact that it is often the educated members of an ethnic group who become the foremost spokesmen for a renewed ethnic consciousness and mobilisation.[3] From earlier visits[4] to Naxi areas and Kunming it was my clear impression that this was in fact the case concerning the Naxi minority. The Naxi who want to get an education have to leave their local villages and go to the city, in most cases Kunming, where approximately 4000 Naxi reside. These Naxi live away from their native area in Han Chinese surroundings where they, nevertheless, tend to stick together. They receive a long education based exclusively on the culture of the majority Han. They experience a contradiction between their affiliation with an ethnic group mainly comprised of peasants and their own position as intellectual Naxi in Chinese society. They are often actively engaged in central as well as local politics. I knew that a number of intellectual Naxi were deeply engaged in what they call 'traditional Naxi-culture' and that they were actively pursuing a self-definition as Naxi, seeking to define a distinctive 'Naxi-character'. My fieldwork research concentrated on the reasons for and the perspectives of the modern revival and reformulation of Naxi customs and traditions in the 1980's: I was curious to discover why a number of Naxi start to use the religious Dongba (or Dobbaq in Naxi pinyin[5]) script in new contexts, to learn to read the Dongba script, to write calligraphy in Dongba characters, to create new versions of what they conceive as being traditional Naxi festivals, music and dances, and to conduct renewed research into the so-called 'Dongba Culture' (*Dongba wenhua*). Furthermore, what was their purpose in establishing a Society of Naxi Culture (*Naxi wenhua xuehui*) and what significance did a Society of this kind have to a small national minority in China?

Historical Sources to the Study of the Naxi Minority

According to official Chinese statistics the Naxi minority (*Naxizu*) constitute 277,750 people,[6] including the approximately 23,000 people who are called Mosuo (or Yongning Naxi) in Chinese and who prefer to distinguish themselves from the Naxi. The principal habitation area of the Naxi is concentrated around the relatively prosperous Lijiang Naxi Autonomous County (established in 1961) in the northwestern part of Yunnan, with the 'capital' of Lijiang inhabited by approximately 50,000 people. The Naxi live in close contact with several other national minorities such as Bai, Yi, Pumi, Lisu, Tibetans, and of course with Han Chinese. Throughout history the Chinese have been rather interested in the Naxi area: the town of Lijiang was situated on the important trade route between South China and Tibet, and the royal Naxi Mu lineage was very open towards incoming Han craftsmen, artisans and scholars. Consequently, the Naxi living on the Lijiang plain in particular have been strongly influenced by Chinese culture and social organization.

A main source for the pre-1949 history of the Naxi are the significant works[7] of the botanist and self-taught ethnographer, Joseph Rock, who lived in the area of Lijiang most of the time between 1922 and 1949, and studied Chinese historical sources relevant for the area, as well as the genealogical chronicles of the royal Mu family in Lijiang. Since the early 1980s several Chinese articles and monographs, based upon fieldwork from the 1950s, have been published on the Naxi minority. As part of the Communist project to classify all citizens of China into different 'nationalities' (*minzu*), numerous anthropologists, linguists, historians, etc. were sent to the minority areas in the 1950s. The purpose of their fieldwork was to make suggestions for classification, and to determine the stage of development of each *minzu*. This was done with a firm theoretical and ideological stand in the evolutionary ideas of Engels[8] (based upon Morgan's *Ancient Society*) which assumed that, on the economic level and depending here upon also on the cultural level, groups of people would always develop into higher and higher stages of civilization. The focus of the research was on economy, and researchers who themselves participated in the fieldwork have confirmed to me that their approach to religion especially was very superficial. Obviously, this was mainly due to the rigid Marxist theoretical framework which treated religious belief as an illusory reflection of social inequality, deemed to disappear with the elimination of the exploiting classes.[9] Because of political obstructions, the results of the large-scale fieldwork were only published from the the beginning of the 1980s onwards. This extensive material provides valuable information about Naxi society before and after 1949, although evidently the outmoded evolutionary ideology behind the fieldwork often makes the presented analysis of the basic data problematic to say the least.

The Naxi minority has been central to Chinese anthropologists especially because of the matriliny found among the Mosuo commoners. It is being argued that the Naxi and the Mosuo historically were one group of people, and that the Naxi in Lijiang developed away from the assumed backward matriliny into what is regarded as the more civilized patriliny. In 1723 a Chinese magistrate was established in Lijiang, due to the system of *gaitu guiliu* which replaced the former local authority, the *tusi*, with direct power of Qing officials. This change never took place among the Mosuo in Yongning who kept their local Mosuo *tusi* until 1956. It is held that this expansion of Chinese (civilizing) influence caused the Naxi, and not the Mosuo, to quickly develop a patrilineal system.[10] The central Qing government is in this respect valued positively as the civilizing center and the agent of change in the backward minority regions (e.g. Gong Yin, 1992: 152). As McKhann shows, there is no historical evidence that the Lijiang Naxi were in fact ever matrilineal, but by maintaining this view Naxi history has been constructed as a proto-example of the Morganian evolutionary theory (McKhann, 1994). Consequently, the Mosuo part of the officially classified Naxi minority has (to their great annoyance) been subjected to numerous Chinese investigations seeking to provide 'insight into the ancient history of mankind' through these 'living fossils' (e.g. Yan & Song, 1983:1-7).

In all Chinese sources the Naxi are described as having a very pragmatic attitude towards religion. They used to employ whatever religious beliefs and practices they found usable. Shamanism, Daoism, Chinese and Tibetan Buddhism were all to be found in Naxi areas at least prior to 1949[11], and the Naxi had their own ritual specialist too, the Dongba, who performed many of the important Naxi ceremonies exorcising demons.[12] The Dongba practised as ritual specialists in the villages, they were not organized in a sect and had no priesthood, monasteries or temples, and what is called Dongba religion (*dongba zongjiao*) in Chinese sources was never *the* Naxi religion per se. The Dongba developed a pictographic script for which the Naxi have become famous in and outside China, and the Dongba manuscripts, recording rituals and legends, contain a rich and very interesting literature as seen in a historic as well as an artistic perspective (see for instance translations into Chinese in *Naxi Dongba guji yi zhu* (An Annotated Translation of the Ancient Naxi Dongba texts) 1-3, 1986). Though there is no doubt that today there are still Dongba practising in more remote Naxi villages and that a few young ones are also being trained,[13] there were already only a very few Dongba remaining by the middle of this century.[14]

Today many Chinese and Naxi Dongba researchers prefer to talk about a 'Dongba Culture' (*Dongba wenhua*) rather than a Dongba religion (*Dongba zongjiao*). The term 'Dongba Culture' is constructed as a mean of bringing together, into one objectified concept, a number of different aspects connected to the Dongba, such as dances, rituals, myths and scripts. The choice of the term *wenhua* reflects an emphasis on scripts and literature, something which (as I shall return to) is highly estimated in China when judging upon a *minzu*'s degree of development.

Most likely the term 'dongba Culture' is also preferred because it is less politically sensitive in China to promote a 'Dongba Culture' than a 'Dongba religion'. Whether, from a historical point of view, it is appropriate to use a comprehensive term like 'a Culture' about the activities of the individual Dongba is questionably and reflects the lack of research on the Dongba activities as seen in relation to local society. The Dongba script, the Dongba rituals, songs and dances have become crucial in the Naxi intellectuals' modern attempts to form a Naxi identity based on a reconstructed distinctive Naxi past, and when I use the term Dongba Culture in the following, it refers to the intellectual Naxi's own modern interpretative use of the term in the sense of a coherent system of Dongba activities.

Minority Identity in China

In the modern nation-state of China, a number of factors have an impact on the formation and transformation of ethnic identities: the ethnic classification of all inhabitants, the minority policy, and the ideology of national unity (*minzu tuanjie*) being very significant ones.

China (like the former Soviet Union) has classified all of its citizens according to an official definition of an ethnic group or nationality: the Chinese term is *minzu* which in fact neither corresponds strictly to the term 'nationality', which would normally imply a people with a nation state, nor to the most common Western use of the term 'ethnic group' where the group in question is expected to have some sort of common ethnic identity or feeling of shared ethnic descent and culture.[15] After years of extensive field-work in the 1950s, the Chinese government decided to officially recognize 56 different *minzu*[16], among which the Han Chinese today constitute 92% and the other 8% (80 million-odd people) is made up by what is most often trans-lated as minority nationalities (*shaoshu minzu*[17]). In theory, the Chinese defined each *minzu* according to four criteria formulated by Stalin: common territory, common language, common economic life and 'a common psycholo-gical make-up manifested in common specific features of national culture' (Gladney, 1991: 66). In the province of Yunnan alone, where the largest number of different ethnic groups is found, more than 260 groups considered themselves qualified to be recognized as a distinctive *minzu* in the 1950's.[18] In Yunnan, however, only 26 different *minzu* (one of them being the Han) are officially recognized today, the argument being that this specific number was reached on the basis of the Stalinist objective, scientific definition. However, publications from the 1980's, as well as personal accounts from some of the people who themselves engaged in the fieldwork of the 1950's, reveal that the figure was reached rather randomly, partly because it proved an extremely difficult task to identify the numerous ethnic groups in China within a relatively limited period of time. Most likely, the State Commission on Nationalities (*guojia minzu shiwu weiyuanhui*) also found that more than 400 different groups in the whole of China were simply too many when considering administrative convenience. Consequently, the objective official classification of people often does not correspond to subjective feelings of ethnicity. Groups of people may, and some in fact do, apply to be reclassified, but this is very difficult to achieve and therefore a significant number of people in China today are in fact dissatisfied with their official *minzu* affiliation.[19] On the other hand, there is no doubt that the official classification has also caused groups of people to gradually change or adapt ethnic identities in accordance with their classification.[20] The Mosuo branch of the Naxi minority is an example of a group of people who wish to be identified independently from their Naxi classification,[21] but apart from this the Naxi generally insist that due to historic reasons they belong to one ethnic group. The official classification of each Chinese citizen obviously supports the Naxi's (as well as other national minorities') feelings of belonging to a distinctive group, of being different from the majority Han.[22] Using the elucidating terms of Kavaraj, communities formerly 'fuzzy' in the sense that they lacked clarity — for example in terms of space and geographical distribution — have been objectified and made into clearly demarcated 'enumerate' communities (Kavaraj, 1993: 4). Identities have been mapped and counted and the relation between minorities and the majority has been firmly consolidated.

The fact that the Naxi are officially recognized as being a distinctive national minority, and at the same time consider themselves as such, probably increases their chances of being taken seriously in a political dialogue with the government. It also makes it relatively easy for them to voice collective political and economic demands and wishes. I shall return to this in connection with the Society of Naxi Culture.

Since the Cultural Revolution, with its attempts to force the cultural and economic assimilation of national minorities, the Chinese government has shown a considerably higher degree of political tolerance towards expressions of ethnicity. This has obviously had a strong impact on the resurgence of ethnic identities among national minorities, and concern is now being raised about the damaging influence the lenient policy eventually will have on the government's attempts to modernize and exert political and cultural influence on the minorities.[23]

In China, national minorities receive special political privileges which in some cases make it attractive to be classified as other than Han. It has often been noticed that the national minorities are allowed two children whereas the Han may only have one, but the situation today is much more complex. There is a certain leniency in the birth-control policy towards national minorities, but the rules differ from province to province and where, for example, Naxi living in the countryside may have two children without any economic sanctions, Naxi in Kunming and the town of Lijiang are now allowed only one. Concerning education, members of national minorities also enjoy certain privileges: they have relatively easier access to higher education because of the minority institutes which educate and train minority cadres. At the Institute of National Minorities in Kunming, 95% of the students belong to national minorities[24] and ideally members of each of the 25 officially recognized minorities in Yunnan are always represented at the institute. The majority of Naxi students at the Minority Institute in Kunming come from the most sinicized Naxi town, Lijiang. Living in close contact with Han Chinese, having easy access to knowledge of Chinese language, obviously makes it easier for them to attend a middle school where all teaching is in Chinese, based on Chinese history, etc. Consequently, they also have a better chance of passing the university entry examination than do the Naxi coming from more remote villages.[25]

From the 1980's onwards, the Chinese government has paid special attention to the modernization of the minority areas which are generally still some of the poorest in China. Naxi farmers and traders in Lijiang Autonomous County are relatively well off today and improved economy, education, tourism, reconstruction of temples, etc., obviously have had an impact on the resurgence of ethnicity and on the educated Naxi's political claim for further influence on development. The national minorities have been granted a higher degree of self-government at all administrative levels under the slogan: 'minorities are the masters of their own house'. However, some Naxi complain that Han Chinese get too much economic power at local village level since they administer the 'transportation bureaus' and 'grain bureaus', etc. Therefore, the slogan is reversed into: 'national minorities manage the household affairs, Han Chinese are the masters of the house.'

The Chinese state's ideal of national unity (*minzu tuanjie*) is still heavily promoted and is in fact not contradictory to the post Cultural Revolution era's higher degree of political tolerance towards expressions of ethnicity and the official promotion and sponsoring of minority festivals, songs, costumes, dances, etc. Expressions of ethnic identity are accepted on a cultural level as long as ethnicity does not imply actual nationalism. That is, as long as it does not interfere with 'a unified China and the socialist economy' (*Minzu Gongzuo* (Minority Work), 1991 no. 5: 1). Religious activities in China have to remain apolitical and preferably individual. Large organized religious movements or sects, constituting a powerful position in a number of people's lives, are more likely to be seen as a potential political danger to the state and its ideals than are diffuse, isolated activities not interfering with other aspects of people's lives. The modern expressions of Naxi identity are, by and large, kept within the politically acceptable framework and as such pose no direct threat to the Chinese government. The Naxi claim no right to political independence, they are not hostile towards Han Chinese in general and they do not conflict with the overall ideal of national unity.

Chinese Media and the Belief in Cultural Evolution

Through the numerous official stereotyped portrayals of happy, colourful, dancing and smiling minority people in the Chinese media, through the sponsoring of certain festivals and selected reconstructions of temples destroyed during the Cultural Revolution, and through the promotion of tourism in certain minority areas, the State tends to neutralize and control religious and other cultural expressions of ethnicity. By creating stereotypes of minorities as being backward and naively happy people, the unequal power relation between minorities and Han is legitimized[26]. Lilley (referring to Morris) remarks that a number of other states in recent years have ceased to force the cultural assimilation of minority groups and 'yet it is clear that this liberal benevolence still domesticates imaginings, attempting to centralize and manage the domains in which ethnic differences may be legitimately expressed' (Lilley, 1990:178). The official Chinese media turn dancing, music, clothing, etc., into products made for other people to look at; dances are performed by specialists and music is performed by professional musicians. History and traditions are manipulated and presented as a kind of primordial and static 'traditional culture'. Tradition becomes a piece of art, an exotic play to be watched, rather than an integrated part of people's lives. The media's characterizations of national minorities mostly supply a stylized picture in which tradition is separated from other spheres of social life and thus becomes harmless. This means that the Chinese official depiction of a certain national minority is often incongruent with the group's perception of itself.

Nevertheless, the official images are still powerful and exert influence on the minority people themselves, as well as on the attitudes of the majority Han.

Chinese television tends to depict the Naxi minority in a popular, folkloristic style where Naxi identity and aspects of Naxi culture are transformed into politically innocent and strictly local cultural expressions. These TV shows support the government's attempt to control and decide upon exactly which religious and other cultural expressions may be accepted and even celebrated, and which may not. The state selects and presents its own version of what it claims to be '*the* Naxi culture'.

In accordance with the evolutionary ideas of Engels and Morgan (as earlier mentioned), the national minorities are generally presented by the media as groups of people who have developed economically as well as culturally since 1949, but who are still relatively backward and need to develop further. Though the Naxi minority in general is not described as being one of the most backward minority groups in Yunnan, it is still presented as being influenced by 'negative left-overs' like, for example, the earlier mentioned matrilineal tendencies in certain areas of the Mosuo.

To most of the Naxi students in Kunming the concept of each *minzu* being either backward or developed was obviously very significant; almost all of the Naxi students I talked to in Kunming told me that they had become much more conscious of being Naxi since they started studying at the Minority Institute. During their primary and middle school education they had learned about Chinese history, geography, religions etc., and all teaching was in Chinese. They had learned nothing about the Naxi. When they arrived in Kunming they were confronted with a number of *minzu* that they did not know at home, and they heard and learned something about the Naxi minority's history, especially from the Naxi teachers at the institute. Important to most of the students was that during this confrontation, through the information from teachers which had caused them to read books on their own initiative, they had learned that they were not as backward as they had previously taken for granted!

During their education, many of the young Naxi had come to find it a hindrance that they were Naxi born in a Naxi area. They found that they were at a disadvantage in terms of language (they had to learn Chinese besides their mother tongue) and, most importantly, they had come to regard the Naxi as being backward in their economy, education and culture. One student, who grew up in a remote border area where very few other Naxi lived and who had never learned to speak Naxi, told me that when she first moved to Lijiang she would tell people that she was Han Chinese. She, as well as quite a few of the other students, had been ashamed of being Naxi. However, when they had learned about the Dongba religion and the Dongba script, and realized that many Chinese and foreign researchers were interested in these aspects of Naxi culture, they, in their own words, ceased to feel uncomfortable being Naxi. One of the most influential factors was that during their meeting with all the other *minzu* at the Minority Institute and from reading the Chinese evolutionary descriptions of the stages of development of the Naxi, they had come to conclude that the Naxi minority was in fact rather developed compared to many other minorities:

Before I always thought the Naxi were terribly backward. I was unhappy that I was Naxi. Nobody likes to live in a backward place. At *Minyuan* [the Minority Institute] I learned that the Naxi has a very developed culture, a lot of Naxi study at universities, a lot of them are in America, and a lot of foreigners go to Lijiang. We have learned a lot from the Han's culture and therefore we are not as backward as for instance..[thinks]..Yi or Miao. (19 year-old female Naxi student)

It was often proudly singled out to me that the Naxi now have the second highest percentage of university students among all the different *minzu* in China. According to Chinese statistics (often disagreeing on the figures) this is definitely an exaggeration, although the Naxi generally are placed relatively high on the list: one Yunnan statistic ranks the Naxi next to only Hui, Manchu and Buyi (*Yunnan minzu jiaoyu yanjiu* (Research on Yunnan Minority Education), 1989: 90). However, the point is that the statistically high number of intellectual Naxi served as a proof to the students that they were relatively developed and that they did not have to feel embarrassed belonging to an uncivilized minority, a minority without *wenhua*.

A retired teacher at the Minority Institute, He Hongchang, describes in an article what she perceives as a general inferiority complex (*zibeigan*) of many young minority people. She believes that tourism is a potential which might help the young people get rid of this inferiority complex when discovering that Chinese and foreign tourists are interested in their native places and their history (He Hongchang, 1987:15). Several interviewees were convinced that the increasing interest in the 'Dongba Culture' by foreign researchers has a similar impact.

In the case of the Naxi students I interviewed, the majority of them certainly had had an inferiority feeling because of their ethnic affiliation, but most of the students expressed that they were now quite happy and proud of being Naxi. He Hongchang does not analyze the reasons for the inferiority feeling. However, a school system which one-sidedly focuses on Han China, along with the fact that the minorities are constantly told in the different media, in school, etc., that they are backward and need to develop, certainly contributed to this feeling. The tendency of, for instance, the TV programmes is always the same: the more a minority has adapted to Han Chinese culture, the higher developed it is considered.

No matter how much the educated Naxi and the Naxi students are opposed to the idea that the Naxi minority is backward, only a very few of them would question the general perception that each *minzu* can be placed on a hierarchic ladder according to their backwardness or development. They would stress that although the Naxi areas were economically backward, the Naxi, when compared to many other minorities, should be considered a 'developed *minzu*' because of 'its long history', 'own script' and 'its Dongba Culture'. The evolutionary hierarchic way of conceiving the different *minzu* is truly pervasive in China today. The Han community has, pretty successfully, been constructed and presented as a relatively homogenous community covering the vast majority of the Chinese inhabitants, and thus the Han *minzu* is placed at the top of the hierarchy both in respect of numbers and of degree of economic development.

Modern Dongba Culture

For several reasons, which I shall discuss in this section, it is the so-called 'Dongba Culture', with all its different facets, which has become the main symbol of a unified Naxi minority, of outspoken 'Naxiness' as imagined by the intellectual Naxi in Kunming. The 'Dongba Culture' is their pride and it prooves to them that they have no reason to feel inferior to the Han Chinese. Therefore, they use it actively to promote and strengthen the Naxi minority within the Chinese state. Before coming to the Minority Institute in Kunming, the interviewed Naxi students had found that it was completely useless to learn anything about their own historical background. Their history and their ethnic identity was perceived in a very primordial way — they were aware that they were Naxi (and not for example Tibetan or Hui) but it was a 'natural' or 'habitual' part of their life and often not very significant. Furthermore, 'being Naxi' apparently meant 'being Naxi in that particular village' and not part of the larger group of people which the Chinese had classified as Naxi.

Growing up in a Chinese educational system they had, as earlier mentioned, eventually come to find it a hindrance that they were Naxi. Being students at the Kunming Institute of National Minorities, many of them became interested in knowing more about their own background, especially about the Dongba religious practices. None of them (except one) had ever seen a Dongba practising his rituals, in fact Dongba rituals had never had any direct bearing on their lives and they actually did not believe in the use of religious rituals. Nevertheless, they now realised that the 'Dongba Culture' could help them to eradicate their complex feelings of inferiority and to define a Naxi identity. Quite a few of the Naxi students now wanted to become researchers of 'Dongba Culture' after they had graduated. The Naxi teachers and the well known Naxi researchers specializing in the 'Dongba Culture' strongly supported this wish.

In the Naxi 'capital' of Lijiang particularly the Dongba script has also had a modern revival: the State financed Research Institute of Dongba Culture in Lijiang receives students who learn to write Dongba script, it translates texts and has opened a small exhibition hall of Dongba relics and materials. In a small community like Lijiang this certainly influences people's knowledge and consciousness of the Dongba: a number of individual Naxi have learned to write calligraphies in the Dongba script and put these on display in small shops mainly for tourists; in Naxi villages matchboxes bear a print of a small Dongba character; and restaurant owners (especially those serving tourists) write Dongba characters on their signs. One of the more interesting recent uses of the Dongba script are modern paintings incorporating the old Dongba characters. Here the characters are not used for writing calligraphies, but are given new life as individual figures expressing different aspects of 'Naxi life'. Besides their artistic value these paintings serve as a neo-traditionalist expression of a modern Naxi identity. One of the artists said about his own paintings:

We Naxi have to use our own tradition and our Dongba Culture. I paint to express the traditions of the Naxi, to express myself and to show that Naxi culture is just as great as Han Chinese Culture.

Most of the Dongba painters and the people connected to the Institute of Dongba Culture in Lijiang are educated Naxi who have been living in Kunming for a longer period of time and who, during this period, have developed an interest in their own minority. However, it is obvious in the town of Lijiang that the interest in different aspects related to the Dongba is also manifest among local non-intellectuals. More and more Naxi in Lijiang are able to make profits by promoting the 'Dongba Culture' which fascinates the incoming flow of tourists as well as foreign and Chinese researchers. Although the Dongba rituals are no longer in active use in Lijiang, many aspects of the 'Dongba Culture' have gained new life, meanings and forms.

However, it would be wrong to conclude that the main reason for this is tourism (foreign and Chinese), which since 1986 has been steadily increasing in Lijiang. My interviews pointed to several reasons why the 'Dongba Culture' has become so important to the modern formulation of ethnic identity among intellectual Naxi especially. One reason is the Chinese fetishistic obsession with scripts: the Chinese character system is indeed a traditional pride of the Chinese, its ancientness is indisputable, its relative continuity is praised, and writing is a valued form of art. Minorities who have developed their own form of script are also placed relatively high in the evolutionary hierarchy. It is therefore not surprising that script comes to occupy a most relevant position in the intellectual Naxi's attempts to solve individual feelings of inferiority to the Han, to give positive meaning to the definite classification as Naxi, to give history relevance in an effort to strengthen political influence and make the Naxi minority more visible. This is supported by the numerous foreigners and Chinese interested particularly in the Dongba script.

Furthermore, many Naxi, especially intellectuals, have come to regard what they call 'Dongba Culture' as a symbol of their Naxiness, partly because they see 'Dongba Culture' as something typical only of the Naxi minority. By insisting upon the historic existence of a distinctive 'Dongba Culture', symbolizing the Naxi minority today, they are able to distinguish themselves (as a group) from other minorities and the Han. Finally it is not without significance that 'Dongba Culture' can be promoted in a way that is not politically controversial. Since Dongba rituals are only alive to a very limited degree in Naxi daily life, it is perfectly acceptable for the Chinese government to support research and promotion of 'Dongba Culture'. The Dongba script is 'just' a religious script and a historic relic; it is not a device which could ever replace Chinese characters. 'Dongba Culture' becomes a powerful symbol in the ethnicity of the intellectual Naxi, precisely because of its ability to solve individual identity problems and direct attention towards the Naxi as a distinctive minority people, while at the same time being politically inoffensive — something which increases chances for financial and ideological support from the Chinese government.

The Society of Naxi Culture

One concrete outcome of some of the intellectual Naxi's wish to extend their political influence on questions related to the Naxi, as well as their wish to strengthen the cohesion of the Naxi in Kunming, was the establishment of the Society of Naxi Culture in Kunming in 1986. The goals and activities of this society reflect some of the intellectuals' hope to provide meaning to a modern common Naxi identity based upon common roots and history.

The Society has around 200 members, most of them are Naxi intellectuals and cadres. None of the students I interviewed were members of the Society, though they would virtually all attend the annual Sanduo festival arranged by it. The aims of the Society are many-sided, the main ones being to promote modernization (cultural and economic), to work for 'intellectual development' in the Naxi areas where a considerable number of Naxi are still illiterate, to unite Naxi researchers with people preoccupied with more concrete work beneficial for the Naxi (like for example establishing factories in Naxi areas), and to promote the education of Naxi scholars researching subjects related to the Naxi minority (Guo Dalie, 1987: pp. 24-25).

The Society of Naxi Culture is very explicit about its ambition to intensify a common Naxi identity. Ideally, it wishes to unite Naxi from all areas, in spite of cultural and economic differences, in a strong communal feeling. Guo Dalie, head of the Society, writes about the ethnic consciousness of the Naxi in general:

The Naxi minority has a strong ethnic self-consciousness and it loves its own native places very much. This is a very great spiritual resource and within the given limits it is even more powerful than other resources. Ethnic consciousness is able to deal with matters in which administrative and economic methods are insufficient, because it possesses the drive of the lofty thought of dedicating oneself to one's own *minzu*. This one factor is an excellent forte of the Society of Naxi Culture. (Guo Dalie, 1987:23)

The Society's encouragement of a common Naxi identity has unto now especially been indicated by two activities of a cultural nature: the celebration of the Sanduo festival by all Naxi living in Kunming, and the attempt to reform the traditional Naxi female costume:

Minority clothes are a hallmark of the minority: it is by the clothes that you first recognize a certain minority. It is also an important factor in relation to the inheritance and continuation of a minority's traditional culture. The Naxi minority's costumes are rich and colourful. In Yongning and Baidi the Naxi women's costumes are beautiful, tasteful and extremely rich in distinguishing features. Although the costume of the Naxi women in Lijiang is dignified, very simple and unsophisticated, but nevertheless in good taste, the problem is that it is too heavy and clumsy and lacks the feeling for colours and practicability of the present era. Therefore, during recent years more and more young Naxi women do not want to wear their minority clothes. If this continues the Naxi minority's costumes may disappear. This has raised anxiety among a number of Naxi people. (Guo, Dalie, op. cit.)

In 1986, the Society of Naxi Culture formed a small group which was to think up some modified designs of the Naxi costume. In 1987, at the torch festival in Kunming, they presented five different modern Naxi costumes from which one was chosen as being the best modern version of the traditional Naxi dress. However, the dress was not well received in Lijiang where the local people apparently found the entire undertaking rather useless. Neither did any of the young female students I interviewed find it necessary to reform a costume which they would only wear at major festivals anyway. Unsurprisingly, the reason for this was not so much that the costume is impractical and colourless, but simply that the young, educated Naxi women are just as interested in fashion and modern clothes as are the young Han Chinese. The Society of Naxi Culture is especially concerned that the Naxi women living in the town of Lijiang tend to prefer modern clothes to the traditional Naxi dress. Almost all young Naxi women in the countryside wear the same Naxi costume as their mothers and grandmothers, whereas the Naxi men, just as the men of many other minorities, have already taken over Han Chinese clothes. The Society of Naxi Culture does not question this, nor does it try to change the men's clothes. The general attitude seems to be that, if anyone, it is the women who ought to stay traditionally dressed, that it is the women who in this respect represent what is perceived as traditional Naxi culture, while the men represent modern society. In respect to this preoccupation with costume, it seems that the influence of the Chinese stereotyped images of minorities manifests itself. Indeed, costume is extremely important in most Chinese presentations of minority people and clothes are taken as one of the main components of ethnic minority identity. Costume identifies a minority for the Han and it proves, to the Han, the exotic nature of the minorities as well as their backwardness.

Another example of the very conscious way in which the Society of Naxi

Culture expressed Naxi identity and attempted to strengthen the Naxi identity of all Naxi living in Kunming was the establishment in 1987 of the Sanduo festival in Kunming:

The Naxi minority celebrates several festivals but none of them has the form of a unitary *minzu* festival. The Society finds that a minority festival is a symbol of the minority. It is a celebration where the *minzu* concentrates on expressing its flaming, bold and unrestrained feelings and it is a form of that *minzu*'s age-old traditional cultural heritage. At the same time, it is the best occasion for every *minzu* to make extensive economic and cultural exchanges. (Guo Dalie, 1987: 23)

Again, I would argue, the influence of the general Chinese perception of what constitutes minority culture reveals its pervasiveness among minority people themselves. Each minority is expected to have a kind of 'national festival' (*minzu jieri*) which by and large has remained unchanged through history. The central TV news will show some minutes from the festivals of selected minorities (especially the most colourful and exotic ones!) — that is, the festivals which are judged to be the minority's national festival per se.

The Society of Naxi Culture found that it lacked this celebrated minority signifier, and thus it chose the Sanduo festival deliberately as being *the minzu* festival of the Naxi. From 1987 onwards it has been held every year, gathering a large number of the 4000-odd Naxi living in Kunming together. The reason for choosing precisely the Sanduo festival to symbolise a unified Naxi minority is that Sanduo is an important traditional protection deity of the Naxi and of no other ethnic minority. The society wanted a celebration which in a symbolic way would distinguish the Naxi minority from the other *minzu* thus intensify a common Naxi identity and the general cohesion of the Naxi in Kunming. Hence, the content of the Sanduo festival is much more symbolic than the celebrations in Lijiang where Sanduo is in fact worshipped by many people.

This conscious choice of the Naxi festival reflects the need of some intellectual Naxi to express their ethnicity in a surrounding where they are otherwise not being noticed as Naxi. Furthermore, the festival is an important occasion for exchanges between Naxi of different occupations, all concerned with their native Naxi areas. It is a cultural forum where collective demands for increased political influence in Naxi areas may be communicated and intensified. As such, the Sanduo festival is a unifying cultural symbol as well as an indirect powerful medium for dialogue with the government.

Ethnic Identity and Internal Stratification

Our self-consciousness as Naxi is very strong. We may look like Han Chinese and our ways of arranging marriages and funerals etc. may be similar to the Han Chinese, but inside we are very different. I feel very comfortable when I'm in company with other Naxi and when I'm speaking the Naxi language. Naturally, my best friends are Naxi. Therefore, it is extremely important to preserve the Naxi language. It is the most important factor of Naxi identity, but to our children here in Kunming, it is probably most important that they become fluent in Han language (*hanhua*). (From an interview with a 35 year old college graduate in Kunming)

Most of the educated Naxi in Kunming certainly did voice a very strong consciousness of and pride in being Naxi. The long term education received in Chinese, based exclusively on subjects related to Han Chinese China, had generally not caused the Naxi to feel that they were like the Han Chinese majority, nor to wish to assimilate with the Han Chinese. Rather, it seemed that they had become much more conscious of not being like the majority Han, but being Naxi: having a different language, history and cultural heritage. Nevertheless, the Naxi from the town of Lijiang had adapted especially well to the Chinese school system. They were all very much aware of their close historical relation to the Han Chinese which had caused the Naxi minority to be rather well integrated into the modern Chinese state. They all realised that the Naxi minority was a very small group of people which could try to obtain certain advantages within the Chinese system, but which was never, and would never become, a politically radical pressure group demanding autonomy.

On the surface and to the outsider, it was often striking how the intellectual Kunming Naxi's perception of being Naxi contradicted their actual lifestyle. Almost all of the Naxi in Kunming were very concerned about the preservation of the Naxi language; they preferred to speak Naxi among friends and some said that they would never come really close to somebody if they had to speak Chinese to them. The emphasis on language as an ethnic marker, and as a basic reason for 'difference', probably reflects the fact that precisely language was the most 'visible' difference between Naxi and Han in Kunming. Two students, who grew up in areas where no other Naxi lived, now felt very unfortunate that they were not able to speak Naxi or dance Naxi dances. Being officially classified as Naxi (having at least one Naxi parent) made it obligatory also to have a Naxi identity, and this meant at least speaking Naxi. Although she would have very much liked to, one of these students did not attend the Sanduo festival in Kunming simply because she did not feel she was a 'real' Naxi. However, most Naxi parents in Kunming in fact only taught their children Chinese. Some explained this by the fact that they were married to a Han Chinese, but most found it necessary for their children's future education. Most of the students (none of whom had children) planned only to teach their children Chinese while very few intended to teach them both Naxi and Chinese. All argued that the Naxi language was useless when living outside a Naxi area, and that even when going back to Lijiang it was better for the children career-wise to become fluent in Chinese. Still, quite a few of the same interviewees in Kunming regretted that many young Naxi parents living in Lijiang also wanted to educate their children in Chinese. Since Lijiang is the most concentrated Naxi region, the Naxi in Kunming found that this endangered the survival of the Naxi vernacular language.

Although the educated Naxi, living in Kunming, consciously want to keep alive all aspects of what they consider as 'typical Naxi culture', it is obvious that with regard to language, religious beliefs, contents of festivals and choice of clothes, they differ very much from most local Naxi living in Naxi areas. Although the focus of my fieldwork was on the intellectual Naxi and I did not do systematic research among Naxi peasants[27], there is no doubt that in local Naxi areas the different dialects of Naxi are spoken and only very few understand Chinese. Virtually all the peasant women wear the traditional Naxi dress, local Naxi festivals are celebrated, as are a number of festivals shared with other *minzu* (like for example the torch festival of the Yi), different deities are worshipped and it is not done as a conscious demonstration of 'Naxi Culture'. Interviews with students from Lijiang showed that before they came to Kunming they were generally not aware of which *minzu* their friends belonged to since local Pumi, Bai, Hui etc. most often spoke Naxi to them. In Lijiang the Naxi was the majority and it was only during confrontation with the Chinese school system that they started comparing themselves with an image of the Han Chinese as a group.

Most local peasants I talked to were not aware of the existence of the Society of Naxi Culture and those who were found it very hard to understand the aims and purposes of the intellectually dominated Society. Because of a very significant difference in education, occupation and life style, most local peasants felt closer to, for example, Bai or Tibetans in their own village than to these far-away, intellectual Naxi. The opposition between the Naxi peasants and the intellectuals of the Society of Naxi Culture is evident: the Society in

Kunming want to reform the Naxi dress in order to make it more attractive to the young Naxi women in the town of Lijiang, but they themselves would only wear it on special occasions. They celebrate Sanduo but do not, in fact, believe in deities at all; they carry out a celebration in the name of Sanduo, but they do not make offerings to him. They do not perform religious rituals which are now practised in public once again in numerous Naxi villages, after having been kept rather secret during the Cultural Revolution and the period just after. They are concerned with the consequences of the adoption of more and more Chinese words into the Naxi language, but their own children may never learn to speak Naxi at all. Generally, the educated Naxi saw no contradiction in this attitude. To them it was the perception of being Naxi which was most important, along with the concrete attempts to influence development at all levels in Naxi areas, to strengthen the local Naxi's feeling of a conscious and common Naxi identity and improve their level of education.

Most of the educated Naxi I talked to insisted on the existence of a strong common feeling of community among all Naxi regardless of occupation, educational level or geographic area. They had a primordial perception of their own ethnicity and of the ethnicity of other Naxi. Feeling Naxi was to them something 'natural', something every Naxi was born with, but also something which may be altered or strengthened through conscious efforts, especially by the educated members of the minority. Many of the Naxi intellectuals saw themselves as representatives of the Naxi minority in the Chinese state. While living away from the Naxi areas they were still deeply concerned about their own minority's economic development and rights as a minority group. They had their own ideas of the prospects of development in the Naxi villages which did not necessarily correspond with the viewpoints of the Naxi actually living in and around Lijiang. Several interviewees in Kunming complained that the peasant Naxi were too satisfied with their present economic situation and therefore, they were an obstacle to the prosperous development of the Naxi minority. They were criticising the peasants for not taking part actively and enthusiastically in the project of modern change, for clinging to more traditional structures and modes of life. Obviously, in this respect, the creation of, and insistence upon, a meaningful common Naxi identity is a rather ambiguous undertaking for the small group of intellectuals. The Society of Naxi Culture, as well as the interviewed educated Naxi, generally saw no contradiction between the strong urge for economic development and the conscious attempts to maintain what they perceived as 'typical Naxi culture'. Their ambition was to promote a strong economic development, based mainly on industry and tourism, in the hope and belief that this development would also lead to a higher intellectual level of all Naxi and to a higher degree of ethnic consciousness in the local areas. At the same time they saw a potential for economic development in the Naxi identity itself: ethnic consciousness was, so to speak, the precondition for encouraging and engaging the Naxi peasants in the struggle for economic progress. They firmly believed that their wishes for a prosporous development of the Naxi areas were in the interest of all Naxi and that it was only ignorance which produced local resistance against more rapid development.

Besides the belief that all Naxi are first of all Naxi, and as such constitute a culturally homogeneous group in spite of differences in occupation, education, income, cultural habits, etc., the intellectual ideal of a homogenous Naxi minority was also manifested by the educated Naxi's attitude towards the Mosuo branch of the Naxi. All interviewees in Kunming, without any exceptions, were convinced that for historic reasons the Mosuo formed a natural part of the Naxi. They acknowledged that the Mosuo had very different customs, wore different clothes and spoke a different dialect, but they did not approve of their attempts to be distinguished as an independent minority group. The matrilineality of the Mosuo was generally perceived in accordance with the dominant evolutionary ideology: it was seen as a more backward stage of Naxi society which the Lijiang Naxi had long outgrown. Many Naxi regarded their grandmother (mostly the paternal one) as head of the family, but at the same time they would stress that Naxi women were suppressed by the men, mainly because they had to do far the largest part of all work. This was seen, not surprisingly especially by the Naxi women, as a very negative aspect of Naxi life and several of them spoke positively about the Mosuo women´s status. However, because the Mosuo generally was considered as a rather backward part of the Naxi, in terms of economy and culture, it was most often the position of the Han women which was regarded as the most desirable. Whereas the educated Naxi insisted that the Mosuo had to remain part of the Naxi, many local Naxi in Lijiang tended to look down upon the Mosuo. They found it quite irrelevant whether the Mosuo were officially classified as Naxi or not. The numerous Chinese scholarly and popular books describing the Mosuo people as being on a lower evolutionary stage of development seem to have influenced the perceptions in Lijiang as well as among the Mosuo themselves who have now become reluctant to allow anthropologists and social researchers into their area.

The very few Naxi students who came from remote Naxi villages and had never been to Lijiang obviously also felt that they differed very much from the Lijiang Naxi. They were not interested in being reclassified as other than Naxi, but they rejected the idea that they felt a natural spiritual fellowship with the Naxi from the town of Lijiang in particular:

I once participated in the Sanduo festival in Kunming, but this festival is celebrated according to the customs of the Lijiang Naxi which are different from the customs in my village. We all go to the temple and burn incense and the people there actually believe in him. However, it is good that a Sanduo celebration is held here in Kunming. It gives the Naxi an opportunity to be together [...] I would never start talking to some Lijiang Naxi I did not know, only if they were Naxi from Sanba. The Lijiang Naxi are very different from us. I feel closer to the Tibetans and Bai from my area than to them. (From an interview with a 22 year old student)

Conclusion

A large number of educated Naxi especially, who are or have been living in Kunming away from their native Naxi villages, are today giving voice to a strong sense of ethnic identity. They articulate their own version of what they conceive as 'traditional Naxi Culture' and see themselves as representatives of a united and culturally homogenous Naxi minority. They acknowledge the existence of cultural and economic variations in different Naxi areas, but consider these of lesser importance as compared to the common history, culture and psychology which they insist is relevant to all the people who are officially classified as Naxi; 'We are all Naxi in our hearts'.

The influence of a centralized, rational and non-religious Chinese, communist education has contributed to making the intellectual Naxi seem rather indistinguishable from Han Chinese in Kunming. However, ethnic identities have been mapped and counted in China, and they have been objectified to a degree which leaves no escape even if one were desired. It is not sufficient to be Chinese (*Zhongguoren*): you have to have, per definition, a *minzu* identity at the same time. It is clear that sentiments of general commonness with other Naxi in regard to language, history and cultural traits are very strong among many of the intellectual Naxi. They, as an intellectual elite, are certainly not making up an ethnic category called Naxi, but they are choosing their past and formulating ethnicity by defining a specific Naxi culture. In its form the intellectual Naxi's version of Naxi traditional culture may not seem so different from the official media's simplifications and idealizations of selected cultural aspects. They are both occupied with costume, festivals and scripts. However, to the intellectual minority members it obviously makes a world of difference that they themselves articulate the meanings and contents of ethnic identity on the basis of what they consider to be of historical relevance. To intellectual Naxi, and probably to many other intellectual minority members in China, it is of utter importance to prove and show that they are not part of the Chinese version of minorities as being backward and uneducated, that they are not 'little brothers' to be helped by the Chinese, but rather older brothers within their own *minzu* who are very capable themselves of representing the interest of the *minzu* and guiding economic and cultural change.

The Naxi minority is regarded as a very well integrated minority in China. They have a rather good record of literacy and a relatively high percentage of educated members and cadres. They are generally not hostile towards Han Chinese, they do not demand political independence: modern expressions of Naxi identity are, by and large, kept within the politically acceptable framework and as such do not directly challenge Chinese government policies. In this respect the Naxi obviously differ from a number of other minorities in China today. Unlike for example the Dai minority, the Naxi do not have a traditional educational system based upon religion. They readily accept the centralized Chinese schooling system, whereas the Dai are resistant to government pressure towards educating Dai boys in official schools rather than in traditional Buddhist monasteries. The Naxi of Lijiang have long been living in close contact with Han Chinese and their language (especially in Lijiang) is heavily influenced by Chinese. They do not have a strong common religious foundation making them reluctant to accept secular education and communist propaganda against so-called religion and superstition. Furthermore, they have no objections against the central government's project of promoting the unity of the nationalities (*minzu tuanjie*) — there is no contradiction in being Naxi and Chinese. For Naxi intellectuals in Kunming, the political connotations of a modern Naxi identity (based upon sentiments of common culture and objectified in an identity corresponding to the official classification) is mainly expressed in their wish and attempts to gain control over political decisions regarding economic and cultural development in their native Naxi areas within the Chinese state. Because of their relatively high number of intellectuals and cadres, and due to their non-confrontative strategy, the Naxi intellectuals often manage to find acceptance for their political demands within the framework of Chinese political praxis. This, in turn, may well nurture spiralling demands for more influence and self-determination in Naxi areas in the future.

References

Anderson, Benedict (1983): *Imagined Communities: Reflections on the Origins and Spread of Nationalism*. London: Verson Press.

Barth, Fredrik (ed.) (1969): *Ethnic Groups and Boundaries: The Social Organization of Cultural Difference*. Boston: Little Brown.

Bentley, Carter (1987): 'Ethnicity and Practice', *Comparative Studies in Society and History*, 29, 1.

Chien Chiao, Tapp, Nicolas (eds.) (1990): *Ethnicity and Ethnic Groups in China*. Hong Kong: New Asia College, Chinese Univ. of Hongkong.

Comaroff, John L. (1987): 'Of Totemism and Ethnicity', *Ethnos*, 52.3.4.

Crossley, Pamela K. (1990): 'Thinking about Ethnicity in Early Modern China' in *Late Imperial China*, 11, no. 1.

Dongba Wenhua Lunji 1, 2, (1985 and 1991) [Anthology on Dongba culture]. Yunnan Renmin Chubanshe.

Dreyer, June Teufel (1976): *China's Forty Millions*. Harvard University Press.

Erbaugh Mary S. (1992): 'The Secret History of the Hakkas: The Chinese Revolution as a Hakka Enterprise' in *The China Quarterly*, December.

Friedman, Jonathan (1992): 'The Past in the Future: History and the Politics of Identity', *American Anthropologist*, 94.4.

Gong Yin (1992): *Zhongguo tusi zhidu* [the *tusi* system in China]. Yunnan Minzu Chubanshe.

Guo Dalie (1987): 'Naxi wenhua xuehui de tedian he gongneng' [The Characteristics and Aims of the Society of Naxi Culture] in *Minzuxue yu Xiandaihua*, 1.

Guo Dalie (1983): 'Lüelun Naxizu xinli suzhi tedian ji qi bianyi yinsu' [A Brief Account of the Special Psychological Makeup of the Naxi and its Varied Factors] in *Minzuxue Yanjiu*, 5. Minzu chubanshe.

Guo Xiaolin (1990): 'Review of Chinese Research on the Yongning Naxi Matriliny', *The Stockholm Journal of East Asian Studies*, vol. 2.

Hagendoorn, Louk (1993): 'Ethnic categorization and outgroup exclusion: cultural values and social stereotypes in the construction of ethnic hierachies' in *Ethnic and Racial Studies*, 16:1.

Hansen, Mette Halskov (forthcoming): 'Education and Ethnic Reactions: Naxi intellectuals in the Chinese province of Yunnan', in Brødsgaard & Strand (eds.): *Reconstructing Twentieth Century China: Discourses of State, Society and Nation*.

Harrell, Stevan (ed.) (1994): *China's Civilizing Project*. Seattle: University of Washington Press.

Harrell, Stevan (1990): 'Ethnicity, Local Interests, and the State: Yi Communities in South West China', *Comparative Studies in Society and History*, vol. 32, no. 3.

He Hongchang (1987): 'Lüelun fazhan minzu diqu lüyouye de zhongyao yiyi' [A Brief Account of the Basic Meaning of Developing Tourism in Minority Areas], *Minzuxue yu Xiandaihua*, 1.

Hobsbawm, Eric and Terence Ranger (eds.) (1983): *The Invention of Tradition*. Cambridge: Cambridge University Press.

Jackson, Anthony (1979): *Na-khi Religion*. Mouton.

Kaviraj, Sudipta (1993): 'Religion, Politics and Modernity'. Paper presented at seminar on 'ethnicity and nationalism', Sandbjerg, Denmark, May 1993.

Keyes, Charles F. (1976): 'Towards a New Formulation of the Concept of Ethnic Group' in *Ethnicity*, 3.

Keyes, Charles F. (ed.) (1981): 'The Dialectics of Ethnic Change', in Keyes (ed.): *Ethnic Change*. Seattle: University of Washington Press.

Li Jinchun & Wang Chengquan (1984): *Naxizu* [The Naxi Minority]. Yunnan Minzu Chubanshe.

Li Jinchun (1991): 'Qiantan Naxizu tong Hanzu de tonghun' [A Discussion of Intermarriage between Naxi and Han People] in *Minzuxue yanjiu*, No. 10. Minzu chubanshe.

Li Guowen (1991): *Dongba wenhua yu Naxi zhexue* [Dongba Culture and Naxi Philosophy] Yunnan renmin chubanshe.

Lijiang Naxizu zizhi xian gaikuang (1986) [A Survey of The Lijiang Autonomous County]. Yunnan minzu chubanshe.

Lilley, Rozanna (1990): »Afterword: 'Ethnicity' and Anthropology« in Wijeyewardene (ed.): *Ethnic Groups across National Boundaries in Mainland Southeast Asia*. Singapore: ISAS.

Luo Zhufeng (ed.) (1991): *Religion under Socialism in China*. London: M. E. Sharpe

McKhann, Charles (1989): 'Fleshing out the Bones: the Cosmic and Social Dimensions of Space in Naxi Architecture' in Chiao Chien & Tapp, N. (eds): *Ethnicity and Ethnic Groups in China*. Hong Kong: Chinese University of Hong Kong.

McKhann, Charles (1994): 'The Naxi and the Nationalities Question' in Stevan Harrell (ed.) *China's Civilizing Project*. Seattle: University of Washington Press.

Minzu Gongzuo [minority work] 1991, No. 5.

Mueggler, Erik (1991): 'Money, the Mountain and State Power in a Naxi Village' in *Modern China*, 17, No. 2.

Naxi Dongba guji yi zhu 1-3 (1986) [An Annotated Translation of the Ancient Naxi Dongba texts]. Yunnan minzu chubanshe.

Naxi shehui lishi diaocha 1, 2, 3, (1986 and 1988) [A Survey of the Social History of the Naxi Minority]. Yunnan Renmin Chubanshe.

Naxizu jianshi [A Short History of the Naxi Minority] (1984). Yunnan Renmin Chubanshe.

Ranger, Terence (1993): 'The Invention of Tradition Revisited: The Case of Colonial

388SOCIAL ENCOUNTERS

Africa' in Ranger and Vaughan (eds.): *Legitimacy and the State in Twentieth Century Africa*.

Rock, Joseph F. (1947): *The Ancient Na-khi Kingdom of Southwest China*, vol. 1, 2. Cambridge, Mass. Harvard University Press.

Rock, Joseph F. (1963): *The Life and Culture of the Na-khi Tribe of the China-Tibet Borderland*. Wiesbaden.

Scott, George M. (1990): 'A resynthesis of the primordial and circumstantial approaches to ethnic group solidarity: towards an explanatory model' in *Ethnic and Racial Studies* 13, no. 2.

Song Zhaolin & Yan Ruxian (1983): *Yongning Naxizu de muxizhi* [The Matriarchal System of the Yongning Naxi]. Yunnan renmin chubanshe.

Sun Ruoqiong (ed.) (1990): *Zhongguo shaoshu minzu jiaoyuxue gailun* [An introduction to the education of Chinese minorities]. Beijing: Zhongguo laodong chubanshe.

Sun Hongkai (1992): 'Language recognition and nationality', *International Journal of the Sociology of Language*, No. 97.

Wellens, Koen: forthcoming study on Pumi/Xifan minority.

Xinan minzu diqu jingji gaikuang [A general survey of the economic situation in the southwestern minority regions] (1986). Sichuansheng minzu yanjiusuo.

Yunnan shaoshu minzu shehui lishi diaocha ziliao huibian, 1-5 (1987). Yunnan Renmin chubanshe.

Zhongguo minzu tongji (1992). Zhongguo tongji chubanshe.

Zhou Yaowen (1992): 'Bilingualism and bilingual education in China' in *International Journal of the Sociology of Language*, 97.

Notes

1. This article, and the M.A. thesis upon which it is based, has been made possible through assistance, suggestions or critical comments from especially Wang Ningsheng, Harald Bøckman, Koen Wellens, Stevan Harrell, Stig Thøgersen and through financial support from the Carlsberg Foundation. Obviously, I am very grateful to all the Naxi in Kunming and Lijiang who agreed to be interviewed.
2. My main method of research was interviews with a total of 25 Naxi students, teachers, and researchers living in Kunming. Some were formally arranged with the help of the Yunnan Nationalities Institute, some were informal, and often I would meet with the interviewee several times. During the interviews there were only the interviewee and myself present. Each interview would last between two and four hours. Furthermore, I talked informally to a large number of Naxi in the County of Lijiang. All the interviews were conducted in Chinese, which is only the second language to most Naxi.
3. For example Comaroff, 1987. Scott has argued that although higher-class individuals are generally more likely to identify according to their class affiliation, experiences of opposition often lead to resurgence of ethnic consciousness (Scott, 1990:166).
4. Between 1986 and 1988.

6. *Zhongguo minzu tongji,* 1992.

7. Part of which have been translated into Chinese.

8. As mainly presented in Engels: *The Origin of the Family, Private Property and the State,* 1985 [1884].

9. Recent Chinese research on religion in China reveals a more sophisticated and open-minded approach to religious questions in a socialist country. For instance: Luo Zhufeng (ed.), 1991.

10. See e.g. *Naxizu shehui lishi diaocha, 2* [Investigations into the social history of the Naxi], 1986. The anthropologist Anthony Jackson, basing his argument mainly on Rock's works, suggests that this result was due to forced sinicization.

11. See e.g. *Naxizu shehui lishi diaocha,* 2, 1986: 63.

12. There is still a lack of qualified research on the question of Bön religion in Naxi regions, the relation between Bön and Dongba, and on the Tibetan influence on the Naxi in general.

13. see e.g. *Zhen Chuan Naxizu diqu minsu he zongjiao diaocha,* 1990 [An Investigation into the Customs and Religion in the Naxi areas of Yunnan and Sichuan]. This was also revealed to me by personal accounts from Naxi living in areas outside the Lijiang plain.

14. We still lack research as to the reasons why the importance of the Dongba waned in the 20th century.

15. E.g. Keyes 1981, Harrell, 1989.

16. One of these, the Jinuo, only gained recognition in June, 1979.

17. In Chinese texts the word *minzu* in itself often refers only to the national minorities.

18. *Yunnan shaoshu minzu shehui lishi diaocha ziliao huibian* [A compilation of research materials concerning the social history of the minorities in the province of Yunnan] 1, 1987: 1.

19. See also Harrell, 1990 and Harrell (ed.), 1994.

20. See e.g. Gladney, 1991, Harrell, 1990, and Wellens in a forthcoming study about the Pumi/Xifan minority.

21. Several Mosuo told me in 1991 that they had applied for being reclassified as new national minority called *Mosuozu.* I have no official confirmation of this.

22. It is becoming more and more clear that the term 'Han', which is most often taken for granted, is just as problematic and disputable as most other defined *minzu* within China. See for example the recent discussion about Hakka and Han identity among prominent communist leaders in Erbaugh, 1993.

23. See for example *Zhongguo shaoshu minzu jiaoyuxue gailun* (An Introduction to the Education of China's National Minorities), 1990: 267.

24. The remaining 5% is constituted by Han Chinese who have been brought up in the most remote border areas (mostly because their parents were sent there as cadres) without good possibilities of middle school education.

25. See Hansen (forthcoming).

26. See Hagendoorn 1993:33-36 summarizing the discussion of the concept of stereotype.

27. Firstly my time for fieldwork was limited and secondly part of my agreement with the Yunnan Institute of National Minorities was that I would confine my research to Kunming and the town of Lijiang. However, I did talk informally to a large number of Naxi outside the town of Lijiang. Furthermore, I am indebted to Koen Wellens for information about rural Naxi society.

Liu Shaoqi and the Sinification of Leninism

Graham Young

Among the most significant areas of 'cultural encounters' in modern China has been the assimilation of foreign-derived political concepts, as several generations of Chinese have sought to grapple with new and, at least initially, alien understandings of politics and their application to Chinese practice. In terms of political consequence, for much of this century the most important encounter has been with currents of political thought identified as 'Marxist', to the extent that 'Marxist' concepts have prevailed over other concepts — either in the sense of eliminating them, or in providing the framework for their definition (e.g., 'democracy'). The predominance of 'Marxism', of course, has been a function of the establishment and maintenance of political hegemony by the Chinese Communist Party (CCP). This type of encounter, therefore, has been shaped not only by the contents of a foreign-derived current of political thought but also by its mediation through the CCP's political role.

As Dirlik has demonstrated, the early development of the CCP was not greatly informed by understanding of Marxism. The CCP was founded and became active 'before there was any significant appreciation of Marxist theory, or its application in revolutionary analysis'. And Dirlik further notes that 'Bolshevik organization obviated the need for theoretical enquiry and analysis. The radicals who founded the Party became Communists before they were Marxists, and once they had done so, an organizationally defined ideology became for them a substitute for theoretical analysis'.[1] In its later development, the CCP came to devote much greater attention to formulating the ways in which Marxism was relevant to, and could be applied or adapted in, its own political practice. Most notable in this respect was the 'Sinification of Marxism' during the late 1930s-early 1940s.

By addressing both the Party's assimilation of Marxism and its linkage to specifically Chinese political activity, 'Sinification' was a self-conscious step away from the early deficiencies in theoretical analysis Dirlik identifies. Nevertheless, that effort was still closely constrained. The CCP still needed to take account of externally-imposed strictures of Marxist-Leninist doctrine, as expressed in contemporary Soviet formulations. Most importantly, the interpretation of revolutionary theory was inseparable from issues of operations of the CCP organisation — including the establishment of authority of some Party leaders as opposed to others, the induction of members and cadres into an orthodoxy, and the role of the organisation in political activity. There certainly was no notion of a recourse to Marxism which might be turned against the Party. In other words, despite the Party's attention to generating greater competence in 'theoretical analysis', Sinified Marxism remained an 'organizationally defined ideology'.

Indeed, we can go further to suggest that during this period the linkage between Marxism and the Party organisation was, in fact, reinforced in the CCP. This was effected through another process of systematically assimilating universalist political concepts and adapting them to the Chinese environment — a process which might be called the 'Sinification of Leninism'. Liu Shaoqi was among the most prominent contributors to this endeavour, especially through a series of systematic expositions on the character of the CCP during the 1930s and 1940s. At one level, Liu's treatment of Leninism was rather straightforward, as he repeated and elaborated standard Soviet-derived formulations concerning organisational structures and principles. It is this more narrow connotation of 'Leninism' which is often associated with the notion that Liu was the 'organisation man' of the CCP. And the effort to propagate those structures and principles was itself challenging enough, given the inconsistency with Chinese political cultural traits and lack of experience with modern political party organisation. But Liu also sought to add another dimension of universalism — not simply using or adapting general formulations, but also defining the CCP according to its integral and necessary role in world historical processes. The overall thrust of Liu's treatment of organisational doctrine was to establish a corporate identity of the Party, as the bearer of revolutionary tasks which were illuminated by Marxism. Thus, the two processes of 'Sinification' were complementary not only in that together they included both the 'Marxist' and 'Leninist' dimensions of the Party's self-designation but also in the sense that this broader interpretation of Leninism was inseparable from the Party's role as the vehicle of Sinified Marxism.[2]

Liuist Leninism

As with any discussion of the Marxist-Leninist party as 'vanguard', Liu began from standard assertions concerning the party's connection to the uniquely progressive qualities of the proletariat — including abilities in organisation and discipline, thorough commitment to revolution, and congruence of its own interests with those of all labouring people.[3] The Communist Party, as 'the highest and concentrated expression of the character of the proletariat', crystallised such characteristics, distinguishing itself not only from other classes and their parties, but also from the masses of the proletariat itself.[4] Liu's reference to such standard formulations confronted the obvious difficulty that the CCP, as the supposed vanguard of the proletariat, was composed mainly of peasants. One response was to emphasise the Party's efforts in mobilising urban workers, despite its necessary shift of focus to the countryside from the late 1920s. Liu also argued that the social origin of its membership could not be the sole factor determining proletarian character, pointing to the Labour parties of Europe as examples of parties which were not authentically proletarian despite their memberships.[5] More generally, Liu's works contain two inter-related themes on which his claim for the CCP's role as proletarian vanguard was based: identification with the world historical mission of the proletariat and the revolutionary movement to fulfil that mission; and orientation towards the guiding revolutionary theory of Marxism.

Consistent with the general proposition that the proletariat's own liberation could be achieved only by the liberation of all, Liu saw the interests of the Chinese proletariat as necessarily identical to the interests of all in China.[6] Beyond that, he considered the Chinese revolution as part of the 'world-wide, final revolution' with the objective of realising Communism, and encompassing a century of joint struggle and sacrifice by countless millions of people throughout the world.[7] Thus, for Liu, the Chinese revolution could not be understood simply in terms of defeating immediate enemies, such as Japanese imperialism, or even of fighting for goals such as national liberation. These had to be related to universal objectives transcending the Chinese situation, and to the world-wide movement for realising these objectives. The democratic revolution in China differed from precedents in other countries precisely because it was 'a part of the world proletarian revolution'.[8]

It was then an easy step for Liu to move from this understanding that the Chinese revolution was inherently proletarian to an assertion of the CCP's fundamental character. The Party's proletarian credentials were established by its development during the period of world revolution, after the October Revolution, by its bringing the universal Communist cause to China and providing leadership as part of this world historical current.[9] But the Party was uniquely fitted for this task only because of its grasp of Marxist-Leninist theory, which provided revolutionary guidance both generally in its universal validity and specifically in its adaptation to particular circumstances. Thus, Liu saw both the general and the specific aspects of Marxism-Leninism as important in defining the Party's character. That is, he accepted the 'Sinification of Marxism' notion that Marxism-Leninism provided a methodology for devising revolutionary policy, condemned any tendency for the separation of theory and practice, and commended those who 'are not satisfied to memorise the principles and conclusions of Marxism-Leninism but are firmly determined to take the standpoint of Marxism-Leninism, to grasp the Marxist-Leninist method, to put them into practice, and are active in directing all revolutionary struggles, transforming reality and at the same time transforming themselves'.[10] But, as the reference to Party members' personal transformation suggests, Liu's concerns went beyond the use of theory for practical guidance. He saw that study of theory was also intrinsically important. Assimilation of Marxism-Leninism allowed members to become suitable parts of a proletarian vanguard through their understanding of and commitment to the universal proletarian historical mission as well as to more immediate revolutionary objectives. They could then overcome the limitations of social origin, especially by countering the corrosive effects of 'petty-bourgeois ideologies' manifested among peasants.[11] Liu saw a necessary link between the ability to use theory, in the sense of guiding practical activity, and the fostering of ideological standards. Only those who could 'take the proletarian standpoint' and 'adopt the ideals of the proletariat as their own' could have a proper grasp of Marxism-Leninism.[12]

In sum, Liu portrayed the Communist Party as not only a mechanism for applying the guiding theory but also the incarnation of proletarian interests and an intrinsic part of a universal movement for realising those interests. Thus, he effectively saw the Party as the embodiment of the revolution, suggesting what might be termed an 'organismic' conception of the Party. He himself referred to the Party as 'a unified organic whole' (*tongyi de youjiti*).[13] And he developed the analogy of Party members constituting the cells of a human body, noting that the healthy development of the cells strengthens the whole body, and vice versa, although 'generally speaking, the whole determines the parts'.[14] His emphasis on 'the whole' indicated not only his concern for integration and coherence but also the view that the Party was an entity transcending its constituent organisations and membership. It was an organism which embodied the universal revolutionary process in the specific Chinese situation.

Organisational Principles

Liu's organismic conception was basic to his prescriptions concerning the Party's activities, but his attempts to reconcile it with the exigencies of political practice also led to ambiguities and tensions in his treatment of many aspects of leadership doctrine. Although all of those aspects cannot be considered here, two which warrant attention are his formulation of organisational principles and his discussion of institutionalised as opposed to personalised leadership (bearing upon the role of the Party leader).

As the 'organisation man' interpretation has pointed out, a common theme in Liu's writings was that organisation in itself is a source of strength. In standard Leninist fashion, Liu related this issue to the proletariat's strengths in organisation and discipline, which should be crystallised in the Communist Party. Thus, the Party is 'the highest form of proletarian organisation', consisting of 'the most advanced, most organised, most disciplined' of the proletariat.[15] 'Definite organisational form and definite rules' were necessary to establish the Party as 'a collective whole'.[16] Nevertheless, while strong organisation had intrinsic merits, any organisational question was subordinated to the Party's role in revolutionary processes. Liu explicitly criticised the tendency to divorce organisational questions from political and ideological questions, and made it clear that organisational unity alone was not enough. 'The content and substance of the Party's unity is the uniformity in ideology produced from Marxism. This kind of ideological unity is most basic; without it, the Party's unity is impossible.'[17] Since the interests of the proletariat were revealed only through Marxist-Leninist theory, then it was the understanding of theory which defined the character of the Party. But Liu also saw that the relationship between ideological and organisational matters was reciprocal: 'Only if there is first ideological uniformity can organisational uniformity be guaranteed; but organisational uniformity, on the other hand, can help, promote and to a certain degree consolidate ideological uniformity'.[18] Liu was concerned not simply with the need to impose organisational coherence and order; the more fundamental level of ideological uniformity was the basis of and cement for the Party organism, and organisational procedures had to serve that uniformity.

Liu preferred to emphasise this sort of reciprocal relationship, but his more systematic exposition of leadership doctrine revealed many ambiguities, especially when he faced the difficulty of potential conflict between strict adherence to organisational rules and the Party's fundamental rationale of defining 'correct' revolutionary direction. While his subtle analysis of the concept 'democratic-centralism' was far from a mere assertion of organisational rules, Liu demanded that obedience to the Party organisation should be 'unconditional and absolute'. Thus, he criticised those who raised conditions for obedience to their superiors, such as qualifications, intellectual ability, age, educational level, standing within the Party, or personal relationships.[19] Such conditions were impermissible and, in fact, irrelevant. Obedience was a relationship with the whole Party organisation and could not be personalised, by either the leader or the led. Those in leadership positions were not to be considered as individuals but as component parts of an organic whole.

These strictures raised few problems of consistency with Liu's general analysis (even if they did conflict with political practice). More testing was his rejection of the view that obedience to superiors or the majority was on the condition that they be 'correct in principle and politics'. He insisted that, once a decision was made, it had to be carried out even if it was wrong. And he gave as examples Marx, Lenin, and he himself, in the support of revolutionary activities which they saw as mistaken.[20] Liu's works suggest several grounds for rejecting a 'correctness' condition. First, and most obviously, he resorted to the notion that organisation has intrinsic merits. If members refused to carry out directives and decisions, 'there will not be a Party'. But he appeared to recognise the weakness of this position: '... this seems to be rather crude, but to organise several hundred thousand Party members and maintain the Party's unity, what can we do if we do not use rather crude methods?'[21]

Secondly, Liu argued that the proper organisational procedures — democratic-centralism, intra-Party struggle and minority rights to reserve opinions — were more likely to lead to correct definition of direction and to provide means for correction of mistakes. 'Collective leadership is the gathering together of the experience and intellectual power of the whole Party. It collects the best opinions and plans of the whole Party and turns them into one resolution and one programme'.[22] Generally speaking, the views of the majority were more correct than those of the few. This might not be so always, since 'only a few wise, talented and far-sighted people can discern the development of the objective matters and the far progress of history'. But even in these cases, the few should follow the majority so as to ensure unity in organisation and action, while continually pressing to have the wrong decision reversed. Any disagreement had to be 'according to definite organisational procedures'.[23]

Thirdly, Liu demanded individual subordination in terms of the Party's character as embodiment of the revolution. He claimed that inner-Party disputes were likely to be on less important issues, since the conclusions on such fundamental matters as the nature of Chinese society and the Chinese revolution had already been agreed.[24] Reliance on this general argument was also demonstrated by Liu's discussion of the particular contrary example of Lenin's split with the Second International. Liu claimed that, while Lenin was justified in this action, no member of the CCP would be justified in emulating him. 'First of all, that was Lenin, this is you'. To disobey the CCP organisation would be to depart from 'Leninism and the revolution'. And Lenin had created the split only after a long period and when it had become clear that the Second International was 'bankrupt' in Marxist terms.[25] Here Liu presented a notion of 'correctness' more fundamental than that applying to specific policies. As the embodiment of the revolution, the Party remained the repository of correctness, even when it made specific mistakes. And unconditional obedience was justified according to this more fundamental correctness. Only if that were infringed could disobedience be permitted. Thus, the only exceptions to unconditional obedience which Liu allowed were when higher-level authorities had 'shown anti-Party conduct' or were found to be betraying the Party and acting as enemy agents.[26] While he provided examples from CCP history, and insisted that such charges would have to be well substantiated, he left the possible manifestations of such conduct as rather vague. Nevertheless, Liu's position was that only in the extreme case in which the Party ceased to be the embodiment of the revolution could its unity be broken.

Liu's emphasis on obedience clearly entailed a strict attitude to Party discipline which, as he noted, was enforced through compulsion and penalty for violation. But he also argued that discipline in the Communist Party was based on 'voluntary subordination' and should not be 'mechanical'.[27] By this he meant that the fundamental basis for discipline was the ideological awareness of members, their understanding of the Party and its role, and their willingness to subordinate themselves to these wider objectives. Thus, punitive measures were inferior to methods such as criticism and discussion because they had less 'educational significance'.[28] Unity and discipline derived from 'true uniformity in the Party in ideology and principle and the consciousness of Party members' rather than punishment (and, Liu remarked parenthetically, if discipline could be maintained only through punishment, 'then the Party is at a criticial point').[29]

Liu thus saw the process of criticism and self-criticism, of intra-Party struggle, as crucial in strengthening Party organisation through the fostering of ideological unity. And such struggle should be restricted to matters of 'principle', which Liu defined as 'questions of our methods of observing and handling problems according to the general rules of the development of things'.[30] Far from merely emphasising organisational discipline, Liu asserted that all Party members had the duty to engage in criticism and self-criticism, to resist actively any mistaken tendencies or opinions, to avoid unprincipled harmony.

One difficulty in Liu's position was the definition of 'principle'. When he suggested that 'questions of daily political affairs and questions of a purely practical nature' should not be matters of intra-Party struggle, it was by no means clear how principled and practical questions differed. Liu sometimes implied that this was a distinction between means and ends, suggesting that compromise was appropriate on the 'practical' questions of means to shared ends, which were not amenable to compromise.[31] But he could not properly rely on that distinction, since he saw principle in terms of both 'observing' and 'handling' problems according to 'general rules of development'. In his own terms, he faced difficulties in the notion of uniting theory and practice.[32]

Liu also suggested another basis for compromise, in terms of a hierarchy of principles: 'our rule is that the part submits to the whole, the temporary submits to the long-range, and the small principle submits to the greater principle.' He suggested that there should be compromise over questions of principle which were 'neither very important nor urgent'. The justification for this was not only in terms of the needs of the practical struggle, but also of maintaining the Party's solidarity.[33] Such a position again reflects Liu's organismic view. His discussion of principle was not always linked directly to practical activities, as he focussed on the integrative role of principle or ideological uniformity and the integrity of the Party itself as the embodiment of the revolution. Hence, he tended to see questions of principle as at least partly abstracted from practice, and sought to preclude any dispute which could detract from the solidarity of the Party. But, by the same token, major questions of principle were of crucial importance, since they were central to the ideological uniformity on which Liu's view of the Party as the embodiment of the revolution was based. Liu suggested, therefore, that if there were members who persisted in mistakes in principle, then they would finally have to be expelled from the Party. And if a majority developed an inconsistent principled position, there would be no choice but to split and form a new Party.[34] Unity in principle was fundamental, and had to underlie any form of uniformity in organisation and action. If any 'cells' became incompatible with the 'body' because of lack of unity in principles, then they would have to be removed.[35]

Institutionalised versus Personalised Leadership

The subordination of individual to Party organisation was also clear in Liu's discussion of the moral qualities of members and the treatment of interests. In striking contrast to accusations directed against him during the Cultural Revolution, the core or Liu's discussion of necessary qualities of Party members was an ethic of sacrifice. Good Communists sought to carry out the most arduous work, never fearing difficulties, dangers or personal loss. And the aim of a Party member could not be individual reputation or glory, although this would follow for those devoted to the revolutionary cause.[36]

There was nevertheless some ambiguity in Liu's works, concerning the extent to which he acknowledged the legitimacy of personal interests. On one level, Liu recognised that a Party member might have individual interests, and demanded that, in the case of conflict, they be subordinated to Party interests. Again, this should not be merely a case of obeying the organisation, but should be done consciously and voluntarily.[37] But Liu also cast doubt on the very notion that Party members should have individual interests. He claimed that no member could have any success independent of the Party's success, and that 'the Party member's individual interests and development are incorporated within the Party's interest and development'.[38] In Liu's view, the Party member was no longer an ordinary individual, but a 'general representative of the class'.[39] In effect, he sought to obliterate the distinction between the interests of the Party and the individual, insisting that 'the Party's interests are the concentrated expression not only of the interests of every Party member but also of the interests of all workers and of mankind's liberation'.[40] The optimum, therefore, was that a Party member should have no interests apart from the Party's revolutionary activities.

Liu's treatment of the relationship between individual and organisation was most pertinent to those holding responsible Party positions. His formulations were, as Sullivan's extensive and detailed analysis shows, consistent with long-standing themes in CCP leadership doctrine. In particular, he continued the emphasis on the institutional rather than personal basis of leadership, which emerged in the Party's early years, and in the 1930s-1940s was expressed by other Party figures, such as Peng Zhen.[41] Hence, while asserting that all Party members had to strive to be active in revolution, Liu repudiated the role of 'heroes'.[42] Individual contributions should not be ignored, but the credit for any success should be attributed to the Party. Achievements might be partly the result of individual effort, but the principal reasons were the direct help of the Party, its strong position overall, and the legacy of a century of collective effort for the Communist cause, which had created whatever favourable conditions existed for current revolutionary struggle.[43]

As noted above, Liu developed the analogy of Party members constituting the cells of a human body. One of the flaws Liu noted in the analogy was that the body could not grow another brain once it was removed, but the Party could continue even if its leaders were removed, since it could replace one Central Committee with another.[44] This qualification in fact strengthens Liu's organismic notion. His stress was on the Party as a single organic entity in which the whole was paramount and the parts (even the most important parts) had to be defined as only elements of the whole. Accordingly, Liu strictly distinguished the Party's collective leadership on the basis of democratic-centralism from other forms such as 'individual centralism' or 'dictatorship'.[45] In countering the tendency to personalise leadership, he was most concerned with the dangers of 'patriarchism' (jiazhangzhi), and insisted that any position of leadership was conditional upon obeying the organisation and the majority.[46]

Liu's repudiation of personalisation of inner-Party relations faced some obvious difficulties of conflict with political practice. He clearly was challenging the importance of guanxi as a cultural trait which remained salient in Communist Party operations. His depiction of 'unprincipled struggle' included factional activity and all promotion of individual or group interests rather than the interests of the whole Party. Any unity forged from personal relationships rather than principle was impermissible. All matters within the Party had to be raised formally for principled discussion, excluding other extraneous factors.[47] 'Unprincipled struggle' necessarily undermined the ideological uniformity on which the Party's organismic character was based and, hence, the Party's fundamental rationale.

The other obvious difficulty Liu faced was the role of the leader, as by the 1940s Mao's clear political predominance seemed to conflict with the subordination of individual to organisation. Nevertheless, there were abundant examples of Liu's praise of Mao.[48] There were two main ways in which Liu tried to reconcile emphasis on Mao's individual qualities with the animus against personalised or heroic understandings of leadership. First, he claimed that good Party leaders themselves complied with subordination to the organisation. No Party member should 'stand outside or above the Party to lead it and drive it forward. Lenin and Stalin (sic) both stood inside the Party to lead it and drive it forward; each played his role as a Party member inside the Party.'[49] Similarly, according to Liu, Mao was scrupulous in observing Party organisational procedures and was a conscientious student of the masses. As well as being leader, Mao was also 'an ordinary member of the Party'.[50] Rather than considering how Mao's role as leader might conflict with principles of collectively governing the Party's operations, Liu preferred to see Mao as a model in observing those principles.

Secondly and more importantly, Liu sought to justify the position of the dominant leader by linking it with the Party's role as bearer of the proletarian historical mission. Consistent with his metaphor that Party members are like the cells of the human body, Liu maintained: 'We obey the Party, the Central Committee and the truth, not individuals'. Nevertheless, although he asserted that the reason for obedience to leaders was that they had done good work within the organisation and 'represented the truth',[51] much of Liu's discussion suggests a closer relationship between Mao and historical mission. His article celebrating the Party's 22nd anniversary claimed that a particularly noteworthy feature of the Party's history was that the Chinese revolutionary forces had been able 'to find their own leader, Comrade Mao Zedong'.[52] This was extended to a Mao-centric interpretation of Party history:

The history of the Chinese Communist Party should be the history of the development of Marxism-Leninism in China; it is also the history of the struggle between Chinese Marxist-Leninists and all groups of opportunists. Objectively, this history has developed with Mao Zedong as the centre.[53]

Liu's report on the 1945 Party Constitution claimed that, as a 'creative and talented Marxist', skilled at combining Marxism-Leninism with practice, Mao had 'raised the ideology of the Chinese nation to an unprecedented height of reason and pointed out to the suffering Chinese nation and people the only correct, complete and clear road towards thorough liberation — the road of Mao Zedong'.[54] Mao's writings, were 'the highest expression of the wisdom of the Chinese people and their highest theoretical attainment', 'one of the greatest achievements in the history of the world Marxist movement,' and so on. The Chinese revolution could succeed only when it followed Mao's line and his leadership. Relating this to the Mao-centred version of Party history, Liu asserted: '... the true history of our Party, and the correct revolutionary direction of the Chinese proletariat and people, were located where Comrade Mao Zedong was; and they continued, existed and developed with Comrade Mao Zedong as the representative and the centre.'[55]

Such statements may still be seen in terms of affirming Mao's special contributions to the Party as an organisation. Nevertheless, they are striking in the extent to which Liu's vigorous repudiation of personalised leadership in the Party has been stretched to accommodate celebration of one individual. Just as he asserts consistency between Mao's behaviour and organisational principles, so Liu prefers to assume consistency between the Party's role as bearer of proletarian mission and Mao's role as the 'centre' and architect of 'the road of Mao Zedong'.[56] Hence, he avoided confronting the possible challenge to the Party organisation posed by identification of Mao individually with revolutionary process and historical mission. That challenge did not fully emerge until the Cultural Revolution, but it is ironical that it was prefigured in Liu's wrtings of the 1940s, even if he preferred to ignore it.[57]

Party and Masses

One common accusation later directed against Liu was that he, in contrast to Mao Zedong, denigrated mass political activity with the view that 'the masses are backward'. While expressing the need for mass activity obviously necessary for any Marxist-Leninist revolutionary, it was the case that Liu was generally less enthusiastic than Mao concerning the heroic and creative qualities of the masses, and he was careful to insist that the Party should be clearly distinguished from the mass movement both theoretically and organisationally. Liu's analyses of the mobilisation of a mass movement often dwelt on difficulties and inhibitions. In terms of organisational coherence, he argued that any organisation of the masses had to be based on their own consciousness and activism, as an organisation produced through pressure could not succeed. Discipline within a mass organisation was also to be based on the consciousness of the members themselves.[58] The problem was that the masses, because of their low political and cultural levels, did not understand the need for organisation. Hence, leadership was necessary to convince them of this need, thereby transcending the simple expression of immediate mass desires. Liu also pointed to the limited scope of mass concerns. The masses had to be organised according to their own demands, which produced different types of organisation — political, economic, and cultural. But, Liu suggested, the masses would likely be most concerned with immediate economic interests. By contrast, the political was the highest form of all organisation, and only the people with the highest political consciousness could join the political party of a class. Hence, political organisation could not be the principal form of mass organisation, and a political party could not be included within the scope of mass organisations.[59] All such assertions were consistent with the standard view of the proletarian qualities which found concentrated expression in the Party. Other types of political organisation were suitable for uniting the masses only temporarily and on specific issues. The task of leadership was to generalise and extend the limited demands which initially provided the basis for mass organisations.

Liu's comments are clearly informed by the assumption of a basis of Party leadership, intrinsically valid apart from connection to the mass movement. But this should not be used to depict Liu as an advocate of vanguard separateness out of line with the mass character of the Chinese revolution. As many have emphasised, the Chinese Communist revolutionary movement in the 1930s-1940s varied significantly among base areas and other arenas of Party operations, and one key to CCP success was precisely the ability to adapt to particular local conditions, in the ways in which Liu's attention to the mass movement advocated. Hence, Liu's views should not be seen as conflicting with a Mao-derived 'mass line'. On the contrary, Liu was a principal contributor to the formulation of principal themes of the 'mass line', revolving around the methods of mass mobilisation and the manner in which the CCP might exercise leadership.[60] Liu did not neglect the importance of mass activity, but did emphasise that such activity had to proceed with guidance and direction from the Party. That was consistent with the orthodox Leninist view held uniformly by Party leaders at the time, and it was only later, when

the notion of mass activity directed against the Party organisation was entertained, that Liu could be seen retrospectively as denigrating the masses.

A Liuist Legacy

Liu's formulation of leadership doctrine helped to meet an important need in
the development of the CCP and its political activity. While he took part in
articulation of the 'mass line', his main contributions clearly concerned the
character of the Party organisation, the style of its internal political activity,
and the basis for participation and commitment among cadres and members.
He sought to weld a distinct organisational ethos within the CCP, which had
to counter inconsistent political cultural influences, and to establish the
grounds for internal legitimation, as both prerequisite for and complement of
the legitimation of the Party's wider political role. His 'Sinification' of
Leninism assimilated the general Soviet-derived orthodoxies of leadership
doctrine, translating and extending them with specific reference to Chinese
circumstances. At the same time, he located CCP activity within a framework
of universal historical mission. This then became a basis for reinforcing the
Party's corporate identity, which was important in an environment necessarily
involving dispersion and locally-based variations among Party activities. Liu's
organismic notion, with its constant emphasis on the collectivity of the Party
organisation, sought a focus of integration and coherence beyond the mere
application of organisational rules.

While other Party figures dealt with these matters, Liu's contributions had
the greatest authority because of his standing as the highest-ranked person,
next to Mao, within the Party Centre. With the focus on internal legitimation,
the primary audience consisted of Party members and cadres, as shown by
his prominence in myriad inner-Party manuals and training materials. The
ambiguities of his position did not hamper its utility (at least, until the
Cultural Revolution) because, as noted above, when Liu confronted
difficulties and inconsistencies he responded in a way which emphasised
Party collectivity and solidarity. The orthodox interpretation of lessons to be
derived from Liu could vary over time, of course, and sometimes included
rather one-sided emphasis on particular aspects — as, for example, the later
extension of Liu's notion of subordination of individual to the Party to the
demand that members should become 'docile tools'.[61] Nevertheless, the
principal message of complete identification of the Party with historical
process and mission persisted.

That obviously changed with the Cultural Revolution. It is not difficult to demonstrate that Cultural Revolutionary attacks grossly distorted Liu's position, largely through exploiting his ambiguities. Thus, for example, his distinction between 'principled' and 'unprincipled' struggle was used to claim that he advocated the 'theory of intra-party peace'. Similarly, in contrast to his ethic of sacrifice and subordination of individual interests to those of the Party, Liu was accused of advocating 'joining the Party to climb up' and 'merging private and public interests'. Such accusations were, of course, not merely isolated misunderstandings of what Liu had said. Rather, they were constituent parts of the Mao-centric view of the Party which reached new heights during the Cultural Revolution. On one level, that involved an attempt to distinguish Mao's ever-correct and consistent revolutionary line from the various contributors to an opposing incorrect and pernicious line throughout the Party's history, of which Liu was supposed to be the most important example. More fundamentally, there emerged the notion that the Party emanated from Mao. Hence, Mao's role was not justified according to his position as Party leader. The reverse applied, with the notion that the Party was authentic or legitimate only to the extent to which its operations were consistent with Mao's 'line', Mao Zedong Thought, and Mao's personal role. An immediate implication was that all former Party organisational rules and procedures could be challenged, on the grounds of inconsistency with Mao and his 'line', as demonstrated in the attacks upon Liu's supposed advocacy of 'slavishness'. And the role of the Party organisation itself could be repudiated on the same grounds. Hence, the potential contradiction between Party and leader, which Liu had recognised but had preferred to gloss over, was fully realised. Liu and his understandings of the Party were both victims of the type of Mao-centrism which he himself had helped to foster in its early stages.

The more recent official treatments of Liu have rescued him from wilful distortion, and thereby restored him as an authority on the Party organisation. Nevertheless, Liu's works are patently anachronistic — not merely in the sense of reference to the very different political circumstances of earlier periods, but also in the expression of fundamental orientations to the role of the Communist Party which are no longer salient. His demands on matters such as organisational procedures and forms of political activity may always have been too stringent to be met by most CCP members. Now they may be so far from prevalent types of behaviour within the Party that they no longer serve even as credible models. Most generally, within the current orientation of the CCP there are only the faintest echoes of Liu's understanding of the Party as the bearer of a universal proletarian historical mission. Liu may have been restored as an authority, but his role is almost entirely decorative as his organismic notion appears irrelevant to current CCP practice and can now be of little use in the Party's efforts at self-legitimation.

Notes

1. Arif Dirlik, *The Origins of Chinese Communism* (Oxford University Press, New York, 1989), p. 269.
2. As Søren Clausen has reminded me, the term 'Leninism' is itself certainly problematic. On the one hand, there are issues concerning the interpretation of Lenin's own political thought. On the other hand, there are many strands of post-Lenin thought which have attempted to use Lenin in such a way as to claim title to 'Leninism'. In the following discussion I do not attempt to deal with these issues; the focus is on Liu's treatment of themes of political organisation and leadership, which can be associated with the term 'Leninism' for purposes of convenience, while recognising that a different focus would necessarily consider that association more critically. Thus, there is no attempt to assess the relationship of Liu's views to Lenin's thought, nor to compare Liu with other variants of 'Leninism' (such as contemporary Stalinist orthodoxy or other CCP views).
3. 'On the Class Character of Man' (1941), in *Liu Shaoqi Wenti Ziliao Zhuanji (Special Collection of Materials on Liu Shaoqi)* (Taibei, 1970), p. 98. (Hereafter cited as *Liu Collection*); 'On Open and Secret Work' (1939), in *Liu Collection*, p. 69.
4. 'On the Class Character of Man', in *Liu Collection*, p. 98; 'On the Cultivation of a Communist Party Member' (1939), in *Liu Collection*, pp. 27-8.
5. 'Report on the Revision of the Party Constitution' (1945), in *Liu Collection*, p. 149.
6. 'Oppose All Bad Tendencies Within the Party' (1941), in *Liu Collection*, p. 116; 'A Letter to Chinese Workers on the 2nd Anniversary of the War of Resistance' (1939), *Collected Works of Liu Shao-ch'i* (3 Vols, Hong Kong, 1968-69), I, p. 149 (Hereafter cited as *CW*); 'Leadership is the Crucial Issue of the National United Front' (1936), in *Selected Works of Liu Shaoqi*, Vol.1 (Beijing, 1984), pp. 58-9 (Hereafter cited *SW*).
7. 'Speech at Yancheng Training Course for Security Personnel' (1941), in *Liu Collection*, p. 85; 'Oppose All Bad Tendencies Within the Party', pp. 120-21, 123.
8. 'Speech at Yancheng Training Course for Security Personnel', p. 85.
9. Hence, he saw the CCP as 'one of the best branches of the world Communist Party' — 'On the Cultivation of a Communist Party Member', p. 44. In 1948, Liu repeated the view that the Chinese revolution was an intrinsic part of the world revolution in urging cadres to study other countries. By this time, though, Liu put more emphasis on the achievements of the CCP, referring to the influence the Chinese revolution would have elsewhere: 'Speech Delivered to the First Class of Students of the Institute of Marxism-Leninism' (1948), *SW*, pp. 412-13.
10. On the Cultivation of a Communist Party Member', pp. 29-32 (quotation p. 29). 'On the Liquidation of Menshevik Ideology in the Party' (1943), in *Liu Collection*, pp. 131-33.

11. 'On the Class Character of Man', p. 98.
12. 'On the Cultivation of a Communist Party Member', p. 32.
13. 'Report on the Revision of the Party Constitution', p. 165.
14. 'On the Cultivation of a Communist Party Member', p. 54.
15. 'On Intra-Party Struggle' (1941), in *Liu Collection*, p. 101.
16. 'On the Cultivation of a Communist Party Member', pp. 53-4.
17. *Ibid.*, p. 54.
18. *Ibid.*
19. *Ibid.*, pp. 58-9; 'Oppose All Bad Tendencies Within the Party', p. 124.
20. 'On the Cultivation of a Communist Party Member', pp. 64-5.
21. *Ibid.*, pp. 57-8.
22. *Ibid.*, p. 56.
23. *Ibid.*, p. 57.
24. *Ibid.*
25. *Ibid.*, p. 58.
26. *Ibid.*, p. 60.
27. 'Report on the Revision of the Party Constitution', p. 169.
28. 'On Developing Democracy' (1944), in *Liu Collection*, p. 140.
29. 'On Intra-Party Struggle', p.111. See also 'The Party and Its Mass Work in the White Areas' (1937),*SW* 1, p. 76.
30. 'On Intra-Party Struggle', p. 108.
31. E.g., *ibid.*, p. 109.
32. To take one example, concerning the principle of not attacking cities in the then military environment, Liu suggested that an attack on a city, which was occasioned by special circumstances, did not involve a question of principle. It became such only if the attack on a city followed from advocacy of the principle of attacking cities! ('On Intra-Party Struggle', p. 109) This implied a separation between action and the theoretical understanding of 'general rules of the development of things'. The principle became something which could survive even in the face of action which contravened it. And Liu provided no criteria for demonstrating at what stage such contrary action raised the question to the level of principle. Cf. Frederick Teiwes, *Politics & Purges in China: Rectification and the Decline of Party Norms 1950-1965* (White Plains, New York, 1979), pp. 27-8.
33. 'On Intra-Party Struggle', p. 109.
34. 'On the Cultivation of a Communist Party Member', p. 54.
35. Liu's discussion of principled struggle was further complicated by his prescription for handling unprincipled disputes. He suggested that summary treatment should be avoided because it would leave people dissatisfied and the dispute would continue. In such cases, there should be an attempt to achieve unanimity on the basis of principle, and then see whether the dispute still remained. If it did, then the dispute had been raised to the level of principle and had to go through a process of struggle before it could be resolved. ('On Intra-Party Struggle', p. 112) This implies that even disputes not involving principle nonetheless had an underlying principled basis — that there was a 'correct' resolution in every case. Thus, Liu tended to undermine his own principled/unprincipled distinction. He seems to have been unaware of this implication, however, and preferred to

demand that Party members should avoid all disputes not involving principles, so that the party's solidarity and integrity were not threatened.

36. 'Be a Good Party Member, Build a Good Party' (1940), in *Liu Collection*, pp. 77-81; 'Oppose All Bad Tendencies Within the Party', pp. 119-20; 'On Enjoyment and Happiness', *CW*, I, pp. 90-92.

37. 'On the Cultivation of a Communist Party Member', pp. 38-9; 'Oppose All Bad Tendencies Within the Party', p. 123.

38. 'On the Cultivation of a Communist Party Member', p. 39; 'Be a Good Party Member, Build a Good Party', pp. 78-9, 81. See also Lowell Dittmer, *Liu Shao-ch'i and the Chinese Cultural Revolution: The Politics of Mass Criticism* (Berkeley, 1974), pp. 189-90; Michael Luk Yan Lung, 'The Career of Liu Shao-ch'i, with Special Reference to the Growth of His Power and the Development of His Political Thought, 1921-1949' (M. Phil., University of Hong Kong, 1974), pp. 252ff..

39. 'On the Cultivation of a Communist Party Member', p. 39.

40. *Ibid.*

41. Lawrence Sullivan, 'The Evolution of Chinese Communist Party Organization and Leadership Doctrine, 1921-1949', a paper presented at the Conference on 'New Perspectives on the Chinese Communist Revolution', Leiden, 1990, *passim*.

42. 'On the Cultivation of a Communist Party Member', p. 55. See also 'Oppose All Bad Tendencies Within the Party', pp. 120-23.

43. 'Oppose All Bad Tendencies Within the Party', pp. 121-2.

44. 'On the Cultivation of a Communist Party Member', p. 54.

45. 'On Developing Democracy', p. 138.

46. 'Oppose All Bad Tendencies Within the Party', pp. 124-5. Apart from recognising organisational constraints, those in leadership positions were also obliged to be exemplary in the moral qualities of membership, including greater willingness to sacrifice for the Party's cause. Nevertheless, Liu also argued that there had to be a division between leaders and led, and differences in treatment of people according to their positions. 'Egalitarianism negates any difference in authority and in treatment.' And ignoring the differences between leaders and led resulted in 'ultra-democracy, negating the organisational character'. But despite these differences, people should have the 'democratic spirit', by which Liu meant that they should not consider themselves 'higher' than others because of their positions. While organisation implied hierarchy, Liu attempted to counter this with the promotion of attitudes suggesting that all differences are only temporary or contingent, that 'mankind is basically equal'. ('Democratic Spirit and Bureaucratism', in *Liu Collection*, pp. 83-4; 'The Party and Its Mass Work in the White Areas'[1940], p. 75).

47. 'On Intra-Party Struggle', p. 108; 'Oppose All Bad Tendencies Within the Party', p. 126.

48. In contrast to earlier arguments which used Cultural Revolution hindsight to trace antagonism between Mao and Liu back to the pre-1949 period, Frederick Teiwes has demonstrated their close links from the late 1930s: 'Mao and His Lieutenants', *The Australian Journal of Chinese Affairs*, Nos. 19+20, 1988, pp. 56-60, and 'The Formation of the Maoist Leadership: From the Return of Wang Ming to the Seventh Party Congress', a paper presented at the Conference on 'New

Perspectives on the Chinese Communist Revolution', Leiden, 1990, pp. 16-19. Cf. Raymond Wylie, *The Emergence of Maoism: Mao Tse-tung, Ch'en Po-ta, and the Search for Chinese Theory 1935-1945* (Stanford, 1980), pp. 112-14, 158-9, 205-7, 275-9.

49. 'On the Cultivation of a Communist Party Member', p. 54.
50. Report on the Revision of the Party Constitution', p. 147.
51. 'On the Cultivation of a Communist Party Member', p. 59.
52. 'On the Liquidation of Menshevik Ideology in the Party', p. 130.
53. *Ibid.*, p. 133.
54. 'Report on the Revision of the Party Constitution', p. 147.
55. *Ibid.*, pp. 152-4.
56. Liu's position may be seen as deriving from explicit political calculation, not only in acknowledging Mao's political predominance but also in the sense of expanding bases of support for the Party. While a more abstracted commitment to the Party and its mission might apply among some in the Party (the more politically sophisticated, or those who could be given more extensive inner-Party training), a specific individual provided a clearer focus of commitment for lower-level Party members and the Party's mass constituency. See Sullivan,'The Evolution of Chinese Communist Party Organization and Leadership Doctrine, 1921-1949', pp. 63ff.
57. Frederick Teiwes suggests a further level of irony in that in the early 1940s Liu himself criticised other Party leaders in a way prefiguring the Cultural Revolution: 'The Formation of the Maoist Leadership', pp. 18-19.
58. 'Several Basic Principles for Organising the Masses' (1939), in *Liu Collection*, pp.10-12. See also 'Various Questions Concerning Fundamental Policies in Anti-Japanese Guerrilla Warfare' (1937), *CW* I, pp. 46-8.
59. 'Several Basic Principles for Organising the Masses', pp. 12-14.
60. See Luk, *The Career of Liu Shao-ch'i*, ch. 6.
61. *What Kind of Ideals Should Communist Party Members Have?* (Beijing, 1958), especially pp. 1-12.

Creative Borrowing. How the Chinese Appropriated Dualism and Transmuted It

Flemming Christiansen

It is a common perception that the West looks to the East and *vice versa* for intellectual inspiration, a perception carried by much evidence both historically and in recent times. The nature of this cultural cross-fertilisation is the object of incessant appraisal both in the East and the West. Taking the example of a western theoretical concept that has been taken up in China, this contribution posits that the western concept in the Chinese context achieves a structure fundamentally alien to its western roots, but at the same time, as a borrowing, performs a useful and dynamic function within the Chinese intellectual framework.

To demonstrate this assertion, the contribution examines the Chinese debate on dualism, a concept borrowed from a specific western context.

Dualism as a concept is central to neo-classical development economics. In the transition to industrialisation there occurs an imbalance between the 'traditional' and 'modern' sectors of the economy. This imbalance is based on the 'unlimited supply of labour' from the agricultural sector, which means that industrialisation can develop in an environment of low wages (the Lewis model). The theoretical development of neo-classicist economy focused on the various exchange mechanisms which conditioned economic growth and the emergence of modern industry. The mechanics of development were structured by supply and demand of the main factors labour, capital, raw materials, food and purchasing power between agriculture and industry. Agriculture, at the starting point, was seen as a closed, non-commoditised and self-sufficient sector yet to be broken up and commercialised by industrial development. Industry, being dynamic and more efficient, would have advantageous terms of trade with backward agriculture, extracting surpluses from agriculture in order to develop further. Predatory exploitation of agriculture would, however, mean that supplies from agriculture would dry out and adversely affect industrialisation, so the equilibrating forces of the economy would in the long-term uphold terms of trade that would ensure development. Political intervention and similar 'economically irrational' behaviour would be ironed out by the forces of the economy, which regulate supply and demand. The unequal relationship with agriculture would terminate when agriculture was fully commoditised. The theoretical framework is normally referred to as the *Lewis-Ranis-Fei Model* after the three main authors who devised the theory; the *Todaro Model* is an extension of the model which explains the issue of labour migration, interpreting — in economic terms — why rural-urban migration took place even if there was urban unemployment. The main axiom of this neo-classicist theoretical framework is that the forces of economy rule above all other factors: That supply and demand meet in the market place, and that political, social and other constraints or imbalances imposed on the market will eventually be dissolved or evened out by the equilibrating forces of the economy. The models were characterised by two fundamental assumptions: (a) the market forces regulated the flow of resources in the economy, political control merely being a variable in the equation; (b) the process of development was basically a domestic affair, international influences being variables that could be accommodated in the equations.

The development of the Chinese economy since 1949 certainly poses itself as a serious challenge to the neo-classicist school of thinking. The flow of resources between agriculture and industry did not take place in the market place during most of the 45 years that have so far elapsed since Liberation, but was the field of excessive state control. For most of the time prices and quotas were fixed by direct state intervention, labour recruitment and migration were heavily regulated by the state, and most of the features presumed in the models simply did not come true.

There are two possible reactions to this in the western tradition of science paradigms. Either the anomaly is solved by methods from the extant theory, or the theory is rejected as irrelevant or insufficient as an explanation.

The neo-classicist school has largely ignored the socialist world during its existence, and has, perhaps with some glee, been able to celebrate its collapse as a proof of the universality of the forces of the economy. The anomaly of socialist state control of the economy could still be examined in the model as a calculation of how the economy would have behaved if there had been a free market, thereby also indicating the magnitude of political manipulation of the socialist economy, which is regarded as inherently perverse by neo-classicists.

Some would perhaps choose to reject the neo-classicist account as irrelevant since the Chinese economy during all these years did not base itself on a market economy. One could argue that the economy of the reform era developed a 'socialist market economy' strongly harnessed and manipulated by state intervention. The predictions of the neo-classicist models have not been honoured by the events in China, and so at least in the Chinese case the theory is insufficient as an explicatory framework.

The Chinese, however, did neither of this. They embraced the models of the neo-classicist school in order to create an explanatory framework for Chinese economic development. The Chinese 'dualism' discourse borrows some key arguments from the neo-classicists and uses them creatively. The discourse gained its own dynamic and logic, distinctly different from the neo-classicists'.

I will here analyse the process of borrowing from a structural perspective: Which elements played a role in the transformation of Western 'dualism' into Chinese 'dualism'? More specifically one could ask whether it is a case of code-switching. Code-switching is when speakers of one language use elements of a foreign language in their speech, for example to negotiate a specific status in relation to the people they communicate with.

One could also ask whether it is a case of integral incorporation of a foreign concept into the Chinese discourse. If this were the situation, the foreign concept loses it original value and is sudordinated the conventions of the Chinese discourse.

Finally, one could regard the phenomenon as a convergence of discourses. In that case the borrowing is a symptom of a process by which the value patterns and conventions of discourse in China and the West come closer to each other and promise to eventually amalgamate into a new discourse, common to China and the West.

As will be evident from the following, the second explanation is valid: Dualism was subsumed under the hegemony of dialectical materialism.

Contextual factors

From the end of the 1970s it became fashionable among Chinese intellectuals and scholars to examine and adopt *foreign* scientific methods and theoretical notions which were seen as *advanced*, *objective*, and *superior* when compared to the domestic intellectual landscape which had been stymied by ideological imperatives, petty politics and subjectivity during the Cultural Revolution.

There was especially a proclivity for 'hard science' methods which were politically 'safe,' given the fact that they made no ostensible claims on the political reality. The claim of political 'neutrality' for science and technology is universal and makes it possible to transplant it into cultural contexts in which it is fundamentally strange.

Its coexistence with other types of cultural expression and daily life is conducted in the form of code-switching, in which the 'foreign' elements are called upon and generally known among peers, but not felt to be integrated elements of one's own discourse. The ability to master the 'foreign' discourse and use it in code-switching practice gives status and establishes a corporate identity of academics. The code-switching is most conspicuous when concepts and notions are left untranslated as foreign words when they are used in the domestic context, but code-switching is also possible with a translated vocabulary, the only condition being that those who are part of the discourse agree to regard it as exclusive and 'foreign,' and consciously manipulate the terms of the discourse.

Apart from being an identity generating status marker, the use of a 'foreign' discourse also has the function of enabling communication with foreign scholars. Here, however, another communicative problem arises. While the 'foreign' discourse adapted by the Chinese scholars is likely to be complete and well understood by them in its explicit embodiment, they are unlikely to be familiar with its cultural subtext and associative context. Their communication with their foreign opposite numbers, therefore, is limited to the technical and explicit and meets a limit in cultural rapport.

This limitation means that the Chinese and the Western scholars are likely to have fundamentally diverse value patterns related to their common field of scholarship, and that although the trappings, symbols and structures of academic discourse may seem similar in China and abroad the social, cultural and economic contexts are fundamentally different. To illustrate this, one could think of the classical example of diplomacy, where the representatives of several countries agree on a principle, but each have their own interpretation of the principle. Although all are aware of the discrepancy in interpretation, the formulation of the principle has done the trick.

V. S. Naipaul has in *Among the Believers* derided the unprincipled use of Western science and technology in fundamentalist Islamic countries. These countries, he opines, are not aware that the foreign technology carries its ideology of modernisation with it. Like a Trojan horse, Western science and technology will bring destruction to the old, ideologically pure ways.

Whatever the situation may be in the most conservative Islamic countries, I do not think the situation is similar in China. The cultural subtext of 'foreign' discourses in China is not likely to seep into China, but in the process of borrowing scientific concepts, these are gradually incorporated into the body of Chinese discourses.

The example of dualism is an accentuated example of this.

Dualism in China

While the Western discourse on dualism was conceived in the 1950s and 1960s, the major Chinese debate began in the 1980s. Tan Xiongwen in his student textbook *Development Economics* (Fazhan jingjixue), and Tao Wenda in a different reader with an identical title, introduced the Western concepts of development economics, including the Lewis-Ranis-Fei Model (see e. g. Tao Wenda 1988, 91ff). Lewis's seminal article on the unlimited supply of labour from 1954 had been published in Chinese in 1984 in *Selected Contemporary Foreign Economic Articles* (Xiandai guowai jingjixue lunwen xuan) by Shangwu Yinshuguan along-side other crucial articles of the neo-classicist tradition. Among educated Chinese economists and social scientists in the 1980s the neo-classicist tradition was well-known, and it was part of university curricula.

The concept of dualism in the Lewis version was referred to as 'shuangyuan jiegou' (Tao Wenda 1988, 91) and 'eryuan (jingji) jiegou' (Rural Economy Group 1990, 49-65), the two expressions being virtually synonymous, like 'double system' and 'dual system,' but in the main vocabulary of the debate *eryuan* was the dominant expression. The dualism concept was not particularly prominent in any debates until the end of the 1980s. It was regarded with the same technical, slightly revering attitude as most other foreign concepts, but only having marginal, if any, relevance for China. Mastering this concept in itself did not give much status, unlike more sophisticated branches of 'foreign' science.

However, in 1988 and 1989 a short-lived debate broke out, which explicitly linked on to the Lewis-Ranis-Fei Model, and which reformulated the content of the model to make it fit with the Chinese reality. This debate is interesting because it shows the process of borrowing 'foreign' concepts, where the 'foreign' concept is subsumed under the Chinese discourse and looses the rigorous connotations it has in the Western context.

The Case of Rural and Urban Development in China

The Chinese lack of a market place should have deterred people from using the dualism model to describe the Chinese development. However, it could in a circumspect way give an important indication of what had 'gone wrong' in China.

Under the conditions of rural-urban dichotomy in China, the rural-urban barrier thwarted the transition of the dual economy to unification, i. e. the transfer of the rural surplus labour force, while conversely reinforcing the dualist tendency in the wake of the increasing industrialisation, exacerbating the lopsidedness. (Rural Economy Group 1990, 61).

Exactly the point that the state had used non-market measures, rather than the market economy, to accomplish the building of a *heavy* industry was at the core of the problem. The heavy industry is capital intensive and labour extensive, so under conditions where the income per head of the population was low and agriculture was the absolutely dominant sector of the national economy, a régime of the 'countryside aiding the cities and agriculture supporting industry' was chosen (Rural Economy Group 1990, 60).

To develop the high accumulation rate and resource capacity needed for heavy industry, securing the incessant flow of resources and capital to the cities from the countryside, the Chinese 'established a set of mechanisms of economic interaction which were characterised by rural-urban segregation, including state monopoly of trade and marketing, household registration and state labour allocation' (Rural Economy Group 1990, 60).

The dualism thus instituted was an 'economic structure,' whose 'modes and mechanisms of interaction were dissimilar to the general pattern of dual economy in developing countries described by the economist Lewis' (Rural Economy Group 1990, 60). Li Xiangchang (1989, 3-4) is even more emphatic, saying that it is wrong to conceive of dualism simply as a 'general transitory phenomenon during industrialisation,' and he focuses on the separation or mutual alienation of the economic structures. Qi Haodong (1989, 26) does not blame the 'dual economy' as such for the lack of coordination between rural and urban China, but ascribes it to the 'intervention of supraeconomic forces' which created serious friction in the rural-urban relationship. He instead urges that the unbalanced interaction mechanism be converted into an advantageous interaction mechanism of the dualist economy.

The use of the neo-classicist dualism concept obviously was limited to borrowing it by analogy. The fundamental axioms of the neo-classicist models were fully recognised and understood (while some authors do not address the origin of the concept at all, their formulations do not reveal serious lack of knowledge about it), but dualism in the Chinese context was deliberately and distinctively formulated as an alternative or parallel to the model, characterised by state control of the economy. The analogy lay in the transfer of production factors from the countryside to the cities to fund industrialisation; one type (according to the original model) was carried out by the market, the other (according to the revised Chinese model) by state control.

The Chinese debate focused on the nature of rural-urban dichotomy and its mechanisms as a protracted unbalanced relationship between rural and urban China, and not very strongly on how the production factors were transferred. This was conceptualised separately and formed a different discourse, that of the 'scissor's gap.'[1]

The underlying tenor of the discussion was that the policy of heavy industrialisation, copied from the Soviet Union, and motivated by the ambition of 'casting off poverty and taking in the developed countries of the world in a relatively short period of time' (Rural Economy Group 1990, 60), was unrealistic and wrong. It had created an intractable cleavage in the Chinese economy that had to be solved in some way.

Within this conjecture, dualism stood for both (a) a divide in Chinese society, but also for (b) a field within which this split could be solved. From this follows that most of the contributions were concerned with the nature of possible solutions rather than the understanding of how the cleavage came about.

In itself it is remarkable that the dualism model does not essentially add to the ideas promoted by Mao Zedong in his famous speech from 1956 on the 'Ten Great Relationships,' namely that prudent consideration should be made with regard to the relative development of the various sectors of the economy. The striking point, of course, is that the political inertia of the Chinese state in terms of economic organisation did not allow for a balanced development as suggested by Mao, and while 'walking on two legs' was one of the prominent slogans of the 'Great Leap Forward' in the late 1950s, signifying the simultaneous development of agriculture and industry, this notion was not followed in the practice of Chinese development. Within the scope of Mao Zedong's concept, the same mechanisms could be analytically approached as in the 'revised' dualism model. Why, then, would the development economists in the 1980s start using the neo-classical models?

In the following I will argue that there were two discourse levels, one at which the dualism model could provide a conceptual framework that was inherently meaningful (although far from all participants in the debate took up this point); and at another level, where the 'revised' model was at harmony with dialectical materialism as a discourse tradition.

At the first level, the Lewis-Ranis-Fei model provided a critical tool to explain the rise of rural industry in China in the 1980s, unveiling some of the fundamental structures of economic interaction in the reforming society. At the second level, the dual structures created and reinforced by state intervention did conceptually coincide with the notions of 'unity of opposites' and 'main contradictions' which have such a prominent place in everyday Chinese thinking. The following discussion of some of the many contributions to the debate is intended to explain these two levels of conceptual borrowing.

The aim is to illustrate that the 'foreign' concept of dualism was not borrowed lock, stock and barrel, but was used creatively and by analogy in a domestic discourse; to this end the process of borrowing was based on the precondition that the 'foreign' concept could serve within the domestic tradition of discourse.

The Rise of Chinese Rural Industry

The understanding of Chinese dualism by the Chinese rural economists and observers was based on the realisation that the division of China into rural and urban societies was drastic and disruptive to development. There was a general acceptance that the rural-urban divide was created by state intervention. Its disturbing effect on development could most clearly be perceived in the fact that urban industry was not able to absorb rural labour, while the agricultural sector remained flooded with underutilised labourers and was technologically backward; there was no illusion that a continuation of the division in its extant forms would bring any growth in the economy or would bring the rural labour surplus into work.

The difference between industry and agriculture in the context of China de facto was equated to the mutual alienation of the rural and the urban economies. The Chinese debaters agreed that state imposed structures were responsible for this, including the household registration system, the unified marketing and procurement systems as well as the labour allocation system. These were crucial for upholding negative terms of trade for agricultural products, which in Chinese debates are referred to as the 'scissor's gap.' The whole structure of rural 'ownership by the labouring masses' (i. e. collective ownership)[2] and the 'ownership of the whole people' (i. e. state ownership) to mainly urban assets, as well as the jurisdictional division of China created several, partly overlapping borderlines between rural and urban China between the mid-1950s and the end of the 1970s, some still being maintained at a less pronounced level in the early 1990s. The division was cultural, economic and social and constituted a sharp segmentation of the population in 80 per cent peasants and 20 per cent urbanites. The details and technicalities of the segregation shall not be discussed in detail here, but some of its effects are worth noting:

(a) urban industrial production could produce in a soft economic environment since the capital transfer from the country-side took place as a 'hidden' tax, defined as a low price for agriculture and a high price for industrial goods sold to the countryside. The outcome was that the state authorities could not allocate the revenue in the most appropriate way, but had to accept that inefficient enterprises gained just as much benefit as efficient ones;

(b) the rural population remained in the countryside, and migration was minimal, as was the transfer of rural labour to large industry in the cities; some recruitment of peasants for urban industry took place, but was off-set by the 'sending down' of school leavers to the country-side between 1962 and 1978;

(c) while nominal wages for urban labour remained low (but higher than rural incomes), the total consumption expenses of an urban worker to be carried by the work units were very high, covered by (a) basic wage; (b) work related allowances (butie); (c) bonuses (except during the Cultural Revolution); and (d) free or subsidised housing, medical care, old age pensions, child care, schools, foodstuffs, heating, drinking water, electricity, leisure activities etc. In addition, most public utilities were strongly subsidised by the state's coffers, e.g. including local and long-distance transport and social support schemes in neighbourhood committees.

These factors meant that the generation of occupational opportunities for peasants in the urban sector posed a problem. It entailed direct state investment that was not commensurable with the productivity increase, i.e. production could not cover the capital and consumption related expenses of additional workers.

The state, in order to solve the problem of low or negative returns from industrial investment could, of course, make a further recourse to the main sources of income for the urban sector by regulating fiscal proceeds and the hidden transfers from agriculture via the 'scissor's gap,' but such a procedure would depend on agriculture's capacity to carry the increased burden, and with increasing overloading of agriculture with surplus labourers due to the demographic increase and the continued lack of labour transfers to the urban sector, such a policy would not be sustainable for long.

One possible consideration was, of course, to do away with all barriers between agriculture and industry or the countryside and the cities to let the market forces pitch the workers' incomes in industry at a level reflecting their real productivity. Such a neo-classicist recipe would not be viable, since the institutions of a market economy did not exist, and also because suddenly upsetting living standards of urban workers would cause serious dissatisfaction and political unrest.

Job creation outside the state sector, however, was a feasible option, and in 1970 the Chinese state began, on a small scale, to create job opportunities in rural collective, non-agricultural enterprises. Between 1978 and 1983 the sector started a rapid expansion which has not yet ended in the early 1990s.

This is exactly where the Chinese dualism debate takes its point of departure. The idea is that the agricultural and non-agricultural elements of the rural economy react in ways similar to those characterising the dualism model. In the formulation of Liu Songsheng and others (1988), the 'dualist cycle' has to be overcome by obeying the objective laws of rural development, in order to create a modern economic system. This process should follow a three-phase pattern, (a) the accumulation phase, where agriculture creates investment for non-agriculture; (b) the non-agricultural feed-back phase where non-agriculture helps modernise agriculture in terms of technology, and through government intervention creates favourable conditions for the development of 'large agriculture,' i. e. agriculture in a broad sense;[3] and (c) a balanced development phase where agriculture has reached a high technological level and develops with high productivity per agricultural worker and where farm incomes exceed non-agricultural incomes.

The authors focus on three main constituent elements: (a) the evolution of the agricultural mode of production, in which the peasants should be urged to switch from pure agricultural production into partly non-agricultural, partly agricultural activities; however, due to the limiting effect of part-time agriculture for long-term development, the authorities should

give technological aid and regulate agriculture so as to achieve specialisation
and management of scale; (b) the development of agricultural technology at
increasing levels, following the overall needs of the development of
production structures; and (c) urbanisation in various steps, following the
overall agricultural development.

The problem has also been analysed as a set of contradictions (Wu
Weidong et al. 1988) in a 'triple economic structure,' namely the contradictions between (a) rural industry and urban industry; (b) rural industry
and traditional agriculture; and (c) traditional agriculture and urban industry.
The development of Chinese rural economy, therefore, is seen as a movement
away from a 'dual structure' into a 'triple structure.' Since the laws of the
economy are supposed by the authors to reign in the long-term, the above
mentioned contradictions will gradually and simultaneously decline.

Li Xiangchang also sees the role of rural industry in this light:

Rural industrialisation can certainly not be explained in a simple manner as peasant
behaviour; from a more fundamental point of view, it is the result of the concerted
performance of all sorts of social forces under the lopsided dual structure. It has
emerged with a perspective negating the original model of urban industrialisation,
and is created in sharp contradiction vis-a-vis urban industrialisation. (Li
Xiangchang 1989, 4).

Li Xiangchang's argument is that the only way to solve the problem of
dualism is to create conditions for 'local consumption' (jiudi xiaohua) of the
surplus agricultural work force in rural industries, stepwise transferring them
into still larger urban centres. Deng Yiming (1989) in a slightly different way
reaches the same conclusion. He argues that the double dual structure must
be simplified by incorporating the rural non-agricultural enterprises into the
system of 'national' (quanguo) non-agricultural enterprises. A restructuring
of the distribution of economic activities is also necessary, so that more
processing of agricultural products takes place in the country-side. Deng
Yiming's proposal is to gradually abolish the formal structures determining
the extant dual structure, e.g. the household registration system, and to
increase state subsidies to farmers.

The Chinese debate, as it is evident, centers around the question of long-
term development of agriculture, and in most participants' opinion the state
plays a crucial role in solving the dualist structure, while the underlying
market forces are recognised, but given a subsidiary role.

The theory of dualism and its transmutation in China gives an interesting view of how a concept can change focus and be used creatively to solve a theoretical problem within a new discourse context.

Dualism and Dialectical Materialism

The dualist theory was attractive because it formulated an imbalance in the economy as a pair of opposites. While the western concept was linear towards 'economic take-off,' the Chinese debaters saw the opposites in terms of dialectical struggle. From the 'sharp contradiction' of city versus countryside grew a new element, a new contradiction, namely that between agriculture and rural industry. To understand the development and to further the solution of the contradictions, it was necessary not to focus one-sidedly on one element, but to understand both sides, grasping the principle of the unity of opposites. No fundamental change, for example, could be achieved by putting emphasis on only one aspect at a time.

The ultimate solution would be the total unification of the opposites. This would only occur when rural industry had developed into a modern sector, when a large majority of the population was urbanised and when agriculture had reached a high technological stage.

However, none of the contradictions mentioned here were 'main contradictions.' They were all subsidiary contradictions to the main contradiction, and as such were not to be the focus of the 'struggle of life and death' which characterises the main contradiction, i. e. agriculture was not to subside in order to secure development, but its weight was to be shifted within the dynamic development of the dialectical struggle.

The main contradiction, where the absolute opposites struggle fiercely, had been declared by Zhao Ziyang at the Thirteenth National Congress of the Chinese Communist Party in Autumn 1987. It was the contradiction between the backward condition of the Chinese economy on the one hand and the aspirations of the Chinese people for an advanced and modern material and cultural civilisation. The tasks of the Chinese Communist Party for the coming 50 to 100 years had been set with the view to overcome backwardness, furthering economic development with all means available.

Within the scope of this task, it was important to examine how development of the economy could be achieved. Within Chinese dialectical materialist thinking the most important step would be to look for the material constraints between major elements of the economy, perceiving of them as opposites and contradictions that had to be solved. Once the mechanisms of these contradictions had been fully understood, it would be possible to regulate the relationship between them in order to gradually solve them.

The constraint created by dualism, as outlined above, seriously constrained the overall development of the Chinese economy. A vast array of perceived problems, including the existence of a huge rural surplus labour force, low agricultural productivity, low industrial productivity, the emergence of rural industry, bottlenecks in the distribution of goods, price inflation, backward technology in agriculture, could be comprehensively understood with reference to the dualist concept, and each problem could be formulated as a set of opposites or a contradiction in its own right.

Within the Chinese realm of thought, cognizance would have to rely on the formulation of contradictions like this, and only the formulation of contradictions would give a guideline for which action should be taken. Action would, under all circumstances, be political action, government intervention. Even the imposition of laissez-faire rule in part of the economy would only be seen as political action.

The 'objective laws of economy,' in the Chinese dialectical materialist understanding, do not contradict this view of cognition, they condition the nature of contradictions and determine the type of intervention that is needed.

In conclusion, I hold that the Chinese use of the Lewis-Ranis-Fei model in 1988 and 1989 was a form of creative borrowing which by no means marked the importation of yet another western, Aristotelian or linear logic into China. It was introduced by analogy to serve a function in the conceptualisation of an opposition within the framework of Chinese dialectical materialism.

Some Reflections

It could, of course, be asserted that dialectical materialism is a poor theoretical construction of dubious import, mainly exploited to give false credibility to despicable political objectives. Dialectical materialism is undoubtedly a pliable intellectual matrix which alows for frequent reformulations of the 'main con-tradiction.' Werner Meisner has claimed that the 'dialectical materialism' debate was merely a coded, allegoric controversy on whether or not the Communist Party should enter the second united front with the Guomindang in the 1930s (Meisner 1990; Christiansen 1991). One point of criticism prevalent in the western understanding of dialectical materialism is that it as a system of thought does not rely on a proper definition of its concepts, and that these concepts are hazy, overlapping and subject to constant change; in this way dialectical materialism is felt to be unacceptable in western philosophical discourse, a point made strongly by Meisner (1990, 3).

The most damaging attack on dialectical materialism, of course, is that redefinitions of the 'main contradiction' do not reflect developments of thought inherent to the theory, but rest on mere political expediency.

Dialectical materialism, however, could also be described in positive terms as a flexible tool for rationalising practical issues, deeply engendered in Chinese behaviour. Its formalised expression in the Chinese political ideology may prompt some people to openly distance themselves from it, but left with few other customary and socially accepted forms of reasoning, their intellectual intercourse will still be characterised by dialectical materialism.

Chinese philosophers like Liu Changlin (1990) claim that the Chinese possess a structure of cognizance distinct from the west, and while Liu Changlin shrewdly places himself in a position critical of simplistic political dogma, he unfolds an analysis which is characterized by dialectical materialism. He seeks back into history in an effort to reconstruct the cultural roots of dialectical materialism, seeking to disengage it from its political shackles.

It merits serious consideration that dialectical materialism is popular in China, is plausible in its context, has credibility among its users, and gives guidance on what to do and what not to do. It is, in other words, a socially accepted pattern of social intercourse with a reality *sui generis*, on top of which an edifice of official political discourse is erected.

The example of dualism gives an impression of the clash of culture that can occur when a western notion is borrowed into the Chinese context. In this contribution it is demonstrated how dualism is creatively borrowed and incorporated dynamically into the Chinese discourse which is totally alien to the western assumptions underlying the dualism concept.

References

Christiansen, Flemming (1991), 'Philosophy, Politics and the Origins of Chinese Communism.' *Journal of Communist Studies* Vol. 7, No. 4 (December) pp. 557-61.

Deng Yiming (1989), 'Lun Eryuan Jingji Jiegou Shiqi Nongye Zengzhang yu Jiuye Jiegou Zhuanhuan' [On Agricultural Growth and the Transformation of the Occupational Structure in the Period of the Dual Economic Structure], *Zhongguo Nongcun Jingji* No. 7, pp. 15-25.

Li Xiangchang (1989), 'Lun Shuangchong Eryuan Jiegou yu Nongye Fazhan' [On the Double Dual Structure and Agricultural Development], *Zhongguo Nongcun Jingji*, No. 2, pp. 3-16.

Liu Changlin (1990), *Zhongguo Xitong Siwei* [Chinese System Thinking], Beijing: Zhongguo Shehui Kexue Chubanshe.

Liu Songsheng, Lu Yixiang and Liu Baojin (1988), 'Shelun Shehuizhuyi Chuji Jieduan Nongcun Jingji Fazhan de Guilü' [On the Laws of Rural Economic Development During the Primary Stage of Socialism], *Nongye Jingji Wenti*, No. 5, p. 43-46.

Meisner, Werner (1990), *Philosophy and Politics in China. The Controversy over Dialectical Materialism in the 1930s*. London: C. Hurst, 230 pp.

Qi Haodong (1989), 'Lun Woguo 'Eryuan Jingji' Yunxing de Lishi Xiandai he Weilai Juezhe' [On the Historical Reality of the Functioning of the 'Dual Economy' in Our Country and the Options for the Future], *Zhongguo Nongcun Jingji*, No. 7, pp. 26-32.

Tao Wenda (1988), *Fazhan Jingjixue* [Development Economics]. Beijing: Zhongguo Caizheng Jingji Chubanshe (2nd edition 1990).

Rural Economy Group (1990), *Biewu Xuanze — Xiangzhen Qiye Yu Guomin Jingji de Xietiao Fazhan* [There Is No Alternative — The Coordinated Development of Rural Enterprises and the National Economy] edited by Guowuyuan Yanjiushe Nongcun Jingjizu and Zhongguo Shehui Kexueyuan Nongcun Fazhan Yanjiushe. Beijing: Gaige Chubanshe.

Wu Weidong, Feng Yuhua and Jia Shenghua, 'Woguo Sanyuan Jingji Jiegou Wenti Chutan' [Some Issues of the Triple Economic Structure in Our Country], *Nongye Jingji Wenti*, No. 5, pp. 52-56.

Notes

1. The scissor's (*jiandaocha*) gap denotes a price-fixing mechanism, whereby the calculated cost of production of agricultural goods is set at a lower level than it should according to Marxist price theory, and where the price of industrial goods for agricultural use are set higher than they should. In this way the state can levy a hidden 'tax' on agriculture. This mechanism could operate because the state had a total monopoly of procurement and sale, and all prices were determined by price commissions.

2. The ownership structure in the country-side was different from urban collective ownership in one important respect: It was based on the population having 'agricultural household status' living in a clearly defined jurisdiction (production brigade or administrative village), while the urban variety was organised like workers' cooperatives.

3. The term 'large agriculture' (*danongye*) is used to encompass agriculture, forestry, irrigation and water power, orchard management, animal husbandry, aquaculture, and similar activities. The term agriculture (*nongye*) in Chinese normally only designates cultivation (grain, industrial crops and vegetables).

China—EC Relations: From the Strategic Game to the Game of Global Competition

Clemens Stubbe Østergaard

When the Italian Foreign Minister Gianni de Michelis visited China in 1991 ago as a member of the EC-troika, he proposed the conclusion of a political agreement with China, similar to that between the EC and the United States and the EC and Japan.[1] It has not materialized. De Michelis also stressed China's role in the 'necessary' construction of a 'new multi-polar world order' which includes a 'reorganization of North-South relations'.

EC-China relations originally developed on the basis of Chinese political goals and European economic aims. After 1982-83, both of these motivations lost their dynamic effect on the relationship, which did not progress as expected. In recent years, Chinese goals have been mainly economic, while political considerations have played an increasing role in the EC policy towards China. These asymmetries and other inertia-factors have ensured that the relationship has not developed much beyond trade regulation and technical cooperation (Boardman, 1981; Kapur, 1986).

Even the new environment presented by the end of the Cold War and the changes in European integration do not seem to have brought any improvement. To what degree can this be explained by recent developments in, and EC relations with, the rest of the Asia-Pacific region?

First, the paper will look at other possible explanations of the lack of diversification in relations. Turning to the Asia-Pacific region, it then discusses the new international environment there, before singling out a number of changing relationships of the European Community with the region. An attempt is made to determine how these new factors influence EC-China relations, and finally we look to the future in search of potential common interests which might form the basis for increased political cooperation between China and the EC.

Systemic and Actor-Level Explanations

Trends in the International Political and Economic Systems
There could be several explanations of the single-track relations of the 1990s. At the level of the international system, fundamental systemic changes in the global power structure are drawing Europe and China away from each other. The same effect can be derived from the main trends of globalization and regionalisation in the international economic system. In addition, fundamental conceptual and doctrinal changes weaken or damage relations.

Structural Change

The most obvious systemic change is that from *bipolarity to multipolarity* (Buzan, 1991).[2] It was a development that China had looked forward to for many years, since it would mean increased room of manoeuvre. When it came, it was a disappointment, because at the same time the international agenda had shifted from strategic to economic interests. This played to Japanese and Newly Industrialized Economies strengths in economics and Science & Technology, rather than to China's military and strategic capabilities. In addition, an informal security community seemed to form among the major centres of capitalist power, Europe, Japan and the United States. It was supposed to be able to meet challenges to the new 'order' and it made it more difficult for China to influence this, in a sense, uni-polar structure. For this reason China would not want by its actions to strengthen such a security community. For the EC side, the apparent strength of the centre-coalition lessened interest in the periphery/Third World and its economic deterioration. The move from bipolarity had several other consequences. The inherent demise of the Soviet threat removed a mutual strategic interest from the EC-China agenda. The increasing importance of regional politics and conflicts also caught the attention of both parties.

In the international economic system, the main new phenomenon was an apparent confirmation of *economic tripolarity*. That is, a trilateral regime of cooperation and free trade between three large markets, underpinning and stabilising inter-capitalist rivalry in the world system. This does of course carry the danger of an erosion of the open world economy and the formation of blocs — the certain losers being developing countries and the former East bloc. In the present context, it has on the one hand the effect of directing some EC attention to Japan rather than to China. On the other hand, a broader pattern of increased economic competition between Europe, Japan and the US will further sharpen interest in resource exploitation and overseas markets, thus promoting interest in relations with China.

Globalisation and Regionalisation

Other important trends were globalisation, regionalisation and the rise of non-state actors in the system. *Globalisation* (Simon, 1991),[3] entailing global competition, global firms, global networks of production and distribution, could be a dynamic factor for increased interaction between Europe and China. A key question for China at present is whether it can become a strategic player in the game of global competition. The basis of its strategy for attaining this goal is the expansion of exports to the United States and Europe to finance technology acquisition and reach the position of a partner in relationships with multinational corporations. This leads to strains in the trade relationship with EC.

Transnational companies have become a much more dominant feature of the international economic system, and lately the multi-nationalisation of Japanese companies has augmented their role. Transnational business alliances are a strong element of the 'tripolar' economic structure. A transnational industry coalition was the driving force behind the Single Market Process and Europe 1992 (Sandholtz and Zysman, 1989), but it can be argued that in the 1990s transcontinental strategic alliances between multinationals in US, Europe and Japan are seen as the most effective way to cope with the globalisation of markets, the changes in the production process and the costs and risks of large scale Research & Development (Østergaard, 1993). EC-China relations may thus be superseded by the multinational companies' (MNC's) transactions within and between themselves. But it would clearly be vital for China to be able to take part in R & D at this level, and perhaps its own transnational corporations will be a key (Ye, 1992: 131).

Regionalisation also weakens the EC-China tie, as areas within China are pulled into the various networks, transborder relationships and mini-regions forming in the Asia-Pacific region.

Conceptual and Doctrinal Change

The systemic changes are related to a major *conceptual change* or agenda shift already hinted at (Guo, 1990). With the end of the Cold War, economic, societal and environmental issues have risen on the international agenda. As economic factors rise to prominence, security is seen as much in economic as in military terms. Science and technology is increasingly regarded as the key to power, rather than territory and acquisition (Zagoria, 1991). By the same token, borders are becoming less important to economics. This conceptual change will tend to detract attention from the need for political cooperation between China and EC. In the economic area, as we have seen, it leads to conflict.

A final area of change could be called *doctrinal*. First, the end of the Cold War has seen the near-total demise of other ideologies than liberal capitalism, with its canon of political pluralism and market economics. There is in particular no ideological division in the security community of the centre. Secondly, the West tends to want to spread its political system, economic model and ideology of capitalism to other countries, producing a countermovement as other civilisations react to the pressure. The most evident example is Islamic fundamentalism, but even the gradually transforming remnants of communism in Asia could be provoked. Thirdly, new international norms are promoted and become universal, as Western institutions and regimes appear victorious (Buzan, 1991).[4] There are some positive aspects of this doctrinal change, which relies more on negotiation and bargaining. But if it is not administered with pragmatism and a respect for other civilisations, it will encumber even EC–China relations.

Situation and Interests of the EC and China

Quite apart from the effect of larger trends in the international system, changes in the *situation and interests of the two actors themselves* may also be possible explanations of the thinness of relations. Discussing the EC, it is as always important to remember the distinctions between government elites in the member states, Community institutions and European industry elites.

For the *European Community*, three factors seem important when evaluating relations with China. The first one is the lack of a common security and foreign policy. After the Single European Act, and until the Maastricht Treaty takes effect, the Twelve may develop a common position, but are limited to diplomatic action through the Presidency. The Community can, for more concrete action, support the positions of the Twelve's European Political Cooperation (EPC), using the commercial, economic and financial means at its disposal. This is controversial because it often means a break with established principles and interests, it is costly and it can easily be perceived as encroaching on the foreign policy prerogatives of member states. It is important to distinguish between, on the one hand, the Community's economic activities, which are based on a transfer of authority to the Community, and on the other hand the EPC which remains inter-governmental. One is highly organized, while the other is less structured and lacks staff and means. Thus economic and political dialogue has had very different degrees of structure and institutionalisation. The latter often resulted from external demands or from a crisis, but the possibility was there for a political agreement (Flaesch-Mougin, 1991). The Commission and the Euro-pean Parliament have sought to extend their authority by introducing political 'touches' to external economic policies, for instance around human rights and democratisation which they knew would be likely to be consensus-issues. In the case of EC-China relations, this has given a certain tension. And in general, the possibilities for political dialogue have not been good (Hill, 1991).

After the Maastricht Treaty, the system will be transformed, allowing for a common foreign policy. While the 'common positions' (article J.2) is a continuation of the EPC, the 'joint action' of article J.3 in part V of the treaty is more ambitious, the level of commitment being higher, though still not comparable to that of the external policies of the Community, e.g. trade, fishery, and agriculture where commitment has a judicial character (Petersen, 1993). Subject areas suggested for 'Joint action' are: the CSCE process, disarmament in Europe, non-proliferation and economic aspects of security policy, in particular transfer of military technology to third countries and weapons exports. Other possible fields are the CIS and Eastern Europe, the Balkans, Mahgreb, the Middle East, and development cooperation.[5] Insti-tutionally, the Council will be responsible for policy-making, the EPC Secretariat merging with its bureaucracy, and the Commission being fully associated with the CFSP including implementation and external representation. The Presidency remains responsible for day-to-day business, and the unanimity-principle generally prevails, though — in a break with the inter-governmentalist approach — qualified majority voting is foreseen in certain cases. It remains to be said that defense policy is included in the CFSP for the first time, article J4 linking it to longer term development of a common defense policy, even a common defense.

These developments may well make the EC-China relationship more substantial. It could also be hypothesized that member states have postponed increased bilateral political relations while expecting the Community to undertake them in the future.

The second factor militating against an upgrading of relations has surely been the very *preoccupation of Europe* with the process of revitalized integration, underway since 1983. This inward turning was further worsened by the agenda of German reunification, and then by the need to cope with East European hopes for association or membership. Deepening and expansion of integration has left little surplus capacity among politicians and bureaucrats. Nor, it seems, has the transnational industry coalition had sufficient interest in China to offset this. While some of the pressure may relent after the successful ratification of the Maastricht Treaty, new issues of integration are waiting, while new potential member states approach the Community. Even Kazakhstan, bordering on China, has asked for membership (Nisbet, 1992).

Thirdly and finally, the unrelenting *protectionism* of the EC will continue to create stresses in trade relations with China, souring other types of relations. Trade policy drives EC foreign economic policy in the Asia-Pacific region. And, in the words of Louis Emmerij, 'no other actor in the international trading system ... deviated so widely from the principles of free trade as has the Community' (Emmerij, 1990). There are indications that the EC has been somewhat more protectionist than either the United States or Japan, EC non-tariff barriers being especially discriminatory against the manufactured exports of middle-income industrializing countries (Rudner, 1992:26). Disenchantment with the EC and its demands regarding anti-dumping measures, safeguards, reciprocity requirements, local content, etc. is not limited to China, but there have certainly been trade frictions since the European trade surplus of the 1980s turned into a deficit which has doubled every year since 1987, reaching $12 billion in 1991.[6] The talk was of China's tariffs and non-tariff barriers, import-taxes, import-licensing restrictions, problems in currency allocation for imports forming a de facto import quota, etc.

The lack of a common foreign and security policy, the blinkers of deepening and widening integration, and the dominance of tough trade policies have all set limits to the development of EC-China political relations.

China's situation and interests have also not been conducive to closer ties with the EC. Time, trade and peace remain essential to Chinese policy. And in a sense China, like the EC, is preoccupied.

The need to gain *time*, while increasing its overall strength through economic development and particularly through stronger science and technology, is central for China. The situation is favourable, except for the perceived trend of consolidation of a capitalist 'centre' consisting of US, Japan and Europe. Such a development leaves very little room for China in the management of world affairs, and it is only natural to counter it by exploiting the undoubted contradictions between the three actors which approach a tripolar dominance of the world. A weak point in the tripolarity is the realization of Europe's role as a single or unitary actor, and so China also stresses — and exaggerates — disunity and turbulence in Europe at present. Diplomatic efforts are not expended on the EC, but rather on securing the support of the countries of the South as a base for regenerating China's foreign policy. It might, finally, also make sense for China to await a stronger bargaining position before making political deals with Europe.

Economic relations are becoming a necessity. Using official Chinese statistics, the EC is the fourth-largest *trade* partner of China with 10.5 per cent of total value of import and export. Germany, Italy and France are the main partners. If export via Hong Kong is included, much larger figures are reached, and the EC estimated that the deficit in bilateral trade was $9.3 billion in 1992. Since 1979, the EC states have given government credits for 649 projects to a total of $9.34 billion. There are about a thousand Sino-European joint ventures entailing contractual investments of about $8 billion. Important development assistance has been in agricultural extension, food aid, fishery projects, pharmaceutical science, and subsidized wheat sales.

Peace is a necessity too, and with the preoccupation of the great powers with economic affairs the situation is good for China's independent foreign policy. There is no need to try to establish closer security links with Europe. With the end of the bipolar situation, China's security problems are in the regional conflicts, be they territorial, ethnic, etc. In short, a regional security complex where Europe cannot be of much help, except perhaps regarding sophisticated weaponry to cope with the quasi-arms-race going on in the Asian region.

This leaves two main ways in which the EC is interesting. China needs it as a market and a source of assistance, technology and investment and thus is dependent on acceptance of Chinese exports.[7] And Europe might be necessary as a counterweight to a possible US hegemony, which seems, however, to be a more and more unlikely scenario.

The configurations of the national and international situation of each of the two actors may change or be modified. One of the characteristics of the era is the speed of change itself, the *transitory character* of developments. This goes for the other actors too. The international situation has a particularly transitional character because every single one of the five main powers in a multipolar world will be going through painful structural reforms for years or decades to come. Europe while trying to adapt to 1992, German reunification and events to the east of it, China and Russia going through transformations towards market economies, Japan and the US forced to solve the imbalances in and between them. If just one of these enterprises falters, global stability is threatened once again.

The Asia-Pacific Context for EC-China Relations

General Trends of the Region
Turning to the Asia-Pacific region, we find a stable situation where, in China's view, all forces are balanced, interdependent and mutually constrained, in a high-growth economic context (Xin, 1993: 10). I will argue that recent developments in, and EC relations with, the rest of the Asia-Pacific region can supply part of the explanation for the lack of life in EC-China relations.

First of all, there are some important economic and political trends to be found in the new international environment in East- and South-East Asia. Some of them are autonomous and long-term phenomena, others are derived from the Single Market Process and the end of the Cold War. Together they have resulted in the rise to economic and political importance of other actors in the region than China, attracting increased interest from the EC. This interest is in part a recognition of the sustained 6-7 per cent growth in BNP of the region and the global economic importance of several actors, such as Japan, Taiwan and Asean. In part it is of a defensive nature, arising from worries about Asia organising, be it in the form of Asean, AFTA, APEC or EAEG, or about Japan squeezing Europe out of the Asia-Pacific region.

Well-known *long-term trends* have been those of liberalisation and privatisation commencing in the mid-80s, as well as that towards democratisation starting in 1986. The tendency for Japan and the newly industrialized economies of South Korea, Taiwan, Hong Kong and Singapore to form an economic coalition working towards a 'soft institutionalization' of an open and loose regional economic regime has also developed since the mid-80s (Inoguchi, 1992). By now, many fully integrated networks of production have been built up by Japanese corporations like Sony, Mitsui and Mitsubishi, forming a division of labour covering the whole East Asian region (Tokunaga, 1992). Inter-regional trade has consequently increased dramatically in recent years, supported by the transformation of political alignments permitting new axes of economic cooperation. Trade among Asian countries grew by 23 per cent in 1991, while export growth to the rest of the world expanded only by 14.8 per cent.[8] Regionalisation has not stopped globalisation, partly because of the need to compete globally, partly because transnational corporations based outside the region seek the technological and manufacturing skills it offers. The overall result of these trends is a dynamic region, incorporating up to four different tiers of economies and containing mini-regions of especially high economic activity (Johnson, 1991).

The effects of a revitalized European integration (and the end of the Cold War) were somewhat preempted by the increased intra-regional trade and investment. But since Europe was an increasingly important market — EC's share of Asian exports was 16.8 per cent in 1990, and its share of Asean's exports rose by 31 per cent from 1989-91 — the nations in the region fought against protectionism, GSP-differentiation, EC agricultural policies (the Cairns Group) and also presented a 'united front' against EC attempts at condition-ality.[9] Fears of protectionism led Asean to accept larger regional organisation from 1989 and the result, Asia Pacific Economic Cooperation (APEC) in turn led the EC to complain about the procedure and the fact that the EC was not invited to participate in what it was feared might become a rival economic bloc based on exclusionary trade policies (Crone, 1992). The Asean Free Trade Agreement, which commenced on the same day as the European Single Market, has not been the object of EC criticism (Vatikiotis, 1993).

The upshot of these trends in the new international environment has been a *change in EC relations* with individual actors in Asia. Growing importance has been accorded to Japan, both because of its position as the second largest economy in the world, and because of its beginning independence in foreign policy (Østergaard, 1993). Closer relations have been sought with Asean, in spite of Indonesian-Portuguese altercations over East Timor. Beginning relations to Taiwan have developed since 1990, and finally Vietnam receives a high degree of attention. In the following, we shall look at these four EC-partners in more detail.

Factors Interfering with or Weakening EC-China Relations
In what ways could the relationship of the European Community with the rest of the Asia-Pacific region theoretically interfere with the EC-China relationship? Primarily through competition for resources, functional substitution and value-fulfilment.

Competition for *resources* refers to two kinds: attention and money. First, it is important to remember the small number of officials engaged in Asian Affairs in Brussels. Though, in principle, Asian Affairs are all in Directorate General 1, at least three Commissioners claim political influence. The Secretariat of the European Political Cooperation is diminutive, too. Principles of rotation often assure that expertise does not grow beyond a certain point. I am not arguing that this is comparable to a single-issue foreign ministry, but I am saying that the recent higher activity in a wider Asian context must detract from planning and actions related to China. Money is scarce, too, and the greater overall dynamism in Asia has brought about a globalisation of EC external cooperation policy as a response to intensified trade and investment relations with developing countries in Asia. In spite of the increased funds set aside in 1992, there is competition and recent grants to Russia will make this worse. From 1990 to 1992, the EC provided 44.8 per cent of all aid to the countries of Eastern Europe and 73 per cent of that to the CIS.[10]

Functional competition refers to fields where other nations in the Asia-Pacific area can replace the function China has had in relation to the EC. Markets for exports are important, and only about 1 per cent of EC exports goes to China. Other countries may be more suitable markets for European goods, or may offer 'packages' of massive expansionary spending.[11] Resources in a wide sense must also be included. An obvious one is low-cost disciplined and educated labour power. Finally, in a security context EC institutions or governments may, rightly or wrongly, perceive that China's strategic functions can be replaced by other states or groupings in the Asia-Pacific. Some even go as far as to designate new 'poles' in the region.

Competition on *value-fulfilment* refers to the new-found stress of the EC on principles such as human rights and democracy (Østergaard, 1990; Østergaard, 1993). It has been made possible by the end of the Cold War, and it is part of the zeal described above for universalizing liberal capitalism and political pluralism. It has of course led to much discussion about political conditionality on trade and aid, and it means that the position of a number of other nations in Asia is improved relative to that of China. From 1984 to 1989, the EC had committed 35 million ECU for 16 projects in the rural sector, food aid of 100 million ECU and some aid in energy and education, as well as science & technology. It reacted to the events in China in June 1989 by proposing the postponement of examination of new credits from the World bank, as well as of almost all its own new projects.[12] When it decided, in October 1990, to 'gradually' resume appraisal of new projects, it introduced the study of the human rights record and participation in the life of society as a guideline.[13] The gradual resumption of cooperation has focused on the poorest regions of China and is supposed to be guided by close monitoring of the human rights situation. The 1991 level of commitments did not exceed that of 1988. At the Lisbon EPC Ministerial meeting in February 1992, it was decided that new cooperation programmes should concentrate on good governance, poverty alleviation, minorities, environmental protection and promotion of economic reforms.

Some Important Cases: Japan, Taiwan, Asean and Vietnam
Let us look at the cases of Japan, Taiwan, Asean and Vietnam, with the above three categories in mind. EC ties with South Korea could also be considered, when the commission has completed its thorough review on upgrading relations, commenced in 1993.

Japan
The image of a tripolar world has placed EC-Japan contacts on the mutual agenda as the so far weakest link in a triangle with the US in a pivot position. Japan in particular has sought to counterbalance its political dependence on the US, and has wanted to see Europe as a unitary actor. Europe was reticent for a long time, but from 1991 the Commission made a weak attempt to take the initiative for a new external bargain with Japan. As US hegemony diminished, there were more opportunities for the Community and Japan to find positions of common interest in opposition to American economic and political views and actions, and an informal foreign policy network grew up around these important institutions and regimes. But it was perhaps only the vicissitudes of the Gulf Crisis, and the influence of the Europe-oriented Deputy Foreign Minister Hisashi Owada, which finally led to the preparation of an EC-Japan Joint Declaration to strengthen political dialogue. In the process, the President of the Commission in June 1991 visited Tokyo for the first time in five years, 'playing the statesman, not the car salesman', as a participant observer noted. Some saw the declaration as averting attention from the economic issues, while the Japanese were humiliated by French attempts to impose managed trade as the price of political dialogue.[14] This contradiction has always been a feature of relations, and the main impression is that a new phase has been reached. The declaration foresaw a battery of formal elements in the foreign policy network:

1. Existing regular consultation mechanisms, in specialised areas.
2. Annual summits between the president of the EC Council and Japan's Prime Minister.
3. Annual meetings between the Commission and the Japanese government at ministerial level to continue.
4. Semi-annual consultations between the foreign ministers of the Community and the Commissioner responsible for external relations (troika) and the Japanese foreign minister.
5. Briefing of each other's representative, by the presidency on EPC (following ministerial political cooperation meetings), and by Japan on the government's foreign policy.
6. Regular review of implementation, through the above fora.

On top of this, Jacques Delors created a special task force to find areas of cooperation,[15] Commissioners pay regular visits to Tokyo, as do members of the European Parliament. Considering the exigencies of the EPC framework, this is a large amount of institutionalisation. The Commission clearly wants to expand its foreign policy role. There is even a certain similarity between it and Japan: The two are in many ways at a similar stage of taking up their responsibilities on the world stage and both are trying to translate economic clout into international political influence, with an internal structure stretched to capacity. They have both begun to do something about it, Japan by organising a new powerful policy coordination bureau in the MFA, the Commission by nominating Hans van den Broek as 'Foreign Minister'.

While Japan thus definitely competes for the diplomatic resources of the EC, its market is also potentially very well-suited to European high quality products competing with similar American ones. The rise by 69 per cent (from $18.5 to $31.2 billion) in Japan's trade surplus with EC in 1992 will tend to sour relations, but the recent injections of hundreds of billions of dollars into the economy makes it likely that European industry will be attracted. As regards strategic thinking, no one in Europe has introduced this consideration, but implicitly Japan is part of the 'security community' described above, primarily in the capacity of financial backer.

Taiwan

Since France vetoed diplomatic relations in 1964, the EC has not had official ties with Taiwan.[16] Beginning with a freight tax agreement in August 1990, this has been changing. The European Chamber of Commerce in Taipei was treated by the Taiwan government as official representatives.[17] An agreement on the monitoring of textile exports to EC was also reached in mid-1991 and talks on intellectual property rights held in November that year. This was termed 'informal contacts', and officially there were no negotiations, but they continued when a delegation of ministerial officials went to Brussels half a year later.[18] In January 1991, the French Minister for Industry paid an official visit to Taiwan and in April 1992 the vice-chairman of the Commission Martin Bangemann as the first high-ranking EC official.[19] The EC for the first time agreed to accept Taipei as the venue for trade talks later in the year, which was regarded as 'a political breakthrough' by Taiwan authorities.[20] The talks were led by the Deputy-Director General of the General Directorate for External Relations and included discussions on GATT. At the end of the year, Commissioner Bangemann's Deputy Chief of Cabinet visiting Taipei hoped to promote substantive relations and pragmatic bilateral ties between Taiwan and the EC.[21]

All in all, considerable resources were spent on the Taiwan relationship, to the implicit detriment of China–EC relations.

Taiwan has increasingly formed a market for European goods, after setting itself the goal of establishing a better balance in its foreign trade, which until 1990 was dominated by US and Japan by over 50 per cent. The goal of 20 per cent of trade to be with Europe was reached in 1989, while equality with the US share of trade is aimed for in the year 2000, and at the moment Europe is Taiwan's third largest partner.[22] The introduction of the 6-year National Development Plan of US$300 billion also greatly excited European industry, especially subjects like mass rapid transit, electrical power generation, aerospace, environmental protection and financial projects.

The European Parliament recently reminded the EC of the strategic and political importance of Taiwan, suggesting that the EC strengthen relations and help it develop into 'a balancing power to check Japan's economic domination as well as play a role in the power structure of the entire West Pacific area'.[23] This is not a widely backed view, but it calls to mind France's severely criticized sale in late 1992 of sixty Mirage 2000 jet-fighters to Taiwan. The French have a particular optimism on Taiwan, seeing it as major economic power in the Far East and encouraging China to benefit from 'triangular operations' between itself, Taiwan and external actors.[24]

Taiwan may thus be said to 'compete' with China on both resources and functions. As for principles or values, the democratic developments since 1986 have given Taiwan significant good-will in Europe. However, the development sketched out above would not have been possible without the end of the Cold War, the weakened situation of Chinese foreign policy in the wake of June 1989, and the competition in that same foreign policy between the goals of Chinese reunification and that of obtaining foreign capital and technology for modernization.

The Association of South East Asian Nations

The case of *Asean* may also be analyzed using the categories of competition for resources, functions and values. Europe's relations with the association's member countries have a colonial history, but it was not until Great Britain joined the EC that cooperation was sought. The 1980 agreement was the basis of relations for a decade, and regular ministerial meetings were held for a group-to-group dialogue, while bilateral relations have also been stepped up. The meetings involve foreign ministers and contain a political section discussing 'hot spots' particularly in Asia. They have been marked by both consensus and criticism, ending with a joint declaration and a press conference, but may be followed by meetings of for instance economy-ministers and the EC. In 1992, the Commission was busy preparing a new and broader 'Third Generation' EC/Asean agreement, of the kind signed with certain Latin American countries.[25] Asean is an important recipient of EC development assistance. In January 1992, the EC agreed to increase its aid budget for Asia by 55 per cent to $2 billion in the 1992-1995 period.[26]

The importance of the Asean market of 320 million people is mirrored in the great efforts made by the EC to convince the countries that '1992' is not detrimental to Asean's exports, and in EC's increased cultural diplomacy. In the course of two decades, the gross national product of Asean was multiplied by nine. The continued growth and dynamism of the region is based on the stability resulting from perceived Vietnam and Cambodia settlements and thus is part and parcel of the end of the Cold War. It is also a consequence of the Japan-led international division of labour in the region. This very aspect has made it increasingly difficult for the EC to compete with investment and market-shares of Japanese and US firms cooperating in the area.[27] The Commission welcomed the decision to create the Asean Free Trade Area, seeing it as compatible with GATT. As regards resources, Asean may be seen to compete with China, and in the area of potentiality, Indonesia should not be overlooked with its huge population and many raw materials.

Strategically, there have been attempts to posit Southeast Asia as a 'pole' of the new political and economic world order. In the context of European Political Cooperation, the Twelve have found that the internal strengthening of Asean gives hope for 'the emergence of a strong new pole of stability in Asia, in the context of a multipolar world'.[28] A Chinese analyst has taken a similar view, finding a pattern of a quadrilateral and five sides or parts with significant impact on peace and stability, Asean constituting a side or part due to its improved political, strategic and economic status giving it a greater say in Asia-Pacific affairs (Chen, 1991). Needless to say, the EC could run the risk of being involved in China-Asean conflicts, for instance around the Spratly Islands. It should certainly also be aware of the dangers of militarization of this region which is so vital to world trade.

Regarding principles, Asean has stood up very clearly against EC attempts to impose conditions. In July 1991, the EC said future ties must address human rights and environment, but Asean replied that no group should impose its standards of human rights and environmental issues or try to make them conditions for trade and investment.[29] Conditionality was unacceptable. This has prevented a replacement of the 1980 agreement with an economic pact, and it was a major contentious issue at the latest ministerial meeting in Manila in October 1992, when a compromise was reached to defuse the conflict between Indonesia and Portugal over human rights violations in East Timor.[30] Overall, however, the governments are democratic and the market economy reigns, putting Asean a good deal closer to EC sets of values than China.

To sum up, Asean has competed for both attention and money. As a group it may have found it easier to establish a political dialogue with the EC. It can to a degree substitute for the functions of China in European perceptions, and it is closer, though not in total agreement, regarding values. It may have appeal as a counterweight to China, consisting of more manageable states, perhaps proceeding towards an economic and security community.

Vietnam
Vietnam is taken up as a case because its development is so recent, not because EC links with it are strong. It has attracted the attention of the EC since its reform-policy started, and the country's constructive relations with Asean raised the hope of a Chinese-style future. It naturally competes for funds, though Japanese banks give big loans. In some aspects, the EC–China and EC-Vietnam relations are comparable: both are a case of assisting reform of a socialist system with large potentials as a market and for investments, possessing a disciplined labour force and off-shore oil resources. Since

Vietnam relinquished its plans for hegemony over South East Asia, it has the possibility of integration with Asean in the longer term. It competes for attention and money and offers some of the market and resource functions available in China. In addition, it meets with preferential attitudes from France and from Great Britain. The result has been generous development assistance and negotiations on diplomatic relations. Ten million ECU were allocated for aid in the 1993 budget.

Analysis of the three cases would seem to support the view that the rise of other actors in the region may have contributed to the emaciation of the EC–China relationship by diverting attention and providing substitutes for the general objectives sought by the EC. The greater picture of a change from the Strategic Game to the Game of Global Competition has reinforced this trend by strengthening the role of economic factors.

Concluding Remarks

The above analysis may present a too pessimistic view of the present and future of EC–China relations. One might stress the successful solution of trade problems, the great strides made in relations since 1989, the sea-trade breakthrough in 1992,[31] or the many examples of successful technical cooperation or joint ventures. The main concern here has been the lack of diversification of ties and the limbo of political relations, and for perspective we will consider some scenarios which might regenerate or initiate relations. First, some drastic eventualities:

1) The collapse of the reform process in the CIS, particularly in Russia, but also in the world's fourth largest nuclear power, Ukraine, could lead to chaos and a centrifugation of refugees, or it could lead to a post-Yeltsin junta setting its sights on expansionism.
2) The birth of a universal Islamic fundamentalist movement in Central Asia, creating fears for both Xinjiang and Turkey, would create common EC–China political interests. The effects of a civilisational Cold War, possibly even seen as functional by the West in its attempts to achieve cohesion in its own camp, would be more difficult to evaluate.
3) A nuclear-armed Japan, perhaps in combination with a neo-isolationist United States, might give Europe and China a common political interest.
4) Catastrophic changes in climate or environment would of course tend to drive the world together — or apart.

Leaving such apocalyptic scenarios, some important issues for cooperation could help bring together the EC and China:

1) If the multinational corporations develop to become a law unto themselves and ally freely across borders, only international cooperation will succeed in enforcing for instance competition regulations.
2) Cooperation around issues of narrowing the ever-worsening North-South gap, or in modernising the CIS could draw on China's successful reforms and Europe's particular vulnerability to the dangerous consequences of failure.
3) A deterioration of Sino-Japanese relations, or dissatisfaction with the growing dependence on Japan, might give Europe appeal as a 'third option' between the superpowers US and Japan. The attractions of European pragmatism compared to the US could be a factor. In a more pluralist China of different regions, some of them might also see a particular interest in cooperation with Europe and its Eastern European economic area.
4) Finally, the big balance-of-power play that China, as a permanent member of the Security Council, is intent on being part of, needs contacts and information and relationships of influence. To exercise its diplomatic skills, China needs to keep good relations with the EC, too. At the moment, there is enough reason to preserve a friendly situation and to involve China still further in the management of interdependency.

References

Boardman, Robert (1981): 'Guns or Mushrooms — Relations between EC and China 1974-1980', *Politica*, Vol. 13, no. 1, pp. 50-79.

Buzan, Barry (1991): 'New Patterns of Global Security in the Twenty-First Century', *International Affairs*, Vol. 67, pp. 431-51.

Chen, Qimao (1991): 'International Pattern in Asia-Pacific Region: Brewing Changing', *Korean Journal of International Studies*, Vol. 22, no. 3, Autumn, pp. 327-45.

Crone, Donald (1992): 'The Emerging Politics of Pacific Cooperation', *Pacific Affairs*, Vol. 65, no. 2, Spring, pp. 68-83.

Emmerij, Louis (1990): 'Europe 1992 and the Developing Countries: Conclusions', *Journal of Common Market Studies*, Vol. 29, no. 2, p. 250.

Flaesch-Mougin, Catherine (1990): 'Competing Frameworks: the Dialogue and Its Legal Bases', in Geoffrey Edwards and Elfriede Regelsberger (eds.) *Europe's Global Links. The European Community and Inter-regional Cooperation*. London: Pinter Publishers, pp. 27-42.

Guo, Changlin: 'The New International Environment and Northeast Asia', *Korean Journal of International Studies*, Vol. 21, no. 4, Winter, pp. 523-38.

Hill, Christopher (1991): 'The European Community: Towards a Common Foreign and Security Policy?', *The World Today*, Vol. 47, no. 11, pp. 189-93.

Inoguchi, Takashi (1992): 'Japan's Foreign Policy in East Asia', *Current History*, December, pp. 407-12.

Johnson, Chalmers (1991): 'Where Does China Fit into a World Organized into Pacific, North American, and European Regions?', *Issues & Studies*, Vol. 27, no. 8, August, pp. 1-16.

Kapur, Harish (1986): *China and the EEC: The New Connection*. Dordrecht. M. Nitjhoff.

Nisbet, Stephen (1992): *Reuter General News*, March 2.

Norgaard, Ole et al. (eds.) (1993): *The European Community in World Politics*, London: Pinter.

Petersen, Nikolaj (1993): 'The European Union and Foreign and Security Policy', in Norgaard et al. (eds.) (1993) pp. 9-30.

Rudner, Martin (1992): 'European Community Development Assistance to Asia: Policies, Programs and Performance', *Modern Asian Studies*, Vol. 26, no. 1, pp. 1-29.

Sandholtz, Wayne and John Zysman (1989): '1992. Recasting the European Bargain', *World Politics*, Vol. 40, no. 1, pp. 95-128.

Simon, Denis Fred (1991): 'China in the World Economic System', *Proceedings of the Academy of Political Science*, Vol. 38, no. 2.

Tokunaga, Shojiro (ed.) (1992): *Japan's Foreign Investment and Asian Economic Independence. Production, Trade and Financial Systems*. Tokyo: University of Tokyo Press.

Vatikiotis, Michael (1993): 'Market or Mirage', *Far Eastern Economic Review*, April 15, pp. 48-50.

Xin, Hua (1993): 'Six Characteristics of the World Situation in 1992', *Beijing Review*, January 11-17.

Ye, Gang (1992): 'Chinese Transnational Corporations', in *Transnational Corporations*, Vol. 1, no. 2, August, pp. 125-33.

Zagoria, Donald (1991): 'The End of the Cold War: Its Impact on China', *Proceedings of the APS*, Vol. 38, no. 2, pp. 1-11.

Østergaard, Clemens Stubbe (1990): 'Swans Scolding the Tiger? Scandinavian Foreign Policies towards Democratization in China 1976-1990', *Cooperation and Conflict*, Vol. 25, no. 1, pp. 171-94.

Østergaard, Clemens Stubbe (1993): 'From Strategic Triangle to Economic Tripolarity. Japan's Responses to European Integration', in Nørgaard et al. (1993).

Østergaard, Clemens Stubbe (1993): 'Values for Money? Political Conditionality in Aid: the Case of China', *European Journal of Development Research*, Vol. 5, no. 1, pp. 112-34.

Notes

1. *Agence Europe*, May 22 and 23, 1991.
2. Though anything from three to seven poles is offered by analysts.

3. Defined as 'increasing integration of and coherence of markets and industries'.
4. This includes the promotion by the centre-countries of non-nuclear proliferation and control of conventional arms trade.
5. *Report to the European Council in Lisbon,* June 1992. In the framework of the EPC, the Twelve welcomed China's decision, in principle, to accede to the Treaty on Non-Proliferation of Nuclear Weapons. *Agence Europe,* August 30, 1991.
6. 'Western Europe', *Reuter General News,* March 13, 1992. This includes exports through Hong Kong, in contrast to the official Chinese statistics on trade.
7. It is symptomatic that most of the 11 'recommendations' in Xiao Yuankai: Zhongguo he Ougongti guanxi fazhande fenxi, [Analysis of the developing relations between China and the EC] *Xiou Yanjiu,* vol. 10, no. 6, 1992, regard developing trade and economic relations with Europe.
8. ADB figures, quoted in *China News Digest,* Global edition, April 17, 1993.
9. *Bangkok Post,* November 2, 1990, p. 15; Far East, *Reuter Economic News,* February 16, 1990; *Financial Times,* February 16, 1990, p. 6; *Far East Reuter General News,* November 19, 1992; *Business Times,* Singapore, November 6, 1992; Western Europe, *Reuter General News,* September 23, 1992; *Business Times,* Singapore, July 17, 1992.
10. *Information,* April 15, 1993.
11. There is of course a wide differentiation in the export-profiles of member States, and Italy for instance regards China as a vital market, among the top regions of the world in the future (*South China Morning Post,* January 22, 1993).
12. *Declaration on China,* Annex II SN 254/1/89, p. 26, European Council Meeting, Madrid, June 26-27.
13. 'Abusive treatment', *Far Eastern Economic Review,* January 3, 1991, pp. 8-9.
14. An EC trade official remarked: 'The French are letting their mistrust and suspicion of Japan sour our hopes for a better relationship', *Far Eastern Economic Review,* August 1, 1991, p. 13. In fact, Japan's gains on the world stage may be French (and British) losses. And the Japanese economy grew with 'one France' between 1986 and 1992.
15. See 'Delors Calls for Team to Strengthen EC-Japan Relations', *Asahi News Service,* May 24, 1991.
16. *Agence Europe,* August 30, 1990. There was a Textile Accord between the EC and the 'Republic of Taiwan' from 1970 to 1973, but it was discontinued. Insofar as it was a consequence of China's diplomatic problems during the Cultural Revolution, there could be a structural similarity to the situation in 1990 when Taiwan again rose in status vis-a-vis the EC.
17. 'ROC to Have Multilateral Meeting with EC Representatives on 6-year National Development Plan in October,' *China Economic News Service,* June 5, 1991.
18. *Reuter General News,* October 31, 1991.
19. *China Economic News Service,* April 11, 1992.
20. *Agence Europe,* September 8, 1992.
21. *China Economic News Service,* December 10, 1992.
22. A realistic Taiwanese assessment of the effects of the Single Market is in Philip Liu: 'European Single Market — a Mixed Blessing for Taiwan's Economy,' *Business Taiwan,* January 11, 1993.
23. *China Economic News Service,* December 4, 1992.

24. *Le Monde*, April 28, 1991.
25. *Agence Europe*, January 30, 1992, February 5, 1992, March 27, 1992.
26. *Far Eastern Economic Review*, June 4, 1992. There are complaints from the European Parliament that the money is unused or badly spent, probably because senior EC policy makers are indifferent to Asia's trade and aid interests, concentrating instead on the traditional areas of Africa, the Caribbean and Latin-america.
27. *Neue Züricher Zeitung*, September 12, 1991, p. 15.
28. *Agence Europe*, February 15, 1992. French Premier Michel Rocard predicted closer ties based on many common interests, including the maintenance of a free trading system (*Japan Times*, November 12, 1990, p. 1).
29. *Far East, Reuter General News*, July 22, 1991.
30. *Agence Europe*, October 31, 1992.
31. The EC-China Maritime Trade Agreement in August 1992, giving each operator the right to trade freely within respectively the EC and the PRC (*Lloyds List*, September 29, 1992, p. 5).

Current Western Perceptions of Chinese Political Culture

Søren Clausen

In the last few years, the field of contemporary China studies has witnessed a major outpouring of studies related to Chinese political culture. The cultural approach to Chinese politics has always played an important role since contact was established between China and the West, but modern political culture studies in the strict sense, after proud beginnings in the 1960s and 1970s, during the 1980s increasingly appeared as a dead end with few dedicated practitioners and believers. However, a number of trends and events in the late 1980s, with the 1989 Democracy Movement as the single most significant factor, changed the situation. Veterans of Chinese political culture studies have returned to the field with revitalized energy, and, more significantly, a new generation of China scholars has explicitly challenged earlier assumptions and methods and suggested new departures for Chinese political culture studies. In the introduction to one of the pivotal 'new school' books on Chinese political culture from the early 1990s Elizabeth Perry proudly proclaims that:

... As adherents of the neoculturalist perspective, we let our defense rest upon the belief that this approach differs significantly from many previous efforts to explain Chinese protest in cultural terms and offers a more credible, and thus longer-lived, means of interpreting political change (Perry 1992a:4).

The purpose of this essay is to survey and discuss some examples of the contemporary crop of Chinese political culture studies and to look at the new departures in the field within the wider framework of a general discussion of the political culture approach. Why did the first generation studies of the 1960s and 1970s experience frustrations and setbacks in the 1980s? What are the causes that have recently produced a new flowering, and which new ideas and methodologies have shown themselves? Finally, have the basic problems and dilemmas of the political culture approach as they manifested themselves in the first generation studies been surmounted with the new generation of studies, or does the political culture approach remain hampered by significant theoretical and methodological problems? It will be argued that recent civil society debates, advances in social survey studies related to Chinese political culture, as well as a more sophisticated use of the culture concept itself, all have contributed to produce genuine advances in the field. But fundamental aspects of the approach remain open to debate, since the study of political culture is itself a 'cultural encounter'.

The first generation of Chinese political culture studies[1]

The modern social-scientific concept of political culture, an outcome of inter-disciplinary efforts in the 'melting pot' of American social sciences after WWII, reflected the dramatic events of the 1930s and 1940s — the advent of fascism, World War II, and the emergence of a large number of new nations following the conclusion of the war. What went wrong in those countries that became fascist, in spite of having democratic constitutions? And what about the new nations in Asia, Africa, etc...: is it possible to transplant democratic institutions into those countries? The dissatisfaction with existing concepts and methods was discussed at a series of meetings in the late 1950s between a group of politically-oriented anthropologists and a number of political scientists, led by Gabriel Almond; the single most significant outcome of this intellectual cross-breeding was the publication of *The Civic Culture*, by Gabriel Almond and Sydney Verba, in 1963. This study, which is one of the most influential works of modern political science to this day, used the sample survey method to make a systematic comparison of attitudes and values relevant to a stable democracy in five countries (USA, Great Britain, Germany, Italy and Mexico), measuring factors such as 'citizen competence', 'subject competence', and 'participation' (and concluding, not too surprisingly, that the USA and Great Britain scored far better than the other nations).

The Civic Culture was soon followed by another major work, *Political Culture and Political Development*, by Sydney Verba and Lucian W. Pye. Whereas *The Civic Culture* was still very much within the confines of the familiar Western political world, *Political Culture and Political Development* took a full step towards making the concept universally applicable to all nations, and this is the reason why Pye's definition has become one of the most-often quoted definitions of political culture:

In any operating political system there is an ordered subjective realm of politics which gives meaning to the polity, discipline to institutions, and social relevance to individual acts. The concept of political culture thus suggests that the traditions of society, the spirit of its public institutions, the passions and the collective reasoning of its citizenry, and the style and operating codes of its leaders are not just random products of historical experience but fit together as a part of a meaningful whole and constitute an intelligible web of relations (Pye and Verba 1965:7).

The intellectual currents that met in the formulation of the political culture approach can be summarized in four points:[2]

1) European sociology, particularly the works of Max Weber; in all of Weber's works, the power of values to create or change social institutions (as in *Capitalism and the Protestant Ethic*) is emphasized, that is, the subjective categories are of prime importance. In the US, Talcott Parsons led in introducing the Weberian approach to American sociology.

2) Social psychology can be traced back to Sigmund Freud's attempts at social generalization based on the psychoanalytic theory; Wilhelm Reich's studies of fascism in the 1930s deserve mention, even though they are often forgotten nowadays. The major work *The Authoritarian Personality* (1950), by a group of researchers led by Theodor W. Adorno, describes the social forces that make fascism possible — forces that are by no means confined to Germany and Italy; a similar line of argument can be found in Hannah Arendt's *The Origins of Totalitarianism* from 1951.

3) Closely associated with social psychology is the psychoanthropological approach of the 1920s and 1930s, the works of Bronislaw Malinowski, Ruth Benedict, Margaret Mead and Harold Laswell. The distinctive feature of this approach is its preoccupation with the effects of early childhood socialization in the formation of politically relevant attitudes and behaviour.

4) Finally, the development of the sample survey research method was catalytic in forming the concept of political culture; with the vastly improved techniques for handling large numbers of data, it finally became possible to conduct empirical studies, in keeping with the tradition of objective, quantifiable and verifiable social science, in fields that were hitherto only open to subjective impressions, intuition and the like.

These four approaches formed the basis of political culture studies as the field came to be defined in the mid-1960s. The pioneering works of the 'Founding Fathers' (Almond, Verba and Pye) opened the field for a wave of studies of the political culture of Western democratic societies, communist societies, and Third World countries. In the early 1970s, studies of the political culture of 'developing nations' were quite prevalent; from the late 1970s onwards studies of 'communism and political culture' came to the fore, to the extent that Almond in 1983 declared political cultural analyses of the 'second' (Communist) world as 'a test of the explanatory power of political culture theory' (Almond 1983:127).

The relevance of the political culture concept to studies of communist countries is evident: there exists a fairly large discrepancy between official norms and actual citizen attitudes, hence the need for a theory that allows us to 'look behind the curtain'; also, the communist countries are 'laboratory societies' that bring out possible tensions between official and 'private' values more clearly than is usual. Archie Brown has argued that:

the possibilities of discussing sensibly the harmony or dissonance between values, on the one hand, and political structures, on the other, are perhaps greater in the case of Communist societies where there has been (a) a radical break in the continuity of political institutions, and (b) an unusually overt and conscious attempt to create new political values and to supplant the old (Brown 1979:12).

A latent bias of the political culture approach in communist studies is noticable: it may degenerate into a search for 'weak spots', since the political culture of the population is assumed to be a stable historical heritage, latently hostile to the ideology imposed on it from above. As Lowell Dittmer has remarked, 'there seems to be a tendency in Western social science to resort to a concept of culture whenever attempting to understand systems that are alien, hostile, or apparently irrational' (Dittmer 1983a:51).

In a survey of the first generation of Chinese political culture studies, one person stands out: Professor Lucian W. Pye. He was not only among the 'Founding Fathers' of political culture studies, he was, indeed still is, the most prolific writer on Chinese political culture, having written several major works on the subject between 1968 and 1988. As a man born and raised in China, deeply impressed with 'the revolutionary findings of modern depth psychology' (Pye and Verba 1965:8), and imbued with infinite optimism concerning the new-found political culture concept (in his first major study he wrote about 'the great challenge to political science...for which the concept of political culture holds such great promise' (Pye and Verba 1965:9)), it was only natural that he should turn his energy to the psycho-cultural study of China. In *The Spirit of Chinese Politics* (1968) we find the Chinese mentality analyzed and the implications for authority and political life discussed; in *China: An Introduction* (1972) the psycho-cultural dimension occupies only a secondary position in a general survey of modern Chinese history; in *Mao Tse-tung: The Man in the Leader* (1976) Pye resumed his psychological approach, this time in the study of the formation of Mao's personality; *The Dynamics of Chinese Politics* (1981) really has much the same scope as *The Spirit of Chinese Politics*, but with a much more detailed analysis of how power operates at the top level of Chinese politics. In 1985 came the magnum opus *Asian Power and Politics: The Cultural Dimensions of Authority*. It is an attempt to compare several Asian countries in the matrix of the psycho-cultural approach, an endeavour which, to a critic of Pye, would seem self-defeating from the outset; how can one understand the great differences between, say, China and Japan, if one starts from basically the same psycho-cultural setting ('dependency', 'deference to authority', 'suppression of aggression', 'personal relations', etc...)? In *The Mandarin and the Cadre: China's Political Cultures*, from 1988, Pye concentrated his arguments once again on the case of China in an attempt to structure a more dynamic, bipolar theory of Chinese political culture. In this sense the last-mentioned work belongs to the 'new wave' of political culture studies.

A student of Pye, Richard H. Solomon, came out with the single most comprehensive and ambitious Chinese political culture-study in 1971: *Mao's Revolution and the Chinese Political Culture*. In scope and concepts, it follows very much in the footsteps of *The Spirit of Chinese Politics*; it differs methodologically, however, in basing itself on a psychological sample survey. It differs also in its conclusion concerning the question of continuity versus discontinuity in Chinese political culture. Where Pye tends to see continuity (the communist style of leadership as very much a product of the expectations of the common people, that is, political culture), Solomon finds a sharp contrast between traditional political culture and the political culture that Mao tried to instill in the Chinese people.

Apart from Pye and Solomon, not many other major monographs have been devoted to the study of Chinese political culture. Alan P.L. Liu's *Political Culture & Group Conflict in Communist China* (1976) differs from the other studies in the field, since the structure examined by Liu is the officially desirable — at the time of his writing — political culture, as exemplified by Red Guard behaviour, not a semi-autonomous sphere of attitudes and values shaped outside the reach of the propaganda machine. Alternatives to the psycho-cultural approach associated with the names of Pye and Solomon are found in the works of Andrew J. Nathan (e.g. *Nathan 1985*), Jack Gray (e.g. *Gray 1979*) and Lowell Dittmer (e.g. *Dittmer 1983a* and *1983b*), to mention a few of the most prominent writers. In fact, a large number of studies on China from the 1970s and 1980s are relevant to the topic if we look beyond the political culture concept in a strict sense. Studies of participation are clearly important since participation is one of the main variables in Almond and Verba's study of political culture. From J. R. Townsend's *Political Participation in Communist China* (1969) and Martin King Whyte's *Small Groups and Political Rituals in China* (1974) to Andrew Nathan's *Chinese Democracy* (1985), there is broad agreement on the fact that China indeed has a political culture characterized by a very high level of participation. This does not imply democracy in the Western sense, however. In Nathan's words, 'Chinese democracy involves participation without influence' (Nathan 1985:227). Equally relevant are works on Chinese education and political socialization as well as a whole range of sociological close-up studies. The political culture approach has rarely been explicitly used in such works, since it has come to be seen by many China scholars as too closely associated with the psycho-culturalist school of thought.

A dividing line in political culture studies gradually became apparent during the 1970s and 1980s. The 'Civic Culture' approach essentially sees poltical culture as a positive factor that cushions social conflicts by means of toleration and moderation and provides stability to institutions by means of democratic values; it is a recipe for successful modernization. The psycho-cultural approach, in contrast, is a tool for diagnosis of a failed or warped modernization process; it sees culture as a dark shadow on the path to modernity. The bifurcation of political culture studies also reflects a fundamental frustration of the early efforts at formulating a social-scientific approach to political culture: the ambition of structuring a *universal* approach gave way to the realities of a heterogenous political world where basic differences remained much more stubbornly entrenched than had been envisaged by the development optimism and convergence thinking of the 1960s. The methodological gap in political culture studies related to Western societies and Third World/communist societies respectively tended to widen rather than narrow.

As regards studies of Chinese political culture, this bifurcation became the Scylla and Charybdis of methodology for the first generation of studies. A 'Civic culture' approach was frustrated by the basic unavailability of empirical material in the form of attitude surveys; emigré interviews could make up for some of the deficiency, but major problems regarding representativity and interpretation remained. The alternative psycho-cultural 'Pye' approach pointed towards a static perspective of changelessness; the interpretation of all the dramatic swings and changes of Chinese 20th century history as functions of unchanging mechanisms of primary child socialization appeared equally frustrating and futile.

The other alternatives all contained equally frustrating contradictions. Taking the Party-defined political culture as a point of departure (e.g. Liu 1976) dissolved some of the problems regarding empirical study as well as the interpretation of psychological patterns, but it also took the teeth out of political culture as a concept for investigating the dynamics of the relationship between leaders and people. Solomon's focus (Solomon 1971) was clearly on that relationship, but his method for interpretation of interview data left the question of identification of *politically relevant* attitudes unanswered.

During the 1970s and 1980s the political culture approach to contemporary China studies did not quite live up to the expectations of the 1960s. Obviously, in epochal events like the Cultural Revolution, the subjective dimension of political life in China must be important, but avenues to the study of it were blocked. The approach fared best in surveys of modern Chinese history (e.g. Nathan 1985) and in psychological portraits of individual leaders (e.g. Pye 1976), but the unavailability of social survey data precluded a genuine sociological breakthrough, while the still-towering influence of the classical sinological approach cast a shadow of changelessness on the psychological interpretation of Chinese political culture. For reasons that are not very obvious Chinese political culture never figured large in the bourgeoning literature of 'Comparative Communism' in the 1970s and 1980s and the field was thus denied some of the methodological sophistication associated with comparative communist studies. The rather few studies that did connect China with the comparative communism approach were also among the more successful (e.g. Gray 1979, Dittmer 1983b). In fact Lowell Dittmer's 1983 essay on 'Comparative Communist Political Culture', which distinguishes between polical culture as independent, dependent and intervening variable and focuses on the interplay between symbolic and dynamic aspects of Chinese political culture, foreshadowed the new wave of political culture studies in the late 1980s and early 1990s.

The origins of the 'new wave': Chinese political culture rediscovered

A number of trends and events in the 1980s contributed to setting the stage for a new upsurge in attention towards Chinese political culture. Some of these contributing factors were of a global nature, affecting the perception of Chinese society by the outside world, while other factors were specifically related to developments in China.

In a very general sense the 1980s experienced a resurgence of the culture concept in the West, in social life as well as in the social sciences. The modernizing ethos of mainstream social and political discourse as well as the radical counterdiscourse of the 1960s and 1970s produced a reaction that found its clue in the culture concept. The 1980s saw a floodtide of official reverence for 'culture', a renewed effort at enlisting the energies of 'tradition' and 'popular culture' and exploring the secret lore of 'local culture' and 'ethnic culture'. Social critique gave way to 'black culture', 'gay culture' or 'youth culture'. In the social sciences the abstractions of mainstream functionalist theory as well as the Marxist-inspired counterdiscourses likewise gave way to a fascination with the 'depths' of culture studies, thus transcending the conflictual approach to society implicit in both mainstream and critical 1970s discourse. The culture approach paved the way for focusing on long-term continuities, on the significance of language, rituals and symbols, and offered a way to look at what keeps societies together rather than at what pulls them apart.

In China a similar 'awakening' to the culture concept took place during the 1980s, only in a much more striking way, culminating in the 'culture fever' (*wenhua re*) debates of the second half of the decade. In China the reaction against the earlier mode of social discourse implied a break with the hegemonic Maoist language of 'struggle', and joining up with the 'culture fever' thus had implicit political significance regardless of what views one actually took in the debates concerning the merits and demerits of traditional Chinese culture. These debates also covered some ground regarding the impact of traditional culture on contemporary Chinese political culture (e.g. Wang He 1987, Zi Zhongxun 1987).

A second factor contributing to the the new wave of Chinese political culture studies was the emergence of *social surveys* in China during the second half of the 1980s. Public opinion studies on a national level using a scientific sampling method were the outcome of the beginnings of urban reform in 1984, as the complexities of the reforms required better tools for understanding developments in society (Rosen 1989:157). The first series of nationwide large-scale surveys was launced in 1985 by the *Tigaisuo* (The Economic System Reform Research Institute) founded in 1984 by Zhao Ziyang and associated throughout its existence with the technocratic, reformist tendency in the leadership. The *Tigaisuo* conducted a total of 14 surveys from 1985 to 1989, and its activities were soon matched by a number of other public opinion institutes, some of them private or semi-private. The most important of these was the dissident think-tank 'Beijing Research Institute for Social Science and Economics' (*Beijing Shehui Jingji Kexue Yanjiusuo*) led by Chen Ziming and Wang Juntao,[3] which published a *Yearbook on Chinese Political Science* and conducted the first nation-wide survey on 'The political culture of Chinese citizens' (Bonnin & Chevrier 1991:585). Some of the results from this survey were published in a 1989 book by Min Qi entitled 'Chinese political culture: The socio-psychological elements that obstruct democratic politics' (*Zhongguo zhengzhi wenhua: Minzhu zhengzhi nanchande shehui xinli yinsu*) (Min Qi 1989). The political culture approach was rapidly catching on among Chinese social scientists, and the concept was discussed in a number of scholarly journals in 1987-1989 (e.g. Chen 1987, Xu 1989). A Beijing pilot study for another national survey was conducted in December 1988 (a brief description of this survey is found in Nathan 1990, pp. 197-98) by Shi Tianjin, who became a coworker of Nathan's in one of the most comprehensive recent Chinese political culture surveys (Nathan & Shi 1993). The Chinese social scientists involved in these surveys, the reform-oriented employees of the *Tigaisuo* as well as the dissidents of the semi-private institutions, suffered massive persecution with the 1989 crackdown on the Democracy Movement. Some, such as the *Tigaisuo* leader Chen Yizi, were exiled, while others were jailed and sentenced to long prison terms, such as Chen Ziming and Wang Juntao. The repression did not mean the end of social-scientific surveys in China, however, and Stanley Rosen has kept track of post-Tiananmen surveys that continue to document the political estrangement among China's youth that had already manifested itself clearly in the 1986-1989 period (Rosen 1989a, Rosen 1992). Social surveys have continued in China after 1989, as well as scholarly debates on the political culture approach, and most recently Western scholars have managed to join in the organization and interpretation of political culture-related social surveys in cooperation with Chinese colleagues (e.g. Nathan & Shi 1993, Hjellum 1994), the results of which will be further discussed below.

A third ingredient in shaping new avenues to the study of Chinese political culture was the emergence of the *civil society discourse* in some East European countries during the 1980s (see Keane 1988, Miller 1992). The civil society concept can be traced back to the founding fathers of classical liberal thought, particularly John Locke's *Two Treatises on Government* from 1690, and it appeared in the works of Ferguson, Mill and Tocqueville as a key concept for understanding the self-determination of society vis-à-vis the state. Other approaches to the concept surfaced in the works of Hegel, Marx and Gramsci, and the concept, since it serves as a core element of the self-image of capitalism and modernization, naturally has invited dispute throughout (for excellent surveys of the civil society concept in modern Western political philosophy, see Giner 1985, Andersen 1994). In post World War II sociology the concept on the one hand became associated with the liberal approach of Almond and Verba as discussed above while on the other hand playing a role in critical European sociology, as in Jürgen Habermas' influential 1962 work *Strukturwandel der Öffentlichkeit* ('The Structural Transformation of the Public Sphere').

The introduction of the civil society concept in East European dissident thought provided a powerful weapon for recasting the roles of state and society; the concept offered a way to focus on non-official activities and ideas as the body of a society-to-be and a moral community with much of the legitimacy lacking in the structures of the state. With the privatization and decentralization of the Chinese economic reforms as well as the escalation of ideological estrangement and dissident ideas during the 1980s, the civil society approach naturally presented itself as a framework for conceptualizing the energies of Chinese society *beyond* and *against* the power of the Party-state. This approach has in recent years become one of the most important intellectual frameworks for understanding Chinese society, manifesting itself in hundreds of books and articles, some of which will be discussed below. In relation to the study of Chinese political culture the civil society approach suggests the outline of structures and trends in that amorphous body. However, the actual development of civil society in China is far from clear, and approaches to understanding it differ widely.

The catalyst for the above mentioned trends towards a more sophisticated, empirical and dynamic approach to the study of Chinese political culture was of course the 1989 Democracy Movement. The events of 1989 demonstrated beyond any trace of doubt the growing chasm between official China and popular ideas/values. No longer can the Chinese Communist Party pose as the spokesman and sole representative of 'the Chinese people', and no longer can Chinese society be understood as simply the product of state and Party policies. The course of events in 1989 as well as some of the demands raised by the protesters — freedom of the press, improvement of the legal system, etc. — contributed to confirming a civil society perspective for Chinese society. In other ways, however, traditional Chinese modes of public behaviour appeared to play a very significant role. The moralistic discourse of all forces involved in the events, the separation of social strata from each other in the demonstrations, and a host of other phenomena all suggest a reenacting of traditional Chinese values and structures to an extent that surprised many Western observers. The 'message' of 1989, in terms of political culture, is far from simple.

In a wider sense the reawakening of Western attention towards the cultural dimensions of politics in the wake of 1989 is only natural. Major surprises in China's modern transformation tend to invite cultural explanations, while periods of stability attract structuralist modes of analysis, elite studies and the like. The post-1989 fascination with a cultural approach to Chinese politics may very well turn out, in a long term perspective, to be a brief fire fanned by temporary confusion. The long term outcome depends on China's future development and on what the 'new wave' of political culture studies has to offer.

Approaches to the study of Chinese political culture

The dynamic turn of psychoculturalism
In a survey of the new wave of political culture studies related to China it should be noted that the impulses pointing towards new departures in the field have also manifested themselves *within* the most prominent approach of the 1960s and 1970s, i.e. the psychoculturalist approach associated above all with the name of Lucian Pye. The standard objection to Pye's early works has been directed against the circularity and statism of the argument: Pye made Chinese political culture appear as an inescapable iron cage, since even the most radical attempts at revolutionizing China only served to underscore the heavy hand of tradition. The change of political climate in China since 1976-1978 added to the pressure against the 'classical' psychoculturalist line of argument; pragmatic modernization and cautious pluralization seemed to

demonstrate that the iron cage is not hermetically closed. Pye's 1988 work *The Mandarin and the Cadre: China's Political Cultures* took up this challenge in suggesting a dynamic view of Chinese political culture involving *two* contradictory and competing political cultures:

Yet the fundamental polarity of China's traditional cultures was between the orthodoxy of Confucianism and a heterodox blend of Taoism, Buddhism, and more localized belief systems. The traditional Chinese contrast was thus between an elitist high Confucian culture that glorified the established authority of the better educated and rationalized their claims of superiority on the basis of possessing specialized wisdom, and a passionate, populist heterodox culture that glorified the rebel and trusted magical formulas to transform economic and social reality (Pye 1988:39).

This line of argument allows Pye to present Dengist pragmatism and Maoist radicalism as equally 'Chinese': 'The China, or the political culture, of Maoism once seemed to be the very essence of the 'Chinese revolution' and to capture what was most distinctive about China's drive to find a place in the modern world. Yet Deng Xiaoping's China, or political culture, also seems quintessentially Chinese, even though it is totally different from the first' (Pye 1988:37). At the bottom of things, however, the two cultures are as related as yin and yang, and they are the twin products of the same basic psychological mechanisms: '... the intensity of the clashes between the two cultures is a function less of the degree to which they differ and more of the fact that representatives of each culture can recognize the attractions of the other in themselves and thus feel the need to resist the other aggressively... [t]he paired alternative values have their roots in the traditional Chinese political cultures, but they are sustained by central contradictions generated by the Chinese socialization processes' (Pye 1988:43).

A number of polarities in the Chinese psychological setup are examined, providing examples of how the same basic yearnings and drives give rise to radically different and opposing values, such as the example of 'Egalitarian Brotherhood versus Formal Respectability':

The sum effect of the Chinese problem with intimacy is to produce powerful cultural sentiments that resonate to the ideological appeals of either brotherhood or formal respectability. It also helps to explain how a people, who at one time can be swept away in oceanic feelings of egalitarian comradeship — as during the Cultural Revolution — can in another mood become self-centered within their own feelings of righteousness. In short, a dialectical tension in the psyches of individual Chinese centered on questions about intimacy gives resonant support to two quite different ideological approaches in the political realm (Pye 1988:49).

A number of other such polarities are similarly dissected in the book, and Pye suggests that they all relate to a core problem of Chinese culture, 'the problem of self identity in a culture that gives ambiguous instructions about the relationship of the self to others' (Pye 1988:70). The seedbed that produces both of China's political cultures is one of ambiguity regarding both individual and collective: 'There is thus in Chinese culture no distinct concept of the self except in terms of the other, which is generally a collectivity. Yet there is no strong bonding, no easy outpouring of feelings to the very people who give one one's identity... The result is the paradox of widespread egotism by people with fragile egos' (Pye 1988:71). The source of this tension in the relationship between Self and Other is found in the early socialization process, particularly in the 'sharp contrast between the highly indulgent and nurturing treatment common in the first years and the demanding discipline and outside controls imposed in subsequent years' (*ibid*). The basic expression of this psychological conflict is the *repression of aggression*, and Pye thus closes his argument at the note on which he had started — with 'The Spirit of Chinese Politics' — two decades earlier.

The first chapter of 'The Mandarin and the Cadre' is a spirited and sometimes angry refutation of Pye's critics, and the problem of *explaining change* is addressed head-on: 'Indeed the central thrust of the rest of this book is precisely the relationship of Chinese culture to the modernization of China, and therefore we shall be demonstrating how culture can explain change' (Pye 1988:26). The suggestion of a bipolar set of political cultures, reminiscent of the approach taken by Jack Gray in Gray 1979, does not relieve Pye's critics of their duties, however. At best the iron cage of Chinese political culture has been supplied with two compartments that allow the prisoners temporary — and illusionary — change of positions. But the iron bars, shaped by the peculiarities of the Chinese socialization process, remain in place. Examples drawn from the depths of Chinese history are as valid and relevant for the argument as the most recent events; the effects of a century of war, revolutions, breakup of tradition and social change dwindle in this perspective, and Pye has in actual fact demonstrated how culture can *defeat* change rather than 'explain' it.

As always, Pye's approach works better with failure than with success, and the events of 1989 provided the ideal occasion for airing the psychocultural arguments. In his 1990 article on 'Tiananmen and Chinese Political Culture' (Pye 1990) Lucian Pye eloquently uses the Tiananmen protests as point of focus for a recapitulation of:

... a host of well-established conclusions about Chinese political culture. These include such themes as the sensitivity of authority to matters of 'face', the need for authority to pretend to omnipotence, the legitimacy of bewailing grievances, the urge to monopolize virtue and to claim the high ground of morality, the drive to shame others, an obsession with revenge, the inability to compromise publicly, and so on and on (Pye 1990:331).

The Tiananmen events also gave Pye an opportunity to give 'change' a solid kick: 'The conventional wisdom... is that a 'Chinese revolution' has been going on for the last 150 years. Yet, for most of that time the country was getting nowhere and the ways of thinking of the majority of the Chinese people had not greatly changed...' (Pye 1990:332). We are back to Changeless China and vintage Pye; indeed the 1990 article is among Pye's most striking works. The reactions of the students to the death of Hu Yaobang on April 15, 1989, which served as a catalyst for the protest movement, are described in terms of: '[T]he rule in China is that when the situation is hopeless, take hope... for the heroic is always flavoured with a touch of the tragic' (Pye 1990:333). The ensuing stage of demonstrations and sloganeering is related to the Chinese rule of: 'Don't analyze, just moralize'. To avoid accusations of selfishness the students had to constantly escalate their demands in the direction of abstract, lofty ideals. The reactions of the authorities during that early stage were equally bound by the code of claiming moral superiority, thus making practical solutions and a defusion of the confrontation impossible: 'Since there is no way of compromising in a battle of shaming, the struggle in China could only intensify' (Pye 1990:341). The use of foreign-inspired modes of protest, such as the hunger strike, are seen as 'reinforcing traditional Chinese symbolism' (Pye 1990:343), thus strengthening the students' appeal among the people of Beijing. In the final showdown the authorities 'relied on the traditional Chinese tactic of surprise and deception (Pye 1990:345),' and the aftermath has demonstrated 'the heightened importance of revenge, always a driving force in Chinese politics' (ibid.). In conclusion, '[t]he Chinese style of politics has again obstructed national progress' (Pye 1990:347) in the 1989 disaster by reducing both government and protesters to puppets in the iron hand of Chinese political culture.

It appears that since the late 1980s there has been a resurgence of the respectability and popularity of psychoculturalism; if this is true, it may be less a function of theoretical upgrading than of factors external to the approach: the 'culture craze' in China as well as in some fields of China studies in the 1980s serves as the broad background, and the Tiananmen protests of 1989 are the main catalyst. But critical questions regarding the methodology of psychoculturalism remain valid: on what basis are facts ascribed 'significance'? In the case of 1989, all innovative, alien or non-traditional features of the movement are very quickly relegated to secondary importance. And other critical questions should be asked as well: Can leadership and opposition really be described as products of the same mold? How about the effects of reform and decentralization and the emerging forces of social autonomy? And how is the timing and popularity of the protests to be understood: why would massive discontent and protest surface after a decade of unprecedented material gains and liberalization? Clearly the politically relevant attitudes of all sections of the Chinese people are now in a process of change, but that process is invisible from the psychoculturalist perspective.

The civil society approach
The civil society approach to contemporary China is the most far-reaching alternative to the theses of psychoculturalism, since its first assumption is the relative *otherness of society* vis-à-vis the state and the implicit potential for escaping the 'iron cage' of political culture. The civil society approach also implies the possibility of reactivating the 'Almond dimension' of political culture with its focus on adult socialization, institutions, and change. The literature related to civil society is quite voluminous, and some systematic surveys and discussions of the approach have already appeared. In a special issue of *Modern China* devoted to debating the validity of the civil society approach in China studies Heath B. Chamberlain surveys much of the existing literature and suggests a distinction between three approaches to the issue:

1) Civil society as 'solidarity at the barricades'. This view, which draws inspiration from the sudden emergence in the spring of 1989 of a new collective, anti-government 'spirit' uniting millions of citizens, was prevalent in a number of studies produced in the immediate wake of Tiananmen but has since dissipated as the dust settled; in Chamberlain's words, '[i]f... we mean to measure progress away from one mode of social existence to another,

surely we need more than a series of snapshots taken during the heat of a revolutionary movement' (Chamberlain 1993:202).

2) The second category of studies focuses on the more enduring features of 'counterstructure' or 'institutionalized autonomy' of social relations vis-à-vis the state. Attention has mainly been directed at the dissident intellectual stage of the 1980s, but again enthusiasm has waned in the early 1990s; as the 1989 events showed, the Chinese state and Party leadership is perfectly capable of crushing *institutionalized* autonomy, and at the same time the events also demonstrated the enduring closeness of the relationship between the educated elite and the state. In Chamberlain's words, '[t]he intellectuals' vision of civil society is not so much '*counter*structure' as it is '*alternate* structure' — a way of organizing and staffing the state apparatus diffently, rather than challenging it altogether' (Chamberlain 1993:203).

3) The third approach takes a longer-range historical perspective in seeing the first signs of a Chinese civil society appearing already in late imperial and republican times; the economic reforms of the 1980s have paved the way for the reemergence of these long-submerged features of Chinese modernity. (It is specifically this approach which is the main topic of the 1993 special issue of *Modern China*.) Again, Chamberlain's critique is to the point: regardless of what one thinks of the pathbreaking works in this field such as William T. Rowe's two studies of Hankou in the late imperial period (Rowe 1984, Rowe 1989), Mary Backus' study of elite activism in Zhejiang (Rankin 1986) and David Strand's study of social life in 1920s Beijing (Strand 1989), '... the putative link between the 'public sphere' of a century ago and civil society of today is very tenuous indeed' (Chamberlain 1993:204), and the approach tends to conflate civil society with 'society' pure and simple.

Chamberlain's critique aims at preserving the theoretical substance of the term *civil* in 'civil society', i.e. 'civility' as something more than just opposition to the state. Indeed he suggests focusing more attention on the part played by the state — also in positive terms — in the changing relationship between society and citizen, and recent studies of the Chinese workplace are mentioned as examples of this. Chamberlain's line of argument is further elaborated in a recent review article (Chamberlain 1994).

In a 1993 study of the new social organizations that have sprouted in the wake of the economic reforms Gordon White has also surveyed the state of civil society studies related to China. White distinguishes between two main approaches, that is, (1) civil society as a particular type of political relationship between state and society based on the principles of citizenship, rights, representation and the rule of law, and (2) civil society as *intermediate social organizations* (White 1993:65). The first usage of the concept, roughly equivalent to the Chinese term *gongmin shehui* ('society of citizens'), is obviously rather remote from contemporary Chinese political realities, and attention is commonly being directed towards the second approach, which can be divided into three subgroups:

a) Civil society as comprising *all* nongovernment social organizations including 'uncivil' Mafia-like groups, nationalist or religious organizations, kinship units as well as modern organizations such as trade unions, chambers of commerce and professional associations. This approach, which is connected with the the Chinese term *minjian shehui* ('society of common people') conflates civil society with society in general, much like Chamberlain's third category.

(b) Civil society as 'bourgeois society', i.e. an autonomous sphere of economic activity based on private property and regulated by markets. This approach harks back to Hegel and Marx, and it is connected not just to captialism but to modernity in general. It is associated with city life, and the Chinese equivalent is *shimin shehui* ('the society of city-people').

c) The third usage of the civil society concept refers to organizations which arise in opposition to the state, with the 1980s Polish Solidarity as the global model example. Most studies of civil society in China, according to White, take this approach and the mass mobilization of 1989 as the main case study. White's own study, in contrast, focuses on the rise of new intermediate organizations in the wake of the economic reforms, i.e. an approach directed towards the second subcategory of 'bourgeois society'.

Finally, in this brief overview of civil society debates Barrett McCormick's 1991 discussion of 'The Impact of Democracy on China Studies' (McCormick 1991) deserves mentioning; McCormick distinguishes himself from both Chamberlain and White by his generally optimistic attitude to the civil society approach as a promising alternative to mainstream policy analysis.

There are striking differences and disagreements among the various debaters on Chinese civil society. Very optimistic accounts have been produced by Larry Sullivan (Sullivan 1990), Thomas Gold (e.g. Gold 1990a, Gold 1990b, Gold 1994) and McCormick, Su Shaozhi & Xiao Xiaoming (McCormick, Su & Xiao 1992) to mention some of the most enthusiastic debaters. But even the optimists are not talking about quite the same thing. Sullivan's 1990-text is based on a Rousseau-inspired analysis and suggests that '[i]n one fell swoop, Chinese urban society, particularly in Beijing, was transformed from a 'sheet of loose sand' (*yipan sansha*) into a cohesive civil society capable of maintaining social order and even assuming the everyday functions of government without 'central' control' (Sullivan 1990:127). Sullivan's text is the prototype of the 'solidarity at the barricades' approach and particularly focuses on the *instant nature* of civil society: 'Civil society and the resultant capacity to express the general will as sovereign authority could literally come at a moment's notice, just as it did in China in spring 1989' (Sullivan 1990:129). Gold, in contrast, is a supporter of the 'historical approach' and argues for a 1989 *resurgence* of a civil society that the Chinese Communists had never quite managed to destroy despite four decades of efforts; even the Marriage Law of 1950 and the introduction of compulsory schooling is seen as motivated by the Communists' desire to break up the resistance of family and society (e.g. Gold 1990a:24). As for the current 'resurgence' of civil society Gold takes the all-inclusive approach criticized by both Chamberlain and White, regarding any non-government-led institution or activity as a 'base' for civil society in China. McCormick, Su & Xiao also support the thesis of long-term growth of civil society in China ('[i]f the growth of civil society is a long-term trend which began over a century ago and is still underway, then the Leninist state established in 1949 can be seen as an interruption rather than the inevitable and unavoidable expression of Chinese culture...', McCormick, Su & Xiao 1992:182) and take a generally optimistic view of the prospects for civil society in China, but still they are less all-inclusive than Gold in the analysis of the potential 'bases'.

A somewhat more cautious and balanced optimism can be found in a large number of recent books and articles such as Andrew Nathan's 1990 book 'China's Crisis' (Nathan 1990) and in the works of David Strand (e.g. Strand 1990), Elizabeth Perry (e.g. Perry 1993b), Martin King Whyte (Whyte 1992) and Michel Bonnin and Yves Chevrier (Bonnin & Chevrier 1991). A more sceptical position can be found in Frederic Wakeman's discussion of the 'historical approach' (Wakeman 1993) and in Andrew Walder's recent studies of the role of workers in the 1989 protests (e.g. Walder 1992, Walder & Gong 1993), while Richard Baum has argued to the effect of a 'virtual lack of civil society' in China (Baum 1992:493). Generally speaking, the enthusiasm of 1989-1990 has tended to give way to more cautious attitudes regarding the potential for civil society in China.

For the purpose of this essay it might be useful to structure the different approaches taken by recent studies of civil society in China along a continuum from 'minimal' definitions of the concept involving little or no conscious opposition against the current structures of the Party-State to more exclusive definitions involving a measure of awareness, opposition or dissidence.

1. A number of studies relate civil society to dysfunctions *within* the structures of the state as well as to various forms of unintentional 'disorder' engendered by the economic reforms. In the stimulating 1988 study by Vivienne Shue, *The Reach of the State: Sketches of the Chinese Body Politic*, the civil society concept is not explicitly used, but her line of argument has served as an inspiration for others who do see civil society as related to inherent contradicitions and shortcomings of the Party-State. Shue's argument demonstrates how *local government*, historically as well as in present-day China, has come to function in some ways as a representative of local social interests, not neccessarily due to political disagreement but rather as a function of its conflicting duties and structural position. The most original part of Shue's argument, however, is the hypothesis that '... in some respects, the socio-political changes accompanying the 'liberal market' reforms of the 1980s may impair the ability of peasant communities to oppose inimical state actions and policies. Ironically perhaps, the 'reform' order may render some rural villagers more rather than less vulnerable to the designs of outside powerholders' (Shue 1988:77). (The changes of China's 'Body Politic' since Shue's time of writing, with the ongoing buildup of political-economic power at the provincial and local levels, have not brought out Shue's premonitions in a literal sense, but her line of analysis has highlighted an oft-forgotten dimension of the dialectic between state political power and market forces.)

Mayfair Mei-hui Yang's 1989 article on 'corporateness' in a Chinese factory runs on parallel tracks to the Shue argument; her study documents the processes on the factory floor of developing ideas and practices commensurate with the local interests of the enterprise. She suggests that Chinese enterprises are 'at the same time entities of the state and entities of civil society (Yang 1989:39)', and that 'enterprises in China increasingly are seeking relief from the societywide functions they serve for the state and from state administrative linkages (Yang 1989:59)'.

The Yang article opened the door to studies of emerging civil society as a function of the structural transformation of Chinese workplaces. The study of changing worker attitudes has been carried on particularly in the works of Andrew G. Walder mentioned above; Walder has documented the proliferation of contradictions and discontent in the workplace as a consequence of the economic reforms (e.g. Walder 1992), and his study, with Gong Xiaoxia, of the Beijing Autonomous Workers' Association in 1989 has shown that worker demands in the Tiananmen protest took a turn distinctly different from the student agitation (Walder and Gong 1993). Walder's argument about rising contradictions within the workplace runs counter to Yang's 'corporateness', and he is also much more cautious about employing the civil society concept. Gordon White, in the article discussed above, is also cautious about civil society, but the idea of focusing on 'intermediate organizations' (whether invigorated versions of the traditional 'mass organizations' such as the Labor Unions, Women' Federation and the Communist Youth League, or the new-type economic and professional associations that have sprung from the reforms) appears promising. Anita Chan's 1993 study of growing trade union autonomy in the Post-Mao era is an in-depth study of one such 'intermediate organization' (Chan 1993).

Dorothy Solinger's 1992 study of China's floating population as a potential form of civil society (Solinger 1992b) takes a somewhat different direction; like the other studies of the 'dysfunctional' approach she directs her attention towards the unplanned, unwanted consequences of reform, but China's internal migrant population is a very surprising candidate for the honourable position as vanguard of the civil society and makes sense in that role only as a harbinger of *uncontrolled* social development. Solinger suggests that if one emphasizes separation from the state as a crucial feature of civil society, one 'might pinpoint this group as a kind of sprout of civil society. They are recruited into the cities largely by private, personal agents. They organize themselves in a rudimentary way by way of locale of origin. They burden the city and its facilities, cause crime and (very occasional) violence, bring excess offspring. And they tamper with the administrative integrity of the city, making hay of urban bureaucratic coordination and inciting graft' (Solinger 1992a:30). Solinger proceeds to conclude, however, that China's transients in fact pose no serious challenge to the state, since 'they contribute at least as much to the state as they take from it, in both manifest and latent guises' (*ibid*) by manning the most undesirable job functions in China's semi-bankrupt state enterprises, etc. This conclusion makes good sense, but bringing the civil society concept into the matter perhaps less so. If disorder is the main criterion, would an earthquake not count as a contribution to 'civil society'?

2. Closely related to the 'dysfunctional' approach there is a large body of

literature related to the civil society potential of emerging *private business* in China. In fact some of the works discussed above, such as Yang 1989 and White 1993, bridge the two groups. As for the significance of the private entrepreneurs, the support of the *getihu* (private businessmen) for the 1989 protests has been noted by some observers (e.g. Østergaard 1989). Thomas Gold has also emphasized the role of private businessmen as a base for civil society (e.g. Gold 1990b:148-49). K. E. Brødsgaard takes a rather optimistic view of the level of autonomy attained by private entrepreneurs (Brødsgaard 1994), but this view is contradicted by some other studies (e.g. Solinger 1992b, Bruun 1993), which emphasize the webs of *guanxi* connecting local entrepreneurs with local officialdom; in Solinger's words, '[u]rban economic reform in China has not yet led to the emergence of what is popularly called 'civil society' among the business class (Solinger 1992b:121)'; Solinger argues that in fact the reforms 'have merged, if under vastly shifted conditions, the entities we call state and society' (Solinger 1992b:136). At the 1994 annual AAS Conference in Boston a session on the 'Shifting Boundaries of Public and Private' signalled frustration with using the civil society approach in relation to the economic reforms in China and suggested an alternative framework labeled 'quasi-public, quasi-private'. This concept seeks to capture the interpenetration of state and society and the two-way nature of the economic reform process: while government organs move towards a profit orientation one can also see a *'danwei-ization'* ('unit-ization') taking place in the private sector, through which private enterprises assume some forms and characteristics normally associated with state-owned enterprises. The session squarely criticized the civil society approach:

We have also found the civil society model to be wrong, or at least highly biased, in its stress on the *autonomy*, or sought after autonomy, of societal groups from the state. The civil society model tells us that groups in society want, more than anything else, autonomy from the state. Our research has found that quite to the contrary a wide range of societal groups actively seek to integrate themselves more effectively into the bureaucracy, to develop good connections with state officials, to lobby for state-controlled scarce resources, to compete for a larger share of the state pie, and in a myriad other ways seek to capture and gain a good position within the still powerful bureaucracy (AAS 1994:24-25).

3. A third group of civil society studies related to China focuses on changes in popular attitudes and mentality. Lawrence Sullivan's ebullient endorsement of the 1989 protests as the expression of the 'general will' of the people has

been mentioned already; an equally rosy image of the Tiananmen movement is found in N. Kutcher's essay 'Time of Songs and Tears' which distinguishes between an 'inner movement' imbued with the loftiest moral qualities ('a new community on the square', Kutcher 1991:120) and the 'outer movement' involved with confrontation and vulnerable to the morally degrading influences of manipulation and politics. On a more down-to-earth note, C.S. Østergaard in the immediate wake of Tiananmen examined the changing attitudes of various groups and segments of the Chinese population (Østergaard 1989). Martin King Whyte's balanced 1992 essay on 'Urban China: A Civil Society in the Making?' also directs its main focus on values, ideas and attitudes. Whyte observes that the Cultural Revolution inadvertently served to sow the seeds of civil society: Firstly, through the antibureaucratic thrust of the Cultural Revolution and the revelations about abuse of power, etc.; secondly, through the temporary release of many individuals from their bureaucratic supervisors; and, thirdly, because of widespread political alienation produced by the traumatic experiences of the Cultural Revolution (Whyte 1992:86-88). Whyte cautiously concludes that there is 'some basis for optimism that a nascent civil society will survive to provide potential for a more democratic China in the future' (Whyte 1992:97).

4. Civil society as embodied in the work and activities of critical, dissident intellectuals is a prominent approach to Chinese civil society which has found expression in a large number of studies, most of which describe the intellectual evolution of individual dissidents. Michel Bonnin and Yves Chevrier in 1991 published a most useful study of the institutions of intellectual dissent that emerged during the 1980s; they have shown that the *idea* of an autonomous civil society was clearly present among many such dissident intellectuals, but they also caution against 'the enduring traditions in the intellectuals' own political culture and political vision' (Bonnin & Chevrier 1991:569). The dissidents managed 'to grow social roots while not directly challenging the state and taking advantage of growing divisions in the power elite' (Bonnin & Chevrier 1991:587); but when the showdown came the 'absence of an in-depth political integration of the social coalition arrayed against the state' became crucial (Bonnin & Chevrier 1991:592). However, the authors find that after the repression of 1989-1990 developments conducive to social autonomy have resumed.

Other observers of the Chinese intellectual stage have arrived at even less enthusiastic evaluations. Geremie Barmé's 1991 essay on the Chinese Diaspora deplores the proclivity of Chinese intellectuals for the 'quick fix', 'totalistic solutions' and a 'movement mentality' (Barmé 1991:103-05). Timothy Cheek argues that very few Chinese intellectuals have completed the transformation from 'priest-rentiers serving the cosmic state' to 'professionals salaried in a bourgeois society' and that '[f]ew Chinese intellectuals argued for a fundamental restructuring of the political order before May 1989; many dissidents simply demanded the right to fulfill the kind of mandarin role that Chinese states (imperial, nationalist, and communist alike) have promised the intelligentsia: that of acting as advisers to those who govern' (Cheek 1992:125). Possibly the strongest criticism of this nature has been made by Elizabeth Perry with her 1992 statement that 'the very people who launched the Tiananmen protests — urban intellectuals — were perhaps the greatest fetter on its further development' (Perry 1992b:148). Perry argues that a host of traditionalist features — 'emperor worship', deference to state authority, contempt of ordinary citizens, Confucian moralism, etc. — all served to destroy the innovative potential of the protest movement.

5. The 'historical approach' to Chinese civil society, which claims that sprouts of civil society emerged already in late imperial and republican times, may attach itself to the four other approaches discussed above; it is a significant part of the general contemporary trend towards a China-centered history (in contrast to earlier paradigms of 'tradition — modern transformation' and 'impact — response', cfr. Cohen 1984); the paradox that this implies is that it generously allows Chinese civilization to produce, on its own accord, a perfectly Western trajectory of history... (The intellectual challenges of this paradox are intelligently discussed by, among others, William T. Rowe in the 1993 special issue of *Modern China* dedicated to the civil society debate; Rowe 1993.)

The civil society approach is directly relevant to the study of Chinese political culture since it points in the direction of the *structures and dynamics* beneath the flimsy surface of the manifestations of political culture. In a larger perspective it reconnects the study of Chinese political culture with the mainstream sociological 'Almond approach' of civic culture. The study of Chinese civil society has its own measure of flimsiness, however. This is determined by the present nature of Chinese society, but also by inherent contradictions in the theoretical concept of civil society, to be further discussed below.

Social surveys
One of the enduring obstacles to a sociological mainstream study of Chinese political culture during the 1960s and 1970s was the unavailability of empirical data based on social surveys. The emergence of Chinese sociology in the 1980s, particularly the flourishing of social surveys since 1986 mentioned above, changed the situation. Chinese sociological studies of political culture are outside the scope of this survey of Western perceptions; in actual fact, however, a number of Chinese sociologists in the late 1980s readily accepted the foundations of Western empirical political culture studies as expressed in the preface to Min Qi's 1989 study mentioned earlier, which draws directly on Gabriel Almond and dedicates the book to 'comrades working to establish 'civic culture' in China' (quoted from McCormick, Su & Xiao 1992:198). The level of *political tolerance* has been studied by Chinese researchers, and Min Qi's book arrived at negative conclusions. In one of the surveys of this study respondents were asked whether they supported the expression: 'I firmly disagree with your viewpoint, but I will defend to the death your right to express it.' The majority of respondents were unable to understand the statement (Min Qi 1989:123, quoted from Rosen 1992:175). A rather more optimistic appraisal of Beijing citizens' democratic aspirations was arrived at in Shi Tianjian's 1988 study, which found that 77 percent of respondents were interested in politics and 79 percent disagreed with the proposition that: 'If we implement democracy in our country now it will lead to chaos' (Nathan 1990:197-98). The empirical foundations of these studies are not above doubt; the methodological problems of Chinese 1980s social surveys are discussed in Rosen & Chu 1987 and Rosen 1989a. According to Nathan & Shi, 'all the Chinese studies on which we have information, including Min Qi's, were methodologically flawed in terms of sampling, question formulation, and interview techniques' (Nathan & Shi 1993:97).

In the early 1990s two empirical studies of Chinese political culture based on collaborative efforts between Western and Chinese social scientists have appeared. These studies must be assumed to have better methodological foundations than earlier Chinese studies. In very general terms they point in the same direction: there is empirical evidence that the politically relevant attitudes of the Chinese differ significantly from popular attitudes in countries with well established democratic traditions and that the prevalent Chinese political values to a certain extent act as a blockage for democratization in China. The 1990s Western-Chinese collaborative studies thus tend to confirm the more pessimistic preliminary 1980s empiricial studies, Western as well as Chinese (e.g. Nathan 1985, Min Qi 1989).

Torstein Hjellum's 1994 study is based on two surveys carried out in 40 cities by the National Research Centre for Science and Technology for Development. The first survey was carried out in 1988, and the second, with 2,395 respondents, in 1991. (A third survey was conducted in late 1993, but the data from this survey have not yet been analyzed.) The surveys were not originally designed for a study of political culture, but many questions serve the purpose. The method for selection of respondents was that of random sampling, but in actual fact better educated people were overrepresented in the surveys. Most questions were of the multiple choice type with a choice between three, four or five options. The middle category has been chosen for most of the questions by 30-50 percent of respondents, in some cases up to 60 percent. The implications of this are unclear, since the middle category answer might reflect unwillingness to answer what may have been perceived as a sensitive question, or a lack of understanding of the question, rather than just a neutral position. A number of in-depth interviews were conducted in Beijing in 1993 to check the validity of the survey methodology. One of the most valuable features of the Hjellum study is that it allows comparison over time and between different age groups. A comparison of the 1988 and 1991 data yields insights into the effects of the Tiananmen events on political attitudes. Furthermore, the survey data group respondents into young, midage and old, which makes it possible to study generational differences in political attitudes. Among the main conclusions of the study:

— The reform decade has not changed people's mentality in the direction of formulating group interests; a pragmatic *guanxi* approach remains as powerful as ever.

— Most people feel that the quality of government is important, and half the respondents also emphasize the entitlement to political participation.

— The achievements of the reform decade are generally positively evaluated. Positive answers also predominate as regards 'democratization' (in 1988, 46 percent of respondents agreed that the extent of political democratization had improved, and in 1991 the figure had risen to 50 percent; in-depth interviews indicated, however, that many respondents do not associate with 'democratization' anything comparable to a Western understanding of the concept).

— Critical views of the government regarding moral quality, efficiency, openness and public order predominate.

— As for political rights the surveys were hampered by a very high frequency of middle category answers, indicating that many respondents either did not wish to state their opinion or did not understand the questions. The level of satisfaction regarding various 'rights' (such as 'the right to vote', 'freedom of speech', etc.) registered a moderate drop from 1988 to 1991.

— Young people are clearly much more critical of the government than older people, and, likewise, better educated citizens tend to be more critical than others.

Hjellum's overall conclusion is that Chinese political culture is characterized by traditional orientations and that 'Westernbased optimism on behalf of civil society and a growing democratic pluralism in China seems to be considerably exaggerated' (Hjellum 1994). Widespread dissatisfaction is fully compatible with traditional orientations ('subject political culture' in Almond's terms), and there are few signs of a 'participatory political culture' pointing towards democracy.

The survey results regarding the level of satisfaction with 'rights' are very difficult to interpret, and the methodology of the surveys may be faulty in this respect. How should one evaluate answers to questions regarding 'rights' that the Chinese citizens, simply put, do not have? What does it mean that, for example, five percent of respondents are 'very satisfied' with their 'right to join different kinds of mass organizations' and their 'freedom of assembly and procession', while a roughly equal number are 'very dissatisfied'? Hjellum's in-depth interviews in fact indicate that meaningful interpretation of the data is almost impossible; 'satisfaction' regarding a certain 'right' may be the expression of an acceptance of the de facto lack of the right in question rather than a positive evaluation of the situation. There is no easy approach, however, to data that may help reveal popular Chinese attitudes to sensitive issues such as political rights.

In 1993 Andrew Nathan and Tianjian Shi published some results from a 1990 social survey conducted in China in cooperation with the Social Survey Research Center of People's University of China. The survey questionnaire was designed in the United States and pretested in Beijing in 1988. 3,200 people selected by random sampling were interviewed. The survey is, in the authors' words, 'not only the first scientifically valid national sample survey done in China on political behaviour and attitudes, but the only valid national-level sample survey on the political behaviour and attitudes of the general populace ever done in a Communist country' (Nathan & Shi 1993:97). Most questions were adapted from Almond and Verba's *The Civic Culture* and the *International Social Survey Program* (ISSP) to allow cross-national comparison. The general conclusion of the study is that 'while some of the attitudes associated with democracy are less prevalent in China than in some other countries, Chinese political culture today is neither especially traditional nor especially totalitarian' (Nathan & Shi 1993:98). Three dimensions of political culture are examined:

1) Regarding the perceived impact of government, Nathan & Shi find that '[i]t is striking that so few Chinese citizens perceive their government as having an impact on their daily lives' (Nathan & Shi 1993:99). Approximately 72 percent of Chinese respondents stated that both national and local governments had no effect on their daily lives (compared with, for example, 10 percent of Americans in Almond and Verba's classic study). This finding is also remarkable in its total disagreement with the surveys that Hjellum's study is based on. According to those surveys, 71 percent of respondents in 1988 agreed with the statement that it was 'most important' to have a satisfactory government and only two percent answered 'not so important' or 'not important at all'. In 1991 the percentage of respondents agreeing with the 'most important' answer had dropped to 49 percent, but this is still a very long way from the Nathan & Shi results. Part of the discrepancy, but not all of it, may be ascribed to the urban and educational bias of the surveys used by Hjellum. The Nathan & Shi study found that the perceived impact of the national government varies substantially with the level of education: among respondents with some university level education the 'no effect' percentage was only 36.1.

2) Political efficacy refers to beliefs regarding citizens' competence to understand and participate in politics ('internal efficacy') as well as beliefs about the responsiveness of the government ('external efficacy'). As for 'internal efficacy' nearly 50 percent of the respondents felt that they understood the 'important issues facing their work unit' very well or relatively well, compared to 19.9 percent for local issues and 17.9 percent for national-level issues (Nathan & Shi 1993:106). Chinese respondents scored lower than citizens of other countries but did not lag far behind Italians and Mexicans as they appeared in *The Civic Culture*. Regarding external efficacy a majority of Chinese respondents thought that they would be treated equally by a government office, higher than the Italians and Mexicans of the 1960s. Interestingly, the Nathan & Shi study found a curvilinear relationship between education and expectations of bureaucratic fairness: respondents with some primary education have a higher level of confidence in the

bureaucracy than uneducated people, but the level of confidence *falls* with higher levels of education. Nathan & Shi point out that a cultural attitude normally considered conducive to democracy may also help to buttress authoritarianism: 'The relatively high Chinese figures on output affect dovetail with findings from the 1988 Beijing survey that many Chinese citizens have developed a range of techniques for exerting influence on the bureaucracy despite the authoritarian nature of China's political system. This sense among ordinary people of having access to the system may help explain why political dissatisfaction among intellectuals has not struck many sparks among the broader population, especially in the rural areas where the less-educated are concentrated' (Nathan & Shi 1993:111).

3)Political tolerance is an important part of a democratic culture. As Pye has stated on many occasions, Chinese political culture is very low on political tolerance and high on 'hatred and revenge'. In this case the empirical data fully confirm the observations of psychoculturalism: Chinese score far lower on tolerance than people from a number of Western countries. Less than 20 percent of Chinese respondents were willing to allow deviant views to be expressed at meetings and around 10 percent would allow it in teaching situations or in publications. Education is positively correlated with tolerance, but 'at each level of educational attainment, Chinese respondents are less tolerant than people in other countries' (Nathan & Shi 1993:112). It should be noted, however, that the question used to test political tolerance among Chinese took the 'Gang of Four' as the example of deviant views; considering the effects of fifteen years of propaganda since 1976 it may be a bit like asking for 'sympathy for the Devil'.

Nathan & Shi's findings are accompanied by a careful discussion of the limitations of the study and of the social survey approach in general. The disadvantages include 'the inability to go back in time except under special circumstances, the technique's flattening or simplifying effect on the cultural attributes which can be measured, and the intrinsic inability to identify attibutes which are or might be culturally unique, except in a trivial sense' (Nathan & Shi 1993:97). In the conclusion the authors note that political culture is but one of the several sets of conditions that affect the prospects for democracy (Nathan & Shi 1993:114).

The findings of Nathan & Shi generally conform to the — much more preliminary — results of Nathan's earlier 1985 survey. The discrepancy between the Hjellum study and Nathan & Shi regarding the perceived impact of government is disturbing, and there are also dissonances between the 1988 pretest survey in Beijing conducted by Shi Tianjian concerning popular attitudes towards democracy and the 1993 study. On balance, however, these recent surveys have contributed much towards establishing an empirical basis for understanding Chinese political culture. Nathan & Shi correctly point out that the survey results, structured along universal dimensions of analysis, are in a sense an artifact of the approach — just like the findings of cultural distinctiveness are equally an artifact of the interpretive approach [i.e. psychoculturalism]. A more basic problem, though, is the evaluation of the *implications* of the survey results for an understanding of how the system operates and predictions regarding its durability. If similar surveys had been conducted in the Soviet Union and Eastern Europe prior to 1989, would they have enabled social scientists to predict the collapse of the system? It is an inherent contradiction to examine the significance of 'politically relevant attitudes' for political systems that are designed to ignore such attitudes. It may safely be assumed that Chinese political culture in fact involves a complex structure of enduring as well as more volatile 'layers' of politically relevant attitudes, and that periodic outbursts of unrest may quickly and radically alter the internal setup of this attitudinal structure. Thus, the recent advances in empirical studies of Chinese political culture have not obliterated the need for a deeper understanding of cultural dynamics in China.

Neoculturalism

The term neoculturalism, proudly proclaimed by Elizabeth Perry in 1992, does not signal a unity of views or methods. What is reflected in the new generation of political culture studies is rather a general and gradual transformation of the approach to culture studies during the 1980s. It follows that the 'new generation' is not in any way sharply demarcated from earlier approaches, and in fact a number of the studies surveyed above give expression to the ideas of neoculturalism in varying degrees.

The emerging line of thinking has been aptly summarized by R.G. Fox in a recent study of nationalism:

Culture, we are coming to think, is not a heavy weight of tradition, a set of configurations, a basic personality constellation that coerces and compels individuals. Culture is a set of understandings and a consciousness under active construction by which individuals interpret the world around them... Similarly we have drained off much of the necessity and teleology of the nation-building literature. National culture is not an inevitable output of infrastructural investment. It is a contingent product, of history, of struggle... (Fox 1990:10).

Within China studies, a similar refocusing of the culture concept has been expressed by Helen F. Siu: 'Instead of upholding the prevailing image of a reified China enshrouded with primordial sentiments, one may see how advocates on different ends of the spectrum have negotiated their respective positions to generate a complex, open cultural process' (Siu 1993:27). Several recent studies of Chinese nationalism and cultural identity embody the new 'active approach' to culture. A number of essays reflecting the approach were published in the 1991 special issue of *Dædalus* entitled 'The Living Tree: The Changing Meaning of Being Chinese Today' and in the 1993 issue entitled 'China in Transformation'; other essays appeared in a 1993 volume on *Cultural Nationalism in East Asia* (Befu 1993). A fine example of this line of studies is Arthur Waldron's study of the establishment of the Great Wall as a key Chinese cultural symbol in the 20th century (Waldron 1993). Waldron has highlighted the interplay between China and the West in this process as well as the conflicts between various groups regarding the interpretation of the Wall, which can be used to signify imperial power as well as impotence towards China's nomad neighbours, grandeur as well as social injustice and misery on the part of the hard-working builders, nationalist pride as well as embarrassing xenophobia.

In political culture studies, the 'active approach' to culture implies looking at political culture as a historical creation under constant change rather than a changeless psychological framework: 'Political culture is a historical creation, subject to constant elaboration and development through the activities of the individuals and groups whose purposes it defines. As it sustains and gives meaning to political activity, so is it itself shaped and transformed in the course of that activity' (Keith Baker, quoted in Perry 1992a:10). The approach may serve studies of how certain forms of political discourse are shaped in modern history, utilizing and manipulating cultural values in the process. A recent example of this is Peter Zarrow's 1990 study of *Anarchism and Chinese Political Culture*, which argues that 'anarchism proved to be a useful tool to robe and manipulate Chinese culture' (Zarrow 1990:156.). Adherents of the approach are particularly interested in symbols, rituals, theatrical forms and other such features that embody the meeting point between historically transmitted cultural forms and the active use of these forms for the political purposes of the hour. In the most optimistic versions of neoculturalism, the Chinese people are transformed from helpless victims of tradition into resourceful guerrilla warriors adept at putting cultural capital to good use for their own purposes; an example of this might be Edward Friedman's recent studies of the emergence of a Southern Chinese cultural identity (e.g. Friedman 1994). Jeffrey Wasserstrom and Elizabeth Perry's 1992 volume on *Popular Protest and Popular Culture in Modern China* sets out on a similar note to examine the 'multitude of available cultural repertoires' and the 'fluidity and flexibility of cultural practice' (Perry 1992a:5). Some of the essays employ the metaphor of *performance*, such as Esherick & Wasserstrom's examination of the 1989 events as 'political theater': 'Some public rituals are always necessary, and in those events, there is always the danger that students or other actors will usurp the stage and turn the official ritual into their own political theater' (Esherick & Wasserstrom 1992:51). But in the final analysis, who usurps whom? Several contributors to the 1992 Wasserstrom & Perry volume in fact end up with conclusions centered on 'the heavy burden of the past', 'the fetters of tradition', etc. Innovative trends in cultural analysis cannot undo the fact that the forces of authoritarianism won out in China in 1989. Post-1989 government efforts to promote cultural nationalism are certainly a case of 'invention of tradition' (to borrow the term of Hobsbawm and Ranger's influential 1983 book) and involve a fair amount of fiction; but for the moment these efforts are backed by power. As for the enterprising 'cultural guerrillas' of 1989, there is no doubt that using the cultural weapons arsenal caused a number of self-inflicted wounds: the political language of the protest movement kept students separate from other social groups and prevented the development of political dialogue, to mention two of the most obvious problems. If the focus is shifted too radically in the direction of seeing culture as creative activity above all, the other side of the coin — culture as conditioning — takes revenge. At best the 1989 events were a case of 'a tradition that was being lived as well as exploited', to borrow David Strand's elegant formulation (Strand 1990:2). Wasserstrom's Afterword to the 1992 volume explains how the neoculturalist approach differs from the psychoculturalism associated with Lucian Pye in its emphasis on differences between pre- and post-1949 China as well as in treating culture as a more fluid and less deterministic force. In the same breath, however, Wasserstrom very honestly acknowledges that:

... Pye's version of events [in 1989] in fact has a good deal in common with many of those presented in earlier chapters [of this book]. Like Pye, most contributors to this volume have highlighted the continuities linking the imperial, Nationalist, and Communist periods of Chinese history. Like Pye, many of us have focused our attention on the way in which cultural factors — patterns of interaction, rituals, beliefs inculcated through education, ideas concerning how the world should work and how one finds one's place in it — shape protest and repression. And, like Pye, many of us have emphasized the need to take the symbolism of the movement very seriously (Wasserstrom 1992:271).

Our survey of Chinese political culture studies thus ends where it began, with a student of China's political culture whose views are as stubbornly persistent as are apparently many features of the object of study.

Concluding remarks

The political culture concept has come a long way in China studies. From the early beginnings of psychoculturalism, Sinology-inspired extrapolations of philosophical principles and shaky empirical studies based on emigré interviews, the approach has evolved into a plethora of civil society studies, large-scale social surveys and sophisticated neoculturalist deliberations. Political culture has evolved from being seen as the dead imprint of the past, of Communism or of basic socialization patterns, into a complex and dynamic structure involving a multifaceted cultural capital that is actively appropriated by the Chinese people.

Yet some basic problems of the approach persist. There is a fundamental ambiguity in the use of the political culture concept in relation to non-Western, nondemocratic societies. The study of political culture was originally designed to examine the subjective underpinnings of democratic institutions as a way to evaluate the stability of those institutions (i.e. *The Civic Culture*). In the case of nondemocratic societies the approach begs a definition of orientation: are we looking for features of culture that serve to bind the ruled to the rulers, or the opposite, political culture as a reservoir of potential resistance to autocratic rulers? The third option at this fundamental level is the open-ended approach which looks at political culture as a realm of symbols, values and attitudes that may be exploited in various ways by both rulers and ruled, and in fact by many different groups and segments of society. Pye's psychoculturalism could be seen as an example of the first option, the civil society supporters — but in a sense also Solomon — as an example of the second option, and neoculturalism as the embodyment of the third. Social survey results may be interpreted within any of these basic orientations and yield very different conclusions according to the choice made. The choice of basic orientation is determined by political changes in China, of course, but changes outside China also affect the outlook of observers.

The recent popularity of the civil society concept is a case in point. The immediate source of nourishment for the approach obviously is the adoption of the concept by a number of East European dissident writers during the 1980s as a tool for delegitimizing state socialism, but there may be deeper levels of motivation at play for Western followers of the approach than just solidarity with oppressed liberal dissidents. China has always served as a screen for psychological projections of the Western mind; it is the stage for our worst nightmares as well as for our fondest dreams. In retrospect, the adoration of Maoism by Western leftists in the 1970s appears to have served a surrogate function as compensation for *defeat at home*. In a similar vein, it could be argued that liberal hopes regarding the emergence of a Chinese civil society are motivated — subconsciously, perhaps — by the apparent collapse of civil society at home: the atomization of Western societies, the emergence of a new, unruly underclass in the ghettoes, the public disgust with politics, etc.

It is worth remembering that Jürgen Habermas' 1962 *Strukturwandel der Öffentlichkeit*, from which many contemporary followers of the civil society approach draw inspiration, treats the 'public sphere' as a *historical category* associated primarily with the 18th and early 19th centuries; the second half of Habermas' book deals with the 20th century *degeneration* of civil society and the public sphere. Salvador Giner's excellent discussion of civil society theories in a similar way concludes that:

Traditional Marxian — including Gramscian — notions of civil society are bound to become increasingly outdated. They may soon be as outdated as those cherished by the nostalgic neoliberal thinkers of today already are.... Accordingly, those who still subscribe to these views would do well to use them only to understand bygone situations. Confined to the past, they will no doubt continue to prove most enlightening (Giner 1985:264).

The current popular use of the civil society concept rests on at least three faulty assumptions:

1) Civil society is treated in a reified way rather than as a category belonging to the history of ideas. Civil society theory may be seen as the reflection of enlightenment philosophy in the sphere of social thought. It embodies the vision of universality and reason as the guiding principles of society. Historically, in the course of modernization various interpretations of the vision emerged and clashed. We may distinguish between a conservative line of thought which identifies civil society with local community and values

to be protected against the onslaught of modernization, a liberal version identifying civil society with market freedom and the rule of law, and finally a leftist version regarding civil society as the home of reason and social justice to be protected against rapacious capitalism. Contemporary political discourse in the West still contains echoes of these competing schools of thought, but as a core ideology of modernization civil society was superseded by nationalism already in the late 19th century.

2) In the current use of the civil society concept one can also see the shadow of the 'political development' line of thinking prevalent in the 1960s. Regardless of the present sorry state of civil society in the West, one may argue that China, along with the former state socialist countries in the East, has 'reached the stage' of market capitalism and the accompanying civil society structures. The very rapid collapse of anything resembling civil society in the former Soviet Union and East Europe after 1990 has greatly frustrated this line of thought, but there are still lingering hopes about the eventual emergence of more regular 'market economy cum civil society' structures. The blind spot of this kind of thinking is that it clings to an identification of civil society with the nation-state. Examining the history of ideas, however, it appears that it was precisely this identification which caused the demise of civil society ideology a century ago; the vision of a society governed by reason, civility and humanism was killed by nationalism, and if the concept is to regain some of its enlightenment potential today, the first step is to discard the identification with the nation-state. Civil society today, if the term is to have any substantial meaning, is a global enterprise with regional, national and local branches. It is tied to neither market nor state. Amnesty International, human rights groups and environmental protection movements may serve as examples of such a contemporary global civil society.

3) The third 'blind spot' of current civil society discourse has to do with the *role of the state*. Heath B. Chamberlain's suggestion to 'bring the state back in' when discussing civil society in China has already been noted above. Yves Chevrier has argued along related lines:

The failure to modernise, so far, has been to a large extent a failure to bring the state back in, or better still, a failure to build a modern state out of the maze of bureauratic networks and informal influences that make (or should we say undo?) the Chinese state... China's archaic political structure and social organization make central power too strong where it should give more leeway to autonomous social forces, and too weak locally where it should be strong enough to rein in bureaucratic interests in order to support a modern market economy resting on an emancipated society under the rule of the law (Chevrier 1992:14).

The fact that 'society' is tied to the 'state' in a thousand ways is a two-way problem. In today's developmental states, 'rolling back the state' is much less of an issue than the problems regarding institutionalization, legalization, efficiency, combating of corruption, etc.

The study of political culture, thus, is part and parcel of the ideological constructs of the contemporary world and the approach is fraught with problems of interpretation. Nevertheless, with China slowly edging closer to the brink of systemic change, a better understanding of the subjective dimensions of Chinese political life is as important an item on the agenda as ever. On the basis of this survey of political culture studies related to China some of the more promising avenues to a better understand appear to be:

— Further refining of the social survey instruments. Much has already been achieved in the field of social surveys since the mid-1980s; further progress will depend among other things on the ability of researchers to shape questionnaires in a way that will help highlight attitudes particularly relevant to the Chinese political setting and thus throw more light on the structure of attitudes with its enduring as well as volatile aspects. The limits to such efforts are of course dictated by political climate and bureaucratic goodwill.

— Focusing on the impact of actual political experiences, i.e. on political culture as a *process* rather than as one polarity in a dialectic of 'structure' versus 'culture'. M.K. Whyte's analysis of the impact of the Cultural Revolution as a significant factor shaping current ideas and values, as discussed above, might serve as an example of this. An even more obvious example might be the threads connecting the protest movements of 1976, 1978, 1986 and 1989: the way the movement of 1989 developed was to a high extent conditioned by the nature and fate of the earlier movements, with 1976 as (in a larger perspective) a victory for the protesters and 1978 as (at least in some ways) a 'draw'.

— New and refined concepts are needed that may help transcend the ideological simplifications of 'state' and 'society'. The concept of 'local society' discussed by Andrew Walder in a number of recent articles might be an example of this (e.g. *Walder 1994*).

References

AAS 1994: The Association for Asian Studies, *Abstracts of the 1994 Annual Meeting*, Ann Arbor, Mich.: Association for Asian Studies.

Adorno, Theoror et al. (1950): *The Authoritarian Personality*.

Almond, Gabriel and Sydney Verba (1963): *The Civic Culture. Political Attitudes and Democracy in Five Nations*, Princeton, N.J.: Princeton University Press.

Almond, Gabriel (1983): 'Communism and Political Culture Theory' *Comparative Politics*, Vol. 16, no. 1,

Almond, Gabriel and Sydney Verba (1989): *The Civic Culture Revisited*, Newbury Park, Cal.: Sage [original ed. 1980].

Andersen, Heine (1994): 'Det civile samfund i teoretisk lys' [The theory of civil society], *Social Kritik*, no. 29, pp. 14-28.

Arendt, Hannah (1950): *The Origins of Totalitarianism*.

Barmé, Geremie (1991): 'Traveling Heavy: The Intellectual Baggage of the Chinese Diaspora', *Problems of Communism*, Jan.-April 1991, pp. 94-112.

Baum, Richard G. (1992): 'Political Stability in Post-Deng China, Problems and Prospects', *Asian Survey*, Vol. 23, no. 6, pp. 491-505.

Befu, Harumi (ed.) (1993): *Cultural Nationalism in East Asia. Representation and Identity*, Berkeley: University of California Press.

Bonnin, Michel and Yves Chevrier (1991): 'The Intellectual and the State: Social Dynamics of Intellectual Autonomy During the Post-Mao Era', *China Quarterly* No. 127, pp. 569-93.

Brødsgaard, K.E. (1994): 'Urban Private Business and Entrepreneurs in Haikou City' in Brødsgaard & Strand (eds.), *Reconstructing Twentieth Century China* (forthcoming).

Brown, Archie and Jack Gray (eds.)(1979): *Political Culture and Political Change in Communist States*, London: Macmillan.

Archie Brown (ed.) (1984): *Political Culture and Communist Studies*, London: Macmillan.

Bruun, Ole (1993): *Business and Bureaucracy in a Chinese City: An Ethnography of Private Business Households in Contemporary China*, Berkeley: University of California Press.

Chamberlain, Heath B. (1993): 'On the Search for Civil Society in China' *Modern China*, Vol. 19, no. 2, pp. 199-215.

Chamberlain, Heath B. (1994): 'Coming to Terms with Civil Society', *Australian Journal of Chinese Affairs*, no. 31, pp. 113-17.

Chan, Anita (1993): 'Revolution or Corporatism? Workers and Trade Unions in Post-Mao China', *Australian Journal of Chinese Affairs*, no. 29, pp. 31-61.

Cheek, Timothy (1992): 'From Priests to Professionals: Intellectuals and the State Under the CCP', in Jeffrey N. Wasserstrom & Elizabeth J. Perry (eds.)(1992), pp. 124-45.

Chen Kuide (1987): 'Zhengzhi wenhua yu bijiao zhengzhixue' [Political culture and comparative political science], *Dushu*, no. 6, pp. 29-37.

Chevrier, Yves (1992): 'Tiananmen Viewed from Post-Socialism: the failure and challenge of modernisation in the PRC', *Forum for a Better China*, no. 3, pp. 12-14.

Clausen, Søren (1991): 'Chinese Political Culture: A Discussion of an Approach', *The Stockholm Journal of East Asian Studies*, vol. 3, pp. 39-77.

Cohen, Paul A. (1984): *Discovering History in China. American historical writing on the recent Chinese past*, New York: Columbia University Press.

Dittmer, Lowell (1983a): 'The Study of Chinese Political Culture'. In Amy A. Wilson, Sidney L. Greenblatt and Richard W. Wilson (eds.), *Methodological Issues in Chinese Studies*, New York: Praeger, pp. 51-68.

Dittmer, Lowell (1983b): : 'Comparative Communist Political Culture.' *Studies in Comparative Communism*, Vol. 16, 1983, pp. 9-24.

Esherick, Joseph W. and Jeffrey N. Wasserstrom (1992): 'Acting Out Democracy: Political Theater in Modern China' in Jeffrey N. Wasserstrom & Elizabeth J. Perry (eds.)(1992), pp. 28-66.

Fox, R.G. (ed.)(1990): 'Introduction' *Nationalist Ideologies and the Production of National Culture*, Washington DC: American Anthropological Association, pp. 1-14.

Freud, Sigmund (1930): *Civilization and its Discontents*.

Friedman, Edward (1994): 'Reconstructing China's National Identity: A Southern Alternative to Mao-Era Anti-Imperialist Nationalism', *The Journal of Asian Studies* Vol. 53, no. 1, pp. 67-91.

Giner, Salvador (1985): 'The withering away of civil society', *Praxis International*, Vol. 2, pp. 247-67.

Gold, Thomas B. (1990a): 'The resurgence of civil society in China', *Journal of Democracy*, Winter 1990, pp. 18-31.

Gold, Thomas B. (1990b): 'Party-State versus Society in China' in J.K. Kallgren (ed.), *Building a Nation-State: China after Forty Years*, Berkeley: University of California Press, pp. 125-51.

Gold, Thomas B. (1994): 'Bases for Civil Society in China' in Brødsgaard & Strand (eds.)(1994) (forthcoming).

Gray, Jack (1979): 'Communism and Confucianism'. In Archie Brown and Jack Gray: *Political Culture and Change in Communist States*, London: Macmillan.

Hjellum, Torstein (1994): 'Changes in Political Culture in China During the Modernization Period Since 1978' in Kjeld Erik Brødsgaard and David Strand (eds.)(1994) (forthcoming).

Keane, John (ed.)(1988): *Civil Society and the State*, London: Verso.

Kutcher, Norman (1991): 'China: The Time of Songs and Tears', *Problems of Communism*, Jan.-April 1991, pp. 119-25.

Liu, Alan P. (1976): *Political Culture and Group Conflict in Communist China*, California Santa Barbara: Clio Press.

McCormick, B.L. (1991): 'The Impact of Democracy on China Studies', *Problems of Communism*, Jan.-April 1991, pp. 126-32.

McCormick, B.L., Su Shaozhi and Xiao Xiaoming (1992): 'The 1989 Democracy Movement: A Review of the Prospects for Civil Society in China', *Pacific Affairs*, Vol. 65, No. 2, pp. 182-202.

Miller, Robert (ed.)(1992): *The Development of Civil Society in Communist Systems*, Sydney: Allen and Unwin.

Min Qi (1989): *Zhongguo zhengzhi wenhua: Minzhu zhengzhi nanchande shehui xinlie yinsu* ['Chinese political culture: The socio-psychological elements that obstruct democratic politics'], Kunming: Yunnan Renmin Chubanshe.

Nathan, A.J. (1985): *Chinese Democracy*, New York: Knopf.

Nathan, A.J. (1990): *China's Crisis: Dilemmas of Reform and Prospects for Demorcacy*, New York: Columbia University Press.

Nathan, A.J. and Tianjian Shi (1993): 'Cultural Requisites for Democracy in China: Findings from a Survey' *Daedalus*, 'China in Transformation', Spring 1993, pp. 95-123.

Perry, Elizabeth J. (1992a): 'Introduction' in Jeffrey N. Wasserstrom & Elizabeth J. Perry (eds.)(1992), pp. 1-13.

Perry, Elizabeth (1992b): Elizabeth J. Perry: 'Casting a 'Democracy' Movement: The Roles of Students Workers, and Entrepreneurs', in Jeffrey N. Wasserstrom & Elizabeth J. Perry (eds.)(1992), pp. 146-64.

Perry, Elizabeth J. (1993): 'China in 1992 (1993): An Experiment in Neo-Authoritarianism', *Asian Survey*, Vol. 33, No. 1, pp. 12-21.

Pye, Lucian W. and Sydney Verba (1965): *Political Culture and Political Development*, Princeton, N.J.: Princeton University Press.

Pye, Lucian W. (1968): *The Spirit of Chinese Politics*, Cambridge, Mass.: MIT Press.

Pye, Lucian W. (1972): *China. An Introduction*, Boston: Little, Brown.

Pye, Lucian W. (1973): 'Culture and Political Science: Problems in the Evaluation of the Concept of Political Culture'. In Louis Schneider and Charles M. Bonjean (eds.) (1973): *The Idea of Culture in the Social Sciences*, Cambridge: Cambridge University Press, pp. 65-76.

Pye, Lucian W. (1976): *Mao Tse-tung. The Man in the Leader*, New York: Basic Books.

Pye, Lucian W. (1981): *The Dynamics of Chinese Politics*, Cambridge, Mass.: Oelgeschlager, Gunn and Hain.

Pye, Lucian W. (1985): *Asian Power and Politics: The Cultural Dimensions of Authority*, Cambridge, Mass.: Harvard University Press.

Pye, Lucian W. (1988): *The Mandarin and the Cadre. China's Political Cultures*, Ann Arbor: Center for Chinese Studies, The University of Michigan.

Pye, Lucian W. (1990): 'Tiananmen and Chinese Political Culture. The Escalation of Confrontation from Moralizing to Revenge' (1990): *Asian Survey*, Vol. 30, no. 4, April 1990.

Rankin, Mary B. (1986): *Elite Activism and Political Transformation in China: Zhejiang Province, 1865-1911*, Stanford: Stanford University Press.

Rosen, Stanley and David S. K. Chu (1987): *Survey Research in the People's Republic of China*, Washington, D.C.: United States Information Agency.

Rosen, Stanley (1989a): 'Value Change Among Post-Mao Youth: The Evidence from Survey Data' in Perry Link, Richard Madsen, and Paul G. Pickowicz (eds.), *Unofficial*

China: Popular Culture and Thought in the People's Republic, Boulder: Westview Press, pp. 193-216.

Rosen, Stanley (1989b): 'Public Opinion and Reform in the People's Republic of China', *Studies in Comparative Communism*, Vol. 22, nos. 2-3, pp. 153-70.

Rosen, Stanley (1992): 'Students and the State in China: The Crisis in Ideology and Organization' in Arthur Lewis Rosenbaum (ed.), *State & Society in China. The Consequences of Reform*, Boulder: Westview Press, pp. 167-91.

Rowe, William T. (1985): *Hankow: Commerce and Society in a Chinese City, 1796-1889*, Stanford: Stanford University Press.

Rowe, William T.: »The Problem of 'Civil Society' in Late Imperial China« *Modern China*, Vol. 19, no. 2, pp. 139-57.

Schneider, Louis and Charles M. Bonjean (eds.)(1973): *The Idea of Culture in the Social Sciences*, Cambridge: Cambridge University Press.

Shue, Vivienne (1988): *The Reach of the State; Sketches of the Chinese Body Politic*, Stanford: Stanford University Press.

Siu, Helen F. (1993): 'Cultural Identity and the Politics of Difference', *Dædalus*, Spring 1993, pp. 19-42.

Solinger, Dorothy J. (1992a): *China's Transients and the State: a Form of Civil Society?* Hong Kong: Institute of Asia-Pacific Studies, 1992.

Solinger 1992b: Dorothy J. Solinger: 'Urban Entrepreneurs and the State: The Merger of State and Society', in Arthur Lewis Rosenbaum (ed.), *State & Society in China. The Consequences of Reform*, Boulder: Westview Press, pp. 121-41.

Solomon, Richard H. (1971): *Mao's Revolution and the Chinese Political Culture*, Berkeley: University of California Press.

Strand, David (1989): *Rickshaw Beijing: City People and Politics in the 1920s*, Berkeley: University of California Press.

Strand, David (1990): 'Protest in Beijing: Civil Society and Public Sphere in China' *Problems of Communism*, May-June 1990, pp. 1-19.

Sullivan, Laurence (1990): 'The emergence of civil society in China, spring 1989', in Tony Saich (ed.), *The Chinese People's Movement, Pespectives on Spring 1989*, New York: M.E. Sharpe, pp. 126-44.

Townsend, J.R. (1969): *Political Participation in Communist China*, Berkeley: University of California Press.

Wakeman, Frederic (1993): 'The Civil Society and Public Sphere Debate, Western Reflections on Chinese Political Culture', *Modern China*, Vol. 19, No. 2, pp. 108-38.

Walder, Andrew G. (1992): 'Urban Industrial Workers: Some Observations on the 1980s', in A.L. Rosenbaum (ed.), *State & Society in China, The Consequences of Reform*, Boulder: Westview Press, pp. 103-20.

Walder, Andrew G. (1994): 'The decline of communist power: Elements of a theory of institutional change', *Theory and Society*, No. 23.

Walder, Andrew G. and Gong Xiaoxia (1993): 'Workers in the Tiananmen Protests: The

Politics of the Beijing Workers' Autonomous Federation' *Australian Journal of Chinese Affairs*, No. 29, pp. 1-29.

Waldron, Arthur (1993): 'Representing China: The Great Wall and Cultural Nationalism in the Twentieth Century' in Befu (ed.) (1993), pp. 36-60.

Wang He (1987): 'Traditional Culture and Modernization — A review of the general situation of cultural studies in China in recent years', *Social Sciences in China*, Vol. 2, pp. 9-30.

Wasserstrom, Jeffrey N. & Elizabeth J. Perry (eds.)(1992): *Popular Protest and Political Culture in Modern China: Learning from 1989*, Boulder: Westview Press.

Wasserstrom, Jeffrey N. (1992): 'Afterword: History, Myth and the Tales of Tiananmen', in Jeffrey N. Wasserstrom & Elizabeth J. Perry (eds.)(1992) pp. 244-80.

White, Gordon (1993): 'Prospects for civil society in China: A case study of Xiaoshan city', *Australian Journal of Chinese Affairs*, No. 29, pp. 63-87.

White, Stephen (1979): *Political Culture and Soviet Politics*, London: Macmillan.

Whyte, Martin K. (1974): *Small Groups and Political Rituals in China*, Berkeley: University of California Press.

Whyte, Martin K. (1992): 'Urban China: A Civil Society in the Making?', in A.L. Rosenbaum (ed.), *State & Society in China, The Consequences of Reform*, Boulder: Westview Press, pp. 77-101.

Yang, Mayfair Mei-hui (1989): 'Between State and Society: The Construction of Corporateness in a Chinese Socialist Factory', *Australian Journal of Chinese Affairs*, No. 22, pp. 31-60.

Xu Wanmin (1989): 'Sanzhong quanhui yihou woguo zhengzhi wenhua fazhan de jiben quxiang' [The basic trend in the development of political culture in our country since the Third Plenum] *Shehui Kexue* 1989, No. 1, pp. 20-23.

Zarrow, Peter (1990): *Anarchism and Chinese Political Culture*, New York: Columbia University Press.

Zi Zhongxun (1987): 'The Relationship of Chinese Traditional Culture to the Modernization of China. An Introduction to the Current Discussion'. *Asia Survey*, Vol. 27, no. 4, pp. 442-58.

Østergaard, Clemens Stubbe (1989): 'Citizens groups and a nascent civil society in China: towards an understanding of the 1989 student demonstrations', *China Information*, Vol. 4, no. 2, pp. 28-41.

Notes

1. The survey of the first generation of Chinese political culture studies is based on *Clausen 1991*.
2. Cf. Almond's 'The Intellectual History of the Civic Culture Concept', in *Almond and Verba 1989*; Lucian W. Pye's 'Culture and Political Science: Problems in the Evaluation of the Concept of Political Culture', in *Schneider and Bonjean 1973*; and the chapter 'Political Culture and Political Science' in *White 1979*.

3. The significance of dissident sociology in late 1980s China is described in *Rosen 1989* and *Bonnin & Chevrier 1991*. Bonnin and Chevrier present a carefully balanced analysis of the degree of 'autonomy' on the part of the dissident groups and organizations.

Biographical Notes

Harumi Befu received his Ph.D. from the University of Wisconsin, and is now professor of Anthropology at Stanford University. Recent publications include *Cultural Nationalism in East Asia — Representation and Identity*, Berkeley, University of California, Department of East Asian Studies, 1993 (editor).

Bei Dao, a writer and poet, is founder and general editor of the foremost Chinese language literary periodical in the West, *Jintian*. His poetry is translated into many languages. He has been living in the West since 1989 and was a lecturer at the Department of East Asian Studies at the University of Aarhus 1990-92.

Vibeke Børdahl, mag.art., Ph.D., was Associate Professor of Chinese language and literature, Department of East Asian Studies, University of Aarhus, Denmark, 1972-1982. Currently research fellow at the Danish Research Council for the Humanities, Department of Asian Studies, University of Copenhagen. Monographs and articles in the field of Chinese literature, literary criticism, literary history, dialectology and oral storytelling. At present working on the monograph: *The Oral Tradition of Yangzhou Storytelling*.

Flemming Christiansen, MA, University of Aarhus, Ph.D., Leiden University, teaches Chinese Politics at Manchester University in Great Britain. His main field of research is Chinese rural development and rural policy in China. He presently coordinates a research project on Chinese sustainable agricultural policies in ecologically sensitive areas in China, which is financed by the European Commission. His recent works include: *'Market Transition' in China*, Modern China, vol 18, no 1, 1992 and *The Legacy of the Mock Dual Economy: Chinese Labour in Transition 1978-1992*, Economy and Society, vol 22, no 4, 1993.

Søren Clausen graduated from the University of Aarhus, Denmark, in political science and Chinese. He is Associate Professor of modern Chinese language, history and society at the Department of East Asian Studies, University of Aarhus. He has published mainly in the fields of contemporary Chinese politics, Chinese Marxism and economic thought, modern Chinese history.

Recent publications deal with Chinese political culture, Chinese historio-graphy and issues relating to Chinese identity.

Wenwei Du earned his Ph.D. degree in Chinese & Comparative Literature at Washington University in St. Louis, the United States of America. He was Chinese lecturer at the Department of East Asian Studies 1992-94. As Assistant Professor of Chinese, he is now teaching at Vassar College. His research areas are Chinese drama & theatre and East-West literary relations. He has been writing essays in these directions.

Bjarke Frellesvig earned his Ph.D. degree at the University of Copenhagen and is Assistant Professor of Japanese language and linguistics at the Department of East Asian Studies, University of Aarhus. He is the author of *A Case study in Diachronic Phonology: the onbin sound changes in Old Japanese*, 1994, as well as several articles on Japanese and general linguistics. At present he is working on the prosody of Kyoto Japanese, diachronically as well as synchronically.

Mette Halskov Hansen is a Ph.D. student attached to the Department of East Asian Studies, University of Aarhus. Her dissertation is a comparative study of the relationship between education and ethnicity among the Jinuo, Naxi and Dai minorities in the Yunnan Province in Southwest China.

Susanne Juhl graduated from the Department of East Asian Studies, University of Aarhus, in 1988. She has been Assistant Lecturer of Classical Chinese, and is now writing her Ph.D. thesis entitled *An Empirical Investigation and Analysis of the Social and Cultural Conditions in the Nothern Liang*.

Greg Kulander is a Ph.D. student attached to the Department of East Asian Studies, University of Aarhus. His dissertation is a study of how Chinese agricultural universities have contributed to the development of the human resource base in Chinese agriculture during the 1980s and 1990s. He has previously written on human resource development in the Chinese agricultural extension system.

Wendy Larson, Associate Professor of Chinese Language and Literature at the University of Oregon, publishes on modern literature, women writers and feminism, contemporary theory, and film. She also translates contemporary fiction and poetry, and is working on an anthology of post-1985 poetry. Larson is the author of *Literary Authority and the Modern Chinese Writer: Ambivalence and Autobiography*, Duke University Press, 1991 and is presently completing a manuscript on women and writing in modern China.

Knud Lundbæk was formerly Professor of medicine at University of Aarhus. He is now Emeritus Professor and Research Fellow at the Department of East Asian Studies specializing in the history of sinology. His publications include: *T.S. Bayer (1694-1738) — Pioneer Sinologist*, London and Malmö, 1986 and *Joseph de Prémare (1666-1733), S.J. — Chinese Philology and Figurism*, Aarhus 1991.

Gunner Bjerg Mikkelsen graduated in Chinese and history of religions from University of Aarhus in 1993, and is now writing his Ph.D. dissertation on the introduction of Manichaeism into China.

Kirsten Refsing, dr.phil., Associate Professor of Japanese and head of the Department of Asian Studies, University of Copenhagen. Research areas are Ainu and Japanese language and culture; at present she is working on a project about cross-cultural marriages.

Marie Roesgaard graduated from the Department of East Asian Studies, University of Aarhus, in 1989 and in 1994 completed her Ph.D. dissertation on Japanese educational reform.

Roy Starrs is Associate Professor of Japan Studies at the Department of East Asian Studies, University of Aarhus. During the 1994-95 academic year he is conducting research in Japan as a Japan Foundation Fellow for a new book on the theme of 'nation and tradition in Japanese literature'. His main interests lie in comparative literature and culture, as reflected most recently in his study of Nietzschean philosophy in Mishima's novels, *Deadly Dialectics: Sex, Violence and Nihilism in the World of Yukio Mishima*, co-published by the Japan Library in England and the University of Hawaii Press in the U.S.A.

Stig Thøgersen is Associate Professor of modern Chinese language and society at the Department of East Asian Studies, University of Aarhus. He is author of *Secondary Education in China After Mao: Reform and Social Conflict*, 1990 and *The Making of a Chinese City. History and Historiography in Harbin*, 1995 (with Søren Clausen), as well as several articles on Chinese education and local history, and translations of Chinese prose and poetry. He is presently working on the modern history of education in a county in Shandong province.

Anne Wedell-Wedellsborg is Associate Professor of modern Chinese language and literature at the Department of East Asian Studies. She is currently with the Centre for Cultural Studies at the University of Aarhus. She has published monographs and articles in the field of modern Chinese literature and literary criticism, history of literature and the democracy movement, as well as translations of contemporary Chinese poetry and prose. Recent publications include: *Inside Out. Modernism and Postmodernism in Chinese Literary Culture*, Aarhus 1993, (ed. with Wendy Larson).

Graham Young is Senior Lecturer in Politics, University of New England, Armidale, Australia. His major research interests have been the Chinese Communist Party and Chinese Communist political thought. His most recent publication is *China Since 1978: Reform, Modernisation and 'Socialism with Chinese Characteristics'*, co-authored with Colin Mackerras and Pradeep Taneja, 1993.

Clemens Stubbe Østergaard is Associate Professor at the Department of Political Science, University of Aarhus. He is Co-Chairman of East Asian Area Studies, University of Aarhus. His main research interests are international relations in Asia-Pacific, Chinese rural problems and political corruption, Japanese politics. Recent publications include *Remaking Peasant China. Problems of rural development and institutions at the start of the 1990s*, Aarhus 1990. (ed. with J. Delman and F. Christiansen); *From Strategic Triangle to Economic Tripolarity* in Nørgaard et al. (ed): 'The European Community in World Politics', Pinter 1994; *Values for Money? Political Conditionality in Aid — The case of China* in Sørensen (ed): 'Political Conditionality', 1993.

Index